PRAISE FOR

PARCELLS

"One thing you want with books like this is locker-room dish, and enough scenes are tantamount to the crazy stuff you see in a classic football insider's account like Roy Blount Jr.'s *Three Bricks Shy of a Load*."

—COLIN FLEMING, *BOSTON GLOBE*

"*Parcells: A Football Life*, written with Nunyo Demasio, is well worth it, especially the part that deals with his time with the Patriots, a behind-the-curtains look we so seldom get."

—BILL REYNOLDS, *PROVIDENCE JOURNAL*

"Anyone who appreciates NFL history, plus any longtime fans of the Giants, Patriots, Jets, Cowboys, and Dolphins, is going to want to run out to your local bookstore to buy *Parcells*."

—BEN VOLIN, *BOSTON GLOBE*

"Impossible to resist."

—*NEWSDAY*

"A win for longtime fans of the coach."

—*NEW JERSEY STAR-LEDGER*

"A football historian's delight. There are several enlightening details into one of the NFL's most successful coaches of the modern era."

—*ATLANTA JOURNAL-CONSTITUTION*

"*Parcells* provides a fascinating behind-the-scenes look at NFL life on and off the field."

—BOOKREPORTER.COM

"If there's anybody in the business that aspires to be a head football coach in this league, I think they'd serve themselves well to read [this] book because he tells everything: the interworking of these organizations [and] how they work in the league and itself. It's a pretty eye-opening book."

—JIM CALDWELL, HEAD COACH OF THE DETROIT LIONS

PARCELLS

A FOOTBALL LIFE

Bill Parcells

AND

Nunyo Demasio

THREE RIVERS PRESS
NEW YORK

Library of Congress Cataloging-in-Publication Data
Parcells, Bill, 1941–
    Parcells : a football life / Bill Parcells, Nunyo Demasio.
       pages cm
    Includes index.
    1. Parcells, Bill, 1941– 2. Football coaches—United States—
Biography. 3. New York Giants (Football team) I. Demasio,
Nunyo. II. Title.
  GV939.P35A3   2014
  796.332092—dc23
  [B]   2014027830

ISBN 978-0-385-34637-5
eBook ISBN 978-0-385-34636-8

Printed in the United States of America

Book design: Barbara Sturman
Cover design: Christopher Brand
Cover photograph: Joe Robbins/Getty Images

10 9 8 7 6 5 4 3 2 1

First Paperback Edition

To Mickey Corcoran,
a perfect role model for an aspiring young coach.

To Dorcas Demasio,
a special woman who started calling her oldest son a
writer several years before he officially became one.

Contents

PARCELLS

A FOOTBALL LIFE

1

Tucked between two volcanic areas in southwestern Italy, the coastal city of Naples at the turn of the twentieth century was among the poorest regions in Europe. Baldassare Naclerio was thirteen when his family moved from Naples to New York City in 1900, part of a tidal wave of Italian immigrants flooding the United States in search of economic opportunity. Like many others embracing assimilation, Baldassare Americanized his first name, becoming Harold.

The Naclerios lived in the upper Manhattan neighborhood of Harlem, which wouldn't become an African-American enclave for several more decades. Within months of his arrival, Harold used his woodworking skills to find employment as a cabinetmaker. Several years later he met Julie Ferrioli, another native of Naples. The two teenagers fell in love, married, and moved to tiny Wood-Ridge, New Jersey, to raise a family. Perched atop a hill, their house was weather-beaten yet cozy, with a small yard and garden that Harold kept immaculate.

Harold found a full-time job with the American Bell Telephone Company. He supplemented the family income with part-time employment as a mechanic and barber while applying woodworking and masonry skills on his home. By age nineteen, Julie Naclerio had a brood of three, which would grow to five and include an energetic, outspoken girl named Ida. After graduating from high school, Ida decided against attending college and landed a job at Lever Brothers, a Britain-based soap manufacturer with subsidiaries in several countries. Of Ida's $5 weekly salary, she contributed $3 to her parents for expenses; like most women of her generation, her best hopes lay in marrying the right man.

On August 10, 1913, Charles O'Shea was born to an Irish couple in Cambridge, Massachusetts. Within a few years the boy's father died in his sleep and his mother succumbed to the influenza epidemic of 1918. The deadliest in history, the pandemic killed up to 50 million people worldwide, including an estimated 675,000 Americans. Orphaned at age five, Charles was adopted by his aunt Esther St. George. When she married a man whose surname was Parcells, her nephew also took the last name. After purchasing two rooming houses on a downtown block, the family moved to Hackensack, New Jersey. Lucinda Whiting, a black cook and maid at the establishment, helped raise Esther's quiet nephew, doting on him so much that he came to view her as a mother.

Charles grew up to be a six-foot-one, wiry teenager with blazing speed, ramrod posture, and an incongruous nickname: "Chubby." During the late 1920s, Chubby's athleticism and passion led him to become a three-sport phenomenon at Hackensack High. Also academically inclined, Charles was pursued by several top colleges, and the 195-pounder accepted a football scholarship from Georgetown University, where he would also run track and play basketball. For most of his college football career Charles was coached by Jack Hagerty, who had once played for the New York Giants, helping them capture the 1927 NFL title.

At Georgetown, Hagerty discarded the Notre Dame Box, a single-wing offense that had flourished during the 1920s under Knute Rockne, the Fighting Irish legend, in which the running backs lined up in a box formation. Instead Hagerty installed the single-wing offense used by the Giants, based on a long snap and four backs: tailback, fullback, quarterback (blocking back), and wingback. The line was unbalanced: two players lined up on one side of the center and four on the other. The formation, which resembled a wing, emphasized chicanery more than power. Playing in this Giants-style offense, Charles Parcells became one of the top halfbacks in the East. He was also versatile enough to line up at quarterback and to make point-after kicks.

When Charles Parcells graduated in 1935 he entered Georgetown's law school, where he earned his Juris Doctor before taking a job as an agent for the Federal Bureau of Investigation. On returning to Hackensack he met Ida Naclerio in nearby Wood-Ridge. Ida's diminutive size belied her forceful nature. Often heard before being seen, the boisterous Italian woman provided a dramatic counterpoint to the tall, reserved Irishman. Where Ida turned the smallest issues into melodrama, Charles was quick to shrug and smile. The soft-spoken G-man was smitten, and after an ardent courtship he persuaded Ida to marry him. The couple moved to Hackensack, where Ida loudly worried about her husband's safety as a law-enforcement officer. Those concerns were only heightened by the birth of their first child.

Duane Charles Parcells arrived at Englewood Hospital in New Jersey on August 22, 1941. Astrological signs for the newborn indicated that he would be ambitious, autocratic, caring, excitable, generous, proud, strong-willed, and destined for big things. From Napoleon to Barack Obama, Leos have tended to be natural leaders, energetic taskmasters to whom others gravitate for guidance; those born between August 15 and August

22 are considered particularly hotheaded and impatient. Fond of the spot-light, they turn sullen when upstaged. Complex and volatile, Leos can be egomaniacal one moment and grounded the next, cocksure yet thin-skinned; despite being detailed-oriented, they are better at organizing the lives of others than their own.

Duane "Bill" Parcells's earliest memory places him in the backseat of the family car on the Pennsylvania Turnpike. His younger brother Don is cry-ing as their father barrels through the turnpike's dark tunnels, but three-year-old Duane feels only excitement. Their father's FBI job has taken the family to Des Moines, Iowa, then Joliet, Illinois, which means occasional road trips east, like this one, to see relatives. In time, Charles will capitu-late to Ida's badgering and return to New Jersey, taking a job at the United States Rubber Company as director of industrial relations, commuting to the company's office in midtown Manhattan.

Charles and Ida decided to settle in suburban Hasbrouck Heights, slightly north of Wood-Ridge and south of Hackensack. Charles paid $8,000 for a gray-and-white, single-story house on Columbus Avenue, where he converted the attic into a bedroom for Duane and Don. Only a few blocks away in the quiet, tree-lined neighborhood, Frank Sinatra lived with his wife, Nancy, and their newborn girl. Singing for the Tommy Dorsey Orchestra, the Hoboken native had established himself as one of America's most popular vocalists. The white exterior of Sinatra's seven-room clapboard home was often smeared with red-lipsticked messages from infatuated girls. On sunny days Sinatra and his wife walked their baby stroller past Charles Parcells's new home.

When Duane turned five Charles bought him a Rawlings baseball mitt and a Louisville Slugger, knowing that his boy didn't need to go far to use them. Across the street from their home sat a one-acre lot dubbed Army Field, just a few miles from the swamplands that would become the home of Giants Stadium. "Don't confuse it with anything like a park," Parcells says. "There were just patches of grass out there." But for Duane and his pals, the lot was a field of dreams where they gathered after school. Al-though most players were older than Duane, the five-year-old joined in with them right away. His brother Don, twenty-one months younger, got into the action several years later for a similarly early start.

Blacks were a rarity in Hasbrouck Heights, an otherwise diverse com-munity. Italian-Americans composed the largest ethnic group, along with families from Poland and Ireland. At a time of social tension among those groups, Army Field promoted camaraderie. Duane's interactions with blacks were limited to visits with his great-aunt in Hackensack. Most of her roominghouse employees were African-American, and had worked there for decades. Charles taught Duane to treat them like family. Lucinda Whiting, who had helped raise Charles, was paid the same deference as Esther Parcells herself.

Despite being fond of Lucinda, Ida, who hardly knew any blacks while growing up, didn't quite share her husband's racial outlook. "My mother comes from an Italian background, where there's a lot of prejudice," Parcells says. "My father? None, because he was raised a little bit by a black woman. I'm not trying to tell you that I'm devoid of prejudice, but he raised me with the philosophy 'Every man is your equal. Every man is your brother. You take people for who they are.' And that served me well in my lifetime because I've gotten along with all kinds."

Duane began attending Euclid Elementary School, only a few blocks from home. One day, an older boy, scowling, approached him in the sandbox: Danny Astrella was displeased to find his usual spot near the swings occupied, and by a new kid at that. Duane, bigger than most boys his age, declined to move. Danny, even more of an exception in size and strength, shoved Duane and punched him in the face. When Duane stepped forward to counterattack, Danny flipped him on his back, swiftly ending the scuffle.

Duane cried all the way home. As soon as Ida saw her son she turned apoplectic, vowing to find the perpetrator the next day, but when Charles returned from work and heard about the incident, he calmed his wife and went upstairs to speak with his downcast son.

"You weren't looking for trouble, were you, Duane?"

"No, Dad, I wasn't."

"You should never look for trouble, but if it comes your way, you have to be ready to deal with it."

"I tried real hard, Dad, but I couldn't do much. He's bigger, older, and stronger than me."

"Well, that may be, but you're going to have to go back out there tomorrow."

"No, Dad!"

"Well, if you don't go tomorrow, you're going to keep hiding from this kid. You have to go face him. Don't go looking for trouble, but go."

The next day Duane reluctantly returned to the scene of his beating. When Danny approached him Duane's heart raced, but he stood his ground. To Duane's surprise, Danny just walked on by. Seeing the benefits of confrontation, Duane embraced the approach. Most kids, even older ones, wilted in the face of his increased assertiveness. Inevitably this new mind-set led to more fisticuffs with Danny, but before long the two boys became best friends. Every morning they'd meet with several other kids at a candy store five blocks from Bill's home for the walk to school.

Duane Parcells disliked his first name because it was unusual. That sentiment was confirmed during the fourth grade, when a substitute teacher took attendance. "Duane Parcells? Duane? Is *she* here?" The gaffe embarrassed Duane, but had no effect on his sense of his own masculinity. By the fifth grade, the future Tuna weighed 160 pounds and was one of the neighborhood's most imposing boys.

As big as you are, there's almost always someone bigger. In this case Richie Jones, a herculean eighth grader, dwarfed even Duane. "He was a monster," Parcells recalls. One day Richie came to Army Field with a couple of hulking classmates. Normally football teams at Army Field were evenly matched, with as many as ten players on a side, but this time Richie and his two buddies skewed the talent level so drastically that a new agreement needed to be made: Richie and company would play together—against everyone else. Duane and his teammates became swarming Lilliputians against the zany power offense. "It was one of the most fun games I ever played in my life," Parcells recalls, laughing. "It took eight of us to get Richie down. And when he'd fall it was like a sequoia going down. If you were underneath him, it hurt."

A sense of innocence and safety permeated daily life in Hasbrouck Heights. Mothers patronizing the local butcher shop often left their babies in carriages outside the store. Drug use appeared to be nonexistent, and violent crime seemed restricted to New York City. Paradoxically, the sense of law and order in Hasbrouck Heights was partly due to the Mafia.

Parcells says of his childhood: "I wouldn't trade it with anybody. I could go anywhere. You knew who the bad guys were. You just couldn't go completely crazy."

Duane tested that limit a few times. Once, while visiting his great-aunt in Hackensack, he scaled the side of the church next door until he reached his goal: the steeple. He perched there, grinning at bewildered pedestrians, one of whom recognized Duane and related his daredevil antics to Charles Parcells. As usual, Charles didn't need to raise his voice to get through to his son. "He steered the ship at our house," Parcells says. "My mother was more in operations. She dealt with the nuts and bolts—the day-to-day battle."

Duane inherited Ida's explosive temperament, leading to frequent battles between the two. She often said about her son, "*Gli piace mescolare la pentola,*" which translates from Italian into, "He likes to stir the pot." Unabashedly confrontational, Ida didn't hesitate to beat Duane for misbehaving. Parcells recalls, "She was a good-hearted woman with a short fuse. I got that from her." He adds, "I *do* like to stir up trouble. I believe that sometimes chaos and confrontation are the real mothers of invention, not necessity."

Ida occasionally tied up her son with a cord and walloped him. One of Duane's worst punishments came after he stole a pack of cigarettes from his father and took them to school. Although he didn't smoke, possessing them made him feel cool. When Ida discovered the cigarettes in her son's coat pocket, she pinned him to the floor and pummeled him with her fists. If Duane resisted, Ida used whatever was within reach to restore order. She once broke a plate over his head. "She wasn't abusive," Parcells stresses. "She threw things here and there to get me to snap out of it when I was young."

Charles generally spared the rod, unless he heard one of his boys giving lip to Ida. Then he took the perpetrator, usually Duane, out to the back-yard for a spanking.

Due to Charles's long workdays, during the week his family didn't spend much time together outside the home. Special entertainment consisted of Ida driving her children to nearby Teterboro Airport. With scarce air traf-fic, it gave cars access right up to the runway, where the Parcellses parked to watch the planes taking off and landing. Duane's quality time with his father also involved aircrafts. The pair took occasional trips to the Hack-ensack River, east of Teterboro, to observe the single-engine seaplanes navigate the water on their slender pontoons. Charles would park his car close to the dock, from where father and son watched the action.

On the first such trip Duane spotted oil tanks emblazoned "Hess" across the river, prompting him to ask his father about the name. Charles gladly provided the colorful, Horatio Alger story: A Jewish boy, Leon Hess lived down the road in Asbury Park, helping his Eastern European father dig and sell clams in summertime. During the Great Depression the family saved enough money, $24, to buy its first oil-delivery truck. As a teenager, Leon acquired five more trucks before buying the oil refin-ery he would parlay into a billion-dollar company. Charles Parcells, who preached meritocracy and drive to his kids, appreciated Hess's life story.

Ida also took her boys to Bischoff's, a popular ice-cream parlor in Tea-neck that featured employees in white hats and black bow ties, concoct-ing exotic combinations of forty available flavors. Duane's favorite sundae, the Broadway Flip, included chocolate sauce, almonds, and pecans. It cost thirty cents, although Ida often talked her way into a discount.

The longest family outings occurred during summer visits to the Jersey

Shore, where Charles joined the family on weekends. Ida would rent a garage apartment a few blocks from the beach. Don and Duane built sandcastles and swam for hours. Nightfall was the only thing that prompted their departure.

Ida was a shrewd negotiator who refused to pay retail. She began by feigning ignorance about the price. After the salesperson announced the amount, whatever it was, Ida unleashed a derisive response: "Ha!" She claimed that a nearby competitor was selling the same product for much less. To the embarrassment of her children, Ida wouldn't let up until the price was markedly reduced. The boys disliked going shopping with her, but Duane would never forget the effectiveness of her methods. He learned the benefits of actively collecting information, and selectively giving it.

One extreme case of Ida's bargaining, giving insight into a personality trait of her oldest son, occurred at a clothing store in nearby Carlstadt, New Jersey. Its owner, Mutchie Marcatelli, was a longtime friend of the family acquainted with her penny-pinching ways. So when Ida inquired about a fancy coat costing $800, Marcatelli preemptively offered her 50 percent off.

Automatically, Ida said, "Ha!"

After a stunned moment, Marcatelli rallied. "Mrs. Parcells, you can have the coat. Take it as a present from me."

Ida responded, "Ha! What do you think I am? A charity case?"

Confounded, Marcatelli asked, "What do you want to pay for it?"

"I'll give you two hundred and fifty dollars."

"Sold!"

In Hasbrouck Heights, organized sports like Pop Warner football and Little League baseball were embryonic. Video games didn't yet exist, and television was just entering the picture (most channels were test patterns). With so much time on their hands, boys naturally focused on sports. By the time Duane turned nine, Army Field had given way to Cape Cod homes, and most of the town's athletic fields were near the Meadowlands, southeast of town. Duane often chose to make the hilly three-mile ride on his bicycle to a playground near Teterboro Airport. "Coming home was a bitch, pedaling up all those hills," Parcells recalls.

The alternative was playing in the neighborhood. Depending on personnel and mood the choices included curb ball, step ball, and punch ball (whacking a ball with a closed fist). The kids often just grabbed a soft red rock nearby and used it to mark out first, second, and third bases on the asphalt. The fire hydrant on Duane's side of the street was home plate. Curb ball required only the Spalding High-Bounce, a lively pink rubber ball, and, of course, a curb. "We played it all over the place," Parcells says. "You only needed two guys and a street that wasn't busy."

A perfect pitch against the edge of the curb produced a home run. Balls hitting just below that ended up as grounders, and if the defense didn't field the dribbler cleanly, a runner ended up on first base. Danny and Duane, generally on opposing teams, often had heated arguments involving the rules. "If there was a controversy, Parcells was right in the middle of it," says George Swede, whose backyard touched Army Field. "And he knew his rules."

Duane possessed excellent hand-eye coordination, while Don was the more gifted athlete, inheriting his father's physique and speed. Charles had kept his sports scrapbooks hidden away, never mentioning his athletic exploits to his boys. Aside from buying essential equipment, Charles didn't push them toward sports. Regardless, his two kids, especially Duane, fit into the town's sports-crazy culture like a hand in a baseball glove. "I loved getting up to bat," Parcells says, "or putting the ball in the bucket, or tackling some guy."

The National Basketball Association, founded in 1946, was in its infancy, and the NFL's heyday was on the horizon, so baseball, the national pastime, was Duane's favorite sport. With Charles regularly bragging about his Yankees, who had won five straight World Series titles from 1949 to 1953, Duane's rebellious streak prompted him to become a Red Sox fan. Boston was the only team preventing the Yankees' baseball hegemony.

At night Duane frequently used his Bendix radio to tune in to baseball games, unlatching the toaster-sized gadget to turn it on. While Ida and Charles thought their older son was asleep, he lay under the sheets in the dark, spellbound by the night-game broadcast. As an adult, he would use his uncanny memory to ace baseball trivia quizzes involving that era.

When Duane was nine, Hasbrouck Heights created a baseball team for kids ages eight to twelve in the Bergen County Peewee League. After tryouts Duane was named to the squad for his first organized competition. The Peanuts, who wore gray uniforms with red trim, played against neighboring towns. Their archrival was Lodi, which was slightly west of Hasbrouck Heights and a tad more blue-collar. From April to August the Peanuts hopscotched throughout Bergen County playing more than thirty games. "It was like *The Bingo Long Traveling All-Stars and Motor Kings*," jokes Parcells, referring to the blaxploitation comedy about ex–Negro Leaguers barnstorming through the Midwest in the 1930s.

Generally, Duane's teammates were as many as three years older than he was, which usually meant they were more polished. Duane, whose primary attribute as a second baseman was strong fielding, batted toward the bottom of the lineup. "I was an easy out," he says. His first hit came on a swinging bunt that produced a roller down the third-base line. "I can remember it like it was yesterday. I couldn't beat out anything, because I was so chubby. But I *did* beat it out. That's a hit; that counts. Box-score readers don't know whether or not it was a frozen rope to center field." The next year, however, Duane's hitting improved markedly, and he moved up a few spots in the lineup. By his final season he had become one of the team's best players with a .600-plus batting average, and in one game he smashed three homers.

Around that time, Duane visited Yankee Stadium for his first professional sporting event: Charles took his two boys to watch the Bronx Bombers face the Washington Senators. From the first moment Duane was transfixed. The Yankees' blue pinstripes were pristine, and the crisp, white boundary lines contrasted sharply with the emerald field. "I couldn't believe what I was seeing," Parcells says. "It was so green. I was just awestruck."

Duane experienced a similar feeling when he attended his first Giants football game on December 5, 1954, as part of a group of Boy Scouts. He watched from the Polo Grounds bleachers as New York defeated Pittsburgh, 24–3, in front of 16,856 spectators. The memory remains vivid for its pageantry: The Steelers, quarterbacked by Jim Finks, wore gold helmets and black jerseys with gold numerals. Charlie Conerly guided the Giants, in their blue helmets and matching jerseys emblazoned with white. Parcells says, "The seats weren't very good, but it was the whole display that really got to me."

The thirteen-year-old was hooked.

The tremendous popularity of television overlapped with the start of the New York Giants heyday, which ran from 1954 to 1963. The Parcells family bought their first TV set in 1950, and Duane, his bedroom festooned with team pennants, watched the New York Giants religiously. His favorite show was the team-produced *Quarterback Huddle,* hosted by Marty Glickman and broadcast on CBS. Duane sat cross-legged in front of the TV while Glickman interviewed heroes like Charlie Conerly, the winning quarterback in the 1956 NFL championship; defensive back Emlen Tunnell, the first black to make the Giants and the Hall of Fame; and defensive tackle Arnie Weinmeister, also elected to Canton despite a brief career. "It was pretty hard to be in New York in those days and not be a Giants fan," Parcells says, "unless you were Communist."

By the time Duane entered the eighth grade, two new siblings had joined him and Don: Doug was born in 1953, and Debbie arrived a year later. After three boys, Charles and Ida were especially pleased that their newborn was a girl. These new additions to the family compelled Charles to look for a larger home. He found it ten miles away in another suburban town, Oradell, a short drive to the George Washington Bridge. Charles paid almost $10,000 for the new split-level brick ranch, its driveway lined with oak trees. Like other towns in North Jersey, Oradell had been a farming community before giving way to an onslaught of middle-class families wanting to live relatively close to New York City.

"I liked Hasbrouck, but hey, there wasn't any family vote on the move," says Parcells, whose school year at Franklin Junior High was disrupted. "I was apprehensive, but you gotta do what you gotta do."

Duane Parcells began attending Oradell Junior High, where he shared a striking resemblance with a fellow eighth grader named Bill. The two were constantly mistaken for each other, but Duane didn't mind. At least "Bill" could never be confused with a girl's name. So he never corrected his schoolmates, and within a year virtually everyone except his parents called him Bill.

Ida didn't find out about the unofficial name change until she saw it in the local paper's sports section, where her son often appeared, being one of the best baseball players in summer youth leagues. Ida and Charles were more amused than angry. In college Charles himself had tweaked his first name to Charley. Duane's parents didn't force him to revert, though they continued using his given name. Occasionally Ida mocked her son by calling him Willie—never Bill.

Despite the frugal example provided by his mother, Bill Parcells was a spendthrift, constantly borrowing money from his brother Don to blow on baseball cards and accessories for his English racer bike. After Bill's freshman year in high school, his father required him to get a summer job. Bill worked as a janitor at a local junior high school, saving enough to buy a blue-and-cream 1956 Ford, even after Charles made it clear that his son would be responsible for all costs. Whenever the car had problems that Bill couldn't fix himself, it sat in the garage. Regardless, Bill continued to wash and wax it.

In the summer of 1956, William "Mickey" Corcoran was named basketball coach of River Dell High, the new regional school in Oradell that would count Bill Parcells among its students. Corcoran had played basketball at Saint Cecilia High for Vince Lombardi, who was also the school's assistant football coach. Lombardi's first year as head coach in 1939 coincided with Mickey Corcoran's sophomore season. At five-ten and 130 pounds, with a tough Irish face that made him seem bigger, Mickey was a cocksure and instinctive point guard. The coach lived one block from Corcoran's family in Englewood. Occasionally after practice, Lombardi instructed Mickey to telephone home for permission to travel to Sheepshead Bay, Brooklyn, for a meal made by the coach's mother, Matilda. On their drives into New York City, coach and player spoke mainly about strategy.

During Mickey's basketball career at Saint Cecilia, the Saints won slightly more than they lost. But Mickey experienced the genesis of Lombardi's motivational legend. A temperamental disciplinarian, Lombardi had sharp mood swings that caused fellow coaches to nickname him Mr. High-Low. Despite being Lombardi's favorite player, Mickey was often the target of his vitriol. "Tear your butt and then pat you on the butt," Corcoran recalls. "Knock you down, and then pick you up. The man understood how to handle people." Lombardi inspired Mickey to become a coach.

Months before classes commenced that fall at River Dell High, Corcoran started gauging prospective players. In the first session, Corcoran rolled out two basketballs, instructing his charges to perform layup drills at both ends of the court. At six-foot-two and 190 pounds, a sophomore stood out: Duane "Bill" Parcells was the biggest boy on the court. But the oversized underclassman also caught Corcoran's attention with his unusual behavior.

Taking a bounce pass and darting down the left lane, Bill used his left hand to kiss the ball off the glass. As he jogged to the back of the rebounding line, the blond, blue-eyed boy paused for a long moment, hands on hips, to stare at his new coach. "It was as if he was looking to give me *his* approval," Corcoran recalls, chuckling. "He wanted to know if I knew what the hell I was doing as a coach. He looked me over pretty good every chance he got."

Despite lacking speed, the über-competitive power forward was easily Corcoran's best player. He had a feathery touch, a nose for rebounds, and exquisite timing in blocking shots that more than compensated for his unspectacular leaping ability. Bill's nifty post-up moves demonstrated the agility of a smaller player.

The first time Charles Parcells picked up his son after basketball practice, he approached the new coach to introduce himself. As usual, Bill was the last player on the court, taking extra shots after practice. While Bill gathered his belongings out of earshot, Charles Parcells and Mickey Corcoran talked. Charles said, "Every once in a while, Duane gets out of line. So I just want you to know you have my permission to kick his ass if you need to."

Corcoran smiled. He had already been planning on instilling in his players the hard-nosed principles he had learned under Lombardi, but he felt further empowered by Charles's blessing. "After that I had all I needed to coach him," says Corcoran of Parcells. "His father and I were on the same page."

During the college basketball season, Mickey Corcoran took some of his players into New York City to watch the Columbia Lions and Fordham Rams play at home. Occasionally, Corcoran, well-connected with college coaches in the area, traveled with his crew as far away as West Point. At the basketball games, Bill made sure to sit next to Corcoran. While teammates relaxed, Parcells whispered questions about strategies and decisions. In almost a decade as a coach, Corcoran had never met such a cerebral player.

However, Bill also had an emotional side, which sometimes got the better of him. During one practice, when his sweet jumper turned sour, he drop-kicked the basketball at the ceiling. Corcoran yelled, "Parcells, you're gone," and Bill wasn't allowed back without an apology.

Bill's hair-trigger temper was even worse in games. River Dell faced Park Ridge during a winter contest that Corcoran's Golden Hawks led by 17 late in the first half. As a loose ball flew out of bounds, a Park Ridge player pointed at Bill as having touched it last. The referee concurred, giving possession to Park Ridge. Bill ran over and screamed in the official's face: "What are you listening to him for?" The official blew his whistle, signaling a technical foul. Corcoran reacted by taking Bill out of the game. Bill stewed on the bench as River Dell's lead dwindled from 17 to 12 to 8. "If I put him back in and we win," Corcoran explains, "he's going to have me by the balls for three more years."

Corcoran kept Bill on the sidelines while River Dell's lead evaporated, sending the game into overtime. The Golden Hawks lost by one point, and in the locker room afterward, Corcoran blasted his top player. "Parcells, you weren't worth the two points you cost us on that technical foul you drew. If you ever get another one, you're not going to play another minute for this team." Back home that night, Bill sat silent and stone-faced at the dinner table. Without finishing his meal, he headed for the basketball hoop mounted in the backyard and shot baskets in the cold.

Charles Parcells exploited Bill's obsession by requiring high grades for participation in sports. So, despite spending countless hours on the gridiron, diamond, and court, Bill forced himself to study enough for stellar grades. Parcells says of his father's academic condition: "It was kind of like the sword of Damocles was hanging over my head. I was the Damocles of northern New Jersey."

In Coach Corcoran's two-hour practices, ninety minutes were spent on defense. Corcoran preached that a strong defense allowed a team to successfully compete against opponents with superior talent. River Dell players who didn't demonstrate intensity on defense didn't last on Corcoran's Golden Hawks. He believed that zone defenses were relatively ineffective, so the team played man-to-man exclusively, and players were schooled to fight through picks. A sharp strategist who often seemed one step ahead of his counterparts, Corcoran explained to his team that every game contained the key to triumph. Finding it was the difference between winning and losing, so he stressed tireless preparation for specific game situations.

One of Corcoran's coaching gifts was diagramming plays without providing superfluous information that risked overloading his players. Perhaps the best example occurred during a game in Bill's junior season. The score was tied late in regulation, and River Dell had possession when Corcoran called a timeout with eight seconds left. In River Dell's huddle, Corcoran told Bill that he would get the ball at the extended foul line, the imaginary line from the free-throw line to the sideline.

Then River Dell's coach broke down the play. He anticipated that the defender of the offensive player throwing the pick would slide over to guard Bill. After Bill received the ball, Corcoran added, another defender would attempt a double-team. "He didn't say another word," Parcells recalls of Corcoran. "My job was to get the ball in the basket, but he solved a lot of problems for me: *how* I'm going to get the ball and *where* I'm going to get the ball. That's great teaching, and great motivation."

Bill came off a screen as scripted, catching the ball on the wing with his back to the basket. He turned around before the double-team could get there, and splashed a jumper over the shorter defender who had switched on the screen. The Golden Hawks erupted in jubilation at the game-winning shot. As word of Bill's exploits got around town, he began hearing comparisons to his father. His interest piqued, Bill asked his dad about his storied past.

Charles turned cryptic. "That's ancient history." So Bill poked around and discovered his father's old scrapbooks, with news clips detailing Charles's three-sport stardom at Hackensack High. Bill knew that his father had played college football at Georgetown, but he was surprised by the degree of his success. A photo in the *New York Times,* published October 28, 1934, showed the sinewy and elusive halfback darting past a defender to gain nine yards on rain-soaked turf at Yankee Stadium. At the future home of the New York Giants, roughly 15,000 spectators had witnessed Charles Parcells set a school record for punt returns: 197 yards.

Given his long hours and commute to Manhattan, Charles Parcells didn't attend many of Bill's games. Regardless, the corporate lawyer was so concerned about placing undue pressure on his son that his rare appearances stayed under wraps. Coach Corcoran occasionally snuck Charles in through a field-house door before tipoff, and Charles took a seat that minimized his chances of being seen by Bill. "I didn't know it at the time," Parcells says, grinning, "but he was in cahoots with Mickey Corcoran so I wouldn't know when he was at the games."

Charles played dumb as Bill became one of the top scorers in Bergen County. There was only one occasion when Charles made pointed remarks about his son's performance. After Bill's uncharacteristically lackadaisical play against an inferior opponent, the Golden Hawks lost by 12 points. Charles told Bill, "If you're gonna go down there and do that, you might as well give up the game." Bill was stung, but he saw his dad's point.

"He was coaching his son to be somebody," Parcells says, "to be motivated, to not be an excuse-maker. The expectations were that you were to work hard. You don't get notoriety or medals for that. That was his expression. 'You don't get any medals for trying. It's results that count.'"

Charles's laid-back persona masked his high standards. Even as Bill excelled in school or sports, his father warned his boy: "Success is never final but failure can be."

He had regular sayings, many of which he coined, to highlight life lessons for his children.

When Charles heard too much whining, he said: "The complaint department is on the fourth floor." The family, of course, owned a three-story home. Detecting self-pity, Charles responded: "Too bad, so sad." When things turned irrefutably gloomy, Charles provided perspective with wry humor: "It's always darkest before it goes pitch-black." If a friend did something stupid or offensive, Charles explained the reason for keeping that person in his circle: "A friend is someone who knows all about you, and likes you anyway." Charles, whose duties included contract negotiations with his company's union, often explained away inanity: "Never discount stupidity as a factor, because it's always in there somewhere." He considered inflexibility to be a human failing, and stressed the importance of being open to alternative ideas: "It doesn't cost you anything to listen."

Charles used these maxims so often that Bill memorized them, decades before he spread them to the NFL and beyond. Bill retained a few sayings from Ida, too, mainly Italian proverbs. After Bill did something inappropriate for the umpteenth time, she'd say, *"Il lupo cambia il pelo ma non il vizio,"* which means, "A wolf may change his fur but not his bad habits."

Despite his many positive attributes, Charles, of course, had imperfections. Of these, the biggest was binge drinking. Charles joined Alcoholics

Anonymous, but complained to his family and close friends about the organization's name: "It's one word too long." In a six-degrees-of-separation town like Oradell, plenty of people knew of his personal demons.

An admirer of his dad's smarts and strong will, Bill was confounded by Charles's struggles with the bottle. "My dad was very remorseful after he drank. I asked him to explain it to me several times when he was sober," Parcells recalls, "and he had a difficult time." As he tried to overcome his alcoholism, Charles warned his oldest son, "Don't go there. Don't start. It's dark, and it's miserable."

Don Parcells lacked his brother's overall passion for sports. While Bill starred in the three sports, Don was lukewarm about baseball and basketball. "He couldn't throw it in the ocean in basketball, but he could play defense," Corcoran recalls. "If I said to Don, 'You're playing this guy tonight,' he'd shut him down. He was quick as a cat." Don preferred track, where he thrived in the sprint and quarter-mile. But powerfully built at six-foot-one and 190 pounds, he enjoyed football almost as much as his brother did.

Although Bill was built like a lineman, his take-charge personality helped earn him the starting quarterback role for River Dell. The head football coach, Tom Cahill, was a disciplinarian who advocated a strong running game. In Bill's senior season, his younger brother Don earned a varsity spot as a sophomore. Blending speed and toughness, Don was named starting fullback late that same season. One of Bill's favorite moments in high school occurred against Ramsey High. Late in the scoreless game, Bill handed off to his brother deep in Ramsey territory. Don barreled up the middle and bowled over a linebacker before shifting into high gear for the winning touchdown.

"I couldn't believe what I saw," Parcells says. "He looked like a missile. I would have rather have had him than pretty much all of my teammates."

Being married to a Bergen County sports legend didn't spur Ida Parcells's interest, and she rarely attended her children's games. An exception occurred on Thanksgiving Day in 1958. River Dell football served as part of the traditional family gathering. So Ida sat in the stands with her husband. She barely understood the basics of football, yet she knew enough to cheer as her son Bill orchestrated a drive, with Don contributing, that placed the Golden Hawks near their opponent's goal line. "Of course, having viewed that one game, she knew *everything* about football," Parcells recalls, chuckling. "She could collect information quickly."

As usual, Coach Cahill sent in the offensive play from the sideline. But this time, after assessing the defense's formation on third-and-goal, Bill ignored the coach's orders. His quarterback audible was executed poorly, and River Dell failed to score. When Bill returned to the sideline, the coach beelined over to his quarterback. Aware of Bill's parents seated right behind the Golden Hawks' bench, Cahill wrapped his right arm around Bill's shoulders and redirected him so that the two faced the field.

"Bill, the next time you make a call like that, your fat ass is going to be on the bench for the rest of your career, which fortunately isn't too much longer."

"But, Coach, I saw something in the defense."

Cahill snapped. "Dammit. When I tell you to run a play, you run it!"

When Ida saw her son later that night, she said, "Wasn't that nice of Coach Cahill to console you like that?"

During the late 1950s, Vince Lombardi, now offensive coordinator of the New York Giants, moved from Englewood to nearby Oradell, just a few blocks from the Parcells family. Big Blue's assistant coach became casual friends with Charles, and Bill often played football with Vince Jr. at a local playground. Some of Bill's pals were tight with Lombardi's son, and used the connection to obtain Giants tickets, but Bill never received any free-bies. However, Vince Jr. did give Bill a face mask that belonged to Giants fullback Alex Webster. Elated by the gift, Bill wore it in pickup football games at the park.

A neighbor with Giants season tickets took Bill to the 1958 playoff classic between the Giants and Browns. Bill's vantage for the Snow Game was behind Yankee Stadium's 344-foot sign. He went bonkers after Pat Summerall, a future friend, won the game, 13–10, with the improbable 49-yard field goal. Bill couldn't land tickets for the iconic championship game between the Giants and Colts, so he accepted an invitation to join high school friends ice-skating at Lake Hopatcong in Jersey. But while his pals ice-skated during the cool afternoon, Bill left to access his car radio nearby. He sat in his '56 Ford for more than three hours, riveted by Marty Glickman's play-by-play. When the Colts prevailed 23–17 in overtime, Bill started to cry. He was mute the rest of the day. "I died," he recalls.

After World War II, semiprofessional baseball became popular in the tri-state area. Local teams traveled to South Jersey and New York City. Most semipro players ranged in age from their late twenties to early thir-ties, but after completing his junior year at River Dell High School, Bill was already one of the area's best players. Skilled at pitcher, catcher, and first base, he considered himself good enough to join their ranks. One day, after watching the Oradell Raymonds taking batting practice, the sixteen-year-old approached their player-manager, Larry Ennis, to inquire about joining the team.

Having watched several of River Dell High's baseball games, Ennis was familiar with Bill's abilities, mainly as a catcher. So Ennis didn't hesitate to make the teenager the youngest player on the Raymonds. Despite his age, Bill earned the starting job at catcher thanks to his sure hands, quick release, and powerful arm. "He wasn't interested in dominating players not as good as he was," says Ennis. "He wanted a challenge, and he related to the older guys real well." Bill was reminded of his age the first time the team went out drinking after a game and Ennis told the bartender, "Just Cokes for this guy." By the end of the season, though, the kid was batting cleanup.

"If he was coming out of high school now, he would never be in football," Corcoran says. "He would have signed a *huge* baseball contract. What a prospect he was. Holy cow."

The Philadelphia Phillies considered signing him out of River Dell in the summer of 1959. One of the club's scouts invited Bill for a tryout as a catcher. But Charles nixed any possibility of a Major League contract. He told his son: "You are definitely going to college. When you get out of college, if you want to go play, you can go play. Not now."

Parcells says of his father's verdict: "I wasn't on the same page, but I understood what he was saying."

Although college baseball scholarships were atypical at the time, Seton Hall—prodded by Corcoran—tried to entice Bill by offering him a chance to play two sports, baseball and basketball. But Bill had zero interest in attending college in the metropolitan area, which included Fordham, from which he had also received a basketball offer. Bill wanted a football scholarship, discouraged by his father's ban on professional baseball without a degree.

Bill was recruited by football powerhouses such as Auburn and Clemson, but he turned them down after Charles encouraged him to focus on schools with the highest level of academics. Bill looked into the Ivy League before accepting a scholarship offer from Colgate, a small school in upstate New York with a sterling academic reputation. One factor in his decision was a desire to remain in the Northeast, but not too close to home.

Ida gave her son an elephant figurine as a going-away gift. She instructed Bill to place it facing his bedroom door, so that the statuette could bring in prosperity and happiness.

2

Bill Parcells packed his belongings into his 1954 Ford Fairlane, and drove to Colgate University, reaching the rural town of Hamilton, New York, in half a day. Colgate's football program lacked the cachet of others that Parcells had turned down, but the Red Raiders offered something he found intoxicating: a relatively tough schedule in Division I, with occasional games against ranked teams. As a member of Colgate's freshman team, Parcells scrutinized the varsity, coached by Alva Kelley, and often attended their games.

When the season began, he quickly discovered the downside of a demanding schedule as the Red Raiders lost six straight before eking out a 16–13 victory against Bucknell on November 7. The following week, Syracuse humiliated Colgate, 71–0, behind sophomore halfback Ernie Davis, who would lead his team to the national title. The Red Raiders didn't earn their second victory until the season finale at Brown, Alva Kelley's previous team. By this point, Parcells regretted his decision to attend Colgate. "I hated the place," he recalls. "I was looking around all the time and thinking the same thing over and over: 'These guys don't want to win.'"

Parcells joined Colgate's baseball team, playing catcher in the spring of 1960. Late in the season, he was contacted by the same Philadelphia Phillies scout who had tried to sign him out of high school. Charles happened to be on campus, visiting Bill. When he learned of Philadelphia's renewed interest, Charles reiterated his position: a college degree had to come first.

With baseball still on his mind, Parcells returned to Oradell for his summer break. After greeting everyone, Bill told his six-year-old brother, Doug, to grab a Wiffle ball and bat for some backyard action. Although Doug was a natural right-hander, Bill Parcells taught his sibling to bat lefty. "His thinking was this: if I hit lefty instead of righty, I would save a step and a half running to first base," recalls Doug Parcells, who has an athletic complex in Oradell named after him for decades of service as the town's recreation director. "And that was it. I was converted. To this day I can't even swing a bat right-handed, all because of Bill and that step and a half. He also thought it would be better because, hitting lefty, the right-hander's curve came in to you."

After agonizing about whether he should return to Colgate for his sophomore year, Bill drove back to Hamilton, New York, for football camp in the fall of 1960. But it took only two practices to confirm his distaste for the Red Raiders program. He quit the team and the school. That same day Bill returned to Oradell and sought out Mickey Corcoran, who scolded his former star for relinquishing a football scholarship without having an alternative.

When Bill dropped the bombshell on his parents, they got upset.

Charles asked, "What are your plans now?"

Deadpan, Bill replied, "Join the marines."

Charles was in no mood for wisecracks. "You either go back to school somewhere this semester, or my financial support ends right now."

Corcoran made several exploratory phone calls on Bill's behalf, including one to Wichita State University. "I've got this young man who can play, if you think you might want him." After Corcoran described Bill's stellar history at River Dell High, Wichita head coach Hank Foldberg agreed to provide the former Colgate student with free tuition and books for one semester, if he tried out for the football team. Bill Parcells left the Northeast for the first time since he was four years old, unaware that he wouldn't move back to the Garden State for nearly two decades.

The largest city in south-central Kansas, Wichita was a magnet for young people in the area, yet to a Jersey native it felt alien. Wichita players were formally known as Wheatshockers, although virtually everyone called them "Shockers." Given that his scholarship hung in the balance, Bill decided to set aside his baseball dreams and focus on making Wichita's football team. In the Missouri Valley Conference, the Shockers faced schools with well-regarded programs such as Arizona State, Boston College, New Mexico State, and Tulsa. By joining the Shockers, Parcells would be competing against some of the nation's top players, including several NFL prospects.

The player who was once recruited by top teams like Alabama and Clemson easily earned a spot on Wichita's roster. Parcells only practiced with the Shockers during the 1960 season as their new coach, Hank Foldberg, guided the school to an impressive 8-2 record, including going undefeated, 3-0, in the conference.

Freshman Judy Goss and a friend were strolling across campus one day when Goss's female companion discreetly pointed out Bill Parcells. "I think he's cute. Don't you?"

Goss agreed. "Hmm. He *is* pretty cute."

The feeling was mutual. Parcells had spotted Goss at a student party the previous week but hadn't yet mustered the nerve to approach her. When he discovered that she worked part-time as a secretary in the school's sports information office, he began regularly stopping by her desk to chat on his way to the locker room. Although Goss wasn't into football, the two found an excuse to speak almost daily. Their conversations, occasionally flirtatious, led first to dating, and then to a serious relationship.

Goss stayed close to her man as much as possible. She and a female friend became WuShocks, the team's twin mascots, wearing a black outfit with a shock of wheat as headgear. "We just ran around, jumping up and down, acting like cheerleaders," Judy recalls. "I got into it because Bill was playing football."

As the Shockers set out to repeat their previous year's success, Parcells's versatility made him a key backup. Being one of the team's biggest athletes at six-two and 235 pounds, Parcells played mostly offensive tackle, defensive end, and linebacker. Once again the Shockers won eight games while going undefeated in the conference, earning them a place in the Sun Bowl at El Paso, Texas. It was only the third bowl game in Wichita's history, and its first since 1948. Although the Shockers lost to Villanova, 17–9, in a game televised nationally on ABC, Parcells was delighted with his first experience in big-time college football.

On learning that Bill Parcells had never even been on a horse, teammates decided that he needed to culturally assimilate. A group of players took him to a ranch rodeo near Tulsa, Oklahoma. This was no cowboy bar with a mechanical bull; it was the real deal. Despite his death grip on the animal's bucking rope, Parcells lasted only a moment, far short of the eight-second standard, before being violently tossed off. Fortunately for the bull-riding wannabe, the animal's horns had been blunted, limiting its goring ability. But, as Parcells recalls, "that sonofabitch could have killed me. I was off in about three seconds. Those were the days: I thought I could do anything."

Parcells even thought that he could outwrestle a bear. The cockamamie idea came to him one day when he was walking down a street in Wichita. Following the sounds of hooting and hollering, he came upon a crowd of spectators gathered around a makeshift boxing ring. Parcells couldn't believe his eyes: a man was fighting a brown bear that weighed several hundred pounds while people cheered. The bear had no claws, and a muzzle covered his mouth, yet the encounter was still lopsided.

The reason for this insanity? A nearby sign made it clear: "Pin the bear, win a new car." No longer the owner of a vehicle, and without funds to buy one, Parcells lingered. The rules declared that the first contestant to lift the ursine off his hind feet, or pin him on the mat, would win the car. In superb condition at 235 pounds, Bill felt he had as good a shot as anyone. So he signed up and was scheduled to fight a few days later.

Parcells spent much of the next forty-eight hours in the crowd, scouting his future opponent. Before every match, to the audience's delight, the bear guzzled Coca-Cola from a sixteen-ounce jar given to him by a handler. Far more interesting to Parcells was one contestant who came close to winning by wrapping his arms around the bear, although he couldn't quite lift the animal off the ground. Parcells considered himself fortunate to be fighting the bear at night, when it was probably tired after a full day in the ring. However, the new car didn't go to the big, blond, curly-haired football player; he gave it his all, but he couldn't quite pin the bear.

After deciding to earn money in a saner way, Parcells took a part-time job managing Pizza Hut, a new restaurant near campus. The original Pizza Hut soon moved to a new location across the street from Wichita State's campus. Unlike its current incarnations, this was a full-service restaurant with a menu that included beer, pasta, salad, and sandwiches. Since the establishment kept staff to a minimum, Parcells became a jack-of-all-trades: bartender, cook, host, waiter. The restaurant did a brisk business, and its young manager impressed his bosses with his business savvy and strong work ethic.

Coming off two impressive seasons guiding the Shockers, Hank Foldberg was lured away by Texas A&M and replaced by Marcelino "Chelo" Huerta. The new coach put Parcells on the first unit in his junior season and named him co-captain. On the gridiron, Bill behaved like a coach himself, giving teammates pointers while exhorting them. However, an avalanche of injuries contributed to Wichita's going 3-7 and winless in their conference. The team's struggles made Parcells cantankerous for most of the season, but he still found ways to have a good time.

Wichita's football players often boxed for fun, using a makeshift ring in the women's basketball gym. In these sparring sessions Parcells was known for a quick left hook that made teammates reluctant to go against him. But his dance moves outside the ring gained even more notoriety. The Shockers kept a phonograph in the trainer's room, which abutted the locker room, and players often listened to their favorite songs while changing. Just before spring practice in 1961, Bill put on a 45 rpm record of "The Twist." He had learned the dance in Oradell while on summer break following his first year at Colgate. As the catchy music blared he introduced the Twist to his teammates, saying, "Chubby Checker does this at the Peppermint Lounge in New York City."

"Of course, a lot of us Midwesterners, we hadn't even seen it," recalls Ron Turner, Wichita's former end, selected by Philadelphia late in the 1962 NFL draft. "It's kind of hard to imagine him doing the Twist there in his jockstrap in the locker room, but he was quite the dancer. He was a little overweight, but he was well-coordinated and a really good athlete."

. . .

Now an upperclassman, Bill Parcells was considering following in his father's footsteps by attending law school, but the physical education major also felt a powerful tug toward athletics. Mickey Corcoran was an exemplar of coaching as a livelihood, and Parcells wanted to remain active in sports. "I'd always liked the life," Parcells says. "I used to bitch about practice, but the truth is I wouldn't have known what to do with myself without it once my classes let out."

Meanwhile, Bill was having a stellar senior season as the Shockers went 7-2 and captured a share of the Missouri Valley championship. Parcells was among the top players on a team ranked second in the nation in total offense. His most impressive game occurred in Wichita's season finale, on November 30, 1963, versus conference rival Tulsa. Parcells led the Shockers to an upset victory, 26–15, against a team that included quarterback Jerry Rhome and wideout Howard Twilley, who would become one of the best tandems in college football history before going on to noteworthy NFL careers.

Parcells harassed Rhome all afternoon, finishing the day with four sacks and twenty tackles, many near the line of scrimmage, while smothering Tulsa's running game. It was among the best defensive performances in Division I that season. "You can hit someone hard on every play," says Len Clark, a former Wichita defensive tackle, "but there's a difference between hitting someone hard and punishing them. Bill punished Tulsa that day."

After the season Parcells was named to the College All-Star team, a group of the nation's top seniors scheduled to face the defending NFL champions. He also earned an invitation to the Blue-Gray Classic, which showcased seniors, often NFL prospects, whose teams failed to make a bowl game. Amid the accolades, the Detroit Lions selected Bill Parcells as an offensive tackle in the seventh round of the 1964 NFL draft. The event lasted twenty rounds, making Parcells today's equivalent of a late third-round choice. The NFL consisted of only fourteen teams, and Parcells was the eighty-ninth player selected out of 280 prospects.

That year's draft was unusually flush with talent. A record eleven future Hall of Famers were selected, including Florida A&M wideout Bob Hayes, who went to the Cowboys one spot ahead of Parcells. Two future Hall of Famers were chosen *after* Parcells: Cleveland picked Morgan State tailback Leroy Kelly in the eighth round. And because of a five-year naval commitment, Heisman-winning quarterback Roger Staubach wasn't selected until the tenth round (128th overall).

Four Shockers were drafted, including quarterback Henry Schichtle, Parcells's fellow co-captain, who rewrote Wichita's passing records before going to the Giants in the sixth round. "I was sick," Parcells says, half-jokingly. "That was *my* team. I kept thinking, 'Why couldn't it be me?'"

December 3, 1963, a local newspaper in Wichita published a story headlined "Five Shockers Picked in National Grid Draft." The article came with a photograph of each Shocker: Parcells—shown from the waist up—had curly blond hair and grinned in his number 70 jersey. The other teammates were receiver Bob Long (fourth round, Packers) and tackles David Klein (fifth round, Browns) and Steve Barilla (twentieth round, Lions). Long would become a key player on Lombardi's Packers who made pro football history by winning three straight championships, including the first two Super Bowls, in 1967 and 1968.

A month after being drafted, Parcells decided against playing in the Blue-Gray Classic in Montgomery, Alabama, since it fell too close to Christmas. Instead, he focused on the second annual Challenge Bowl: the National All-Stars versus the Texas All-Stars on January 4, 1964, in Corpus Christi, Texas. The game featured the best players from Southwestern states, particularly Texas, versus top seniors in the rest of the nation. Parcells describes the Southwest Challenge Bowl as being "kind of a second-class all-star game." But among Parcells's teammates was Ohio State fullback Matt Snell, who would go on to play a key role in the Jets' iconic 16–7 victory over the Baltimore Colts in Super Bowl III. Parcells considers Snell to be that game's true MVP, not quarterback Joe Namath, for amassing 121 rushing yards on 30 carries in the ball-control offense of the Jets.

Al Davis of the Oakland Raiders coached the National All-Stars; the Texas contingent was guided by Frank "Pop" Ivy of the Houston Oilers in an event that used AFL coaches because of sponsorship by the upstart league. As an avid Giants fan, Parcells knew little about the AFL, which was in its fourth year of existence. But at practice for the National All-Stars, Parcells was fascinated by his first exposure to a pro coach. With his dark, slicked-back hair, Al Davis stalked the field and barked instructions with a gravitas that belied his slender physique. His distinct voice combined an adopted Southern accent with his native tongue of Brooklynese. Parcells clung to every word while scrutinizing Davis's mannerisms.

Earlier that year, Davis, who grew up in the Flatbush neighborhood of Brooklyn, had been lured from the Los Angeles Chargers. The thirty-three-year-old was the youngest person in the history of professional sports to simultaneously hold the positions of coach and general manager. Davis's Raiders leapfrogged to a 10-4 season after their previous record of 1-13, earning him the AFL's award for Coach of the Year.

During a Wednesday practice, five days before the 1964 Challenge

Bowl, Bill Parcells broke his right hand. The linebacker didn't seek treatment until the next day, when it swelled "like a baseball under my goddamn skin." Parcells had assumed that he had broken a bone, but the team doctor discovered he had fractured four. Parcells was a starting linebacker, so Davis needed to know his status; without Parcells, Davis would need to fly in another player as soon as possible.

Davis walked into the trainer's room where Parcells's arm was being set in a cast, and asked, "You gonna play, or not?"

The doctor interjected, "I wouldn't play if I were you."

Parcells replied firmly, "Oh, I'm playing."

Davis smiled tightly, pleased by his linebacker's resolve. Parcells, twenty-two, viewed the Challenge Bowl as the coda to his college career, and couldn't imagine missing it just because of a few broken bones. He was also motivated by income: $800 for each member of the winning team, and $600 to the losers. Players who sat out weren't paid. It was good money, especially for a recent college graduate whose wife was pregnant with their second child. Besides, Parcells, who'd wed Judy in 1962, wanted to spend as much time as possible around Davis. After an intense practice, the Raiders coach stopped at the team hotel lobby to relax, plopping into a free seat next to Parcells. The moment gave Parcells the opportunity to talk football with Davis for almost an hour. "From then on," Parcells recalls, "I was hooked on him."

Parcells played with typical ferocity for virtually the entire game while wearing the cast. Matt Snell rushed for four touchdowns as the National All-Stars won, 66–14, at Buccaneer Stadium. Afterward Al Davis slipped an extra hundred dollars into Parcells's pocket.

Before graduating from college in the spring, Bill Parcells gave Pizza Hut notice that he was quitting with an eye to coaching. Dean Pryor, Wichita's backfield coach, had been named head coach of Hastings, a tiny college in south-central Nebraska. Pryor had told Parcells that if he didn't make Detroit's NFL roster, he should join Hastings's four-man staff as a defensive assistant. It already included Don Boyette, Parcells's ex-teammate at center, as an offensive assistant. The salary was meager at $3,000, and the seasonal job involved only six months of work. But as Pryor pointed out, the gig provided the start to a coaching career one notch above high school. Parcells was delighted to have the opportunity in his pocket.

Impressed with Parcells as an employee, Pizza Hut tried to reverse his decision to leave. Dick Hassur drove in from Topeka, where he had opened its first franchise in 1959, and promised Parcells an annual salary of $15,000, plus the lucrative possibility of owning a franchise within five years, which could lead to a princely income of $100,000. Flattered by the offer, Parcells told Hassur that although he enjoyed working at Pizza Hut, football was his passion. And assuming he didn't make the NFL as a player, Parcells planned to leave for Hastings. "It's funny how life turns out," Parcells says. "I probably would have been a millionaire by the time I was thirty. Who knows?"

Bill Parcells reported to the Detroit Lions training camp in the summer of 1964, hoping to make the team as a guard. The Lions, a good club during the early 1960s, were coming off a 5-8-1 season with extenuating circumstances: Detroit's star defensive tackle Alex Karras and Packers halfback Paul Hornung had been suspended indefinitely for placing bets on NFL teams. The league also fined five of Karras's teammates $2,000 each for betting on games in which they didn't play. The gambling controversy cast a pall over a team that in 1962 had gone 11-3, including a Thanksgiving rout of the title-bound Packers.

After several practices, Parcells believed that he was making a solid showing, but with time running out on Dean Pryor's offer, Bill needed a candid breakdown of his chances. "I had to survive," Parcells says. "I needed to know what I was going to do." Parcells explained his situation to George Wilson, Detroit's head coach, who told him to wait until the final preseason game, more than a month away. Bill phoned Judy in Wichita to convey Wilson's equivocal response. The rookie decided to remain with the Lions for a few more practices. But on July 22, Parcells bolted camp after a morning session, two weeks before Detroit's first preseason game against the Redskins. He was allowed to keep the $2,000 signing bonus from his $10,000 contract.

Looking back, Parcells describes himself as being "just average" for an NFL prospect. Although he was versatile, smart, and tough at six-three and 240 pounds, most NFL players were a notch above him. "I wasn't overly big, and certainly not overly fast," Parcells says. "I was just kind of an in-between guy who played several positions. But when it got down to doing something specific consistently well, I just didn't have enough ability." As a seventh-round pick of the 1964 draft, Parcells was a sure bet to make the AFL, where his former teammate, Miller Farr, flourished after going undrafted by the NFL. However, the upstart league was still years away from its heyday. After long discussions with family and friends, Parcells determined that chasing a pro career was too risky financially. Except for stars and top draft picks, NFL salaries weren't yet astronomical. "I shouldn't say 'security' when talking about coaching," Parcells says about his decision, "but that's what it was."

Before reconnecting with Judy and their toddler, Suzy, in Wichita, Parcells phoned Dean Pryor to accept the coaching job at Hastings. Packing would be simple: the school couldn't afford to pay its football assistants beyond the season, so Bill and Judy would leave most of their belongings behind, where they lived, near her parents. "Contract labor," Parcells jokes. He was heading into the hinterlands of college coaching, where perhaps the town's most successful businessman owned a car and tractor dealership. "I think it was a dead heat," Parcells says, "as to whether he sold more cars or tractors."

Hastings College, a liberal arts school, had about one thousand undergraduates, and the nearby town had a population of roughly twenty-five thousand. Parcells needed to make a big adjustment not just to his new career but to an environment where, in the fall, pheasant hunting seemed to generate as much excitement as football. Invited to participate in that other popular sport for the first time, Parcells joined Dean Pryor and a local boy as they waded through a creek that reached Parcells's thighs. Pryor and the kid rousted some nearby pheasant for Bill, whose first shot struck one, sending it fluttering to the ground. Pryor encouraged him to finish the job, but Bill didn't have the stomach for it. So the boy wrung the pheasant's neck while Parcells watched in disgust.

It was the last time he agreed to go pheasant hunting.

Back on campus, the twenty-three-year-old coach embraced his new job, learning how to organize drills and formulate strategies to help players develop. "It was like a kindergarten in coaching," Parcells says. "You're learning how to do it." Only a few weeks removed from NFL training camp, Parcells was intense and hands-on. If he was displeased with his unit, he took a defender's spot on the field while Pryor ran the play again. Without pads or helmet, Parcells manhandled offensive players as he showed the defensive unit the way he wanted them to execute. "He'd just rip them apart," recalls Terry Petersen, a defensive back under Parcells.

Taking a breather wasn't permitted during or between drills. After one scrimmage play a defender came up hurting though uninjured—a crucial difference to Parcells. When the player asked to take a break, Parcells screamed, "Get this guy off the field! Get that equipment off him and put it on somebody that can go!" That fire-and-brimstone approach galvanized his players, who recognized the unusual fervor in a temporary coach. By noon, if Parcells decided that his practice plans for the day weren't sharp enough, he'd skip lunch to iron out the details. Dean Pryor was delighted by his new hire.

Hastings football consisted of some thirty players, including the twelve-man junior varsity, which Parcells oversaw. Pryor's third assistant was Dr. Lynn Farrell, the school's athletic director, who helped out with the football team until the basketball season, when he transformed into the hoops head coach. "It was a very different era," Parcells recalls. "Everybody did everything." The all-for-one ethos spurred Parcells to cut grass on the gridiron, construct lockers, clean equipment, and operate the Ditto machine, a forerunner to the photocopier. After practices, Parcells washed the team's uniforms with Cold Power. "I was a coach and I loved it," Parcells says. "I couldn't get enough."

Eager to increase his knowledge of the game, Parcells spent substantial time studying college football's heavyweights. "There were six of them," he says, "who were, like, *it*." Like most followers of the sport, Parcells was particularly enamored of Ohio State's Woody Hayes and Alabama's Paul "Bear" Bryant. "A bigger-than-life guy," Parcells recalls of Bryant. "It's hard for me to describe who that would be like today. There's no one like that." The neophyte also scrutinized John McKay (Southern California), Ara Parseghian (Notre Dame), Darrell Royal (Texas), and Bo Schembechler (Miami University in Ohio before he became legendary at Michigan). Parcells even researched Bud Wilkinson's career after the Oklahoma icon retired in 1964 at age forty-seven. "He was the king," Parcells declares.

Parcells had entered high school as Wilkinson became football royalty with 47 consecutive victories, an iconic mark set from 1953 to 1957 that has never been seriously threatened. Wilkinson's record during seventeen seasons at Oklahoma is embedded in Parcells's memory—145-29-4—the same way that Joe DiMaggio's streak remains alive for baseball fans. Bill Parcells, the man who would coin the phrase "**You are what your record says you are**," says of Wilkinson's .826 winning percentage, "That's all you needed to know."

Charles Burnham Wilkinson was also known for a 3-4 defense, often dubbed the Oklahoma defense because it was his signature. Parcells studied Wilkinson's version of the hurry-up offense, designed to "just wear your ass out."

"There wasn't any Internet; there wasn't any television," Parcells says of Wilkinson's tenure, which included three national titles and thirteen consecutive conference championships. "And for me, all the way in New Jersey, to hear about this Oklahoma coach, it was a testament to his greatness."

Judy Parcells became a stay-at-home mom while pregnant with her second child. Knowing their budget was tight and their stay only temporary, the family rented a tiny apartment on the bottom floor of a dental office one mile from the school. The rent was $62.50. "Obviously, we weren't eating steak and shrimp at the time," Judy says.

The painted cinder-block walls made it difficult to hang pictures, and the only two window wells were near the ceiling, making it difficult to glimpse the outside. The mattress took up most of the bedroom, Suzy's crib occupied what little space remained, and the low ceiling forced Parcells to stoop in order to reach the bed. "It was like living in a tomb," he says. Despite their spartan existence, Judy considers the experience in Hastings as a high point in their marriage. "We didn't have two cents to our name, but I've often said to him that it was probably our best time together," says Judy. "We were young, and didn't know any better. Life was simple then. He probably wouldn't see it that way—as our best time. I'm sure he wouldn't. But I would go back to those days."

When asked to respond, Parcells actually agrees with Judy that Hastings marked the best period of their marriage, but he offers a somewhat different reason: "We went from an uncertain path to at least knowing how we were going to be able to raise a family. Hastings was a first step toward a career path."

Parcells used the car for work, so Judy became a pedestrian much of the day, pushing Suzy in the stroller. Mother, daughter, and future child headed to one of several local parks or to the modest downtown. Judy became close friends with Dean Pryor's wife, Betty, who also had a toddler, and the two mothers often hung out together while their husbands coached.

Home games were played in A. H. Jones Stadium, capacity circa two thousand. The Broncos faced other small private schools in America's heartland with names like Chadron State, Colorado School of Mines, and Doane. Their crowning game was the Mineral Water Bowl, played at Roosevelt Field, a high school stadium in Excelsior Springs, Missouri. "But I thought I was coaching in the Rose Bowl every week," Parcells says. "Believe me." One victory would come against Colorado College, whose starting tailback was someone named Steve Sabol. As part of the postgame ritual, the future NFL Films president and Parcells documentarian shook hands with Hastings's defensive coach.

After a season-opening win, the Broncos played at home against a formidable opponent: Nebraska Wesleyan, their rival based in Lincoln, 106 miles away. In the previous season the Prairie Wolves had almost gone undefeated while capturing the conference title. Their best weapon in the red zone was a bootleg, in which the quarterback moves with the ball toward the sidelines, often after faking a handoff. Sprinting parallel to the line of scrimmage, the quarterback either runs upfield or throws a pass. The purpose of the play is to confuse the defense by moving the signal caller from his usual position behind the center, often causing defensive backs to abandon their assignments in anticipation of a scramble.

After scouting Nebraska Wesleyan's offense, Parcells focused on thwarting its favorite play. During the week leading to the game, Parcells spent a substantial part of every practice and player meeting discussing the bootleg. Primary responsibility would rest with perhaps the best Bronco: Jack Giddings, who played fullback on offense and safety on defense. Giddings was the original Bill Parcells Guy: smart, tough, hard-working. "A coach's dream," Parcells says. With Giddings anchoring the defense, Parcells was convinced that the Wolves wouldn't score in their typical fashion.

The test came early, as the Wolves drove the ball down the field and into the red zone. Near the goal line Nebraska Wesleyan turned to its favorite weapon. After the snap the Wolf quarterback faked a handoff, scampered toward the sideline, and then suddenly stopped and planted his feet to throw toward the receiver Giddings was covering. It was just what the defense had drilled for, but to Parcells's surprise—and dismay—his talented safety was out of position after biting on the routine bluff. The tight end, Giddings's man, was wide-open for the pass. Touchdown.

As Giddings jogged to the Bronco sideline, Parcells seethed. "I wanted to kill Giddings," he recalls. Not waiting for his player to reach the bench, Parcells charged toward him. Inches from the player's face mask, the coach screamed, "How many goddamn times do we have to practice something?!"

Giddings looked down at the ground.

"What does it take for you to learn?"

Giddings remained silent.

"Goddamn it," Parcells screamed. "I went over this with you."

When the two men got back to the bench, Parcells continued his expletive-filled rant until Dean Pryor walked over to his assistant. "Leave the guy alone, Bill."

"But Coach, we worked on the damn play a hundred times in—"

Pryor, voice raised, cut Parcells off. "Well, you obviously didn't go over it enough, because he didn't get it." The teachable moment was the first time that Pryor had ever scolded his assistant, and it happened in front of a bench full of players.

"That cut like a knife to the heart," Parcells remembers. "But it was one of the best lessons I ever learned." Regardless of the mistake made by a player, his coach shared responsibility for any lack of execution. The onus falls on the coach to foster an environment conducive to learning—and *retaining*—instruction. Over the decades, Parcells would convey this same lesson countless times to his coaches when they blamed a player for not following instructions.

Fast-forward almost forty years after "The Lesson." NFL legend Bill Parcells is coaching the Dallas Cowboys, when Jack Giddings telephones to touch base. Parcells doesn't even say hello.

Knowing that it's Giddings after a receptionist transfers the call, Parcells asks, "How come you didn't cover the tight end?"

Giddings retorts, "You didn't go over it enough."

"We went over it *six* or *eight* times."

"I needed *eighteen* times."

The former Hastings Broncos coach laughs, but in fact Parcells's painstaking approach may have overwhelmed Giddings. The rookie coach didn't yet realize that expounding on every complex variation of a play, and how to defend each one, was often unnecessary and even detrimental. "Time and trouble," Parcells says, "have taught me that there is a fine line between what a player can handle under pressure and what he can't."

Despite the loss to Nebraska Wesleyan, Hastings won its next four games. Parcells's defense proved stingy, especially against the run: the Broncos were allowing offenses only an average of roughly one hundred yards. With two games left in the season, Hastings remained ranked among NAIA teams.

In a contest with postseason ramifications, the Broncos played a home game against their other rival, Kearney State. The Lopers were 5-1, averaging 43 points in three previous games. Parcells's unit faced a formidable offense anchored by its top player, lineman Randy Rasmussen. One of three NFL players in Kearney State history, Rasmussen would be a Jets starting guard in Super Bowl III.

In a hard-fought affair, the Lopers defeated Hastings, 30–20, squelching any chances of the Broncos appearing in the Mineral Water Bowl. By far the most despondent member of the Broncos, the voluble defensive coach turned mute and ashen-faced. Pryor's spouse noticed that her husband's defensive assistant looked physically ill after the game. "My wife didn't think Bill would stay in coaching," Pryor recalls, "after the way he reacted to that game. It hurt him so bad to lose."

Parcells's mood improved after Hastings won its season finale to finish 7-2, a winning prelude to his coaching career. After the final game, Parcells and Judy packed their modest belongings into a six-by-eight U-Haul trailer and set off on the return trip to Wichita.

The Hastings job wouldn't come open again until nine months later, in the fall of 1965. Given the paltry salary and the impending arrival of a second daughter, Dallas, returning to Hastings seemed unlikely. Parcells fantasized about landing a coaching gig that paid a living wage, but given his limited connections, this seemed far-fetched. Once again his thoughts turned to law school. As the son of an attorney, Parcells was confident about his chances at obtaining a Juris Doctor, but he figured that he should bolster his academic credentials with graduate classes at Wichita. Uncertainty about his ability to afford law school revived another option: returning to Pizza Hut. Though disappointed by his departure, the restaurant's executives had left room for Parcells to return.

"I had to do *something* to earn a living," Parcells recalls. As he mulled over his options, the head-coaching dominos that would shape his next several years brought news of an opportunity. After a 4-6 season at Wichita, Marcelino Huerta, the Shockers coach who took over before Parcells's junior year, was dismissed. Huerta was replaced by one of his assistants, George Karras, who caught wind that Parcells was back in town and contemplating grad school after a brief coaching stint. Some Shocker boosters urged Karras to hire the school's former defensive force.

Karras made Parcells an offer he couldn't refuse: a *full-time* coaching job, overseeing the defensive line and assisting with the linebackers. When word eventually trickled east to Oradell that Duane "Bill" Parcells, its high-strung former star, was embarking on a coaching career, Richard O'Toole, who had played football three years behind Parcells at River Dell High, was one of the residents bemused by the development. "Bill was a rare bird," recalls O'Toole, who played football for Brown University. "When I heard he was getting into coaching, I remember thinking he was heading into oblivion. I mean, what were the odds [of stardom]?"

The Dallas Texans were charter members of the AFL in 1960, the same year that the NFL's Dallas Cowboys came into existence. Both teams played their games in the Cotton Bowl while attempting to become the main pro football attraction in town. Although the Texans captured the AFL championship in 1962, they struggled to draw fans, even more so than their crosstown rivals. So owner Lamar Hunt relocated to Kansas City in 1963, changing the franchise's name to the Chiefs.

In the summers of 1965 and 1966, Parcells and one of his colleagues, Lew Erber, made the relatively short trip to Liberty, Missouri, where the Kansas City Chiefs held training camp at William Jewell College. The two Shocker assistants showed up to watch a pro team run its practices. Coached by Hank Stram, the Chiefs were among the best teams in pro football. And Parcells discovered teaching methods by observing his sessions, focusing on how the future Hall of Fame coach and his staff taught technique. "When you watch another man coach," Parcells says, "you come away with something."

Tom Cahill left River Dell High School in 1959, the same year Bill Parcells graduated, after being hired by Army's athletic director, Earl "Colonel Red" Blaik, to coach freshman football and baseball. The development was quite a compliment to Parcells's ex–football coach.

Red Blaik had been one of the most influential coaches in college football while guiding the Black Knights from 1941 to 1958. His team captured consecutive national championships in 1944, 1945, and 1946, but his impact went beyond a 121-33-10 record that included six undefeated seasons. Blaik mentored scores of assistants who went on to become successful coaches, including two future legends, Sid Gillman and Vince Lombardi. He was among the first college coaches to implement a two-platoon system, with one unit playing strictly offense and the other defense. Blaik also pioneered using game film to chart an opponent's tendencies, examining every snap.

In May 1966, Blaik elevated Cahill to head football coach after Paul Dietzel, discouraged by the institutional constraints of coaching at Army, left abruptly for South Carolina, taking five assistant coaches with him. Given a one-year contract, Cahill scrambled to fill several vacancies. The obscure head coach and his new staff, however, guided the Black Knights to a surprising mark of 8-2, capped by a victory over archrival Navy. Both losses came against nationally ranked teams, Notre Dame and Tennessee. More important, Cahill had led Army to its best season since Blaik's 1958 team went undefeated. The development was a dramatic turnaround after two seasons slightly under .500. Cahill was named college Coach of the Year, and rewarded with a multi-year extension, which also covered most of his staff.

Nevertheless, Bob Ward, Cahill's defensive coordinator, who doubled as the unit's line coach, accepted the top job at Maryland, his alma mater. One of the best linemen in Terrapin history while playing both ways from 1948 to 1951, Ward succeeded Lou Saban.

Knowing Cahill's need for a replacement entering the 1967 season, Mickey Corcoran telephoned his former basketball lieutenant. "I've got the perfect guy for you."

On hearing Parcells's name, Cahill reacted with silence. He knew first-hand that Parcells had been one of the best and smartest athletes in Bergen County, and his brother, Don, had graduated from West Point in 1965 after three seasons playing football for the Black Knights. But Cahill was also familiar with Parcells's hyper personality. The coach had flashbacks of the hotheaded forward who kicked basketballs when things didn't go his way, and the cocksure quarterback who occasionally ignored sideline instructions. He could only assume that Parcells, twenty-five, lacked the maturity to coach, especially at a program like Army's, which emphasized leadership and disdained recalcitrance.

After the brief pause, Cahill said, "Bill Parcells? Gee, I don't know. Why do you think I should hire him, Mickey?"

Corcoran responded incredulously to his fellow Irishman. "Why? Do you have to ask, Tom? Billy's one of us! He's a Jersey guy!"

Cahill wasn't convinced, so he mulled things over for a few days while Corcoran continued to prod. Finally, he agreed to take a chance on his former quarterback, naming Parcells Army's new defensive line coach. The team's youngest assistant, Parcells would be among colleagues who possessed extensive experience, in sharp contrast to his situations at Hastings and Wichita.

Just before the beginning of each season, Army's coaches spent two weeks on a retreat at Bull Pond, a fishing camp in a mountainous area eight miles southwest of campus. The tradition had begun in the 1940s, when Red Blaik arranged the getaway for his staff, some military brass, and a handful of sportswriters like the renowned Red Smith of the *New York Herald Tribune*. From late July to early August, the campers slept in a two-cabin compound that included a mother lodge. They gathered nightly to view team highlights and movies on a projector. Despite the emphasis on relaxing and bonding, substantial time was spent discussing the upcoming season.

A perennial guest was Tim Cohane, the author and former sports editor of *Look* magazine. During the 1948 retreat, Cohane convinced Blaik to interview Vince Lombardi, a fellow Fordham alum and obscure assistant coach, for an opening at offensive line coach. Cohane had been the school's publicist when Lombardi played for the Rams. The writer kept on attending the annual get-togethers even after Blaik retired as coach a decade later. Erudite, with a gruff personality, Cohane didn't go long without lighting up a pipe or tucking into a glass of scotch.

Parcells had always been intrigued by the written word. And with access to a top sportswriter, he wanted to exploit the opportunity to get pointers. One afternoon, Bill was getting ready to go for a swim in the pond when he spotted Cohane on a stationary raft alone, reading a book. Seizing the moment, Bill swam out to the barge and clambered on board.

Parcells interrupted Cohane: "Tim, I want you to teach me to write."

Cohane glanced up at Parcells, grunted, and kept on reading.

Parcells waited for a moment and reiterated: "Why don't you teach me how to write?"

Realizing Parcells's sincerity, Cohane said, "All right, go back to the cabin and write me something about Bull Pond."

Parcells excitedly swam ashore and got to work. The writer wannabe used several fancy adjectives from the strong vocabulary that had helped get him into Colgate. He put great thought into describing the nearby mountains and picturesque scenery in extensive detail. After a few hours, Parcells was satisfied with the two pages filled with purple prose.

He returned, taking care to keep his handiwork high over his head as he side-stroked back out to the raft. Handing Cohane the handwritten sheets of paper, Parcells silently awaited Cohane's verdict.

Cohane grunted every few seconds as he read, which Parcells considered a bad sign. His pessimism was confirmed when Cohane shook his head, and said, "This is horseshit!"

Parcells felt crushed.

Cohane, still reading, added, "Now, it's punctuated correctly and all, but it's horseshit."

"Why?"

"You're not telling me anything. Be precise, direct, and to the point. Why did you come here?"

"To have a good time with my friends."

"So go to your cabin and don't come back until you've written about that. The first sentence should say something like: 'Bull Pond is a place where I go each summer with my friends.'"

Parcells went ashore to revamp his essay. He kept the flowery sentences to a minimum before returning to the raft a couple hours later.

Cohane didn't grunt while reading Parcells's second take, offering some tepid praise.

"Well, that's better."

It was a nonfootball lesson Bill Parcells would never forget: be straightforward in written communication just as well as with the spoken word.

. . .

Some of Cahill's concerns about hiring Bill Parcells surfaced early, even as the Black Knights won their first two against Virginia and Boston College. Parcells drove his players harder than any other Army football coach. He concedes that he was "impulsive, aggressive—maybe a little off the reservation," but fellow coaches reined him in.

Still, Parcells's strengths, including his high energy and ability to galvanize, trumped his flaws. Ultimately, Parcells's unit performed well, reassuring Cahill that he had made the right decision in hiring his former quarterback.

The players related to Parcells, who was only a few years older than some of the upperclassmen, yet his demanding style and captivating persona helped affirm his authority.

Just as he had at his previous jobs, Parcells had a habit of lining up for snaps to aggressively demonstrate what he was looking for. Defensive linemen hung on to Parcells's every instruction and strove to gain his trust. The Black Knights relished playing for him, despite his tendency to be harsh. "They aspired to be Bill's guys," recalls Steve Yarnell, a former defensive lineman who became one. "Bill had something about him: magnetism, personality. You're drawn to him."

The charismatic coach was consumed by his job. Following a 10–7 home loss against Duke on October 7, Parcells sat by himself on his living-room sofa, scowling. Suzy, now four years old, walked in and climbed up next to her dad. But Parcells was beyond even the reach of his cuddly daughter. So Suzy contorted her face, imitating his grimace.

Mickey Corcoran visited from Jersey to see how Parcells was faring. While watching football practice, Corcoran took pride in the fact that Parcells exuded command and leadership, even through the inflection in his voice. The once-rebellious high school star was a natural teacher. Corcoran smiled as he watched Parcells get down in the dirt to demonstrate for his players. River Dell's coach left West Point impressed by Parcells and pleased that his recommendation was panning out.

Army's student-athletes faced exacting academics and military training, so the maximum daily time allotted to football, except for games, was ninety minutes. Although this constraint posed a challenge for Army's coaches, it ensured that little time was wasted on the field; Cahill's staff focused on the most important matters. "It taught me that I probably did better with less time than I did with more," Parcells says. "It forced you to decide on what exactly was important, and I always remembered that. A lot of coaches say, 'More [time] is always better.' I found that not to be true as I matured as a coach."

As the Black Knights won six straight, Parcells's outlook on special teams shifted dramatically. An adherent of Blaik, Cahill stressed special teams more than his counterparts did. Despite a tougher schedule, Army again went 8-2, dropping its finale to Navy. And Parcells saw the significant difference a strong special teams unit could make. Perhaps the quickest way to revitalize a program, he realized, was by strengthening special teams.

The Black Knights were invited to play in the Sugar Bowl, but the Pentagon reiterated its stance barring Army from any postseason games. The Vietnam War was dividing the nation, which apparently factored in Army's decision not to embrace the spotlight of a bowl game. The Pentagon said that permitting the Black Knights to play "would tend to emphasize football to an extent not consistent with the mission of the academy, which is to produce officers."

After the season, Army hired two new assistants, Al Groh and Ray Handley, who helped the varsity in spring practices and coached the plebes in the fall. Cahill continued to generate accolades for being a stellar leader, but at one point he responded to all the praise by saying, "What is a great coach? A great coach is somebody who has good assistants, and is smart enough to let them coach."

In this environment, Parcells learned the importance of a strong supporting cast. He considers his Army stint to be his formative coaching years, describing the decade that followed as the "gypsy years, the blur years."

Bill Parcells and his family lived on Bartlett Loop, a row of brick buildings that housed Army's coaches, their names on green boards outside the front doors. Parcells, Judy, and their two girls shared a duplex home in a two-family housing unit. For Judy, West Point represented the first time she had lived away from home. Except for the harsh winters, the Kansas native enjoyed the military culture and scenic surroundings along the Hudson River.

Charles and Ida Parcells weren't far away—only about forty miles, or less than an hour by car. On rare occasions, they attended Army home games. But it was only after the season ended that Judy, her spouse, and the kids visited Oradell for relatively long stretches, giving her a chance to better get to know her parents-in-law. Like virtually everyone who met them, she was intrigued by the sharp contrast in personalities. Judy had never been around any woman like Ida, whom she found to be "volatile" and a bit intimidating. Judy concluded that her husband's personality came from Ida. "She would give you the shirt off her back if you asked her for it," Judy says, "but she never let you forget it, either."

During the summer, Parcells visited Peekskill Military Academy, where the Jets held training camp. To reach Peekskill, a small town in Westchester County, Parcells and his colleagues took Bear Mountain Bridge over the Hudson River. They made the trip for the opportunity to observe the AFL team coached by Weeb Ewbank and quarterbacked by Joe Namath. Parcells enjoyed scrutinizing one of pro football's top coaches. Ewbank had led the Baltimore Colts to NFL championships in 1958 and 1959. His first championship came in the so-called greatest game ever played, the overtime thriller against the Giants that so devastated Big Blue fans, including one high school student in Oradell, New Jersey, glued to his car radio.

In 1963, Bobby Knight, a recent graduate of Ohio State, accepted a job as an assistant coach for Army's basketball team. Knight's talents were so prodigious that in two years he was promoted to head coach at the age of twenty-four. When Parcells joined Cahill's staff, Knight was entering his third season as head basketball coach. Although Parcells lived around the corner from Knight, they first met in West Point's main gym, where Bill was playing a pickup basketball game that included some of Knight's assistants. After a break in the action, Knight and Parcells were introduced to each other, and right away realized they were kindred spirits.

Like Parcells, Knight had starred in high school basketball, baseball, and football before attending college. Knight, who was only one year older than Parcells, accepted a basketball scholarship from Ohio State. One of his professors was Woody Hayes, who taught a popular English class in addition to coaching the Buckeyes football team. Knight was a backup forward on the Ohio basketball team that captured the 1960 NCAA Championship, led by future Hall of Famers John Havlicek and Jerry Lucas. Although basketball became his primary focus, Knight still loved football, just as Parcells remained passionate about basketball even after his decision to coach on the gridiron. Knight wanted to talk football, Parcells hoops. Both coaches remained avid baseball fans, giving them a tie-breaking topic for vigorous discussions.

They became fast friends. Ambitious, with type A personalities, Knight and Parcells both seemed to take defeat worse than their counterparts. When Army's basketball team lost a home game, Knight usually visited Parcells at home, remarking half-jokingly that he wanted a place to hide. The two stayed up late, discussing key aspects of the game. Knight saw Parcells's analytical mind as a valuable asset. The basketball coach was impressed by Parcells's ability to deconstruct the athleticism of hoopsters as well as gridders, and his painstaking attention to detail.

The two bright twentysomethings studied their top contemporaries and shared an appreciation for sports history. Parcells was impressed when Knight spoke about the impact on him of three gridiron greats: Red Blaik, Vince Lombardi, and Paul Brown. Knight was born in Massillon, Ohio, where Brown had coached high school football during the 1930s before becoming the most innovative and influential coach in pro football history. "The Thomas Jefferson of football," says NFL historian and documentarian Steve Sabol. "You can say George Halas is the George Washington: he founded the league. But Paul Brown gave the game a scope and a shape, a language and structure."

One afternoon Knight invited Parcells to the Catskill Mountains for dinner with basketball coaching great Clair Bee. The septuagenarian was in retirement after an influential career, highlighted by a historic run at Long Island University in Brooklyn. From 1931 to 1951, Bee's team had won 83 percent of its games, setting an NCAA Division I record. But his overarching contributions included the 1-3-1 defense and the three-second rule. At dinner with Bee, Parcells noticed a striking shift in Knight's behavior. Army's outspoken basketball coach said little and listened raptly. Mostly he asked questions, prompting further insights from Bee. When the evening came to an end after hours of conversation, Knight thanked Bee profusely for his time.

The friendship between Knight and Parcells grew as they spent time together: Knight's basement or Parcells's living room provided the backdrop for conversations that ran deep into the night. They assessed the methods of coaches in all sports and traded ideas about subjects like motivation and strategy. Maniacal about preparation, the two Army coaches agreed that the mental aspect of any game was just as important as the physical. Knight espoused the same philosophy that Corcoran had passed on to Parcells in high school: defense and playing smart maximized the chances for victory. "You'd better guard 'em," Knight stressed. "And you'd better take good shots."

Parcells enjoyed watching Knight conduct practices, noticing that Knight avoided using some traditional basketball drills. Knight explained that he only used drills that he believed truly served a purpose, regardless of what was popular with other coaches. Parcells found Knight's contrarian outlook smart and bold, especially for a young coach.

Despite his youth, Knight was already one of the best coaches in Army basketball history. Following his rookie season, when he guided Army to eighteen victories, he was courted by Florida, but decided not to go. Still, Knight only signed one-year contracts, which gave him the most career flexibility. In the spring of 1968, Wisconsin offered Knight a higher-profile head coaching job when John Erickson left to become general manager of the NBA's Milwaukee Bucks. Upon returning from his visit to Wisconsin, Knight went to Parcells's house, where the two men discussed the new opportunity into the early morning. By the time Knight headed home, Parcells was convinced that his pal would resign as Army's head coach.

Indeed, Knight had all but done so, after asking Wisconsin not to reveal his decision until he informed his superiors. However, when Wisconsin leaked news that Knight would be its new coach, he telephoned the school to officially decline. Parcells was delighted that Knight was signing his fourth one-year contract with Army, knowing it meant he'd be spending more time with his buddy.

They often played pickup basketball at West Point's main gym, with its upper-level track encircling the courts below. Because there were so many participants, the contests were typically half-court, make-'em-take-'em, with the winner being the first team to score ten baskets. Among the regulars was Arthur Ashe, who joined West Point in 1966, fulfilling his military service after graduating from UCLA as an ROTC member. Ashe oversaw West Point's tennis program while competing as one of the world's top players. Parcells also played hoops with Major Norman Schwarzkopf, an academy instructor in his early thirties.

In their early games, Parcells and Knight played on opposite sides. Having similar physiques, they ended up defending each other, two aggressive players who knew how to exploit their size in the paint. Their matchup often devolved into heated arguments over disputed foul calls. So, in time, they hatched a plan to consistently play on the same team: One of them would volunteer to be one of the two "captains" who picked players. Knight would make Parcells his first choice—or vice versa.

During the mid-sixties, America's involvement in Vietnam was expanding under President Lyndon Baines Johnson, and by 1968 Army's head coaches faced an increased challenge in guiding their sports programs. Opposition to the war had reached a fever pitch. Students occupied buildings on college campuses, and protesters around the nation were chanting, "Hey, hey, LBJ, how many kids did you kill today?" The acrimonious atmosphere made athletic recruiting more difficult than ever for the Black Knights, and it hadn't been easy before: along with academic requirements similar to those of the Ivy League schools, West Point required a five-year commitment to the military. Parcells supported Knight by occasionally traveling with him on recruiting trips.

Meanwhile, Don Parcells faced far graver concerns, deep in the jungles of Vietnam, where he was serving as a captain in the Twenty-Fifth Infantry. One night his brigade came under heavy mortar fire, forcing him into a foxhole, where shrapnel tore one of his legs open. Bleeding profusely, Don knew that he would die soon without a miracle in the form of a rescue helicopter reaching him. It materialized within a few moments, and a medical officer on board applied a tourniquet to Don's leg as the chopper lifted off to get him further treatment.

Don recovered from about ten shrapnel wounds, and after returning to the United States he was awarded the Purple Heart for soldiers wounded or killed in battle. Don then served as an instructor at Fort Sill, an army post in Lawton, Oklahoma, where he lived with his wife and infant son. "I'm very lucky," Parcells says, "that I didn't lose him in Vietnam."

Several officers with ties to the football team aided the coaching staff. Major Joe Bishop, a physics instructor and former Black Knight, worked closely with Parcells. Only six years younger, Parcells enjoyed his time with the major, whom he considered part of the staff. But on July 17, 1968, Bishop left for Vietnam to fulfill a tour as an operations officer. A few months later, Parcells was saddened to hear that Bishop had died on September 19 after his military aircraft crashed in Nha Trang, a coastal city of South Vietnam. When the accident occurred, Bishop's combat group was returning from a field inspection. Parcells thought about Bishop every day. The tragedy reinforced Parcells's appreciation for just how lucky his brother had been to survive his combat experience.

Bill Parcells couldn't help but be influenced by West Point's culture and rich history. He relished Army's structure and gained a deeper appreciation of the military experience. Formally established in 1802 after playing a key role in the Revolutionary War, West Point became the nation's first and most prestigious service academy. Its alumni, "The Long Gray Line," included Presidents Ulysses S. Grant and Dwight D. Eisenhower, as well as several renowned generals from Robert E. Lee to George S. Patton. Six years before Parcells arrived, the central campus was designated a national landmark, with its imposing monuments and neo-Gothic architecture, including spired buildings and barracks surrounded by massive stone. During somber funerals for soldiers at West Point, planes roared above the ceremonies. Parcells and Judy enjoyed watching the cadet parades. Their patriotism, already strong, only increased.

Army's offensive line coach, Bob Mishak, a West Point graduate who had played for Blaik, recommended a bestselling war novel to Parcells: *Once an Eagle* by ex-marine Anton Myrer chronicled an Army officer's rise from cadet to general, overcoming countless obstacles by sticking to his values. Published in 1968, the 1,312-page book became a classic among military personnel. Parcells was particularly taken with a passage about inflexibility, perhaps because it eloquently expounded on his father's adage **"It doesn't cost you anything to listen."** Parcells memorized it for future use. **"Inflexibility—it was the worst human failing; you could learn to check impetuosity, you could overcome fear through confidence and laziness through discipline, but rigidity of mind allowed for no antidote. It carried the seeds of its own destruction."**

In the late 1960s, football scouting required teams to exchange their game films, and each school assigned a coach to the task. Parcells was Army's film-exchange coach, and the person holding the job for Navy was a scout named Steve Belichick, who was more than twenty years older than Parcells.

Belichick was a graduate of Western Reserve, where he had played fullback under Bill Edwards in a single-wing offense that emphasized the position. On graduating in 1941, Belichick used his connection to Edwards, the new Detroit Lions coach, to land a job as the team's equipment manager. When the Lions struggled early, Belichick made the case that he was just as good, or mediocre, as the Lions' fullbacks, so Edwards signed the five-foot-eleven, 193-pounder for the rest of a season. Belichick mostly blocked for All-Pro runner Byron White, the future associate justice of the Supreme Court. But one of his professional career highlights was a 65-yard punt return for a touchdown against the Giants. About a decade later, Steve Belichick would name his newborn son, Bill, after his ex-coach, partly in gratitude for being granted the opportunity to live his NFL dream.

Following that one season, Steve Belichick left football to serve in World War II, after which he coached at Hiram, Vanderbilt, and North Carolina. Steve Belichick joined Navy's Midshipmen in 1956, when he gave up coaching to specialize as a scout. In 1962, he penned *Football Scouting Methods*, which became a classic in the profession. That year, Steve's ten-year-old son, Bill, started analyzing game film with him. "I'm sure if he had been a fireman," Bill Belichick says, "I would have been pulling those hoses behind him." Bill Belichick spent substantial time with his dad at the Naval Academy in Annapolis, Maryland. During the early 1960s, its star quarterback, Roger Staubach, enlisted the boy to catch his passes. Gradually, Steve's son assumed various duties for Navy's program with the blessings of its coaching staff.

The Army-Navy Game, which dates to 1890, codified one of the most enduring rivalries in college football. Traditionally the annual contest marked the season finale for both service academies. Plenty of scouting went into the game, which occurred at a neutral site, usually Philadelphia because of its equidistance to West Point and Annapolis. Through numerous interactions, Steve Belichick and Bill Parcells came to know and like each other. Both men were diligent and indefatigable in their jobs. Parcells noticed that Belichick showed unusual expertise in special teams, especially the kicking game. Professorial in his spectacles, Steve Belichick often wore a blue baseball cap emblazoned with "N" in gold. His precocious son met Parcells while traveling with Steve on scouting trips.

On November 30, 1968, at Philadelphia's John F. Kennedy Stadium, Army defeated Navy 21–14, concluding a 7-3 season.

During the NFL season, the Green Bay Packers, coached by Charles Parcells's former neighbor Vince Lombardi, were televised weekly in New York State. So on Sundays, Bill Parcells went over to Knight's basement to watch their games. During one telecast Lombardi, angered by Green Bay's shoddy tackling, yelled: "What the hell is going on out here?!" Knight started to use the line on his players long before Lombardi highlights would turn it into a famous phrase.

Early in 1969, Bill Parcells visited Bobby Knight's basement to watch Super Bowl III. The pre-merger contest pitted the New York Jets, the AFL champions, against the Baltimore Colts, the NFL champions. As a Jersey native, Parcells was rooting for the Jets, whose training camps he attended in the summer. Knight was going for the Colts, largely because of Tom Matte, an ex-quarterback at Ohio State who had become a Pro Bowl runner for Baltimore. When New York started to move the ball early behind runner Matt Snell, Knight and Parcells looked at each other and agreed that an upset was possible. But the coaches didn't talk much, engrossed in what would be one of the biggest upsets in sports history.

Parcells was spending so much time around Knight that he was turning into a de facto basketball assistant. After football season Bill scouted upcoming basketball opponents in the New York metropolitan area, including Fordham, Rutgers, Seton Hall, and St. John's. Knight provided Parcells with instructions on what to look for. And the football coach turned basketball scout attended the games, took notes, and reported his observations back to Knight. The hoops coach dubbed his volunteer assistant "Walter" because of Parcells's fondness for the name of a high school basketball scout in New York City, Walter November. "Walter" even attended Army's road games when his schedule permitted. In one game he got so frenzied that he constantly elbowed Knight by accident, which resulted in his being banished to the end of the bench, next to Knight's son Tim.

On February 14, 1969, Parcells was back in his usual seat next to Coach Knight when Army visited Rutgers in New Brunswick, New Jersey. Cahill, who had known Knight since the early 1960s, also attended the critical game at the College Avenue Gymnasium. A small number of cadets sat at the end of the bench, additional support for their school in hostile territory. Behind their tough point guard Mike Krzyzewski, a senior and captain instructed not to shoot, Army was pushing to reach the National Invitation Tournament (NIT). At this point in time the National Collegiate Athletic Association (NCAA) Tournament invited only twenty-five teams to play, leaving plenty of strong contestants hoping to play in the NIT at Madison Square Garden. And occasionally a top team spurned the NCAA's invitation. Knight had already guided his teams to two of Army's four NIT appearances.

The College Avenue Gymnasium, nicknamed "the Barn," was set up with balcony-style seating on three sides of the court. The fourth side, opposite the benches, had no seats. That quirky setup gave the 3,200-seat arena one of the most intimate settings in college basketball. "A band-box gym," Parcells says. In a physical, defensive battle, Rutgers prevailed 49–47. Several fans rushed the floor, precipitating a skirmish involving cadets, spectators, and Rutgers players. Order was restored only after police officers got involved.

Army's players headed to the tunnel as fans booed and heckled. One spectator, leaning from an overhang, threw a punch at Knight, barely missing the stone-faced coach as he walked, oblivious, toward the visitors' locker room. But Parcells, a few steps behind Knight, saw the swing, so he cocked his fist and sent the fan reeling. Parcells kept walking, but after Knight finished his postgame comments to his players, Parcells came over to him and whispered, "I've got to talk to you."

Knight directed Parcells to a quiet corner.

"Listen, while you were walking off the floor, some guy took a swipe at you. He missed, but I reached up and punched him. I think the cops are coming after me."

Knight instructed his players to surround Parcells as Army's group left the building. Parcells crouched within the cluster of basketball players while cadets lined the perimeter, and everyone walked to the team bus. "We got him out of there with his own honor guard," Knight jokes.

Spending so much time with Bobby Knight only strengthened Bill Parcells's desire to become a head coach. Parcells would keep absorbing the best methods and habits whenever and wherever he could, in order to reach that goal.

4

The war continued to disrupt recruiting by Army's Black Knights. In 1969, Cahill's team dropped to 4-5-1, his worst record in four seasons as head coach. With formidable teams such as Nebraska, Notre Dame, Penn State, and Tennessee on Army's schedule, the future looked bleak. After the season, Florida State head coach Bill Peterson courted Parcells to join the Seminoles, one of the better programs in college football, coming off a fourth consecutive winning season.

On taking over in 1960, Peterson had propelled Florida State to prominence, going 55-38-11 with four bowl appearances before he contacted Parcells. At a time when college offenses tended to be conservative and run-oriented, Peterson used a wide-open passing attack. But, being a colorful character, he was known almost as much for his frequent malapropisms: "We're going to throw the football come high or hell water." Or, "We're not going to be any three-clouds-and-a-yard-of-dust kind of team."

For all his mangling of the English language, Peterson was spot-on in hiring coaches on the rise. The large group included Don James, who would make his mark at the University of Washington, after being Peterson's defensive-backs coach, then defensive coordinator; Bobby Bowden, the future Florida State legend, who was wideouts coach from 1963 to 1965; and Joe Gibbs, decades before NFL glory, who oversaw the offensive line from 1967 to 1968.

Peterson targeted Parcells as another outstanding young coach and urged him to fill an opening overseeing Florida State's linebackers. Despite enjoying his time at Army, where he had been elevated to defensive coordinator, Parcells was drawn by the opportunity to work for a big-time program without institutional constraints. Though reluctant to part from his pal Bobby Knight, Parcells left Army to join the Seminoles for their 1970 season. While the Black Knights continued a downward spiral that led to Cahill's dismissal, Florida State enjoyed a 7-4 season as Parcells continued to grow in his profession. He learned important things from offensive-line coach Al Conover, an energetic and affable twenty-nine-year-old who showed an uncanny ability to maximize talent, especially by using props.

Just before a November 14 game versus Virginia Tech, Conover homed in on the Hokies mascot, the Gobbler. As Peterson gathered the more than fifty players for their pregame talk, Conover slipped out and returned with a wild turkey, which he unleashed in the room. The gobbler strutted around wide-eyed as the Seminoles howled in delight. "He would go to the far reaches to provide motivation," Parcells recalls. "This turkey was in there, walking around, bobbing its head. Half the players had never seen one before."

The motivational madness paid off as the Seminoles trounced Virginia Tech, 34–8, on their way to another winning season. Despite spending only one year on the same staff as Conover, who would leave for Rice, Parcells was influenced by him. Florida State's linebackers coach saw how Conover balanced toughness and geniality to spur his linemen, adjusting the mix to fit their personalities. That uncanny knack was one that Parcells intended to develop. "He could be a taskmaster and he could be a teacher," Parcells says of Conover. "He also could be playful and have some fun with the players. I liked that."

After the season, Steve Sloan joined Peterson's staff as an offensive coordinator. From 1962 to 1965, Sloan had played quarterback for Bear Bryant at Alabama, mostly backing up Joe Namath until the sensation entered the 1965 AFL and NFL drafts. One of Sloan's top wideouts was Ray Perkins, and the talented tandem helped Alabama capture national championships in 1964 and 1965. The Atlanta Falcons, an expansion team, selected Sloan near the middle of the 1966 draft. And after a brief career as a backup, the former All-American returned to Alabama in 1968, when Bryant hired him to oversee quarterbacks. The position placed Sloan on the radar as a promising college coach. Knowing Sloan's ties to Bryant, Parcells frequently grilled the twenty-seven-year-old about his experiences under the football demigod.

At Florida State, Parcells became close friends with the team's wideouts coach, Dan Henning. The Bronx native was easier for Parcells to relate to than most Floridians. During the off-season Henning went with Parcells to visit his parents in Oradell, New Jersey. One afternoon Henning and Parcells went off to play golf and didn't get back until after Ida fell asleep. The next morning, she roused them from their beds.

"So where were you boys last night, and what the hell were you doing?"

Her son explained that they'd gone out for a few drinks after golf. Henning remembers thinking to himself, "We're grown men—with kids." Later, when Ida wanted intelligence from Parcells about her other kids, she demanded his presence in the kitchen and closed the door. Henning sat in the living room, worried about his buddy. Ida didn't open the door until she was satisfied with her son's information. "The only thing that was missing," Parcells says, "was the lamp that interrogators shine in your face."

Around this time, Parcells read Bill Libby's *The Coaches*. The 247-page volume profiled seventy-two coaches in sports ranging from auto racing to track and field. Parcells had already studied a handful of the college football coaches highlighted, such as Bear Bryant, but the book also interviewed coaches like Red Auerbach, Paul Brown, Leo Durocher, Mike Holovak, Tom Landry, Vince Lombardi, Billy Martin, Ara Parseghian, Adolph Rupp, Bill Russell, Casey Stengel, and John Wooden. The book jacket teased, "In their own words, the men who have to call the shots tell what it takes to survive in the world's most insecure profession." The preface detailed the job's unique challenges, and pressures, while describing seemingly every style and persona, including the religious, the fraud, the laid-back, and the dyspeptic; Parcells, who perhaps fit in the latter category, was so stirred by the preface that within days he laminated a condensed version. "Once I read it," Parcells explains, "I knew I needed to keep that for the rest of my life."

Steve Sloan, Florida State's offensive coordinator, moved to Georgia Tech for a year at the same position before being named Vanderbilt's head coach in 1973. At twenty-eight years old, Sloan, who seemed destined to replace Bear Bryant, was the youngest head coach in college football. And his clean-cut looks made him appear to be even younger. While Sloan was assembling a formidable group of coaches, Parcells telephoned him to express interest in overseeing Vanderbilt's defense. Sloan regarded his former colleague highly and gladly gave him the job. Rex Dockery, a sharp offensive coach, came with Sloan from Georgia Tech as Parcells's counterpart.

During the first half of the twentieth century, the Vanderbilt Commodores were one of the most dominant teams in the South. Home games took place at 34,000-seat Dudley Field, the first stadium below the Mason-Dixon Line built exclusively for football. The head coach for most of that stretch, Dan McGugin, was an innovator revered by followers of Southern football who retired in 1934 with a .762 winning percentage. But those glory years were a distant memory by the time Steve Sloan, a native of Cleveland, Tennessee, arrived. Football was no longer emphasized at Vanderbilt like it was at other Southeastern Conference schools. Facing fierce weekly competition from teams like Alabama, Auburn, Georgia, and Mississippi, the Commodores were coming off their thirteenth consecutive losing season, finishing 3-8 under Sloan's predecessor, Bill Pace.

The academically rigorous school, with alumni that included two vice presidents of the United States, had targeted Sloan to turn things around.

The new staff faced a herculean challenge trying to lift a football program stuck at the bottom of the SEC. Parcells's duties included running the off-season conditioning program, which spanned six weeks. Strength-and-conditioning coaches didn't yet exist. Parcells was chosen because the staff felt that he was best suited for the job. Other assistants were given responsibilities including film exchange, recruiting, and high school relations.

The first thing Vanderbilt players noticed about their new defensive coordinator was his demeanor: it was as if he was looking for a fight. The day before spring practice commenced, Parcells made an unprecedented request of Reno Benson, the student equipment manager. Parcells told Benson, "Listen, we start working out tomorrow. Get me some five-gallon buckets with sand, and set them in each corner of the gym."

"What are we going to do with them, Coach?"

"Don't you worry about that. They'll be used."

While Benson positioned the buckets around the main gym at the McGugin Center, several players asked Benson what they were for, but the equipment manager was unable to enlighten them. They found out within the hour, when players were rushing to the buckets to vomit from the intensity of the workout. Parcells intended to get the Commodores into optimum shape while purging the program of its losing culture. Being in top condition, Parcells preached, paid dividends in the fourth quarter. "Guys cursed him every single day," recalls ex-linebacker Preston Brogdon, whose twin brother, Paul, was Vanderbilt's tailback. "But we were a different team physically after going through it."

Parcells also caused some tears with a demanding approach that challenged the players' resolve. More than a dozen Commodores quit, unable or unwilling to handle the increased demands. "Football's not for everybody," says Parcells, who ran weekly boxing sessions for players. "It's a hard game; it requires sacrifice. You've got to have some toughness to play it."

A few days into the off-season program, Parcells introduced an activity he'd picked up at Florida State that he believed would foster toughness: stick fighting. As the Commodores gathered around a ring to watch the first two contestants, Sloan observed and Parcells, whistle dangling from neck, served as referee. He patrolled the ring to cajole, police, and determine a winner, but virtually no rules existed beyond one simple goal: gain sole control of the stick. Occasionally the combat was so fierce that it ended with broken noses and black eyes. The winner was permitted to depart and head to the showers; the loser was forced to remain in the ring to face the next contestant. When a fight went on too long without a result, Parcells declared a tie and sent both players out of the ring winners, a nod to their competitiveness.

The Darwinian contest occurred every Thursday, following a forty-five-minute workout for conditioning and agility. Stick fighting after an intense workout, Parcells believed, taught the Commodores never to quit on the gridiron. He even goaded the equipment manager into practicing: occasionally Parcells inserted Reno Benson into the scout team offense to take snaps versus the first-team defense. And the fact that Benson wasn't a player didn't exempt him from running wind sprints at the session's conclusion.

"Really, it was a blessing," Benson recalls. "I loved every minute of it."

Steve Sloan spent much of the off-season program observing his new players and checking on their grades. Then he called for a team meeting at the McGugin Center. In preparation for the gathering he had instructed Benson to paint three bricks: white, gold, and black. Each one was placed on a table in front of the meeting room at the facility's lower level.

Sliding the white brick forward, Sloan told his players, "This first brick represents some of you guys who go to class and get up in the morning for team breakfast. You show up, but when you come over here for the off-season program, we can tell that football is not important to you. We've already lost some white-brick guys: you're doing the right things, but you can take or leave football. I don't want a lot of these white bricks."

Sloan pushed the next brick forward. "Now, you guys that this black brick represents, you're doing exactly what we want in football. You love the game; you love the off-season workouts, and the competitiveness of this program. And that's good. The problem is that a lot of you are cutting class, you're missing breakfast, staying out late, drinking, and messing around. You're not doing the right things off the field, and I don't want that either."

Sloan slid the final brick toward his players. "Now, this gold brick here represents the guy that goes to class, he's doing the right thing, he's using his tutors, and his grades are good. He's well-rounded. He comes over here in the afternoon for the off-season program and he's busting his tail; he's lifting those weights, he's competitive, and he loves football."

Sloan concluded with emphasis. "I want twenty-two of these gold bricks."

After the speech the coaches headed back to their offices on the upper level. As Sloan walked up the stairs, his defensive coordinator trailed him. When they reached the top of the staircase, Parcells said, deadpan, "Hey,

Steve, all of those black bricks you got on offense? I'll take them over on defense if you'll give them to me."

Sloan recalls of Parcells: "He had a lot of funny one-liners, and believe me, he could fire them off one after the other, using the humor to soften his sarcasm and criticism." So despite Parcells's combative style, many players, including those on offense, gravitated toward him. He could be fun to be around when in the mood. Occasionally after practice, Parcells instructed a player to find four teammates interested in half-court hoops. The three-on-three contests were based on rough-and-tumble Jersey rules that gave Parcells an edge: when a player went up for a jump shot, Parcells might bump him on the chest, and if the shooter cried foul, the coach would respond, "Hey, that wasn't a foul. I didn't hit you hard enough."

The hard-fought contests could go on for hours.

Bill Parcells oversaw a physical, ball-hawking 5-2 defense that befitted his personality. Rex Dockery installed a veer offense, featuring option runs that helped control the clock. Alternating at quarterback, Fred Fisher and David Lee read the movement of defensive players, and distributed the ball accordingly on pitches and handoffs. Vanderbilt's fortitude seemed to have benefited from Parcells's steps in the off-season. The Commodores uncharacteristically won two straight for a 3-2 record going into their first SEC game, a home contest against Vince Dooley's Georgia Bulldogs. On a chilly October afternoon, most everyone in the homecoming crowd of only 16,789 was painfully aware that Vanderbilt had lost twelve consecutive games against SEC opponents.

Georgia, at 3-1-1, was a heavy favorite, led by star quarterback Andy Johnson, who often dashed to the perimeter for big gains, and shifty tailback Jimmy Poulos. Any chance for an upset, or even a competitive game, rested on a strong effort from Joe "Buffalo" Reynolds, a linebacker whose athleticism made him one of Vanderbilt's best players. To Parcells's chagrin, however, Reynolds rarely maintained his intensity throughout an entire game.

In the first half, the talented linebacker confirmed the negative side of his reputation: on a crucial third-down play Reynolds's lapse permitted Johnson, a future runner for the New England Patriots, to sprint for a first down. Apoplectic, Parcells ordered the linebacker off the field. As the player trotted back to Vanderbilt's sideline, Parcells stopped him with enough force to rip the shoestring holding his shoulder pads together. Parcells gave Reynolds a tongue-lashing before the brawny linebacker slunk away to repair his equipment.

Georgia led 14–3 at halftime, thanks to Johnson's scoring run and touchdown pass. But Vanderbilt's defense responded with a strong effort in the second half as Reynolds maintained his focus and intensity. The Commodores allowed only two first downs while intercepting Johnson twice. With about five minutes left, Hawkins Golden, a soccer-style kicker, booted his third field goal, giving Vanderbilt a 15–14 lead. The Commodores held on for an 18–14 shocker as Golden finished the game with a school-record four field goals. It was Vanderbilt's first three-game winning streak since 1963, and its sole victory against Dooley's Dawgs.

The Commodores finished the season 5-6, the most victories they'd had in five years. And with players suddenly showing an unfamiliar swagger, Vanderbilt seemed poised for further improvement. "We had as much talent as other teams in the SEC," says Walter Overton, an ex-wideout who became a Tennessee Titans executive. "We just had to believe that we could win. It was all about mental toughness. That's where Sloan, Parcells, and that staff came in. They galvanized and harnessed every one of us to the task at hand."

At the outset of its next season, in 1974, Vanderbilt looked galvanized, jumping to a 2-1 start. Sloan's team faced an early gauge in its next game: home versus Florida, ranked eighth and undefeated at 4-0. For Parcells and senior quarterback David Lee, this first game against Florida as members of the Commodores held extra significance. Lee's reasons were personal, and while coaching at Florida State from 1970 to 1972, Parcells had acquired a distaste for its interstate rival: his Seminoles had lost all three games versus Florida, including a 42–13 spanking in Parcells's final season.

The Monday before the Seminoles visited Dudley Field, Parcells strung up a stuffed alligator from the ceiling of the trainer's room. As Commodore players chatted while being taped for practice, Parcells strolled in. The room quieted down before he suddenly leaped into the air and headbutted the Gator. While it swung from the ceiling, Parcells walked out of the room without a word. Players reacted with alarm and amusement.

Parcells repeated the act every morning leading up to game day.

As team captain, David Lee had developed a Friday morning ritual of stopping by Parcells's office for a chat. The morning before the big game, Lee walked in as usual.

Parcells collared him. "Lee! Come here, sit down."

The quarterback obliged.

"Is the team ready? How do the players seem to you? Are we ready to go?"

Lee responded with an anecdote from three days earlier. As team captain he had called a meeting in the players' dormitory, where, for the first time, he detailed the reasons for his personal animosity toward the Gators. A native of Pensacola, Florida, Lee had been one of the top high school players in the state. After participating in an all-star game in Gainesville as a junior, Lee and his father visited Florida's football office, where Gator coach Doug Dickey promised him a full scholarship. During his senior season, Lee dislocated his right shoulder and missed several games. When Lee returned to Gainesville for an official visit, he was stunned by Dickey's parting remarks.

"David, I'm gonna call you next week and let you know whether or not we're going to extend you a scholarship."

Lee, taken aback, said, "Coach Dickey, you've already offered me a scholarship."

Dickey responded, "I know, and I'm going to call you next week and let you know for sure."

Lee steamed. "Hey, Coach, don't call me. I can go somewhere else to play."

Hearing the story, the Commodores roared at Lee's response. When he had finished, safety Scott Winfield rose and said, "Let me tell you what the Gators did to me." And after Winfield aired his grievance, kicker Mark Adams, a Pensacola native and Lee's best friend, went next: "Well, them sonofabitches didn't even send me a questionnaire." By the time Adams finished, the dormitory rocked with whooping and cheering.

Parcells grinned. His team was ready.

The coach balled his right hand into a fist before extending it to reveal a scuffed copper bracelet.

"Lee, you know what this is?"

"Yeah, it's a copper bracelet."

"I only wear this in special, special situations. One time I wore it at Army. We hadn't beaten Navy—we beat Navy."

Parcells paused as if giving Lee time to appreciate the powers of the amulet.

"Lee, I'll tell you what I'm gonna do. I'm going to let you wear it during the Florida game."

Lee, in a polite tone, said, "Coach, I think I'll just wear my wristbands, but I really appreciate it."

Zipping pinpoint passes, David Lee guided Vanderbilt to a surprising 24–3 lead over Florida en route to a 24–10 victory at a delirious Dudley Field. Lee's vengeful tour de force dropped the Gators from the top ten in national rankings, and catapulted the Commodores into prominence for the first time in decades. Parcells's defense in a conference full of high-powered offenses had helped transform Vanderbilt. His unit played with a blend of ferocity and discipline. "They would just knock you out," Sloan says.

The unit stayed strong as the Commodores defeated several tough opponents, including Mississippi, 24–14, the first time Vanderbilt had done so since 1951. In their next game at Dudley Field, the Commodores faced Parcells's former team Army. Steve Belichick traveled to Vanderbilt to scout the Black Knights for the Army-Navy game. He brought his kid, Bill, one semester away from obtaining an economics degree at Wesleyan, where he played tight end and center. Father and son visited Parcells before the game, and the Belichicks watched Vanderbilt trounce Army, 38–14, cementing a shift in the fortunes of both programs. In a season of milestones, Vanderbilt finished 7-3-1, earning an invitation to the Peach Bowl. Seven Commodores were named to the All-SEC team, including receiver Barry Burton, who also made the All-America squad. Steve Sloan was named the conference's Coach of the Year.

The Peach Bowl pitted Vanderbilt against the Texas Tech Red Raiders, who had been ranked as high as ninth in the nation during the season. Before the game at Atlanta–Fulton County Stadium, Red Raiders coach Jim Carlen announced he would be leaving for South Carolina. But the Commodores also faced distractions: David Lee had scheduled his wedding one week before the game, based on the assumption that Vanderbilt's season would be over: the bowl invitation was only the second in school history. Also, Texas Tech was secretly courting Steve Sloan as Carlen's replacement. Coming off Vanderbilt's first winning season since 1959, Sloan was a hot commodity.

During the Peach Bowl, televised nationally on ABC, Lee appeared uncharacteristically discombobulated, and the contest, a defensive struggle, ended up tied at 6. By the time the team returned to Nashville, rumors were flying about Sloan's imminent departure. Commodore fans bombarded him with telegrams, and camped out in front of his home. To their relief, on New Year's Eve Sloan announced his decision to stay. But the following day Sloan stunned the city by reversing his decision.

Rex Dockery agreed to join him in the move to Texas Tech. Sloan also wanted to poach Parcells, but knowing his defensive coordinator's strong desire to be top dog, Sloan recommended him for the opening. Already impressed by the thirty-four-year-old assistant, Vanderbilt asked him to be its head coach. It was a great moment for Parcells, the realization of his dreams after sixteen years as an assistant, yet the defensive coordinator felt torn. Although Vanderbilt's academic credentials were a plus, the school lacked the football tradition and institutional commitment of most conference teams. Because of the distinct recruiting disadvantage in the SEC, Parcells believed that Sloan had made a shrewd move by taking a better gig after a brief, successful stint.

Parcells had a habit of speaking to himself, especially before making a big decision. And in choosing whether to lead Vanderbilt in 1975, he stood at the biggest crossroads of his career.

Parcells #1: Okay, who are you gonna beat?

Parcells #2: Well, that's the question.

Parcells #1: You gonna beat Tennessee? You gonna go down the road with ninety thousand people in the stands and beat the *Volunteers*?

Parcells #2: Probably not.

Parcells #1: You gonna beat Alabama? You gonna go into Birmingham or Tuscaloosa and beat *Bear Bryant*?

Parcells #2: Probably not.

Parcells #1: LSU?

Parcells #2: Probably not.

Parcells #1: Georgia?

Parcells #1 (quickly added): Don't even bother answering that one. You know you're not going to beat Georgia, don't you?

Parcells #2: Yeah, I know.

Parcells and his doppelgänger went through the SEC roster of teams, including Auburn, Florida, Kentucky, Mississippi, and Mississippi State. Parcells couldn't identify one program Vanderbilt would consistently defeat. The only lesser football programs were William & Mary and perhaps Tennessee-Chattanooga. Without a drastic change in recruiting trends, or institutional priorities, Parcells would not only be hard-pressed to maintain Sloan's success, but might end up with only a few wins per season. Becoming Sloan's successor, Parcells concluded, had almost no upside.

His career aspirations made the decision excruciating, but soon after the New Year, Parcells departed Nashville ahead of his family for an early start overseeing Sloan's defense at Texas Tech. The new staff included wideouts coach Mike Pope, who had coached three seasons with Parcells at Florida State, and a defensive assistant, Romeo Crennel, lured from Western Kentucky. "The next thing I knew," Parcells says, "I was in the middle of nowhere—Lubbock, Texas, is the state capital of nowhere—watching the wind blow and wondering just where the next city was, exactly."

Not long after Parcells's departure, his wife got help from some friends with what was becoming an all-too-frequent ritual: packing their belongings into boxes after the family's patriarch found a new job. Movers arrived early in the morning and spent several hours loading items into a moving van. Judy vacuumed, dusted, and mopped the empty house. "Leaving it spic-and-span," Dallas Parcells says.

By now, Suzy and Dallas had a baby sister, Jill. The three girls and the family's golden retriever, Buckles, squeezed into Judy Parcells's red Gremlin, a small two-door hatchback. Popular during the early 1970s, it looked like a sawed-off station wagon, with its two bucket seats in the front and a rear bench seat designed for three passengers. The family's three suitcases couldn't fit inside, so Judy strapped them to a luggage rack and set off on the two-hundred-mile drive to a motel in Memphis, the first of three legs before reaching their new home.

Judy had been driving for less than a mile when Suzy, riding shotgun, glanced in the rearview mirror and shouted, "Mom, the bags just flew off the car." As Judy pulled over to the shoulder, the girls looked back and saw their clothes strewn all over the road. A passing car pulled over to help, and its driver turned out to be the football coach at the local high school where Judy regularly ran on the track for exercise. Judy set off again a half hour later with the luggage secured by rope. The skies opened, and a blinding rainstorm stayed with the family all the way to Memphis. The next morning, the motel clerk told Judy that a tornado had swept through town overnight.

After another seven-hour drive, Judy Parcells arrived at her sister's home in Oklahoma City for a brief visit before setting off on the five-hour drive to Lubbock. About 150 miles out, Judy looked in her driver's-side mirror and had a horrifying feeling of déjà vu. One of the three suitcases had fallen off, although this time it stayed closed. Judy drove at a crawl the rest of the way as everyone in the car wondered what might happen next. When the family reached its new home without any more drama, night had fallen, and Bill Parcells was still at work. Texas Tech's new defensive coordinator got home late, as usual, to find that his hectic first days at work hadn't been quite as eventful as his family's wild ride.

The Red Raiders were considered just a notch below the elite football programs, although in 1973, only two years before Steve Sloan's arrival, Texas Tech went 11-1 to earn a national ranking of eleventh. The team capped its impressive season by defeating Tennessee, 28–19, in the Gator Bowl. As members of the Southwest Conference, the Red Raiders faced tough opponents like Arkansas, Baylor, Houston, Rice, Texas, Texas A&M, and Texas Christian. Sloan's new school appealed to him by being heavily invested in its football program. The home field, Jones Stadium, contained

50,500 seats, more than twice the number needed to accommodate the student body.

Parcells brought the same approach that he had used to help jump-start Vanderbilt. But several Red Raiders bristled at Parcells's hard-charging style and disparaging remarks. Upperclassmen in particular, having experienced the 11-win season, hesitated to buy into Parcells's methods. His linebacker-oriented schemes contradicted what the returning Red Raiders had been taught.

Another factor contributing to the incompatibility stemmed from cultural differences between a Northeastern-bred coach and a defense full of Texan athletes. "We didn't understand much about him when he first arrived," recalls former safety Greg Frazier. "He was very brash—what we would define as a Yankee. He really didn't quite understand how to get the most out of his boys from Texas. His idea of motivating was to embarrass you, try to goad you into doing better." Former defensive end Richard Arledge put it more bluntly. "His first year, he hated us. And in our view, he was a New York asshole. He was a grab-you-by-the-face-mask-and-degrade-you type of guy."

One incident in practice highlighted the chasm. The offense on the opposite end of the field was engaged in a spirited session; the defense was sluggish despite its coordinator's prodding. Suddenly, Parcells screamed: "You guys make me sick! Just get the hell off the field!" The defense, surprised for a moment, obeyed with more alacrity than they had shown all day. Arledge recalls, "I think he was expecting all of us to say something like, 'Coach, come on; we'll do better. Give us another chance.' Well, you never saw [so many] guys disappear so fast in your life. He just kind of stood there gasping. We were gone. It was terrible."

For the first time in his career, Parcells found himself struggling to rally his players. Before kickoff for the inaugural spring game, players milled around in the locker room or sat by their stalls. Parcells went from locker to locker, shoving each player he came across, or slapping their shoulder pads. "All right, are you ready?" The Red Raiders had never experienced anything like it; most of them acknowledged that they were ready, but Parcells was unaware of defensive tackle Billy Bothwell's habit of sitting in silence to psyche himself up. When Parcells nudged Bothwell, he rose from his seat and pushed back—hard. Caught off guard, Parcells tumbled to the floor. Defensive assistant Romeo Crennel attempted to defuse the awkward situation, saying, "I think he's ready, Coach."

As players watched to see what would happen next, Parcells picked himself up and walked past Bothwell to the next locker, where he continued to bump and slap until he had laid hands on every Red Raider.

"I really don't think he was angry," Frazier recalls, "because if nothing else, he knew Bothwell was ready to play."

During the season, however, the defense performed inconsistently as Texas Tech struggled to stay above .500. Parcells's misery increased with each loss, limiting his opportunities to show his lighter side. Unlike at Vanderbilt, where he organized basketball games with players, Parcells kept his distance off the field. He drove his Red Raiders even harder, with little to show for it.

Texas Tech finished 6-5, a doubly disappointing mark given the high expectations. An alarming number of defensive players seemed increasingly antagonistic toward Parcells. Realizing that the defensive coach's talents would be squandered if his players rebelled, Steve Sloan held meetings with the defense, especially its rising seniors, attempting to smooth things over. But the onus remained on Parcells to calibrate his approach. "He was probably trying to figure what direction to take as a coach," Sloan recalls. "West Texas was still mostly cowboys then, and it was a different kind of life than he was used to."

Despite the commanding presence on the gridiron, Parcells came across as shy off it. He disliked speaking in front of large groups and preferred to socialize with no more than two people. Parcells declined invitations to staff parties and outings, making it difficult for colleagues to penetrate his personal shield. Some coaches were surprised the first time they spotted Parcells on the tennis courts across the street from the football facility. But he became an almost daily presence, displaying a deep repertoire of shots and excellent hand-eye coordination. Sloan's staff knew of Parcells's successful football career at Wichita, but his colleagues were unaware that he remained a well-rounded athlete.

In the off-season, Ray Perkins, a wideouts coach for the New England Patriots, visited Lubbock as part of his duties scouting the western part of the country. During his stay, Perkins spent substantial time with his ex-teammate under Bear Bryant; Sloan introduced the former All-American wideout to Parcells. Perkins spoke with a Southern drawl acquired growing up in Petal, a tiny town on the bottom tip of Mississippi. He and Parcells might as well have come from different planets, but the two men were straight-talking coaches with strong work ethics and reputations for toughness. Perkins thoroughly enjoyed their brief conversation.

Entering 1976, Parcells started playing pickup basketball with the Red Raiders, interactions that brought a thaw as the coordinator and his players got to know each other better. Off the court Parcells held one-on-one meetings with several players, discussing his defensive philosophy and, for the first time, seeking their input. In the rare instances that Parcells offered wiggle room at practice—say, skipping a drill—the beneficiaries were seniors. Soon players who had tuned out Parcells realized that the coordinator was a first-rate coach. Upperclassmen went out of their way to help new teammates acclimate to Parcells's sharp edges. His zingers never stopped flying. When one underclassman cornerback kept getting burned, Parcells started calling him "Toast." But by the start of the season, players were buying into Parcells's style as much as his system. The defense showed promise as it began to shed its old habits. And its coordinator didn't hesitate to take little-used offensive players and convert them into defenders, revealing a knack for putting athletes in situations that maximized their abilities.

Texas Tech's defense turned miserly as the Red Raiders won their first eight games to once again challenge for the Southwest Conference crown. Quarterback Rodney Allison was turning into a star as Texas Tech went 10-1, reaching as high as fifth in the national rankings. The Red Raiders tied for the Southwest Conference crown, garnering an invitation to the Astro-Bluebonnet Bowl against seventh-ranked Nebraska. Texas Tech lost, 27–24, at the Houston Astrodome, but the resurgent Red Raiders still ended the season ranked thirteenth. Sloan was named conference Coach of the Year, while Allison captured MVP honors. The success affirmed Parcells's methods, cementing a reversal in his relationship with players. By now, "he really had the players in the palm of his hand," Sloan recalls. Despite the new dynamic, the unrelenting coach still struck fear in his players. When he stepped on the field or walked into a meeting room, the air seemed to get thicker.

Romeo Crennel discovered one reason that Parcells was ornery at practice. Before the coaches left their offices for one session, Crennel spotted the defensive coordinator placing a pebble inside his right sneaker, sliding his foot in, and tightly tying the laces. Parcells used the pebble as a "training mechanism" for staying alert. "Whenever I stepped the wrong way, it reminded me, 'Hey, be on top of this; pay attention,'" explains Parcells, who had started the peculiar habit at Florida State. "It was like having a little bell on your wrist: every fifteen seconds, it goes off." After practice Parcells placed the small stone on his desk with the rest of the collection· from the practice field. His choice of stone size depended on his mood.

The assertive defensive coordinator was sometimes just as hard on fellow coaches at practice when they made mistakes. "Sometimes I had to try not to be afraid of him myself," Sloan jokes. A head coach in assistant's clothing, Parcells intended to accept the next offer for the top job.

· · ·

During spring practice Parcells noticed a man sitting in the stands, scrutinizing the defense. His face was weather-beaten, and he wore a brown jacket emblazoned with a white "B."

Occasionally, when the opportunity presented itself, the man stepped forward to question Parcells about his schemes. After a few exchanges, he told Parcells in a bass-heavy drawl, "You know, you're a pretty good coach."

Seeing the stranger at practice for several days, Parcells approached him to get his name and exchange pleasantries. Gordon Wood confirmed Parcells's guess that he was a high school football coach.

Parcells said, "I notice you're here every day. Where are you coming from?"

Wood responded, "Brownwood."

Parcells knew that the central Texas town was a three-and-a-half-hour drive away. "Are you staying in a hotel here?"

"No, no. I just drive back and forth."

Parcells was flabbergasted to learn that Wood was one of the winningest coaches in the history of high school football, which was like a religion in the Lone Star State. By amassing more than three hundred victories while coaching in a sports coat and tie, Wood had become a Texas icon. Most of the wins came with the Brownwood Lions, a team he had transformed into a dynasty. Wood's stature gave him friends like Bear Bryant and Lyndon Johnson. Once, when Bryant was asked why he quit Texas A&M for Alabama in 1958, he responded, "I had to leave Texas. As long as Gordon Wood was there, I could never be the best coach in the state."

Despite a secure legacy, Wood was willing to drive almost seven hours round-trip to sit in the white-hot sun for the slim chance of gleaning something useful from an obscure defensive coordinator. Parcells had prided himself on a relentless work ethic, but Wood's actions provided an aha moment: succeeding at the highest levels in coaching required long-term zeal, although that went against human nature. "It was a revelation to me," Parcells says. "I was just a young guy, and he'd already been an established, super coach. That's what impressed me so much: he was still hustling."

Parcells struck up a friendship with the super coach, who had picked cotton as a child to support his family. Wood solicited the young coordinator's ideas while Parcells picked the older man's brain.

By 1977, players liked Parcells enough to give him a nickname, Coach Pretty, for the careful way he combed his curly blond hair. Although the moniker was affectionate, the players were too intimidated to utter it in his presence, so Parcells didn't find out about it until decades later. The Red Raiders won five of their first six games for another promising start, but quarterback Rodney Allison suffered a serious injury in the third game versus Texas A&M. The absence of the early candidate for the Heisman Trophy kept the Red Raiders from being a ranked team once again. Yet Texas Tech finished at 7-4, earning an invitation to the Florida Tangerine Bowl in Orlando, Florida, a forerunner to the Citrus Bowl. There the Red Raiders were trounced, 40–7, by Florida.

Sloan accepted his latest head-coaching offer, joining Mississippi for a return to the SEC. With change in the air, Sloan's hard-nosed defensive coordinator was courted by the Air Force Academy in Colorado Springs for its head-coaching gig. This time Parcells didn't need to talk to himself in order to figure out if he should take the gig. Despite what he knew were the special challenges of coaching at a service academy, this seemed like the opportunity he'd been waiting for.

5

At Air Force, two former Army colleagues were reunited with Parcells. Al Groh was hired as defensive coordinator from North Carolina, where he had been overseeing linebackers, including an underclassman named Lawrence Taylor starting to draw attention for his otherworldly athleticism, like once leaping to block a punt before landing on his neck and then rising unscathed. Ray Handley was already in place as an offensive assistant under Air Force's previous head coach, Ben Martin. In addition to Ken Hatfield, lured from Florida to run the offense, Parcells brought on Tom Backhus as offensive line coach. Backhus had played for Woody Hayes during the late 1960s, culminating with a 1969 Rose Bowl victory over Southern California for the national championship. After hiring Backhus, Parcells wasted no time before insisting on a favor: he asked Backhus to arrange a meeting with Woody Hayes in Columbus, Ohio. Parcells was giddy when his new assistant quickly set up the appointment with one of the six great coaches he had studied since joining the profession.

One morning early in 1978, Backhus and Parcells arrived at Ohio State's main campus, where the rookie head coach found himself seated across from a legendary counterpart. For several hours, Wayne Woodrow Hayes described his philosophy regarding staff structure, practice setup, and maximizing talent. Hayes stressed the importance of the field-position game, and urged Parcells to take great pains in preparing his team for the elements whenever it was necessary. "If you're gonna play in the Atlantic, you gotta train in the Atlantic!"

Although the sixty-five-year-old was among the best tacticians in football history, he rarely delved into strategy during the conversation. He complained that sports journalists were generally "rotten bastards" and "divisive."

The young coach sat spellbound by a peer who embodied success, power, and knowledge. "It was *heaven*," Parcells recalls. "*Heaven*."

After joining Ohio State in 1951, Hayes had built the program into a football power, capturing national titles in 1954, 1957, and 1968. Parcells was struck by Hayes's passion, even in his twenty-seventh season as Buckeyes coach.

Most of his staff members were off campus handling recruiting duties, but Glen Mason, his new outside-linebackers coach, happened to be one of the few assistants around. Occasionally, Mason, who had played the position for Ohio State the previous season, stepped into the office, interrupting the conversation with a team matter for Hayes. One time when his assistant coach walked in, Hayes said excitedly, "Mason, you ought to listen to some of this."

The squat and square-jawed coach did some considerable listening, too. He asked Parcells several questions about his personal and professional background. Hayes showed patience and grace, in stark contrast to his off-campus image as someone whose occasional rages on the field revealed a dark side, and had even prompted game suspensions.

Time flew by for both men, so the Ohio State coach suggested dinner at a restaurant roughly one mile away. Despite bitter-cold weather, Hayes decided to walk. Parcells worried about freezing, but his companion, wearing a red short-sleeve shirt and a matching tie, seemed oblivious to the temperature. Hayes was known for acts of self-flagellation: pacing the sidelines during a football game, he would occasionally bite into the heels of his hands until they bled. The habit was even more masochistic than Parcells's pebble in his right shoe.

Patrons stared at Hayes when he entered the restaurant, which featured a framed picture of him on the wall. Over dinner Parcells marveled at Hayes's polymathic range as the older coach offered informed opinions on the economy, politics, war, and pop culture. "People thought he was a Neanderthal," Parcells says. "But he was well-read, and politically astute." Hayes particularly enjoyed military history that detailed battlefield tactics, and devoured biographies of American generals. Finding parallels between football and war, the amateur historian sprinkled his gridiron speeches with military terms and quotes from George Patton. Hayes even named a passing scheme after Curtis LeMay, the air force general who served in World War II.

After a long day in Hayes's presence Parcells hadn't had his fill, so the young coach requested permission to return to campus the next morning for one last conversation before heading to the airport to catch his return flight to Colorado. Hayes obliged with another engaging discussion. Around noon, knowing his time was running out, Parcells said, "Coach Hayes, one of my last questions has to do with handling the media. Can you give me any advice on that?"

Hayes paused for a long moment, the first time Parcells had seen him look stumped. Only months before his get-together with Parcells, Hayes had charged at an ABC cameraman who was recording the coach's explosive reaction to a fumble, leading to probation by the Big Ten.

The Ohio State coach finally replied to his visitor, "Young man, I think you should consult someone else on the matter."

Then Hayes quickly added, "It's a war you can't win, but you can win a few battles. So screw 'em when you can."

Hayes's humility only added to the young coach's reverence.

Back at Colorado Springs, Parcells was eager to try reviving a program that had gone 10-32-2 over the previous four seasons. He was familiar with the constraints of coaching at a service academy, but he had also received indications from Air Force that his team's course loads would decrease slightly during football season.

The new job was a career achievement on many levels. Parcells's salary of roughly $40,000 was easily an employment high. The family lived in a split-level home in the foothills of the Rocky Mountains, with a deck that offered a bird's-eye panorama of the city; in the morning, looking southwest gave a sublime view of Pikes Peak. His wife and three daughters enjoyed their new friends and scenic surroundings in northern Colorado Springs. The married couple had come a long way from a tiny basement apartment carved out of a dentist's office in Hastings, Nebraska.

The Parcells era at Air Force started on a high, with a 34–25 victory at Texas–El Paso. The Falcons' next game, on September 16, was at Boston College's Alumni Stadium. Tim Cohane, the sports journalist who had given Parcells a one-day writing tutorial on a West Point retreat, phoned the coach to ask for a favor. Cohane was teaching a journalism class at Boston College, and he wondered if Parcells could write something about his team to be shared in class. A couple of days before the game, Cohane received a letter from Parcells. The sardonic professor appreciated the humor.

Before reading the note in class, Cohane told his students, "This is the guy who had one day of class with me, and this is what he remembered. It's pretty good."

Parcells's note read, "Dear Tim. You told me to be precise, direct, and to the point in all of my literary enterprises. My team is slow and friendly."

In front of an audience that included Charles and Don Parcells, the Falcons defeated the Eagles, 18–7, in Chestnut Hill, Massachusetts, for a second straight victory, but Parcells's team indeed turned out to be slow and friendly. Air Force lost five straight, and eight of its last nine, without showing any glimmers of hope. Its penultimate game was a 42–21 loss to Georgia Tech at Falcon Stadium, where in windy, snowy weather, Parcells watched Eddie Lee Ivery set an NCAA record by rushing for 356 yards. As the rookie head coach trudged off the wet field, he said to those around him, "This job is going to take a while." But by the end of Air Force's

3-8 season, which included two decisive losses against Army and Navy, Parcells felt disillusioned. Contrary to the administration's pitch in hiring him, Air Force's football players faced the same exacting academics and military training as other cadets. The confluence of those demands and the requirements of their hard-charging coach proved untenable.

Parcells felt further demoralized several weeks after the season when Woody Hayes's career ended in disgrace. At the Gator Bowl on December 29, Ohio State trailed 17–15 late when Buckeye freshman Art Schlichter gambled on a pass. Clemson defensive tackle Charlie Bauman intercepted it before being pushed out of bounds at Ohio State's sideline. When the defensive lineman glared at the Buckeye coaches and players, Hayes stepped up, shoving his right forearm against Bauman's throat. The sixty-five-year-old's response triggered a skirmish that led to his ejection. The next day Hayes was dismissed by athletic director Hugh Hindman, his former player and assistant.

"I was saddened when he punched the kid from Clemson," Parcells says, "because I know what he did for so many players and so many kids. The thought that he would be remembered for that one incident upset me. He was such a good man."

Parcells was familiar with the legend's progressive side: Hayes was among the first major college coaches to recruit black players. The early group included lineman Jim Parker, whose talents contributed to Hayes's first national championship in 1954, before Parker went on to have a Hall of Fame career with the Baltimore Colts. Hayes also bucked convention by starting large numbers of African-American players and hiring black coaches. Deeply committed to academics, he taught classes that stressed vocabulary to freshman athletes. Hayes was well-regarded by faculty members, even some of those who criticized college sports. "He was what a coach is supposed to be," Parcells says. "He was a disciplinarian; he was demanding. But he also had a great sense of values, and he imparted those to people. In the short time I was with him, I learned a lot."

Realizing that an institutional shift at Air Force was far-fetched, Parcells found himself yearning for another top coaching assignment. But unable to find any safe landing spots, he charged forward in an effort to overcome his program's entrenched constraints. In late February of 1979, Parcells flew to California on a recruiting trip, which only reinforced his distaste for wooing high school kids. But on returning to Colorado, Parcells was surprised to receive a long-distance call from someone he barely knew: Ray Perkins, the new head coach of the New York Giants. Hired after being offensive coordinator of the San Diego Chargers for one season, Perkins was assembling a staff. He wanted to know if Parcells had any interest in flying east to discuss a crucial position: linebackers coach.

"I would have walked," Parcells says.

Their conversation years earlier, and Parcells's reputation for defensive acumen, had left an impression on Perkins. The new Giants leader sensed a kindred spirit who could help him resuscitate a moribund franchise.

For ten years, from the mid-1950s through the early 1960s, the New York Giants had been perhaps pro football's best team, capturing the hearts and minds of fans in the New York area and beyond. Season tickets were treated like heirlooms. Throngs of supporters traveled beyond the seventy-five-mile television blackout zone to watch games in motel rooms. Those glory years kicked off just after Parcells became an ardent fan in Hasbrouck Heights, and didn't end until after the 1963 season when he turned his attention to coaching.

The twelve-team NFL was divided into the Western Conference and Eastern Conference. During that decade-long heyday, the Giants won the Eastern Conference six times, and captured a championship in 1956 under Jim Lee Howell. Over that span no team produced a better regular-season winning percentage (.702), although the Browns, Colts, and Packers each captured two titles. After that, Giants fans had to suffer through fifteen years of putrid play, interrupted only by flashes of mediocrity. Making matters worse, the other New York team, the upstart New York Jets, stunned the Baltimore Colts to claim Super Bowl III in January of 1969. Seven months later, in a highly anticipated exhibition game, the Giants faced their metropolitan rivals for the first time. The stage for the preseason contest was the Yale Bowl in New Haven, Connecticut. Jets coach Weeb Ewbank declared that the winner would own "bragging rights for New York." And fans of both clubs behaved as if it were Super Bowl IV. The segment of the NFL community that considered the Jets championship victory to be a fluke was certain its view would be confirmed with a loss against the mediocre Giants.

That preseason game on August 17, 1969, had been enough of a draw for Army's defensive coordinator, Bill Parcells, to drive from West Point to Connecticut. As a college coach, he hadn't been keeping track of the Giants nearly as closely as he had during childhood. "I was on my own gypsy trail," he says, "on the Greyhound tour of college coaching. But if you followed football at all, you knew that coaches came and went with the Giants, and so did the general managers."

Having switched his allegiance to the Jets after spending time observing their training camps as an Army coach, Parcells was pleased that Gang Green led 17–0 to enter the second quarter. Wellington Mara, the Giants president and co-owner, reportedly tried phoning in a play from the coaches' booth. But no one answered on the sidelines in a game in which Joe Namath threw three touchdown passes and the Giants lost, 37–14.

By the end of preseason, Giants coach Allie Sherman was fired.

Giants Stadium was unveiled in 1976 in East Rutherford, a ten-minute drive from Bill Parcells's hometown of Hasbrouck Heights. But New Jersey's first major-league sports venue was no salve for long-suffering fans. Perhaps the franchise's lowest point occurred on November 19, 1978, when the Giants, uncharacteristically in the playoff hunt at 5-6, hosted the Philadelphia Eagles.

During the game's waning moments, the Giants held the ball and the lead, 17–12. With 31 seconds left to play, Eagles defensive back Herman Edwards congratulated tailback Doug Kotar at the line of scrimmage. The Giants eschewed the routine fall-down, a precursor of the knee, that would have run out the clock. Instead, quarterback Joe Pisarcik bungled a handoff to fullback Larry Csonka, causing the ball to jar loose. Edwards scooped up a serendipitous bounce for the Eagles and scampered 26 yards into the end zone. Big Blue fans dubbed the ignominious moment "The Fumble," while the Eagles faithful called it the "Miracle of the Meadowlands."

For his role in the surreal loss, Pisarcik needed a police escort to retrieve his car. Offensive coordinator Bob Gibson, who had instructed Pisarcik to hand off the ball, was fired after the game and never coached again. Fans organized bonfires to get rid of their season tickets, and Wellington Mara was burned in effigy. Those spectators who kept their tickets used them to enter Giants Stadium and throw lemons on the field. A plane overhead flew a banner that read "15 Years of Lousy Football—We've Had Enough."

In the six seasons before Perkins courted Parcells in 1979, Big Blue went 23-62-1. The Giants hadn't made the playoffs since 1963, while producing only two winning records. Off the field, co-owners Wellington Mara and Tim Mara, Wellington's nephew, underwent the most infamous family feud in sports. Despite a string of feeble drafts, the animosity prevented agreement on virtually anything, even a general manager. The disarray in the once-proud franchise prompted the league's involvement, leading to the arrival of former Baltimore Colts executive George Young on Valentine's Day 1979. The forty-nine-year-old GM was balding and spoke in a high-pitched voice that belied his rotund size. He boiled down his choice of a new head coach to Ray Perkins and Dan Reeves. But Young was more comfortable with Perkins, who had played for Baltimore from 1967 to 1971, when Young was a Colts executive and assistant coach.

• • •

For Bill Parcells's interview, the Giants arranged a reservation at the Sheraton in Hasbrouck Heights, a location that allowed Parcells to spend time with family and friends before his big talk with Perkins. During the interview, Perkins expounded on his plans for the defense. He wanted to revamp the 4-3 scheme that the Giants had used for decades, replacing it with a flexible 3-4, featuring a strong linebacking corps trained by Parcells.

Perkins never mentioned Parcells's ties to the area, but Big Blue's head coach was familiar enough with his candidate's background to be aware of the storybook twist: Parcells, who had last lived in the Northeast in 1969, was finally coming home to a plum gig with the Giants.

As the discussion drew to a close, Perkins asked, "So what do you think?"

Parcells responded, "When do we start?"

The head coach and his new linebackers guru shook hands.

After accepting Perkins's offer, Parcells placed a long-distance call to Judy conveying his excitement. Her tone of voice was neutral, though his tin ear didn't detect it. Parcells flew back to Colorado, where he announced his departure. The decision to bolt Air Force after one season generated criticism in the local papers. Nonetheless, the program followed Parcells's recommendation to hire his offensive coordinator, Ken Hatfield, as his replacement; Al Groh would also stay on, as Hatfield's defensive coordinator.

Reunited with Judy, Parcells saw how unhappy she was with making yet another move. Over the past fifteen years, she had been a trouper, traversing the country with her husband while he took on seven football jobs: Parcells had been a Bronco (Hastings), Shocker (Wichita State), Black Knight (West Point), Seminole (Florida State), Commodore (Vanderbilt), Red Raider (Texas Tech), and Falcon (Air Force). In almost every case, he had left the family behind while Judy dealt with the logistics, which included packing and finding new schools for her daughters. But this time, after Bill Parcells's best job offer yet, she was balking.

He tried to sway her: "Honey, I can't *not* take this job. I don't know when I'm going to get another pro offer. You know how they talk about opportunity knocking? Well, in my case, it's kicking down the damn door."

Judy responded "Bill, I just don't know if I can move again."

Another complication was that the economy in the Denver area had slumped, which made selling the house challenging. But within a few days, in late February 1979, Parcells put it on the market and boarded a Jersey-bound flight so he could join Perkins's staff for March minicamp. On the plane, Parcells recognized one of the passengers: Bill Belichick, who had been hired by Perkins from the Broncos to oversee special teams. For the twenty-seven-year-old, it was a step up from Denver, where he had been an assistant special-teams coach and defensive aide. The new colleagues expressed exuberance about joining Perkins. Parcells added that he was particularly glad to be leaving Air Force.

After arriving in New Jersey, Parcells and Belichick checked into the Sheraton, where they both planned to stay for the next few months. Parcells was the fourth assistant named to Perkins's staff after Ernie Adams (special offensive assistant), Ralph Hawkins (defensive coordinator), and Pat Hodgson (receivers coach). The head coach and his other assistants were already at the Hasbrouck Heights hotel, preparing for their first minicamp. Belichick, who aspired to become a defensive coach, asked Perkins about helping with the linebackers. The head coach responded that the decision was up to the new linebackers coach, Bill Parcells, who gladly obliged Belichick's request.

The staff turned to the daunting task of transforming the culture of a team inured to losing. "It was like *F Troop* there," Adams recalls, "absolutely out of control." Perkins oversaw long, grueling practices that evoked Bear Bryant; unlike the Crimson Tide legend, Perkins was merciful enough to permit water, but he showed Bryant's disregard for injuries that didn't involve broken bones or hospital stays.

Parcells was just as tough as Perkins, though more likely to smile. The former Air Force coach seemed at home among his new Giants colleagues. By day, Parcells was blissfully consumed with helping coordinator Ralph Hawkins install a 3-4 defense while preparing for April's draft. But Parcells's exuberance evaporated when he returned to his hotel room at night and called Judy for an update on her mind-set and the prospects for selling the house. Neither situation had changed. Judy reiterated her stance against moving east, noting that the girls were ensconced in Colorado Springs. Suzy and Dallas were attending Air Academy High, one of the state's top schools, and Jill went to Air Academy Junior High School at the base.

Before her children became teenagers, Judy had mostly enjoyed the itinerant lifestyle of a coach's wife, living in the Midwest (Kansas and Nebraska), Northeast (New York), and South (Florida, Tennessee, Texas), then the Rocky Mountain state of Colorado. She says of the first several relocations: "During those years, there was always something exciting. And I couldn't wait for the next move."

Judy had never been outside the Midwest until 1966, when the couple left Wichita for West Point. She had marveled at the spectacular panorama of the campus's barracks, massive buildings, and cliffs overlooking the Hudson River. And she loved the patriotic display of the cadet parades, marching-band music blending into the roar of military planes in formation just above. Before the latest move, Judy had relished the flat country that surrounded Lubbock, Texas, for its reminders of Kansas prairies back home. But after settling in Colorado Springs, she hadn't expected the next move for at least a few years. The thrill of zigzagging the nation while Parcells chased his football dreams had dissipated. The older girls, Suzy and Dallas, didn't want to relocate and leave their friends yet again. Suzy, the eldest, would be a high school senior in the fall. More fundamentally, however, Judy suspected her husband of infidelity.

"It was a bad time," she says. "So why should I pack up and go through that headache all over again? It was just going to be the same old thing once I moved to New Jersey."

Parcells concedes the point. "Most of those problems at home were my fault; I take the blame for that."

Judy had been compliant throughout her marriage; her decision to take a stand came during a wave of feminism sweeping the nation. Her stance helped Parcells grasp the gravity of the situation, and forced him to make the toughest decision of his life: either remain with the New York Giants and likely trigger the dissolution of his family, or walk away from the NFL opportunity knocking after fifteen years of toiling.

The next morning Parcells walked into Perkins's office, explained his predicament, and resigned. Perkins responded by saying, "Listen, I'm sorry for both of us, but I understand. Let me ask you this: Do you think you can stay through the minicamp for our veterans we've got coming up?"

"Sure."

Parcells phoned Judy afterward and said, "I'm coming home."

"What?!"

She was stunned—and delighted. That phone conversation was brief, as Parcells explained to Judy that he needed to stay on another couple of months, but that she should pick him up from the airport the day after veterans minicamp ended in late May. Reflecting on his friend's decision to quit coaching for family, Bobby Knight says, "I frankly think it took a helluva lot of guts to do what he did. A lot of guys talk about doing what he did, but they never do it. I've felt in life like I was at that point, but I never took the step that Parcells did."

Parcells counters, "There was nothing heroic about it. But I figured I owed Judy one. She had been on the same Greyhound, seeing-America-the-hard-way tour I'd been on. Sometimes somebody hands you your dream and you've got to hand it right back."

The career ramifications, however, weighed on Parcells. Quitting a plum rookie assistant position in the NFL after less than four months seemed like career suicide, and during his final days with the Giants, Parcells was at his crabbiest. Before one practice, offensive lineman Brad Benson lumbered into the training room for treatment. Parcells came in moments later and plopped into the whirlpool. When another defensive player asked Parcells for specifics about the upcoming workout, the departing coach snapped, "How the hell do I know? I have as much say around here as a fart in a hurricane."

Bill Parcells asked Bill Belichick to drive him to the airport for his flight to Colorado. Parcells's resignation had been so abrupt that some defensive players were unaware of the development until they returned for training camp in August. "Just as quickly as he came, he left," defensive end George Martin recalls. "I didn't know what the whole situation was about."

Parcells checked out of the Sheraton, and although the half-hour drive to Newark International Airport was mostly silent, Parcells expressed his regrets about leaving. He told Belichick how much his family enjoyed Colorado, and explained their reluctance to join him in yet another move. When the two coaches reached Continental's terminal, Belichick asked Parcells if he had his plane ticket. Parcells confirmed that he did, but what he thought to himself was, "Yeah, I've got my ticket out of the business."

After takeoff Parcells plugged in headphones and selected a country music station. Then the Giants assistant—the *former* Giants assistant—wept quietly during the four-hour flight. "I was leaving a place where I really wanted to stay," Parcells recalls. "I had to do what I had to do, but I really wasn't sure what was going to happen."

Parcells couldn't fathom a professional life that didn't include football. Although Judy was thrilled about his decision, her feelings were tempered by a new concern: for the first time in their relationship, no one was bringing in a weekly paycheck. Soon after she met him at the airport, Judy asked, "What in the world are we going to do for money?"

It was June 1979, and the Parcells family had enough savings to last through October; with a penurious approach, the money *might* stretch until the New Year. Parcells believed that taking a job in sales might generate the least culture shock. He was used to selling things, most recently a new defensive scheme to veteran stars like Harry Carson. Now the former coach would try to find something else to peddle. Exploiting some connections with Air Force, Parcells went on a calling spree. And after a tip he applied for a job with Gates Land, a land-development company that sold property in master-planned communities. Parcells told its president, David Sunderland, that his family wanted to stay in one place and that the company's long-term prospects were appealing. Sunderland was sold, and Parcells got the job.

"He didn't sit around with a long face, saying he wished he was back on the football field," Sunderland recalls. "He wasn't in a blue funk. He was focused and energetic and committed to results."

Cheyenne Hills went on to become the city's first master-planned community before the term "new urbanism" was coined in the early 1980s. Cheyenne Mountain, as it's known now, has tens of thousands of residents, including some who bought property from a full-throttle salesman named Bill Parcells.

Judy sought gainful employment, too, for the first time. "That was pretty scary, no one in the family having a job," she says. "So I had to go out and get one right away." After searching the classified section of the *Colorado Springs Gazette-Telegraph,* she parlayed her experience as a receptionist at Wichita's athletic department, where she had first met Parcells, into a job as a legal secretary.

Before Bill Parcells chose his family over football, his internal clock had been regulated by the sport. He automatically woke before dawn, leaving the house early to fully engage in the minutiae of preparation. Even after a twelve-hour workday, football dominated his mind. Anything unrelated to the sport, including his children, was considered a distraction, as the week's rhythm culminated on Saturdays, win or lose. Parcells grew accustomed to, perhaps even reliant on, the fluctuations of the football season. Following a respite in the off-season, the whole cycle began anew.

After a jarring start in his new reality—"at first he was lost," Judy remembers—Parcells found his footing. His mornings free, he ate breakfast with his wife and daughters for the first time. And on weekends, Parcells took the family on recreational activities in the mountains. Despite having cut his umbilical cord to football, Parcells seemed to thrive during the first few months of his new world. But in late July, the start of NFL training camp, he began suffering withdrawal pangs. "Reading the sports pages every morning," Parcells recalls, "was like getting knifed."

Within a month he took a tiny step back toward the NFL. He obtained a job with Al Davis's Raiders writing scouting reports on their AFC West rivals, which he could do by attending Broncos home games. Parcells bought a pair of season tickets for end-zone seats at Mile High Stadium, where he and Judy tailgated outside before kickoff. But Judy was unaware that her husband's note-taking was part of an NFL dalliance. Parcells found the job stimulating, especially after his experience at Giants minicamp. "It kept me interested," he says of the part-time gig. "I started thinking more about pro football, understanding it better."

But one game per week wasn't enough for an ex-coach whose genetic markers might as well have been yard markers. So on Saturday afternoons, Parcells attended Air Force home games with Judy. Parcells was uneasy about returning to Falcon Stadium, but the desire to watch his old team trumped any discomfiture. At worst, "maybe somebody would give me the Forgotten but Not Gone Award," he says.

Under the pretext of earning extra income, Parcells became a color commentator for radio station KRDO-AM, which broadcast local high school football, *Denver's Game of the Week*. On Friday nights Parcells showed up at the press box in Garry Berry Stadium wearing an overcoat with a flask in his pocket. He didn't always drink the coffee served to media members. His partner, play-by-play announcer Jeff Thomas, was a prominent local broadcaster. Parcells's self-described style was "blathering idiot." With the side jobs, Parcells's annual earnings increased to about $45,000, more than even the Giants salary he had relinquished. Yet he grew more despondent. "I turned into a damn yuppie," he says. "I was dying. I was dying to coach."

At home Parcells put on a happy face, but after seventeen years of marriage, Judy didn't need to be told that her husband disliked his new life. The telltale sign was that he became increasingly temperamental. One Sunday afternoon, the couple was watching an NFL game on TV. As the announcers described the action, Judy blurted, "This is beginning to drive me nuts."

Parcells, engrossed in the game, responded, "What was that, honey?"

"You're driving me nuts, Bill. I think it's time you thought about getting back into football."

Parcells snapped to attention. He had been fantasizing about hearing those words since he had stepped off his Continental flight from New Jersey.

The next evening, the couple was sitting at a restaurant bar, watching *Monday Night Football*, when Judy reiterated her thoughts, this time even more unequivocally.

"We've got to get back to football."

Parcells responded, "I'm going to do it, honey, and someday I'm going to be a head coach in the NFL. And I'm going to win a Super Bowl."

"God, you haven't even got a job, and you're saying this?"

6

In mid-October of 1979, Parcells punched the digits he had contemplated dialing so often during his football purgatory. When Ray Perkins picked up, Parcells said, "I want to come back."

Perkins replied, "I figured you would, sooner or later." Perkins added that the Giants were playing in Kansas City on October 21. Parcells responded that of course he already knew their schedule.

Perkins asked, "You want to have breakfast?"

Parcells flew to Kansas City to meet Perkins at the team hotel the morning of the game. He enjoyed running into some Giants players in the lobby. At breakfast Parcells reiterated his desire for an NFL return, hopefully with Big Blue. Perkins was candid. "I don't have anything right now. And I'm not sure I'll have anything after the season. Let's stay in touch, and if I hear anything about other teams, I'll let you know."

But Parcells became intent on obtaining a coaching job as soon as possible. In December, he put his home up for sale, and found a buyer committed to moving in on February 13. Parcells turned to his college connections, first phoning Steve Sloan, who was still at Mississippi. Sloan responded that he would get back to Parcells promptly with a sense of the college opportunities. After hanging up, Sloan began spreading the word that his talented ex-lieutenant was seeking employment.

The next day, Stanford head coach Rod Dowhower phoned Parcells. "I hear you're looking."

"You bet."

Ray Handley, who had joined Dowhower's staff when Parcells left Air Force, strongly recommended his former boss, so Stanford's head coach flew to Colorado Springs to meet Parcells, and during the get-together the two men reached an agreement; the new defensive coordinator merely needed to visit the school before making things official. Parcells flew into Palo Alto, and it took him only a few minutes to declare Stanford's campus, including its buildings with red-tiled roofs dotting exquisitely manicured greenery, the most beautiful one he had ever seen. Parcells was convinced that Judy and the kids would be equally enamored of the surroundings. While he was still in Palo Alto, however, the possibility of working there evaporated as big news hit campus. Dowhower was leaving Stanford: he had accepted an offer from the Denver Broncos to be their offensive coordinator.

Parcells's disappointment eased slightly after he flew back to Colorado Springs and heard a message from Sloan about another possibility. Mississippi's defensive coordinator position was open, and it had Bill Parcells's name on it. The former real-estate agent wanted the gig, but Sloan gave him extra time to make certain, knowing that Parcells had cast a wide net. His expertise with the 3-4 scheme appealed to NFL coaches like Fritz Shurmur, New England's defensive coordinator. So Perkins contacted the Patriots, where he had coached offense for four seasons under Chuck Fairbanks, to tell them that Parcells would be an excellent hire for their opening at linebackers coach.

Perkins phoned Parcells to tell him that the Giants still had no openings, but that he should call Ron Erhardt, who needed a linebackers coach. Parcells was skeptical; he didn't know the Patriots head coach. "I've got this offer from Steve at Mississippi."

Perkins responded, "Call Erhardt."

"This Mississippi thing is solid. I still really haven't coached in the pros. I probably don't have a chance to get the New England thing."

"Call Erhardt."

When Parcells contacted Erhardt, the Patriots coach told him to come up to the Boston area for an interview. On Thursday, February 7, Parcells flew to Boston before driving to Foxborough, where the Patriots headquarters was located. After the interview, Parcells asked how many people were up for the job. Erhardt told him that he was the first of several candidates, and that a decision would be made by Tuesday, February 12. Parcells conveyed a sense of urgency. "I can't hold up Steve Sloan at Mississippi, and I have to be out of my house in, like, twenty minutes."

He returned to his hotel room still uncertain about his future, but within a few hours Erhardt telephoned with an offer. When Parcells informed Sloan, the Ole Miss coach said, "Give 'em hell. You've always belonged in pro football anyway."

The next few days were a whirlwind. On Friday, one day after the interview, New England announced Parcells as its new linebackers coach. Over the weekend Judy flew to Boston to look for a home. On Monday the family agreed on a place in Norfolk, Massachusetts, a rural town on Boston's periphery, and Judy returned to Colorado to deal with the move. Suzy was only three months away from graduating at Air Academy High, so she stayed behind, moving in with the family of Al Groh, Air Force's defensive coordinator, who had known Parcells since they were at Army.

• • •

At Patriots training camp, Parcells used the same razor-tongued intensity he'd employed as a college coach. During one practice, defensive back Rick Sanford offered a lame excuse after botching an assignment, and Parcells yelled, "Who do you think I am? Charlie the Tuna? I believe anything?" Parcells was alluding to the naive and affable cartoon mascot for StarKist, the canned tuna company, who was an icon of pop culture during the 1960s and 1970s. Parcells's retort spurred laughter from the Patriots players, and from that day forward he was known as "the Tuna," or "the Big Tuna." His linebackers plastered Charlie-the-Tuna logos on a helmet, and each week during training camp one defensive player was chosen to wear the helmet at practice. Coincidentally, the nickname somewhat described Parcells's physique: like a real tuna, the Big Tuna was stout in the middle, tapering off at both ends.

Bill Parcells would also pick up something in New England far more important than a catchy moniker: formative training in how to evaluate personnel. The GM, Bucko Kilroy, and the director of college scouting, Mike Holovak, were both former NFL players well-regarded for their abilities to assess talent.

Kilroy had starred as a two-way lineman for the Philadelphia Eagles, helping them capture the 1948 and 1949 NFL Championships. Some years after he retired because of a knee injury, the Redskins hired him as a personnel director in 1962, making him one of the league's first full-time scouts. Kilroy showed great skill at spotting talent—for example, by using Washington's first two picks in the rich 1964 draft to select two future Hall of Famers: halfback Charley Taylor, third overall, and defensive back Paul Krause, eighteenth. That was the same draft in which an offensive tackle named Bill Parcells was chosen eighty-ninth by Detroit.

Until the late 1940s, football scouting lacked sophistication: it was mostly regional; and because of time constraints, coaching staffs focused on gathering available film on prospects. Some clubs resorted to plucking players off the college All-American list. The least myopic organizations also researched black-owned newspapers, such as the *Baltimore Afro-American*, the *Pittsburgh Courier*, and the *Amsterdam News*, based in the Harlem section of New York City.

Although the Dallas Cowboys weren't founded until 1960, the franchise was instantly at the forefront of personnel evaluation, thanks to the innovative duo at its helm: chief scout Gil Brandt and GM Tex Schramm. Brandt espoused targeting the best available athletes, even if they were basketball players or track stars. And he was among the first scouts to search for kickers in soccer leagues outside the United States, particularly Latin America.

Schramm attended the 1960 Winter Olympics in Squaw Valley, California, where he was intrigued by an IBM computer that compiled statistics, including medal standings and record times; the Cowboys executive believed the technology could be used to organize scouting data. On returning to Dallas, Schramm contacted IBM to explore his brainstorm and enlisted help from Salam Quereishi, one of its computer programmers from India. Their get-togethers were challenging because of the programmer's thick Indian accent and the GM's gruff manner, but they went beyond the standard metrics of height, weight, and speed to create five categories—agility and quickness, explosiveness and strength, mental alertness, character, and competitiveness—rating prospects from 1 to 9.

The heavy expense of the nascent system prompted the need to share costs with other interested NFL organizations, so Schramm chose two teams from the Western Conference, who were therefore not direct competitors: the San Francisco 49ers and the Los Angeles Rams. Over the next four years, each club contributed a total of roughly $300,000 to create a computer model to be used in evaluating players. While awaiting the finished product, the group formed the first scouting combine: code name Troika.

After the innovative system was implemented in 1964, the raw data was shared among the three teams. Depending on each club's philosophy, critical factors were weighted differently. The computer also distilled information to create one list of the fifteen best college prospects. Atop the page was a cocksure, gunslinging quarterback at Alabama: Joe Namath.

Meanwhile, Gil Brandt was taking notice of astute moves being made by Washington's top scout, Bucko Kilroy. After the 1965 season Brandt lured him to the Cowboys. As computer technology evolved, Dallas tweaked the value placed on certain qualities. In 1965, the Cowboys counted speed as 14.6 percent of a tight end's grade. The next year, the attribute dropped to 11 percent. Kilroy helped refine their scouting system, filling the roster with talented players who blended size and speed. By his second year in Dallas, Tom Landry's Cowboys began their record streak of twenty winning seasons.

Kilroy's scouting genius increasingly gained attention, and in 1971, New England's Upton Bell, the league's youngest GM, enticed Kilroy to leave Dallas. The thirty-three-year-old was the son of Bert Bell, the founder of the Eagles, who had once employed Kilroy while serving as the NFL commissioner. Kilroy brought two protégés with him from Dallas, Dick Steinberg and Tom Boisture. After upgrading New England's scouting system, they infused the team with talented players and hired Mike Holovak, their onetime coach and a former star fullback at Boston College, as Kilroy's top college scout for the newly renamed New England Patriots.

When Parcells joined the Patriots that season, Ron Erhardt tutored him about pro offenses, and defensive coordinator Fritz Shurmur educated him on the NFL's brand of two-gap defense. In this scheme, the defensive player is responsible for both sides, or gaps, of an offensive blocker. By contrast, the one-gap defense requires accountability for the space between two offensive players—for example, the guard and the center.

Nonetheless, the ambitious young assistant quietly ached to learn about building a team. He intuitively understood that for all the importance of coaching, football is in many ways a personnel-acquisition business. The greatest coaches got the most out of a team regardless of its skill set, but boosting a club's talent level elevated the chances at success. Vince Lombardi's Packers were stacked with *eleven* future Hall of Famers, all acquired by an obscure GM, Jack Vainisi. Regardless of the era, winning organizations generally have top personnel departments that employ a distinct philosophy for acquiring talent.

Erhardt's staff of eight assistants all helped to evaluate college players. In personnel meetings, scouts read their reports aloud. While college linebackers were being assessed, Parcells took notes and listened intently, knowing he would be required to provide an opinion based on the disseminated information. Kilroy barely interacted with Parcells through normal channels. In between practices and meetings, however, Parcells sought out the GM, peppering him with questions about building a team. The interest was atypical for an assistant coach, particularly one in his first NFL season. Impressed by such passion, Kilroy responded with kindness, spending substantial time providing a primary education about scouting in pro football. Parcells confirmed many of the principles during separate conversations with Holovak. "They gave me a great foundation," Parcells says of Kilroy and Holovak. "I was fortunate to be exposed to those people and that system in the beginning."

Kilroy's first, and most important, lesson was the need for a personnel philosophy. Lack of guidelines for targeting talent usually led to failure. Parcells learned that roughly half the league's teams had no blueprint for talent acquisition.

The rookie NFL assistant didn't bring attention to the private lessons. Decades later, when informed about Kilroy's influence on Parcells, Erhardt expresses surprise: "I never heard that before. Evidently, Bill knew something that we didn't know. I don't remember him saying anything about Bucko." But Erhardt adds quickly: "Bucko always had time for you. There were a lot of us that would talk to him about personnel."

Kilroy was well-organized, although one might not suspected it given the way his crinkly white shirts often hung from his suit pants. Barrel-chested and tall with a slapdash appearance, Kilroy stood out upon entering a room in his size 17 triple-E shoes. "A big ol' Irishman," Parcells recalls. Kilroy had a quick-trigger laugh, unleashing giggles like machine-gun bursts. Despite his sharp mind, the bespectacled scout with snow-white hair tended to utter "Bucko-isms," malapropisms such as talking about "collision" between teams when he meant "collusion," or a "re-thread" player instead of a "retread." Some trades fell through, Kilroy explained, because they were "cost-prohibited" versus "cost-prohibitive."

After enlightening Parcells about the fundamentals of personnel evaluation, Kilroy delved into his intricate system for gauging talent. The Patriots stressed size and speed while also recognizing the five so-called critical factors of football skill, from agility to competitiveness. The sum of those qualities helped determine if a prospect had the desired makeup. Emphasis on certain qualities varied based on position, like a quarterback's poise, or a wideout's ability to run after the catch. "Bucko gave me the critical-factor exposure," Parcells says, "and I grabbed hold of that quick. I still have copies of his breakdown, and I would never let them go."

Kilroy's complicated approach to assessment was known in NFL parlance as a "typing system," with alphanumeric scores that classify, or *type*, each prospect with precision. Grades help determine if a physical drawback will inhibit NFL success and, just as important, whether the ostensible disadvantage clashes with the team's personnel philosophy.

The numerical cutoff for NFL consideration is a 5.5, which equates to a late-round pick at best; 9.0 or higher signifies a player bound for the Hall of Fame. Kilroy wrote down the requirements for a prospect's meriting a 9.0 to 9.9: "A first-year starter, Pro Bowl–type player. Must be a dominant impact player immediately. Ability to change outcome of the game. Must have 9 athletic ability. Must have height-weight-speed ratio of 7 or higher. Cornerback and wide receivers must have playing speed of 8 or higher."

It's rare for an athlete to earn a 9.0; the mark usually occurs once in a generation. Entering the 1980 draft, Oklahoma tailback Billy Sims was graded an A9 by Kilroy and Holovak. As a college senior Sims led the nation with 1,896 rushing yards while scoring 22 touchdowns. He validated the rare grade by making the Pro Bowl as a rookie. Sims would end up being the only prospect to earn an A from any team connected to Parcells.

Most NFL teams today use numeric-only assessments, which Parcells considers flawed although simpler than the alternative, which is adding a typing system of letters from A to K. Each letter is assigned a maximum number, from 2.0 to 9.9, and once letters are put together with numbers, NFL scouts have what they need to visualize a prospect. In the typing system, K, the lowest letter grade, means that the prospect has only one redeeming feature. The highest number that can go with a K grade is a 3.9, so K-type players have virtually no shot at getting drafted.

Parcells's intelligence allowed him to grasp the system's complex coding and contingencies in only one season. "A: He's got it all, great. B: He's got it all, great. C: He doesn't have it all; he's short, but he's great. D: He's got it all, but there's one circumstance that you're a little leery about. E: He's got size and speed, but he's an underachiever. F: He's got everything but speed, meaning toughness and size. F's are usually linemen. G means he's a good player. You can give him up to a 6.9, but he's like a C; he's short. H: You can only give him a 6.4 'cause he's a projection. I: Size and speed; he's like a D, only he's not as good. J: He's got size, but he doesn't have bulk, he needs to fill out. K: One redeeming feature."

To better understand the complexities of the system, Parcells came up with maxims. "I's and D's before G's and C's." Or, as Parcells explains, "That means take the size before you take the shorter guy."

Despite the intricacies of his system, Kilroy considered talent acquisition to be an inexact science involving intuition almost as much as information. No one in league history matched his experience as player, coach, and scout. He often dipped into this deep reservoir spanning generations to compare athletes. Kilroy taught this comparative mind-set to Parcells, whose extraordinary memory would become an asset in evaluating personnel. If a prospect didn't evoke a past successful player, there were reservations. But when an athlete conjured a good player from the past, scouting interest rose.

Kilroy also taught Parcells that some prospects who didn't fit New England's personnel philosophy might thrive on another team. "So we always had a special category of players," Parcells says. "We called it: 'Well, they're good, but they're not for us.' They don't fit our prototypical standards. We try not to compromise those."

Parcells began developing precise preferences: defensive linemen who were boxy, strong, and physical, yet possessed quickness; tall linebackers who were heavier, thus bulkier, than the average; defensive backs who were terrific tacklers. The common quality was toughness. Parcells's template was strikingly similar to Lombardi's. As early as 1962, Green Bay's three starting linebackers, led by Ray Nitschke, were all six-foot-three and 235 pounds, close to the size of the team's defensive ends. And Willie Wood, the star Packers safety, was among the surest tacklers in NFL history.

Parcells's bigger-is-better philosophy would transfer to the offensive side as a right tackle who was at least six-foot-six and 315 pounds. Besides those basic metrics, Parcells wanted offensive linemen with long arms and wide buttocks. His ideal runner was a relatively big, punishing back with a north–south mentality.

After George Young was named Giants GM in 1979, he was intent on learning the system by poaching New England's front office. Dick Steinberg was one of Kilroy's top scouts, so Young offered Steinberg a job as Big Blue's personnel director. Steinberg declined because of a simultaneous offer from the New Orleans Saints. Undeterred, Young courted Kilroy's other protégé, and Tom Boisture accepted the job in 1980 to become Young's right-hand man. Boisture taught Young the system in New York around the same time that Parcells was quietly getting lessons on it in New England.

Erhardt's Patriots went 10-6 to finish runner-up in the AFC East. Nonetheless, for the second straight season, they missed the playoffs by just a game. New England scored 441 points, a club record that would stand until 2007, eclipsed by an offense featuring quarterback Tom Brady and wideout Randy Moss. Seven of Erhardt's Patriots were voted to the Pro Bowl, including linebacker Steve Nelson.

7

Despite New England's postseason absence, Parcells enjoyed his experience learning the pro game. His contributions, including a key role in Steve Nelson's breakout season, affirmed confidence in Parcells's ability to coach at the highest level. He was eager to prepare for the 1981 draft and to better familiarize himself with the Boston area, but those plans were disrupted by a phone call from Ray Perkins. Only two years after Parcells had suddenly quit his new job as the Giants' linebackers coach, a decision he feared would result in being blackballed, he received an even better offer: Big Blue's defensive coordinator.

Following a 6-10 record in his first season, Perkins's Giants went 4-12 as injuries decimated the roster. Big Blue was outscored by 176 points while both the offense and defense proved anemic. Perkins was so convinced that Parcells would transform New York's defense, and help turn the Giants into winners, that no interview was necessary. In the telephone conversation, he offered Parcells defensive carte blanche and reiterated his goal from their first go-round: "Mold a linebacking corps that I can build a defense on."

The Patriots linebackers coach immediately informed Erhardt about his new opportunity. Before departing New England, Parcells made copies of Kilroy's grading scale and placed them in a black plastic folder. The typing system would serve Parcells well for the rest of his career.

Parcells signed only a two-year deal, which tied him to the remainder of Perkins's contract. Although its length wasn't ideal, Parcells was pleased about getting a raise: his first child, Suzy, was headed to college in the fall, and the second, Dallas, was only months from being a high school senior.

Parcells would earn his salary and more if he could turn around a defense that had allowed 425 points, an average of 26.5 per game, while ranking next to last in the 28-team league. With an interception-prone neophyte at quarterback in Phil Simms, and no standouts at tailback or wideout, Big Blue averaged 15.5 points for the league's third-worst offense. Parcells noted that Perkins's Giants record (10-22) was similar to that of his two predecessors, both of whom had been fired. If Big Blue floundered in 1981, Parcells surmised, Perkins's entire staff would be dismissed. Yet he chose to focus on the positive: the potential recognition he'd get for revitalizing Big Blue's defense.

The New York Giants joined the NFL in 1925, five years after the league's creation. Their addition fit with the NFL's desire to reach bigger markets and gain more revenue, while dispelling the notion that it was a small-town endeavor. At the time, the NFL consisted of one division with twenty clubs, including several obscure ones based in Ohio: the Akron Indians, Canton Bulldogs, Columbus Tigers, and Dayton Triangles. Other teams included the Duluth (Minnesota) Kelleys, Hammond (Indiana) Pros, Pottsville (Pennsylvania) Maroons, Rock Island (Illinois) Independents, Chicago Bears, and Green Bay Packers, and clubs in Cleveland (Bulldogs) and Detroit (Panthers). The league champion was determined by the best record. In their first home game, the Giants lost to the Frankford Yellow Jackets, based in their namesake neighborhood of Philadelphia, who would capture the NFL title in 1926 by going 14-1-2. Their mark included two 6–0 victories versus the Giants within hours during a season in which back-to-back games were common. The Giants earned the 1927 championship with a record of 11-1-1.

By the time the NFL became a two-division league in 1933, many of the smaller teams had disbanded: only ten clubs remained. In the first championship game pitting Eastern and Western finalists, the Bears defeated the Giants, 23–21. After a stellar stretch from 1955 to 1963, the Giants went into a free fall. When Bill Parcells was named defensive coordinator, Big Blue had endured eight consecutive losing seasons while averaging four victories. Within the organization, pressure to reverse course was immense.

"For the most part, Ray Perkins treated everybody the same: the coaches were just like the players. We were all shit in Perkins's eyes," recalls ex-linebacker Harry Carson, the club's fourth-round pick in 1976. "Everybody was a dog. The assistant coaches felt the pressure, and as they say, shit rolls downhill."

Big Blue's decision on its top pick in the 1981 draft, second overall, was monumental for the franchise. The New Orleans Saints, coached by Bum Phillips, held the first selection. The prevailing notion was that the Giants would choose whoever remained of the top two prospects: North Carolina linebacker Lawrence Taylor and South Carolina tailback George Rogers. Giants GM George Young considered Taylor, an All-American with extraordinary athleticism, to be the best linebacking prospect he had ever evaluated. With a rare blend of size, speed, and power at six-three, 237 pounds, Taylor fit the ideal prototype at his position, leading to a grade of B8.2 in the Giants typing system. Young even suggested that Taylor's physical gifts surpassed those of Dick Butkus, the legendary linebacker who had excelled with the Bears from 1965 to 1973.

Young, a secretive person, was characteristically coy about his draft preference. Despite his effusive praise, the GM never quite publicly committed to Taylor while New Orleans remained open to the possibility of drafting Rogers, winner of the Heisman Trophy. As head coach of the Houston Oilers in 1978, Bum Phillips had used their top overall pick on Earl Campbell, who turned out to be one of the best runners of all time. But since subterfuge was typical of the draft, especially one without a unanimous top choice, the order of the first two selections maintained suspense.

New York's roster was already deep with linebackers. And the talented veterans on the unit remarked that using the team's top pick on Taylor would be superfluous. Taylor's agent declared his client's contractual goal of $250,000 per season, or $750,000 over three years, which would make him among the league's highest-paid defenders. Some Giants veterans hinted that they wouldn't suit up in 1981 at a salary lower than that of a rookie's. Offended by such sentiments, Taylor responded that the Giants should avoid drafting him so that their linebacking corps wouldn't be disrupted; he hoped to be chosen by the Cowboys, although they would need to trade up from their twenty-sixth overall choice. Young deemed the public tit-for-tat and speculation irrelevant.

The 1981 NFL draft was held in the basement ballroom of the New York Sheraton. Ed Croke, the Giants public relations director, was the team's representative at the televised event. Sitting at a table assigned to the Giants, Croke's main duty was to relay their choice. Handing a card to NFL commissioner Pete Rozelle was each team's way of making a selection, which was then announced from a podium. At Big Blue's draft war room in Giants Stadium, Young phoned Croke. "Listen. Get two cards. You're gonna write down two names: 'George Rogers, running back,' and 'Lawrence Taylor, linebacker.' Just keep 'em in your lap. Whichever one Bum Phillips takes, get that second card in as fast as you can."

Rozelle announced New Orleans's selection, George Rogers, delighting Big Blue's front office and its fans. Scores of supporters among the spectators on the ballroom's balcony chanted Taylor's name. Rozelle had set aside the customary fifteen minutes for the Giants to make a choice, but within seconds Croke retrieved the alternate card from his lap and sprung from his seat to reach Rozelle. The commissioner announced the second overall pick as Giants Nation cheered triumphantly.

Several weeks later, when Taylor reported to minicamp, Harry Carson reached out to him, arranging a sit-down for a long talk to reduce any animosity. The rookie wore number 56 because of his admiration for Thomas "Hollywood" Henderson, a flashy linebacker who had helped the Cowboys reach three Super Bowls between 1975 and 1979, winning one in 1978, before being released mainly because of cocaine abuse.

As a North Carolina Tar Heel, Lawrence Taylor played on the defensive line before moving to outside linebacker. By the end of his college career he was one of the best linebacker prospects in decades. Parcells expressed astonishment that one-third of Taylor's tackles as a senior occurred behind the line of scrimmage. The reasons for the statistic came to life on the first snap of Giants training camp in Pleasantville, New York. Taylor attacked the ball like a cheetah. In no more than two steps, the six-three, 237-pounder seemed to be at full speed. Yet he possessed the strength of a sumo wrestler, power-rushing more effectively than defensive linemen who were at least fifty pounds heavier. Much of Taylor's strength came from his lower body, from his buttocks to his knees. The linebacker shed tight ends Gary Shirk and Dave Young, two of the biggest Giants on the field, as if they were flyweights. Taylor matched his physical gifts with an ultracompetitive spirit that aimed at dominance. Suddenly it seemed confounding that New Orleans had bypassed Taylor, even for a star runner like Rogers.

Taylor finished his first intrasquad game with four sacks and a fumble recovery. The performance was so otherworldly that even a passerby ignorant of the difference between a fumble and a sack could tell that he was the best player on the field. Over the years Giants veterans had witnessed ballyhooed prospects with terrific physical attributes that didn't make it in the NFL, but the rookie linebacker from North Carolina eased any tensions with his new teammates by living up to the hype while showing a willingness to work hard.

Perkins gave Bill Belichick permission to use Taylor on his special-teams unit. Giants coaches reviewed practice daily on film, and they sat riveted and amused by the special-teams footage, watching intrasquad opponents steer clear of Taylor. He played with kamikaze ferocity, yet he had an uncanny knack for avoiding injury. After almost a week of scrimmaging, Perkins sidled up to Parcells. The typically dour head coach grinned. "I came to camp wondering if he was everything he was cracked up to be."

Parcells said, "So?"

"Well, he's everything he's cracked up to be."

They both laughed.

Parcells said, "No shit. I gotta get this kid into the *game*."

Perkins nodded, agreeing that the standard approach of keeping error-prone rookies from starting didn't apply to Taylor. Early in preseason, the rookie was promoted from backup to the Giants' fourth linebacker in their new 3-4 scheme.

The 3-4 defense was invented in the late 1940s by Oklahoma Sooners coach Bud Wilkinson, whose career Parcells had studied intensively as a college assistant. The base formation consists of a nose tackle between two defensive ends (the "three"), plus two inside linebackers flanked by both outside linebackers (the "four"). Before this, NFL linebackers didn't need to be particularly athletic, big, or powerful. Their main duty was supporting the run defense and adjusting to the pass.

As college coaches entered the NFL, though, the position evolved; during the 1970s, when the so-called Oklahoma defense reached the pros, the unconventional alignment began propelling linebackers to stardom. Now they not only had responsibility for stopping the run; they had to pass-rush like defensive linemen and contest passes like defensive backs. The wide range of duties required linebackers to be among the best athletes on the field. "They became attackers," Parcells explains. "Hell, they became assassins, like Lawrence Taylor."

For decades before Parcells was hired as Giants defensive coordinator, the club had generally used a 4-3 defense. Created by Tom Landry during the 1950s when he was the team's defensive coordinator, the alignment typically placed four defenders at the line of scrimmage and three linebackers behind them. Parcells's planned change was "earth-shattering," recalls former defensive end George Martin, who had played exclusively in the 4-3 since joining the Giants in 1975.

Perkins expected the change to spur an aggressive defense while exploiting the increasingly athletic pool of college linebackers. But Parcells intended to revamp the defense's mind-set as much as its alignment. The main objective was to force the ball carrier to the perimeter, just as Parcells had taught his initially resistant Texas Tech unit to do.

Making the change even more drastic, Parcells also implemented the two-gap approach, which was foreign to most of the Giants. As a former Wichita linebacker, Parcells had played in the system before using it as a college coach. The two-gap system in the 3-4 alignment was brought to the Patriots, if not the NFL, by Chuck Fairbanks during the 1970s. His defensive coordinator, Hank Bullough, made key contributions to enhance the two-gap system, so NFL coaches now referred to the 3-4 version of it as the "Fairbanks-Bullough" defense. Introducing the two-gap approach to the Giants, Parcells required his defenders to play head-on instead of focusing on one assigned gap. "It's not, 'I got this gap, and you got that gap. And how come you weren't in your gap?'" Parcells says. "I don't like that. We *all* got these gaps. We *all* got the ball carrier."

New York's defense had a strong veteran presence, linebackers set in their ways, so Parcells faced an early challenge. Instead of dealing with compliant student-athletes, Parcells now encountered "a different breed of animal," as former linebacker Harry Carson recalls. When the Giants defense was informed of the seismic shift from the 4-3, some players grumbled, unhappy that the new coach was altering their traditional scheme. Oblivious to the barbs, Parcells exuded confidence as he explained his changes. First he expounded on how the 3-4 would play to the defensive unit's strength. Although the Giants had allowed an average of 26.5 points the previous season, their starting linebackers made a terrific threesome of seasoned players: Harry Carson sandwiched by Brian Kelley and Brad Van Pelt.

A fourth-round choice in 1976 by way of South Carolina State, Carson was among the league's top linebackers, earning Pro Bowl status in 1978 and 1979. Van Pelt, a second-round pick in 1973 out of Michigan State, had garnered five consecutive Pro Bowls from 1976 to 1980; although he didn't fully exert himself at practice, Van Pelt performed fiercely in games. Kelley, a graduate of California Lutheran, had been chosen in the fourteenth round during the same draft as Van Pelt. These incumbent linebackers had never won more than six games in a season, yet they regularly performed with fervor. Taylor's dazzling performances from day one compelled Parcells to make him a starter, too. The defensive coordinator also envisioned having rookie linebacker Byron Hunt, a ninth-round pick via Southern Methodist, in the regular rotation by midseason.

Parcells's detailed breakdown of the new scheme often took place in one-on-one talks with leaders of the defense. Each day Parcells pulled a veteran aside to convey some particular aspect of his reasoning. He might discuss how a player's forte factored into a lineup change, for instance. "Fireside chatter," Martin says of the conversations. Previous Giants coaches had never deigned to explain their alterations, and as the defensive boss, with influence in management decisions to jettison players, Parcells could have taken the same approach. But his inclusive approach helped minimize player resistance while promoting an understanding of his logic.

Although Parcells had never played in an NFL regular-season game, his success as a college linebacker gave him currency with Giants players. Parcells's most important attribute, though, was his expertise, conveyed by sharp teaching skills. He stressed fundamentals such as tackling and blocking to veterans surprised to be learning so many new things. "He was the first educational coach I had in my entire career," says George Martin, who was in his seventh season when Parcells arrived.

Parcells compares arranging—or rearranging—personnel for the 3-4 to working on a jigsaw puzzle. Brian Kelley switched to inside linebacker next to Harry Carson. Taylor was placed at outside linebacker, while fellow rookie Byron Hunt and Brad Van Pelt shared the opposite spot. George Martin and Gary Jeter, a Pro Bowl alternate in 1980, were capable defensive ends, but for the system to work, Parcells needed to find a nose tackle. The search was complicated by injuries and players who weren't the right fit, but by early in preseason, Parcells had targeted a rookie defensive end: Bill Neill, drafted in the fifth round of the twelve-round draft. Parcells revealed his brainstorm at Big Blue's first meeting of scouts and coaches to discuss players, where his idea was met with a chorus of skepticism.

One scout noted about Neill, "He's never played there."

Another declared, "He can't do it."

George Young was more diplomatic: "He doesn't look like he's physically suited to the job."

Parcells grew upset at the sentiment, and glanced at Perkins to gauge his take. The head coach's silence kept the idea from being officially rejected. Parcells had already jolted his defense with several changes, including moving the speedy Beasley Reece from strong safety to free safety, but Parcells believed that the derision regarding Neill stemmed from politics. The chances of the midround pick being released jumped substantially if his switch to nose tackle failed, and scouts didn't want to sully their draft class.

Parcells listened to the skeptics for a few more minutes, hiding his disgust that no solutions were being offered. After everyone had said his piece, Parcells calmly told the gathering that he understood that it was his first Giants training camp, and he meant no disrespect. Then Parcells added in a forceful tone, "Unless any of you guys got a better idea, I'm going to move the sonofabitch there tomorrow."

The packed room turned silent. In the absence of counterproposals, the topic of nose tackle was closed. The next morning Bill Neill switched positions as the final piece of the 3-4 puzzle. His backup was Jim Burt, an undrafted free agent via Miami on his way to earning a roster spot by playing with abandon on special teams.

The 4-3 was the only defensive scheme Harry Carson had played in since entering Wilson High in Florence, South Carolina, in the late 1960s. He exuded the confidence of someone voted the NFC's top linebacker for two consecutive seasons, but under Parcells the sixth-year veteran needed to make perhaps the biggest adjustment of anyone: becoming one of two starting inside linebackers while performing within a system that required tighter discipline. In their first lengthy conversation, Parcells told Carson, "I think you've got an awful lot of talent, you've got good instincts, and you're *very* visible out there. But I'm not sure you're a good linebacker."

Surprised, the elite linebacker stared for a few seconds at the neophyte NFL coach.

"What do you mean?"

"You rely too much on your instincts, and as good as they are, they're not enough to make you one of the best in the game, which is what you should be—not because some player vote says you should go to the Pro Bowl, but because you really are."

"You just tell me where to start."

The star linebacker's openness impressed Parcells, who wanted Carson to correct some bad habits involving technique and positioning. Carson had always crowded offensive linemen, engaging them as soon as possible before stuffing the hole. His starting point was no more than three yards from the line of scrimmage, but Parcells instructed him to play as much as five yards back. The adjustment felt strange during the first several practices, leaving Carson frustrated. But Parcells just kept reassuring Carson that he possessed the quickness to start farther back before the snap. Carson overcame his discomfiture through repetition, embracing Parcells's challenge to take his game to the stratosphere. "That's the thing about Parcells," Carson says. "You can be good, but he'll find a way to break you down and build you back up to make you even better."

Lawrence Taylor's dominance in college had allowed him to intimidate coaches and teammates, so Parcells knew it was important to set boundaries early in his relationship with the rookie linebacker. At six-three and 250 pounds, Parcells was slightly bigger than his linebackers, even Taylor. The defensive coordinator's imposing frame added heft to his instructions, and played a part in sometimes instilling fear.

Parcells stood eye to eye with Taylor, saying, "Lookit, I'm going to say what's on my mind, Lawrence. I won't bullshit you. So don't try to bullshit me."

The rookie linebacker nodded in agreement. For all Taylor's prodigious talent, Parcells believed he could improve significantly. Taylor had spent most of his college career terrorizing offensive players near the line of scrimmage, but the linebacker, who had a limited understanding of passing defense, was open to learning the pro game. Although he was supremely confident, if not arrogant, on the field, he was a good listener during practice. "I didn't have to be a genius to know that he was going to be the horse and me the world's biggest jockey," says Parcells, a horse-racing aficionado. "He shut up and paid attention."

Taylor grasped football concepts quickly, showing an intuitive feel for the game and the way each athlete on the field contributed to every play. Parcells had granted Bill Belichick his wish to assist with the linebackers and occasionally the special-teams coach tested them on their knowledge of the playbook. A party animal, Taylor found it unnecessary to study as assiduously as his teammates did; he could still ace Belichick's tests, and was often the first to finish.

The Giants played a preseason game against Chuck Noll's Steelers, quarterbacked by Terry Bradshaw. After eleven pro football seasons and two straight Super Bowl MVPs, Bradshaw thought he had seen it all, but by the end of the exhibition contest, Pittsburgh's quarterback realized that he had never faced anyone quite like Taylor. "He dang near killed me," Bradshaw says. "I just kept saying, 'Who is this guy?' He kept coming from my blind side and just ripped my ribs to pieces."

In the preseason games that followed, when offenses directed running plays away from Taylor, he showed a knack for splitting a double team, chasing the carrier across the field, and tackling him for a loss. Taylor displayed awesome power, speed, and instinct, plus he seemed to be indefatigable. The linebacker often fought off a tight end with one hand before determining the ideal moment to pounce. "He was a football superman," Parcells says. Teammates joked that his locker should be replaced with a phone booth. With Green Bay visiting the Giants in week five, the Packers focused on neutralizing Taylor. Offensive coordinator Bob Schnelker warned his players what they'd be up against. "Guys, let me tell you. I've seen Butkus, I've seen Nitschke, I've seen the best. He's better than all of 'em."

The Packers won the game 27–14, handing New York its third loss in five games, but the rave reviews of Big Blue's top draft pick only increased. Supreme athleticism often enabled Taylor to recover from botched assignments or technical errors in time to make crucial plays.

New York's next game, on October 11 versus the St. Louis Cardinals in Giants Stadium, suddenly became crucial. After starting out with promise, Perkins's team seemed headed for another dismal season. During first-quarter action, Parcells called for his right outside linebacker to retreat for pass coverage on the snap. Instead Taylor stormed the quarterback for a sack that caused a fumble, recovered by the Giants. When Taylor returned

to the sideline, Parcells asked, "Lawrence, did you know you were supposed to drop back in that defense?"

Taylor replied, "Oh yeah, I forgot."

In the second quarter, Parcells called the same defensive play. Inexpli-
cably, Taylor once again charged past the line of scrimmage to hammer the
quarterback for another fumble. This time defensive end George Martin
snapped up the pigskin, sprinting to the end zone for a touchdown. The
crowd roared as Taylor strolled to the sideline, where he was mobbed by
teammates. Amid the din, Parcells approached the linebacker and stared
at him without comment.

Taylor broke the silence by slapping his temple with an open palm. "I
did it again, didn't I?"

Parcells repressed the urge to smile, and tried to sound stern. "Yeah,
you did. You know, Lawrence, we don't even *have* what you just did. It isn't
in our playbook."

Taylor smiled. "Well, Coach, we'd better put it in on Monday, because
it's a dandy."

New York's 34–14 victory prompted the defensive coordinator to revamp his relatively vanilla playbook. Previously it had called for the outside linebacker to rush on one of three passing situations, but Parcells now
let Taylor attack on two of every three. The modification unleashed the
"football superman" for quarterback-rattling moments that lifted the defense as New York won three straight. On October 18, Big Blue trounced
the Seahawks, 32–0, for its first shutout in three seasons. Then a 27–24
victory over Atlanta gave New York a 5-3 record at midseason, in stark
contrast to the previous season's midseason mark of 1-7.

Parcells was positioning Taylor on the left, middle, and right side of
the defensive alignment, and even in a three-point stance at defensive end.
Officially Taylor was a weak-side linebacker lining up on the side without
a tight end, but his unorthodox rushes were disrupting conventional formations. Opponents tried to adjust by taking drastic measures. Redskins
head coach Joe Gibbs created a single-back, double-tight-end formation,
hoping to keep Taylor at bay with the extra, heavyweight blocker. Washington's offense used formations with blockers who slid toward Taylor:
"Fifty-six is the rover; find the rover."

Parcells was not just an excellent teacher; he was a quick learner, too. He
stood out on the coaching staff for his masterly grasp of human behavior,
with an uncanny knack for getting the most out of each individual. "He
knew which players he could put the needle to," recalls Dave Jennings, a

Pro Bowl punter at the time, "and which ones were sensitive and couldn't be dealt with like that." Sometimes, though, Parcells kept a player off balance with contradictory approaches: The coordinator might berate someone throughout practice for lackluster effort, but after the session ended he would walk up to the dismayed defender and put an arm around him, saying, "You know I really love you, right?"

Parcells knew that such maddening methods wouldn't necessarily work on a budding superstar who performed fiercely with every snap, but he was intent on prodding Lawrence Taylor to sustain, if not increase, his production. So Parcells exploited Taylor's ultra-competitive nature by invoking the other top linebacker of the 1981 draft. Hugh Green was chosen seventh overall by Tampa Bay after a stellar career with the Pittsburgh Panthers, where he finished second to George Rogers in voting for the Heisman Trophy. Within earshot of Taylor, Parcells praised Green, who was playing well as a rookie. "That's the kind of linebacker I'd want on my team."

The remarks irritated Taylor, despite his performing at a higher level than Green. Taylor responded as Parcells guessed he would—by maintaining his high level of performance with occasional superhuman flourishes.

Despite coaching with an edge, Parcells also found ways to bond with his players. He enjoyed banter and repartee, even when he was the butt of it. The main thing that kept the defensive coordinator in a nasty mood was losing. Stars and backup players alike yearned to satisfy their hard-to-please boss; his overarching desire was to find athletes he could trust on the field.

New York's promising record at midseason was undermined by three consecutive losses, bringing familiar angst to the team's long-suffering fans. Parcells's defense contributed to the skid, allowing an average of 27.3 points against the Jets, Packers, and Redskins. In the 30–27 loss against Washington, quarterback Phil Simms, New York's first-round pick in 1979, separated his shoulder in a season-ending injury. Perkins was forced to start rookie Scott Brunner, a sixth-round pick.

Things looked bleak for the 5-6 Giants as they traveled to Philadelphia for a November 22 game. The Eagles were 9-2, including a 24–10 victory over Big Blue in their season opener. In the five years since Dick Vermeil had taken over as head coach, the Eagles had never lost to Big Blue.

The air was nippy a few hours before the 1 p.m. kickoff at Veterans Stadium as Vermeil strolled on the field. Despite temperatures in the low thirties, Vermeil relished the relative solitude. Spotting the opponent's defensive coordinator going through a similar pregame ritual, Vermeil decided to walk over and introduce himself. "Bill, I don't know if I should like you or hate you, but I'm certainly going to congratulate you because, boy, this New York Giants defense has really changed from what it was when I started coaching against your team."

After Vermeil's introduction the opposing coaches chatted for a few minutes. Several hours later Parcells's unit justified the compliment by stifling an offense that had scored 90 points the previous two games. New York's skid against Philadelphia, dating to 1975, ended with a 20–10 victory. "I started respecting him even more," recalls Vermeil, chuckling.

Including the upset versus Philadelphia, Big Blue won four of five during the stretch run as Parcells's defense tightened the screws: opponents scored an average of only 10.8 points. The linebacking corps lost Pro Bowler Brad Van Pelt to injury, yet rookie Byron Hunt filled in with no drop-off. By late in the season, Perkins was making adjustments to the offense based on Parcells's unit. Going into a game, Perkins would ask for his outlook on the defense. If Parcells felt that it was particularly vulnerable, Perkins emphasized ball control. When Parcells foresaw his players stifling an opponent, Perkins was inclined to open up the offense for Scott Brunner's passing. Big Blue's defense began to dictate the team's style, or chances to win, in each game. "Mickey loved it," Parcells says of the Giants' new identity. "He'd been telling me about how defense wins games since I was fourteen."

Perhaps the unit's most impressive showing came in the regular-season finale against Tom Landry's Cowboys, who were vying for the NFC's top seed. In a 13–10 overtime victory decided by Joe Danelo's field goal, the Giants held Dallas to its lowest output of the season, improving to 9-7. The late-season flourish propelled Big Blue to its first playoff appearance since 1963. Returning to Philadelphia for an NFC wild-card game, Big Blue upset the Eagles for a second time, 27–21, as Brunner tossed three touchdowns and Rob Carpenter amassed 161 rushing yards.

New York's roller-coaster of a season ended in the divisional round with a 38–24 loss to Bill Walsh's 49ers, the postseason's top-seeded team. San Francisco assigned guard John Ayers, the team's best blocker, to Lawrence Taylor, who finished with only three tackles, including a sack against quarterback Joe Montana. Nonetheless, the linebacker became the first rookie in NFL history to be named defensive player of the year, helping Parcells's unit transform into one of the league's best.

With its unique, pass-crazy offense, San Francisco went on to capture the franchise's first Super Bowl, 26–21, over Forrest Gregg's Cincinnati Bengals. Big Blue finished the season allowing 257 points, a striking improvement from 425 points the previous year. By guiding the Giants to their first postseason in almost two decades, Perkins was rewarded with a contract extension, and the resurgent franchise even earned an appearance on *Monday Night Football*'s 1982 schedule.

When Ray Perkins was hired by the Giants in 1979, he invited the team's beat writers to his home for an informal gathering. Dave Klein of the *Newark Star-Ledger* asked for Perkins's thoughts on Alabama's head-coaching job if it ever became available.

"I'd walk to Tuscaloosa for it."

Replacing Bear Bryant wasn't on Perkins's mind three years later, when Big Blue's 1982 preseason started ominously. Quarterback Phil Simms hurt his knee in another season-ending injury, tailback Rob Carpenter was holding out for a new contract, and, worst of all, Lawrence Taylor suffered an injury and was expected to miss at least the first four games. Undermanned, the Giants lost their first two games before the season was halted by a players' strike. When they agreed to return for a nine-game schedule two months later, the silver lining for Big Blue was Taylor's recuperation and Carpenter's having signed a new deal.

After losing its first game after the strike, Big Blue won three straight as the defense gave up a total of only 27 points. A December 11 victory over Philadelphia in a rare Saturday game improved the Giants to 3-3. With only three games left, they were in postseason contention, but everything was suddenly overshadowed by Perkins's stunning revelation: he was leaving the Giants to coach at Alabama.

Bear Bryant was planning to end his twenty-five-year tenure in late January of 1983, but Perkins told his players that management might want him to step down immediately. If so, Perkins informed his assistants, one of them would likely replace him. Both offensive coordinator Ron Erhardt and offensive line coach Bill Austin had NFL head-coaching experience: From 1966 to 1968 Austin had coached the Steelers, prior to Chuck Noll. When Vince Lombardi died on September 3, 1970, near the start of his second season in Washington, Austin had filled in for his ex-coach. Even so, Parcells, with a strong recommendation from Perkins, believed he had the best shot among Giants coaches.

Although disappointed by Perkins's impending departure, George Young understood the pull of the Alabama job, especially to Bear Bryant's ex-wideout. "All those former players, they're like the followers of Muhammad," Young told reporters. "And each of them wants to be the one anointed to take his place." So the GM took pride in the fact that Alabama targeted Perkins over other possibilities such as Steve Sloan at Mississippi.

One night soon after the bombshell, Parcells was the last coach leaving Giants Stadium. George Young was sitting in his office with the door ajar when he spotted Parcells walking by. The GM yelled for the defensive coordinator to drop in. Parcells grinned in the hallway before entering Young's office with a serious demeanor. During the next hour and a half, Young asked questions about the Giants that went beyond the defense, but the GM didn't reveal his thoughts about replacing Perkins.

When Alabama made things official on December 13, Perkins telephoned Young, who was in Tulsa, Oklahoma, attending a meeting of the United Scouting Combine, a personnel-evaluation event. After speaking to Perkins, the GM decided to cut his trip short. At 10:30 p.m., Parcells received a call at home from Young, who was awaiting his return flight at the Tulsa Airport.

"I want to talk to you Tuesday after work."

Parcells replied, "Well, I want the job." Tuesday, an off day for players, was hectic for coaches, who were busy reviewing film and preparing a game plan. Parcells arrived at his usual start of 6 a.m. and worked until 7 p.m., when he headed down the hall to meet Young. He exuded confidence. "I knew I wasn't there for a social visit," Parcels recalls. "I thought I would either come out of there with the job or say something that would eliminate me from consideration."

In a discussion that stretched three hours, Young complimented the coordinator on the defense's turnaround, and conveyed the organization's desire for continuity. At Young's suggestion, Parcells took a few minutes to read the organization's corporate bylaws, which put the head coach under the GM's supervision. When Young broached the topic of Perkins's staff, Parcells felt momentum moving his way, and seized it.

"There are going to be a few guys on the staff I don't want to retain."

Young replied, "That's completely up to you. Let's just talk about any moves you make before you actually make them."

"Fine."

Finally, Young wrote down some figures for a prospective multiyear contract, averaging $125,000. He also promised to insert language giving Parcells the same authority held by Perkins, including significant input in the draft.

Young asked, "Would these terms be satisfactory to you?"

Parcells replied, "Do you want me to accept those terms?"

"This is a ballpark figure."

"Is it the going rate?"

"Pretty close."

Switching gears, Parcells said sternly, "Now, George, you're not going to write anything in that contract that says I have to socialize or play golf, are you?" Young laughed at the remark, but when Parcells showed no sign of levity, the GM realized it wasn't a joke. Young moved past the potential sticking point by replying that the last place he wanted to find his head coach during the season was on a golf course.

Parcells preferred not to sign a new contract until his current one expired on February 28, 1983, so to seal their agreement, the new head coach and the GM shook hands. Young was pleased that he'd settled on Perkins's replacement so quickly, minimizing distractions for the upcoming Redskins game. Also, Young wanted to avoid losing Parcells to another club by waiting until after the season.

Young had first heard Parcells's name mentioned in early 1979, soon after being hired as Giants GM from the Miami Dolphins. In his final day there as personnel director, Young was cleaning out his desk before leaving for a California-bound flight to interview Perkins. Dan Henning, the Dolphins quarterbacks coach, swung by to strongly recommend someone as an assistant coach.

"There's a guy you ought to be interested in named Bill Parcells."

Henning insisted that his ex–Florida State colleague would be Big Blue's best assistant. Because Young respected Henning, he made a mental note of the remarks. The GM, though, didn't want to force anyone on his new head coach. After hiring Perkins, Young never mentioned Parcells as a prospective candidate. But as the two discussed the key job of linebackers coach in early 1979, Young was pleased to hear that Perkins was targeting the head coach of Air Force.

The new Giants head coach drove home to Upper Saddle River, New Jersey, and greeted his wife with the news. Judy Parcells was thrilled for her husband. Parcells phoned his oldest daughter, Suzy, at Idaho State University, and then called his father in Oradell. "The name 'Parcells' may not be an asset around here anymore."

Bill Parcells's crack alluded to the criticism inherent in being the Giants head coach. Charles Parcells was a popular man in Bergen County, where his friends included mayors, judges, and the like. Jokes aside, Charles grasped the significance of his son's new position, and he was characteristically laconic and even-keeled.

"Good luck."

In a separate conversation, Bill Parcells told Ida excitedly, "Hey, Mom, I'm going to be head coach of the Giants."

She responded, "When are you gonna get a *real* job, like your brother the banker? Aren't you tired of those gymnasiums?"

Even as Parcells rose in his profession, Ida saw little value in coaching.

Instead she constantly bragged to friends and relatives about her other son, Don, being managing director at Marine Midland Bank.

After informing his other close relatives, Parcells phoned Bobby Knight. Before hearing the news, Knight mentioned that the football head-coaching job at Indiana had just come open, and he'd been planning to call Parcells to gauge his interest. Parcells replied, "Thanks, but under the circumstances, I'm glad you didn't. I'm going to be coach of the Giants."

The Hoosiers coach was thrilled. Parcells told Knight that he had various options for structuring his new contract, so Knight suggested that Parcells visit Bloomington in a few weeks to discuss it. As Parcells's salary increased, the financial aspect of the profession became increasingly important to him.

The next day the Giants held simultaneous press conferences announcing Perkins's departure and Parcells's ascension. Before reporters arrived in the press lounge, Harry Carson stopped by the podium to offer Parcells his congratulations. When Parcells toggled the face of his new nameplate, Carson laughed at the inside joke. As defensive coordinator Parcells had reminded his players about their expendability by noting the convenient design of locker-room nameplates.

Parcells put the twin developments of the day in perspective when he told reporters, "For Bill Parcells, coaching the New York Giants is what Alabama is for Ray Perkins. I would have done this for free." During the press conference, linebacker Brian Kelley passed by and interjected: "All right. Way to move in, Tuna. I mean *Sir* Tuna." Parcells grinned amid laughter from reporters and club officials.

Kelley's lighthearted "*Sir* Tuna" contained an element of uncomfortable truth. Parcells's new title demanded a level of deference. In the defensive coordinator's meeting room, where expletives flew both ways, Parcells had seemed as much colleague as boss. Those loose interactions would have to end. "That was the biggest thing that we had to come to grips with," Carson recalls. "Instead of, 'Bill, you arrogant asshole,' or 'Bill, you dick,' we had to call him 'Coach Parcells' and extend him a certain degree of respect."

The defense understood that the move would help maintain continuity for a franchise that finally seemed headed in the right direction, but some players were concerned that Parcells's new responsibilities would alter their relationship. "We didn't want to share Bill Parcells," George Martin explains. "We felt he was ours alone. We were upset when he was named head coach because now we had to share him with that sorry offense. How dare they!"

Many NFL pundits felt that the Giants needed an offensive-minded coach to become a championship-caliber team, but George Young pointed out that some of the top contemporary coaches came from defensive backgrounds, including Tom Landry, Chuck Noll, and Don Shula. "I'm not looking for a genius coach," Young told reporters. "I'm not saying that Bill isn't one. What I am saying is that we are not in the genius business. If you're asking for a messiah in this business, forget it. That happened a long time ago."

Naturally, Phil Simms hadn't spent much time with Bill Parcells, yet the fourth-year quarterback knew the defensive coordinator well enough to imagine he'd make a good head coach. During downtime at Giants headquarters, Parcells and Simms had occasionally sat next to each other and talked. Once, Parcells described his ideal quarterback as strong-armed, unflappable, and confident. Simms was so psyched by the talks that when the quarterback arrived home he excitedly told wife, Diane, "He's talking about me!" Simms had viewed Ray Perkins as forbidding, and he had watched enviously as Parcells balanced toughness and tenderness with his defensive players. So while acknowledging the outgoing Perkins's tremendous contributions to the organization, Simms was pleased with the change. "I need some stroking," he told reporters.

Parcells was eager to assume control for the upcoming critical game in Washington on December 19, but with the Giants in playoff contention, Young instructed Perkins to keep his lead role for the team's final three games, all of which were on the road. The club needed to win at least two contests to make the postseason, and Young wanted to avoid throwing Parcells into the tail end of a topsy-turvy season. Despite being a lame duck, Perkins commanded respect for having guided the franchise to its first playoff appearance in almost twenty years.

Their chances for a postseason berth dimmed when the Giants lost to the Redskins, 15–14, on a snowy afternoon at RFK Memorial Stadium. With four seconds left, Mark Moseley's 42-yard field goal wobbled over the crossbar after being tipped. The kick sent the Redskins into the playoffs while giving Moseley an NFL record for 21 consecutive field goals.

During the flight to St. Louis for a December 26 game, Parcells and Perkins sat next to each other in the plane's front row. Perkins mined Parcells for insights from his fifteen years coaching college football, while Parcells bombarded Perkins with inquiries about the Giants organization. "I was already grateful to Ray," Parcells says, "for taking me by the scruff of the neck and dragging me back into pro football. Now I was grateful to him for leaving."

The Giants lost to the Cardinals, 24–21, in a game that all but mathematically ended their postseason hopes. Perkins's team won its finale, 26–24, versus Philadelphia to finish the season 4-5. And the transition period from Perkins to Parcells came to an end. After the game, the former defensive coordinator spoke candidly to the media about impending changes involving Giants assistants: "I don't view them as my coaching staff; I view them as Coach Perkins's staff." Ultimately, Parcells retained five assistants, the roots of his coaching tree: Ron Erhardt (offensive coordinator), Bill Belichick (linebackers coach), Romeo Crennel (special teams), Pat Hodgson (receivers), and Lamar Leachman (defensive line).

8

Bill Parcells opened his first practice as Giants head coach on April 29, 1983, with his father at his side. Inside the team's facility at East Rutherford, New Jersey, near where he raised his boy, Charles Parcells listened while the franchise's thirteenth coach addressed players in a rookies-only session. The NFL newbies included linebacker Andy Headen, safety Terry Kinard, defensive end Leonard Marshall, offensive tackle Karl Nelson, kicker Ali Haji-Sheikh, and cornerback Perry Williams. Parcells boomed, "You're not on scholarship anymore. No one's going to wake you up in the morning, but just like any other guy in business, I'm interested in production and reliability. I don't want guys who I have to get out of jail, or don't know where they are."

Parcells was no longer defensive coordinator of a team that barely missed the playoffs in the previous, strike-shortened season. He was the popular choice among Giants players to lead a franchise with high hopes of re-creating its 1981 playoff appearance. Later, in Perkins's old office, Parcells experienced a surreal moment viewing a group photograph of himself among the head coaches entering the 1983 season: Tom Landry stood next to the Giants' new leader, with Chuck Noll nearby. The former Hastings assistant had reached the upper echelon of his profession.

Parcells hired Bobby Knight's son Tim to work as one of the Giants ball boys, joining two of Vince Lombardi's grandsons for the plum gig. One day at practice, Parcells was flattered when Tim told him, "You coach just like my father." While the firebrand basketball lord had already captured two NCAA Tournament titles, Parcells was just getting started as an NFL head coach. At training camp Parcells began tweaking the club in his image, and Giants veterans started calibrating their collegial approach.

The first hint of trouble came a few weeks before the regular-season opener. The new head coach faced a quarterback quandary—a choice between the talented yet oft-injured incumbent, Phil Simms, and the unspectacular though reliable backup, Scott Brunner. "There are a lot of things a new coach doesn't need," Parcells says, "and a quarterback controversy is one of the big ones. It's just like stepping into a pile of shit."

Simms had been drafted seventh overall in 1979, out of Morehead State in Kentucky. When Pete Rozelle announced his name on draft day at the Waldorf-Astoria, Giants supporters unleashed boos, viewing the blond, blue-eyed quarterback as an unsexy pick. They were unfamiliar with Simms and his public school of 7,200 in a rural area between Lexington, Kentucky, and Huntington, West Virginia. Even the Giants' representative at the draft, promotions director Tom Power, wasn't up to speed. When the surprise choice was relayed to him via telephone from the organization's draft bunker at Giants Stadium, Power wrote "Moorehead" on the card that he handed to Rozelle for the official selection.

In four seasons with the Morehead State Eagles, Simms completed only 48.9 percent of his passes in a ball-control offense that never reached a bowl game. Nonetheless, his powerful arm and school-record 5,545 passing yards made the relatively obscure quarterback an NFL prospect. New 49ers coach Bill Walsh, who lacked a first-round pick, targeted Simms with San Francisco's second-round choice, twenty-ninth overall. But after Simms was drafted early by New York, San Francisco switched gears and went after a Notre Dame quarterback named Joe Montana.

Young's unpopular choice looked promising as a rookie, winning 6 of 11 starts in a season the Giants went 6-10. He was runner-up for Rookie of the Year, earned by tailback Ottis Anderson, who had been drafted by the St. Louis Cardinals one spot after Simms. The Giants quarterback showed even more promise in 1980 before separating his shoulder with three games left. A similar injury early during the 1981 season again forced Scott Brunner into a starting role.

Brunner was a heady if unspectacular quarterback, adroit at reading coverage. He came from a Division II team, the Delaware Fighting Blue Hens, having led them to the 1979 national title in his only season as starter. In 1980 the Giants plucked Brunner in the sixth round of a twelve-round draft. In 1981, while Simms was sidelined, Brunner was steady enough for Big Blue to reach an elusive playoff appearance. He guided the Giants to the upset victory at Philadelphia before their rollicking ride ended on the road against the Montana-quarterbacked 49ers.

In the 1982 preseason, Perkins had been inclined to stick with Brunner as his starter. It was a difficult choice for the coach who had convinced management to draft Simms. After an exhibition contest against Pittsburgh, Perkins informed his staff of his leanings. Before that decision was handed down, however, Simms suffered a season-ending knee injury, a setback that made Perkins's decision moot, postponing the quarterback controversy.

Since he had joined the Giants in 1981, Parcells had seen more production from Brunner but intended to name Simms the starter if the quarterback reprised his earlier promise with a strong preseason. When both quarterbacks responded with so-so performances, Parcells faced his first major decision. Parcells sought input from his staff, but no assistant offered strong support for either candidate. In the absence of compelling evidence, the typically assertive coach turned wishy-washy.

When the Giants head coach called for each of his quarterbacks to visit his office the next morning for a decision, Simms assumed he would reclaim the starting job, especially after having undergone a grueling rehab. Plus the fifth-year veteran believed that being "a meat-and-potatoes guy" made him Parcells's type of quarterback. Before leaving home for Giants Stadium, Simms told his anxious wife, "It's going to be me, don't even worry. I just can't imagine it going any other way."

As Simms walked down the hallway toward Parcells's office, he saw Brunner stepping out. The incumbent didn't scrutinize his challenger's facial expression for any hint of a decision. Exuding confidence, Simms moved toward the seat opposite Parcells, who was skimming a Red Sox trivia book while wearing a white golf shirt emblazoned with the baseball team's logo.

"Hey, Coach."

Before Simms's butt hit the chair, Parcells responded, "Phil, I've decided to go with Scott."

Stunned, Simms said, "Excuse me?"

Parcells reiterated his decision.

"You've got to be kidding me."

While Simms trembled with rage, Parcells offered an explanation. But the erstwhile starter felt betrayed.

Shaking his head, Simms blurted, "Trade me!"

"Is that really what you want?"

Simms, known for being a good soldier, responded loudly, "Yeah, that's what I want."

"We'll see what I can do about it."

The Brunner-quarterbacked Giants split their first four games, the last of which was an impressive 27–3 victory over Green Bay. But on October 2 against San Diego, Big Blue's defense imploded in a 41–34 setback. Five days later, on October 7, the Giants experienced a more profound loss when running-backs coach Bob Ledbetter died of a brain hemorrhage. The forty-nine-year-old had suffered a stroke two weeks earlier, on his birthday.

Ledbetter, whom Parcells had met through Dan Henning, was in his first year with the Giants, having spent the previous six years as running-backs coach for Walt Michaels's Jets. When Michaels hired him in 1977, Ledbetter was the first black coach in Jets history. A burly man with a reputation for inspiring players, Ledbetter brought a toughness to his job that he had developed as an army master sergeant during the Korean War.

Two busloads of players traveled from Giants Stadium for Ledbetter's funeral in Fort Salonga, Long Island, where they were joined by an equal number of Jets. Parcells struggled to get through the next few days. A moment of silence for Ledbetter preceded the national anthem at Big Blue's next home game, against Philadelphia. But after an emotional start, the Giants seemed headed for their second straight defeat as Ron Jaworski's 18-yard pass to wideout Mike Quick gave Philadelphia a 14–6 lead in the third quarter.

Faced with the prospect of a 2-4 record, Parcells decided to yank Brunner, and the passed-over Simms made the most of the opportunity. He completed four of his first five throws, and Butch Woolfolk's seven-yard run capped a drive that cut Philadelphia's lead to 14–13. The impressive display filled Giants Stadium with hopes of a comeback victory, but on Big Blue's next offensive series, Simms demonstrated his tendency to be brittle. After he took the snap on third-and-short, his right hand struck the massive arm of defensive end Dennis Harrison. Screaming in pain, Simms looked down and saw bone protruding from his throwing thumb. It was Simms's third consecutive season-ending injury.

"I felt bad for him," Parcells says, "and worse for me."

The upshot, beyond a 17–13 loss to the Eagles, was that Parcells turned back to the quarterback whose tepid production had compelled a switch. Naturally, Brunner's confidence, and the offense's faith in him, had nosedived. The Giants didn't win again for another six weeks. The skid was only interrupted by an October 24 game against the St. Louis Cardinals that ended in a 20–20 tie. Quarterback Jeff Rutledge started for Big Blue in the team's rare appearance on *Monday Night Football*. "One of the ugliest games," Parcells recalls, "of all time."

Two of Parcells's daughters, Suzy and Dallas, were away at college. So in Upper Saddle River, New Jersey, only his youngest daughter, Jill, and wife, Judy, were home to feel the brunt of the losses—from Parcells, who was miserable to be around, and from critics, whose clamor increased with each setback. On most Monday mornings during the season, Jill complained to her mother about feeling under the weather, and asked for permission to stay home from school. She hid the true reason for wanting to miss classes after the weekend, anticipation of her schoolmates trashing the Giants and her father, but Judy saw the correlation right away. "It was hard for me, too," Judy recalls, "because I knew what she was dealing with. Bill was working so hard, yet not getting the results he wanted."

Judy and Jill couldn't even enjoy a basic perk of being related to the Giants head coach. Parcells had four season tickets for the mezzanine balcony, across the 35-yard line, at Giants Stadium, where an overhang protected the seats from rain and snow, but it did nothing to shield Parcells's wife and daughter from hecklers. During one home game a man sitting in the level below railed incessantly. In a strident voice laced with curses, the fan criticized Parcells's coaching ability along with his girth. By the fourth quarter Jill had reached her limit. Moments later Judy watched with nervousness and pride as Jill poked the spectator, demanding an end to the diatribe. The act wasn't surprising coming from Jill, whose nickname was "Chip," as in "off the old block": among the Parcells girls, she had inherited her father's assertiveness.

Mother and daughter watched the final quarter of the loss in relative peace.

In late October, a few weeks after Bob Ledbetter's death, Charles Parcells underwent double-bypass surgery at Columbia-Presbyterian Medical Center in Manhattan. Despite requiring a transfusion, the operation seemed to go smoothly. But when Ida returned to Oradell after paying Charles a visit, she began complaining about sharp back pain. Ida phoned Parcells one morning, telling him that it had become so excruciating that she couldn't get out of bed. Parcells arranged for a doctor to see her, but with the pain unabated the physician instructed Ida to immediately visit a local hospital for further testing.

The bad news turned worse. Diagnosed with malignant bone cancer, Ida was admitted to Memorial Sloan Kettering in Manhattan, perhaps the nation's top cancer facility. However, the disease had progressed so far that she was given only a few weeks to live. "I had the feeling," Parcells recalls, "that the world was coming down on my head."

Parcells decided to keep the prognosis from Charles while he was still in the hospital. Released in early November, Charles first went to visit Bill and Judy in Upper Saddle River, when Parcells finally revealed the severity of Ida's condition. Charles returned to Oradell distraught. Fortunately, he didn't stay home alone because his daughter, Debbie, had been living with her parents. After only a few days Charles developed a blood infection and was rushed to nearby Hackensack University Medical Center. "It was one thing after another, and I didn't handle it well," Parcells says. "But what are you going do? They're not going to cancel the football games. In this business, you don't ever stop. You can't stop. You've just got to keep going. When it comes down to it, I'm an it-is-what-it-is kinda guy. You've got to be able to deal with it. The poor-me syndrome is very damaging psychologically, and it loves company."

In his scarce free time, Parcells shuttled between hospitals, seeking good news and finding none. Back at work, hopes of a turnaround proved equally elusive. On November 27, the Giants lost 27–12 to the Los Angeles Raiders, dropping to a record of 3-9-1, a painful reversal for an organization with playoff aspirations. Simms's broken thumb seemed to have triggered an epidemic on the gridiron, as the Giants rarely finished a game without at least one additional injury. Waves of players landed on the injured-reserve list, which meant a minimum of four missed games, including such key performers as Pro Bowl linebacker Harry Carson and tailback Rob Carpenter. As healthy offensive players, particularly quarterback Scott Brunner, showed a tendency for carelessness and turnovers, frustration and anger boiled into the open. Linebackers Brad Van Pelt and Harry Carson demanded to be traded, and Lawrence Taylor complained publicly about the team's regression.

Amid these challenges, another issue simmered. A few weeks into the season, Parcells had discovered an undercurrent of drug abuse on the team: several players were cocaine and marijuana users. Thanks to an innocent childhood, Parcells had virtually no experience with drugs, but he was convinced that marijuana and cocaine were hindering his team's performance. Although his father had been an alcoholic until reaching sobriety in midlife, Parcells knew little about substance abuse. What he discovered led him to conclude that when the season ended, players linked to drug use would be given a chance to break their addiction, or be jettisoned.

Beyond the not-so-secret drug problem and injury epidemic, declining productivity among some veterans made Parcells's Giants a far different team from the one for which he had worked as defensive coordinator. Too many players lacked the kind of esprit de corps that had been so useful during tough stretches. This mountain of problems would have been challenging for even an established coach, but Parcells's inexperience only made the situation worse. The witty Jersey native found almost nothing to quip about as the season wore on.

Although his parents were in grave health, Parcells refrained from discussing their situations. When reporters inquired about his personal tribulations, Parcells offered only the basics while emphasizing that off-the-field difficulties didn't reduce his commitment to the Giants. He veered off script only slightly in a postgame conference following a November 27 road loss to the Los Angeles Raiders. "I think I have this game in perspective. It's very, very important, and it's my job. But I understand what place it occupies in the world. It's important for me, but it's not the only thing."

Nonetheless, in early December, Parcells received stunning news that put his job front and center. Parcells's agent, Robert Fraley, telephoned to tell his client that the Giants were secretly courting someone to replace him. George Young had contacted Howard Schnellenberger, head coach of the powerhouse Miami Hurricanes, to gauge his interest in Parcells's job. Agents representing coaches weren't yet the norm, and Young avoided them whenever possible, so he was unaware of Schnellenberger's connection to Parcells's agent. The coincidence was perhaps the only bit of luck during the Twilight Zone of a season.

Parcells couldn't believe that he was being judged after less than one injury-marred season. "I didn't exactly want to run into George Young's office and give him a hug," Parcells says, "when I found out that in addition to all the bad things that were happening in my life, he was scouting Howard Schnellenberger's future plans when he said he was scouting games." Still, Parcells knew that Young's shenanigans could take place only with the blessing of Big Blue's owners.

Young and Schnellenberger had a long-standing relationship. In 1968, Young started his NFL career by joining the Baltimore Colts as a scout. Young got the job largely through Don Shula, Baltimore's head coach at the time, but when Shula switched to the Dolphins in 1970, Young stayed with the Colts. After Schnellenberger was hired as Baltimore's head coach in 1973, he appointed Young as his offensive coordinator.

Future Giants GM Ernie Accorsi, working in Baltimore's front office, urged Young against a switch to coaching: "You're nuts." With Baltimore struggling, Schnellenberger and his staff were dismissed less than two years later. Using their ties to Shula, Young and Schnellenberger landed with the Dolphins in 1975, Schnellenberger as offensive coordinator and Young back in the personnel department. When Young moved to the Giants as GM in 1979, Schnellenberger departed the Dolphins to coach the University of Miami.

Using a pro-style offense not yet standard in college, and the disciplinarian approach of his mentors Bear Bryant and Don Shula, Schnellenberger led the Hurricanes, unranked since the 1960s, to national prominence. In 1983 the football team, quarterbacked by Bernie Kosar, was heading to a 10-1 record, top-five ranking, and invitation to the Orange Bowl. Given Parcells's struggles and Young's relationship with Schnellenberger, the college coach became an alluring candidate. During the 1983 season, the former colleagues spoke face-to-face a few times.

Parcells says, "I never met Howard Schnellenberger, but to his credit he told my agent, 'These guys are offering me the job, and I'm not going to take it. You need to tell Bill that that's what they're doing.' So he was really a coach's coach, and I've admired him for that."

Aching for a second chance in the wheelhouse, Parcells was uncertain how to handle the explosive intelligence. The embattled coach turned to one of the NFL's most successful and controversial figures: Raiders chief Al Davis. Parcells considered him to be among the smartest men in pro football, and their connection dated back to 1964, when Parcells played for Davis in a college all-star game. Upon joining the NFL sixteen years later, Parcells had reached out to him.

Through Parcells, the Raiders boss was reminded of his younger self, and grew fond enough of Big Blue's head coach to become a sounding board. One of Davis's conversation starters was asking sardonically, "Am I speaking to the coach of the New *Yawk* Giants? The cradle of professional football?" When Parcells brought up the Southwest Challenge, Davis's remarks about vividly remembering him were met with skepticism.

On being told about the Schnellenberger situation, Davis advised Parcells to avoid making any rash decisions or stupid remarks to the press, and to focus on coaching. "Let me handle it," Davis said.

Then one of the shrewdest men in football did his thing. Jimmy "the Greek" Snyder was a popular analyst on CBS's *The NFL Today,* which aired on Sundays as a lead-in to the day's football games. In an era before ESPN and the Internet, much of the league's news came from NFL pregame shows, particularly Snyder's. On Sunday, December 11, 1983, a few days after Parcells phoned Davis about his predicament, Jimmy the Greek dished hot news to his national audience: Howard Schnellenberger had been approached by the New York Giants to replace Bill Parcells. Snyder deemed it shameful that the team was ready to dump its talented head coach before his first season had even come to a close. For three consecutive weeks, Snyder reported on Parcells-related news. The analyst contended that although Schnellenberger was flattered by the Giants' courtship, he had a handshake agreement with Donald Trump to coach his New Jersey Generals of the United States Football League.

Snyder's public admonishments, and Schnellenberger's apparent lack of interest in replacing Parcells, forced the Giants to reconsider. In a *New York Times* article the next day, headlined "Young Is Angry," the GM refused to discuss Snyder's reports. "Bill is the coach. I don't want to comment on anything that speculative." The speculation grew even more frenzied when Schnellenberger called a Monday press conference to address his future. The forty-nine-year-old coach stated that he would be joining neither the

Giants nor the Generals. "After listening to them," Schnellenberger said, "I told them that my desire was to move this football program along and try to win the national championship."

Among Parcells's players the rumor had turned into a running joke. After one practice offensive tackle Brad Benson inked "Schnellenberger" on a piece of trainer's tape before heading to the tunnel at Giants Stadium to locate the head coach's parking spot; there Benson stuck the tape over the nameplate for Parcells's blue Cadillac. Someone removed it before the beleaguered coach had a chance to laugh, or cry.

In 1978, Dick Vermeil guided Philadelphia to its first playoff appearance in eighteen seasons. The milestone was spurred by the so-called Miracle at the Meadowlands, New York's tragicomic loss to the Eagles on November 19, 1978, which had led to Big Blue's hiring George Young and Ray Perkins, then to the Bill Parcells era. Citing burnout, Vermeil retired in 1982, two years after leading Philadelphia to its first Super Bowl appearance, and joined CBS as an NFL analyst. Vermeil had envisioned a bright future for Parcells based on Big Blue's transformation under the young coordinator.

Late in 1983 Vermeil visited Giants Stadium in preparation for a broadcast. It was one day earlier than normal, but Vermeil wanted extra time with Parcells to encourage the rookie head coach suffering through a disastrous season. "He was getting his ass beat badly," Vermeil says. "I really thought the guy was going to be a great coach, but boy was he depressed. He said, 'You know something? I think they're going to fire me. They're going to run me out of New York real soon.'"

In a season filled with bad news, more was yet to come. On December 12 Parcells received word that Rex Dockery, his colleague at Texas Tech and Vanderbilt, had been killed in a plane crash in Lawrenceburg, Tennessee, that left no survivors. Dockery, forty-one, was on the flight with three others as part of his duties as Memphis State head coach. "You know how many single-engine planes I was on with this guy?" says Parcells, whose fear of flying preceded the crash. "Probably fifteen."

Four days after Dockery's death, news came in that Doug Kotar had died of brain cancer at age thirty-two. Undrafted out of Kentucky, Doug Kotar had earned Big Blue's fullback job during its 1974 preseason. A tough, inside-outside runner with good hands, the five-eleven, 205-pounder moved more like a pickup truck than a sports car while amassing 3,600 rushing yards, among the most in team history. Kotar's death was expected, yet it cast a pall over the organization during the waning days of the season.

The Giants went as a team to Kotar's funeral in western Pennsylvania, but the head coach didn't make the trip: it coincided with his mother Ida's funeral on December 16, one day before the football season ended. Doctors considered Charles's health too tenuous to permit him to leave Hackensack University Medical Center to attend his wife's funeral. Parcells and his siblings could only pray that one parent would make it out of the hospital alive.

Nearly a year earlier, in January 1983, only three weeks after Parcells's promotion in New York, Dan Henning had been named head coach of the Atlanta Falcons. The symmetry was gratifying for the close friends and former college cohorts. After learning about Parcells's dicey situation, Henning guaranteed him a coaching position with Atlanta if he got fired. Things had turned so dark late in the season that Parcells was considering quitting the Giants. Parcells concedes: "Don't think it didn't cross my mind to throw up my hands and say, 'Who needs this?'"

Henning helped dissuade him. In one of their phone conversations, Henning asked Parcells, "Hey, what's the worst thing that can happen to you?"

"What do you mean?" Parcells replied.

"Just what I said. What's the absolute worst thing that can come out of this?"

"Well, the worst thing that can come out of this is that I get fired."

"Big deal."

The friends erupted in laughter.

For the talented and driven Giants coach, the stakes were certainly higher than Henning implied, but Parcells's resurrection after living through football limbo in 1979 showed that he was more than just a survivor. The conversation with Henning helped bolster his resolve. "It was the same thing Al Davis kept telling me in the dark days," Parcells recalls, "except that Dan uses nicer language."

In the gloomy final week of the 1983 season, Parcells and George Young finally met to discuss the coach's status. Although neither man mentioned back-door maneuverings, Howard Schnellenberger was the elephant in the room. When Parcells asked whether he would be retained in 1984, Young suggested that the two wait until after the season finale to discuss the future.

After burying his mother, Bill Parcells traveled to Washington, D.C., to coach his team at RFK Memorial Stadium on December 17. The finale against the Redskins encapsulated the season. New York's defense, led by Lawrence Taylor, performed as if it were in playoff contention, and the

Giants took a 19–7 lead during the third quarter. However, the Redskins parlayed two New York fumbles by Jeff Rutledge into points en route to a 31–22 victory. That coda gave the Giants, *Bill Parcells's* Giants, a 3-12-1 record for the franchise's worst mark since 1974. Despite an NFL-high twenty-five players on the injured reserve, the team's most jarring statistic was its league-worst 58 turnovers: 31 interceptions and 27 lost fumbles. Brunner threw 22 interceptions and 9 touchdowns. Parcells had named Jeff Rutledge the starting quarterback for the final two games, to no avail.

Big Blue's offense lacked competence in football basics: passing, catching, blocking. The unit finished ranked twenty-fifth in the twenty-eight-team league, averaging 16.7 points. The defense, New York's strength, dropped to a ranking of sixteenth after allowing an average of 21.7 points. Inevitably, some sports pundits called for a head-coaching change, citing the team's decline after Ray Perkins's departure. On the other hand, Parcells's supporters contended that the team lacked even one above-average offensive lineman, or a quarterback who could stay healthy: reporters dubbed Simms "Phil Ouch." The Giants weren't devoid of talent, though. Four players made the Pro Bowl: linebackers Harry Carson and Lawrence Taylor, cornerback Mark Haynes, and kicker Ali Haji-Sheikh. Although the running game slipped after Rob Carpenter's injury, rookie Butch Woolfolk rushed for 857 yards, and wideout Earnest Gray caught 78 passes, tying the NFC best, for 1,139 yards.

One year and a couple of days after the Giants introduced Parcells to the media as their new head coach, his return was uncertain. "What was supposed to be the best year of my life," Parcells says, "turned out to be the worst. The year I spent out of football in Colorado was a picnic compared to 1983."

By the season's end, Parcells understood that he had compounded his buzzard's luck with serious mistakes as a head coach. Operating under the assumption that NFL head coaches were supposed to have a big-picture mentality, he had delegated too much authority to his assistants, an approach that was out of character. Although players had shown Parcells more deference in his new leadership role, too much coziness remained from his time as defensive coordinator, a problem exacerbated by his efforts to avoid being pretentious. "I had some other things going on, too. That's no excuse for doing a poor job, which I did," Parcells says. "I didn't really approach being head coach like I should have." Regardless, the hard lessons learned from his rookie season would be for naught if the franchise dismissed him. Suspense mounted as management met to discuss the team's future. On the Friday following the season's last game, word finally came from on high. The Giants had decided to commit to Parcells for the 1984 season.

About one week later, January 2, Howard Schnellenberger's Hurricanes handed top-ranked Nebraska its sole loss of the season, 31–30, in the Orange Bowl. The game, one of the most memorable in college football history, gave Miami its first national championship.

Years later, several months after the Giants won their first Super Bowl, George Young finally admitted that the organization had contemplated firing Parcells as a rookie head coach. In a *New York Times* article on September 6, 1987, Young said, "When you're 3-12-1 and in the third-to-last game we had 51,000 no-shows, you have to think about those kinds of things."

Parcells believes that the GM was under pressure to save his own job. Young tended to be conservative and risk-averse, traits that had led to his choice for Ray Perkins's replacement. Parcells has "probably" forgiven Young, or at least come to terms with the GM's shenanigans. "As I got older, I realized that these guys are businessmen," says Parcells. "This may be the most important lesson I've ever learned in sports. We're all part of the assembly line: owners, commissioners, coaches, and players. And when they ask you to get off the train, it stinks. 'You mean *me*? You want *me* off after all I've done?'

"Like Brett Favre. He saw it right in front of him [in 2008]. It stung, and I don't blame him. He busts his ass for the Green Bay Packers. He goes out there every Sunday, hurt, tired. He's been a great player. That franchise owes him a tremendous amount, but he's still not entitled. You are *never* entitled.

"And that's what I learned. No matter whether you're an owner, commissioner, player, coach, or general manager, you're *never* entitled. As time went forward, that insight served me well, because I gained a great understanding of management, of what had to be done, a greater understanding of where you are in the pecking order. After one year, I knew where I was: win or get fired. That took a lot of the diplomacy out of my attitude."

Linebackers coach Bill Belichick was being courted by the Minnesota Vikings, who had just hired Les Steckel to replace Bud Grant as head coach. New defensive coordinator Floyd Reese wanted his football pal to oversee the Vikings secondary. The pair had spent two seasons with the Detroit Lions in the mid-seventies, and in 1979, Reese declined Ray Perkins's offer to come with Belichick to New York.

When Belichick informed Parcells about Minnesota's interest, the response revealed the head coach's tenuous situation, despite his official reprieve. "George Young is trying to screw me, so we might all be gone soon. If you want to go, and you get the right offer, you ought to take it."

Belichick heeded Parcells's advice and traveled to Minneapolis to spend a day with the Vikings. He came so close to accepting an offer that it was announced on local TV. But after sleeping on his decision, Belichick declined the offer in the morning when Reese came by to pick him up.

Since joining the Giants in 1981, Parcells had incrementally expanded the role of his ambitious assistant. Although Belichick was only eleven years his junior, Parcells felt a paternalistic responsibility, often describing him to Ray Perkins as being like a son. The Nashville native enjoyed the East Coast, especially Nantucket, the island south of Cape Cod, Massachusetts, where he aspired to own property. So, despite the uncertainty in New York, Bill Belichick viewed working under Parcells as an ideal situation.

The good news regarding Parcells's job was tempered by his father's condition, but by late January 1984, Charles had shown surprising progress. After he'd gone three weeks without a violent reaction, doctors expressed guarded optimism that the infection was finally under control. If no setback occurred within several days, Charles would be sent home.

Parcells departed for Mobile, Alabama, for the Senior Bowl, where NFL coaches and scouts gathered annually to evaluate top college seniors. One week later he debarked from an afternoon flight to Newark International Airport, planning to head directly to Hackensack Medical Center. Enthusiastic about his father's imminent release, he hadn't even changed out of his coaching clothes after watching the final workout at Mobile that morning. Parcells wore tan slacks and a New York Giants sweater while clutching a duffel bag emblazoned with the team logo. It was unusual for him to wear team gear in public. "But I didn't give a shit," Parcells says. "I was just trying to get back to New Jersey."

After the twenty-mile drive to the hospital, Parcells hurried to the nurses' station.

"Mr. Parcells, I wouldn't go in there if I were you."

"Why not?"

"Your dad has been very upset. He's sleeping now."

"What's the matter?"

The nurse explained that Charles had suffered yet another extreme reaction, preventing doctors from releasing him as hoped. With Charles still gravely ill and sullen, she urged his son to postpone the visit. Parcells declined, walking past her to find the door to his father's room open. Charles was asleep, with his back to the entrance, tossing in discomfort. His son stood in the doorway, silently watching from a few feet away. After a few minutes, unwilling to disturb his father, Parcells left the hospital to head home.

"That was the saddest day. That was my lowest point," Parcells recalls. "I think things are kind of taking a turn for the better. And then this happens. I was despondent."

The Parcells clan believes that Charles's infection stemmed from a blood transfusion during his bypass, and circumstantial evidence supports the theory. His renowned heart surgeon, John Hutchinson III, performed operations on several high-profile patients, including Arthur Ashe in 1979 and 1983. When the tennis legend revealed his bombshell about contracting HIV, he contended that it came from an ill-fated blood transfusion during the second bypass—in 1983. At the time, scientists hadn't created a test to screen blood for transfusions. "I can't definitely say what happened," Parcells says of his father's blood transfusion. "But the blood he got seems to have been contaminated, because he got some kind of infection in the process."

Two days after his son's visit, Charles was transferred to Columbia-Presbyterian Medical Center for an emergency operation. Doctors warned the family of the strong possibility that he might not survive. A day before the surgery, his sons, arriving together, gathered at the hospital. When Bill, Don, and Doug entered Charles's room, their father was sitting on the edge of his bed, upright, as if defiant of his condition. He perked up further as his boys provided updates on their lives. For several minutes Charles Parcells resembled their familiar father, the soft-spoken yet gregarious former athlete. "I don't know if he was just putting up a good front," Parcells says, "but he certainly didn't seem to be."

The FBI agent turned attorney expressed satisfaction about his marriage, his four children, his career, and his rich life experiences. Charles instructed his oldest son to serve as executor of his will, if necessary. He asked his boys to look out for their little sister, Debbie, the family's black sheep.

Finally, Charles said in a firm tone, "Don't worry about it. I'm ready to go. If this is it, then this is it. It's been great. It's—"

Bill Parcells interrupted. "Dad, we'll see you when you come out."

The three sons wished their father luck, but two hours after surgery, Charles lapsed into a coma caused by hemorrhaging. He was placed on life support, and doctors gave him little chance of recovery. The next morning Charles Parcells died, only six weeks after his wife's passing. "They think the infection settled in his aorta. They didn't know," says Bill Parcells, anger in his voice decades later. "The doctors couldn't tell him what the hell was going on."

Former defensive end George Martin recalls Parcells's tumultuous season. "Looking back now, I wonder how he stood up under the pressure, especially given the deaths of both parents in such a short period of time. I looked at Bill that year, and it was like seeing a friend suffer and you're helpless to lend him a hand. We gained tremendous respect for each other, as a result of the ordeal we all went through that year, but particularly for Bill. He weathered that storm like no one I ever saw."

9

Linebacker Carl Banks didn't dare wipe the sweat dripping down his face and into his eyes. The rookie's only concession was blinking; he feared being caught looking away, even momentarily. On the opening day of training camp, in July 1984, Bill Parcells had gathered his team into a semicircle at practice. As he addressed the Giants players, his white-hot glare matched the heat in Pleasantville, New York. Although management had kept Parcells on, for him the distress of nearly losing his job to Howard Schnellenberger lingered. The second-year coach knew that his reprieve came only because the Miami Hurricanes coach passed on his job. Parcells told his players, "I'm going to be fired if I don't win."

It was less a win-one-for-the-Gipper plea than a matter-of-fact remark. Fallout from the 3-12-1 meltdown meant that players and coaches needed to win for each other. In his speech Parcells promised to become the authentic, if rawer, version of the former defensive coordinator, instead of the conflicted head coach, and failed actor, of 1983. Parcells's right shoe contained a pebble, the quirky habit to sustain alertness, and crabbiness, that he had shelved as a rookie head coach.

"I really wasted my first year," Parcells admits. His ideas about the new position hadn't meshed with his personality. So the second-year coach abandoned his own preconceived notions and decided to lead on his own aggressive terms. He recalls, "This is what I actually said to myself, and I'm not making this up: 'I don't know who these people are that are trying to get me. But they're not getting me. I'm getting *them*.'"

His demeanor shifted from tough yet affable to almost exclusively acerbic. Players, especially on defense, were forced to shed any sentimentality left over from Parcells's former role. "That's when," he says of 1984, "I got my reputation for being brusque, but I was fighting for my professional survival. You're not politically correct and you're not as sensitive to other people's feelings when you're fighting for your own life. I got a little overzealous, a little overaggressive, a little dissatisfied with *anything*. Even when we were doing well, I was on their asses."

The hard-ass approach could have caused a backlash, particularly from veterans, but one factor preventing a player rebellion was the nucleus that had grown accustomed to Parcells since 1981. It included defensive tackle

Jim Burt, linebacker Harry Carson, and defensive end George Martin. Being able to see past the nastiness, the incumbents helped new team-mates acclimate. And once in a blue moon, Parcells offered kudos that boosted morale.

His first two major moves occurred several months before training camp. Disturbed by the previous year's inordinate number of injuries, Par-cells decided to add a strength-and-conditioning coach. He interviewed several candidates before choosing Johnny Parker, who had been working for the University of Mississippi after stops at South Carolina, Indiana, and Louisiana State. The decision was influenced by Bobby Knight's rec-ommendation during a phone conversation when the Indiana basketball coach told his friend, "It's not work for this guy. He *loves* it."

One aspect of the 1983 season that Parcells had hated was the lack of unity among teammates, especially when the Giants struggled. Parcells believed that a new weight room would contribute to conditioning while fostering camaraderie; now players interested in weight lifting were forced to use a cramped, windowless area with cinder-block walls in the bowels of Giants Stadium. NFL locker rooms were often open to the media, guests, and other members of the organization. But weight rooms were generally limited to players and coaches, creating an intimate haven that Parcells viewed as part clubhouse and part frat house.

He presented a proposal for a modernized weight room to George Young, who received approval from ownership. The new facility, which greatly expanded and revamped the hole-in-the-wall, cost more than $200,000. It was supervised by Johnny Parker, who made sure it became an exclusive domain for players, Parcells says, by all but issuing "secret de-coder rings" for admittance.

In spring 1984, Parker unveiled his first off-season program, focusing on weight lifting and running. Parcells was pleased that some thirty play-ers showed up for the voluntary workouts. As he had envisioned, the new facility helped Giants players become less injury-prone. Just as important, it served as a social hub where players and coaches got to know each other better.

Management mended fences with Parcells by supporting his weight-room plan and his desire to revamp the roster. In his mind he sorted players into two groups: those he planned to develop, and those who lacked a champi-onship mentality. Parcells also noticed that the roster was getting athleti-cally old at a few key positions.

During the off-season, Parcells, with Young's cooperation, jettisoned more than twenty Giants through trades or releases. The castoffs included several talented players who he felt were stifling the club. Among these were two significant departures, popular linebackers Brian Kelley and Brad Van Pelt. The thirty-two-year-olds had been with New York since being drafted in 1973. Parcells had good relationships with both veterans, but he felt that their playing habits were too ingrained for the changes he wanted to make. Van Pelt, who had lobbied for a trade, was dealt to the Minnesota Vikings for Tony Galbreath, a thirty-year-old fullback with superb pass-catching ability; Kelley was traded to the San Diego Chargers for a tenth-round pick. Their departures marked the dismantling of the "Crunch Bunch," the linebacking corps considered to be one of the NFL's best and perhaps its hardest-hitting. The unit had been something that Giants fans could take pride in during the team's dismal seasons.

Harry Carson recalls Parcells's mind-set at the time. "He recognized that he had to do things his own way, and it couldn't be about friendship. It's like the whole Mafia thing: It's nothing personal; it's business. In order for him to keep his job he was going to have to get the best people on the field to play the game the way he wanted."

George Young had replenished the linebacking corps in the 1984 draft. Carl Banks was the third overall pick out of Michigan State, and Gary Reasons from Northwestern State was plucked in the fourth round. The Giants had obtained the pick from Denver by trading Scott Brunner, which also decreased the chances of another quarterback controversy. Big Blue's other first-round choice, twenty-seventh overall, was offensive tackle William Roberts (Ohio State). Quarterback Jeff Hostetler (West Virginia) came in the third round, and a seventh-round pick brought wideout Lionel Manuel (Pacific) to give the Giants a terrific draft class. But one new addition, undrafted on graduating from the Naval Academy in 1979, epitomized Parcells's type of player.

After serving a five-year tour of duty, Phil McConkey made a belated attempt to become an NFL receiver/returner. Beyond his extensive layoff, McConkey faced a challenge in his shrimpy size. He had shown enough talent in high school to make New York's all-state team as a runner and receiver, but his five-ten, 145-pound frame kept him from getting any scholarship offers from major colleges. So McConkey joined the Naval Academy, where he thrived, including on October 7, 1978, during the Midshipmen's 38–7 road rout of Bill Parcells's Air Force Falcons. In the first half McConkey produced a 19-yard end-around plus a 36-yard catch, helping Navy to a 23–0 lead. That season Navy won the Commander-in-Chief's Trophy, which went to the season's best service-academy team.

By 1983, McConkey was twenty pounds heavier, but still a wiry 165 pounds when Parcells invited him to Giants camp. Big Blue's interest was spurred by several recommendations, including one from Steve Belichick, who was still a football scout at Navy. McConkey owed one more year of service to the navy as a helicopter pilot for nuclear weapons transshipment, but he obtained a leave of absence to attend camp.

During the opening practice McConkey played like the Energizer Bunny. His speed and tirelessness made most of his teammates look like they were moving in slow motion. Although the undrafted military pilot wouldn't be discharged until 1984, Parcells offered him a contract that included a $3,500 bonus. McConkey balked, explaining that he wanted to explore playing for his hometown Buffalo Bills.

Parcells didn't relent.

"How about I throw in another thousand?"

McConkey replied, "Done deal."

Returning to the club in summer 1984, McConkey noticed a stark difference in Parcells. "He now wanted *his* guys," recalls McConkey. "Guys who only wanted to know where and when: where the game was, and when it was going to be played. He wanted guys who, if the game was going to be played on the Brooklyn Bridge at midnight against the Jersey City Destroyers, would show up ready to play."

The ex-pilot entered camp as a long shot to become one of Parcells's guys, listed at the bottom of the depth chart for wide receivers. McConkey survived the first few cuts, lasting through the preseason finale. However, a slew of players were going to be released after a game against the Steelers, so McConkey's situation remained dicey.

About four hours before the opening kickoff, Parcells walked into the locker room. He headed toward McConkey, pulling up a stool next to the nervous dervish. "Hey, kid, I want you to know you've done a great job. I want you to go out there tonight, relax, and have a great game."

Parcells's remark signaled that McConkey had made the regular-season roster. McConkey's punt-return and kick-return skills had propelled him past the other bubble players.

That preseason moment would be just about the only time in 1984 that Parcells eased pressure on McConkey—or any other Giant. Whenever McConkey shagged punts during practice, Parcells stood at his shoulder, scrutinizing technique and shouting commentary. Virtually no catch met Parcells's standards. "Now, you've got to understand something about Parcells," McConkey says. "He never caught a punt in his life, but he is the absolute expert on catching punts. He critiques every catch, and it's never good enough."

Parcells's favorite punt drill required the returner to corral at least three punts almost simultaneously. Parcells first employed it in the early 1970s as linebackers coach under Bill Peterson at Florida State. As pigskins fell from the sky only seconds apart, the returner was forbidden to place any on the ground. Each returner placed the first catch somewhere against his body, moments before snagging the next ball, and then the third. Dropping the punt wasn't an option. "It was against the law," McConkey remembers, "punishable by beheading if you let that ball hit the ground." The drill taught the returner to put himself in the proper position while maintaining full concentration on the ball. To keep balls from dislodging, the recipient needed to make sure each punt was headed toward the ideal part of his body, the middle of the chest. Sometimes Parcells simulated punted balls by standing near the returner and using an underhand motion to toss footballs and wisecracks.

McConkey's dexterity and hand-eye coordination were such that he was able to catch up to four balls in the drill. Teammates were wowed, but Parcells, who had seen a player in college snag five pigskins, responded nonchalantly. The head coach's perfectionism motivated McConkey to further sharpen his skills. McConkey recalls one time when Parcells insisted on the team practicing in a gale with thirty-mile-per-hour winds. The experience helped train the ex–navy pilot for the notorious winds at the Meadowlands.

As Giants defensive coordinator, Parcells had frequently sought off-the-gridiron information about his players, and as head coach he spent even more time mining their personal sides. His research methods included conversations with players' friends, former coaches, and agents. Parcells seldom offered information regarding his own private life to players, or anyone else, but he accumulated considerable personal info from players themselves in random conversations. Those exchanges spiked during off-season minicamps because of extra downtime. His favorite setting for non-football exchanges was the weight room, but casual interactions also took place in meeting rooms and the locker room.

During the season Parcells went out of his way to have as many lengthy one-on-one discussions as possible. The habit included practice-squad members, the least-recognized players on the team. The head coach's superb memory allowed him to create a mental dossier on each player, and he used innocuous tidbits or sensitive info as fodder.

In Harry Carson's case, Parcells unearthed a childhood nickname; during one preseason practice in 1984, Parcells walked over to the veteran linebacker and whispered it into his ear. Carson shuddered, then stood stock-still. Parcells declined to reveal his source to the stunned linebacker. For the rest of the season Parcells only used the nickname in private moments.

"To this day, I don't know how he did it," Carson says. "I didn't want him yelling it out to the whole team. It got my attention, and for a while, he hung it over my head. But the funny thing was that it told me that the guy cared enough to really dig into who I was."

Decades later, Parcells and Carson still refuse to divulge the nickname.

The second-year head coach didn't hesitate to approach his counterparts for pointers on the pro game. Parcells felt that Seattle's Chuck Knox designed rushing offenses better than anyone, so the Giants coach befriended Knox, who had won multiple Coach of the Year awards, and questioned him about strategies. Parcells also increasingly consulted Al Davis about a range of issues faced by head coaches. The Raiders chief, whose franchise was coming off its third Super Bowl victory, provided the viewpoint from management or ownership. Regardless of any problems, Davis stressed that Parcells should focus on winning, not excuses. "Just do your job."

Despite having a better handle on being a head coach, Parcells knew that his job was at risk if the club's drug issues weren't addressed. He began to tackle the team's problem of marijuana and, to a lesser extent, cocaine abuse. Lawrence Taylor's travails would become well-chronicled because of his stature, but the elite linebacker was just one of a number of substance abusers on the Giants when Parcells took over. The team-wide problem was an albatross for the second-year head coach, and he steeled himself to deal with it.

In the early eighties, league rules policing drugs were inchoate, just like those in the nation's workplaces: the NFL was a few years away from establishing a policy. It wouldn't be until 1986 that Commissioner Pete Rozelle hired Dr. Forest Tennant, a UCLA professor who was running methadone clinics in Southern California, to oversee a centralized program that included warnings, counseling, suspensions, and a lifetime ban with the ability to appeal after one season.

However, Parcells didn't wait on the league office or Giants management to address the problem. He responded with self-education, persuasion, and vigilantism. When the Giants head coach attended the annual owners meeting in Palm Springs, California, during the off-season, he visited the Betty Ford Clinic in nearby Rancho Mirage. The fourteen-acre facility was named after the former First Lady, who overcame her addiction to painkillers and alcohol a few years after Gerald Ford departed office. Returning east, Parcells registered as an outpatient at Fair Oaks

Hospital in Summit, New Jersey, to learn more about drug addiction and methods to combat it. The private treatment center also offered a nation-wide hotline service (1-800-COCAINE) run by Jane Wright Jones, its associate clinical director.

An addiction expert specializing in cocaine, Dr. Jane Jones was quoted frequently in newspapers and made presentations at conferences on the subject. Jones, who also had a private practice as a psychiatrist in Engle-wood, became an invaluable resource and ally to a coach seeking a crash course. Whenever Parcells encountered a player showing signs of mari-juana or cocaine abuse, the coach sent him to see Jones. A black woman in her thirties with a disciplinarian streak, she connected well with many of Parcells's players. After counseling sessions, Jones relayed her general insights to Big Blue's head coach.

By leaning on Jones's expertise, Parcells discovered that cocaine abuse had exploded in recent years, causing a spike in health and social problems. Twenty-two million Americans, roughly one in ten, had tried cocaine. An estimated five million were considered habitual users. In 1984 the price of the drug was plunging, making it affordable to an even larger market. Ac-cording to Jones, in 1983 one gram of cocaine cost between $100 and $125, but by the end of 1984, it sold for as little as $70. And that year, emergency rooms reported twice as many cocaine-related incidents as in prior years.

Jones explained cocaine's allure to a coach whose worst vices were cigarettes and beer. The drug offered the promise of enhanced strength, sexuality, sociability, and intelligence. After addiction took hold, however, users eventually lost the euphoria along with the ostensible benefits. So-called cokeheads suffered chronic fatigue, migraines, seizures, paranoia, and depression that occasionally led to suicide. The drug cost some users their job, income, spouse, and friends, and if they became criminals to support their habit, it could also cost them their freedom.

To illustrate cocaine's pernicious attraction, Jones often cited a study involving rhesus monkeys: given the option of pressing levers for cocaine or for life's basic necessities, including food, water, and sleep, the animals chose the cocaine, dying within a month of drug-induced convulsions.

One important approach to combating drug use, Parcells learned, fit nicely with his personality. A primary tenet of Fair Oaks, since renamed Summit Oaks Hospital, put it this way: "Confrontation is often required, and is an integral part of treatment, especially in the case of addiction where denial exists." Dr. Jane Jones elaborated: "Bill, you can't be a Good Samaritan. You've got to threaten their jobs, make it consequential. Don't say, 'I'm trying to be a good guy, and help you with your problems.' They lie. They just want to get drugs, so you've got to bust their balls."

Parcells fully intended to confront players he suspected of drug use and, if necessary, force them to take tests not authorized by the league. His plan would exceed the collective bargaining agreement, which detailed the contractual rights of players. Knowing this, Parcells felt compelled to gain the support of defensive lineman George Martin, the Giants representative to the players union. A team co-captain, Martin held substantial pull among teammates, who often sought his advice, particularly regarding league issues.

In a meeting between the two men, Parcells said, "Look, we've got a problem. The New York Giants. *We* have a problem. Now I'm going try and solve this problem. And you can either help me solve it, or we can fight about it."

Martin responded, "No, Coach, I'm going to help you solve it, 'cause I agree. I think we *do* have a problem."

"I want to get drugs off my team. You want drugs on the team?"

"No, Coach, I don't."

However, one prickly issue still concerned Martin: the racial dynamic. Parcells had targeted some players based partly on circumstantial evidence, including behavior. Almost all of them happened to be black. Martin, a black player, asked Parcells, "Can't we catch some white guys doing drugs?" The loaded question brought the conversation's tensest moment, as the head coach and defensive end stared at each other for a few seconds.

Parcells had earned a reputation for connecting with black athletes, a noteworthy quality because of its rarity in white coaches. He traced his genuine ease among blacks to his many childhood interactions with employees of his paternal grandaunt's rooming business, including Lucinda Whiting, who had helped raise his father. In a league with vestiges of racism, Parcells understood Martin's concerns, but struggled to come up with a response.

Finally Parcells said, "We're only catching white guys drinking beer right now. We're catching only black guys smoking marijuana. That's what we're catching right now."

During another long pause, Parcells anxiously awaited Martin's verdict. The defensive end asked, "Well, how are we going to do this?"

Parcells exhaled. "I'm going to start testing these guys, and we're going to have some casualties."

"Okay, I'm with you."

Parcells realized the significance of winning over the team's union representative. Their heart-to-heart conversation, plus Martin's follow-up actions, forged a lifetime bond. "He could do no wrong after that," Parcells says of Martin's support. "If it weren't for him, you would never have heard of me, because he supported me in ways that the average player wouldn't have done. But his intelligence allowed him to realize that it was for the greater good."

Aware of just how unusual this alliance was, Martin visited Hazelden, a well-regarded drug rehab center in Minnesota, to learn about the boundaries of confidentiality and support. "There were some very delicate situations," recalls Martin, who became president of the D.C.-based players association in 1987. "Do I say, 'Well, I'm going to be a hard-liner; the players haven't agreed to that, so I've got to call down to D.C. and get permission?' No, I was concerned about the individuals getting better. You can sit down, and you can collectively bargain rules of engagement. But if you've got a guy who's in need of treatment, who may be in denial, sometimes those rules have to go out of the window."

So Parcells began confronting alleged drug abusers, concluding his meetings with an ultimatum: provide urine samples for testing, or find another team to play for. "I made sure they understood we were going to do something about this," Parcells says, "whether they wanted to or not." Parcells's methods lacked both NFL authority and uniformity. A bit player who failed a drug test might escape being dumped, while a starter might be dismissed. In general, Parcells gave players an opportunity to rehab with the club's assistance, but tolerance for multiple chances was applied on a case-by-case basis.

Parcells confronted one talented player showing signs of drug abuse by asking, "How much cocaine do you use?" Skeptical of his answer thanks to outside intelligence, Parcells bellowed, "Go downstairs, get your shit, and get outta here."

Another private confrontation occurred with a backup defensive back. Parcells screamed at him, "How much pot are you smoking?"

The player responded, "I'm not smoking."

Parcells snapped. "Go! If you want to be screwing around, screw you. Get out. I'll get somebody else."

"Well, uh, I'm smoking a little bit."

"Well, that shit is stopping now. We're gonna test you every week, and if you're not clean in a month, you're out."

The defender stayed clean enough to appear in all sixteen games. Still, by season's end, the Giants had released at least ten players suspected of drug abuse, mostly pot smoking. Former defensive lineman Leonard Marshall says, "You can probably make a guess about which guys were doing stuff by just looking at the roster the next year [1984], and the year after [1985], and figuring out which ones were gone: guys who could still play football, but no way could they play for Parcells anymore."

Entering the 1984 season, the Giants needed to upgrade their receiving corps. Parcells was interested in an undrafted free agent, but before making an offer, the Giants gave him the requisite physical examination, which revealed traces of marijuana. Parcells told the wideout, "Okay. I like you very much as an athlete. But you've got one problem."

"What's that?"

"Well, you smoke pot."

Parcells went on to stress that a Giants contract depended on the club being given carte blanche to drug-test.

"If you don't want to agree to allow me to test you, I'm not telling anybody about the marijuana, just go find some other team. I don't give a shit."

Like virtually everyone else who faced Parcells's terms, the receiver acquiesced. And he didn't test positive for marijuana, or anything else, that entire season.

Lawrence Taylor first tried cocaine at a party during his rookie season. He began using it recreationally during his second NFL season, in 1982, and by 1984 he was hooked on perhaps the most addictive form of the drug: crack. Taylor often rationalized his abuse by stressing that it didn't keep him from stellar performances on the field or otherwise impact his life. Following Big Blue's disastrous season in 1983, Taylor made the All-Pro team for the third consecutive time, and despite switching to inside linebacker in place of an injured Harry Carson, Taylor recorded nine sacks. Regardless, Parcells, who felt that Taylor had underachieved, decided to bring the issue to a head.

The coach and the star linebacker lived only three blocks apart in Upper Saddle River, so Parcells organized a meeting at Taylor's home that included the athlete, his parents, his wife, his agent, and his business adviser. When the group gathered at Taylor's dinner table, Parcells took charge.

"Everybody here?" As he took attendance, Taylor's mother began to weep. Then Parcells glared at Taylor. "Here's the deal, Lawrence. You say this stuff isn't affecting your life. Well, your business guy, he says he can't get hold of you to make a decision. Your agent, he's fed up with you. Your wife's fixing to leave your ass. Your boss is getting ready to suspend you. And I haven't even gotten to your mother and father."

Parcells glanced at Taylor's parents. "Your mother's over there crying. Now, I want you to tell me again that this shit isn't affecting your life. I want you to tell me right now. Come on."

Parcells stared at the superstar, waiting for an answer.

Taylor responded by bursting into tears.

• • •

Parcells realized that his vigilante approach would inevitably come to the attention of league headquarters, so the second-year coach made a pre-emptive phone call to NFL commissioner Pete Rozelle. Parcells explained the situation during a brief conversation, and Rozelle offered his tacit approval; the league planned to catch up.

Concern about the consequences of drug abuse heightened during the 1980s, coinciding with Parcells's crackdown. The government responded with an antidrug campaign, and introduced employee testing. On September 15, 1986, President Ronald Reagan signed an executive order requiring federal agencies to create a drug-testing system. Within a few years private-sector companies standardized the monitoring of illicit drugs, mainly by urinalysis.

A nanogram, one-billionth of a gram, is the microscopic measurement used to ferret out drug residues. The standard positive level of detection (LOD) for cocaine is 150 nanograms per milliliter. Bill Parcells's threshold was substantially lower: *any* number of nanograms discovered in the team's annual physical examination placed a player under *his* microscope. Although Parcells was pushing the legal envelope at the time, he had no regrets about being ahead of the curve. "It helped our team so much to clean up as best we could what was a pretty serious problem," Parcells says. "Now, we didn't save them all. But we saved a lot."

The trade of Scott Brunner made Phil Simms the prohibitive favorite to start at quarterback. Jeff Rutledge was Simms's competition, and after losing his leading role the previous season, the oft-injured quarterback took nothing for granted. He returned to the Giants with increased intensity and edginess. "Simms's attitude was a little like mine for '84," Parcells says. "He didn't give a shit what anyone thought."

The sixth-year quarterback badgered Johnny Parker to allow him to join the offensive linemen's weight-lifting program. Parker, who hadn't yet designed one for quarterbacks, capitulated. Lifting less weight per set than his linemen, Simms otherwise adhered to their program. He turned into such a workout fanatic that he and Parker became close friends. Parcells loved his veteran quarterback's determination, and by the third preseason game, the head coach had seen enough to name Simms his starter.

The regular-season opener marked Simms's first start in almost three years. New York's season began auspiciously as the Morehead State product amassed 409 passing yards in a 28–27 victory over Philadelphia. Simms produced the highest passer rating (157.6) of his career. Then the

Giants defeated Dallas, 28–7, for their first 2-0 start since 1968. Once again Simms resembled a franchise quarterback, "as long as he stayed out of the emergency room," Parcells says.

The offensive line, with its infusion of new personnel, needed time to mesh. Two key additions were Chris Godfrey and Karl Nelson. Godfrey had gone undrafted out of Michigan in 1979 before playing one season for the Jets, followed by a stint with the USFL's Michigan Panthers. Nelson was a third-round selection in 1983 via Iowa State. With New York's offensive line gaining synchronicity at a glacial pace, Parcells grew even more concerned about Simms's staying upright, but the head coach admired his quarterback's reluctance to complain, even when his protection turned porous.

Despite the early success, a slump dropped the Giants to 4-4, placing the season, and Parcells's head-coaching career, at a crossroads. Among the setbacks was a 33–12 loss against the Los Angeles Rams at Anaheim Stadium. Sensitive to his uncertain future, Parcells decided to shake up the offensive lineup, benching tailback Butch Woolfolk for Joe Morris, while promoting Phil McConkey to third-down receiver. Parcells wasn't sold on Morris as an NFL talent because of his five-seven frame and shortcomings as a blocker and receiver. Yet Woolfolk's poor play following two splendid seasons gave the coach limited options at tailback.

Morris excelled as Big Blue won five of its next six games, including critical victories over the Cowboys, Redskins, and Jets. The tailback, who started out playing guard in high school, possessed a low center of gravity and uncanny vision that had helped him break the records of Syracuse greats like Jim Brown, Larry Csonka, and Floyd Little. He seemed capable of moving sideways faster than defenders ran forward. Although Morris remained a mediocre blocker and pass catcher, the Giants often used offensive sets that hid those weaknesses as he became one of the league's top runners.

Meanwhile, Phil Simms stayed clear of the emergency room while setting club records for passing yards (4,044), completions (286), and attempts (533). Zeke Mowatt, an athletic tight end in his second season, became Simms's favorite target. His primary wide receivers were Earnest Gray and rookies Lionel Manuel and Bobby Johnson.

The defense turned stingier in the second half of the season with linebacker Carl Banks emerging as a major talent; he and fellow rookie Gary Reasons bolstered a linebacker corps that no longer contained Brian Kelley and Brad Van Pelt. The holdovers remained an imposing group, however, including Harry Carson, Andy Headen, Byron Hunt, and Lawrence Taylor. On the defensive line, Leonard Marshall and Jim Burt became starters alongside George Martin. And the defensive backfield began to solidify, with safeties Kenny Hill and Terry Kinard supporting cornerbacks Mark Haynes and Perry Williams.

With Parcells's 9-5 Giants seemingly playoff bound, their catastrophic previous year felt like a distant memory. Big Blue, though, lost its final two games against the St. Louis Cardinals and the New Orleans Saints. The 9-7 mark left the Giants second in the NFC East, but it was good enough to earn Bill Parcells's team a wild-card berth.

The Giants traveled to Anaheim Stadium for a first-round game against John Robinson's Los Angeles Rams on December 23, 1984. Having blown out Big Blue during the regular season, the Rams were heavy favorites. But in the first quarter the Giants took a surprising 10–0 lead soon after defensive back Bill Currier recovered a fumble at Los Angeles's 23-yard line. The Rams ended up losing five fumbles, undermining Eric Dickerson's 107 yards rushing, which included a 14-yard score in the third quarter. Dickerson's touchdown cut Los Angeles's deficit to 13–10, but kicker Ali Haji-Sheikh increased the lead with his third and final field goal as Big Blue upset Los Angeles, 16–13, advancing to the divisional round.

Mickey Corcoran was at Parcells's side when the game ended at Anaheim Stadium. As the two walked off the field, heading toward the tunnel, Corcoran told Parcells, "Bill, God put you on this earth to be a coach."

Parcells's upstarts visited San Francisco next, in a matchup that evoked the 1981 postseason. Bill Walsh's 49ers were coming off a first-round bye, having been the first-ever NFL club to win fifteen regular-season games. The dominant, well-rounded team stopped a rejuvenated Big Blue, 21–10, before going on to capture another Super Bowl by defeating Don Shula's Dolphins.

Regardless, the road triumph over the Rams signified a pivotal moment in Parcells's career; his tremendous professional growth that season peaked with the surprising victory. "I said to myself," he recalls, " 'Okay, Parcells, you can do this. So let's try to do it well.' " In 1984, Parcells's players and staff not only withstood his unvarnished approach, they seemed to thrive on it as his image morphed into a type A caricature: acerbic, aggressive, cantankerous, demanding, irascible, unrelenting, and wisecracking. Parcells complains of the portrayal, "The media took it and ran, and they never let it go."

The resurgent season helped reduce the strain between Young and Parcells, though tensions occasionally surfaced. Still, in a sharp reversal from the previous season, management rewarded their coach with a revamped four-year contract. Parcells had been among several first-year head coaches in 1983, but after a rocky start in 1984, his prospects rebounded with Big Blue's progress. Meanwhile, most of his counterparts, including confidant Dan Henning, were fired.

10

For at least two seasons the outside world knew Bill Belichick as the Giants linebackers coach. But Parcells, swayed by Belichick's coaching prowess, had given him a much bigger assignment: overseeing the defense. The quiet promotion in 1983 showed Parcells's regard for the former special-teams coach. The job was one of the most demanding, especially given Parcells's background. Yet the head coach granted his young defensive coordinator autonomy within basic parameters.

"Look, here's what I want you to do. I don't really care how you get it done, but I want it done."

Parcells had withheld the formal title in order to gauge how the baby-faced, reticent coach handled the job, and to shield him from public scrutiny. Early on, Belichick, younger than some veterans, had encountered resistance from players. Several members of the defense, particularly the cocksure, talented linebackers he inherited, saw him as a technocrat and neophyte. They noted his lack of playing experience as a pro, and dismissed his football résumé at tiny Wesleyan with its Division III program.

The five-ten coach's soft monotone, which stood in stark contrast to Parcells's frequent thunderclap, didn't help matters. "It would put us to sleep," Harry Carson says. No one nodded off more at meetings than Lawrence Taylor. Occasionally he awoke to find Belichick staring at him. One time the riled linebacker snapped, "You either get me now or you get me on Sunday." Players dubbed the defensive coordinator "Voice of Doom" or used Parcells's shortened version: "Doom."

Moments before kickoffs, Taylor sometimes tried to tweak "Doom" by pretending that he had forgotten the instructions emphasized all week. But with his uncanny feel for the game, the linebacker excelled in his assignments. Despite Taylor's inattentiveness during Belichick's meetings and his cursory reviews of the playbook, the defensive coordinator relished coaching him on Sundays. Belichick knew that Taylor was not just an extraordinary physical specimen but perhaps the smartest defensive player on the field.

Defense remained the forte of the resurgent Giants as Belichick, who never quite understood his nickname, produced exquisite game plans. "We didn't lose a beat," recalls Romeo Crennel, his replacement as special-teams coach. Belichick's skill as a tactician won the respect of his players, gradually erasing their doubts that he was a worthy successor to Parcells. The unit and its young coordinator adjusted to each other.

Steve Belichick, still scouting for Navy, was proud that his son was quietly overseeing Big Blue's defense. He was particularly grateful that his ex-counterpart was protecting Bill Belichick from potential media criticism. During trips to the New York area, Steve attended Giants practices in East Rutherford, where Parcells didn't hesitate to solicit his services.

"You want to watch, or you want to work?"

"I want to work."

"Okay, well, here are two guys we're looking at. I want to know what you think of them."

Parcells's vigilantism in 1984 had helped markedly reduce Big Blue's drug problems, and going into the 1985 season, optimism permeated the organization. However, substance abuse on the part of the team's best player remained an issue. Lawrence Taylor's teammates knew that he drank too much; in fact, he bragged about it. The star's cocaine addiction, however, went undetected by most.

Behind the scenes, Parcells kept trying to exploit his bond with Taylor, but by 1985, drugs had consumed the linebacker's life, causing it to spiral out of control. He was using cocaine and its powerful derivative, crack, three times a week now, as opposed to a couple times a month, as he had the previous year. Bingeing on as much as an ounce a day, Taylor often left his wife, Linda, and their two kids at home to cruise for cocaine in dangerous neighborhoods, spending more than $1,000 daily on drugs, booze, and prostitutes. Occasionally he showed up for meetings of the defense wearing sunglasses, reeking of alcohol and mouthwash.

Although Taylor could still be dominant on the field, his performances had become erratic, compounded by opponents who were now geared to protect against him. At times the linebacker seemed to want to be somewhere other than the gridiron, and like many cocaine users, he grew increasingly paranoid. "I knew that I was no longer 100 percent," Taylor admits. "But I also knew that my 75 percent was better than most guys' 100 percent." Taylor lifted teammates and fans by performing his best on key snaps or defensive stands that could shift a game's momentum. "When it was third-and-four," Belichick recalls, "he was a lion."

Belichick's position became official in 1985, when Parcells revealed it to the media. Despite his discomfiture with interview sessions, Belichick began to reap public accolades for his unit's exploits. Parcells praised

Belichick for his smart game plans, but the head coach never stayed satisfied with any aspect of the team, let alone the defense. Just as he did with his players, Parcells constantly pressed his staff. He made each member, even the lowest man on the totem pole, feel as if the outcome depended on his efforts. "The best thing about working under Bill was that he treated everybody fairly," Romeo Crennel says. "The worst thing was that he treated everybody the same by getting on their ass. He pressured you to get it right."

Parcells occasionally upbraided Belichick in the head coach's office over defensive flaws, but the head coach also didn't hesitate to express his concerns at the water cooler. Such exchanges often led to consequences for the rest of the defense. Belichick told his players, "If I have to take it, you have to take it. Shit runs downhill." Of course, the coordinator's pitch and slight frame never quite evoked the same kind of fear as the head coach's did.

Parcells often questioned the decisions of his staff, and when he did he expected precise, cogent responses. Belichick confidently defended his ideas and explained his reasoning, but sometimes the coordinator felt like he was in a no-win situation. After Parcells criticized one plan, Belichick responded, "Well, okay, we don't have to do that. So what do you want to do? What's the alternative?"

"Well, I'm just telling you what you're doing is screwed up."

"How do you want to change it?"

"I don't know, but it's screwed up and you need to get it fixed."

Once, against the Cowboys offense at Texas Stadium, Parcells was caught off guard by Belichick's exotic blitz on a first down. Parcells, speaking into his headset, snapped at his defensive coordinator: "What the hell are you doing?"

Belichick replied into his headset, "I'm giving them a different look."

"No, you're not. You're showing these 76,000 people how smart you are. You're being a circus act." Then Parcells muttered, "You need those X's and O's guys during the week, but on the sidelines, they're not worth a damn."

In another tense moment, a snippy remark by Belichick caused Parcells's face to contort. Parcells yelled, "Don't you start giving me any shit, Belichick, or your ass will be out in the parking lot."

With his old-school sensibilities, Parcells disdained flamboyant schemes. Belichick might like an unconventional blitz scheme, such as a 2-4-5, that emphasized speed, whereas Parcells preferred standard packages that stressed physicality. He considered some of the intricacies in Belichick's game plan superfluous. As Romeo Crennel recalls, "Parcells would say many times, 'You geniuses on defense, you got all this shit in here that we don't need.' Parcells would just rather line up and let the players beat the other guys."

Beyond not always seeing eye to eye, "Little Bill" and "Big Bill" often failed to look at each other during their heated exchanges, so it took players a while to realize that the head coach and his deputy were at loggerheads. "Bill [Parcells] is standing there with his arms folded, and he's listening to everything that's taking place," Carson recalls. "Belichick is calling the defensive signals, and he calls something that Parcells doesn't like. You look over at them and figure that Belichick is talking to somebody upstairs, and Parcells is talking to somebody upstairs. But the reality is they're talking to one another through the headsets. They're going at it."

The angry exchanges didn't linger during the week. To let off steam, Belichick and Parcells sometimes played racquetball at Giants Stadium. Belichick, a former player in Wesleyan's well-regarded program, won most of their one-on-ones. Whenever Parcells lost, he angrily lit up a cigarette and continued to unwind that way.

After reaching an agreement with the players association, the NFL introduced its drug program in 1985, which allowed urinalysis only during preseason; teams could seek permission for additional testing by showing "reasonable cause." Taylor's first NFL urinalysis took place in the summer of 1985. Cocaine showed up in his system, triggering a warning from the league and counseling. The Giants asserted their right to impose more tests during the regular season, but Taylor circumvented his team's tests by obtaining urine from drug-free friends or teammates. He collected the sample in an aspirin bottle that he hid in his athletic supporter. Then, in the bathroom stall used for urinalysis, Taylor emptied the clean urine into the test container.

Despite his troubles, Taylor was among a coterie of players Parcells consulted about team issues. The rest of Parcells's "board of directors" were relatively drama-free veterans that included linebacker Harry Carson, fullback Maurice Carthon, defensive end George Martin, and quarterback Phil Simms. Parcells saw in Taylor many ideal qualities, including his seemingly indomitable will, high threshold for pain, clutch performances, and sense of fair play. The coach loved that his linebacker genuinely didn't care about individual statistics: Taylor was outraged by losses and reacted with glee after victories. "The whole notion of losing," Parcells says, "was like somebody wanted to stab him."

Lawrence Taylor being a once-in-a-generation player, the Giants never considered trading him. The organization seemingly tolerated Taylor's foibles during the week for the sake of his riveting performances on Sundays.

This apparent double standard irked a few players, and might have diluted Belichick's authority. A minority of New York sportswriters seized on the dynamic, criticizing Parcells for ignoring Taylor's substance abuse.

"That's anything but the truth," Parcells protests, anger in his voice. "And that hurts you because they portray you as, 'All he cared about was the game.' I did the best I could, it just wasn't good enough. I wasn't the general manager or the owner. I couldn't do anything I wanted to do.

"Taylor and I had a special bond; we came together. I think he got away with a bunch of shit. But first of all, I'm not just throwing my best player away. I'm trying to help my best player. Some of the guys I got rid of, I tried to help them, too."

Harry Carson believes that Parcells had little choice in his handling of Taylor: "You're dealing with grown-ass people. You can only do so much. It's not like he [Taylor] was a juvenile, and you could put twenty-four-hour surveillance on him. Bill did all that he could. Lawrence had to take responsibility for himself. Bill may have had special rules for different people; Lawrence wasn't the only one."

Parcells's customized approach galvanized his players to have an even better season than 1984's breakthrough. In 1985, Big Blue's stingy defense supported a run-heavy offense starring Joe Morris, the league's touchdown leader, and guided by Phil Simms, whose timely gunslinging would lead to his first of two Pro Bowls. Setting a team record for rushing yards, the Giants finished 10-6, their most victories since 1963, to capture a wild-card berth. For its first playoff home game in twenty-three years, Big Blue faced Bill Walsh's defending champions, who had also won ten games.

While capturing two Super Bowls in the past four years, San Francisco had opened those triumphant postseasons with victories over Big Blue, spurring a cross-coast rivalry between franchises whose leaders took diametrically different approaches. The Giants head coach espoused physical, run-oriented football, and conducted grueling practices with players wearing pads regardless of heat and humidity. Conversely, San Francisco's relatively laid-back commander used a creative, pass-crazy offense, and oversaw minimal-contact practices where players wore shorts while focusing on the precisely timed routes essential to his scheme.

During the week leading up to December 29, reporters peppered Parcells with questions about Walsh's unconventional system, so brilliantly quarterbacked by Joe Montana. Unloading the ball quickly, using only three- to five-step drops to avoid sacks, the superstar didn't rely on additional blockers, instead using the full complement of five receivers. In general, NFL offenses established the run to set up the pass. But Walsh had turned tradition on its head with a ball-control offense that emphasized throws to set up the run. The counterintuitive approach controlled the clock with short completions that acted like long handoffs.

In 1971, Bill Walsh had been promoted to quarterbacks coach for the Cincinnati Bengals under the legendary Paul Brown. New starter Virgil Carter was a sharp passer with mobility but he lacked a strong arm for deep throws. So Walsh designed a novel system that relied on quick, short throws while spreading the ball across the width of the field. In the tailor-made offense, Carter led the league in accuracy (62.2 percent) and was third overall in passing, though Cincinnati finished 4-10. In his first three seasons, the Brigham Young product had completed only 49.7 percent of his throws.

Walsh took over the two-win 49ers in 1979, and he implemented his system after drafting Montana. The third-round pick lacked a powerful arm, yet showed a masterful touch on medium-range passes while expertly reading coverages. Despite being one of the league's worst running teams, San Francisco won its first Super Bowl in 1982 by controlling the clock with the pass. The 49ers captured another Super Bowl in 1985, though with a terrific running attack behind Wendell Tyler and Roger Craig.

Parcells respected Walsh for turning the 49ers from chumps into champions, a task that the Giants leader hoped to emulate in New York. Since first reading *The Coaches* in the early 1970s, he knew that far more than one style, or system, could be used to bring success. But Parcells, who had learned to prize repetition and execution over complexity and super-fluousness, grew fed up with the attention being lavished on the "genius" and his system. The taskmaster viewed Walsh's imitators as wannabes who mistook complexity for smarts.

On a nippy afternoon at Giants Stadium, Parcells's team jumped ahead 10–0 as San Francisco repeatedly failed to exploit drives into Big Blue territory. The 49ers cut into the deficit with a field goal in the second quarter, but in the third period, Simms extended the lead on a scoring pass to tight end Don Hasselbeck. It would be the last touchdown catch by the father of future NFL quarterbacks Matt and Tim. Joe Morris, showcasing the benefits of the traditional approach to offense, rushed for 141 yards. And the Giants kept Walsh's 49ers from scoring a touchdown for the first time ever, smothering Montana with four sacks. The 17–3 outcome gave Parcells's team its first postseason victory over the 49ers, snapping a five-game skid against them.

In the Giants locker room, Parcells beamed as reporters swarmed for his postgame Q&A. Even before the back-and-forth began, he sneered, "What do you think of that **West Coast Offense** *now*?"

The moniker would stick to Walsh's system forever. San Francisco's coach was annoyed, since his design had nothing to do with the West Coast. He would insist that the name be changed to "Walsh Offense" or "Cincinnati Offense," to distinguish it from other offenses that had originated in the geographic area. Nonetheless, Walsh's protestations were to no avail.

Big Blue's next game, against Mike Ditka's Chicago Bears in the Windy City, would feature the league's top two defenses. The Giants were still heavy underdogs, given that Chicago also had a potent offense led by superstar runner Walter Payton that had helped the club to one of the best records in NFL history at 15-1.

Early on, the game at Soldier Field seemed headed for a tight, defensive struggle as Big Blue's defensive unit served up punishing hits to match the haymakers of coordinator Buddy Ryan's group. But any chance for an upset evaporated midway through the first quarter of a scoreless game, when Sean Landeta attempted a punt from New York's end zone. Exhaling little white clouds in the eighteen-degree weather, Landeta lowered the ball with his right hand, but when he swung his kicking foot the pigskin only grazed his instep, skipping a few yards to his right. Recognizing the blunder, he spun around to search for the ball, but Chicago's Shaun Gayle scooped it up and sprinted five yards for a touchdown.

Landeta thought to himself, "This is unreal. How could this happen?" When he trotted forlornly to the sideline, Parcells didn't reveal any displeasure. As if discussing a harmless play in practice, the head coach calmly asked his pudgy punter how the gaffe had occurred. Landeta claimed that the sixteen-mile-per-hour wind had swept the ball away to one side. Although the punt would live in NFL infamy, Parcells said nothing further, turning to face the field, and exhorting his defense.

Landeta punted eight more times without incident, but the Giants proved to be overmatched in a 21–0 loss. In a game of bone-crunching hits, Morris was knocked unconscious by lineman Richard Dent's tackle, while being held to only 32 yards on 12 carries; Simms was sacked 6 times by a bullying, blitz-crazy defense that made it seem as if more than eleven Bears were on the field. Buddy Ryan's unit lived up to its reputation as New York's offense went 0 for 14 on third and fourth downs. Conversely, Chicago's offensive line didn't allow a sack against a unit that had led the NFL in that department.

The Bears went on to shut out the Los Angeles Rams before routing New England in Super Bowl XX. That year Chicago was considered one of the best teams the league had ever seen. But being derailed by history didn't ease Parcells's pain.

. . .

Giants coaches graded their players after each season by meticulously analyzing every play via game film. For 1985, Taylor ranked third among his
team's defensive players, and eighth on the roster. He was still splendid
enough to be named an All-Pro, just as he had every year since his rookie
season, and the fifth-year veteran was widely regarded as perhaps the best
linebacker ever. However, this was the first time Taylor graded out as anything less than the team's top performer in the assessment by Parcells's
staff.

Coming off the shutout loss to Chicago, Parcells implored Taylor to
seek professional help for his drug abuse, and made arrangements to protect the linebacker's privacy. In February 1986, Taylor entered a rehab facility at Houston Methodist Hospital, where Parcells discreetly checked
in on him. When unsubstantiated reports surfaced that the linebacker was
undergoing treatment for cocaine and alcohol abuse, Taylor confirmed his
situation in a statement read to reporters by Tom Powers, the Giants' promotions director.

Then Taylor bolted the clinic.

The linebacker had decided that he could overcome addiction on his
own, using the formidable willpower that helped him dominate football
opponents. Taylor played golf religiously, barnstorming courses around the
country. "My therapy, not recommended for anyone else, was mainly to
enjoy myself as much as I could," he says. "The golf course was my detox
tank. I got free of the pressure cooker that was New York for a while."

Taylor seemed to be drug-free when the Giants tested him weekly during the season. And for the first time since 1983, the linebacker performed
as if he was in total control of his incomparable abilities. He rushed the
passer on 70 percent of defensive snaps, regularly battering and bruising
quarterbacks. Big Blue won five of its first six games, playing with a swagger epitomized by Taylor. Parcells's 3-4 defense was being dubbed the "Big
Blue Wrecking Crew," as Taylor, Carl Banks, Harry Carson, and Gary
Reasons, who was talented enough to start as a rookie in 1984, formed the
best quartet of linebackers in recent memory. The defense also featured
a powerful front line, with Leonard Marshall and George Martin sand-
wiching nose tackle Jim Burt.

During the fast start, Parcells felt that his team was missing something
important: Phil McConkey's sure-handedness and fearlessness on punt
and kickoff returns. The Giants had made the difficult decision to release
McConkey late in training camp because of the availability of younger,
faster, taller wideouts. The Packers then claimed the thirty-year-old off

waivers, which allows the team with the worst record first dibs on available players. Now a serious knee injury to Lionel Manuel, the team's top wide-out, spurred Big Blue to search for a receiver. After the first four games, Parcells persuaded Green Bay to give up McConkey by offering a pick in the draft's twelfth and final round.

Then Parcells telephoned McConkey. "Those Packers sure drive a hard bargain, Phil."

"What are you talking about?"

"I had to throw in a couple of clipboards and a blocking dummy to get you back."

Despite the familiar skewering, McConkey was thrilled about return-ing to the Giants.

"Bill, the grass is greener my ass."

When McConkey rejoined the team for his first practice, Parcells in-sisted that the receiver put that quote on the locker-room chalkboard. The remark wouldn't be erased for the rest of the season.

Lawrence Taylor barely spoke to Phil Simms during their first few years together on the Giants. The linebacker bought into the perception that the oft-injured quarterback lacked toughness and had a sense of entitlement. "I didn't really want to talk to him," Taylor recalls. "As I saw it, he was one of those guys you see on TV that drink tea with their pinky up." The chill-iness between the two extended into the 1985 season, with Simms jealous of Taylor's relationship with the head coach. Parcells often rode Simms to a boiling point that occasionally prompted him to lash back, raising eyebrows among teammates fearful to ever try. Simms believed that the linebacker's star power shielded him from Parcells's vitriol, but Parcells dismisses his ex-quarterback's take, saying of Taylor, "I coached him just as hard as any other player. Maybe more, because my expectations for him were out of sight. I was on his ass. I was also caring."

The headstrong tendencies of both coach and linebacker led to con-flicts that occasionally turned physical. One practice session extended into the early evening because of Parcells's dissatisfaction with his defense's ex-ecution. As the unit focused on pass rushing, Taylor failed to follow in-structions on technique with enough precision to satisfy the head coach. When Parcells became exasperated enough to get in Taylor's face and upbraid him, the linebacker stepped closer, brushing up against Parcells while complaining about his unreasonable demands. Further angered by Taylor's reaction, Parcells nudged his rebellious linebacker.

"You sonofabitch, I'm tired of you."

Taylor stepped forward, returning the push.

Realizing that the argument was getting out of hand, several players stepped in to separate the combatants. Linebacker Carl Banks grabbed Parcells. "Come on, Bill. You know he's your boy."

Another player, doing the same with Taylor, implored, "Come on, L.T., you know he's your daddy."

Regardless of such clashes, Taylor always stood immediately to Parcells's left during the national anthem on game day. The linebacker maintained the ritual even when the two men weren't speaking. It was so ingrained that Taylor sometimes scrambled to find Parcells and position himself in time for the national anthem. "That was his way of telling me: 'Hey, I'm with you now,'" Parcells recalls. "And I always loved that about him, because whether it was one o'clock Sunday or nine o'clock Monday, he was there. And in that moment all of that other stuff wasn't important. We could get back to fighting and arguing after the game."

The Giants had won three more consecutive games entering a November 16 contest at the Metrodome versus the Minnesota Vikings. But Big Blue's 8-2 record couldn't mask the struggles of Simms and his wide-receiving corps, hampered by injuries to Lionel Manuel and Stacy Robinson. "We got to a point," Simms says, "where we were awful. We couldn't complete passes. We couldn't get it down the field at all."

Simms heard boos from fans and read criticism from sportswriters who felt that the team lacked a championship quarterback. His terrific seasons in 1984 and 1985 failed to provide cover. Parcells noticed that without his top wideouts Simms was being uncharacteristically tentative in his throws. During the week of practice, Parcells avoided even the mildest criticism of his quarterback. Instead, several days before New York traveled to Minnesota, Parcells approached the eight-year veteran and advised Simms to ignore the catcalls and negative headlines.

"I think you're a great quarterback, and you got that way by being daring and fearless. So let's go."

On Sunday, heading out of the locker room before kickoff, Parcells reiterated, "Take some chances. I don't care if you throw four interceptions. Just keep throwing it down there."

For much of the game Simms did just that, but with only 72 seconds left the Giants were down 20–19, and he faced a daunting situation at midfield: fourth-and-17. Before breaking the huddle, Simms turned to Bobby Johnson, whose assignment was to line up on the right perimeter. "Bobby, be alert. I might have to come to you late."

On the snap, nose tackle Mike Stensrud breached the line as Johnson sprinted to the first-down marker near Minnesota's bench. Simms scanned to his left and didn't see any possibilities for a long completion. So the quarterback looked right, targeting Johnson near the sideline. As Stensrud wrapped his right arm around Simms's waist, the quarterback sidearmed a fearless spiral before being flung down.

Johnson slowed down at a hole in the defense and turned around to spot the pigskin just as four Vikings led by safety John Harris closed in. The wideout pulled in Simms's pinpoint throw before being pushed out of bounds, gaining an improbable first down at Minnesota's 30-yard line. Picking himself up off the ground, Simms pumped his fists, while Parcells paced the sideline and spoke into his headset as if the completion had gone according to plan. Moments later, Raul Allegre booted a 33-yard field goal for a thrilling victory that kept the Giants atop the NFC East with the formidable Washington Redskins. Simms had thrown for a season-high 310 yards, while completing 25 of 38, none more significant than his final, defining pass.

"From that time on," Lawrence Taylor recalls, "I felt that if we're going to win a championship, it's going to be behind the arm of Phil Simms. He became my man right there."

New York's fourth straight victory improved its record to 9-2. Just as important, Simms's clutch throw, and Johnson's reception, seemed to infuse the franchise with a sense of destiny. Repeatedly winning close games through élan and grit, Parcells's team began to sense a magical season.

The next challenge came at home versus Denver; led by superstar quarterback John Elway and a formidable defense, the 9-2 Broncos topped the AFC West. With a minute left in the first half at Giants Stadium, Denver was ahead 6–3 and threatening to score from New York's 13-yard line. As Elway threw a swing pass to runner Sammy Winder, left defensive end George Martin elevated himself as if he were still a basketball forward grabbing in an alley-oop for the Oregon Ducks. Martin tipped the ball with his outstretched right hand, then corralled it with both arms and sprinted along the long sideline, enthralling the crowd of 75,116. A couple of yards behind, Taylor kept pace as Martin's personal bodyguard while John Elway raced across the field, homing in for a tackle.

Taylor recalls, "I didn't think the old man was going to get all the way downfield, so I said, 'Hey, hey, hey, flip it over here.'"

The oldest Giants player at age thirty-four, Martin froze Elway by feigning the lateral, but a few yards later the ultra-athletic quarterback caught up with Martin at Denver's 45. Elway grabbed Martin's left shoulder to bring him down. But Martin used his free right arm to shove Elway to the sideline. Martin and Taylor found themselves side by side, an ideal opportunity for the linebacker to take possession from his exhausted teammate.

Taylor yelled, "I'm right here. Give it to me."

Martin started to lateral, but saw offensive lineman Billy Bryan converging on Taylor. Gasping for air, Martin held on to the ball while Taylor refocused on blocking. Denver's last hope for a stop belonged to Sammy Winder, sprinting ahead of Martin to try forcing him out of bounds. But hustling cornerback Mark Collins dove into Winder, and as both players tumbled, Martin hurdled over them for a clear path to the end zone.

The defensive end's dramatic run concluded only when Taylor caught him in a headlock to celebrate his teammate's 78-yard return for a touchdown. Even when they hit the ground, Martin clutched the ball, refusing to give it up. The seventh touchdown of Martin's NFL career was the most ever by a defensive lineman. Although the remarkable sequence took 17 seconds, it seemed to unfold in slow motion. "One of the greatest plays," Parcells says, "I've ever seen in football."

Behind Elway's passing and scrambling in the second half, Denver tied the game at 16. But with less than a minute left, Phil Simms repeated his late-game heroics with a 46-yard pass to a leaping Phil McConkey. The connection set up a 34-yard field goal from Allegre, and the Giants triumphed 19–16 for their fourth straight victory by a field goal or less. No NFL team since 1940 had sustained such a nail-biting stretch.

Given such dramatic flourishes, the next game seemed almost routine, despite New York's being down 17–0 to San Francisco at halftime. Still, the *Monday Night Football* contest at Candlestick Park featured another memorable singular effort, this time by tight end Mark Bavaro. Despite a standout career at Notre Dame, Bavaro wasn't rated highly by most NFL teams when he entered the 1985 draft, but because the Giants predominantly ran the ball off tackle toward the outside, they needed a capable blocker at tight end to back up Zeke Mowatt. Ranking Bavaro as the best blocking tight end, Big Blue chose him in the fourth round as the one hundredth overall selection. One of Parcells's scouts, Jerry Angelo, the future Bears GM, told Parcells: "You're gonna love this guy."

By training camp Angelo's prediction proved correct. Typically sparing with compliments, Parcells described Bavaro as his most impressive rookie. During an exhibition game Mowatt suffered a right-knee injury that ended his season, and Bavaro jumped in as a starter for the rest of the year. He turned into not only the league's best blocker, routinely disabling 300-pound defensive ends, but also one of the most difficult pass-catchers to tackle.

Mark Bavaro kept the starting job in 1986, performing with toughness, versatility, and self-effacement. The six-four, 245-pounder was so quiet that for several games in October and November, most teammates didn't notice that his jaw was wired shut; Bavaro had fractured it during a victory versus New Orleans September 28, when he persuaded Parcells to leave him in. The injury would limit the tight end to eating through a straw.

In the third quarter, facing a substantial deficit against San Francisco, the Giants had the ball at midfield. On second-and-10, Mark Bavaro dashed across the middle for a catch at San Francisco's 40. Linebacker Mike Walter, attempting a tackle, ping-ponged off Bavaro's left side, as so many defenders had done throughout the season. Linebacker Riki Ellison dived for another futile attempt. As Bavaro hustled down the field, Ronnie Lott, the star safety known for his fearless hits, wrapped two hands around the tight end's waist at the 32.

Big Blue's man of steel gave Lott a piggyback ride as linebacker Keena Turner hit Bavaro and bounced off. Cornerback Don Griffin tried his luck, but could only slow Bavaro enough for strong safety Carlton Williamson to grab hold. Acting like the Terminator swarmed by overmatched mortals, Bavaro plodded another eight yards before two more 49ers sandwiched him. Finally, Bavaro and four defenders tumbled at the 18-yard line. More than half a ton of San Francisco manpower was needed to halt the indomitable tight end.

Lawrence Taylor says, "I didn't respect anyone in the league more than I respected Ronnie Lott. And to see Bavaro dragging Ronnie Lott, it's like: 'Yeah!'" The Giants wouldn't be stopped either, scoring 21 points in less than nine minutes to triumph 21–17.

The hard-fought comeback kept New York in a first-place tie with its next opponent, Joe Gibbs's Washington Redskins. The Giants traveled to RFK Stadium to face their redoubtable rivals in a rematch after Big Blue's victory earlier in the season. The critical game lacked suspense as Lawrence Taylor, a native of Williamsburg, Virginia, saved his most dominating performance of the season for his father's favorite team. With three sacks and an afternoon harrying quarterback Jay Schroeder, Taylor helped his team to a 24–14 win and sole possession of first place in the NFC East. After the game, Parcells predicted that the Giants and Redskins would face each other again in the playoffs.

Next, Big Blue trounced the St. Louis Cardinals and Green Bay Packers to capture its first division title since the NFL-AFL merger in 1970. The Giants finished 14-2, with nine straight victories, to earn the top seed in the postseason. Showing a tendency to come through in the clutch, Big Blue had won five games by three points or less.

The Giants allowed an average of only 14.8 points, the league's best such mark, behind one of the greatest rushing defenses of all time. Highlighting the NFL's most fearsome group of linebackers, Lawrence Taylor captured every vote for the league MVP award, a rare tribute for a defensive player. With his league-best 20.5 sacks and countless sallies that struck fear in opposing quarterbacks, the linebacker was also named defensive player of the year. On offense Mark Bavaro finished with 1,001 receiving yards, only the eighth tight end in league history to eclipse the thousand-yard milestone. And in turning a once-sputtering franchise into an NFL juggernaut, Parcells garnered Coach of the Year. Still he yearned for more, and the next step was a postseason home game versus San Francisco.

Bill Parcells was fanatical about game-day weather, particularly during playoffs. Before home contests he telephoned Newark Airport or the National Weather Service to gather precise intelligence about such factors as the wind. "If I had had their home numbers," Parcells says, "I would have called meteorologists." But when his team arrived at Giants Stadium to face the 49ers, a much more pressing issue surfaced: the absence of wideout Bobby Johnson.

For home games players checked out of a nearby hotel, and generally took their own vehicles to the stadium. The game-day deadline for arrival was ninety minutes before the opening kickoff, but most players arrived a couple of hours in advance. By the time the Giants finished warming up, with less than an hour to go, Johnson was still AWOL. Leading Big Blue's wideouts in receptions, the five-eleven, 170-pounder was a critical aspect of the team's offensive game plan. In his absence the Giants were left with only three wideouts including Phil McConkey, whose primary job was returning punts. Lionel Manuel had participated in only a few practices after spending a month on the injured reserve with a broken ankle.

Following the 1983 season, Bobby Johnson had been among the players Parcells monitored for drug use. The undrafted receiver via Kansas fell in line while contributing to the team for three seasons. Now, however, as the Giants returned to the locker room before the opening kickoff versus San Francisco, Johnson still couldn't be found. His teammates were furious at the thought that Johnson had chosen a pivotal playoff game to backslide.

A few minutes before New York had to step on the field for the national anthem, Johnson entered the locker room. Before he could try to explain his lateness, Jim Burt, Harry Carson, and Lawrence Taylor shoved the receiver to the ground, cursing and hitting him. As George Martin and Lionel Manuel tried to calm things down, Johnson managed to get back on his feet, but his teammates weren't quite finished punishing him.

Nose tackle Jerome Sally shouted, "Bill! Bill! Get out here!"

Defensive end Eric Dorsey added, "They're killing him! They're killing him! They're killing him!"

Parcells rushed out of his office to the odd sight of Jim Burt ripping Johnson's dress shirt before pushing him into his locker stall. "You better play. If you don't play your ass off, we'll beat you again after the game."

Still struggling to make sense of the bizarre scene, Parcells shouted, "Wait, wait. Whoa, whoa, whoa." The head coach defused the situation, but tensions remained high as the Giants headed to the field. George Martin recalls the fallout from Johnson's last-minute appearance. "Pouncing on him wasn't the answer. Giving him a pass wasn't the answer either. My position was that cooler heads should prevail. Let's put it aside for the moment, and let's go and play. And that's what we did."

Setting aside the brouhaha, the Giants claimed a 14–3 lead in the second quarter. With the outcome far from determined against a potent 49ers offense, Phil Simms faced third-and-15 in San Francisco's red zone. Bobby Johnson's pattern required him to go in motion from the left side and run to the right corner of the end zone. As Simms released the ball, defensive end Dwaine Board and safety Jeff Fuller rammed into him, slamming Simms's head hard against the artificial surface. Lawrence Taylor sprinted over from the sideline, the first Giant to check on his teammate, but Simms declined any assistance, rising gingerly to head for the bench. Nose tackle Jim Burt informed him that Johnson had caught the tight spiral for a touchdown, increasing New York's lead to 21–3, but Simms didn't celebrate the news until trainer Ronnie Barnes administered smelling salts.

On San Francisco's next possession, first-and-20 at New York's 18, Jim Burt bulled his way up the middle to wallop Joe Montana just as the quarterback released a long throw to his left. The ball wobbled well short of its target, Jerry Rice, leading to an interception by Lawrence Taylor. With Rice several yards behind, Taylor sprinted 34 yards for a touchdown. Montana suffered a concussion severe enough to warrant an ambulance to the hospital, becoming the fourth quarterback the Giants had forced out of a game that season.

Jeff Kemp, son of the American politician and ex–AFL star quarterback, replaced Montana, but the offense made no better headway against the wrecking ball of New York's defense. The final score was 49–3, a brilliant performance that saved Bobby Johnson from further locker-room reprisals.

In his postgame remarks, San Francisco coach Bill Walsh told reporters, "We were shattered by a great team," and described Big Blue's performance as being "perfect."

. . .

Reviewing Big Blue's masterpiece, though, Parcells saw chips in the *Mona Lisa*. At the team's next round of meetings he ran through a litany of flaws and declared the final score misleading. Although San Francisco had recorded only one sack, Parcells spent much of practice harping on how the 49ers repeatedly hit Simms. Parcells stressed that Big Blue had no chance of advancing to the Super Bowl without better pass protection.

The criticism left players feeling as if they were coming off a slipshod loss instead of a tour de force that sent them to the NFC Championship. "It almost immediately took the joy out of winning," Simms says. For the rest of the week Parcells's perfectionism, carping, and doomsday scenarios kept players on edge.

This behavior wasn't unusual for the Giants head coach, a firm believer that football success stemmed more from understanding human beings than X's and O's. Parcells wanted to counter what he termed "the psychology of results." He broke this down into four situations.

1. Trouncing an opponent like San Francisco caused overconfidence, which meant he needed to keep his team grounded and focused. "Everybody else is pumping air in them," he says. "Everybody else is telling them how great they are."

2. Losing a close game despite a sharp, spirited effort prompted the team to feel snakebitten. Parcells insisted that regardless of the setback, maintaining intense effort would lead to a winning stretch.

3. A resounding defeat created doubt, so Parcells worked toward the next game while instilling confidence and underscoring a chance at redemption.

4. The worst scenario was a victory after subpar play. Here, Parcells repeatedly reminded his team that its luck would run out without drastic improvements.

"The psychology of results is a powerful deterrent to team success," Parcells says. "It affects everybody: owners, the GMs, the fans, the press. Everybody. The same thing is true for individual performances. Some players are satisfied with performing well, despite their team losing. I don't want those players on my team. The best players I've had, when they played well and we lost, they were miserable. If they played poorly and we won, they were happy we won."

Parcells reined in whoever he deemed was getting inflated by accolades—"the fat-cat syndrome"—by pulling the culprit aside and detailing mistakes overlooked by the media. The coach concluded the jarring conversation by conveying disappointment that the player didn't share his high standards. Conversely, Parcells had an uncanny knack for lifting dispirited athletes like Simms before his virtuoso performance versus Minnesota. Leading up to the NFC Championship, though, Parcells's growling overshadowed any praise for his powerful team.

Parcells's prediction about facing Washington in the postseason came true after Joe Gibbs's team stunned the Chicago Bears, 27–13, at Soldier Field. The Bears had matched the Giants for the league's best record while positioning themselves to repeat as Super Bowl champions. But the Redskins, who finished second in the NFC East at 12-4, proved to be dangerous. The upset victory meant that they would meet their New York nemesis in East Rutherford to determine the NFC Championship.

Ahead of the January 11, 1987, affair, Parcells obtained his detailed weather prognostication. The temperature would be 39 degrees, lowered by wind chill to 29; of more concern to Parcells was a wind forecast at 22 miles per hour. So despite a 4 p.m. kickoff, Parcells, wearing his blue windbreaker and black gloves for the game, arrived on the field at 7:15 a.m. to take in the elements. Over the next few hours he returned to the gridiron three more times to confirm the cold, blustery conditions.

When players showed up for warm-ups about ninety minutes before the game, with Bobby Johnson arriving conspicuously early, the swirling wind easily exceeded the forecast. Redskins punter Steve Cox, known for his ability to handle the elements, struggled to prevent balls from fluttering back toward him. Giants Stadium was notorious for its winter wind, but this was the strongest that punter Sean Landeta, or even Bill Parcells, had ever witnessed in East Rutherford.

About thirty minutes before kickoff, Parcells had his usual meeting with his punter and kicker to discuss the weather. Landeta predicted, "The wind will be a bigger factor than L.T." As the visiting team the Redskins got to select heads or tails on the coin flip, with the winner earning the option to receive the kickoff or defend either goal. Ordinarily teams choose to take the kickoff and start the game on offense, but this time, Parcells gave his co-captain Harry Carson different instructions.

"If we win the coin toss, take the wind and let the Redskins receive."

The Redskins sent five players, led by offensive tackle Russ Grimm, to midfield. As referee Pat Haggerty tossed an oversized nickel in the windswept stadium, the five Redskins yelled "Heads." Tails showed up on the Astroturf, so Carson informed Haggerty that Big Blue would defend the east goal. The decision allowed the Giants, aiming for a fast start, to play the first period with the wind at their backs.

The Redskins didn't go far on their first drive versus a revved-up defense, further aroused by 76,490 enthusiastic spectators. On fourth down, Steve Cox's punt into a gale wobbled to midfield, about a dozen yards short of an awaiting Phil McConkey, before bouncing out of bounds at Washington's 47. The ball had traveled only 23 yards. After several plays, the Giants had moved the ball within field-goal range. Raul Allegre converted a wind-abetted 47-yarder, his longest field goal as a Giant, to open the scoring.

The Redskins struggled on their next possession, causing Cox to punt again, this time from the end zone. As McConkey stood near midfield, the ball fluttered well short of him: the 27-yard punt was barely longer than Cox's first try. Joe Morris's running sparked a drive that had started at Washington's 38, and culminated when Phil Simms stepped up into the pocket, throwing an 11-yard dart to Lionel Manuel in the middle of the end zone. After only two possessions the Giants led 10–0.

In contrast to Cox's punts, Landeta's only attempt in the first quarter traveled 40 yards, and his kicks into the wind were also relatively strong. With Washington struggling to move against gusts of more than 30 miles per hour, New York's lead seemed substantial even before Joe Morris's one-yard scamper into the end zone for a second-quarter touchdown. "The coin toss was probably the biggest play of the game," Gibbs recalls. "And I'm not being sarcastic."

Quarterbacks on both teams maintained little control of any pass that flew more than a dozen yards. In Schroeder's case, the degree of difficulty increased because he was constantly flushed out of the pocket. The alternative, running against the Big Blue Wrecking Crew, was futile, and 76,000-plus howling fans, a record crowd at Giants Stadium, hindered Washington's offense almost as much as the elements. The Redskins were repeatedly forced to punt, and when Cox's kicks did reach McConkey he cleanly corralled the pigskin despite its herky-jerky movements. Parcells's over-the-top drills were paying off. Conversely, Washington's punt returner Eric Yarber too often allowed Landeta's balls to drop, limiting his team's field position.

After another futile Redskins possession with less than four minutes left, thousands of fans started shredding newspapers, programs, and paper cups to fling loose pieces into the wind; spectators also unleashed rolls of toilet paper, creating the atmosphere of a ticker-tape parade.

The Redskins had the ball at New York's 22 on a fourth-and-2 when another Jay Schroeder pass floated away from an open receiver on a short route. With about two minutes remaining, the crowd turned its roar of approval up a notch. Despite potent weapons like wideout Art Monk and tailback George Rogers, Gibbs's team would be shut out for the first time in his tenure.

As Simms killed the clock, Harry Carson went behind Big Blue's bench to grab one of the three Gatorade buckets. Slipping past complicit teammates, Carson snuck up behind Parcells, who swung around just in time to see him looming. Parcells backpedaled, sidestepped, and with a flash of his former athleticism, charged Carson and tried to wrest away the Gatorade. The tables, or bucket, seemed to be turning until punter Sean Landeta grabbed Parcells from behind. To the delight of teammates and spectators, Carson drenched the Giants head coach, who smiled before glancing sternly at the clock.

The ritual would turn into an American sports tradition, the Gatorade shower, for the winning coach moments after a victory. It had apparently started October 20, 1985—when Big Blue defeated Washington 17–3, Jim Burt dumped the liquid on Parcells—but the act became popularized the next season as the Tuna got drenched again and again.

The final tick of the clock in the NFC Championship gave the Giants their first conference title since 1963. Knowing their team was Super Bowl bound for the first time, spectators didn't want to leave the stadium. One mustachioed, middle-aged man pulled out a champagne bottle and poured it into beer cups for everyone sitting in his row. Jim Burt climbed into the stands to embrace his wife and son before ending up exchanging high-fives and hugs with ecstatic fans.

As Bill Belichick, wearing a gray hoodie under his red Giants jacket, walked across the field, he was hoisted off the ground by two of his players. Grinning, the coordinator placed one black-gloved hand atop each player's helmet, and decided to enjoy the ride on their shoulders. The scene would be captured on the front page of the January 12 *New York Times* with a caption that read, "Bill Belichick, the Giants defensive coordinator, being carried off the field after 17–0 victory over the Redskins." Belichick would collect one hundred copies for posterity.

New York's victory marked a changing of the NFL guard. In the previous five seasons, Washington and San Francisco had made it to four Super Bowls, capturing three, but this year's Giants outscored those teams 66–3 in two playoff games. In Parcells's postgame interview, he emphasized his punt returner's performance, noting that Phil McConkey's clean catches had generated a net advantage of 112 yards in field position. "More than any one player," Parcells declared, "McConkey won that game."

Back in the Giants locker room, owner Wellington Mara walked in wearing a ring for the NFL's 1956 championship and a tie clip that marked the franchise's 1962 conference title. Like Parcells and the rest of his team, the seventy-year-old yearned for nothing more than the organization's first Super Bowl victory. Parcells warned his giddy players that they had unfinished business, so no champagne bottles were popped ahead of the trip to Pasadena, California, to face Dan Reeves's formidable Denver Broncos.

11

Bill Parcells relied on Al Davis for guidance in preparing for Super Bowl XXI. Davis's Los Angeles Raiders had missed the playoffs with an 8-8 record under Tom Flores, but the Raiders boss owned three Super Bowl rings, including one as recent as 1983. Heeding Davis's advice that year saved Parcells's head-coaching job during his disastrous rookie stint, and in subsequent seasons Davis's tutelage had helped shape Parcells into one of the NFL's top coaches.

The maverick owner, notorious for his lawsuits against the league, was unpopular in many of the NFL's circles, including among Giants executives aligned with his nemesis, Pete Rozelle. But Parcells felt blessed by Davis's support, and his generosity in sharing his vast knowledge. Parcells saw parallels with another consigliere, Bobby Knight: both were brilliant men often vilified by those who didn't know them well.

Davis recommended that Parcells prepare as much as possible before leaving New Jersey. The Raiders honcho pointed out hindrances at the Super Bowl site, which included logistics and the carnival atmosphere. He also told Parcells, "It's a fine line. You've got to work like hell before you get out there, but don't overwork your players, because a lot of Super Bowl coaches have done that, and they've lost."

Parcells adjusted his plans to achieve the balancing act while keeping the Giants a bit longer on the East Coast. He wanted to modify his team's conditioning for weather in the high 70s to low 80s, so every other practice now included six 100-yard sprints. On alternate days the team ran 60-yard sprints. On the Wednesday ten days before the Super Bowl, Phil Simms had his worst-ever practice under Parcells, and the few passes that reached their targets were dropped. Late in the session, Parcells pulled his quarterback aside. "Listen, can you do me one favor? Can you complete one stinking pass before we finish today so I can sleep tonight?"

Simms completed some passes, but Parcells had plenty of other worries. For one thing, he was unfamiliar with the Rose Bowl, which had been hosting bowl games in Pasadena's warm climes since 1924. So he grilled Giants safety Herb Welch, who had played his home games there as a UCLA Bruin. Welch told Parcells that the end-zone corners were dangerously close to the stands, so receivers executing corner patterns, and defensive backs shadowing them, needed to avoid running into walls. For more stadium insight, Parcells phoned Los Angeles Rams coach John Robinson, who had guided USC from 1976 to 1982. Robinson told Parcells that the field tended to get slick, affecting footing.

Another potential problem involved the week the team would spend in Southern California, which provided players with too many hedonistic temptations during downtime. Bobby Johnson had been toeing the line since going MIA, but Parcells "was afraid he was going to go off the reservation." So the head coach decided to hire someone to chaperone Johnson while the team was in town.

Parcells told the minder, "If he goes to the bathroom, you go with him. If he cashes any checks, I want to know about it."

On Monday, January 19, 1987, the Giants landed in Costa Mesa, south of Los Angeles, to stay at the Westin South Coast Plaza through Saturday. Then they would stay overnight at a Howard Johnson's in Pasadena, a twenty-minute drive to the Rose Bowl. While much of the country was experiencing a cold and angry winter, Southern California was enjoying its usual balmy early-year weather. Only hours after deplaning, Johnson's chaperone called Parcells with news about his charge.

When Johnson arrived in Big Blue's locker room, he was instructed to see Parcells before changing. The receiver walked into the head coach's office.

"Did you just cash a check?"

"Yeah. How'd you know?"

Parcells ignored the question. "How much was it?"

"Five thousand dollars."

"What'd you do with it?"

"I bought a camcorder. I want to record what's happening at the Super Bowl."

"Go get it."

Johnson retrieved the camcorder, and the receipt for $3,238, from his locker stall. Parcells demanded the balance. The startled receiver emptied his wallet, handing his coach almost $1,800. Parcells explained to Johnson that he would get his money back at the week's end. Then the head coach called the chaperone into his office and handed over Johnson's money.

"Give him $100 a day. That's it."

Parcells explains his dictatorial approach: "You think I'm going to go to my owner or the GM with all that bullshit? You think I'm going to consult with them? If I don't just monitor him, it's not going to happen. We're going to the Super Bowl, and I've got this nonsense to deal with."

Later on that first day in California, Parcells conducted one of his lengthiest and most intense practices of the season. The rest of the week went relatively smoothly, as every Giants player avoided trouble. Big Blue's spirited practices went injury-free, and Simms looked his sharpest all season. In a Friday session two days before the game he threw so many consecutive completions that teammates lost count. The warm climate seemed to enhance Simms's accuracy, allowing him to grip the ball more tightly than usual and toss the pigskin precisely wherever he wanted it to go.

At one point, Parcells made an unprecedented request. "Hey, Phil, this is too much. Save some for the game."

Late in the week, the taskmaster decided to adjust Big Blue's offensive game plan to gain the advantage of surprise. Instead of establishing the run, the Giants intended to pass aggressively early. If Simms struck quickly with play-action throws, it would minimize a Denver pass rush led by Pro Bowl defensive end Rulon Jones. Parcells knew that Denver's swarming linebackers, including stars Karl Mecklenburg and Tom Jackson, were intent on stopping Joe Morris, who thrived behind the punishing blocks of fullback Maurice Carthon. Assuming that New York could establish a healthy lead, the offense could then revert to its identity of controlling the clock through methodical running.

On Saturday morning, Parcells declined to have the Giants practice at the Rose Bowl. Big Blue's last loss had occurred on October 19, 1986, at Seattle. The day before the 17–12 setback, which snapped a five-game streak, New York had practiced at the Kingdome. The Giants' only other loss had come in their season opener versus Dallas at Texas Stadium, where the Giants had also practiced the day before. The superstitious head coach detected a pattern that he refused to extend.

On waking at 5:30 a.m. the morning of Super Bowl XXI, Bill Parcells trudged to his hotel window, staring at the morning haze while thinking about the weather. The detailed forecast included a kickoff temperature of 77 degrees and the sun's location at the scheduled start of 3:13 p.m. Parcells didn't want Big Blue's receivers looking into the sun during the first quarter. Wind was going to be a factor, but Parcells wondered how his team would be affected by a potentially slick gridiron and end-zone corners close to the stands.

He contemplated wearing a suit and tie for the game, but decided to dress as he usually did: white sneakers, navy slacks, and a white dress shirt under a gray sweater with "GIANTS" in blue lettering.

On road games, Parcells shared a cab to the stadium with trainer Ronnie Barnes, perhaps his closest friend in the Giants organization. The previous night Parcells had asked Barnes to meet him at the hotel's coffee shop for breakfast at 7:30 a.m. Barnes knew the ex–Air Force coach expected him to get there several minutes beforehand, so when Parcells arrived at the spot at 7 a.m., Barnes was already there, reading the *Los Angeles Times* sports section. Parcells ordered a cheese Danish, his only meal before the game. Barnes read aloud a passage from a sports column by Jim Murray, comparing the Giants to a motorcycle gang, which made Parcells smile.

Barnes asked, "You nervous?"

Parcells replied, "I'm just worried about Elway."

The rifle-armed, fleet-footed quarterback was coming off another prolific season. Elway led the Broncos to an 11-5 mark before they peaked in the playoffs. With Denver down by a touchdown late in the AFC Championship at Cleveland, Elway, already renowned for his fourth-quarter comebacks, delivered an iconic performance. In "The Drive," the Stanford graduate engineered a riveting 98-yard drive to tie the score with 37 seconds left. An encore performance in overtime led to Rich Karlis's game-winning field goal.

Barnes scoffed at Parcells's concerns. "Hell, we're going to chase John Elway out into the parking lot before it's over."

Offensive coordinator Ron Erhardt entered the restaurant. The night before, Erhardt had held a quarterbacks' meeting, and Parcells wanted to know how things went.

"Phil's ready. He's glad we're gonna come out throwing."

"He'd better be."

Parcells asked about backup Jeff Rutledge.

"You know you never have to worry about Rutledge."

At 7:30 a.m., Parcells and Barnes headed outside to hail a cab. Parcells turned to Erhardt, who had coached North Dakota State with great success for seven years.

"Well, it's just like the North Dakota State–Augustana game, right?"

Erhardt, nicknamed "Fargo" after the state's largest city, smiled.

"I think it's a little bigger than that."

The cab carrying Parcells and Barnes got within a block of the Rose Bowl, where a security guard refused to let the vehicle go any farther without the proper pass. Unable to find it, Barnes raised his voice in annoyance, and the guard responded in kind. Attempting to defuse the situation, Parcells leaned over and poked his head out the window.

Smiling, he announced, "I'm Bill Parcells, the Giants coach."

"Yeah, right."

Parcells, exasperated, said, "Hey, I'm the coach of this team."

The NFL Coach of the Year and Barnes were forced to walk the rest of the way. After entering the stadium, Parcells made a beeline to the gridiron. Living up to its reputation, the field was immaculate, early-morning sun sparkling on emerald grass. As he scanned the stadium, Parcells was thinking that just one section could swallow Hastings College's home stadium, with its two thousand seats. "And it wasn't full all the time," he says. But when Parcells walked into the locker room assigned to the Giants, he was surprised at its modest size, and drabness.

Joe Morris, in gray sweats, was the first player to walk in.

Parcells looked at him. "You're not ready to go, are you?"

Morris matched the sarcasm. "Not at all. No, sir, not me."

Parcells pulled up a stool next to Morris's, and the two spoke for half an hour without mentioning the game. Morris shifted the conversation to football, but only to reminisce about his high school career, which included a failed stint at quarterback. Finally, Parcells said, "We're going to come out throwing. We want to loosen them up right at the start."

Morris nodded as Parcells went on. "But we're eventually going to get around to you. And you know I've been on your ass all week about goal-line plays and short-yardage stuff. When we get there, you're going to get the damn ball. And I want you to protect it. Don't let them take momentum."

Parcells's demeanor, though still commanding, was the loosest that Morris had ever seen. The tailback was used to seeing his head coach jittery leading up to games, pacing the locker room, holding a coffee cup. But here, just hours before the biggest game of his life, Parcells seemed focused yet carefree. And his Giants players, favored to beat Dan Reeves's Broncos, took his cue. The atmosphere was relaxed, as if everyone was readying for a scrimmage.

Phil Simms recalls, "Bill had a lot of great sayings. One of them was, **'You can't be afraid to go down in flames.'** It's so true. You can't be afraid of losing, and we were definitely not afraid of losing that day."

Lawrence Taylor liked getting to the stadium later than most teammates. The linebacker had a habit of appearing detached initially, growing more engaged and boisterous as kickoff neared. By the time the Giants took the field, Taylor was usually their most animated player. After arriving at noon, Taylor lay on his back as if to sleep in the bustling locker room, but his eyes stayed open. Parcells smiled at the sight. The linebacker winked back, increasing the coach's self-assurance.

The 101,063 spectators divided the bright stadium into seas of blue and orange as Giants and Broncos supporters wore their team colors. Parcells instructed Phil McConkey to go with his home-game ritual of waving a large white-and-blue towel to rouse spectators before the opening kickoff. In the section of the Rose Bowl dominated by Giants fans, Judy Parcells sat with her three daughters, one son-in-law, three sisters, and their parents. Not far from the group were some ex-teammates from Wichita. Parcells's special guest was former Hastings coach Dean Pryor, who in 1964 gave Big Blue's leader his first job in the profession.

When the Giants trotted onto the field for the introductions, Phil McConkey sprinted over and leaped in front of the Parcells section while waving a white hand towel. The blue-clad spectators roared, making the Giants feel more at home.

Judy Parcells blocked out all the pageantry and players massing on the field to zero in on her husband. "All I could see was Bill," she recalls. "And I was trying to feel what he was feeling."

During the coin toss Parcells maintained his habit of standing at the edge of the 50-yard line. Just as he had in the NFC Championship game, he sent only Harry Carson out for the ritual, while his opponents again used several players. Someone bumped him, and when the coach turned, he saw Neil Diamond, who was about to sing the national anthem, acting jittery.

Parcells said to the singer, "Tell you what, Neil. I'll go out there and sing the national anthem, and you coach these guys the rest of the day."

Diamond smiled. "Bill, you know I'm from Brooklyn, right?"

Parcells nodded.

"I hope you beat the hell out of them."

Parcells felt even more at home.

Moments after the national anthem, Raul Allegre boomed the kick-off as the metropolis-sized gathering, one of the largest-ever at a football game, clamored in anticipation. Elway wasted no time living up to his billing. The fourth-year maestro orchestrated a well-executed drive that set up a 48-yard Rich Karlis field goal to open the scoring and tie Jan Stenerud's Super Bowl record for distance. Simms responded by leading a 78-yard drive, punctuated with a six-yard pass to tight end Zeke Mowatt that put New York up, 7–3.

In Elway's next turn, he completed several short throws to drive deep into Giants territory. And on third-and-goal from the 4, Denver's clever play call, a quarterback draw from a spread formation, reclaimed the lead, 10–7. It was the first touchdown against Big Blue in the postseason.

Simms, however, continued to match Elway's sizzling throws, as if the passers had dipped their right hands into boiling water to see who would pull out first. Both quarterbacks were perfect in the first quarter, with all thirteen passes resulting in completions. The first misfire didn't come until the second quarter, and then only because wideout Phil McConkey slipped after being nudged by a defender.

Big Blue's topsy-turvy approach on offense, passing to set up the run, caught Denver off guard. On the eleven Giants first downs before inter-mission, Simms threw nine times and completed every one while getting excellent protection. As usual, Elway was at his most dangerous outside the pocket. He scrambled while connecting on long pinpoint passes, some-times heaved across his body, which repeatedly put his team in scoring po-sition. Nonetheless, Denver missed opportunities. In the second quarter, Elway led a drive to New York's 1-yard line for a first down. A touchdown seemed inevitable as Elway scrambled on a run-pass option, but Lawrence Taylor burst out of the end zone and dropped Elway for a one-yard loss. On the next play, Harry Carson stuffed fullback Gerald Wilhite's run up the middle for no gain. Denver kept its jumbo-sized offensive set, suggest-ing another rush play, but just before the snap Carl Banks recalled that in their regular-season matchup the Broncos had scored on a pitchout near the goal line.

When Elway tossed the ball left, behind the line, to tailback Sammy Winder, Banks pounced, joined a second later by Carson and cornerback Perry Williams, forcing a four-yard loss. Further deflating the Broncos, Karlis whiffed on the 23-yard field goal attempt, pulling it left to set polar-opposite records in the Super Bowl with the shortest miss. More important, the meltdown kept the score at 10–7, leaving Dan Reeves look-ing glum.

On their next possession the Broncos found themselves in their own end zone, where George Martin sacked Elway for a safety that made the score 10–9. Elway had used a shotgun snap on third-and-12 at Denver's 13, but he failed to find any receivers by the time Martin beat right tackle Ken Lanier.

With less than a minute left in the first half of play, Karlis missed an-other short field goal, this time from 34 yards, giving the Giants a lift as they went into halftime down only one point, the slimmest margin in Super Bowl annals. Throughout New York's magical season the third quarter had been the team's best period, a trend the Giants intended to maintain here on football's biggest stage. At halftime, Parcells urged his team to attack, although with discipline.

Twilight descended, bringing on stadium lights and cool air. On the opening drive of the second half New York seemed to stall at its 46-yard line, with only a foot to go for a first down. During the regular season, the Giants had been perfect on six attempts of fourth-and-1, including one against Denver. But with the team still in Giants territory Parcells sent punter Sean Landeta onto the field to replace Phil Simms. New York also inserted a player with no role on the punt team: backup quarterback Jeff Rutledge.

Landeta awaited the snap while Rutledge assumed a blocking position, standing to the right of center Bart Oates. Suddenly, however, the Giants shifted into a conventional offensive set as Rutledge moved quickly behind center while Lee Rouson and Maurice Carthon darted from opposite spots on the perimeter to crouch three yards behind Rutledge, becoming running backs.

With the 30-second play clock ticking, Rutledge assessed Denver's defense. He looked left and right as Denver's defenders pranced about warily, but they assumed Big Blue was merely trying to draw an offsides penalty for an automatic first down. Denver's inside linebackers didn't clog the middle, which would have caused Rutledge to abandon the play. Instead, the quarterback let the clock wind down and subtly glanced at Parcells, who nodded.

The moment, Parcells says, had called for Mickey Corcoran's great lesson: provide just the right amount of information (what steps to take based on Denver's defense) to put the athlete (Rutledge) in the best position to execute. In front of an international TV audience of 130 million–plus, Jeff Rutledge calmly instructed center Bart Oates to snap the ball. Clutching it to his chest, the quarterback dashed two yards behind right guard Chris Godfrey for a stunning first-down conversion. Parcells smiled tightly at the chicanery's success. Exploiting the new life, Simms guided his team down the field before zipping a risky pass into double coverage. Like most of Simms's throws that afternoon, the location was perfect. Mark Bavaro snagged the ball for a 13-yard touchdown, giving Big Blue a 16–10 lead, and momentum.

Now Big Blue's offense reverted to their ground-and-pound approach as Denver's linebackers, concerned about Simms's aggressive passing, treaded lightly. Late in the third quarter the Giants reached Denver's 45. On second-and-6, Simms pitched left to Morris, who took several steps forward, drawing Denver's safeties, before pulling up behind the line of scrimmage and turning to flip the ball to Simms for a flea flicker. The sandlot trick left wideout Bobby Johnson alone in the end zone, but Simms locked in on McConkey, also open, who caught the ball at the 20 before sprinting to the 3, where ex-teammate Mark Haynes's low hit sent the former helicopter pilot head over heels at the 1. The 44-yard pass was Simms's longest completion of the late afternoon.

On the next play Morris took a pitch from Simms, and with Parcells's warnings ringing in his ears, he clutched the football tightly while following right guard Chris Godfrey. Defenders tumbled like tipped-over dominos as Morris crossed the goal line unscathed. The touchdown gave New York a 26–10 lead with less than a minute left in the third quarter. Several Giants defensive players celebrated as if the game was over. Parcells, conscious of Elway's fourth-quarter mojo, sprinted down the sideline, glaring at the perpetrators, and screaming at them to stay focused.

"Let's go!"

Having settled down in the second half, the Big Blue Wrecking Crew continued to disrupt Elway's rhythm, forcing a slew of misfires that included an Elvis Patterson interception. Lawrence Taylor says of the first half, "It was so hot, nobody could get their breath. In the second half, when the temperature cooled off, we came out and played in our kind of weather." Simms, though, remained on fire, throwing with astonishing precision on a range of passes. He completed all 10 of his second-half throws to set one Super Bowl mark, while the Giants scored 30 points to set another.

With about two minutes to play, and Gary Kubiak in for Elway, the public-address announcer declared Simms the game's MVP. Taylor bear-hugged his quarterback, yelling, "We're the best in the world, for one year." Offensive linemen Bart Oates and Brad Benson doused Simms with a bucket of ice water, cooling him off for the first time all afternoon. Not far away, Carson removed his jersey and pads before borrowing a security officer's yellow shirt to wear as his cover for the inevitable late-game ritual. Grabbing a Gatorade bucket, Carson slipped behind Parcells to unload it. This time he met no resistance. The head coach turned around and smiled as the orange liquid cascaded over him.

A recording of "New York, New York," by Parcells's childhood neighbor Frank Sinatra, blared from the public-address system as several Giants players crooned along. Judy Parcells felt goose bumps remembering her husband's brash prediction when he worked as a Colorado Springs real-estate agent. Since that moment in 1979, she had believed his assertion about one day leading a team to a Super Bowl championship. But the dreamy couple never imagined that it would be the first one in Giants history, and would come so soon after his football sabbatical.

With less than a minute left in the game, Parcells, his arms akimbo, watched Denver's final possession. He was flashing back to his 1964 coaching debut, Hastings's home opener when his defense stifled the Colorado School of Mines, 24–0. "I can't tell you why I thought about Hastings," he says. "I was just thinking to myself: 'My gosh, how things have changed. What a different landscape this is than when I first started.'" The symmetry concluded with a 39–20 victory in which Parcells's much-maligned quarterback finished with the most accurate passing performance, 22 for 25 (or 88 percent), in Super Bowl history.

Judy tried to spot her husband but failed to locate him for a couple minutes amid the throng of photographers and cameramen on the sidelines.

Parcells whispered into the ears of some of his offensive linemen. Brad Benson, Brian Johnson, and Chris Godfrey hoisted Parcells atop their shoulders, enabling Judy to spot her husband raising his right arm in triumph. In one of the happiest moments of her life, and certainly of his, Judy Parcells began to bawl.

Lingering acrimony between the team's co-owners prompted Tim Mara to skip the Vince Lombardi Trophy presentation in the Giants locker room. His uncle and nemesis, Wellington Mara, stood, smiling, at a makeshift podium in the Giants locker room, where Pete Rozelle handed him the trophy. Mara, whose late father, Timothy J. Mara, had acquired the club in 1925 for $500, passed the glistening prize to Parcells.

"Bill, take it away."

Beaming, Parcells raised it high with both hands.

"We buried all the ghosts today," he declared. "They're all gone."

The head coach, all but fired in 1983 while burying both his parents, added, "Bill Parcells is one of the luckiest guys in the world. I don't know why God has blessed me this way."

In the cramped locker room, Parcells gathered his giddy players into a circle, and asked them to hush for an important message. Lawrence Taylor moved to Parcells's left, as if taking his spot for the national anthem, while Mickey Corcoran, in a red cap, smiled from behind his ex-player.

Parcells raised his right arm, pointing his index finger toward the ceiling.

"One thing, fellas. Listen to me. For the rest of your lives men, nobody can ever tell you that you couldn't do it, 'cause you *did* it."

The head coach turned around and walked away, looking more defiant than gleeful. He left his players hollering in approval as the celebration resumed.

The Giants boarded a bus headed to the Westin hotel in Costa Mesa for a private celebration in the hotel ballroom. During the one-hour ride, Parcells observed the scenery while reflecting on each career stop on his road to football nirvana.

The partygoers at Big Blue's bash included celebrities, long-retired Giants, and friends whom Parcells hadn't seen in decades. On a night full of emotion, Charlie Conerly, quarterback of the franchise's previous championship team in 1956, wept while congratulating Parcells.

"I'm so happy for Simms. Hell, I'm so happy for all of you."

Parcells embraced Conerly, one of his heroes as a teenager growing up in Hasbrouck Heights.

The large Parcells contingent also attended the shindig. Jill spent part of the evening with Tom Cruise, a Syracuse native and Giants fan, taking pictures with the actor whose starring role in *Top Gun,* released the previous year, had turned him into a household name. Alcohol flowed, but Parcells made sure to consume only a few beers, knowing he had to attend a press conference the next morning.

Heading home the following afternoon, the Giants boarded a DC-10 plane with flight attendants dressed in Giants uniforms. In fresh blue paint on the exterior of the aircraft's fuselage, a sign read, "Super Bowl XXI Champion New York Giants."

12

Only two days later the additional euphoria in New York, which had celebrated the Mets winning the World Series in October, was disrupted by stunning news: Bill Parcells was contemplating a switch to another team. Two years remained on Parcells's four-year contract with the Giants, worth about $300,000 annually, yet he was open to the idea of becoming Atlanta's head coach and general manager for a substantially richer deal. The revelation startled the Giants faithful and enraged General Manager George Young.

Big Blue's resurrection had eased the strain between Young and Parcells that dated back to the GM's double-dealing with Parcells's job in 1983. The two men had worked effectively together despite their different mind-sets. Whereas Young's demeanor was even-keeled and his approach to decisions maddeningly methodical, Parcells was more mercurial and intuitive. His focus was also short-term: on the next game, or practice, and certainly no more than the following season. "Because that's what a coach is charged to do," he says. "George's view of the franchise was more long-range. I was in survival mode."

The differences were also complementary. Despite Parcells's complaints about Young's conservative bent, the GM's tendency to avoid risk made the head coach rethink some rash ideas. The private, secretive duo shared a football outlook that emphasized tough defense and a powerful running game. Young believed that forcing a prospective player on a head coach was counterproductive, so the GM empowered Parcells in the draft process and avoided interfering in day-to-day decisions. Young agreed to almost all of Parcells's requests involving the team's roster, particularly entering the pivotal season of 1984. The two adhered to Bucko Kilroy's typing system for evaluating talent, although Young placed more value on smallish players like Joe Morris. Both men relished athletes capable of thriving in the Northeast's elements during football season. Working together, Parcells and Young had transformed the New York Giants into a championship team.

However, even the mutually beneficial relationship and a new Super Bowl ring were not enough to erase what Parcells called "the most important lesson I've ever learned in sports," that coaches are as expendable as their players. Big Blue's first championship in three decades provided him with rare leverage in the cutthroat business of sports, and a chance at job security. Mindful of the sobering lessons of 1983, Parcells felt the need to exploit that edge. But didn't Parcells realize that his actions would infuriate the Giants GM? "Well, I figured they might," Parcells replies, "but my feeling about that was: what's good for the goose is good for the gander."

Parcells expounds: "Now, you have to understand that I'm a product of my environment. After one year as head coach the Giants were planning to get rid of me. I'd been in the job four years when we won the Super Bowl, and quite frankly I still didn't know what they thought of me. They did extend my contract after my second year, but it wasn't going to financially benefit me for the long, long term. So here was some interest from another team talking about things that *would* have a long-term effect on my life."

Following a 7-8-1 season, the Falcons had dismissed Parcells's friend, Dan Henning, as head coach. Dick Vermeil and Terry Donahue had declined the club's interest, so Rankin Smith Jr., team president and son of the owner, intended to land the "genius coach" by tripling Parcells's salary in a five-year deal. However Parcells's contract required permission from the Giants for official talks, and George Young emphatically refused to grant Atlanta that clearance. Parcells's agent, Robert Fraley, maintained unofficial contact with the Falcons, but formal discussions meant more leverage in any discussions with the Giants. So Fraley reached out to Pete Rozelle, requesting that the commissioner intervene. Citing league rules, Rozelle declined. He contacted the two owners involved, Wellington Mara and Rankin Smith Sr., to squash the matter.

Blocked from negotiating with Atlanta, Parcells refocused on preparing the Giants for the 1987 season. He found himself craving another Super Bowl title instead of basking in its aftermath. Parcells recalls his mind-set. "It was, 'I'd really like to do this again, so everybody knows it wasn't an accident.' It's kind of a funny thing. You actually want to win *more* than before."

Indiana coach Bobby Knight, winner of two national titles, had warned his friend about this insatiable feeling. Parcells already understood the short-lasting pleasure of winning regular-season games, but capturing the Lombardi Trophy allowed him to identify with Knight's sentiments on winning his first NCAA Tournament in 1976. Even though Indiana also became the sole Division I school to finish the season undefeated, Knight's gratification quickly evaporated. He had tried to explain to Parcells how the desire for a second title felt even keener than the desire for the first.

Knight experienced misery for the next four years, yet winning the 1981 NCAA Tournament only led to an obsession for a *third* national title.

"That feeling takes guys like Dick Vermeil and me and just drives us into the ground," says Parcells, alluding to the former Eagles head coach who retired in 1983 citing burnout two seasons after guiding his team to the Super Bowl. "It's a nonstop gratification-seeking thing. If you're not achieving right now, you're no good."

In March 1987, two months after Parcells's first Super Bowl title, Knight ended another drought by winning his third NCAA Tournament at Indiana. Around that time, Parcells wrote a letter to his returning players. It stressed the challenges ahead, and insisted on attendance for the voluntary off-season program. The letter concluded: "Do you think they are going to cancel next season? The moment is over."

Although the NFL didn't quite cancel the 1987 season, a labor dispute hindered Parcells's pursuit of a second consecutive championship. Owners rejected demands by the players union for free agency and a guaranteed percentage of league revenue, and the impasse stretched beyond the season's first two games. On September 22, a couple of days after Dallas dropped Big Blue to 0-2, NFL players voted to strike. Unlike the 1982 dispute, the league decided to use replacements.

Some clubs had prepared for that worst-case scenario by making extensive plans to work with alternative personnel. The Redskins had scouted bubble players experienced in a one-back offense similar to Joe Gibbs's. The team had made such extensive arrangements that it had a surplus of talented replacement players. The Giants had taken the opposite approach, wanting to maintain unity coming off the franchise's first Super Bowl title. George Young's contingency plan had been to acquire a semi-pro club based in Connecticut, but only two of Big Blue's new players had NFL experience. The roster was composed mostly of castoffs from the United States Football League and Canadian Football League. So in only a matter of days the defending Super Bowl champions, a blend of veteran stars and young talent, turned into one of the league's worst teams.

Adjusting to their new players, Ron Erhardt and Bill Belichick had to drastically streamline their playbooks. To minimize confusion on Parcells's staff, the names of the substitutes were taped onto their helmets. Players were told to bring their own nameplates to their locker-room stalls. Phil Simms's replacement, Jim Crocicchia, brought one that said, "Scab QB," while his backup, Michael Busch, used "Scab QB II." In the same vein spectators at the games, a fraction of the normal number, gave their unrecognizable teams nicknames like Buffalo "Counterfeit Bills," Los Angeles

"Shams," Oakland "Masque-Raiders," San Francisco "Phony-Niners," and Washington "ScabSkins."

Like other labor disputes with much less money at stake, the situation caused flare-ups between striking workers and their replacements. At picket lines some athletes stood in the path of vehicles carrying strike-breakers, attempting to prevent their entry into the stadiums. In Kansas City, Chiefs tight end Paul Coffman and linebacker Dino Hackett waved unloaded shotguns outside of Arrowhead Stadium, and yelled jokingly, "We're looking for scabs."

At an elementary school not far from Big Blue's headquarters, more than twenty Giants players on strike underwent daily morning workouts. Relatively few union members, no more than 15 percent, crossed picket lines, but notable among them were 49ers quarterback Joe Montana, Cowboys tailback Tony Dorsett, and Seahawks wideout Steve Largent. And after two replacement games, both Giants losses, Lawrence Taylor joined his unfamiliar teammates. As he explained to reporters, "The Giants are losing games, and I'm losing $60,000 a week." Backup quarterbacks Jeff Hostetler and Jeff Rutledge, along with rookie safety Adrian White, joined Taylor ahead of an October 19 game in Buffalo.

Such decisions fractured the unity of Giants regulars, but Taylor's celebrity, and his well-known maverick streak, muted criticism. The only player to publicly castigate Taylor was reserve linebacker Robbie Jones, who said, "If you follow Lawrence Taylor, you burn in hell." Told of the remark, Taylor retorted, "I'd rather spend eternity in hell than five minutes with Robbie Jones."

In front of a crowd of 15,737 at Rich Stadium, Lawrence Taylor spent most of his time at middle linebacker instead of his usual spot on the outside right. He drew double-digit penalties from Buffalo's blockers for holding, the only way they could slow him down. The reigning defensive player of the year switched over to tight end for a play in Parcells's new-look offense, but Rutledge, forced to rush his pass by a porous offensive line, threw too high as Taylor broke free near the end zone. Still, Taylor's amazing athleticism enabled him to get his right hand on the ball, which then bounced away. Taylor's hell-bent performance wasn't quite enough in a game marred by 26 penalties, five missed field goals, four lost fumbles, and more dropped passes than receptions. The "Counterfeit Bills" triumphed 6–3 in overtime.

Meanwhile, Washington, exclusively using replacement players, shocked Dallas, 13–7, despite facing veteran starters, including Cowboys quarterback Danny White, tailback Tony Dorsett, defensive end Ed "Too Tall" Jones, and defensive tackle Randy White. The outcome was considered the biggest upset victory in Redskins history.

This football Bizarro World lasted twenty-four days, or three Sundays, at which time the players union voted to end the strike without a resolution. Parcells's Giants found themselves with an abysmal 0-5 record, which included three losses by their replacement squad. As infighting caused by the strike threatened to extend the spiral, Taylor and Jones shared a meal and then played down their public tit-for-tat. Once its regulars were back on the field, Big Blue went 6-4 over the season's final ten games. However, New York's 6-9 record overall left it last in the NFC East—and one of the only defending champions ever to miss the playoffs. Despite strong contributions from its linebacking corps, with Banks, Carson, and Taylor making the Pro Bowl, the defense stumbled. On offense, terrific seasons by Phil Simms and Mark Bavaro couldn't overcome subpar production in the running department. Morris gained only 658 yards behind an injury-riddled offensive line. More than anything, though, Parcells's repeat championship ambitions were derailed by his team's sputtering, surreal start.

The Redskins, whose strike team had gone undefeated, won the NFC East with a record of 11-4. Gibbs's team went on to reach Super Bowl XXII, and trounced Denver 42–10 at San Diego's Jack Murphy Stadium, as Doug Williams became the first black quarterback to play in, and win, a Super Bowl.

Parcells still bemoans Big Blue's front-office decision to limit preparation for the 1987 strike in an effort to prevent divisiveness. "When you start off 0 and 5," he says, "you don't really have a chance in a short season." Former left guard Bill Ard believes that the situation was exacerbated by a demoralized head coach. "The strike year, '87, was a shit year," Ard says; "'87 and '83 had to be his two worst years of coaching."

Following Green Bay's 5-9-1 record in the strike-disrupted season, head coach Forrest Gregg announced he would be leaving the team for his alma mater, Southern Methodist. The Packers dismissed Gregg's staff, rendering wideouts coach Tom Coughlin jobless in January 1988, just when Parcells was looking to fill that position for the Giants. Falcons head coach Marion Campbell recommended Coughlin to Parcells. And Phil McConkey, who had spent a brief stint with the Packers early in the 1986 season, told Parcells, "He's your type of guy."

Parcells arranged for an interview with Coughlin a few weeks later at the Senior Bowl in Mobile, Alabama, but the Steelers were also interested: Chuck Noll had phoned Coughlin to make similar plans. On arriving in town Coughlin met Noll at a restaurant for dinner, after which the free-agent coach visited Parcells in his hotel room to chat. In their first meeting, the two fortysomethings quickly got comfortable with each other.

They were both detailed-oriented disciplinarians from the Northeast who shared Irish ancestry and grew up idolizing the Giants. As a kid in Waterloo, New York, Coughlin had watched Giants games obsessively on his family's black-and-white television, kindling what would be a lifelong fascination. During his first four seasons as an NFL coach, including two in Green Bay, Coughlin had studied Parcells. Coughlin saw the Giants taskmaster as a kindred spirit, and identified with his drill-sergeant streak.

Fifteen minutes into their conversation Parcells made a formal offer. Despite the appeal of the storied Steelers, particularly under Noll, Coughlin accepted it right away. Aware of Pittsburgh's interest, Parcells followed up later that night with a phone call, finalizing plans for his new wideouts coach to visit Giants headquarters.

The next day, Coughlin informed Noll, pointing out his ties to the state of New York, and fondness for the Giants. "I've been thinking about this all my life."

During the 1960s Coughlin had played wingback for the Orangemen in a backfield that included future Hall of Fame runners Larry Csonka and Floyd Little. As a senior in 1967, when Jim Boeheim, the school's future hoops coach, was his residence adviser, Coughlin set Syracuse's single-season receiving record: 26 catches for 257 yards. (If he is selected by the Hall of Fame, that team's entire backfield, with the exception of quarterback Rick Cassata, will have earned that singular honor.)

Coughlin began his coaching career in 1969 as a graduate assistant for his alma mater; and after one year he became head coach of the Rochester Institute of Technology. He returned to Syracuse as an assistant in 1976, staying five seasons before becoming Boston College's quarterbacks coach and de facto offensive coordinator, under Jack Bicknell. During the Eagles' glory years Coughlin's prize pupil was Doug Flutie, who would set the NCAA Division I record for passing yards in a career and capture the Heisman. When Coughlin entered the NFL in 1984 as Philadelphia's wideouts coach, he considered Parcells, busy reviving the Giants, a coach's coach and therefore someone to emulate. So after watching Parcells for years, Coughlin was thrilled by the opportunity to learn up close.

In his first Giants practice Coughlin discovered that Parcells detested scripts, the sequences of pre-planned offensive plays. During 11-on-11 drills that simulated game action, the head coach demanded that his offensive coaches set their scripts aside. Coughlin's sense of Parcells as a domineering leader was quickly confirmed. "He knew exactly what he wanted," Coughlin says, "and it wasn't going to be done any other way." The new assistant was happy to fall in line.

Meanwhile, Bill Belichick, his reputation rising, was starting to express his intention to become a head coach. Parcells regularly called his lieutenant into his office for discussions intended to prepare Belichick by challenging him to make the kinds of key decisions faced by head coaches. He asked Belichick how he would handle, say, a quarterback's injury with the media. If Parcells thought Belichick was wrong, he'd bark, "You need to reconsider that."

Belichick soaked up the head-coaching tutorials.

The Giants were eager to return to normalcy, and to the playoff form they had displayed after the strike. Even hungrier now for another Lombardi Trophy, Parcells put his players and coaches through intense two-a-day practices during training camp. And the Giants, though weary of workouts that included full pads, responded with spirited play.

Big Blue's hopes for a bright season, however, suffered a monumental setback on August 15, when Lawrence Taylor's urinalysis revealed cocaine. Under drug guidelines toughened in 1986, testing positive for the second time, as Taylor had done, triggered an automatic thirty-day ban from the league. Taylor would miss Big Blue's first four games while receiving treatment in an outpatient program supervised by Dr. Forest Tennant, the league's drug adviser. After that the superstar's future would depend on the results of regular testing. Under the revamped policy, offenders were not granted the privilege of privacy for those urine tests; an NFL representative would watch Taylor urinate to preclude any sleight of hand. A third violation would mean a lifetime ban, although there would be one opportunity to appeal after a year.

Taylor's absence cast a cloud over Big Blue's new season as the team started 2-2. Even after his return, the nightmare scenario lingered that one more failed test would end the twenty-nine-year-old's career. However, by playing each game as if it were his last, Taylor galvanized the Giants into winning five of six. The linebacker dominated opponents on the gridiron while passing the league's random drug tests off of it. At 7-3, Big Blue appeared to have overcome its early struggles, but two consecutive hard-fought losses dimmed New York's playoff hopes. Parcells warned his 7-5 team, increasingly hampered by injuries, that it needed to sweep the season's final four games.

The situation seemed especially bleak on November 27, 1988, when the Giants entered the Louisiana Superdome to face Jim Mora's Saints, leaders of the NFC West at 9-3. Injuries had left Big Blue without three Pro Bowlers: Phil Simms, Carl Banks, and Harry Carson. Taylor was another possible scratch with a torn right deltoid, the large triangular muscle that passes up and over the shoulder from the upper arm. The injury made it painful even to comb his hair, but adamant about playing, Taylor strapped on a harness to protect the muscle and keep his shoulder in place. The decision was unsurprising given his reputation for sacrificing his body on the field. The previous year he had played multiple games with a hairline fracture of his right tibia, and with a pulled hamstring that would have put most athletes on crutches. Given his rabid style, the injuries worsened over two games, forcing Taylor to miss his first NFL contest following a streak of 106. His tolerance for pain wasn't necessarily based on the play-offs being at stake. After Taylor suffered a serious concussion during a 1983 game against Philadelphia, trainers hid the linebacker's helmet to prevent his reentry.

At the Louisiana Superdome in 1988, Taylor's torn deltoid seemed to have little effect as he leapfrogged blockers in pursuit of the ball carrier, or rammed his right shoulder into opponents. But after a while the harness loosened, forcing Taylor to sit out some plays to have the gadget retied on the sideline. Ronnie Barnes and a fellow trainer removed his jersey, revealing a long-sleeved, light-blue undershirt with the harness ajar over his upper torso. Taylor rocked in agony, teary-eyed and breathing heavily, as the medical staff tightened his shoulder rig, allowing him to reenter the game.

With the Saints at New York's 24-yard line, Taylor charged the quarterback from the left side of the line, eluding a burly blocker before sacking Bobby Hebert and poking the ball loose with his left hand. Cornerback Perry Williams recovered it, killing New Orleans's promising drive. Later, Taylor lined up at right defensive end in a three-point stance. Although he was triple-teamed, his bull rush collapsed the pocket, causing Hebert to scurry toward the right sideline and throw an incomplete pass. For much of the night Taylor seemed to haunt him, but the Giants would need more than heroic defense to knock off the high-flying Saints.

Jeff Hostetler was a descendant of Jacob Hochstetler, a Swiss-German immigrant who arrived in Berks County, Pennsylvania, in 1738 and established an Amish settlement. Born in Hollsopple, Pennsylvania, on April 22, 1961, Jeff Hostetler became a top athlete at Conemaugh Township High, starring in baseball, basketball, football, and track. In 1979, Jeff Hostetler accepted a football scholarship from Penn State, where his older brothers, Doug and Ron, had played linebacker for Joe Paterno. As a Nittany Lions sophomore, Hostetler, nicknamed "Hoss," seized the starting quarterback job from Todd Blackledge, a highly touted recruit. Although Penn State won two of its first three games, Paterno reinserted Blackledge as a starter. Disillusioned by the decision, Hostetler transferred to West Virginia, against Paterno's wishes.

NCAA rules for switching schools forced Hostetler to sit out the 1981 season. Meanwhile, West Virginia quarterback Oliver Luck, who would become the father of future Colts quarterback Andrew Luck, led his team to an upset victory against Florida in the Peach Bowl. The following year Hostetler replaced Luck, who had graduated, and led the Mountaineers to a 9-2 record, capped by an appearance in the Gator Bowl. Meanwhile, back at Penn State, Blackledge guided the team to a national championship, and after the season, the Kansas City Chiefs drafted Blackledge seventh overall, well ahead of a Pittsburgh product named Dan Marino.

Hostetler continued to thrive in Morgantown, West Virginia, where he dated his future wife, head coach Don Nehlen's daughter. Thanks to his passing accuracy and scrambling ability, Hostetler set a number of single-season school records, including total offense, touchdown passes, passing yards, and completions. During his stellar senior season Hoss was considered a Heisman candidate, and his popularity in Morgantown inspired a record called "Ole Hoss: The Ballad of West Virginia's Jeff Hostetler," sung to the tune of the TV Western *Bonanza*'s theme song.

The Giants selected the six-three, 215-pound gunslinger in the third round of the 1984 draft, but as third-string quarterback behind Jeff Rutledge, Hostetler played sparingly in his first five seasons. He contributed mainly as a holder for kickers, and by preparing Big Blue's defense for mobile passers. Hostetler was so desperate to see real action that he convinced coaches to occasionally use him on special teams. In 1986 the versatile athlete blocked a punt against Philadelphia. Hostetler sometimes practiced as a wideout receiver, too, and broke his leg doing so late that season. After it mended, the Giants considered activating him as a backup wideout for Super Bowl XXI. Early in the 1988 season, Hostetler caught a pass against the Los Angeles Rams, even before he had officially attempted an NFL throw.

Phil Simms's absence due to injury and Jeff Rutledge's banged-up knee gave Hostetler his first NFL start versus New Orleans. Despite the struggles of Big Blue's runners against the Saints, Hostetler performed well. In the second quarter, his 85-yard pass to wideout Stephen Baker gave New York a 7-6 lead. The touchdown was Big Blue's longest pass play since Norm Snead's 95-yarder to Rich Houston in 1972. But at halftime the Giants were down 9–7. As Hostetler walked the tunnel back toward the field, Parcells approached him with a tap on the shoulder. "I'm going to start Rutledge in the second half. It has nothing to do with you."

On Rutledge's first two plays he fumbled the ball on sacks, resulting in turnovers. He also misfired on his first three passes while Hostetler steamed on the sidelines. Fortunately for New York, Rutledge overcame his awful start. New Orleans was leading 12–10 with less than a minute left when Rutledge completed a 32-yard pass to Stephen Baker. The clutch connection set up a 35-yard field-goal attempt. Only 21 seconds remained when Paul McFadden's kick wobbled through the uprights, giving the Giants a rousing 13–12 victory.

Playing in agony, Lawrence Taylor finished the game with three sacks, two forced fumbles, seven tackles, and one deflected pass. In Big Blue's locker room, Parcells embraced Taylor, who then placed his sweaty forehead against his head coach's brow.

Parcells said, "You were great tonight."

Taylor smiled. "I don't know how I got through it."

Parcells still considers the performance Taylor's greatest, and perhaps the best he has ever witnessed as an NFL coach. But one player in the visitors' locker room remained disgruntled. Hostetler wanted to be traded; after spot duty for a half decade, he considered Parcells's decision to yank him despite solid play "the straw that broke the camel's back."

Phil Simms reclaimed his starter's job the next week and led the Giants to a 44–7 victory against the Arizona Cardinals. But just as they had ignored Simms's trade demand in 1983 when he'd lost his job to Scott Brunner, the Giants decided against jettisoning Hostetler. With true free agency still five years away, the Giants were able to keep their talented backup quarterback, who would have been a likely starter on another team.

Big Blue's 28–12 victory over the Kansas City Chiefs improved the club to 10-5. The outcome set up a season finale versus the intrastate rival Jets, with a playoff berth at stake for the Giants. The game also marked just the sixth regular-season game between the only NFL teams to share a stadium. Joe Walton's Jets, whose season was lost at 7-7-1, were officially the home team, but Parcells's team had won eleven straight games in December's frigid elements.

During the first half of play in temperatures in the low 20s, it was Gang Green that looked like the team vying for a postseason berth. The Jets sacked Simms eight times on their way to a 20–7 lead. The bipartisan crowd of 69,770 swayed with the direction of the game. Giants supporters got their chance to turn up the volume in the second half as Simms led a furious rally. His third touchdown pass with about five minutes left gave Big Blue its first lead, 21–20. But late in the game, Jets QB Ken O'Brien drove his team deep into Giants territory. And with 37 seconds left, a 5-yard touchdown pass to wideout Al Toon, the NFL's leading receiver, gave Gang Green a 27–21 victory. Moments after the upset, Jets players pranced around the field. Defensive end Marty Lyons, who had sacked

Simms twice, grabbed his six-year-old son out of the stands and hoisted him on his shoulders for a victory lap.

Despite a 10-6 record and Super Bowl aspirations, Big Blue was now at the mercy of a tiebreaker: having beaten the Giants in head-to-head competition, the 10-6 Eagles captured the NFC East. The Giants also lost out on a wild-card berth, since the 10-6 Los Angeles Rams owned both a better conference record and a victory over Big Blue. So Bill Parcells's team missed the playoffs for the second straight year.

Culminating the frustrating season, linebacker Harry Carson and defensive end George Martin announced their retirement. At thirty-five, the defensive stalwarts were considered senior citizens in the NFL. Carson ended his career as a nine-time Pro Bowler and potential Hall of Famer, while Martin was an unsung cog in Big Blue's machine. However, Parcells viewed Martin as being so integral to the Giants' success that after Super Bowl XXI the coach had cajoled his defensive lineman into delaying retirement. Now, though, that time had come.

The departures of Carson and Martin meant it was time for a reconfiguration of the Big Blue Wrecking Crew. New York's front seven, however, remained a powerful force thanks to talented young players like defensive lineman Erik Howard and linebackers Carl Banks and Pepper Johnson. Most of all, the Giants still had the best linebacker in NFL history. Despite missing the first four games that year, and playing injured for several more, Lawrence Taylor amassed 15.5 sacks, third best in the league. Even more important, the troubled Taylor had abstained from taking drugs.

Another good sign could be found in the excellent group of coaches under Bill Parcells, although he knew that some of them would inevitably command bigger jobs elsewhere. During the off-season Al Groh, Parcells's former Army colleague and Air Force assistant, was hired from South Carolina to oversee the Giants' linebackers, easing Bill Belichick's workload. And Parcells remained on the lookout for talented coaches, in case his ranks were thinned by defections.

Cornerback Harvey Clayton joined the Giants in 1987 after four seasons with the Steelers. At his first practice, Parcells expressed curiosity about a certain technique the cornerback was employing to sharp effect in man-to-man coverage: using his outside arm to tip the cantilever strap of the wideout's shoulder pad, knocking the player off balance. Clayton replied that he had learned it from Tony Dungy, Pittsburgh's defensive coordinator. More football discussions with Clayton convinced Parcells that his new defensive back, though not especially talented, was exceptionally tutored. So only months after hiring Coughlin in early 1988, Parcells placed Dungy on his radar as a future Giants coach.

When news broke of Tony Dungy's dismissal by the Steelers at the end of the 1988 season, Parcells immediately phoned him, seeking a face-to-face meeting to discuss the thirty-three-year-old overseeing Big Blue's defensive backs. Like Coughlin, Dungy had zero previous ties to Parcells. Their interactions were limited to no more than handshakes between coaches during warm-ups. But Dungy had a brief history with the Giants as a defensive back. Going into the 1980 season Ray Perkins had acquired Dungy from San Francisco's Bill Walsh in a trade that included another future head coach, defensive back Ray Rhodes. Dungy spent six months on Big Blue's roster, long enough to meet owner Wellington Mara and his son, John. Dungy, though, didn't last beyond Perkins's training camp. So the cerebral defensive back joined the Steelers to coach their secondary.

Parcells faced plenty of competition for Dungy's services. New 49ers head coach George Seifert, who was replacing Bill Walsh, courted Dungy, as did Marty Schottenheimer, who was in his first year guiding the Kansas City Chiefs. Bengals coach Sam Wyche wanted to hire Dungy, too, but was overruled by owner Mike Brown. Parcells's interest stood out to Dungy because the Giants, only two seasons removed from a Super Bowl title, remained a defensive juggernaut.

A protégé of Chuck Noll, Tony Dungy considered working for Big Blue, a team coming off a 10-win season despite missing the playoffs, an opportunity to broaden his football knowledge in a different system. So the young coach traveled to Giants headquarters at the Meadowlands, arriving in the early morning and making his way to the head coach's office. During a short, pleasant conversation with Parcells the topic of football was barely broached. Dungy inquired about the proximity of Parcells's home to Giants Stadium and the length of his commute.

After the chat Parcells walked Dungy to a meeting room for a group interview with several coaches, including Bill Belichick and Romeo Crennel. Parcells didn't stay for the wide-ranging discussion, which focused on football. As the meeting reached its sixth hour, Parcells's secretary, Kim Kolbe, came in to tell Dungy that a severe storm was moving into the area, and he'd need to depart for the airport right away to keep from being stuck overnight. "We had to cut the meeting short," Dungy recalls, "but we had a lot of fun."

Dungy was surprised and impressed that the football discussion took place without Parcells. Another unconventional aspect of the interview session was its inclusion of offensive coaches while Dungy was being considered for a defensive job. Parcells believed that assistants spent too much time in discrete groups, "their own little empires," and he encouraged them to develop the wider bird's-eye view that had served him well as a rookie NFL coach. "I kind of learned from that," says Dungy, whose coaching tree includes Leslie Frazier, Lovie Smith, and Mike Tomlin. "He [Parcells] wanted to see how I fit in with the group. I'm sure he was going to make the decision in the end, but he didn't want to just tell these guys, 'Here's the new coach, like it or not.' "

Dungy was intrigued by the prospect of joining the Giants, but the small-town native of Michigan was reluctant to move his family to the New York area. In the end, he called Parcells to let him know that he would be joining Marty Schottenheimer's staff in Kansas City.

"This would be a great opportunity, Bill, and I appreciate it. But family-wise, it's not the right move. If you were anywhere but New York, I would have taken the job."

As head coach of one of the NFL's best teams, and staffs, Parcells was almost never turned down by a coaching candidate. He had even lured Tom Coughlin away from the legendary Chuck Noll, Dungy's mentor and owner of a record four Super Bowl rings. So Parcells was surprised by Dungy's decision, and seemed skeptical about the explanation. "At first, I don't think he believed me," Dungy recalls. "But I think that as we got to know each other, he did come to understand that I wasn't BS'ing him. The job was tempting because they were so good. Going there and working under Bill would have been special."

Even without Tony Dungy, Parcells's staff was among the best in franchise history and, it would turn out, in NFL annals. The coaches' locker room included four stalls arranged with nameplates from left to right: "Crennel," "Belichick," "Coughlin," and "Parcells." Giants running-backs coach Ray Handley was a mathematical whiz allegedly not averse to exploiting his aptitude by playing blackjack at Las Vegas casinos. He would secretly count cards, a practice that wasn't illegal but led to his being banned from the premises. In a nod to Handley's math wizardry, Parcells added clock management to his duties.

Hired by Ray Perkins in 1979, Bill Belichick had already contributed the longest stint of any Giants assistant in franchise history. And as his career aspirations intensified, Belichick, on Parcells's staff since 1983, grew weary of some of his boss's traits. Even in a relationship that benefited both men, tension simmered between the head coach and his top assistant. "You could coach with your twin brother," says Al Groh, "and if he's the head coach, eventually you want to be a head coach, too."

Bill Belichick and Tom Coughlin often worked on strategy together during practice. Leading up to games, they shared their detailed perspectives about opponents. The pair were considered the most likely among Parcells's assistants to land head-coaching jobs, if not eventually succeed him. In early 1989 the Browns interviewed Bill Belichick as they looked to replace Marty Schottenheimer, fired after an opening-round playoff loss that overshadowed Cleveland's 10-win season, but the job went to Jets defensive coordinator Bud Carson.

Parcells's coaches had to endure Parcells's roller-coaster moods, stinting praise, bullying, and impatience. Yet those downsides were trumped by his winning ways, expert tutoring, and lasting loyalty. Parcells, who intimately understood the peaks and valleys of coaching, instructed his assistants to keep their summer breaks football-free, a decree intended to prevent burnout. The staff returned for training camp rejuvenated and ready for Parcells's inexorable demands.

Coughlin, as much as any assistant, relished the grind. On Christmas Day, Parcells telephoned the office to retrieve messages, only to have his wide-receivers coach pick up after two rings. Parcells viewed Coughlin as an ideal assistant and a future head coach, thanks to his leadership, intensity, and indefatigability. "Strong like Ajax," Parcells says. As the Giants zoomed to an 8-1 start to their 1989 season without allowing more than 24 points in any game, Coughlin enjoyed the tremendous learning experience. The wide-receivers coach was impressed by Parcells's encyclopedic knowledge of his players, including their personal backgrounds. Coughlin was struck even more by his boss's hyperawareness of players on other rosters. That in-depth familiarity, especially with NFC East personnel, was no accident: Parcells took great pains to study the strengths and weaknesses of opponents. After scrutinizing tape he grilled football people in the know for further insight. Parcells recalls about Joe Gibbs's Redskins, "I knew them cold, what they could do and what they couldn't do. It wasn't, 'Oh, this guy is a good player,' like somebody in the press says."

Parcells's most enlightening lessons, though, involved how to build a team. He tutored all of his coaches in the Kilroy personnel-evaluation system so that the entire staff had the same philosophy on talent assessment. The shared approach, overseen by George Young, helped assistants integrate players into Parcells's schemes. One new weapon was Dave Meggett, drafted in the fifth round, 132nd overall, via Towson University. Parcells had been skeptical about Meggett's future in the NFL given his five-seven, 190-pound frame, until the rookie's explosiveness and versatility made the coach a convert. Meggett led the league in punt-return yards (582), while amassing 577 kickoff-return yards, 531 receiving yards, and 117 rushing yards. He became the first tailback to gain at least 500 receiving yards and 500 punt-return yards. So serious was Meggett as a threat, especially as a third-down back, that he was named a Pro Bowl selection, the only Giants player to earn the accolade that year besides Lawrence Taylor.

Ottis "O. J." Anderson, an eleventh-year veteran in 1989, played like a rejuvenated runner. After three years specializing in short-yardage and goal-line situations, Anderson emerged as Big Blue's featured back after Joe Morris broke his foot. Although Anderson averaged only 3.2 yards per carry on his way to 1,023 yards, his power running fit seamlessly into Parcells's ground-and-pound offense. Anderson produced a career-high 14 touchdowns in 1989, and was named Comeback Player of the Year.

Meggett and Anderson helped the Giants capture their division title with the NFC's second-best mark (12-4) after San Francisco (14-2). Joe Montana, the league MVP, set a passer-rating record of 112.4 in George Seifert's first season replacing Bill Walsh. The Giants and 49ers seemed headed for a showdown to determine a Super Bowl appearance, but first Big Blue faced John Robinson's Los Angeles Rams (11-5) at Giants Stadium. Behind dynamic quarterback Jim Everett, Los Angeles had defeated New York, 31–10, at Anaheim Stadium during the regular season, the largest margin in a Giants loss for the entire year. But the host Giants were playoff favorites, especially with temperatures forecast for the mid-30s.

In a back-and-forth affair the Rams led 7–6 at halftime on a 20-yard touchdown catch by Willie "Flipper" Anderson. Earlier in the season, the UCLA product set an NFL record for receiving yards with 336 versus New Orleans. Despite sharp play from the Giants, particularly O. J. Anderson, they had failed to reach the end zone. In the second half Big Blue's front seven, led by Lawrence Taylor, Pepper Johnson, and Leonard Marshall, hounded Everett as the Giants seized a 13–7 lead. But a pair of Rams field goals, the final one with about three minutes left, forced overtime. The last Giants playoff game to require an extra session had taken place in the 1958 NFL Championship versus the Baltimore Colts, with an outcome that devastated Big Blue followers.

The overtime coin flip went to the Rams, who elected to receive Raul Allegre's kickoff. Within a minute Everett guided Los Angeles to New York's 30. On first-and-15, Flipper Anderson set up on the right side, near the sideline. Single coverage by cornerback Mark Collins required him to disrupt the wideout's route near the line of scrimmage. But on the snap, Anderson sidestepped to Collins's left, avoiding an effective jam. The split-second sequence allowed Anderson to gain a step while sprinting downfield toward the right corner of the end zone. Anderson caught Everett's rainbow pass in stride at the 5, Collins lunging futilely at his waist. As Anderson crossed the goal line the crowd of 76,325 fell so quiet that the whoops by Rams players reverberated in Giants Stadium. Anderson kept sprinting while holding the ball with his right hand above his head. He darted into the tunnel, and didn't stop until reaching the visitors' locker room. Only 66 seconds into overtime, Los Angeles had prevailed, 19–13, for the fastest sudden-death outcome in NFL playoff history. Parcells trudged grimly across the field in his blue Giants windbreaker. "That one," he says of Anderson's catch, "still haunts me."

San Francisco defeated the Rams, 30–3, in the NFC Championship, to reach Super Bowl XXIV at Louisiana's Superdome. There the 49ers trounced Denver, 55–10, the largest margin in the game's history, for their second consecutive title. Joe Montana became the first quarterback to win three Super Bowl MVPs. San Francisco's dominant season and a roster loaded with talent, including backup quarterback Steve Young, prompted predictions of a third consecutive Super Bowl.

The Giants entered the 1990 season as a Super Bowl favorite. The team's playoff heartbreaker against the Los Angeles Rams was considered a fluke. And as the season began, Big Blue confirmed that view, sporting a defense that steamrolled offenses with ferocity and single-mindedness that evoked shades of the 1986 unit.

The defense was among the best ever. And if history doesn't quite repeat itself, the 1990 group proved early that it certainly rhymes. The haymakers sure sounded familiar, even if they came from, say, linebacker Gary Reasons instead of Harry Carson. Once again the Giants possessed the premier front seven in the NFL, essentially Big Blue Wrecking Crew 2.0, and a secondary that wasn't exactly shabby. The unit's mantra was to punish opponents into submission. Defenders relished coming off the field in the fourth quarter saying, "My guy just quit!"

New York's cocksure, bullying defense made up for a less dangerous offense as the Giants racked up victories. Phil Simms looked sharp in directing a smashmouth approach that maximized time of possession and executed with precision. The offense's brute force was epitomized by O. J. Anderson running behind blocking by six-seven, 305-pound lineman Jumbo Elliott. Anderson split snaps with rookie Rodney Hampton, a first-round pick via Georgia (twenty-fourth overall) expected to start by season's end.

Big Blue, with the nickname fitting the personnel better than ever, imposed its will on opponents while winning nine straight for the best start in franchise history. Parcells's team allowed only single digits in four of those games. The offense, though lacking in aesthetics, rarely committed turnovers as Simms posted the league's best passer rating. However, Big

Blue's perfect record did nothing to mute Parcells's complaints. Instead, it only made them louder and more frequent.

With Jeff Rutledge's departure for the Redskins, Jeff Hostetler had taken over as Simms's backup. In practice before a November 18 home game against the Lions, Hostetler quarterbacked the scout team and simulated Detroit's run-and-shoot offense. The system featured motion by receivers to create mismatches and decipher coverage before improvisational routes. Showcasing his considerable talent, Hostetler shredded Big Blue's vaunted defense. At the staff meeting following the session, Parcells mocked Bill Belichick and Al Groh, whose coaching of the Giants' dominant defense was being glorified in the press.

"Okay, you wizards. That might have been the worst football practice I've seen in my life. You guys better go fix it."

A few days later at Giants Stadium, Belichick unveiled a quirky 2-4-5 scheme that completely shut down Detroit's run-and-shoot offense. The Giants triumphed, 20–0, lowering the team's average points allowed to 11. Ray Handley concluded that New York, at 10-0, had clinched a playoff spot, a full week before the NFL's confirmation.

Despite that sizzling stretch, there was still some question as to whether the Giants were the NFC's best team. The defending-champion 49ers matched Big Blue's start victory for victory, inspiring a mantra: "three-peat." No team in league history had ever won more than two straight Super Bowls. The Giants and 49ers were set for a showdown between undefeated teams in two weeks on *Monday Night Football*, but before then Big Blue lost, 31–3, at Philadelphia in a scuffle-filled game that was much closer than the final score indicated. San Francisco's streak was also snapped in an upset by the Los Angeles Rams, 28–17, at Candlestick Park.

As Parcells had expected, his staff was attracting attention for head-coaching openings. On November 28, Boston College fired Tom Coughlin's former boss Jack Bicknell, and courted Big Blue's wide-receivers coach. But with the 10-1 Giants positioned for a Super Bowl run, Coughlin wouldn't entertain the thought of leaving, forcing Boston College to look elsewhere.

Days later, on December 3, the Giants visited Candlestick Park for one of *Monday Night Football*'s most highly anticipated games. In a show of physicality by both defenses, the Giants were down 7–3 in the waning moments of the game. Big Blue was in prime position to score with first-and-goal from San Francisco's 9, but the 49ers made a spirited stand that culminated with a deflected pass in the end zone. After the fourth-down play, Ronnie Lott strutted up to Simms until their face masks touched and spewed expletive-filled taunts. Simms yakked back, bumping Lott before teammates separated the two players. The disappointing outcome gave New York its second straight loss.

The Giants snapped their skid with a 23–15 home victory over the Minnesota Vikings, but in its next game Big Blue faced much stiffer competition from the AFC's top team: the Buffalo Bills, whose record at 12-2 made them seem like inevitable Super Bowl participants versus either the Giants or 49ers. Buffalo's high-powered hurry-up offense, orchestrated by Jim Kelly, overshadowed a badass defense starring sack-master Bruce Smith.

Playing in freezing rain at Giants Stadium in a rare Saturday matchup, New York trailed 14–10 early in the third quarter. After completing a pass to David Meggett, Phil Simms fell, untouched, to the turf while clutching his knee in agony. Simms declined Bruce Smith's help before limping off the field. The freak injury turned out to be a fractured bone, ending the quarterback's season. Jeff Hostetler took the helm, making several sharp throws and scrambling for tidy gains, but Buffalo prevailed, 17–13, handing Big Blue its third loss in four games.

The optimism enveloping Big Blue for much of the season had suddenly evaporated. Without Phil Simms, pundits, if not Giants Nation, turned skeptical about the team's postseason chances. The offense had been middle-of-the-pack even with the MVP quarterback of Super Bowl XXI seemingly headed for one of his best seasons. How could Big Blue go any farther with a backup quarterback who had caught his first pass before attempting one?

Hostetler looked solid in two tight victories against Phoenix and New England to end the regular season, but those nail-biters came against two of the league's worst teams. The Giants were further hamstrung by the loss of Raul Allegre, who had suffered a season-ending groin injury early in the season. In his place was backup kicker Matt Bahr. At 13-3 the Giants had produced one of their best records in franchise history, but unlike the 1986 club that delivered a white-hot finish, Parcells's 1990 team had cooled down the stretch.

Hostetler, twenty-nine, and Simms, thirty-six, were polar opposites at quarterback. Simms was a pure drop-back passer who relied on his powerful arm. Hostetler exploited his mobility, escaping pocket pressure to unleash accurate passes or run for significant yardage. Despite the stark contrast, Parcells believed that revamping the offense just before entering the playoffs would be counterproductive. Instead Parcells inserted bootlegs into the playbook to take advantage of Hostetler's improvisational skills. Suddenly feeling like an outsider because of his injury, Simms failed to offer his replacement any support. Instead the veteran quarterback went incommunicado, leaving the role to third-string quarterback Matt Cavanaugh.

• • •

After going another month without finding a replacement head coach, Boston College renewed its attention to Tom Coughlin. Parcells asked George Young whether he should urge his talented assistant to decline the school's courtship by hinting that Big Blue's head-coaching job would inevitably open up, but the GM said no. In late December, Coughlin accepted Boston College's offer after arranging to stay with the Giants through the postseason.

Despite the fact that a backup quarterback had never won a Super Bowl, Coughlin planned on the Giants having an extended postseason run. He knew that the best defense in the NFL, which had given up an average of only 13.2 points per game, remained intact. And since joining Big Blue in 1988, Coughlin had marveled at Parcells's gift for maximizing his team's chances, despite long odds.

13

Against Mike Ditka's Bears at Giants Stadium, Bill Parcells approved Bill Belichick's plan to mostly use a four-man defensive line instead of a 3-4 alignment. Surprised by the switcheroo, Chicago's offense sputtered as blockers struggled to make their assignments. Big Blue set the game's tone in the second quarter by halting Chicago on the goal line, despite a fourth-down effort. The Giants continued stuffing the Bears, particularly tailback Neal Anderson, who was held to 19 yards on 12 carries.

Jeff Hostetler threw two touchdowns passes against Chicago's renowned defense, while directing a sturdy if unspectacular running game. Rodney Hampton broke his leg in the first half, ending his postseason, so after being displaced late in the season, O. J. Anderson reclaimed his role as New York's featured back. Pounding the Bears with vigor, Anderson accumulated 80 yards on 21 carries, and helped New York dominate time of possession. Hostetler also showcased his running ability, juking defenders near the goal line to score.

During the waning moments of Big Blue's dominant 31–3 victory, Lawrence Taylor and Carl Banks sat next to each other on a sideline bench. With his left arm around his teammate, Taylor remarked, "They said the Giants were dead."

Banks responded, "They stuck a fork in us and said we were done."

Taylor said, "Hey, San Francisco, we're back."

Banks agreed, "We're baaaaack."

The outcome meant a trip to Candlestick for a rematch, this time with a Super Bowl appearance on the line. Since midseason, when both teams were asserting themselves as the NFC's elite, a championship clash had been viewed as inevitable. But with the characteristically cocksure Giants stumbling late in the season, the 49ers seemed destined to make history after losing only two games by a combined 10 points. Its high-powered offense, starring Montana, tailback Roger Craig, and wideouts Jerry Rice and John Taylor, had received much of the spotlight. Nonetheless, San Francisco's hard-hitting defense, sparked by Pro Bowl linebacker Charles Haley and star safety Ronnie Lott, ranked second only to New York's. The 49ers were to be reckoned with on both sides of the ball.

So San Francisco, on a seven-game winning streak in the playoffs, was a heavy favorite against a team using a backup quarterback, the NFL's oldest starting tailback, and a replacement kicker released by one of the league's worst teams. Nevertheless, the Giants, taking cues from their head coach, remained confident, if not defiant. At a team meeting before the club departed for San Francisco, Parcells told the players to consider their travel options: they could plan for two days or seven. Since teams received only one week off before Super Bowl XXV, the NFC champion would fly from San Francisco to the game site in Tampa. At the end of his pep talk, Parcells leaned over and unveiled an oversized suitcase. "I guess you know which one I'm packing for."

Before arriving at Candlestick Park, many Giants players watched the AFC Championship on television early in the afternoon. They marveled as the Bills used their sleek, no-huddle offense to trounce the Los Angeles Raiders, 51–3. With that outcome, the most lopsided AFC Championship ever, the Bills would be playing in their first Super Bowl. Suddenly San Francisco no longer looked like a shoo-in. Whoever captured the NFC Championship would face a formidable opponent capable of racking up big points with fast-break flair.

By contrast the 49ers versus the Giants looked more like a heavyweight boxing championship as the NFC Championship kicked off at 1:06 p.m. local time. During a cool, clear afternoon at Candlestick Park on January 20, the stadium's second-largest crowd ever—65,750—watched muscular, stingy defenses repeatedly deliver body blows to the opposing offense. Wearing Big Blue's all-white uniforms, linebackers Lawrence Taylor, Carl Banks, and Pepper Johnson often blitzed up the middle while San Francisco's wideouts were covered as if by paperhangers. The NFL's second-ranked offense struggled as Joe Montana, league MVP for the second straight year, faced relentless pressure.

As the slugfest continued, the two teams alternated field goals in the first and second quarters to enter halftime tied at 6. The game's only touchdown occurred less than five minutes into the third quarter. After zipping short passes most of the afternoon for small gains, Joe Montana completed a 61-yard touchdown to wideout John Taylor as cornerback Everson Walls gambled and lost, making the score 13–6. Late in the period, Jeff Hostetler guided Big Blue close enough for Matt Bahr's 46-yard field goal, which trimmed the lead to 13–9.

The physical game only intensified in the fourth quarter. Hostetler completed a pass just as 49ers nose tackle Jim Burt plowed headfirst into the quarterback's left knee. The ex-Giant yanked Hostetler's knee, causing it to pop and collapse, sending Big Blue's quarterback to the ground.

When the trainers arrived, Hostetler was lying flat on his back, unable to speak as he writhed in pain. Big Blue feared the worst: Hostetler out for good, leaving the offense with a third-string quarterback, trailing in the final period of the conference championship.

Heading into Big Blue's training camp in 1988, Jim Burt had failed the team's physical after signing a two-year contract. Because of Burt's history of back trouble, including multiple surgeries, George Young and Bill Parcells pressed the twenty-nine-year-old to retire. But Burt, who had gone from an undrafted rookie in 1981 to a Pro Bowler in 1986 through toughness and determination, decided instead on a 1989 football return. He signed with the franchise whose star quarterback he had sent to the hospital in the 1986 NFC Championship. Then Burt helped San Francisco capture its second consecutive Super Bowl. In the NFC Championship one year later, the nose tackle appeared to have dived at Hostetler's knees. But Burt would claim that he had been thrown off balance on the play.

Some Giants on the visitors' sideline, including Parcells, blasted Burt. They considered the below-the-knee hit, a personal foul in today's game, a cheap shot, particularly coming from an ex-teammate. Lawrence Taylor, known for his ferocious yet clean play, screamed at the 49ers on the field, "If that's the way you want to play, somebody else is going to lose a quarterback."

Carl Banks turned to his defensive teammates and said, "Okay, Burt took his shot. If one of us gets a shot at Montana, we've got to end this. It's got to be 'Lights out, Irene.'"

After a few minutes Hostetler's numbness gave way to tingling, and his pain subsided enough for him to rise. To Big Blue's relief, their quarterback limped off the field with only a hyperextended knee, as Matt Cavanaugh, seeing his first action all season, took over.

A few minutes after Hostetler left to have his knee examined, the 49ers took possession. On a pass play from San Francisco's 23, Montana rolled to his right as defensive end Leonard Marshall sprinted past left tackle Bubba Paris, but Marshall slipped while behind Montana, and fullback Tom Rathman shoved him to the ground. Moments later, Marshall rose to resume pursuit of San Francisco's unsuspecting quarterback. Sprinting to his right, Montana stopped to sidestep Lawrence Taylor and wound up to pass just as Marshall launched his six-three, 290-pound frame into Montana's back.

The bone-crunching blow sent Montana flopping to the ground as the ball shook loose. "We thought he'd killed him," Carl Banks recalls. San Francisco recovered the fumble with less than 10 minutes to play, but the damage was done. Montana had broken the pinky on his throwing hand, fractured a rib, and bruised his sternum. The sack was so violent that Montana, struggling to breathe, wondered if he was going to die on the field. The play all but ended Montana's 49ers career. He wouldn't appear in another game for almost two full seasons. In April 1993, with Steve Young established as an elite quarterback, San Francisco traded Joe Montana to Kansas City.

Although the 1990 NFC Championship seemed to be a battle of attrition, Parcells introduced some sleight of hand at a key moment. After Montana's injury, the Giants got to their 46-yard line for a fourth-and-2. Big Blue set up in punt formation, but the 49ers had only ten players on the field, and their call for a timeout to address the oversight came too late. Seeing a sizable opening in the middle of San Francisco's line, Gary Reasons called for a run, having been empowered by Parcells to do so. Stepping in front of punter Sean Landeta to catch the snap, Reasons veered right, darting through a gaping hole that the eleventh man would have filled, and into open space. He sprinted 30 yards before being tackled by punt returner John Taylor. And four plays later Matt Bahr booted a 38-yard field goal, slicing San Francisco's lead to 13–12.

With less than six minutes left, though, San Francisco could virtually seal the outcome with a sustained drive, or a touchdown. Steve Young, in for the injured Montana, threw a 25-yard completion to tight end Brent Jones. But Young, who had excelled in previous seasons as Montana's backup, didn't attempt another pass. Offensive coordinator Mike Holmgren decided to eat as much time off the clock as possible. So the 49ers turned run-heavy for the first time all game.

The decision looked prudent as Roger Craig slashed through punishing tackles to help San Francisco reach New York's 30-yard line. Now, with less than three minutes left, the Giants' situation was dire. The 49ers needed only a couple of first downs to guarantee a victory. Watching on New York's sideline, wideout Mark Ingram got on his knees, placed his helmet between his legs, and clasped his hands. Praying for a miracle, he made the sign of the cross.

On yet another run play, Craig darted up the gut just as Giants nose tackle Erik Howard split a double-team, and dived into the tailback's midsection. To San Francisco's horror and New York's glee, Howard's helmet jarred the ball loose. Lawrence Taylor snagged it in midair, giving the Giants possession at their own 43-yard line.

With 2:36 left, the backup quarterback who had started only six NFL games, including the postseason, focused on taking his team into field-goal territory. On consecutive plays Jeff Hostetler rolled to his right under pressure before completing sharp passes to Mark Bavaro and Stephen Baker. Hostetler's clutch throws and nimbleness helped move the Giants to San Francisco's 24. Instead of risking a turnover, Big Blue bled the clock on some don't-you-dare-fumble running plays. The sequence left Matt Bahr lining up to attempt a 42-yard field goal with four seconds left.

On the sideline the Giants huddled together, many holding hands, others praying. But some refused to watch. Parcells crouched, hands on both knees, watching the action. Matt Bahr, who had missed a 37-yarder early in the fourth quarter, was nervous but confident. Catching the snap cleanly, Hostetler placed the ball down and Bahr boomed a kick that started out straight, increasing confidence. But suddenly the pigskin drifted left, just as it had in his only miss. As Parcells scrutinized the ball's flight, it never quite hooked, sailing a few feet inside the left upright just as time expired. The 15–13 shocker sent the Giants to Super Bowl XXV, as CBS play-by-play announcer Pat Summerall intoned to a national TV audience, "There will be no three-peat!"

Teammates engulfed Matt Bahr, who had briefly played for San Francisco in 1981, taking turns hugging the fourteen-year veteran. Jeff Hostetler knelt nearby. On the sideline Belichick and Parcells grinned and leaped like kids before hugging. The comeback and upset victory were especially improbable since Big Blue had failed to score a touchdown, but the Giants had controlled the ball for nearly two-thirds of the ball game, 38:59. The discrepancy contributed to San Francisco's falling well short of its average of 22 points, on only 240 total yards. The great Joe Montana's production (18 of 26 for 190 yards) was little better than the obscure Jeff Hostetler's (15 of 27 for 176 yards). And Matt Bahr's five field goals were enough to carry the day thanks to a hellacious, bullying defense.

"We hit them in the mouth," recalls Leonard Marshall. "We knocked out quarterbacks, and we knocked out running backs. None of their guys intimidated us. Ronnie Lott tried to intimidate Simms in our first game, but *we* were the bullies in the championship. We beat up on everyone that moved."

In the visitors' locker room Parcells sat in the coaches' corner, grinning as reporters crowded him for comment after the formal Q&A. Smiling, Parcells declared, "Winning is better than sex." His remark would cause a minor stir the next day, his critics deeming it was inappropriate if not disrespectful to women, including his wife. But the head coach was unapologetic.

Because of New York's long odds, Parcells considers the victory over San Francisco one of the greatest conference championships in NFL history, the favorite game of his career. That sentiment was reinforced years later when former NFL referee Jerry Markbreit told Parcells that it was the best game he had ever officiated. Markbreit, who retired in 1999 after twenty-three seasons that included four Super Bowls, noted the remarkable number of future Hall of Famers who played. The game also marked the end of an era. For a number of San Francisco's stars throughout the eighties, Joe Montana, Ronnie Lott, Roger Craig, and cornerback Eric Wright, it was their last meaningful contest for the franchise.

Parcells had arranged for the pilot who had flown the Giants to and from Pasadena for Super Bowl XXI, four years before, to take them again. During the six-hour flight to Tampa, the team rules limiting alcohol loosened, while Giants players shouted over the blaring reggae. Lawrence Taylor, wagering on card games with David Meggett, yelled, "They were saying 'three-peat, three-peat,' but they forgot about the Giants!" The remark spurred laughter, followed by more hooting and hollering.

Parcells seldom ventured to the rear of the team plane, the section that players had dubbed "the projects," but midway through the flight the head coach left his first-row seat and strolled to the back. As he walked down the aisle Parcells chatted and expressed pride in his players. He complimented Leonard Marshall, sitting next to cornerback Perry Williams, for his pivotal sack.

Marshall recalls of Parcells, "He didn't come to 'the projects' often. The little coaches would sometimes come to the back, but he sat up there in the big house."

Parcells got so caught up in the merriment that he ignored his fear of flying. The celebration didn't end until the plane landed in Tampa at 2:30 a.m. eastern standard time. "It was the best plane ride I was ever on," Parcells says, "or ever will *be* on."

On the 3 a.m. bus ride to the Hyatt Regency, however, Parcells turned his focus to the upcoming rematch with Marv Levy's Buffalo Bills and their frenetic offense, which had averaged a league-leading 26.8 points. At least, Parcells thought, the real grass of Tampa Stadium would provide a slower surface for the Bills than their artificial turf. Parcells started to mentally organize the remaining days before the game. "By the time we got off the plane," Parcells recalls, "my mind had done a 180."

Parcells's secretary, Kim Kolbe, who had arrived from New Jersey ahead of the team, was waiting in the hotel lobby at 3:30 a.m. to hand out room keys. Parcells believed that reaching Tampa as soon as possible, several hours ahead of the Bills, would give his team a slight edge in preparation. The first coaches' meeting was scheduled for 7:30 a.m., only a few hours away. Despite fatigue, Parcells slept poorly, his mind racing with thoughts about the Bills.

This Super Bowl pitted the NFL's most dynamic offense against its stingiest defense. For the second straight postseason game, Parcells's Giants were heavy underdogs. Buffalo's starting players included a daunting number of Pro Bowlers, nine, on a team with few weaknesses. Before routing the AFC West champions, the 12-4 Raiders, Buffalo had defeated Miami, 44–34, as Jim Kelly outgunned Dan Marino on a snowy afternoon. No team's offense had ever been hotter going into a Super Bowl.

The accelerated pace of Buffalo's no-huddle offense was designed to disorient and ultimately exhaust opposing defenses. The system had been created that season by Bills coordinator Ted Marchibroda, who had given Bill Belichick his first NFL gig with the Baltimore Colts in 1975. Buffalo's offense performed as if it was in a perpetual two-minute drill—the hurry-up approach that teams use when they're behind late in the game. Marchibroda liked to run the maximum number of plays in the shortest time possible, putting tremendous pressure on defenses, which struggled to make substitutions or set up in proper formation.

Jim Kelly, the NFL's top-rated quarterback, doubled as play-caller, a role typically assigned to coaches. He barked plays as his unit, often using three-wideout sets, hurried to the line of scrimmage. Part of the reason why Buffalo excelled in its innovative system was that it featured first-rate talent at the skill positions: a star passer in Kelly, dangerous receivers in Andre Reed and James Lofton, and a top tailback with pass-catching ability in Thurman Thomas. They all would end up in the Hall of Fame.

Before Parcells began the staff meeting, his coaches were understandably focusing on Buffalo's bazooka-armed quarterback.

Parcells declared, "Kelly's not playing in this game."

Confounded by the remark, some coaches responded, "What?"

"We're not gonna let him play."

The head coach summarized the game plan he had discussed privately with his coordinators. Ron Erhardt's offense, emphasizing O. J. Anderson, would milk the clock in order to minimize Kelly's snaps, hopefully forcing him into impatience. Anderson's smashmouth style on long drives would also wear down Buffalo's defense. "We're just going to pound them to death."

On defense Bill Belichick planned to use an unconventional scheme to disrupt Buffalo's tempo: few linemen while extra defensive backs focused on Kelly's passing attack and pummeled receivers underneath. To unveil the counterintuitive plan, Belichick held a meeting with his unit in a hotel conference room. With the players seated, the coordinator got straight to the point. "I want Thurman Thomas to run for over 100 yards in the Super Bowl."

Several guys looked at each other in disbelief, while others grumbled or cursed the idea. Belichick wasn't surprised by the reaction. His unit took pride in being among the NFL's best at stopping the run. In the previous two seasons, Big Blue had allowed just two tailbacks to reach 100-plus rushing yards in a game.

Belichick insisted. "You guys are going to have to trust me. In order for us to win this football game, Thurman Thomas is going to have to gain 100 yards."

He expounded on his rationale. Hard-pressed to halt Buffalo's offense, Big Blue could minimize big gains with novel schemes using as many as eight pass defenders. Belichick intended to tempt Kelly with open running lanes or force him into throws in front of defenders positioned to pummel his receivers.

The defensive boss expressed confidence in his unit's ability to stop Thomas when it mattered most.

"Are you guys with me on this?"

They grudgingly consented.

The Giants also added an element of gamesmanship. Defensive players were instructed to occasionally kick the ball "by accident" after a referee set it down, and to disentangle themselves from piles as slowly as possible. Last, defenders were encouraged to exaggerate any injuries so trainers would have to spend time getting to the field. While interrupting Kelly's rhythm, the shenanigans would also provide Big Blue's defense with a breather.

Even in Tampa's sunny climes, Parcells made his team practice in pads every day while the Buffalo Bills worked out in shells and shorts. To prepare for Kelly's speedy no-huddle offense, Big Blue's defense practiced lining up as quickly as possible. Belichick's quirky strategy of using only two or three pass rushers showed promise against Big Blue's scout team emulating Buffalo's offense. And after several practices, any traces of player skepticism about Belichick's upside-down plan had vanished.

On Friday the Giants rode to their final practice. As usual, Lawrence Taylor took his seat next to Parcells near the front of the lead bus. During the ride, the head coach made a strange request.

"I want you to start a fight with Jumbo at the end of practice today."

"Why?"

"Just do it."

During the spirited practice session, Taylor riled Jumbo Elliott so much that the offensive lineman ran after him while threatening violence. The six-seven, 305-pounder had no chance of catching Taylor, so he slowed down, shouting, "You bastard." Parcells, who had been watching the action, took the opportunity to yell, "Maybe L.T.'s worried about Bruce Smith ruining this game for us."

Elliott stopped jogging. Enraged now, he swung around and glared at his head coach.

"Bruce Smith won't be ruining a damn thing. I'm going to kick his ass."

After the outburst Taylor understood why Parcells had made his odd request. The massive lineman performed his best when agitated leading up to a game. And with a small margin for error against Buffalo, Big Blue couldn't afford to have Bruce Smith, the NFL's defensive player of the year, disrupt its offense. Circling back after accomplishing his mission, Taylor winked at Parcells, but the head coach remained stone-faced.

Elliott wouldn't find out for several years that Taylor had been in cahoots with Parcells.

The Super Bowl kickoff was scheduled for its latest time ever, 6:15 p.m., but at dawn Parcells was already roaming the hotel lobby. He persuaded Mickey Corcoran, once again his special guest at the Super Bowl, to come down for coffee. And early riser Matt Cavanaugh, the backup quarterback, soon joined them. Within a few hours, Tampa Stadium was humming with unusual activity. Helicopters whirred overhead, and black-garbed SWAT teams and anti-terrorist police in camouflage patrolled the stadium roof, machine guns at the ready. Bomb-sniffing dogs led their handlers. Heavy concrete barriers ringed the arena to prevent vehicles containing explosives from reaching the structure. Tampa Stadium itself was surrounded by a chain-link fence that extended six feet high.

Security measures such as bomb-sniffing dogs were typical for the event. But Super Bowl XXV was taking place only ten days into the Gulf War, heightening concerns about a terrorist attack and generating a showing of patriotism. The security force of 1,700 easily exceeded any ever seen at an American sporting event. At each gate dozens of yellow-jacketed security guards with black handheld detectors would pat down each spectator, setting aside banned items that included miniature TV sets, cameras, radios, and umbrellas.

Around noon, more than six hours before kickoff, Bill Parcells walked into an empty locker room. He was already in game-day clothes, navy slacks with a navy-and-red sweater emblazoned with "Giants" over a red dress shirt. To calm his nerves Parcells lit a cigarette and paced the room, mentally reviewing the game plan as he waited for the first players to arrive.

After a few more hours, 73,813 spectators, many carrying American flags and patriotic signs displaying messages like "God Bless America," began filling Tampa Stadium. Swarms of Giants and Bills fans wearing their team colors—red, white, blue, gray—added to the display of nationalism. The enormous screens behind each end zone alternated images of American soldiers in the battle zone with their compatriots on the home front. When Parcells stepped on the field for warm-ups, he started to grasp just how much America was rallying around the game.

As the sun set behind clouds in the west, temperatures reached the low 70s. Military personnel from different branches lined the field in preparation for the national anthem. Officers held state flags. The Florida Orchestra stood on the gridiron behind Whitney Houston to back up her performance of "The Star-Spangled Banner." Wearing a white headband and matching tracksuit with a red-and-blue print, Houston faced the Giants sidelines. Bill Parcells, about fifteen yards away from the singer, stood to the far left of his players. On the Bills sideline wideout James Lofton thought to himself, "Why can't she turn around and look at us?" He hoped that Buffalo's view of the singer from behind wasn't a bad omen.

Fans waved miniature flags as Houston hit one sublime note after another. Parcells's mind drifted away from football for the first time all day, as the head coach realized he was witnessing a special moment that transcended sports. Houston's soaring notes, graceful yet filled with strength, seemed to speak to the nation. As she sang the final lyrics of the anthem, "O'er the land of the free and the home of the brave," Houston stretched her arms out wide, then up to the sky. At that moment four sleek F-16 fighter jets swooped over the stadium.

"We're talking goose bumps on top of goose bumps," Tom Coughlin recalls.

Parcells adds, "As preoccupied as we all were with getting ready to play, when the national anthem was over we did the only thing you can do after you hear something like that: we applauded." Houston's rendition, prerecorded in anticipation of deafening crowd noise, was instantly ranked among the best-ever performances of the national anthem.

After the Bills received the kickoff, Bill Belichick surprised them by unleashing his quirky 2-3-6 formation: two linemen, three linebackers, and six defensive backs. The striking departure from New York's renowned 3-4 meant that defensive end Leonard Marshall and nose tackle Erik Howard were the only two down linemen, with Lawrence Taylor lining up in an unfamiliar spot as the third pass rusher. Pepper Johnson and Carl Banks were the other two linebackers, supported by six defensive backs. In one variation of the package Johnson sometimes attacked the quarterback while Taylor dropped into pass coverage. In another wrinkle Belichick inserted an extra linebacker and removed a defensive back to create a 2-4-5.

Seeing open space for short throws, Jim Kelly completed two passes on crossing patterns to wideout Andre Reed, but Buffalo was forced to punt without gaining a first down, creating some early Giants confidence in Belichick's risky plan.

Big Blue's offense opened with a jumbo package that presaged its use of brute force: three tight ends fortifying a line anchored by the six-seven, 305-pound Elliott. "Fat slobs," says Mark Bavaro, "picking you up and moving you, and letting you tackle O. J. if you could." Introducing a dollop of David Meggett for a slithery change of pace, the Giants steadily gained enough yardage to take a quick 3–0 lead.

With Belichick's defense more intent on harassing Buffalo's wideouts than its quarterback, New York clogged the deep throwing lanes while targeting Andre Reed for wallops after medium-range receptions. The Giants wanted the Pro Bowl wideout to start hearing footsteps, as the additional defensive backs generated extra hits. Although pummeled after several catches, Reed helped the Bills score a field goal and a touchdown to lead 10–3 in the second quarter.

The Giants took possession for a second-and-9 on their 7 when a pass play seemed headed toward disaster. Anticipating Bruce Smith's attack on the middle of Big Blue's line, O. J. Anderson stepped forward to block him, and Jeff Hostetler, backpedaling, tripped over Anderson's right foot. The quarterback stumbled into the end zone as Smith bulled past Anderson. Struggling to regain his balance while moving to his right, Hostetler sensed Smith closing in from behind. As Smith grabbed his prey's right wrist, Hostetler pulled the ball away. The quarterback used his left hand to gain control, pressing the pigskin against his stomach while falling to the ground. Smith's sack for a safety increased Buffalo's lead to 12–3 with less than nine minutes left in the second quarter, but Hostetler's tenacity and composure had prevented a defensive touchdown, and what might have been an insurmountable lead.

Despite the nine-point deficit, Big Blue's offense stuck to its game plan. On the Giants sideline Parcells implored his offense. "Come on, run with power. Run with power. Let's see some power, Jumbo." After taking possession on its 13, New York used three-tight-end packages, repeatedly handing off to O. J. Anderson for successful power runs. The six-two, 220-pounder meted out as much punishment as he received, using his powerful right arm to whack oncoming tacklers. On one play, linebacker Shane Conlan broke his face mask trying to corral Anderson.

With the Bills focused on Anderson, Hostetler went play-action several times on bootlegs to hit tight end Mark Bavaro running across the field. Fatigued by the prolonged drive in the Tampa humidity, Buffalo's defense, particularly its linebackers, failed to react in time to Hostetler's throws. Showing accuracy, Simms's replacement zipped a 17-yard pass to Stephen Baker, tightly covered in an end-zone corner. The touchdown reduced Big Blue's deficit to two points, and the drive consumed almost eight minutes, leaving Jim Kelly frustrated with only 25 seconds remaining in the half. Although the Bills were leading 12–10 at halftime, their high-speed offense had still not gotten on track.

The Gulf War precluded ABC from broadcasting the Super Bowl's halftime show featuring New Kids on the Block, so ABC News showed a special war report instead, which included an address by President Bush and the First Lady, Barbara. Around the same time Parcells spoke to his players in the Giants locker room. "I was at a Super Bowl four years ago, and some of you guys were with me. We were in the exact same situation then as we are now. The first drive of the third quarter is the most important of the game. We have to do something with it."

Upon receiving the second-half kickoff, the Giants embarked on another run-heavy drive. Jumbo Elliott steamrolled Buffalo's defensive linemen as Anderson ran from behind the left tackle's rump. Grass stains on the back of Bruce Smith's jersey offered evidence of Elliott's powerful blocking. And in a typical sign of fatigue, the Pro Bowl defensive end barely got down into his stance before several snaps.

The Giants sustained the drive, converting four third downs. Perhaps the most pivotal one occurred on third-and-13 from Buffalo's 32. On a crossing route to his right, wideout Mark Ingram snagged a pass eight yards from the line of scrimmage. The drive seemed doomed as Ingram was swarmed by Bills defenders well short of the first down. But the wideout ran through a leg tackle by a diving defender, and pirouetted to his left, spinning free of a would-be tackler who had grabbed him by the shoulders. As yet another Bills player moved into Ingram's path, the wideout faked left and darted right, leaving the defender grabbing air. With only one yard left to go for the first down, Ingram was hit cleanly, but the five-ten, 195-pounder hopped forward on one leg, dragging two defenders with him to Buffalo's 20. Another first down!

Four plays later O. J. Anderson plowed ahead one yard for a touchdown that put New York up 17–12. By bleeding 9:29 from the clock while accumulating 74 yards, New York had produced the most time-consuming drive in Super Bowl history. The fourteen-play sequence changed the tone of the game, and gave Jim Kelly a sense of urgency. But Big Blue's defense continued frustrating the quarterback, switching occasionally to four linebackers for a change of pace. And although Belichick's unit blew some coverages, it prevented Kelly from establishing Buffalo's standard tempo. After having caught seven balls in the first half, wideout Andre Reed struggled. As the Giants had hoped, he lost interest in catching passes that assured multiple savage hits.

A Bills drive starting late in the third quarter showed the potency of their offense in rhythm. Buffalo advanced 63 yards in just four plays, and on the opening play of the fourth quarter Thurman Thomas sprinted 31 yards for a touchdown that gave Buffalo a 19–17 lead.

The Giants responded with another long drive buttressed by Mark Bavaro's catches. But after accumulating 74 yards in 7:24, the Giants stalled at Buffalo's 3. Matt Bahr's 21-yard field goal capped the fourteen-play sequence, giving Big Blue a one-point lead. Buffalo and New York then exchanged unsuccessful drives, keeping the score at 20–19. With the Giants forced to punt from Buffalo's 48, Kelly had one last chance to orchestrate a scoring drive; with 2:16 left, the Bills took over on their 10. Buffalo accumulated substantial yardage against Big Blue's prevent defense, using short passes, run plays, and quarterback scrambles. Kelly darted up the middle several times to exploit open space, and Thurman Thomas's seven-yard dash in the waning moments brought his team to New York's 30. After Kelly's spike to stop the clock, eight seconds remained, enough time for Scott Norwood to attempt a 47-yard game winner.

Norwood's career-best was a 49-yarder, and during the season he had converted a 48-yarder. However, ABC provided a revealing graphic of his career numbers on grass: one of five from distances of 40 yards or more. And the field-goal attempt to decide the Super Bowl would take place on grass.

Matt Bahr approached Parcells with a prediction. "Bill, he's only made one from 47 yards on grass all year. He's going to overkick it."

In one of Tampa Stadium's executive suites, Wellington Mara's wife, Ann, clutched her rosary beads. Just as they had done in the NFC Championship, some Giants formed a circle on the sideline. Jeff Hostetler knelt, biting his fingernails, while Mickey Corcoran, wearing a red cap, chewed gum to the quarterback's right. Across the field the Bills, including head coach Marv Levy, held hands in a long line, awaiting the action.

Bills holder Frank Reich placed the ball down cleanly. Norwood boomed the kick, ensuring it would go the distance, but the kicker knew immediately that it would veer right. As the pigskin sailed a couple of feet wide of the right goalpost, several Giants on the field leaped and threw up their arms. But many of their teammates on the sideline didn't react until a referee in the end zone signaled that the kick was wide right.

As Carl Banks and Pepper Johnson hugged Parcells, the head coach asked his players, "Would you guys take me for a ride?"

Banks responded, "Let's go. Let's take this man for a ride."

Lawrence Taylor joined his two teammates in lifting Parcells onto their shoulders. Smiling, Parcells pumped his right fist in what would become a defining moment in his career, replayed on television countless times over the decades.

Norwood's missed kick assured the Giants of their second Super Bowl in five years, and it placed Parcells in a small group of coaches to capture two Lombardi Trophies, securing his legacy at age forty-nine. In the press box Tom Coughlin was among the Giants coaches leaping, embracing, and slapping each other fives. With four seconds left Jeff Hostetler took a knee, sealing the closest-ever Super Bowl outcome, as Coughlin and his cohort raced to a stadium elevator to reach the field. One Bills coach ended up on the ride down, suffering as Parcells's staff rejoiced.

The Giants controlled the clock for 40:33, a Super Bowl record, compared to only 19:27 for Buffalo, yet they committed zero turnovers. O. J. Anderson gained 102 yards on 21 carries to earn Super Bowl MVP; the Florida native beat out Jeff Hostetler, who completed 20 of 32 passes for 222 yards, concluding the postseason without throwing an interception.

Thurman Thomas accumulated an impressive 135 rushing yards and 55 receiving yards, but part of the tailback's production stemmed from Big Blue's acquiescence. Belichick's defense had permitted only 35 total points over three postseason games. By repeatedly dominating time of possession, Big Blue's offense helped its defense become perhaps the best-rested unit in playoff history. And Belichick, already viewed as a future head coach, bolstered his reputation as a brilliant tactician. His game plan would end up in the Pro Football Hall of Fame.

At the presentation of the Vince Lombardi Trophy, Tim Mara, the Giants co-owner, declared, "Bill Parcells is the best coach the Giants have ever had." Standing in front of new NFL commissioner Paul Tagliabue and to the right of GM George Young, the triumphant head coach raised the Lombardi Trophy with his right hand, sweater sleeves rolled down, as photographers snapped pictures.

After accepting the trophy Parcells was whisked to a makeshift podium inside a tent for a media session. Will McDonough, a prominent football writer for the *Boston Globe* and a friend of Parcells since his first NFL job in 1980, stood a couple of feet away. As journalists hustled in and positioned themselves for the post–Super Bowl Q&A, Parcells leaned over to McDonough and said two words.

"Power football!"

Once the press conference started, Parcells expounded. "They call us predictable and conservative, but I know one thing, having coached this game a long time: power wins football games. *Power wins football games.* It's not always the fanciest way, but it can win games."

A reporter asked if the outcome vindicated Big Blue's style of play. Parcells scoffed, "It's always been vindicated. It's that new stuff that has something to prove."

Compared to new offensive trends like the run-and-shoot and no-huddle, Parcells's grinding approach looked retro. Like Vince Lombardi decades before, Parcells relished big, powerful players on both sides of the ball. He favored bruising tailbacks running behind a massive offensive line. On defense, he concentrated on stuffing the run with beefy, athletic bodies. And whenever receivers caught passes, the head coach preferred them funneled to hulking linebackers who meted out punishment. Even his defensive backs weighed at least 200 pounds. In essence, Parcells wanted his big players to beat up the opponent's smaller players. After Super Bowl XXV, Bills wideout Andre Reed, who had suffered bruises all over his body, conceded that no team had ever hit him so hard. Linebacker Shane Conlan expressed amazement at his face mask breaking as he tried to tackle O. J. Anderson.

Power epitomized Parcells's mind-set in football, if not life. During the playoffs, speculation flared about his possible retirement, which he had occasionally broached, or his departure to another team as a GM and coach. One scenario reportedly involved the Tampa Bay Buccaneers. Parcells had one more year left on a contract averaging $800,000, and the Giants intended to offer him a richer extension. But given his flirtation with the Atlanta Falcons after Super Bowl XXI, the new reports were taken seriously. So during the post–Super Bowl Q&A, Parcells's future with the Giants naturally came up.

He deflected the questions. "The last time we won one of these games, I was in the center of a little controversy. And it didn't allow the team's ownership or George Young to enjoy the victory the way they should have. They are going to be able to enjoy this one."

Parcells returned to the Giants locker room, where players were pouring champagne on each other, shouting to be heard over the din. One of the first players to greet Parcells was Lawrence Taylor. As the coach and linebacker hugged, Taylor, caught up in the moment, kissed him on the lips. Later, Parcells's security chief and ex–Army player, Steve Yarnell, pecked him on the cheek.

Pepper Johnson led a group of players to Jeff Hostetler's locker. As the quarterback changed into his dress clothes, his teammates chanted, "You can't do it. You can't do it. You can't do it."

Hostetler smiled at the sarcastic refrain.

When the locker room finally emptied a few hours later, Jim Steeg, an NFL executive whose duties included Super Bowl logistics, walked through one final time. To his astonishment Steeg found the Lombardi Trophy glistening on a table, surrounded by towels and champagne glasses. The special-events guru placed it in his car trunk before phoning George Young at his hotel to let him know that the NFL's crown jewel had been left behind.

On the second and third floors of their hotel, the Giants' giddy celebration continued into the night. Parcells awoke the next morning on less than an hour's sleep to attend a follow-up press conference for the winning coach. He was asked to describe the feeling of triumphing in the only Super Bowl decided by a point. Grinning, Parcells responded, "Nothing beats winning. Nothing."

He added, "It's like all the Christmas mornings you've ever had wrapped into one."

14

Beyond Tom Coughlin's departure for Boston College, Parcells found himself facing other key losses to his staff. After seven seasons overseeing running backs, Ray Handley, forty-six, informed the organization of his plans to attend law school at George Washington University. And even before the defense's impressive postseason, Bill Belichick was considered a leading candidate for head coach of the Browns. Pundits and Giants fans viewed Belichick as heir apparent to Parcells, assuming the defensive co-ordinator stayed in New York for at least another year. But George Young showed no interest in having Belichick wait out his boss. Instead, the GM disparaged Belichick's potential as a head coach to fellow executives around the league. Young's doubts about Belichick's leadership, particularly his communication skills, made it unlikely that Parcells's lieutenant would ever rise to Big Blue's top job.

Two weeks after Super Bowl XXV, Bill Belichick was interviewed by the Buccaneers and Browns. Tampa Bay needed a successor to Ray Perkins, whom they had dismissed late in the 1990 season while promoting his offensive coordinator Richard Williamson. After twelve seasons as a Giants assistant, one of the longest tenures in franchise history, Belichick accepted Cleveland's offer. At thirty-eight, he became the NFL's youngest head coach, seizing the distinction from the Raiders' Art Shell, forty-four, who also happened to be the league's only black head coach.

In late February, shortly after the loss of Belichick, the Giants also experienced a major shakeup in the team's ownership. After more than a decade of acrimony between Wellington Mara and his nephew, Tim Mara sold the 50 percent share of the franchise held by him, his sister, and their mother. New co-owner Bob Tisch, billionaire boss of Loews Corporation, paid more than $70 million for half the team. Despite Parcells's friendly relationship with Wellington Mara, the head coach was much closer to Wellington's nephew, who was now suddenly gone.

The Giants planned to negotiate an extension of Parcells's contract, possibly three years, for north of $1 million annually. Such an agreement would place him among the NFL's highest-paid head coaches, in a class with Miami's Don Shula and Washington's Joe Gibbs. But with

NFL owners scheduled to vote on approving Tisch's co-ownership in mid-March, the Giants decided to put Parcells's negotiations on hold.

Having contemplated quitting the previous two seasons, Parcells used the time to mull his aspiration of becoming a GM and head coach elsewhere. He consulted his friend Al Davis, who had once held the dual role. The Raiders boss told Parcells he would need a top scout and someone skilled at negotiating player contracts. Robert Fraley, Parcells's Orlando-based agent, believed that Hugh Culverhouse, owner of the woebegone Tampa Bay Bucs, would make an exorbitant offer for Parcells that would include personnel authority. In the meantime, Fraley arranged for his client to audition as an NBC analyst, which could provide him with interim employment.

Parcells compartmentalized, focusing on his duties as head coach by preparing for April's draft. Before Parcells and Young left for the Indianapolis scouting combine, they discussed the staff, which Parcells realigned by adding two new coaches and promoting three. Each of his assistants received a two-year contract, a possible sign that Parcells intended to return.

Linebackers coach Al Groh, forty-six, inherited Belichick's title of defensive coordinator, just as Parcells had envisioned when he hired Groh in 1989. The promotion helped stave off Belichick, who wanted Groh to join him in Cleveland. After being persuaded to delay law school, Ray Handley was named offensive coordinator. Groh and Handley maintained their duties while overseeing key parts of their units: linebackers and running backs. Handley's predecessor, Ron Erhardt, fifty-nine, was elevated to assistant head coach, where he remained an offensive guru with added duties involving defense and special teams.

Parcells also hired Jim Fassel, forty-one, as quarterbacks coach, and Fred Bruney, fifty-nine, as secondary coach. Fassel had been head coach at the University of Utah, and before that, from 1979 to 1983, during John Elway's stint at Stanford, Fassel coached the star quarterback on the same staff as Ray Handley. Bruney had been defensive coordinator for the Bucs. Parcells hired him to ease Al Groh's burden by adding an experienced coach to Belichick's former bailiwick, defensive backs.

Amid all the changes Parcells was making, his own future remained murky. After the NFL approved Tisch's ownership stake in mid-March, the new co-owner mentioned the team's plans to soon discuss reworking Parcells's contract. But Parcells surprised the Giants by asking his boss, George Young, to hold off on any talks.

"I don't really know what I want to do."

The statement was curious, if not ominous, from the team's point of view, but one undisclosed element involved Parcells's health. A daily smoker, he publicly lamented his losing battle of the bulge and high cholesterol level. Similar issues that season had caused Broncos head coach Dan Reeves to undergo an angioplasty, a procedure that mechanically widens blood vessels to the heart that are getting clogged by fatty substances. Parcells had suffered from fainting spells and arrhythmia, an abnormal rhythm of the heartbeat, which he attributed to the stress of his job. Mike Ditka's heart attack at age forty-nine during the 1988 season weighed on Parcells's mind, so after Super Bowl XXV, Bill took a few months to assess his condition. He underwent cardiac stress tests, but when the results didn't reveal anything alarming, doctors concluded that nothing significant was amiss.

However, Parcells, with a former athlete's awareness of his own body, was convinced otherwise. During his daily workouts he occasionally became light-headed, and his heart pounded in an unusual manner. "It felt like it was going right through my chest," he says.

In late April, Parcells participated in the NFL draft and conducted rookie minicamp soon after. But health still dominated his concerns along with subjects like his unresolved contract extension, a new team owner, and his goal of running a team one day. Nearly four months after the Super Bowl, Parcells still vacillated about remaining in New York.

During the second weekend in May he finally decided to quit. A few days later, just a week before veterans' minicamp, he visited Young's office to convey his decision without disclosing a specific reason. The stunning news broke in an article written by the *Boston Globe*'s Will McDonough. That same day, May 15, the team held a press conference. In trying to explain his decision to reporters, Parcells said several times, "I just felt it was time."

He asserted that health didn't factor into his decision, and described any such speculation as "ludicrous." As proof Parcells cited his recent doctor's visit, claiming a clean bill of health. With Parcells's resignation, the Giants announced that Ray Handley would become Big Blue's fourteenth head coach, only one season removed from overseeing running backs. Ron Erhardt had seemed like a natural option given his head coaching experience, but George Young identified with Handley's cerebral nature.

Parcells says, "Far in advance of all this, I asked George: 'You want me to encourage Belichick to stay here rather than go to Cleveland?' He said, 'No.' Before that, I asked, 'Do you want me to encourage Coughlin to stay here?' He said, 'No.' He already had his mind made up about who the coach was going to be: Ray Handley.

"Later on, when that didn't work out, he intimated to the media that had he known that I was going to step down, he would have named

Coughlin the head coach. That's not true. But you have to understand that George was a former schoolteacher. He was an intellectual, like Ray Handley. Ray was very bright. That's who George wanted."

In late May 1991, Parcells felt compelled to undergo another physical. This time, doctors were not so sanguine. Something might be wrong, they told Parcells, although they couldn't pinpoint the problem. Their first recommendation involved the bad habit that Ida Parcells had long implored her son to end: smoking. Showing tremendous willpower, he never lit another cigarette for the rest of his life. Abstaining from nicotine, however, made no difference to the occasional dizzy spells, or explosive heart fluttering.

In late summer, Parcells joined NBC as an NFL analyst and studio host. He signed a three-year deal worth $750,000, and declared that coaching now lay in his rearview mirror. Parcells enjoyed his TV gig, and expressed a desire to become good at it, but reduced stress from the career switch didn't improve his health issues. During broadcasts he endured abnormal heartbeats in the booth, so in early December, Parcells underwent yet another examination, this time by a cardiologist in Ridgewood, New Jersey. Michael Kesselbrenner solved the mystery: Parcells's left anterior descending artery, better known as the widow maker, was experiencing blockage.

Coronary artery disease is still the leading cause of death in the United States. For single-vessel blockage, like Parcells's, doctors prefer to avoid surgery. Kesselbrenner recommended angioplasty, the same procedure Reeves underwent. During the procedure, Kesselbrenner inserted a tube attached to a deflated balloon into Parcells's artery. Then the tiny balloon was inflated, compressing the fatty deposits and widening the artery, before being withdrawn. A couple of days later, Parcells was running painlessly for the first time in recent memory. And with his health concerns set aside, Parcells found himself missing his old job.

By the end of the NFL regular season, ten coaches had been dismissed, the most in some dozen years. The casualties included Richard Williamson of the floundering franchise linked to Parcells's future. And the Buccaneers were preparing an offer to show just how much they wanted him. On Monday, December 23, one day after Tampa Bay finished 3-13, owner Hugh Culverhouse flew in his private plane to Newark Airport before riding in a limousine to Teterboro Airport for a clandestine meeting with Bill Parcells.

The two discussed Parcells's return to the NFL with total control of the Bucs. Culverhouse, seventy-two, felt a sense of urgency because Parcells had another suitor. Green Bay had fired head coach Lindy Infante after a 4-12 season, and Packers GM Ron Wolf had expressed interest in Parcells, his longtime friend. When Culverhouse broached the subject of Green Bay, Parcells stressed his desire to join the Bucs. So for several hours the two discussed what it would take.

During the following twenty-four hours, Parcells grilled Ray Perkins, recently removed from a 19-41 tenure in Tampa Bay. Even before meeting Culverhouse, Parcells had carefully researched the franchise, which had been a black hole for coaches since its inception in 1976, and one of the worst teams in league history. The Bucs were coming off nine consecutive losing seasons. Culverhouse was among the league's most influential owners, serving on several of its executive committees, but the former tax attorney and real-estate investor was infamous for frugality that placed profitability before winning.

The day after meeting Culverhouse, Parcells listed thirty-eight requirements in order for him to become head coach and director of football operations. He sent the letter by overnight mail to Culverhouse, who phoned the free-agent coach to discuss each point. One key matter involved replacing GM Phil Krueger with someone more experienced and well-regarded: former Bears and Lions executive Jerry Vainisi, the younger brother of Jack, Green Bay's GM under Lombardi.

In stark contrast to his reputation for penny-pinching, Culverhouse obliged Parcells on virtually every count, including a five-year, $6.5 million deal that would make Parcells the league's highest-paid coach. Parcells's attorney had approved the contract for his client's signature, so Parcells told Culverhouse that he intended to ink it, but first needed to touch base with the other team that had expressed interest in him, the Green Bay Packers.

Two days later, on December 28, Culverhouse telephoned Parcells to coordinate the announcement of the team's new hire, but to the owner's surprise and dismay, Parcells no longer wanted to join Tampa Bay. Embarrassed, Culverhouse immediately called for a morning press conference at Bucs headquarters. ESPN broadcast it live, expecting Parcells to be announced as Tampa Bay's new coach. Instead, Culverhouse informed the media of Parcells's last-minute decision. "We feel like we've been jilted at the altar," he said, waving the thirty-eight-point document, which included a budget for Parcells's staff ($2.5 million), country-club membership, automobile use, and the types of weights (free versus cable) to be installed at the practice facility.

Hours later Parcells offered a more nuanced version of the development on *NFL Live*, the NBC pregame show where he worked on a crew that included Bob Costas, O. J. Simpson, and Will McDonough. Parcells conceded that both sides had agreed on the list, but the ex-coach added that he had never quite committed himself. "I thought it may be too big a job—too many hats to wear at this time in professional football. There was just something about it in the end that didn't feel right."

Culverhouse predicted that Parcells would coach the Packers, and three days later, Parcells did meet with Ron Wolf to discuss Green Bay's opening, but the buddies didn't reach an agreement. Now, decades later, Parcells explains that his health factored into the decision involving Tampa Bay. "I knew that I was having more than a little problem, and I was gonna have to deal with it. I just didn't know quite what was wrong."

Still, after a full week with no chest pains, Parcells began having serious second thoughts about rejecting an offer that included so much money and power. He telephoned Culverhouse to express renewed interest and to suggest another sit-down. Tampa Bay's owner consented to meeting Parcells in Washington, D.C., on the morning of January 8, 1992. One day beforehand, Parcells lunched with Lou Piniella, the Cincinnati Reds manager. The two had become friends in the late 1980s when Piniella managed the Yankees. He grew up in West Tampa, where he starred in high school basketball before attending the University of Tampa on a baseball scholarship. At one of their favorite eating spots, Parcells picked Piniella's brain about places to live in the manager's hometown.

Culverhouse brought two team lawyers to the sit-down, which hinted that a deal might be reachable. Parcells, who came with Robert Fraley, disclosed that his health had factored into his change of heart, but within the first fifteen minutes of a three-hour conversation, Parcells sensed that Culverhouse, who seemed skeptical of the explanation, was no longer interested. Instead of renewing his full-court press, the owner behaved like the one being courted. To Parcells's chagrin, the meeting ended without Culverhouse's renewing his offer. That same afternoon the Bucs owner issued a statement that the meeting "did not provide him with the comfort level to pursue further discussions."

In February 1992, only six weeks after his angioplasty, Parcells's fears were realized. He started suffering chest pains, signs that his heart issues were far from over. The intermittent aches turned relentless in April, when it became evident that his artery blockage had returned, and Parcells was forced to undergo another angioplasty. Though considered minimally invasive, the procedure expanded the walls of the artery, causing bruising in the lining. When Parcells's artery healed it generated a keloid, a kind of scar tissue, which led to restenosis, a rare condition involving the renarrowing of a blood vessel after angioplasty.

His son-in-law, Jerry Schwille, Suzy's husband, recommended someone who specialized in heart trauma: V. Paul Addonizio, chief of cardiac surgery at Temple University Hospital. Renowned for cutting-edge surgeries while averaging two hundred operations annually, Addonizio fulfilled Parcells's desire for a doctor "used to dealing with trauma, in case something goes wrong." By Parcells's reasoning, a surgeon skilled at complex heart transplants would be at relative ease with a single-vessel bypass.

Parcells's idiosyncrasies prevented him from using the person who had operated on his father, although John Hutchinson was perhaps the top thoracic surgeon in New Jersey. In 1983, Hutchinson, who oversaw the Hackensack University Medical Center, had performed the high-risk emergency surgery on Charles Parcells just days before he died. "I'm definitely not going to that guy; I'm superstitious," Parcells explains. "He did my dad, and that didn't work out the way I wanted it to."

Regardless, coronary bypass remained a last resort. In the meantime Kesselbrenner recommended that Parcells travel to the Cleveland Clinic to undergo an alternative procedure: atherectomy. "You've got nothing to lose, and it just might work."

In late April 1992, on Good Friday, Parcells flew to Cleveland for a third procedure. A device was inserted into the artery and rotated to eliminate blockage. "Kind of like what the Roto-Rooter man does," Parcells says. Although the procedure cleared the artery, its inside walls were bruised again, raising the possibility of more scar tissue. On Easter Sunday, Parcells returned to New Jersey, hoping for a new life. He adhered to a strict new diet, and no longer smoked, but only a few weeks later, in late May, the blockage returned. Parcells suffered shortness of breath and sharp pain in his chest that left him feeling like he might suffer a heart attack at any moment.

Despite having undergone several tests and three operations within six months, Parcells's situation was worse than ever, so on May 29, 1992, he checked into Temple University Hospital for cardiac catheterization, a medical-imaging technique to reevaluate his condition and determine the need for other, more serious options. A tube was inserted into Parcells's body and passed through the blood vessel to the heart, providing precise images of the artery blockage. The results confirmed the need for a single-vessel bypass.

Parcells could still have tried to manage the situation with medication, but the chest pains and the risk of a heart attack would have remained. Parcells consulted with his Jersey-based cardiologist, Dr. Kesselbrenner, who explained the pitfalls of avoiding bypass surgery. "This artery controls 40 percent of the blood flow from your heart. It's 50-50 whether you're going to live if you don't have the surgery. And if you *do* live, things probably won't be the same."

Parcells responded, "Okay, I've got to have the surgery."

He was also informed that the chance of death *during* single-vessel bypass was about 2 percent.

Parcells returned to Upper Saddle River, New Jersey, his thoughts full of impending surgery and the lack of a guarantee despite the great odds of surviving. In four days it would be settled one way or the other.

As a boy, Parcells scaled the spire of a local church for kicks. In high school, he was the quintessential jock, using his body with abandon. During college he entered a contest to wrestle a bear. And in the NFL, Parcells instilled fear in some of the biggest, baddest athletes on the planet. Now, for the first time, Parcells was directly confronted by his mortality. The possibility of imminent death jarred him, as Parcells considered the silver lining of succumbing during surgery. "Fortunately," he says dryly, "I would never know it." Preparing for the worst, he went over the family's finances with Judy at their living-room table. He provided detailed, written instructions that included wishes beyond his will. "In that situation," he explains, "you don't know if you're coming back, so it was time to set my affairs in order with my wife."

Parcells tried to mask his disquietude from his family, assuring everyone that things would turn out fine, but he was determined to keep his daughters from seeing him immediately after the bypass, when he would be weak and connected to a ventilator. "I don't want the girls down there," Parcells told Judy. "Don't bring them in until I'm sitting up."

Late Monday morning, June 1, 1992, the couple drove to Philadelphia. The surgery was scheduled for 7 a.m. the next day. For most of the two-hour ride to Temple University Hospital, Parcells remained mute as his emotions roiled. Unhappy about the need for surgery, he had resigned himself to its inevitability. After silence in the car for several minutes, Parcells reiterated his instructions to Judy for the worst-case scenario, reminding her who to contact about the family's finances. Despite her husband's tough-guy exterior, she detected his angst, especially as Philadelphia neared.

Once Parcells was settled in his hospital room, the only concern he expressed to Judy involved memory loss, a risk of heart surgery. For Parcells, whose memory was preternatural, the only thing worse would be death. During a single-bypass operation, the heart is stopped to allow the creation of a new conduit for blood. In Parcells's case, an artery under his breastbone needed to be grafted to his problematic artery to circumvent, or *bypass,* the blockage, and maintain proper blood supply to the heart. The blood flow would be rerouted by having one end of the clear artery grafted below the clogged section of the vessel known as the widow maker. "Someday people will probably laugh at us for doing this," Addonizio says. "But we literally stitch the new artery to the old one."

To halt the heart without causing death, all the blood needed to be drained from it and funneled through a tube into the heart-lung machine, which temporarily takes over the functions of those organs. Dubbed "the pump," the machine provides respiration while pumping blood throughout the body to maintain circulation and body temperature. After surgery, the heart and lungs resume their normal functions. The downside of the pump is that the longer a patient is on it the more likely it is that complications will occur. Microscopic particles inevitably reach blood vessels in the brain. And the patient may awaken from surgery having forgotten such basic facts as the name of the current president or the most recent Super Bowl–winning coach. In the worst cases, this particulate matter can cause brain damage.

"I always say, 'There's only three kinds of heart surgeons: fast-good, fast-bad, and slow-bad," Addonizio says. "There's no slow-good."

So Parcells instructed Judy to test his memory after he awoke from anesthesia by asking him his address, his birth date, and the phone number of his youngest brother, Doug.

In the late afternoon, Addonizio came to Parcells's hospital room for a meeting in advance of surgery. With Judy present, the doctor provided his patient with a breakdown of the surgery, postsurgical treatment, timeline for his stay assuming no setbacks, and likelihood of complications. Addonizio confirmed that surgery was necessary to avoid the likelihood of a fatal heart attack. Although Parcells had considered a single-bypass operation to be less challenging than other heart surgeries, in certain respects his situation was among the most difficult. The new connection between the rejiggered arteries, called anastomosis, had to be nearly flawless. Technically it wasn't a complex surgery, but the precision required in the linkage made the margin for error almost zero.

Addonizio offers perspective on the low probability of death during surgery. "Keep in mind that for the person who doesn't make it," he says, "it's 100 percent. And 3 percent is pretty high odds compared to, say, the chances of being in a plane crash."

Brooklyn-born in 1948, Addonizio had attended Xavier High, a private school in Manhattan, then obtained a biology degree from New York University. As a teenager Addonizio relished Big Blue's dominance from the mid-fifties through the early sixties. His favorite Giant was quarterback Y. A. Tittle, who won the 1963 league MVP but lost the NFL

Championship for the third straight year. While Addonizio trained to be a doctor, obtaining a medical degree from Cornell University in 1974, he suffered through some of the franchise's down decades. So Parcells was larger than life to Giants fans like Addonizio for returning their team to glory.

The early 1990s was an exciting time for the heart-surgery profession, highlighted by the introduction of the artificial heart, a boon for patients awaiting transplants. Addonizio had performed hundreds of surgeries each year, including some on professional athletes. To manage his intensely pressure-filled job, Addonizio maintained some detachment. "I'm not one of these I-feel-your-pain type of people," says Addonizio, who encourages his staff to lend emotional support. "My job is to do the best I possibly can for the patient."

Therefore, Addonizio failed to detect Parcells's apprehension preceding the bypass. Instead, the doctor was struck by his patient's take-charge mannerism, even in his vulnerable position. With a polite yet booming voice, he asked several incisive questions. Despite the fact that Parcells was talking to the man who would hold his heart in hand, he remained the dominant presence in the room.

"Now, this may seem a bit strange, but the first impression I had was that this was an extraordinarily attractive man," Addonizio recalls. "This is a real man's man, like in the style of, say, a John Wayne. The second impression was that this fellow has tremendous leadership ability. It's not something I can define, but it's something you sense when you're in the presence of certain people.

"It's not as if he was ever mean or demanding. He was a model patient, believe it or not. You would think somebody who's forceful enough to control L.T. would be difficult."

Just before his early-morning surgery, Parcells took a shower to minimize the chances of infection, a significant concern for heart-surgery patients. He was assigned a number, a plastic cap, and a loose gown not designed for privacy. Although Parcells had taken a sedative, his anxiety soared as he was placed on a gurney to be transported to the waiting area of the operating room. The intern handling the gurney turned out to be a player on Temple's football team. And Parcells couldn't resist sizing up his physique, noting the similarities to some of his ex-Giants. Just before strapping Parcells on the gurney, the college student produced a football, a pen, and a sheet of paper.

"Hey, Coach, would you mind signing these for my brother?"

Amused by the timing of the request, Parcells took the pigskin. "Well, if I don't make it out of here, you're going to have the last ball I ever signed. You're going to sell that sonofabitch, aren't you?"

The intern curled his right hand into a fist and tapped the side of the gurney. "Don't worry, Coach, I'll be there when you come out!"

His conviction boosted Parcells's confidence. The famous patient autographed the football and the paper, signing off with, "Good luck." As Parcells was wheeled down the hallway, his gaze largely limited to the banks of fluorescent lights on the ceiling, he wondered if this would be among his final sights. Parcells strained his head sideways, hoping to catch a glimpse of a window to the outside world, but all he could see were brick walls going by. "I was in a bit of a mental battle," he recalls.

Oblivious to his patient's state of mind, the intern moved Parcells along briskly, but when he noticed Parcells craning his neck, he slowed down. Finally, a few yards from their destination Parcells got lucky, spotting a window through an open door that revealed an oak tree, lush with June foliage.

Parcells smiled.

When he entered the OR waiting area, two other patients were waiting on gurneys. One was a policeman from Cinnaminson, New Jersey, an eastern suburb of Philadelphia. Recognizing Parcells, the cop initiated a conversation, revealing that this was his second surgery for a cancerous brain tumor. Ex-coach and cop commiserated for a few minutes until the wall clock registered 7 a.m. Surgery time. The policeman was moved through one door as Parcells was wheeled through another, which opened into a room so vast it looked like a football field, brightly lit for a night game.

Doctor Addonizio had granted his patient's request to bring an elephant figurine into the operation room, which was strapped to Parcells's right ankle. With the trunk curled up, the figurine's head pointed toward the exit door for luck. Parcells owned hundreds of elephant statuettes, sent over the years by fans, including President Nixon, who had learned of the coach's superstition from newspaper articles. But the green-tinted figurine in the operating room was his original and most cherished: Ida's going-away gift in 1959 when her eldest son left home to attend college. Before the surgery, he maximized his chances for success by placing a scapular, the small religious talisman worn by Catholics, on the elephant statuette. "You don't want to tempt fate," he explains, chuckling.

Parcells was in the operating room for less than a minute before the anesthesiologist administered medicine through an IV, causing him to relax before drifting into deep slumber. Soon, an electric buzz saw cut open the front of his chest, making an in-line, vertical incision the length of half his breastbone. The cut sternum was pushed open for access to his heart. Meanwhile, Parcells was connected to the heart-lung machine with a plastic tube to keep his blood circulating while his heart was clinically arrested. In performing thousands of such operations, Addonizio's team had honed its efficiency, skill, and synchronicity. With Addonizio as quarterback, the goal was a successful surgery as speedily as possible. His team considered it a failure to utter a word or, well, an audible, during surgery.

Parcells's operation took twelve minutes of dead silence; it was "fast-good."

Despite performing countless such surgeries, Addonizio says of Parcells's bypass, "I remember his arteries precisely, and the details of the operation—every thought that we had as each stitch was going in [his heart]. That's how important it was to get every little stitch perfect."

As the anesthesia wore off during the late afternoon, Parcells regained consciousness in an ICU room. He could feel the tube in the back of his throat that wound down to the ventilator. Pain radiated from his breastbone, but Parcells's first acute sense was auditory. He heard beeping nearby, plus some distant noises, perhaps voices, which he couldn't identify. He had no memory of the surgery, and wasn't sure if it was over. "I just knew I was alive," he says.

When the nurse assigned to Parcells noticed that he was stirring, she rushed to his side. First she had good news: the surgery was successful. Parcells could expect to be hospitalized for a week, during which time, she assured Parcells, he would receive plenty of help recuperating. Nonetheless, the next several hours were difficult, particularly for a control freak. Parcells needed assistance with even the most basic functions. When Judy visited her husband and saw his condition, she decided to hold off on his memory test for at least another day.

Shortly after surgery, patients often feel depressed. Their sense of vulnerability is heightened, and the long road to rehabilitation hits home. "This is more common for men than women," Addonizio says, "because most of us tend to think of ourselves as immortal. Being in the hospital is not as foreign to women." Although Bill Parcells was grateful to be alive, his feeble state made him despondent. He wondered if he would ever recover enough to coach again.

He was less downcast the next day after being disconnected from the ventilator and allowed to return to his hospital bedroom. When Judy conducted the memory test, he was thrilled to find that his recall was intact.

The fifty-year-old coach was also delighted to hear Addonizio describe his heart as young and athletic.

Friday, June 5, 1992, three days after surgery, Parcells was sitting up in his hospital bed when his daughter Dallas came to visit. Hooked up to his IVs, Parcells wore a navy robe with red-and-white piping on the lapels and cuffs. In an upbeat tone, Parcells said, "It wasn't my time," and told Dallas the story about receiving an autograph request while being wheeled to the OR. One temporary result of the bypass that Parcells complained about was occasionally odd, rapid pulsations in his chest.

"They don't warn you that you're going to have these extra heartbeats."

Later that afternoon, Parcells walked gingerly around his bed a few times. While looking out the window that late spring day, he was interrupted by his first nonfamily visitor: Mickey Corcoran. The sight of his mentor further boosted his spirits.

Parcells hugged Corcoran carefully, saying, "This was a real ass-kicker, Mick. I won't be doing any rebounding for you today."

Corcoran replied, "I can't believe how good you look, Billy. I mean, the surgery was just three days ago."

"It was something. This place, the people here. They're unbelievable." Parcells commented on the irony of receiving world-class treatment in Philadelphia Eagles territory, after having faced so much vitriol at their home stadium.

He told Corcoran, "I'd hear, 'Hey, Parcells, you fat-ass.' That was their way of saying hello."

Corcoran laughed.

Parcells added, "One time, Mark Bavaro was walking with me, and when he heard that he said, 'Don't worry, Bill.' Like he was going to protect me."

Parcells added, "When you wake up in the morning, you don't want to move, but you've got to fight it. Now it feels so good to sweat."

Parcells sat down in the chair next to his bed and sifted through a stack of cards and telegrams.

"Everybody's been great. I got a telegram from Lou [Piniella] that said, 'Never mind getting well soon. Just get me some damn runs!' Then there's one from [Giants safety] Kenny Hill. I used to always get on him. I'd tell him, 'You can't play unless something hurts.' So look what he says in this card: 'Some people can't function unless they create illusionary obstacles to overcome for themselves.'"

Towering above the flowers on the windowsill stood a three-foot elephant figure, trunk raised, facing the door. The gift was from Parcells's boss at NBC, Terry ONeil, the sports executive producer. Nearby was a framed picture of Matt Bahr's last-second field goal for the 15–13 thriller over San Francisco in the 1990 NFC Championship, sent by a Giants fan who had shot it from the upper stands of Candlestick Park. Holding it up and smiling at Corcoran, Parcells said, "The three-peat game."

In preparation for walking the hospital halls, Parcells asked Addonizio for a distance goal. The surgeon responded that the ex-coach should walk for as long as he was comfortable doing so. Following a bypass the heart usually takes about six months to regain its normal strength, he said, but after being bedridden for two days, Parcells was determined to return to normalcy as soon as possible. And, of course, his competitive streak spurred him to try outdoing the average patient.

The next day, Parcells kept track of his distance by counting each step on his way to exhaustion. He briskly walked the halls of his floor for a stretch excessive even for a robust pedestrian: roughly two miles. Sweating profusely, Parcells took deep breaths, causing him to wince in pain.

Addonizio received word of Parcells's foolhardiness, prompting a visit the next morning.

"You know, that wasn't very smart what you did yesterday. But I can see that you're not going to be happy until you go out and run around this hospital ten times. I admire your mentality but you made a mistake. You need to be your own doctor. Don't push things too far, because if you go over the line you're not coming back."

Those remarks, Parcells says, turned out to be the best advice he ever got about his well-being. "I've taken it to heart all these years," says the septuagenarian golfer, who exercises almost daily on a treadmill. "I've always tried to push it, but I never try to cross the line."

Bill Parcells was discharged on June 9, 1992, with an appointment to return in three weeks for reevaluation. Addonizio instructed Parcells to walk twice per day, a stroll in the morning and another in the afternoon. Back in Upper Saddle River, he created a daily rhythm for the regimen: leaving the house by 9:30 a.m. to walk about a mile, or forty minutes; returning home exhausted, and taking a two-hour nap before his next excursion.

The daily trek began on a shaded downhill path, which made his return trip all the more challenging. So Parcells would head back at a snail's pace, sitting on a curb to rest for several minutes before continuing home. The second day, Parcells decided to increase the distance despite considerable humidity, adding a two-block loop that included a leafy cul-de-sac. As he got to the turnaround Parcells glimpsed the first sign of life that morning: a German shepherd, without a leash, darted from a driveway and charged toward Parcells, barking stridently.

During his childhood Parcells had been bitten by dogs. He had also owned them throughout his life. Comfortable with the animals, he understood their body language. "If he's coming right for you with his ears bent back," Parcells says, "he's serious." As the German shepherd approached, Parcells braced for an attack. What was the best defense? Kicking the dog? Was he even physically capable of doing that?

Within seconds, Parcells concluded that his best option, his *only* option, was raising his arms to shield his face and chest, but his sore sternum made this unbearably painful. His heart racing, Parcells didn't move, *couldn't* move. The dog, only a few feet away, abruptly halted and stopped barking. In a surreal scene, man and dog engaged in a staring contest that seemed to last an eternity. The big canine growled but didn't advance. Finally it turned and trotted away.

Parcells recalls, "Now, he must have either figured, 'This sonofabitch isn't afraid of me 'cause he isn't moving' or 'He can't hurt me.' I don't know which one it was. I was just preparing to get bit. That was the most helpless feeling I've ever had in my life. If I'm healthy and that dog comes at me like that, it's going to be a pretty good battle. I might get bitten a few times, but he's in trouble if I can get my hands around his neck."

After the episode Parcells made his way home, where Judy greeted her husband at the door. She noticed he'd been sweating and possibly crying, but assumed that it was related to the aftermath of surgery. When Judy followed her husband into the kitchen, he conveyed the bizarre story.

Judy recalls, "He said it was the first time in his life he had ever felt completely helpless. If that dog had attacked him, he couldn't have fought back. When you go through something major like heart surgery, your system is all screwed up anyway for a while. He was shaking and scared and really upset."

Nonetheless, the next day Parcells decided not to alter his exercise regimen; the route was ideal. He never saw the German shepherd again, as his halting pace picked up, turning into long strong strides. Eventually, Parcells started jogging, and feeling like a new man.

On June 24, 1992, Bill Parcells traveled to Abington Memorial Hospital, forty-five minutes from Philadelphia, for a post-operative visit with Dr. Addonizio. Parcells felt a kinship with his surgeon, recognizing that just as the ex-coach had spent every minute of his day thinking about football, Addonizio was consumed by cardiology. Although Parcells was a famous sports figure, he viewed Addonizio's as being the higher calling.

While waiting for his doctor, Parcells spent several minutes trying to find the right words to express his appreciation. "Thank you" seemed an inadequate way to convey his strong feelings. As Parcells rehearsed a few versions of what to say, Addonizio walked into the room. Having run out of time, Parcells spoke from the heart. "Hey, Dr. Addonizio, you must get a great deal of satisfaction from what you do. People like you don't come along very often. You help mankind. I don't know whether someone's gratitude means much to you. But if it does, I want you to know how much you have mine."

Addonizio responded emphatically. "Of course it does."

At the end of the appointment Parcells was thrilled to get clearance for coaching. Several weeks later, in late July, Hugh Culverhouse sent Parcells a note wishing the ex-coach a swift recovery. The Bucs owner conceded that he hadn't realized the extent of Parcells's health issues until he'd read about the surgery. Parcells appreciated the gesture, and the two men stayed in touch. Within a few months, though, Culverhouse faced his own health troubles in the form of lung cancer. He would die from it two years later at age seventy-five.

With the advent of football season Parcells returned to NBC as an NFL analyst, but his yearning to coach remained, and was stoked on October 25, when the Seahawks faced Big Blue at Giants Stadium. Two days earlier NBC's crew had visited Parcells's old office building in preparation for its telecast, and the ex-coach had engaged in pleasant conversations with Wellington Mara, Robert Tisch, George Young, and his former secretary.

On game day Parcells arrived at the arena at 9 a.m. While heading to the broadcast booth to cover the game with Marv Albert, his play-by-play partner, Parcells ran into Phil Simms in the stadium tunnel. The coach turned announcer couldn't resist needling his ex-quarterback. For the second straight season the post-Parcells Giants were underachieving. After having gone 8-8 in Ray Handley's rookie season, Big Blue entered the Seahawks game at 2-4. Since the roster contained most of the players who had won Super Bowl XXV, blame fell on Handley. As the league's worst team at 1-6, Seattle seemed as if it would offer the Giants a salve.

New York clung to a 6–3 lead at halftime as fans sitting beneath NBC's booth turned around to ogle their team's ex-coach. Soon spectators started chanting, "We want Bill! We want Bill! We want Bill!" The chorus continued into the third quarter as Seattle, owning the NFL's worst offense in more than a decade, scored its first touchdown in four games. As the Seahawks took a surprising 10-6 lead, the crowd changed its tune, booming, "Ray must go! Ray must go! Ray must go!" Several Seahawks players gestured with their arms for Giants fans to get louder, and in a strange twist, the home crowd obliged. Big Blue came back to win 23–10, but the home crowd's vitriol and the team's struggles against a hapless opponent left the Giants feeling like losers.

After the clock ran down, reporters swarmed Parcells to inquire about his desire to coach again, perhaps with the Giants. The NBC analyst responded by comparing coaching to a narcotic, the biggest high of all taking place in the tunnel before a Super Bowl game. Although Parcells expressed sympathy for Handley, he coyly added, "There aren't any vacancies here. The job is not open. I don't anticipate anything in the future."

Several months later the job *was* open. On December 30 the Giants fired Ray Handley after his injury-riddled team finished the season 6-10. His brief tenure as head coach concluded with an overall record of 14-18. As Big Blue fans and players like Lawrence Taylor clamored for Parcells's return, the ex-coach remarked in interviews that he would consider the job if asked. Behind the scenes he took the possibility one step farther by conveying interest to Wellington Mara. However, George Young, empowered to pick the next coach, was still angry about Parcells's flirtation with Atlanta in late January 1987, only days after Big Blue's first Super Bowl victory. The GM had exhausted his tolerance for Parcells's behavior. As Young once said, "Bill knows what defense he'll call during the second series three games from now. But he doesn't know what he's doing in his own life three days from now." More important, Young saw Parcells as power-hungry and difficult to coexist with.

The Giants GM praised the dismissed Handley for "working within the framework of the team." For his replacement, Young was targeting the assistant coach who'd gotten away: Tom Coughlin, who had revitalized Boston College in only two seasons. To the GM's surprise and dismay, however, the forty-six-year-old showed little interest in Big Blue's overtures. Instead, Coughlin signed a sweetened contract to stay at Boston College, citing the desire to cap his efforts with a national championship. The Giants switched gears by pursuing Dallas defensive coordinator Dave Wannstedt, but Chicago preempted them by naming him Mike Ditka's replacement. Underscoring his lack of interest in Parcells, Young pursued, and landed, his third choice: Dan Reeves, who had taken Denver to three Super Bowls in twelve seasons.

Parcells admits about Young, "He didn't want me back. So what? He probably viewed me as something from the past. 'Time to move on.' My youngest brother said, prudently, 'Why would you go back there? You can probably only do worse.' And he was right." As the winner of two Super Bowls in five years, Parcells could still go to almost any other team with an opening, particularly one with lots of room for improvement.

15

Billy Sullivan had less than twenty-four hours to finagle $17,000 to reach his elusive dream: a football franchise in Boston. On Sunday, November 15, 1959, the Massachusetts businessman had received a long-distance phone call from Lamar Hunt, the Texas oil scion. Hunt needed one more team in order to create the American Football League, which intended to compete aggressively with the NFL, whose soaring popularity had come to match that of the nation's pastime.

Sullivan was informed that paying $25,000 by 4 p.m. the next day would land him the AFL's eighth and final franchise, instead of its going to a prospective owner in Atlanta or Philadelphia. With less than $8,000 in cash, Sullivan furiously recruited nine investors, mostly family and friends, persuading each of them to purchase a 10 percent stake. Borrowing the remainder, Sullivan placed it in an AFL bank account just in time to beat the deadline.

During the 1950s, Sullivan, a former public-relations executive, had fruitlessly sought an NFL club for Boston, the nation's largest city without a football franchise. Beantown's previous NFL teams had folded or relocated, prompting local sports fans to focus on a budding Celtics dynasty in the NBA and the storybook twilight of baseballer Ted Williams's career. Red Sox Nation included a rebellious teenager in New Jersey, Bill Parcells, rooting against his father's dynastic Yankees. Massachusetts's football followers, like a kid named Robert Kraft, adopted the New York Giants, whose games were broadcast throughout the Northeastern region.

Boston's first pro football team, the Boston Bulldogs, had arrived in 1929, relocating from Pottsville, Pennsylvania, but they folded after just one season. The void was filled in 1932 by the Boston Braves, who got their moniker by sharing Braves Field with the city's pro baseball team. After one season the football Braves changed their nickname to the Redskins. The Boston Redskins reached the 1936 NFL Championship, but poor attendance during the regular season angered their owner, George Marshall. After his team lost the title game, 21–6, to Green Bay at the Polo Grounds, Marshall moved the Redskins to Washington, D.C. Pro football returned to Boston in 1944 via the Boston Yanks, owned by Ted Collins.

Now Billy Sullivan was filling the void.

• • •

Reflecting Boston's role in American history, Sullivan's new franchise was dubbed the Patriots before their inaugural season in 1960. Sullivan named himself team president before hiring Mike Holovak as personnel director and Lou Saban as head coach. A former *Boston Globe* sports reporter whose father had also written for the paper, Sullivan lacked the wealth to buy a stadium in a league whose team owners included hotel magnate Barron Hilton of the Los Angeles Chargers and oil tycoon Bud Adams of the Houston Oilers. So the Patriots started off by hosting teams at Boston University's football field.

In Mike Holovak's second full season as head coach after Lou Saban was fired, the Boston Patriots reached the 1963 AFL Championship. But Sullivan's franchise lost by 41 points to the San Diego Chargers, marring an otherwise impressive season. After mostly winning seasons in the first half of the 1960s, the Boston Patriots struggled the rest of the decade, while playing in three other "home" stadiums: the Red Sox' Fenway Park, Boston College's Alumni Stadium, and Harvard Stadium, owned by the Ivy League school. The homelessness of the Boston Patriots was contributing to their financial instability.

After the AFL-NFL merger in 1970, the reconstituted league required all twenty-six teams to play in a home stadium with a minimum capacity of 55,000. While cities throughout the nation increasingly provided new buildings for their teams, Boston and Providence declined to do so for the Patriots. Instead, relocation offers flew in from Birmingham, Montreal, Seattle, Tampa, and Toronto. Once again pro football in Beantown seemed doomed. Before the 1971 season, however, Billy Sullivan finally landed a new stadium in Foxborough, a town between Boston and Providence, paying only $7.1 million for a 61,114-seat building. In one of the first such instances, Sullivan sold the stadium's naming rights to the Schaefer Brewing Company for $150,000, spawning its designation for the next dozen years: Schaefer Stadium.

During the off-season the Boston Patriots tweaked their name to become the New England Patriots, officially expanding their representation to the nation's Northeastern corner. In Schaefer Stadium's preseason opener more than 60,000 spectators watched the New England Patriots defeat the New York Giants, but the August 15 contest also revealed significant flaws in the new building. Schaefer Stadium's 800 toilets stopped flushing, drains overflowed, and drinking fountains were inoperable. Those issues were addressed in time for the regular season, but with its messy field and mostly aluminum benches lacking back support, Schaefer Stadium had instantly became the league's worst building.

From 1970 to 1972 the "Patsies," as they were dubbed by disgruntled followers, won a total of just eleven games. By making the postseason in 1976, New England ended a twelve-year drought that stretched back to its infamous AFL title drubbing. This time, in its second playoff berth, the Patriots lost by a closer margin, 24–21, to Al Davis's Oakland Raiders, who would go on to win the Super Bowl.

Boston's sports script flipped in 1978, when the Red Sox suffered the worst collapse in their history, relinquishing a 14-game lead to the Yankees in the AL East; that year Chuck Fairbanks's Patriots won the franchise's first division title in fifteen years. However, distracted by news that Fairbanks had secretly agreed to join the University of Colorado, New England lost its first-ever playoff game at home, 31–14, versus the Houston Oilers. Fairbanks's offensive coordinator, Ron Erhardt, took over the team in 1979, leading it to nine victories but missing the playoffs, one season before hiring Bill Parcells.

Meanwhile, some spectators at Schaefer Stadium were taking the building's name a bit too seriously, earning a reputation for drunkenness and disorderly conduct. On Monday, September 29, 1980, Parcells's fourth NFL game, the Patriots faced the Denver Broncos. Although New England won, 23–14, police arrested about a hundred spectators for hooliganism and other such crimes, prompting *Monday Night Football* to indefinitely ban coverage at the arena.

In 1985 the Patriots captured a wild-card playoff berth under Raymond Berry, the Hall of Fame wideout. New England became the first playoff team to win three straight road games, reaching Super Bowl XX versus Mike Ditka's Bears. But the Patriots' 46–10 loss at the Louisiana Superdome was the worst in Super Bowl history. Three days later, January 29, 1986, the *Boston Globe* published a bombshell revealing that the team was riddled with cocaine and marijuana abusers; the newspaper named six of them. Just as Parcells had done with the Giants in 1984, Berry decided to drug-test his players in a proactive step at odds with the collective bargaining agreement. Despite the scandal, the following season New England went 11-5 to capture the AFC East before losing to Denver in the first round. The Patriots wouldn't reach the playoffs for another eight years.

Although the NFL had grown into a billion-dollar industry by the late 1980s, New England's financial woes were snowballing. A tipping point was the Sullivan family's multimillion-dollar loss from investing in the Jacksons' Victory Tour of 1984, a concert tour that suffered disastrous logistical snafus and cost overruns. Impending bankruptcy forced Billy Sullivan to put his team up for sale. Bidders included real-estate developer Donald Trump; Robert Tisch, the postmaster general; and Robert Kraft, an obscure paper-and-packaging magnate who had once contemplated buying the Red Sox or Celtics.

In October 1988, the Patriots were acquired for $84 million by Victor Kiam, chief of Remington Products, who kept Billy Sullivan on as team president and his son, Pat, as GM. One month later Kiam lost out to Kraft in an attempt to also purchase a controlling stake in what was now called Sullivan Stadium; it had stopped being Schaefer Stadium after the naming rights expired. Kraft, a longtime season-ticket holder who yearned to own the Patriots, acquired a 50 percent stake in the building via a $25 million bankruptcy sale that included the team's lease through 2001. The transaction made Kraft the Patriots' landlord, giving him tremendous leverage in the team's future, especially with regard to any potential sale.

In 1989, the team renamed its home Foxboro Stadium—the "ugh" was left off for the sake of brevity—but failed to escape more ignominy. On September 17, 1989, *Boston Herald* reporter Lisa Olson was allegedly sexually harassed by three players in New England's locker room as she attempted to interview cornerback Maurice Hurst. Victor Kiam responded to the controversy by describing the incident as "a flyspeck in the ocean" and calling Olson a "classic bitch."

Facing a public backlash, including the possibility of a boycott against Remington Products, Kiam apologized in newspaper ads. Nevertheless, Paul Tagliabue, the new NFL commissioner, fined Kiam $50,000 and the three culprits a total of $22,500. The incident stirred a national debate regarding female journalists in the locker room as New England went 5-11. The following season, 1990, the franchise reached its gridiron low, winning only one game under rookie head coach Rod Rust. That disaster led to his replacement, and although the Patriots managed to avoid any more scandals, Dick MacPherson's 8-24 mark over the next two seasons made another coaching change seem inevitable.

Meanwhile, like Billy Sullivan before him, Victor Kiam accumulated enormous debt that necessitated a sale of the franchise. Suitors included Robert Kraft, author Tom Clancy, and Jeffrey Lurie, a Hollywood producer with roots in the Boston area. But in May 1992, Kiam sold the Patriots to the person to whom he owed millions: James Busch Orthwein, an advertising executive based in St. Louis, and the great-grandson of Adolphus Busch, co-founder of Anheuser-Busch.

The ownership change left New England's shrinking fan base disillusioned. Since the late 1980s the NFL had encouraged the Patriots to get with the times by finding a new stadium, giving tacit approval for them to leave town if necessary. Orthwein disclosed his desire to eventually bring a football team to St. Louis, which would fill a void created in 1988 when the Cardinals had left for Phoenix. He broached the possibility of finding a new stadium in the Boston area, or selling the Patriots to land an expansion franchise in St. Louis, the headquarters of his family's Anheuser-Busch company. The twenty-eight-team NFL intended to add two new clubs within a few years. But Patriots followers figured that the most likely scenario involved moving the Patriots to Orthwein's hometown as soon as possible. He'd already chosen a logo and a name for a team there: the St. Louis Stallions.

During the 1992 season, Orthwein acted like an absentee owner as his new team won only two games, while starting four different quarterbacks and playing to sparse home crowds in a decrepit stadium. Although the NFL accepted the possibility of the Patriots moving to St. Louis, it grew alarmed at the deteriorating state of the franchise. And the league office knew exactly who was best qualified to revive a team on life support. In an unusual step that involved Paul Tagliabue, the NFL ascertained Bill Parcells's openness to joining the Patriots, and then strongly recommended him to Orthwein. Contingent on a deal, Parcells even knew where he would live: Norfolk, the Boston suburb he had enjoyed in 1980 as the Patriots' linebackers coach.

Near the end of his team's latest dismal season, Orthwein contacted Parcells for informal conversations. Parcells's pal and TV colleague Will McDonough helped facilitate the connection. After firing Dick MacPherson on January 11, 1993, Orthwein invited Parcells and two other candidates to his winter home in Fort Lauderdale for separate interviews. Parcells's official competition was Mike Ditka, recently dismissed by Chicago, and Buddy Ryan, who had been without a coaching job since being canned by the Eagles following the 1990 season. The meetings, spread out over a weekend, included Orthwein's top two executives on the Patriots: Patrick Forte, the de facto GM and executive vice president of football, and James Hausmann, who ran the team's business side.

Parcells brought a unique tone to his session, grilling the Patriots' triumvirate as thoroughly as it questioned him. Parcells was pleased to hear Orthwein offer more control than the former Giants coach had wielded in New York: ultimate authority in talent evaluation. During the interview Orthwein expressed his desire that the franchise, 9-39 in its prior three seasons, regain relevance within a few years. Parcells responded that merely making the team competitive didn't make the job attractive to him. "But if you're interested in a championship team, I'm your man."

Orthwein loved the cocksure response from the two-time Super Bowl winner. The owner mentioned the likelihood of his selling the Patriots after increasing their value, to pursue an expansion team in St. Louis. Seeing Parcells as an asset in a potential sale and critical to his overarching plan, Orthwein offered him a five-year, $6 million contract with a quirky stipulation. Stepping down before 1998 would cost Parcells more than $1 million beyond relinquishing the remainder of the lucrative deal. The contingency, which could cost Parcells roughly a year's salary, was intended to make it onerous for him to bolt from a new owner.

Parcells requested his own novel provision: marketing rights for non-uniform clothing worn on the Patriots sidelines, home or away. Desperate to hire the legendary coach and bolster the franchise's value, Orthwein agreed. "He didn't know any better," Parcells says. The new head coach would exploit the ancillary income stream by signing a marketing deal with Apex One, an apparel-and-footwear company based in Piscataway, New Jersey. It paid Parcells $200,000 annually for him and his staff to wear clothing, such as winter jackets bearing the team's logo and colors.

Orthwein assured Parcells that he would have final say in personnel, though such power officially remained with upper management. The St. Louis native informed Parcells that he intended to spend most of the season in his hometown. "Carry the ball. You're the boss."

Parcells was suddenly directing a football team that had made the playoffs only six times in thirty-three years. Both its high points, appearances in the 1963 AFL Championship and the 1986 Super Bowl, had ended in blowout losses. The Patriots' headquarters in the bowels of Foxboro Stadium, one of the NFL's smallest arenas, were certainly the league's most dilapidated. Hot water was at a premium as pipes burst, and the locker rooms were cramped and run-down. For Parcells, though, the worst aspect of the franchise involved its roster, full of disgruntled, jaded veterans with little trade value. New players were infected by the team's negative culture, and in public, players often neglected to mention their Patriots affiliation.

Parcells realized that his new team lay near the NFL's equivalent of ground zero. Nonetheless, on January 22, 1993, he awoke in Connecticut pumped up about his first day on the job. A short while later, with Judy in the front passenger seat, Parcells set off on the two-hour drive to downtown Boston for his introduction as the twelfth head coach in Patriots history.

Sensing her husband's exuberance, Judy stared at him. "I haven't seen you this excited in two years."

Excitement likewise engulfed New England. Parcells's press conference at the Westin Copley Place hotel drew a battalion of journalists, including several from New York, plus such luminaries as Massachusetts governor William Weld. Before the Q&A, Weld advocated building a new arena to ensure that the franchise remain in the state indefinitely, noting that Parcells substantially increased the Patriots' value. For the first time in recent memory the team was generating as much attention as the Red Sox. One *Boston Globe* columnist declared the day perhaps the best in Patriots history, as area residents swarmed the ticket window at Foxboro Stadium, propelling season-ticket sales. Knowledgeable fans realized that Parcells's arrival, coinciding with significant changes in player-acquisition rules, marked the dawn of unrestricted free agency. The new era, plus the Patriots' possession of the top overall pick in the 1993 NFL draft, gave the franchise a unique opportunity.

Parcells sat at a podium with Orthwein and his two executive vice presidents, Patrick Forte and James Hausmann. Most of the early questions from reporters involved the Giants, but the new Patriots coach sidestepped questions about why George Young had declined to consider him for Ray Handley's replacement. Instead, Parcells conspicuously praised Wellington and Tim Mara Jr., and Parcells declared that New England would be his final coaching stop. "No doubt. After this, I'm John Wayne."

Orthwein remarked on the likelihood of moving the team unless a new stadium was built in the Boston area. He also introduced a new logo: a stylized head of a minuteman that fans would dub "Flying Elvis," which replaced a uniformed soldier from the American Revolution hiking the ball. Orthwein changed the team's primary colors from red and white to blue and silver. When one reporter asked who had ultimate control of the team's draft decisions, Parcells responded, "I'm going to run everything. I know more about it than anyone else sitting up here." Orthwein agreed, confirming Parcells's unusual clout. Forte would defer to the head coach on personnel decisions after Hausmann made sure that any moves fit within the club's budget.

Parcells wasted no time rearranging the organization's odd football structure. He moved Bobby Grier, New England's incumbent backfield coach, into the personnel department as director of pro scouting; Grier had scouted colleges for the Patriots from 1982 to 1984 before coaching the team's running backs for eight seasons. Then Parcells hired five of his former Giants coaches who had become available after Handley's dismissal: Romeo Crennel (defensive line), Fred Hoaglin (offensive line), Johnny Parker (strength and conditioning), Mike Sweatman (special teams), and Charlie Weis (tight ends).

In a phone conversation exploring the possibility of joining Parcells, Parker asked him, "You really want to do this thing?"

"As bad as I ever did."

Parcells lured his former boss Ray Perkins from Arkansas State as New England's offensive coordinator. Al Groh became defensive coordinator, having held the same position the previous season in Cleveland under Bill Belichick. Even the new secondary coach, Bobby Trott, had ties to Parcells, having been one of his former Air Force assistants. Hoping to re-create the mojo that had captured two Lombardi Trophies, Parcells further targeted some of his ex–Giants players like kicker Matt Bahr and safety Reyna Thompson, a special-teams ace.

Los Angeles Rams coach and friend Chuck Knox soon telephoned Parcells to make sure that one thing had changed. "I know how you are. You're going to plunge into this thing full throttle and kill yourself. You can't do it like you used to." Although Parcells felt that his health issues had been a price worth paying for two Super Bowl titles, he conceded Knox's point. The new Patriots head coach had already made some lifestyle changes since leaving the NFL: no more cigarettes or daily caffeine. Open-heart surgery, and Addonizio's warning about overexertion, had prompted Bill Parcells to pay proper attention to his well-being for the first time in his life.

Bill Parcells plunged into his new job in early February, registering at a motel on the outskirts of Foxborough. He couldn't afford to waste any time, ignoring speculation about the franchise moving to St. Louis as early as 1994. His staff also stayed at the same roadside lodging just off Interstate 95, exploiting the fifteen-minute commute to Patriots headquarters. Parcells awoke daily by 6 a.m., and within fifteen minutes was behind the wheel of his black Cadillac, first stopping at Donut World for his decaffeinated coffee. The short drive on back roads got him to Foxboro Stadium no later than 6:30 a.m., with sunrise still at least a half hour away.

The window view from the head coach's office overlooked the patchy, wintry terrain of Foxboro Stadium. After working for at least fourteen hours, Parcells exited the building and drove into the darkness, reaching the motel, where he ate dinner at the coffee shop. The Jersey native likened that dawn-to-dusk routine, with virtually no glimpse of sunlight, to living in the Lincoln Tunnel. "It was not what you would call a cultural experience."

One typically busy day in late February, Parcells sifted through an overflowing mail bin on his desk, opening a letter from a world-class Frisbee player requesting a tryout. Despite having no football experience beyond Pop Warner, the Patriots wannabe described himself as "sneaky fast." Smiling, Parcells tossed the letter into a trash can, leaving his office to head one flight up for a daily personnel briefing in the war room. He needed more than Frisbee players to lift the franchise from its doldrums.

Charley Armey, New England's director of college scouting, administered the planning hub whose walls contained three poster-sized lists rating draft prospects and NFL free agents, mostly waived players. Every morning Parcells and Armey reviewed the lists before the Patriots head coach decided whether anyone merited a contract offer or tryout. For targeted free agents Parcells gave Armey precise instructions on negotiating strategy. Through the first three weeks of free agency, however, Parcells had signed only one player: center Dean Caliguire, waived twice by Pittsburgh the previous season.

On this morning, Armey told Parcells, "I've got a couple of guys here you might want to consider looking at, Bill."

"I hope so, Charley. You know, there's an old saying that **you judge a trapper by his furs**. So far you've only got one fur." Armey, a front-office holdover who officially reported to Patrick Forte, chuckled, but the high-ranking scout understood the gravity underlying his new boss's remark.

Parcells relished holding sway over his football team, but during free agency the head coach found himself constrained by the owner's frugality. Parcells had wanted to re-sign New England's best player, wideout Irving Fryar, whose contract was about to expire, but James Orthwein declined to exceed the team's budget even to pay market value for top players. So instead of losing Fryar, the first overall selection of the 1984 draft, to free agency, Parcells traded two picks for him. Orthwein also nixed contract extensions to such key veterans as left tackle Bruce Armstrong, tight end Ben Coates, and cornerback Maurice Hurst. That stance threatened to trigger a vicious cycle of losing top talent to teams willing to spend on free agents.

Orthwein's tight budget forced Parcells to sign mostly "hold-the-fort" players, marginally better than those on the previous roster but not the future of a significantly better team. New England would enter the 1993 season with the NFL's second-lowest payroll after the Cleveland Browns, perennial cheapskates. Parcells realized that Orthwein was less interested in a championship team than a competitive one led by a famous coach who improved ticket sales and, ultimately, franchise value. Craving another Super Bowl title, however, Parcells refused to reconsider his goal.

New England faced a monumental and agonizing decision in the 1993 draft, because two outstanding quarterbacks were deemed worthy of being the top overall selection: Drew Bledsoe of Washington State and Rick Mirer of Notre Dame. Parcells publicly left open the possibility of trading down for multiple picks since New England struggled in several areas, including an offensive line that acted like a turnstile, but he intended to base his decision on whatever would improve the franchise soonest. Parcells considered the Patriots' incumbent quarterback Hugh Millen a player who lacked a work ethic, in contrast to backup Scott Zolak. On the last day of spring minicamp, Millen visited Parcells's office to discuss his status. As the player spoke his piece, the head coach thought to himself, "There's no way this guy's going to be my quarterback."

Drew Bledsoe entered the draft following a stellar junior season, earning All-American honors by guiding one of the nation's top offenses. Despite a college career of only twenty-eight games, his passing yards (7,373) ranked second in Washington State history. After graduating from Washington's Walla Walla High, he had been the first true freshman to start at quarterback for the Cougars since 1960. At six-five and 230 pounds, with a powerful arm made more dangerous by his pocket presence, Bledsoe looked like he'd been chosen straight from central casting to portray a star NFL quarterback. Hollywood-handsome, he owned a reputation as the All-American from the laid-back Northwest.

Although Rick Mirer had set Notre Dame's record for total offense yards (6,691), he wasn't as prolific. But Mirer had earned a blue-chip pedigree as an exceptional three-year starter for the storied program. The 49ers, who wouldn't select a player until late in the first round, were so enamored with Mirer that they offered New England their draft slate of seven picks for the first overall position. Bill Walsh, in his second stint at Stanford after retiring from the 49ers, had highly recommended Mirer to San Francisco. Walsh compared the six-three, 210-pounder to another Notre Dame product who had helped him win three Super Bowls: Joe Montana. Given New England's quarterback situation, Bill Parcells declined San Francisco's bountiful proposal, and focused on selecting Mirer or Bledsoe.

Skilled at play-action passing, Mirer showed superior mobility and poise, having experienced more pressure-packed games at Notre Dame. However, few quarterbacks, including those in the pros, matched Bledsoe's arm strength. NFL quarterbacks often struggle to make accurate throws on corner routes, which require pass-catchers to run up the field before turning at a 45-degree angle toward the sideline. The pigskin must travel, say, 40 yards on a clothesline. At predraft workouts Bledsoe wowed scouts by repeatedly unleashing laser-like throws. And with a swashbuckler's presence, he was tough in the pocket.

New England's evaluation of Bledsoe, twenty-one, and Mirer, twenty-three, was so exhaustive that even the two-year age difference was weighed, but the franchise's monumental decision boiled down to the younger prospect's physical gifts. Like other talented quarterbacks, Mirer proved capable of making most throws, but Bledsoe had flaunted the ability to make *all* of them with the strongest arm Parcells had ever seen. New England's coach envisioned the native of Ellensburg, Washington, transforming the team's passing game. Parcells touted Bledsoe to team executive Patrick Forte, who relayed the praise to the quarterback's agent, Leigh Steinberg, during talks about New England's interest. But when Bledsoe flew cross-country to visit the organization, Parcells left the quarterback bewildered by his unflattering remarks.

"You know, most people in the league think that Rick Mirer is better than you are," Parcells said. After the predraft session, Steinberg fumed to the media about Parcells's behavior. "Bill was arrogant, challenging, insulting. I wish I could convey to you the tone of disinterest. It was almost like, 'Why are you here?'"

Parcells responded, "It wasn't my job to impress him. It was his job to impress *me*." But Parcells was impressed enough to remove any drama involving New England's first pick. On the morning of the draft, April 25, Patrick Forte and James Hausmann met Steinberg at the Marriott Marquis in New York to strike a deal. After twelve hours of negotiations, the two Patriots executives and Bledsoe's representative agreed on a six-year contract worth $14.5 million, including a $4.5 million signing bonus.

Mirer went second overall to the Seattle Seahawks. With three selections in the second round, New England picked linebacker Chris Slade (Virginia), offensive tackle Todd Rucci (Penn State), and wideout Vincent Brisby (Northeast Louisiana State). The fourth round brought the Patriots defensive tackle Kevin Johnson (Texas Southern) and defensive back Corwin Brown (Michigan). Kicker Scott Sisson (Georgia Tech) and tight end Rich Griffith (Arizona) came in the fifth round. The next round produced defensive back Lawrence Hatch (Florida). Wideout Troy Brown (Marshall) was plucked in the eighth round to conclude what would prove to be a fabulous draft class.

Drew Bledsoe's predraft visit to Patriots headquarters had given him an early glimpse of Parcells's mind games, stridency, and demanding style. Now the testy head coach refused to use the term that reporters were attaching to Bledsoe, "franchise quarterback," insisting that the former Cougar needed to earn it. Despite Bledsoe's great potential, Parcells bristled at the twenty-one-year-old's being anointed an elite quarterback before he had acquired even the flimsiest body of NFL work. To make matters worse, hyperbole from local pundits was already placing Bledsoe in the same category as Boston's sports icons: Larry Bird, Bobby Orr, Bill Russell, Ted Williams.

The head coach believed that how the quarterback responded to adulation would determine his future. At rookie camp a few weeks after the draft, Parcells warned Bledsoe, "Just remember one thing: I don't want a celebrity quarterback on my team. I hate celebrity quarterbacks. You understand?" He gave Bledsoe his criterion for an ideal quarterback: constantly guiding the offense into the end zone while caring more about winning than individual statistics.

Despite Bledsoe's lucrative contract, Parcells declared the starting job an open competition that included backups Tommy Hodson, Scott Secules, and Scott Zolak. And whenever Parcells felt thirsty during practice, he forced Bledsoe to fetch Gatorade. Phil Simms, entering his final NFL season, predicted that Bledsoe would need skin like an armadillo's to coexist with Parcells, but the same could be said for Bledsoe's teammates, who included thirty new Patriots.

When starting left guard Reggie Redding showed up ten pounds overweight, Parcells released him. Then for six consecutive days, Parcells placed his team on two-a-day drills, for the equivalent of two weeks' worth of practice. "You'd get arrested today if you did that with the new rules," Parcells says, alluding to NFL policies instituted in 2011 that limit practices. Although his grueling schedule went against NFL norms, he felt that New England needed more work than virtually any team in the league. He wanted players who could withstand the physicality of practice, even in sweltering weather, and tolerate hectoring from drill-sergeant coaches. Based on Parcells's experience, some of his athletes wouldn't be able to handle the culture shock, and he wanted to weed them out as swiftly as possible.

He cut linebacker David Howard, the team's second-leading tackler in 1992, for sitting out practice with a toe injury that Parcells deemed minor. Just as players anticipated with relief that a grueling practice was ending, Parcells commanded them to run two 220-yard sprints before finally letting them go.

Despite Bledsoe's awe-inducing arm, Parcells quibbled with the quarterback's throwing motion. He instructed Bledsoe to raise his delivery point a few inches, and gave new wideouts coach Chris Palmer the special assignment of helping the rookie do so. During training camp Palmer and Bledsoe worked together almost daily in the Patriots' fifty-yard bubble facility. As a drill to help Bledsoe hold the ball higher before throws,

Palmer placed several dots of different colors on a net, and the quarterback made sure his right hand was raised above them before unleashing the ball. Bledsoe would stand a few feet from the net before dropping back to pass as Palmer called out the color of the dot that he wanted the rookie to hit. In time Bledsoe altered his throwing motion more to Parcells's liking, but neither the rookie nor the assistant received any kudos from their head coach.

One morning Parcells walked into an office shared by Chris Palmer and Charlie Weis. The head coach tossed a box of Dots, the popular candy, on Palmer's desk. "Here. Maybe you and Bledsoe can share these while he's throwing over the dots." Parcells walked out without saying another word, leaving Palmer feeling mocked despite his efforts. Weis waited for Parcells to walk down the hall before laughing hard.

During his preseason debut Bledsoe showed promise while playing in one half of a 13–7 loss versus the San Diego Chargers. He completed 9 of 21, including a nine-yard touchdown pass to rookie wideout Troy Brown. Bledsoe told reporters that he had expected to perform better, but was generally pleased with his progress. The next day in practice, Bledsoe's first throw went awry. Parcells, who had been scrutinizing the rookie's newspaper quotes, pounced.

"Still happy with your progress, Drew?!"

Drew Bledsoe often showed up five minutes before meetings looking bleary-eyed, a tendency that reinforced Parcells's belief that the twenty-one-year-old was immature, like many young men his age, and oblivious to his enormous responsibilities. In an ideal situation Parcells would have gradually developed Bledsoe behind a veteran, but given New England's dire straits and its rookie quarterback's dazzling talents, Parcells felt compelled to accelerate his learning curve. "I was pretty hard on him. I had to get him ready," Parcells says. "And he wasn't going to get there through osmosis."

Before playing for an easygoing coach in college, Mike Price, Bledsoe had experienced a disciplinarian in high school, Gary Mires, but Mires was nowhere near as implacable and demanding as Parcells. The criticism was worst on Fridays, when the head coach fine-tuned New England's game plan. During simulated action Parcells stood a few feet behind Bledsoe, urging throws while the quarterback scanned the defense. One time Bledsoe stood in shotgun formation, detected an imminent blitz, and smartly called an audible, but it didn't come fast enough for Parcells, who whistled a stop to the action.

"Bledsoe! You don't have time to stand back there and order lobster thermidor for dinner!" Bledsoe, who would never forget the line, recalls, "I couldn't wait until Sunday to get some peace and quiet."

There was a method to the coach's madness. Alluding to the many challenges on game day, Parcells explains, "I'm trying to create a distraction that the players have to deal with." However, the player who had been raised on positive reinforcement and lauded throughout his brilliant high school and college careers chafed at Parcells's relentlessness. Bledsoe often wanted to scream back at his overbearing head coach, but dared not challenge the franchise's leader.

Bledsoe's mother, Barbara, though, had reached the breaking point. She had seen her son berated enough by Parcells, so she visited the head coach's office at Foxboro Stadium to express her concerns. Sitting across from Parcells, Barbara Bledsoe said, "I don't think you should talk to Drew the way you do. It's not going to help him perform better."

Parcells responded politely. "Well, Mrs. Bledsoe, what you need to do is not watch the games, because this isn't high school football. This is professional football, and this young man is getting paid to win games. That's what we're trying to do here."

Parcells acknowledged having a foul mouth made worse by a swift temper, and the combination sometimes left him ashamed of his cruel remarks. He respected Barbara Bledsoe, but felt that an important aspect of his job was applying pressure, often verbally, to her son. "He was in a man's world being asked to do man things," Parcells says. "And my approach was not always what a nurturing mother might give her son."

During their discussion Barbara Bledsoe might as well have been from Venus, and Bill Parcells from Mars. She left the head coach's office without finding common ground, and kept away from practice while publicly criticizing Parcells's approach. But Bledsoe's father, Mac, formerly an offensive coach on Drew's high school team, saw some pluses in Parcells's methods. For one thing, it helped his boy fit in with teammates who resented a rookie earning millions more than they did. So Mac Bledsoe, who years later would author a book called *Parenting with Dignity*, counseled his son to look past the Tuna's biting remarks.

Meanwhile, on the final weekend of August, with training camp nearing an end, Parcells's new home in Foxboro was still under construction. As usual, Judy oversaw the project by herself, but she coaxed her husband into taking a little time to check it out. In their bathroom Judy asked her husband for his thoughts on their new Corian sink tops. Glancing at them, Parcells replied, "If they can block for the quarterback, I like them." As the couple exited the property, Judy asked if he preferred mulch or wood chips for landscaping. Parcells said, "I don't know. If they can run with the ball, I'll take the wood chips."

Their quick visit only confirmed for his wife that after a two-year hiatus, Bill Parcells had fully reverted to his football obsession.

Drew Bledsoe easily won the Patriots starting job with an impressive preseason, completing 60 percent of his passes while throwing five touchdowns and one interception for a 106.0 rating. Once the regular season commenced, though, Parcells's measured outlook on his celebrated rookie proved prescient. As a play-action quarterback Bledsoe struggled, and New England lost 10 of 11 games. Bledsoe showed glimpses of brilliance, but mostly resembled an ordinary rookie. A sprained knee caused him to miss three contests, including the team's sole victory, 23–21, versus the Phoenix Cardinals on October 10.

Bledsoe's low point came at Pittsburgh on December 5, when he threw five interceptions and fumbled four times. Down 17–14 late, he orchestrated a 94-yard drive to Pittsburgh's 1. With a few seconds left, New England needed only 12 inches for a touchdown that would snap its six-game losing streak. On the contest's final play Bledsoe appeared to score on a quarterback sneak, ramming himself against a pile of massive bodies at the goal line. However, the rookie failed to extend his right arm, which held the ball, to ensure that the pigskin broke the plane of the end zone. As time expired game officials ruled that the ball was inches short, and New England fell to 1-12.

Parcells was furious with his quarterback for neglecting to poke the pigskin over the goal line. When Bledsoe returned to the sideline, Parcells yelled, *"Anybody* has enough sense to do that." Parcells knew that he shared the responsibility for not reminding Bledsoe before the play, but with his Patriots record little different from that of his failed predecessor, Parcells used the moment to send a message to his quarterback, whose sense of entitlement seemed to be stifling progress. All of New England's losses during its seven-game skid were close, hard-fought contests except for one, a sign that the team was closer than it seemed to turning the tide.

Parcells told Bledsoe, "You were the fair-haired boy in the NFL going into this year. But next year there will be another fair-haired boy coming out of college. His name is Heath Shuler. And the year after that, there will be another one, and you'll be the guy who's forgotten, unless you wake up and turn yourself around."

Despite the harsh assessment, Parcells's words rang true. With only four games left, Bledsoe had produced seven touchdowns, 13 interceptions, and a completion rate of less than 50 percent. Worst of all, he still hadn't guided his team to a victory. So instead of sulking about Parcells's latest diatribe, Bledsoe took it to heart. For the first time in his football life, the can't-miss quarterback realized that without drastic improvement, he would end up being a bust.

Starting the following day, and throughout the week of practice, Bledsoe showed increased intensity while delivering sharper performances. He also began using Parcells's sniping as motivation. "I realized he was turning up the stress level in practice," Bledsoe says, "just as it would happen in games." In their next contest, the Patriots snapped their skid versus the Cincinnati Bengals, for Bledsoe's first NFL victory in eight starts. New England began to mesh as a team, going on a winning streak that included handing Bill Belichick's Browns a 20–17 loss, and beating the Indianapolis Colts 38–0, as Bledsoe produced a perfect passer rating.

Even during their struggles, the Patriots had been drawing relatively large home crowds for the first time in recent memory, thanks to the optimism generated by the presence of Parcells and Bledsoe. More than 53,000 fans, including businessman Robert Kraft and his two oldest sons, showed up at Foxboro Stadium for their 4-11 team's finale against the 9-6 Dolphins, who needed a victory to make the playoffs. Continuing their improved play, the Patriots led 10–7 at halftime. In a dramatic, high-scoring fourth quarter, the lead changed five times before the period ended tied at 27. In overtime, Bledsoe absorbed a blitzer's wallop while tossing a 36-yard pass to wideout Michael Timpson, delivering New England a riveting 33–27 victory. The touchdown, Bledsoe's 27th completion on 43 throws, was his fourth of the game. More important, the rookie quarterback had guided the suddenly sizzling Patriots to their longest winning streak since 1988.

During his postgame Q&A, Parcells offered rare praise. "How do you like that quarterback? Isn't he something?"

Although Rick Mirer captured the AFC's Offensive Rookie of the Year award, Bledsoe's late-season flourish confirmed New England's draft choice. Bledsoe finished the season with 15 touchdowns and 15 interceptions, completing 50 percent on 2,494 passing yards. Interceptions were not uncommon for a rookie, but only a handful of NFL rookie quarterbacks had ever passed for more yards.

Many in the sellout crowd for the team's last game, though, believed that the franchise's departure was imminent, which made the victory bittersweet. James Orthwein was still CEO of the St. Louis NFL Partnership, created to deliver a franchise to his hometown. After Bledsoe's game winner, spectators chanted, "Don't take our team! Don't take our team!

Don't take our team!" But Foxboro Stadium's dearth of premium seating, increasingly a major source of revenue for NFL clubs, made the building anachronistic. Only a fraction of the seats had chair backs, and the predominant aluminum benches often froze during the winter.

Unsurprisingly, the Patriots generated the least money of any NFL club. Paul Tagliabue deemed the stadium "unacceptable" for the long-term future of the Patriots, signaling he would approve their relocation barring a new or upgraded arena. However, moving the Patriots required their owner to void a lease controlled by Robert Kraft through his stake in Foxboro Stadium. Only a buyout could prevent the team from being legally tethered to the building until 2002, still eight years away. In January 1994, Orthwein offered Kraft $75 million for control of Foxboro Stadium, and the ability to break free immediately, but Kraft declined the proposal. Instead, he countered with his own offer: $172 million for the team itself. This was a stunning sum, given that the Patriots were among the NFL's least valuable teams. It was $32 million more than the previous record paid by Jerry Jones for the Cowboys in 1989.

The proposal proved irresistible to Orthwein. He accepted Kraft's offer, which preempted interest from an investor group that included Paul Newman and Walter Payton. Robert Kraft became New England's fourth owner in six years.

On February 26, his first official day in charge, Kraft announced that the franchise would remain in New England indefinitely, and in Foxboro Stadium for the time being. Despite a snowstorm, fans purchased 5,958 season tickets, even more than on Parcells's arrival, setting the team's single-day record. Patriots supporters were looking beyond their team's league-worst mark over the previous four seasons, guaranteeing that every home game in the upcoming season would be sold out for the first time in the franchise's thirty-four-year history.

Kraft, a Giants fan growing up, had graduated from Massachusetts's Brookline High in 1959, one year before the creation of the AFL and the Patriots. On February 2, 1962, during his school break as a junior at Columbia University, Kraft met a Brandeis University sophomore, Myra, who happened to be the daughter of Jacob Hiatt, a leading industrialist and philanthropist in Worcester, Massachusetts. Their first date ended with a marriage proposal—from Myra Hiatt. Robert Kraft accepted, and the couple married in June 1963, during the same week that he graduated from Columbia. Kraft enrolled at Harvard Business School, completing his studies in 1965. Following a brief stint on Wall Street he joined Rand-Whitney, a paper products company in Worcester owned by Jacob Hiatt.

Kraft showed considerable investment acumen, and in 1968 the owner's son-in-law acquired 50 percent of the company in a leveraged buyout before asserting control of it.

After the Patriots landed a home stadium in 1971, Kraft purchased season tickets for his wife and four boys. His eldest child, Jonathan, was seven years old at the unveiling of Schaefer Stadium. For the next several seasons, the Krafts sat in section 217, row 23, end-zone seats 1 through 6, watching the "Patsies" sputter. The best aspect of attendance for Kraft was family time, but the Newton resident fantasized about owning the franchise and overseeing a winner.

He accumulated the requisite wealth over the next several years, dramatically expanding the size of his private company by acquiring related businesses. The chief of the nation's largest paper company emerged as one of Massachusetts's richest men. By the late 1980s Kraft had earned a reputation for civic philanthropy while occasionally getting embroiled in lawsuits involving his business dealings. In acquiring the Patriots, and preventing them from bolting to St. Louis, Kraft further elevated his stature throughout the Boston area, turning him into a savior.

Robert Kraft focused on learning the business of football while running the Patriots in a fashion similar to his paper-and-packaging empire. He saw the head coach as a company leader who would regularly report to the chief executive officer, particularly on important developments. With his eldest son, Jonathan, as his lieutenant, Robert Kraft placed an emphasis on marketing the team and upgrading Foxboro Stadium in order to generate more revenue. Beyond the stability created by Kraft's commitment, Parcells appreciated the family's willingness to spend money on players. That approach, contrasting with Orthwein's, helped improve New England's roster via free agency in 1994. And Parcells was heartened that Robert Kraft intended to allocate more money to the team's payroll with a cash infusion in 1995.

Parcells's new players included more ex-Giants: linebacker Steve DeOssie, safety Myron Guyton, and guard Bob Kratch. He also hired his ex-fullback Maurice Carthon to oversee New England's running backs. The Big Blue influx prompted playful references to the "New England Giants." Like any other Patriots fan, Robert Kraft revered the team's legendary head coach. Early in his ownership Kraft maintained Parcells's autonomy while making administrative moves that included the departure of several business employees. Nonetheless, Parcells detected some red flags. After paying the most money in sports history for a team, Kraft showed little interest in giving carte blanche to a head coach. Instead, the owner's actions signaled his plan to become proactive in football decisions, specifically personnel matters. And Parcells noticed front-office holdovers angling to influence Kraft by praising all of his ideas.

"When a new owner comes in, people in the organization have their own agendas," Parcells says. "There were lots of voices in Kraft's ear. The year before, I was basically making the decisions because the other people weren't capable of making them. And that's the truth.

"The general manager [Patrick Forte] had no real football experience. I don't know how he ever got there. The personnel director [Bobby Grier] had some experience, but he wasn't down the road far enough. And his experience was just in one area. It was pretty chaotic."

Parcells was also disturbed by Kraft's getting personally attached to Drew Bledsoe. The head coach believed that the owner's behavior would erode the organization's chain of command, while giving the quarterback a sense of entitlement. "That was a major mistake," Parcells says, "to show preferential treatment. The problem was not knowing any better, and thinking, 'Well, this is my franchise.'"

Eighteen players from the previous season were no longer on the roster. With Marion Butts, a former seventh-round pick acquired from San Diego, as the starting tailback, New England lacked a stout running game. And in the absence of the big, strong athletes who had populated Parcells's Giants, defense remained a liability. An advocate of power football to control the clock, limit turnovers, and keep his defense fresh, Parcells found himself on unfamiliar terrain. New England's roster was bolstered by a gifted, strong-armed quarterback who had made strides late in his rookie season. So Parcells repressed his run-heavy proclivity in order to increase his team's chances of winning.

Going into the 1994 season he decided to unleash Drew Bledsoe by installing an offense that emphasized passing. Parcells foresaw an increased role for tight end Ben Coates, who had led New England the previous season in receptions with 53 for 629 yards, while scoring eight touchdowns. Parcells's decision, made decades before the NFL turned into a pass-oriented league, contradicted his image, but it also affirmed his reputation, dating to his college-coaching years, for putting his players in the best situation to succeed. "There's a fine line in this business," Parcells says. "You never have everything you want. And your system doesn't always fit what you have perfectly. So you have to adjust."

Explaining his disinterest in being remembered for X's and O's, Parcells adds, "There's not one single person on earth that knows the circumstances of my teams—players, situations, competition—like me. I did what I thought was best with the players I had *that* year. I have a high regard for people that ran completely different systems: Joe Gibbs, Bill Walsh. I tried to use the people I had in a system that would allow their talents to flourish.

"The sign of a good coach is one who will fit the scheme to the personnel available, at least temporarily, until he can begin to integrate people more in line with his philosophy. What are you going to do? Say, 'Okay, none of these guys are any good for what I want'? Well, who's going to play? You have to play them. They're under contract. You can't build a driveway if you don't have any cement."

Drew Bledsoe instantly flourished, guiding a wide-open offense that produced 35 points in each of New England's first two games. Nonetheless, feeble defensive efforts in those contests against Miami and Buffalo led to narrow losses. The unit improved in its next three games, taking advantage of Bledsoe's explosive freewheeling to spur a winning streak. Maintaining the gaudy offensive numbers, though, proved to be impossible, as New England looked sluggish while losing four straight, in mostly close outcomes that dropped its record to 3-6.

Around this time Kraft seemed to grasp the significance of the lucrative sideline rights Parcells had negotiated with Orthwein. Parcells's shrewdness in negotiating the unprecedented deal was substantially costing the new owner ancillary revenue. The first hint of Kraft's concerns came when he groused to Parcells about the franchise's enormous debt. Every few days, Kraft made similar remarks about bleeding money. "He gave me this sorry stuff," Parcells recalls. "He was driving me nuts with it."

Parcells mentioned Kraft's behavior to his agent, Robert Fraley. Aware of the value of the marketing rights, Fraley urged Parcells to hold on to them tightly unless the owner made a strong offer. Just in case, the head coach and his agent came up with an acceptable figure.

Finally, one day Kraft asked, "Well, what do you want for the sideline rights?"

Parcells responded, "I'll sell 'em to you for $900,000."

"Okay, let's do it."

Parcells agreed to relinquish his marketing rights in exchange for three equal annual payments totaling $900,000: Kraft's first disbursement, $300,000, was scheduled for September 16, 1995. The next payment was due exactly one year later; and the final remittance, $300,000, would be made on September 16, 1997. In obtaining the marketing rights from Parcells, Kraft planned to sign a more lucrative deal with Starter, a sportswear company based in New Haven, Connecticut, that had license agreements with several NFL teams.

New England's aspirations to snap a seven-year postseason drought were on the line when the Minnesota Vikings visited Foxboro Stadium on a chilly afternoon, November 13, 1994. Quarterbacked by Warren Moon, who was enjoying his latest prolific season, Minnesota sported the NFL's top record at 7-2. Its ferocious pass rush was knocking out quarterbacks so frequently that it was being compared to the Big Blue Wrecking Crew.

In the first half Minnesota scored 20 straight points while rendering New England's offense anemic. Parcells was as incensed by his team's lack of urgency as he was by its 20–3 halftime deficit. In the locker room during the intermission, the Patriots seemed shell-shocked. Parcells viewed fiery halftime speeches as being most effective with a self-assured team, and gave them sparingly. In this case, he knew that berating his players, many of whom were inured to losing, would be counterproductive. Feeling some responsibility for New England's lethargy in the crucial game, Parcells gathered his players into a semicircle.

In a calm voice he focused on the top two veterans: left tackle Bruce Armstrong and linebacker Vincent Brown. "You've been here for seven years, Brown. How long are you going to take this? You've been here for eight years, Armstrong. You going to take it for ten? If so, don't call yourselves professional football players. You're just some guys out there passing the time and getting paid." Looking over the rest of the group, Parcells added, "What's it going to take for you guys to wake up? How long are you going to let every team in this league push you around before you fight back?"

Parcells concluded the appeal to his team's pride with a strategic change. He instructed Drew Bledsoe to employ a no-huddle offense, generally used by teams down late in the final period. The conservative coach had never tried a hurry-up system in the third quarter, but with New England's season on the brink and its offense having produced only one first down, the times called for desperate measures.

At the helm of an accelerated offense, Bledsoe returned to early-season form. His rapid-fire pinpoint passing left Minnesota's defense exhausted, and a step slower on each snap. With 14 seconds remaining in regulation time, Matt Bahr's 23-yard field goal tied the score at 20. After New England received the overtime kickoff, Bledsoe completed six consecutive passes, capped by a 14-yard rainbow to fullback Kevin Turner in the left corner of the end zone. Bledsoe started to raise his arms to signal a touchdown for a remarkable 26–20 triumph, but his teammates mobbed him before he could finish the gesture.

The second-year quarterback set NFL records for completions (45) and pass attempts (70) as New England's tailbacks carried the ball only 10 times. He accumulated 426 passing yards, throwing three touchdowns and zero interceptions. Despite throwing so much against a team with a punishing pass rush, Bledsoe had avoided being sacked.

The victory marked a turning point for the franchise. Reinvigorated, New England parlayed the comeback into a six-game streak to keep its slim postseason hopes alive with one contest left: Christmas Eve on the road versus the 9-6 Chicago Bears, who were also striving for a playoff berth.

Even as Bledsoe developed into a legitimate star during New England's dash to 9-6, Parcells remained unappeasable. When the quarterback over-threw a receiver at one practice, Parcells screamed, "Drew, who the hell are you throwing it to? Kareem Abdul-Jabbar?" Bledsoe could never get used to such remarks, deeming them unnecessary. But winning helped make the zingers more tolerable. So despite what Bledsoe considered to be a tense relationship, the two men adulated by Patriots Nation for reviving the franchise were able to get along.

With the playoffs at stake, Parcells's team visited Soldier Field for its regular-season finale. During a defensive struggle the Patriots led, 6–3, late in the final period, when Bledsoe's three-yard touchdown pass to tail-back Leroy Thompson cemented the outcome. New England's 10-6 mark locked them in a wild-card berth—the franchise's first playoff appearance in nine years. Coinciding with a pro baseball strike, an NHL lockout, and the Celtics' poor play, the Patriots' run captivated the Boston area. Parcells's team was the NFL's most surprising, earning him the Coach of the Year award, and further burnishing his credentials. New England's trans-formation, coming only a couple of years after a two-victory season, gave him one of the most gratifying feelings of his career.

The season seemed surreal in more ways than one. A young quarter-back coached by Bill Parcells threw the most passes in NFL history, 691. Drew Bledsoe had amassed 400 completions, four short of Warren Moon's NFL record for a season, while setting a franchise mark with 4,555 pass-ing yards. And at age twenty-two, Bledsoe became the youngest quarter-back ever named to the Pro Bowl. In another historic individual season, Ben Coates caught 96 passes, the most ever by a tight end, for 1,174 yards. The fifth-round pick out of Livingstone College, a tiny, historically black school in North Carolina, also earned Pro Bowl honors.

Nonetheless, in order to advance in the playoffs, Bill Parcells's Patriots would need all of their firepower and more against the last opponent to beat them: Bill Belichick's Cleveland Browns, who owned the league's top-rated defense.

Bill Belichick grew closer to Bill Parcells after departing for Cleveland in 1991. As fellow head coaches they suddenly had much more in common, making their sideline clashes seem like ancient history. During the NFL season they spoke on the phone at least once a week, renewing a friendship that had been at its best in the early 1980s. The frequency of their discussions spiked midway through the 1993 season when Belichick waived quarterback Bernie Kosar, drawing the ire of Browns fans.

The Youngstown, Ohio, native had become the team's most popular player by helping Cleveland reach the AFC Championship three times in four seasons, while setting passing records including consecutive games without an interception. But as Cleveland's new head coach, Belichick considered Kosar a player with "diminishing skills," prompting a switch to Vinny Testaverde. Over the course of lengthy conversations, Parcells urged Belichick to hold steady despite the move's unpopularity with most Browns fans. Belichick had reciprocated the support when Parcells's Patriots initially floundered during his NFL return. Given their bromance, neither head coach wanted to face the other in the postseason, but the football gods gave them no choice.

Leading up to the game, "Little Bill" publicly credited "Big Bill" for helping to mold him into a head coach. Steve Belichick, acknowledging the irony of the matchup, seconded the notion by pointing out several strategies his son had picked up from Parcells: Bill Belichick placed his players under tremendous duress during practice, and often required them to wear pads. Like Parcells, the secretive head coach was occasionally dismissive toward the media. Belichick brought many of Parcells's sayings to Cleveland. Conversely, Parcells praised his former lieutenant for his substantial contributions to Big Blue's past championship seasons. He noted that New England's defensive schemes, implemented by coordinator Al Groh, included several of Belichick's brainchildren.

Despite Cleveland's losing record during Belichick's first three seasons, in keeping with his reputation he fielded strong defenses, run by Nick Saban. The 1994 unit led the NFL in fewest points allowed, 204, or an average of only 12.8 per game, to set a franchise record. Drew Bledsoe had run into Belichick's miserly defense on November 6 at Cleveland Stadium, where the Browns forced him into four interceptions during their 13–6 victory. Bledsoe's heroics during the rest of the regular season had helped his team reach the postseason for the first time since 1986, but in the rematch on New Year's Day at Cleveland Stadium he struggled again, to the delight of 77,452 spectators. On an unseasonably cool afternoon the Browns picked off Bledsoe three times, exploiting New England's reliance on the pass. Conversely, Vinny Testaverde, with terrific support from his tailbacks, delivered a sharp performance on 20-of-30 passing, including 11 straight completions. Despite a 10–10 tie at intermission, Cleveland dominated the second half, giving Belichick his first playoff victory as a head coach.

"In some respects," Parcells says, "I thought I was playing myself defensively."

When time expired in the 20–13 contest, the conflicting emotions created by the matchup manifested at midfield in a heartfelt Giants reunion: Parcells, wearing a winter cap and jacket designed by Apex One, hugged Browns linebackers Pepper Johnson and Carl Banks. Then Parcells shook hands with Belichick, who placed his left hand on his former boss's nape, leading to an embrace, while Johnson and Banks warmly greeted several of their ex-teammates on Parcells's Patriots.

About an hour later Bill Parcells slung an overnight bag over his right shoulder and walked toward the team bus. Although pleased with his team's progress, he grimaced as he considered its flaws. Even before New England's running deficiencies had contributed to its season-ending loss, Parcells realized that big changes were needed. He had never put much stock in Bledsoe's passing records, which came with a league-high 27 interceptions. And Parcells hated his team's rushing average of 2.8 yards per carry, among the lowest in NFL history. After having tailored New England's scheme to his current personnel—the mark of a good coach—Bill Parcells planned to add players who better fit his own football philosophy.

Rookie minicamp opened at Foxboro Stadium in early May 1995 with an oppressive challenge: the 300-yard shuttle was a conditioning test of will as much as heart and lungs. Parcells instructed his new Patriots to line up at the goal line for a version of the exercise made even more hellacious because they were practicing in pads. The rookies began by sprinting to the 25-yard line, where they made an about-face and accelerated toward the goal line for one shuttle run of 50 yards.

Following a three-minute respite, they repeated the pattern, running it a total of six times. As New England's last lineman lumbered across the goal line, the rookies assumed this would put an end to the late-morning practice session. After a strenuous exercise like this, head coaches typically waited at least several hours before conducting any more physical activity. But as his players panted and trembled, Parcells blew his whistle to signal the start of a ninety-minute practice.

Like his new teammates, Curtis Martin Jr., a third-round pick via Pittsburgh, was startled, but Parcells gave the players no time to commiserate. He oversaw a spirited session that left every running back except Martin sidelined by fatigue, with a few minutes to go before practice ended. His whistle dangling from neck, Parcells pointed to Martin and yelled to the offense, "Keep handing it off to him."

The square-shouldered runner gasped for air as he slumped toward the huddle after yet another run. Parcells shouted, "You ready to quit now?"

Martin, sucking for air and sweating profusely, lifted his head.

"Coach, I will crawl over to take the handoff before I quit."

Parcells's scowl hid his admiration as the rookie took another handoff. Running from a dark, traumatic upbringing, Curtis Martin Jr. had come too far to quit.

In 1972, Curtis Martin Sr. completed a four-year stint in the army. Returning to civilian life, the twenty-two-year-old met Rochella Dixon, twenty-five, in his hometown of McKeesport, Pennsylvania. After a brief romance the couple married and moved together to Pittsburgh, where Curtis Martin Jr. was born May 1, 1973. Martin Sr. maintained a marijuana habit that had begun when he was an eighteen-year-old who capitulated to peer pressure.

A few years into a marriage under financial pressure, Martin Sr. became addicted to cocaine and alcohol. Worse, amid drunken rages and drug-fueled outbursts, Martin Sr. began to abuse his wife. Curtis Martin Jr. watched his father lock his mother in the bathroom, burn strands of her hair with a lighter, and poke her legs with lit cigarettes. One time he threw Rochella down a staircase, and in another episode he punched her in the face. The abuse ended in 1978 only because Curtis Martin Sr. abandoned his small family to focus on feeding his drug habit.

Rochella Dixon was forced to raise their five-year-old alone. Mother and son moved to Homewood, where the sibling industrialists Andrew and Thomas Carnegie once resided during the 1880s. Nearly a century later it was one of Pittsburgh's worst areas, known as "Deadwood." Working two jobs, including full-time employment at AT&T, Dixon often didn't return home until 10 p.m. She was unable to afford a babysitter, so she often left Curtis by himself in their apartment. Frightened and lonely, the five-year-old sat by a window for hours, watching street activity outside his two-story building. Some nights Curtis ate "syrup sandwiches," pouring Aunt Jemima syrup on Wonder Bread.

When Curtis turned seven Rochella tied a shoestring with the house key around his neck. She gave him responsibilities like taking the bus a short distance to pay the electric bill. Rochella's mother, Eleanor Johnson, began to help care for Curtis, and in her daughter's absence Johnson assumed a maternal role. She once wrote "Good luck to you" on a two-dollar bill, and gave it to Curtis. He would never spend the gift.

At age ten, Curtis returned home one day to find his grandmother on the floor, dead, eyes staring blankly up at the ceiling. She had been knifed in the chest during a robbery, her blood spattering the peas she'd been shelling. For the next several months, Curtis and Rochella lived in such fear that when one of them showered, the other stood guard.

During the next half dozen years Rochella hopscotched from one menacing neighborhood to the next, desperate to keep Curtis Martin Jr. from meeting the deadly fate of too many people on Pittsburgh's mean streets. As he grew up, more than a dozen of Curtis's relatives and friends, several of them gang members, were murdered. Curtis acquired a sense of fatalism, and occasionally he came close to becoming part of Pittsburgh's macabre statistics.

At the end of one party a fight spilled into the street, leading to gunplay. In a chaotic scene pedestrians ran in every direction. Curtis sprinted across the street to a parked car, ducking behind it next to someone else.

But his decision backfired. The other person crouching behind the car was a gunman busy unleashing a stream of bullets at the other shooter. Curtis didn't know what to do. Run, and the gunman across the street might think he was the adversary. Stay, and he might get shot. Begging God to keep him alive, Martin decided to flee, dashing all the way home. "I don't think," he recalls, "I had ever run that fast before." Over the next several days, Curtis started having nightmares about being murdered, waking in a cold sweat, shivering in fear.

When Curtis reached the tenth grade, Rochella Dixon moved with him to Point Breeze, another hardscrabble area, though somewhat less deadly than their prior neighborhoods. Curtis registered at Taylor Allderdice, perhaps Pittsburgh's best public high school. Most of his classmates lived in its middle-class neighborhood, Squirrel Hill, which included the city's largest Jewish population. Point Breeze, where Curtis lived, was one of nine neighborhoods in western Pennsylvania that supplied a diverse student body to Allderdice High.

Curtis wasn't into sports like many boys his age. He had given up football after playing Pop Warner through the eighth grade. But his gym teacher, Mark Wittgartner, who doubled as the football coach, noticed the boy's exceptional athleticism. For two years Curtis resisted pleas from Wittgartner to join the football team, the Allderdice Dragons, who played on an all-dirt field. The coach predicted that Curtis would win a college scholarship if he played, but Curtis's first thought was, "Man, I don't want to roll around in dirt."

Violence in Point Breeze didn't abate just because Curtis traveled daily to a pristine campus miles away. Whenever her son headed out of the house to socialize, Rochella feared for his safety. So with Curtis entering his senior year, she implored him to try out for football, knowing that less idle time in the neighborhood would decrease her son's odds of falling victim to violent crime. With his mom and his gym teacher on the same page, Curtis agreed. And during spring football practice, Curtis Martin Jr. showed more natural ability than anyone Wittgartner had ever coached. He possessed an unusual ability to elude pursuers through a combination of speed, jukes, and peripheral vision, gifts that dated to his boyhood spent staying one jump ahead of trouble.

Curtis recalls, "I used to always imagine things in my mind. 'I want this person to chase me, and that person to chase me, and then I am going to set it up so they run into each other.' You know, maybe I used to watch too many cartoons, but those were the kinds of things that were always in my mind."

. . .

On his first carry as a high school player in 1990, Curtis Martin dashed 80 yards for a touchdown. With a diamond-studded ring in his left ear, he ran with toughness that invited hard tackles, but more often defenders got used to seeing the green number 29 on the back of his white jersey. Sporting thick eyebrows, a mustache, and a short beard, Curtis sprinted like a man among boys. In memory of his grandmother Curtis tucked her two-dollar bill in his left sock before each game.

In Curtis's sole high school season he was named Pittsburgh's player of the year, rushing for 1,705 yards and 7.4 yards per carry, while scoring 20 times. Despite offers from college powerhouses like Penn State and Tennessee, in the summer of 1991 Curtis accepted a scholarship from Pittsburgh, coached by Paul Hackett. The runner wanted to make it easier for family and friends to attend his games.

Curtis Martin Jr.'s decision invited comparisons to Tony Dorsett, the greatest running back in Pittsburgh's history. Dorsett had helped transform the school's football program, bringing home a national title during his senior year in 1976 and winning the Heisman Trophy before embarking on an excellent pro career. Heightening the comparisons, Martin's freshman roommate was safety Anthony Dorsett Jr., the ex-superstar's son. But Martin didn't feel any pressure. In a city obsessed with the Steelers, Martin had neither attended a football game nor watched one on TV.

Since gridiron glory had come so easily in high school, Martin turned into a slacker. As an underclassman he paid little attention during team meetings, and often fell asleep. Martin's poor habits and more talented competition in college brought consequences, including a serious foot injury that shelved his first year.

Following the 1992 season, Hackett departed to coach quarterbacks for the Kansas City Chiefs, leading to the return of Johnny Majors, who had guided the program during the 1970s. Injuries dogged Martin, limiting him to four starts. He continued failing to meet expectations until his junior season in 1993, when he matured enough to end his lackadaisical ways. Behind a mediocre offensive line Martin rushed for 1,075 yards, scoring seven touchdowns in 10 games as the team struggled. He missed the final game with a sprained shoulder, and the Panthers finished 3-8.

In Pitt's opener for his senior season, Martin showed even more promise, amassing 251 rushing yards during a 30–28 loss to the Texas Longhorns. However, in the next game versus Ohio, Martin left early with a severe ankle injury that kept him out indefinitely. Late in the season, the runner deemed himself healthy enough to play, but the football program

wouldn't clear Martin, preferring that he maintain college eligibility by redshirting the rest of the year. Pitt's staff at the time included three future NFL head coaches: wide-receivers coach Jon Gruden, linebackers coach Marvin Lewis, and quarterbacks coach Mike McCarthy.

Martin, though, made a surprising decision to enter the 1995 NFL draft. Given his lukewarm feelings for football, the move seemed curious. He drew widespread criticism amid predictions that he would end up at the bottom of the draft. In evaluations sought by NFL teams, Pitt's coaches panned Martin. They noted his lack of football passion, perhaps the most damning indictment of an NFL prospect. The five-eleven, 207-pounder was also described as being brittle and unwilling to perform with pain: he had managed to play in only five quarters his entire junior year.

At Kansas City, Martin's former coach Paul Hackett urged the Chiefs to remove Martin from their draft board. His suggestion meant the team wouldn't consider his former player, even in the final round. But Martin's abilities found a believer in Bobby Grier, New England's lead scout, who gave the runner a high grade as an NFL talent. Parcells, intent on diversifying a pass-oriented offense, dispatched Maurice Carthon, his running-backs coach, to Pittsburgh for more intelligence on Martin. "Find out everything you can about this guy. Stay as long as you have to. When you come back, I want to know if he's our guy or not."

From 1985 to 1991 Carthon had been a bruising fullback for Parcells's Giants, a cog in the manhandling, ball-control offense. His punishing blocks while missing only 1 of 76 games created holes for top runners Ottis Anderson, Rodney Hampton, and Joe Morris. Carthon became the only person to play for Parcells and then join his coaching staff. He shared his boss's hard-nosed demeanor, so Mo Carthon's opinion, especially regarding runners, carried weight.

During a face-to-face meeting with Martin, Carthon was struck by the runner's tearful explanation of his injury-marred years. Carthon recalls, "That let me know football meant something to him." After getting back to Foxborough, Carthon told Parcells, "This is our guy, but you're going to be suspicious. He's too good to be true."

Weeks later, Martin traveled to Patriots headquarters for a predraft session with the team, and Parcells met the twenty-one-year-old for the first time. At a workout Martin showed surprisingly soft hands, catching almost every pass thrown at him. Parcells was just as impressed with Martin's humility and earnestness. Following the session, Parcells whispered to Carthon, "Is this guy for real?"

Martin's injury-prone college career kept most organizations from sharing Parcells's enthusiasm. The Cowboys were among the few, assuring

Martin that they would select him in the second round if he was available. For the 1995 NFL draft, Martin gathered with family and friends to watch his fate on TV. Moments before the forty-sixth pick, which Dallas owned in the second round, the group turned giddy in anticipation. But the Cowboys picked tailback Sherman Williams of Alabama.

New England's first selection, twenty-third overall, had been cornerback Ty Law via Michigan. The Pats chose linebacker Ted Johnson out of Colorado in the second round, fifty-seventh overall. By the third round, eight runners had been drafted while Martin remained without a team. Just before the Patriots made their third-round selection, Parcells telephoned the runner. "Son, would you like to be a New England Patriot?"

Martin replied, "Umm, yes sir, I would."

Parcells halted Martin's free fall, selecting him seventy-fourth overall.

After receiving the first check from a rookie contract worth more than $300,000 annually, Martin hired a housekeeper to provide him with nutritious meals, seeing them as an investment in his profession. He worked at Patriots headquarters eleven hours a day, more than any other player. Martin spent much of that time undergoing a rigorous exercise regimen before taking respites in the cold pool and hot tub. Even on off days for players, he repeated the routine before heading home to relax. "A Spartan warrior," Parcells recalls.

Bill Parcells had coached hundreds of players from disadvantaged backgrounds, young black men who had been raised in the ghetto by single moms and overcame lottery-like odds to live their NFL dreams. Martin was different in one striking regard: he had circumvented Parcells's requirement that a player love football. But the rookie made up for it with an insatiable desire to learn. "He was just like a puppy, lapping it up. 'Just give me what you got. Just tell me what to do,'" Parcells recalls. "And when you know he's taking it to the nth degree, that inspires you as a teacher, as a coach. You figure, 'Hey, I've got to give this guy everything I have because he wants it, and he's going to use it.'

"That's when you really have to exercise your own personal discipline, because he's going to try so hard to please you. If I tell him twenty things the first day, he's going to do all twenty and it's going to be a mess."

So Parcells tutored Martin one subject at time, moving to the next only after the rookie showed progress. Parcells praised Martin's instincts and vision, noting the uncanny, split-second maneuvers that enabled him to avoid tacklers. Nonetheless, Martin needed considerable improvement to become Parcells's ideal runner, one who used power as much as speed, and discipline as much as instinct.

Parcells asked if Martin understood play structure: identifying the hole to run through, and recognizing the duties of blockers in creating it. Parcells warned Martin against committing a move merely because he hadn't spotted a hole. Tailbacks who didn't comprehend a play resorted to scampering. Undisciplined runners deviated after the first sign of trouble, and an early decision allowed tacklers time to minimize yardage. Conversely, a move as late as possible, and at the critical moment, hindered the defense.

Parcells quizzed his rookie about the roles played by an offense's kick-out guy and its puller. "Do you even know who these people are?" The kick-out guy blocked a targeted defender, often the first one beyond the point of attack, by sealing him from the inside and pushing him toward the sideline. That inside-out block created a lane for the ball carrier. The puller, a.k.a. the wraparound guy, sealed the other side of the hole. He wrapped around to obstruct inside pursuit. Depending on the running play, a blocker could be a kick-out guy or a puller. A tight end, for instance, might be assigned to kick out the linebacker.

Although Parcells didn't require a purely north–south runner, he demanded downfield-consciousness. Running laterally or, worse, backward, to avoid oncoming traffic angered Parcells. "You've already passed 'em once," he explains. "Don't bring 'em back into the game." Doing so risked leaving the offense with, say, a second-and-11 situation instead of second-and-7. In a sport that often came down to field position, lost yards had a debilitating effect on the offense. "I always tried to tell Curtis, and all the backs I had, that there are a lot of good two- and three-yard runs," Parcells says. "They might not look good to the people in the stands, but they're good when it comes to helping your team win, because you're making positive yards."

Parcells shared a mantra with his tailbacks: "We're trying to run for first downs, not touchdowns. Let's run for first downs first." For the best chance at first downs, Parcells taught his tailbacks to engage a safety as soon as possible. Generally safeties, as the last line of defense, prowled the middle of the field. So Parcells instructed Martin to attack safeties rather than sprint to a perimeter filled with cornerbacks and linebackers.

Martin improved on his fundamentals enough to be named a starter for New England's preseason opener on August 4, versus Detroit at Foxboro Stadium. The reward was especially gratifying to a rookie with a thin football résumé. In the locker room a few hours before his first NFL game, Martin tucked his grandmother's two-dollar bill in his left sock, and as the 7 p.m. start time neared, his five-eleven frame hummed with nervous energy.

When New England took the opening kickoff on the humid night, Martin began to hyperventilate, and the rookie had no time to calm down. Parcells called a run to start the Patriots' offense, then another and another. The kinetic runner responded with shifty moves, producing a couple of first downs. Parcells continued to avoid pass plays, giving Martin the ball seven consecutive times. During the series Martin's jitters eased, but surprised by the flurry of run calls, Martin felt like he was in the dreaded 300-yard shuttle, made harder by the defense's tackles.

Trotting to the sideline after a change in possession, snot dripping from his nose, the runner had trouble staying upright as he gasped for air. Nonetheless, when he got to the bench, he declined to sit.

Parcells walked over. "You all right, son?"

The rookie responded with his breath rasping in his throat. "Yeah. I'm all right. I gotta go back in now, right?" Martin started wobbling toward the field.

Parcells grabbed him. "No, no." Parcells took a few minutes to explain that a starting runner would never know the frequency of run plays during a drive. "Do you have any idea what kind of stamina you will need to do this job?"

Martin nodded.

Parcells said, "Well, there are 56 minutes left in this game. Do you think you can play any more?"

Martin nodded again.

Although Detroit won 30–17, Martin played enough to finish with a game-high 54 yards, on 13 carries, and a boost to his confidence.

Parcells's overbearing approach occasionally caused a steep drop in a target player's performance, sometimes even precipitating his departure from the club. Linebacker Willie McGinest had witnessed the pattern after Parcells drafted him from USC fourth overall in 1994. "When Curtis got there, they knew he could play," McGinest recalls. "So if Bill knows you can play, he's going to start pushing you. Then one of two things is going to happen. You're either going to perform or hit the tank," meaning quit from the pressure.

During one preseason practice, Parcells seemed obsessed with Martin's flaws. Every rush, regardless of yards gained, was deemed subpar. Parcells punctuated a flurry of expletive-laced taunts by screaming: "You're running with your high heels on." Teammates, cringing at the venom, looked to Martin for at least a meek defense. But, as usual, Martin responded to Parcells's hectoring by saying, "Yes, sir." The ex-runner now explains, "I feel like I've had to do a lot to survive while I was growing up. And if

I'm able to deal with that, I can definitely deal with some man hollering at me."

Former cornerback Ty Law recalls, "Curtis was God-fearing, on his own path. He was a little different from the rest of us. He was saved, and reading his Bible all the time. There was nothing that Parcells could say that was going to rile him."

New Patriots players didn't realize that Parcells's harping often signaled the head coach's awareness of talent in need of honing. Silence toward a player usually signified a lost cause, unworthy of attention. Although Martin didn't yet see the dynamic, he intuited the coach's mind-set. Why else, Martin wondered, would Parcells ignore conventional wisdom to draft him in the third round? Why start him in the preseason opener? Martin understood that Parcells required a sturdy, productive tailback, certainly not a dainty one. So the rookie concluded, "There has to be a positive in all this, even if it sounds negative." He became intent on validating Parcells's unspoken faith.

Curtis Martin's progress earned him the starting job for the regular-season opener at Foxboro Stadium. But as New England's 1995 opener approached, the rookie runner questioned his own ability, reminding himself that the September 3 contest against Belichick's Browns would be his first real NFL game.

Martin had a habit of silently praying in the backfield before each snap. On the Patriots' first play from scrimmage, Martin shut his eyes, asking God for a good showing. He was finishing his prayer when Drew Bledsoe yelled hike. Martin hugged the handoff near the 25-yard line as instincts and training kicked in. He took a couple steps forward, not quite waiting for the last moment before sweeping left behind some blockers. Left tackle Bruce Armstrong and right guard Bob Kratch, a puller on the play, created a path that Martin slipped through. After sprinting left to the 35-yard line, he darted right, escaping a futile leg tackle. Martin continued diagonally across the field, leaving several more defenders behind. The rookie then scampered along the sideline to Cleveland's 43-yard line, where he was finally shoved out of bounds. The 30-yard gain, New England's best running play since late in the 1993 season, cleared away Martin's pregame insecurities and jitters.

Despite more such dazzling jaunts, Cleveland led 14–9 late in the fourth quarter. Bledsoe countered by orchestrating a frenetic drive to Cleveland's 1-yard line with 19 seconds left. The Patriots called timeout to decide on the next play: a run up the middle. Parcells told Martin, "Get over the top, and get in!"

Flashback: a goal-line drill in training camp. Parcells instructs Martin to go over the top, then informs the defense what's coming. Unsurprisingly, Martin is halted on his first attempt. Parcells commands the rookie to repeat the play several times until Martin responds by finding different paths over the top.

Back to the waning moments against Cleveland in the season opener: Martin took the handoff, hugging the ball with both arms. The rookie bulled forward, then leaped over burly bodies as if propelled by a pogo stick. Two defenders jumped up to meet him just short of the goal line, pushing him back into the scrum of linemen, but the cat-quick tailback landed on his feet, just as Parcells had taught him, and kept those legs churning. He sprang forward again, extending his arms—and the ball— into the end zone. Cleveland defenders knocked him down, but the damage had been done.

Touchdown. Patriots 15, Browns 14.

Patriot Nation roared as Foxboro Stadium became a sea of gray-and-blue towels.

The game-winning burst brought Martin's total rushing yards to 102, and a media armada to his locker after the game. Reporters jostled for proximity to the rookie hero who had averaged 5.3 yards rushing in his NFL debut. As Parcells headed through New England's locker room, he glimpsed the commotion a few feet away. Parcells boomed, "I don't know why you're all crowding around him. This is just one game. He's just a one-game wonder. Let's see if his ass can keep this up all season, and then you all can come for that interview. You need to get away from him. One-game wonder!"

In the coming days, Parcells used the description so frequently that teammates and reporters picked up on it. As if confirming Parcells's assessment, Martin struggled during New England's next five games, all losses, as the defense gave up at least 20 points each time. With the Patriots constantly trailing, the offense reverted to its dependence on Bledsoe's arm. Getting a limited number of carries, Martin averaged only 37.2 yards, or 2.4 per rush.

However, on October 23 against Buffalo, Martin gained 127 rushing yards, helping to snap New England's skid, 27–14. With his club at 2-6, Parcells was not about to dispense kudos. "Ah, that's just two games." In other words Martin was now a two-game wonder. But on the Sundays that followed, the high-octane performance became a weekly phenomenon. Over a ten-game stretch Martin averaged 108 yards for 4.3 per carry. Martin recalls, "Each time my goal was to get Parcells to say, 'Two-game wonder,' 'Three-game wonder,' 'Four-game wonder,' and so on."

Late in the season Parcells finally revamped the nickname. The Pats were preparing for an 11-on-11 drill and the offense began to huddle while Martin gulped water on the sideline. Parcells asked aloud, "Where's the Boy Wonder?" The new moniker prompted laughter from teammates. It was one of the few superlatives Parcells could attach to a team unable to overcome its horrid start. Overall the defense sputtered and the offense wasn't much better, as New England fell to 6-10, but Martin ended up with 1,487 rushing yards and 14 touchdowns, earning the award for Offensive Rookie of the Year. Having amassed the fourth-most running yards by a rookie in NFL history, he was named to the Pro Bowl. It was the new nickname, though, that gave Martin his biggest rush.

Because he'd been selected in the third round, Boy Wonder earned significantly less money than most starting runners. So he approached management, through his agent, about upgrading his contract. Parcells rebuffed the request.

"Son, if you do it next year, then we'll get back to the table, but anyone can have one good year."

17

In 1977 paper magnate and Patriots season-ticket holder Robert Kraft had struck up a friendship with *Boston Globe* sportswriter Will McDonough, who covered the team. Over the years the men grew so close that their families got together from time to time. McDonough emceed Kraft's fiftieth birthday party on June 5, 1991. By the time Kraft purchased the Patriots in 1994, he considered McDonough among his best friends.

Parcells had first met McDonough in 1980 as New England's linebackers coach. The two bright, brash Northeasterners took to one another through interview sessions and off-the-record conversations. Like Charles Parcells, McDonough, who grew up in the same South Boston neighborhood as his mobster friend Whitey Bulger, was an Irishman. Although Bill Parcells left for the Giants after only one season, he stayed in touch with McDonough, who was establishing himself as a powerful sports journalist. Their relationship deepened as both men rose to legendary status in their professions. When Parcells was named Patriots head coach in 1993, McDonough, who used his unparalleled connections to dispense NFL scoops on NBC-TV, was already part of his inner circle. Parcells and McDonough even shared an agent in Robert Fraley.

While the Patriots were stumbling in 1995, McDonough detected a chasm deepening between two of his best friends. Parcells resented his authority being diminished as Kraft spent more time hatching football ideas with less qualified front-office employees; the dictatorial head coach, fifty-three, bristled at the new way of doing things. Kraft felt that his top employee showed little respect to an ownership family that catered to him. In the increasingly acrimonious atmosphere, Parcells wanted to cut the remaining two years on his contract to one season; however, bolting before it expired on January 1998 would trigger a $1.3 million penalty.

New England's 1995 playoff hopes were long dead when Parcells's team traveled to Indianapolis for its season finale. On December 22, 1995, the night before the game, Parcells gathered his coaches at the team hotel to share important information pertaining to his future and, by extension, theirs. Within a few days Parcells intended to essentially offer Kraft $300,000 to void his contract's final year of 1997.

At 8-7, Indianapolis needed a victory for a chance at the postseason.

Although New England played hard, the Colts won, 10–7, landing them a wild-card berth. A few days later Parcells approached New England's owner with the proposal. Kraft agreed to it, eliminating the final season of Parcells's contract in exchange for having to pay only half of the remaining $600,000 due for his marketing rights.

On January 12, 1996, Parcells signed an amended employment contract without running it by Robert Fraley, viewing it as a simple buyout of his final season. The bilateral option meant Kraft and Parcells would have to jointly agree on the head coach's return for the 1997 season, which seemed as likely as a peace accord between North Korea and South Korea. However, the contract language, written by the Patriots general counsel, included boilerplate wording that prohibited Parcells from coaching for another team in 1997. The amended marketing agreement also failed to specify a new payout date for the $300,000 that Kraft still owed.

In a staff meeting the next day, Parcells provided the upshot of his situation: 1996 would almost certainly be his final season in New England. The momentous development was kept from the public and media, including Will McDonough, so Patriots players and fans remained oblivious to it.

Parcells considered the $300,000 discount on his marketing rights extra money in the team's coffers, so around mid-January of 1996 he urged the Patriots to put it toward hiring Bill Belichick, who expected to be dismissed by the 5-11 Browns. On November 6, 1995, Art Modell had announced plans to relocate the franchise to Baltimore. Cleveland was 4-5 when the stunning news surfaced, and Belichick received assurances that he would be retained to lead the future Ravens. But by the end of the tumultuous season, his overall record had dropped to 36-44 with one playoff appearance in five seasons. And during a tenure spent frequently sparring with the media, Belichick had generated an image that he was miscast as a head coach. On Valentine's Day, February 14, 1996, Modell dismissed the former defensive coordinator.

Kraft didn't share Parcells's view that the marketing-rights agreement gave the franchise more spending money for, say, coaches. However, the owner approved Parcells's idea of immediately placing Belichick on New England's staff. Since Al Groh served as defensive coordinator, Belichick was named coach of the secondary, but Parcells added the title of assistant head coach, reflecting Belichick's true place in the pecking order. "If you're loyal to Bill, he's loyal to you," says Chris Palmer, Parcells's quarterbacks coach at the time. "And if you're one of his guys, you're one of his guys until you go to the grave. There's good and bad in every situation."

With Parcells likely to depart after the season, Kraft now had a qualified potential replacement on staff. The moves involving Belichick and the marketing rights had reduced the animosity between New England's owner and its head coach, but their partnership remained tenuous enough that any perceived slight would risk derailing it. With Kraft bent on removing Parcells's unofficial powers, bitter feelings were bound to resurface. After the 1994 draft had delivered several duds, notwithstanding a burgeoning star in linebacker Willie McGinest, Kraft considered Parcells's abilities as a talent evaluator to be well below his brilliance as a coach. Kraft also expressed a desire that the GM role be held by someone with a long-term stake in the team, instead of a person who essentially coached year to year. So in February 1995 Kraft elevated pro scout Bobby Grier to director of player personnel, reducing Parcells's draft clout. Kraft made himself the tiebreaker if Grier and Parcells disagreed on a player turned up by the team's multimillion-dollar scouting system, but since Kraft had promoted Grier, the move essentially gave draft authority to Parcells's former employee with only five years on his scouting résumé.

Parcells believes that Kraft's decision stemmed from personal reasons rather than personnel ones. "He didn't want me to be the show. Simple," Parcells says. "A couple of owners told him, 'Some of these coaches get too big for their britches. You've got to put them in their place.' So that's what he was doing. He didn't know that putting the wrong guy in his place screws up your football team. But he learned it."

On draft eve, Friday, April 19, Will McDonough telephoned Robert Kraft in his Boston office to gather information for a *Globe* article about possible Patriots choices with their seventh overall pick. Kraft informed him that Parcells and Grier planned to select a defensive lineman—Tony Brackens of Texas, Duane Clemons of California, or Cedric Jones of Oklahoma. McDonough then telephoned Parcells to corroborate the intel. "That's right, one of those three defensive linemen," Parcells confirmed to McDonough. "That's where we need the help. We stink on defense."

A few other league sources, though, told McDonough that Kraft was targeting wideout Terry Glenn, an All-American at Ohio State. Since the owner hadn't brought up the possibility, McDonough ran it past Parcells. "We're not taking a receiver with that pick," Parcells replied. "We're going to get the defensive lineman first, then get the receiver at the top of the second round. There still will be some good ones left." Parcells wanted Muhsin Muhammad, a six-two, 217-pound wideout coming off a breakout season for Nick Saban's Michigan State Spartans.

On draft day at Foxboro Stadium, Bill Parcells and Bobby Grier sat among several Patriots scouts in a bustling war room while the first six selections took place. The developments left New England in a position to draft the player Bill Parcells coveted, defensive end Tony Brackens, with Muhsin Muhammad likely to be available for New England's follow-up pick. But several minutes before the Patriots' turn, Kraft entered the draft room to ask Parcells and Grier to step into another office for a private discussion. Since every scenario involving the selection had already been discussed, Parcells was flummoxed by the last-minute caucus. Once the threesome gathered, Kraft informed Parcells that the Patriots would be using their top pick on Terry Glenn.

Incredulous, Parcells bristled. "We had agreed it was going to be a defensive player." Taking Glenn would violate Parcells's draft principle against selecting a smallish wideout early in the first round. Glenn stood five-ten and weighed 185 pounds, ostensibly making him more injury-prone than a bigger athlete. But Kraft sided with Grier, who wanted the speedy, shifty wideout in order to give New England's offense a deep threat.

Kraft said firmly, "We're going with Glenn."

Realizing he was in a no-win situation, Parcells replied in a snippy tone, "Okay, if that's the way you want it, you got it."

The angry head coach strode out of the office ahead of Kraft and Grier.

New England announced its selection of Ohio State's Terry Glenn, to the surprise of those in the media who knew Parcells's appetite for a defensive player. Embarrassed by the misinformation in his story, McDonough found Kraft in Foxboro Stadium and buttonholed him in an empty room. McDonough asked Kraft why he had lied to him, to which the owner claimed miscommunication. On the draft's eve, however, Kraft had feared that McDonough would relay the organization's true intentions to Parcells, risking a leak to another team targeting Glenn. Despite McDonough's closeness to Kraft, the owner knew that the *Boston Globe* sportswriter and Parcells shared a brotherly bond.

In the draft's aftermath, the owner contemplated firing his head coach, who himself was considering quitting. Each man blamed the other for his unhappiness. Still, with less than a year left of coexisting, neither acted on his inclination. In late April, ESPN reported on Parcells's shortened contract, increasing speculation about his status beyond 1996.

Until the draft Parcells had been reticent with his coaches on specific issues involving Kraft, but during a staff meeting Parcells told them that Kraft's switcheroo was planned in such a way as to humiliate him. Believing that Kraft and his son Jonathan had taken pleasure in it, Parcells vowed to never forget. The episode also damaged the friendship between

Kraft and McDonough, who would give the owner the silent treatment for the next three months.

At a golf club in 1994, Will McDonough had introduced Parcells to his best friend, Joe O'Donnell, a prominent entrepreneur whose main business involved the sale of food in stadiums. As a cub reporter covering high schools in the 1960s, McDonough had selected O'Donnell for the *Boston Globe*'s All-State team in football and baseball. Entering Harvard College in 1964, O'Donnell was the Ivy League school's top player in those sports, and on graduating he was hired as baseball manager of the Crimson. He earned an MBA at Harvard Business School before taking the leap to become its dean. Stepping down in 1976, O'Donnell started a culinary business that expanded into a major food-service corporation, making him one of Boston's wealthiest men.

He was also one of its best connected. O'Donnell's close friends included Mitt Romney, the CEO of leading private-equity firm Bain Capital, and Wayne Huizenga, the Dolphins billionaire owner whose stadium served the concessionaire's products. Meeting New England's legendary coach through McDonough didn't faze O'Donnell. After playing several holes of golf, the threesome ate lunch. Parcells ordered a salad with grilled chicken, O'Donnell a hot-fudge sundae. Staring at the ice cream, Parcells scolded him. "What the hell is wrong with you? What are you eating that for? That's not good for you. You shouldn't be eating that."

O'Donnell scoffed. "You're not serious, are you? You didn't get to be six hundred pounds by eating salad. You must be a serial closet eater. They shouldn't call you the Tuna; they should call you the Whale."

Despite the rapid-fire zingers, or perhaps because of them, O'Donnell and Parcells hit it off. "From that moment," O'Donnell recalls in his thick Bostonian accent, "we've been friends, because he's my kind of guy." Their relationship, based on frankness, flourished enough for the food mogul to quickly join Parcells's normally closed circle.

A few weeks after the 1996 NFL draft, O'Donnell, Parcells, and McDonough met for golf at Oyster Harbors, a gated community on Cape Cod. Heavy rain postponed play, so they ate lunch at the clubhouse, where talk turned to the Patriots and Kraft. Among his pals, Parcells spoke freely. "I don't want any more to do with this guy, but here's what I'm going to do. I'm going to get in the greatest shape of my life. I've already started to lose weight. And I'm not leaving here with a 6-10 record. I'm going to come back and prove I'm better than that.

"I did a lousy job; I know that. But next season we've got a chance to be pretty good. I'm going to have as little to do with this guy as I can, and focus on coaching the team. Then when it's over, I'm out of here. I'm going to retire. This will be my last year coaching."

The Big Tuna shed twenty-five pounds by the opening of training camp, but the slimmed-down version had lost none of his bite. Terry Glenn pulled a hamstring in the first week of practice, and while New England's top pick missed every preseason game because of the injury, Parcells described it to the media as a mild strain. Then, during his daily Q&A at Foxboro Stadium in late August, one reporter asked for an update on Glenn. Smiling, Parcells responded, **"She's making progress."** Laughter from the all-male reporters filled the interview room.

Such zingers from Parcells were par for the course, especially with rookies, but his power struggle with New England's owner had heightened sensitivity about Glenn's situation. After hearing about the jab, Kraft, prodded by his wife, Myra, scolded Parcells in private before following up with a public rebuke on August 27.

"That's not the standard we want to set; that's not the way we do things," Kraft told reporters. Then, in a veiled allusion to his head coach's future, he added, "There was a player last year who gave the finger to the crowd. He's not here anymore."

Parcells's political incorrectness notwithstanding, Glenn was intent on winning over his coach and erasing any doubts about his toughness. The rookie missed New England's season opener, a 24–10 loss at Miami, before making his NFL debut in the next game at Buffalo. With the Patriots down 10–3 in the third quarter, Glenn dove for a 37-yard touchdown reception. Snagging passes in traffic and over the middle, he finished with six receptions totaling 76 yards in a promising performance. However, the Patriots lost, 17–10, an inauspicious sequel to their season-opening loss.

Soon Parcells's status as Patriots head coach triggered another payment due from the $900,000 originally agreed upon for his marketing rights, before the balance had been reduced by $300,000 in exchange for his 1997 departure. So Parcells telephoned Kraft to inquire about getting the final $300,000 sooner than the September 1997 date on their initial payment schedule. But after apparently doing some contractual gymnastics involving Parcells's future status, Kraft refused to pay the remaining monies at all. He contended that voiding 1997 in Parcells's employment contract essentially negated the remaining amount due.

Outraged by Kraft's logic, Parcells went to the law office of Joe Kozol, a top attorney in Boston. Kozol took a few minutes to scrutinize the contract in Parcells's presence before chortling, "The guy owes you." The next day, Parcells telephoned Paul Tagliabue about the matter, but the NFL commissioner declined to take sides. "This is a dispute between you and the owner."

Parcells protested, "No, it's not, Mr. Commissioner. This is an entity that I owned. You know I owned it because you stamped your approval on the contract. I sold it, and I should be paid the amount we agreed on, regardless of my contract status. That has nothing to do with the product I sold."

Tagliabue replied, "Well, he's arguing differently. I guess you can sue him."

Kozol insisted that he would prevail in court, but Parcells heeded his agent, who advised against a lawsuit. Despite his credentials as one of the NFL's top coaches, Parcells concurred with Fraley that suing a team owner wasn't the best idea. Another consideration was Kraft's willingness to drag out legal cases to the point of diminishing returns for litigants.

Parcells now says about Kraft's refusal to pay the $300,000, "That's part of why I left New England. If he took over those sideline rights from me for a fixed amount of money, shouldn't I anticipate being paid that amount? He's my boss, but that doesn't give him the right not to pay his debts to me."

After joining the Patriots in February, Bill Belichick noticed a striking lack of communication between the organization's owner and its head coach. By the season's start Belichick had formed a rapport with Kraft that Parcells never came close to establishing. "I didn't really get to know Kraft that well," Parcells concedes. "And he didn't know the business when he came in." The owner found the new secondary coach engaging and receptive to his football inquiries. Over the course of each week the two spoke for several hours, with Belichick providing the owner with detailed postmortems about the games. The former Wesleyan economics major illuminated Kraft about mathematical principles pertaining to the salary cap. Conversely, the Ivy League–trained owner impressed Belichick with his business savvy and outside-the-box ideas.

With the onset of free agency, they agreed on the concept of attaching a value to each player to construct a team with depth. During one conversation Belichick proposed precise salaries for every spot on New England's roster. Although Parcells held similar views and had tutored Belichick on them, the head coach felt put off by what he viewed as the novice owner further encroaching on his turf.

"People call you a control freak when you want to do it your way," Parcells says, "but I look at it as just having confidence in your own abilities and not wanting anybody holding you back. If I'm the one who's charged with doing the job, then let me do it. And if I don't do it well, then fire me."

So instead of placating Kraft, or tolerating his missteps, Parcells withdrew, leaving Belichick to play the role of intermediary between his two bosses.

After an 0-2 start, the Patriots triumphed in their home opener, beating the Arizona Cardinals 31–0. New England suddenly found its groove, taking three of its four next games, thanks to an improved defense and a diversified offense made potent by the talents of Boy Wonder and Terry Glenn. New England also consistently benefited from good field position, as Dave Meggett re-created the magic from his Giants years with dazzling returns on punts and kickoffs.

Parcells kept Kraft at arm's length while focusing on his daily duties, pressing his players like a steaming iron on wrinkly shirts. New England's hot streak, however, seemed to thaw the frost between owner and head coach. A few days after an October 27 victory over the Bills improved New England to 5-3, Parcells and Kraft exchanged conciliatory words. They agreed that the media reports generated by their clashes were damaging to the franchise, and Parcells surprised Kraft by expressing a sudden eagerness to return in 1997. Parcells said of their differences, "Okay, let's do something about it right now. We can end all of that stuff with a new contract." Caught off guard by the sharp reversal, Kraft balked. "You really don't know what you want to do. So let's wait until the year is over."

Following the conversation, Kraft telephoned McDonough with his new evidence of Parcells's seesaw personality. "Your boy wants to coach again; he asked me about it today."

McDonough replied, "You're kidding me. He has always told me he's finished when the season is over."

"See how this guy changes? He does it all the time."

After hanging up, McDonough called Parcells to convey his befuddlement. Parcells explained several reasons for the change of heart. He was now at his happiest since joining the franchise, and was excited about its future. Feeling good, partly due to a sustained weight-loss regimen, Parcells relished the idea of molding New England's talented group of athletes. Terry Glenn was bolstering New England's receiving corps much the same way that Curtis Martin had transformed the running department as a rookie. With a stronger supporting cast, Bledsoe was having his best season while acting like more of a leader. The offense, less predictable than in previous years, ranked among the NFL's elite.

Meanwhile New England's defense had turned into a solid unit, with contributions from a slew of stout young players, including two talented rookies: linebacker Tedy Bruschi, a third-round pick via Arizona, and safety Lawyer Milloy, a second-round selection out of Washington. Milloy and free safety Willie Clay, a free-agent acquisition from the Lions, gave New England a stingy secondary. Cornerback Ty Law showed strides in his second season, confirming New England's decision to make him its top pick in 1995. He would end up as the best cornerback in Patriots history. Another second-year player, linebacker Ted Johnson, was also contributing to a talented corps led by Willie McGinest and Chris Slade. On special teams Parcells particularly liked rookie kicker Adam Vinatieri, who had been signed as a free agent following a season with Europe's Amsterdam Admirals, of the World League of American Football.

With the second-youngest roster in the NFL, New England seemed poised to become a powerhouse for several years. The upstart team won seven of nine to clinch the AFC East title at 10-5 with one game left. It would take place at Giants Stadium, Parcells's first contest against Big Blue since leaving New York in 1991. A victory in the rare Saturday affair would give the Patriots a precious first-round bye.

On December 16, five days before the regular-season finale, Fraley telephoned Kraft to schedule an appointment for contract talks, but Kraft reiterated that he wanted to hold off until the season's end. Fraley took the decision as a sign that the Patriots would target a different coach in 1997 instead of budging on the contentious issue of GM powers. His client's interest in returning to the Patriots evaporated after hearing the owner's stance. Once again Parcells decided to lead New England as far as possible before coaching elsewhere the following year. Rumors soon swirled that the Jets, headed for the worst season in NFL history, were awaiting Parcells's availability so that they could name him head coach and GM.

On December 21 Parcells roiled in bed at the team hotel near Giants Stadium. His room clock showed 2:08 a.m., but the coach was too anxious to achieve any more shut-eye. He lay awake for a few hours before getting up and heading to Giants Stadium. Parcells arrived at his old stomping grounds by 8 a.m., long before the 12:30 p.m. kickoff. Ignoring temperatures in the upper teens, Parcells paced the windswept field, warming himself with memories.

As game time approached, spectators cheered when they spotted their ex-coach, but after the opening kickoff, the home crowd of 65,387 roared as Dan Reeves's struggling Giants sprinted to a surprising 22–0 lead. New England failed to score until late in the third quarter, when Adam Vinatieri booted a 40-yard field goal. Terry Glenn had suffered a hip pointer in the period, prompting team trainers to suggest that he sit out the rest of the blowout game and save himself for the postseason. But after insisting on being left in the game, Glenn went on to grab a 26-yard touchdown pass early in the fourth quarter, making the score 22–10. Big Blue's lead still looked secure until Dave Meggett, now New England's Dave Meggett, zigzagged a punt return 60 yards for a touchdown with 11:09 remaining. The score stood at 22–17 with less than two minutes left to play, as New England faced fourth-and-7 at Big Blue's 13. On the next play Ben Coates caught a pinpoint throw near the goal line, then bulled past two defenders for a touchdown, prompting teammates to smother their franchise quarterback and tight end on the ground in giddy celebration.

After the dizzying 23–22 victory, Parcells turned toward the crowd behind New England's bench, raising his fist in the direction of Judy and his daughters. Then the emotionally charged head coach hugged Bledsoe, and even Kraft. Back in the visitors' locker room Parcells addressed his players, and called for Terry Glenn to stand in front of the team. Teary-eyed, Parcells praised the rookie for his gutsy clutch performance. "You showed me today that you're a player!" Glenn swelled with pride at winning over his early doubter. By catching eight passes for 124 yards he had set a single-season rookie record with 90 receptions. The Ohio State product totaled 1,132 receiving yards and scored six touchdowns.

Another star of the game, Dave Meggett, delivered the best season of his career, amassing 1,996 all-purpose yards, including 1,369 on punt and kickoff returns, to earn a Pro Bowl selection along with five teammates: tackle Bruce Armstrong, quarterback Drew Bledsoe, tight end Ben Coates, tailback Curtis Martin, and linebacker Willie McGinest. Bledsoe threw 27 touchdowns and 15 interceptions as the Patriots scored the second-most points in the NFL. The defense, Parcells's main concern during the off-season, had improved dramatically and turned stingy late in the year. Led by McGinest, the unit finished ranked fourteenth among NFL teams, compared to tweny-fifth the previous year.

The Patriots had earned a home playoff game for only the second time in their twenty-six-year NFL history. At 11-5, the longtime bottom feeders also claimed the number two seed among AFC teams. Kraft realized that Parcells's departing would anger Patriots followers, even those who had hailed the owner for preventing the franchise's relocation. Making matters worse, Parcells's desire to coach again meant that, barring reconciliation that would include autonomy, he would likely switch to the Jets. The owner grew concerned about being blamed by fans and the media for driving a coaching great away to a division rival. So Kraft insisted that the adversaries remain publicly civil, regardless of Parcells's fate. While on vacation in

Africa, Myra Kraft purchased Parcells a gift of an ivory elephant figurine, trunk up. New England's lame-duck coach also agreed to play nice.

Two days after Big Blue's collapse versus New England, the Giants fired Dan Reeves, ending his four-year tenure at 31-33 with only one playoff appearance. Before being dismissed, Reeves, the NFL's winningest active coach, complained about the organization's power structure. He believed that the team psychologist, whom Young had hired in 1980 partly to offer players counseling, possessed undue influence, particularly in the draft.

George Young spent the next several days interviewing four candidates: Raiders assistant head coach Joe Bugel, Arizona Cardinals offensive coordinator Jim Fassel, Michigan State head coach Nick Saban, and Eagles defensive coordinator Emmitt Thomas. Young targeted Fassel, whom Parcells had hired as a quarterbacks coach in early 1991 before his abrupt retirement, but Parcells's expected departure from New England caused the Giants to consider offering him the job.

Big Blue had gone 46-51 during their post-Parcells years, with attendance dwindling markedly during Reeves's final season. After having ignored Parcells in 1993, Wellington Mara believed that the franchise, in the doldrums again, needed its former head coach to return. His oldest son, John Mara, the team's chief operating officer, concurred. And with the Jets expected to court Parcells, the Giants were sensitive to the instant public-relations advantage Gang Green would gain at their expense. Hiring a new head coach required agreement between co-owners Wellington Mara and Robert Tisch once George Young had recommended a candidate. But the team psychologist, Joel Goldberg, seemed to be successfully dissuading Tisch from letting the organization pursue Parcells. Unless Tisch changed his mind, the two owners would have to settle on another person.

"There was strong sentiment from some people working there who didn't want me back," Parcells says. "Wellington Mara wasn't one of them. He supported my return. That's what I've heard. But my expectations were never really very high."

Curtis Martin locked in his new nickname during his second year by rushing for 1,152 yards and scoring 14 touchdowns. Although he hadn't been an NFL fan growing up, Boy Wonder was psyched about facing his hometown team, the Pittsburgh Steelers, in the playoffs. But Parcells ignored the angle, reminding the runner that it would be his first postseason contest since high school. Pitt hadn't earned a bowl appearance while Martin was at the program, and every significant game of his pro career had occurred in the regular season.

During practices leading to the AFC divisional affair, the shifty runner couldn't avoid Parcells's barbs. Anytime Martin hit the hole without enough oomph, as determined by Parcells, the coach alluded to his postseason inexperience. One time, after Martin flubbed by missing a hole, Parcells said, "Curtis, you're suffering from BGD."

Martin asked, "What's that?"

"That's **big-game disease**, son. You've got it. You don't know how to act in big games. What did you play in Pitt? The Toilet Bowl? Oh, that's right. You didn't even make it to the Toilet. You didn't play *any* bowl game at Pitt."

Parcells also questioned Martin's breakaway speed by invoking Steelers cornerback Rod Woodson, one of the NFL's fastest players. Boy Wonder's career-long run had been 57 yards in an October 16 loss to the Redskins, but Parcells predicted that Woodson would run down Martin to prevent any such gain. "You'll get a 25-yard run when you should have had 50."

Tight end Keith Byars noticed that Parcells's barrage seemed to uncharacteristically ruffle Martin, so the eleven-year veteran pulled the second-year player aside. "Curtis, man, you're going to carry this team." By the end of the week Byars figured that his assurances had soothed Martin, but in New England's locker room before the 12:30 p.m. kickoff, the quiet runner was acting like a man possessed. Byars recalls, "Curtis has got a look in his eye on game day like I'd never seen before. I'm like, 'I hope Bill didn't overdo it.' I'd seen what Bill was doing all week long, but I could only tell Curtis so much. Curtis has got to figure this out on his own. So now Curtis is at a crossroad: Will he step up and play big in the big game, or will he just be another guy?"

Before the game, Kraft approached Parcells to wish him luck. The head coach responded by telling the owner, "I have something you'll appreciate." Parcells reached into his right pants pocket and pulled out a gold pendant inscribed with the Hebrew word *chai*, meaning "life." Parcells's close friend, a Jewish resident of New Jersey named Bobby Green, had given it to him for luck. Parcells always kept the *chai* in his pocket while on the sidelines, noting that one of the two Hebrew letters resembled an upside-down goalpost.

Kraft smiled in appreciation of Parcells's gesture, but the owner flipped the jewelry around and informed his coach, "You're holding it backward. Remember, Hebrew is read right to left."

Temperatures sat in the low forties when Curtis Martin Jr. emerged from the tunnel for warm-ups and jogged into a thick fog engulfing Foxboro

Stadium. Wearing white gloves with matching elbow pads, Boy Wonder swooped both hands together from his sides in a slow, rhythmic clap. Spectators roared after making him out on the mist-filled gridiron.

From the opening kickoff Martin was easier to spot than any other player, running with typical panache. Wideout Terry Glenn parlayed Bledsoe's screen pass into a 53-yard scamper just short of the goal line. Martin capped the drive with a two-yard gallop that opened the scoring. Later in the period, Byars's 34-yard touchdown on a screen pass put New England up 14–0.

Despite his strong early play in the big game, Martin still yearned to refute Parcells's doubts about his breakaway ability. In the second quarter New England had possession on its 22-yard line when Bledsoe pitched right to Martin, who sliced up the middle. Martin zigged toward the left sideline, where Steelers safety Carnell Lake moved to cut him off. Suddenly Boy Wonder zagged right, causing Lake's left hand to slide off his chest as the defender fell to the ground.

By juking the safety Martin had placed all the Steelers defenders in his rearview mirror, and it was off to the races. Martin shifted to a gear that no one, not even Woodson, was going to match. Crossing the goal line for a 78-yard touchdown, the second-longest run in playoff history, Boy Wonder slowed up and high-stepped toward the end-zone seats. Leading with his right hand, which cradled the pigskin, Martin rammed the wall in front of giddy fans who reached down to touch him.

The cathartic sprint increased New England's lead to 21–0, which stayed that way until halftime. During intermission *New York Daily News* columnist Mike Lupica visited Kraft's private suite looking for insight on the NFL's hottest topic: Bill Parcells's future. Kraft used the moment to extend his coach an olive branch in the next day's paper, but the owner's money quote captured the irreconcilable differences at play. "I want to keep him, but I'm not going to give him final say." As part of Kraft's argument for a democratic approach to personnel decisions, he noted the contributions being made by Terry Glenn.

While the rookie wideout was on his way to another terrific game with 69 receiving yards, the afternoon belonged to Curtis Martin, who never let up. Boy Wonder punctuated his performance with a 23-yard scoring run in the final quarter. He ended up with a franchise-record 166 rushing yards, highlighted by three touchdowns. New England's 28–3 victory was dubbed "Fog Bowl II," after the original one that had taken place at Chicago's Soldier Field on New Year's Eve in 1988, when Mike Ditka's Bears defeated Buddy Ryan's Eagles 20–12 in limited visibility.

Perhaps no one was more pleased with Boy Wonder's clutch performance than his supposed skeptic. Willie McGinest explains, "Parcells took a lot of pride in giving kids like us a shot, kids from the 'hood. And he took pride in seeing us excel. He will never say it, but he's the coach most responsible for that."

Once again, Bill Parcells prepared to face a disciple in the playoffs. Tom Coughlin's Jacksonville Jaguars visited Foxboro Stadium on January 12 to decide a Super Bowl appearance. In just its second year of existence, Jacksonville had overcome a 4-7 start by winning five straight for a wild-card berth that had earned Coughlin Coach of the Year honors. He saw Bill Parcells as the person who had taught him far more about football than anyone else.

Among Parcells's disciples Coughlin was the most similar in demeanor and style. Even the Jaguars head coach's office was meticulous, like his mentor's, with a few personal touches, such as a picture of Coughlin and Parcells locking arms. Seemingly alter egos, the two were strong leaders with gruff demeanors. Coughlin's sense of humor was more likely to show up in one-on-one conversations, while Parcells, when in the mood, could leave a group of people in stitches. At a press conference three days before the AFC Championship, Parcells couldn't resist when asked about Terry Glenn's season. Smiling, Parcells replied, "She's doing good." The packed room burst out into laughter at the coach's stubborn political incorrectness. With Glenn now one of Parcells's favorite Patriots, no controversy ensued.

After spurning the Giants in 1993 to remain at Boston College, Coughlin had joined the Jaguars for their inaugural season. The twenty-eight-team NFL decided to add two clubs for its 1995 edition. Charlotte, North Carolina, and former NFL wideout turned owner Jerry Richardson were awarded an expansion team: the Carolina Panthers. With James Orthwein's support, St. Louis was expected to win the other new franchise, but in a surprising decision, the NFL awarded its thirtieth team to Jacksonville, Florida, and shoe businessman Wayne Weaver. Tom Coughlin landed the head-coaching job, which included GM authority, partly because Weaver was impressed by his intensity. Supported by a strong endorsement from Parcells, Coughlin beat out 49ers offensive coordinator Mike Shanahan and Vikings defensive coordinator Tony Dungy.

With their teams in different divisions, Parcells became Coughlin's football consigliere in a role similar to the one he played when Bill Belichick was at Cleveland. The Patriots boss received weekly phone calls concerning Jaguars matters. Despite giving continuing-education lessons, Parcells also picked up ideas from Coughlin. The regular communication persisted after New England and Jacksonville both made surprising play-off appearances after withstanding early-season struggles.

While rooting for each other the ex-compatriots never mentioned the possibility of meeting in the AFC Championship. The Jaguars were heavy underdogs against Mike Shanahan's Broncos, the AFC's top seed at 13-3. However, Jacksonville shocked Denver, 30–27, on the road, for one of the greatest upsets in playoff history, setting up a championship game between Bill Parcells's Patriots and Tom Coughlin's Jaguars. The two kindred spirits had mixed feelings about one of them ending the other's season in a game with such high stakes.

A different story line creating buzz on the morning of the AFC Championship left Parcells furious. The *Boston Herald* published an article based on anonymous sources that read like a legal threat to Parcells: contractually, Kraft could block him from coaching another team in 1997 unless the owner received satisfactory compensation, specifically draft picks. When Will McDonough arrived in Parcells's office at 9 a.m. to tape an interview for NBC's pregame show, the head coach vented. "Imagine, we're here today playing for a spot in the Super Bowl, and Kraft is planting this garbage in the paper. This is unbelievable. This never stops."

McDonough decided to play the role of mediator between his two close friends, urging Parcells to meet Kraft as soon as possible to defuse the situation before the titanic game's 4 p.m. kickoff. Then McDonough persuaded Kraft to head to the stadium early, arranging to see the owner first. Moments like these were the reason that McDonough sometimes generated criticism for being too close to the principals he covered, but with friends like Paul Tagliabue and Al Davis, plus an unequaled Rolodex, the influential sportswriter was the last of a breed who could occasionally act as kingmakers.

Parcells changed into his coaching clothes before sitting behind his desk, disrupting his pregame ritual to wait for Kraft. Around noon McDonough and Kraft walked into Parcells's office together. The owner denied being the source of the story. Regardless, McDonough reminded his two buddies of their vow to take the high road.

Parcells looked up at Kraft standing next to McDonough and made a proposal. "Bob, this is what I'm going to do. When the season is over, I'm going to say that it's time for me to move on, that I've enjoyed my time here. The fans were great. You treated me well. I wish you the best, and I even give you a plug for a new stadium. The next day, you notify Tagliabue that I am free and clear with no further obligations to the New England Patriots."

Parcells extended his right hand across the desk, anticipating a handshake agreement, but Kraft quickly pulled back. Feeling browbeaten, the owner responded firmly, "We shouldn't even be having this conversation. Our agreement is to talk when the year is over."

Just hours before the AFC Championship, relations between New England's owner and its head coach had reached a boil.

Braving a single-digit windchill temperature, 60,190 spectators filled Foxboro Stadium on a gusty afternoon. Jacksonville was forced to punt on its first possession, but things got worse when a high snap allowed New England to tackle punter Bryan Barker only four yards from the end zone. Boy Wonder soon scored on a one-yard dash, his fifteenth straight home game with a touchdown.

Jacksonville's early gaffe presaged sloppiness from both teams. In the second quarter Drew Bledsoe threw an interception that led to a 32-yard field goal by Jacksonville, making the score 7–3. Midway through the period, the Jaguars suffered another special-teams blunder when punt returner Chris Hudson fumbled the ball in Jacksonville territory. New England recovered it at the 19, setting up a 29-yard field-goal attempt.

Then suddenly the stadium plunged into darkness. After an eleven-minute delay because of a power outage that reinforced the notoriety of perhaps the NFL's worst building, Vinatieri's kick made the score 10–3. Both offenses produced mostly feeble drives as New England added another short field goal for a 10-point lead at halftime.

The third quarter brought more of the same as Bledsoe lost a fumble that the Jaguars parlayed into a 28-yard field goal, cutting the score to 13–6. Pro Bowl quarterback Mark Brunell, who had entered the game as the league leader in passing yards, struggled throughout the afternoon while facing heavy pressure, especially from Willie McGinest. Brunell's best stretch came in the final quarter, setting up a second-and-goal at New England's 5. But with less than four minutes left, Patriots free safety Willie Clay intercepted a pass in the end zone by stepping in front of tight end Derek Brown.

Another failed offensive series by the Patriots gave Jacksonville the ball at its own 42 with 2:36 left. However, Patriots linebacker Chris Slade's hit on tailback James Stewart caused a fumble that cornerback Otis Smith scooped up and returned 47 yards for a touchdown to clinch the outcome: a 20–6 victory.

New England's long-suffering fans went bonkers as the fireworks exploding outside the stadium marked the Patriots' propulsion to Super Bowl XXXI versus Mike Holmgren's Packers. Bill Parcells and Tom Coughlin hugged on the field as New England's players held their helmets in the air, acknowledging the full house that had endured the bone-chilling conditions. Before heading to the locker room, the Patriots gathered around Parcells and Kraft for the championship trophy presentation.

Addressing a media throng, Kraft described the victory as among the best moments of his life. He praised Parcells as "the greatest coach in the history of the game," before quickly amending the hyperbole to "in modern times." Parcells became only the second coach after Don Shula to guide two different teams to the Super Bowl. However, animosity lingered from the Patriots' having thrown down the legal gauntlet in the morning newspaper, compounded by the ill-fated meeting just hours before kickoff. With the franchise only one victory away from NFL nirvana, the unfolding drama involving the owner and head coach threatened to divert much of the attention.

18

When Parcells arrived home in Norfolk, Massachusetts, after the game, his mind raced too rapidly for sleep. Obsessed with facing the powerful Packers at the Louisiana Superdome, Parcells drove back to the stadium, entering his office around 3 a.m. He watched game film for a couple of hours before disrupting the sleep of some friends by telephoning them to chitchat. One of them, Lawrence Taylor, retired since 1994, told Parcells that viewing the AFC Championship on TV had caused knots in his stomach just as if he were still a player. Parcells was touched by Taylor's empathy, knowing the ex-linebacker rarely watched NFL games.

Parcells finished his early-morning conversations by 6 a.m. and began preparing for a 9:30 a.m. address to his players. He wanted them to focus on football instead of the inherent nuttiness of a Super Bowl week, with its ticket requests and family members making the trip to New Orleans. To minimize distractions Parcells planned on urging his players to lean on Kraft and the organization to handle any logistics.

The Patriots had enough to worry about going against Mike Holmgren's Packers, the league's most complete team. MVP Brett Favre quarterbacked the NFL's highest-scoring offense, the only unit ranked ahead of New England's. Green Bay's defense, led by sack-master Reggie White, was also formidable, having allowed the fewest points in the NFL. For much of the 1980s both teams had been considered laughingstocks. Green Bay's tide started to turn in 1992 with the arrival of Holmgren and Favre. One year later New England's fortunes shifted similarly when Parcells joined the Patriots and drafted Bledsoe. For this Super Bowl, though, they were 14-point underdogs.

On January 13, 1997, one day after the AFC Championship, Jim Fassel checked into the Sheraton Meadowlands near Giants Stadium, awaiting word from George Young on whether he was going to be Dan Reeves's replacement. New England's Super Bowl appearance meant that if the Giants wanted to hire Parcells, they needed to delay discussions for at least another two weeks, while his contract situation played out. Co-owners Wellington Mara and Robert Tisch hadn't yet green-lighted Young's recommendation of Fassel, a strong indication that Parcells remained a possibility.

At Giants headquarters George Young discreetly called his lieutenant, Ernie Accorsi, into his office before shutting the door. Young had been planning to retire after one more season, ending an eighteen-year tenure with Big Blue that included being named executive of the year more times than anyone in league history. But the GM had no interest in spending his final season with Parcells, possibly with reduced authority. Young told Accorsi, "Look, I'm going down to Wellington right now to tell him that if they hire Parcells, I quit. I'm sure you'll be my replacement."

The remarks surprised Accorsi, since he knew Parcells and Young shared the same football philosophy. The assistant GM was aware of his boss's beef with Parcells after the 1987 Super Bowl, but Young, who characteristically played things close to the vest, had never ripped Parcells to Accorsi. Instead, the GM had been friendly with Parcells the few times that they had interacted after his Giants departure. Young's plan to present the team's owners with an ultimatum exposed his innermost feelings.

He never got a chance to act on his plan. Soon after the closed-door conversation with Accorsi, John Mara entered the GM's office to inform him that Tisch had nixed the idea of hiring Parcells. Relieved by this turn of events, Young responded, "In that case, Fassel is really the best guy out there. Can I offer him the job?"

Mara's reply was less than enthusiastic. "Okay, go ahead."

Young rushed out of his office to head to the Sheraton Meadowlands, but in a roller coaster of events, five minutes later Robert Tisch telephoned the Maras to reverse his veto. He had decided to be open to signing the legendary taskmaster given that the alternative was someone without any NFL head-coaching experience. "If you want to hire Parcells, go ahead," Tisch said.

Mara called the receptionist at the main lobby to find out if Young had left the building. She acknowledged seeing the rotund GM hustling out the door. Since cell phones weren't yet common, Mara called the Sheraton's front desk in an effort to intercept Young, but the Giants owner had no luck. As a final measure Mara asked to be dialed in to Fassel's room. When the Cardinals coordinator picked up, Mara asked if Young happened to be present. Acknowledging that he was, Fassel handed the phone to the GM.

Mara asked softly, "Have you offered the job to Fassel yet?"

Young replied, "Yes, I have."

"Has he accepted it?"

"Yes."

Mara said nothing. He would not retract an offer extended on ownership's behalf.

. . .

On Sunday, January 19, one week before Super Bowl XXXI, the Patriots flew to New Orleans to check into the city's flagship Marriott. By Monday morning, just ahead of New England's first practice in town, the upcoming game versus Green Bay seemed like almost an afterthought as the *Boston Globe* published an explosive story by Will McDonough under a banner headline declaring "Parcells to Leave." Opening up a Pandora's box for the media to dissect, the article cited the reason for Parcells's imminent departure: his poor relationship with Kraft. Robert Fraley had contended that his client was free to coach another team in 1997 without Kraft's receiving compensation, so the article's tone made it seem as if Parcells was being held hostage. And McDonough broached the possibility of a "nasty" court battle after Parcells's contract expired on February 1.

Suddenly, the strained relationship between New England's owner and head coach was out in the open. The sideshow involving Parcells's future turned into the main event, heightened by coverage from a press corps numbering in the hundreds. Speculation about the Jets being his next team shifted to a sense of a fait accompli, as Fraley was quoted calling Gang Green a "topic for maybe someday in the future." Despite going a league-worst 1-15 under Rich Kotite, whose 4-28 tenure prompted his resignation, the Jets had rebuffed several head-coaching and GM applicants during the playoffs.

Taking exception to McDonough's article, Kraft responded with a statement that castigated Fraley for delving into his client's contract only days before the Super Bowl. Kraft reiterated his original agreement to speak with Parcells after the season, and expressed hope for his 1997 return—without GM authority. Of course Parcells would never stay under those circumstances, which kept the situation inflamed for his scheduled press conference on Monday night.

Parcells spent much of the forty-five-minute session being grilled by journalists and criticizing some of them for their assumptions. Deeming his contract status "old news," Parcells angrily denied the existence of a three-year, $10 million deal reportedly waiting for him to run the Jets. Parcells also rejected the notion that he was behind McDonough's story, but some reporters who felt that Parcells didst protest too much kept up their aggressive queries.

Parcells disagreed that the controversy would affect his preparation for Super Bowl XXXI or pose a distraction to his team. Only a few feet away, though, some top Patriots players were being bombarded with questions about their coach's future. They vouched that Parcells had shielded them from his contract situation all season long, but some of them acknowledged the likelihood of his departure based on McDonough's story. Growing weary of the media barrage, Drew Bledsoe scolded reporters for overlooking the game. Green Bay's players similarly expressed fatigue at being asked about Parcells, and complained that their own coach, Mike Holmgren, wasn't receiving his due as one of the NFL's top strategists.

Following the bombshell article, Parcells pressed his coaches and players as hard as ever. New England's practice at Tulane University consisted of two and a half hours of physical contact, with players in pads in near-eighty-degree temperatures. Conversely, Mike Holmgren's practice at the New Orleans Saints facility lasted only an hour, while his Packers wore shorts. Over the ensuing days, though, the media stayed on the theme of Parcells's imminent departure due to differences with Kraft. Some pundits viewed the head coach as an egomaniac and hypocrite who placed his own status above his team's goals. But another narrative cast Kraft as a dilettante who deserved blame for clashing with a legendary coach. Kraft complained to one friend, "This should be a great week for us, but he's sticking the knife in my back and twisting it."

Kraft's sons, who worked as Patriots executives, despised Parcells, convinced that he was trying to make their father look foolish. The owner's family and inner circle occasionally used a demeaning nickname among themselves when referring to Parcells: "Fatty." But on Tuesday, the primary day for media availability, the two men surprised observers by strolling together across the Superdome's gridiron. Kraft smiled as Parcells related some Giants anecdotes from Super Bowl XXI and XXV. Their interaction seemed to contradict the stories dominating Super Bowl coverage, but those who knew the inner thoughts of both men realized they were being frenemies.

During Parcells's Q&A, reporters focused on his relationship with Kraft, but Parcells responded as if the media coverage was much ado about nothing. "Fellas, whenever we see each other, we talk. It's not like we're from some foreign countries or something. It's funny. I get a kick out of this. It's so ludicrous."

Asked to rate the relationship from 1 to 10, Parcells responded, "It's fine." A reporter suggested a 5, but the Tuna didn't bite. "It's fine."

Meanwhile, a sign, "R. Kraft," in the stands of the Superdome alerted the media to his availability. Most owners whose teams made it to the Super Bowl preferred to remain in the background. One exception was Jerry Jones, the Dallas Cowboys kingpin, whose proactive nature had prompted a bitter divorce from Jimmy Johnson after the head coach won a second consecutive Super Bowl in 1994. At a postgame cocktail party

Jones declared that "five hundred coaches" could have captured those Super Bowls with the roster *he* had assembled. Jones later explained his disparaging comments as "whiskey talking," but the inflammatory episode cemented the enmity that had occasionally flared during their partnership.

The parallels to Kraft and Parcells were striking. At Kraft's press conference, the owner said of Parcells, "I'm saying right on the record I don't dislike him; I like him. He's fun to be with most of the time." Kraft credited Parcells with giving him important insight into the NFL, and pointed out that the two even went out for dinner once. But when asked to predict Parcells's return, Kraft declined. "I would say he is mercurial. Whatever he's feeling at this moment, he might feel something different in a day or two."

With media obsession about their fractured relationship unabated, Kraft and Parcells held a joint press conference on Wednesday. Using humor to deflect the press's focus, the pair announced that Parcells had signed a ten-year contract to manage the Kraft family's paper mill. The owner even praised his head coach's choice of a black V-neck sweater. Parcells responded, "Gee, thanks, Bob. My daughter gave it to me for Christmas."

When a reporter asked if the sweater was cashmere, Kraft interjected with more levity. "I don't think Bill's a cashmere type of guy."

However, only a few minutes after the jovial joint appearance, Kraft hinted at his genuine feelings to a *New York Times* reporter, Gerald Eskenazi, who had finagled a one-on-one interview. Providing some background information, Kraft emphasized that Parcells's contract was ironclad in blocking his ability to join the Jets in 1997 without the Patriots receiving steep compensation such as draft picks. Then, smiling, Kraft whispered an off-the-record remark: "He's not as smart as he thinks." Eskenazi was surprised that Kraft would ridicule Parcells to a sportswriter, particularly one from New York. Although the *Times* reporter didn't use the quote, it provided context for his story.

Two days later and forty-eight hours before the Super Bowl, Kraft faxed Paul Tagliabue a copy of Parcells's contract to prove that New England was entitled to compensation if he coached elsewhere in 1997. Kraft suspected that the Jets had struck a deal in principle with Parcells, violating the league's anti-tampering rules covering employees under contract. Weeks later Patriots executives would exercise their legal right to review itemized activity from team-owned phones. According to the club, Parcells's phone usage leading up to the big game revealed several calls to Hempstead, Long Island, the location of the Jets headquarters. Parcells, though, denies telephoning the Jets before Super Bowl XXXI.

• • •

Game day brought windless temperatures in the low seventies as 72,301 spectators headed to the Louisiana Superdome. Parcells maintained his pregame ritual, arriving at the stadium hours before the 5:30 p.m. kickoff. When the Patriots entered their locker room, they felt a sense of normalcy as Parcells interacted with players in his inimitable way. Moments before the national anthem, Willie McGinest, whom Parcells had drafted fourth overall in 1994, approached him on the sidelines. "I hope you don't go, Coach."

Parcells replied, "Regardless of where I am, you're always going to be my guy." The response deflated McGinest, who had been skeptical about Parcells's exiting after leading New England to the Super Bowl.

McGinest recalls, "I always said it wasn't going to happen because I didn't want him to go. But the relationship between him and ownership was dysfunctional. I don't know if Kraft learned from that, but Belichick has control of football operations [with the Patriots]. That's all Parcells wanted."

On Green Bay's second play from scrimmage, wideout Andre Rison executed a nifty route to break free from cornerback Otis Smith, who was left spinning like a top. Brett Favre slung a deep pass to his wide-open receiver for a 54-yard touchdown less than one minute into the game. The situation worsened for New England only two plays later when Drew Bledsoe tossed an interception. Although the NFL's top offense was held to a 37-yard field goal, the Patriots seemed headed for a blowout loss, down 10–0 early.

Even before the significant deficit, New England had placed the onus on Drew Bledsoe to overcome the NFL's best pass defense. Leading up to the Super Bowl, the Patriots put up a strategic smoke screen by publicly emphasizing the need to run the ball. Green Bay expected Parcells to try controlling the clock with the same approach he had used to win the 1991 Super Bowl versus Buffalo. Instead, Bledsoe's aggressive passing off play action delivered an element of surprise similar to Simms's gunslinging in the 1987 Super Bowl versus Denver.

Despite the bleak outlook in the first quarter, the Patriots stuck to their big gun, and Bledsoe rifled several sharp passes while guiding his team to Green Bay's 1-yard line. On the next play, with Green Bay looking for the run, he zipped a short pass to Keith Byars that cut the lead to 10–7.

The score was unchanged when Bledsoe got the ball back with 4:44 left in the period, as he continued to baffle Green Bay with play-action throws, screen passes, and even rollouts. On third-and-1 Bledsoe faked another handoff before passing to Terry Glenn, who dove to Green Bay's 4-yard line, punctuating a 44-yard reception. The highlight-reel play set up Ben Coates's touchdown on yet another pass, giving New England a surprising 14–10 lead.

The combined points were the most in the first quarter of any Super Bowl. Bledsoe's scintillating stretch since his early interception made New England's offensive game plan look brilliant, and Parcells appeared to have a legitimate chance at becoming the only person in NFL history to win Lombardi Trophies for two different franchises. Days before the game, he had joked to a friend, "The price of tuna has just gone up." Bledsoe ended up throwing fifteen times in the period, three more than the previous Super Bowl record set by Joe Montana in 1990 versus Denver.

Early in the second quarter, though, Favre responded with an explosive play from Green Bay's 21. On first down the Packers employed a three-wideout set, and Antonio Freeman beat strong safety Lawyer Milloy off the line of scrimmage to haul in an 81-yard touchdown pass, the longest reception in Super Bowl history. The Packers reasserted their offensive firepower by also scoring on their next two possessions: a 31-yard field goal and 2-yard run by Favre to lead 27–14 at halftime.

New England entered the intermission with only 14 rushing yards on seven attempts, but Boy Wonder, a touchdown machine during the regular season and playoffs, finally scored late in the third quarter. His 18-yard run cut Green Bay's lead to 27–21, once again making the outcome uncertain as Adam Vinatieri prepared to kick off.

Wideout Desmond Howard was coming off perhaps the greatest season ever by an NFL punt returner, parlaying three into touchdowns before scoring on another one in the playoffs versus San Francisco. Against the Patriots he had set up Green Bay's first two scores with punt returns of 32 and 34 yards. At halftime Howard predicted to teammates that the Patriots would avoid putting the ball in his hands the rest of the way to prevent a touchdown return. So as the pigskin from Vinatieri's kick fearlessly hurtled toward Howard inches from the goal line, he felt indignation that New England wasn't avoiding him.

After catching the ball between the hash marks at the 1, Howard burst up the middle of the gridiron. Abetted by wideout Don Beebe's sharp block near the 30, Howard zoomed to his left, past New England's kick-coverage unit. By the time Howard reached midfield, sprinting across from Parcells on the sideline, pursuers might as well have been moving in slow motion. His 99-yard return, a Super Bowl record, came with 3:30 left in the period. Only seventeen seconds after Martin's touchdown, the Packers had reclaimed their 13-point lead, and momentum. The kick-return touchdown, Howard's first in a five-year pro career, all but ended New England's hopes for an upset victory. A 2-point conversion put the Patriots down by two touchdowns, a seemingly insurmountable deficit against a formidable opponent that had recaptured its mojo.

Realizing that the Patriots lacked a commitment to the run, Green Bay's defense had stopped biting on play-action fakes. And on the Patriots' ensuing possession, Reggie White sacked Drew Bledsoe two consecutive times, further demoralizing New England. For the rest of the game the Patriots never crossed midfield. Neither team scored in the final period, making Parcells's future the only drama left.

With a 35–21 victory, Green Bay captured its first Vince Lombardi Trophy in twenty-nine years. And in an outcome determined by special teams, Desmond Howard finished with 244 return yards, tying a Super Bowl mark while setting a record with 90 punt-return yards. He became the first special-teams player to earn the Super Bowl MVP as New England's special-teams unit was outplayed for perhaps the first time all season.

In New England's gloomy locker room minutes after the loss, Parcells addressed his players briefly while owner Robert Kraft observed from the perimeter.

"You can't win games doing the things that we did. We turned the ball over too much, and had very untimely penalties."

Linebacker Willie McGinest flashed back to his exchange with Parcells just before the national anthem and started to cry.

"I was already emotional because we had just lost," McGinest recalls. "And seeing the guy who drafted me, one of my teachers, getting ready to leave made everything bad. He was like another father because I know he genuinely cared about me.

"I didn't know how the Patriots were going to replace him. Who's going to come in now and fill that void? That's what you're thinking as a player. Who can motivate us, do everything he did? I couldn't think of anybody."

Around the same time that the Patriots boarded their team plane for Boston, Parcells took a return flight with family members and Robert Fraley. Two days later, Paul Tagliabue announced that he would mediate the contract dispute. Since targeting Parcells late in the 1996 season, with Belichick as a backup plan, the Jets were patiently awaiting a resolution before officially contacting him. Owner Leon Hess and team president Steve Gutman remained convinced that the best person to resurrect their dying franchise was the coach who had done the same for the Giants and Patriots.

The NFL commissioner wasted little time making a ruling. On

Wednesday, January 29, he issued a statement to the effect that permitting Parcells to coach elsewhere in 1997 without compensating the Patriots ran "contrary to common sense and Massachusetts law." Parcells's contract explicitly barred him from coaching another team or holding a "comparable position" before 1998 unless New England granted permission. So now the remaining issue was whether the Patriots could reach an agreement on compensation with the Jets, who owned the top overall pick in the 1997 draft. Pointing out Parcells's three Super Bowl appearances in twelve years, Kraft publicly established steep requirements for a deal. "I'm speaking now to the Jets. If you have an interest in Bill, please don't trade the number one pick. That must be part of the solution."

On Thursday the Jets telephoned Kraft, but failed to reach a deal. Regardless, Parcells scheduled a press conference for the following day at Patriots headquarters to announce his departure. When his contract expired on Friday, January 31, 1997, he delivered a letter to Kraft in his office, expressing his desire to discontinue employment. Because only a mutual decision could trigger a 1997 return, the step voided the fifth year of his contract.

As Parcells headed for his press conference, Kraft stopped him and said, "You know we can still work something out for you to stay."

But the head coach politely declined, and kept walking to an auditorium packed with sports journalists. Parcells explains why he passed on Kraft's last-minute olive branch: "I was mentally in a different place. I don't mean with a different team. I mean just a different mental frame of mind."

Dressed in a suit and tie, Parcells held a one-hour Q&A that amounted to his resignation. He described Kraft as being supportive overall since purchasing the team in 1994, but crystallized their incompatibility by quoting an unnamed person. "A friend once told me, **'If you're going to cook the meal, they ought to let you shop for the groceries.'** I guess that best explains our philosophical differences."

Responding in a subsequent press conference, Kraft quipped, "I think our groceries are pretty good. They're fresh."

Despite their differences, Parcells considers his split from the Patriots the biggest regret of his career. He left a young team that had four players who were stars or budding stars at an offense's critical positions: quarterback (Bledsoe), tailback (Martin), wideout (Glenn), and tight end (Coates). Plus in McGinest the Patriots had a top player for perhaps a defense's most importance piece: pass rusher.

"I was reluctant to leave," Parcells says of New England. "We made it to the Super Bowl. I had a really good young team, and we had a lot of good football in front of us. But for the owner and myself it was an untenable situation. I'm not saying I wasn't part of the problem, because I was. But I wasn't solely responsible. There are some things I did that I can look back on and say, 'Hey, if I had to do it again, I would do it differently.' And there are some things he did that I won't forget either, that I don't look at very kindly, that really precipitated the breakup.

"I wish it had worked out differently. I just didn't feel like I had much recourse. I felt like it'd be better if I left, though I didn't feel great about leaving, especially since this was a team I had worked hard to build up, because it was really rock bottom when I got there."

Kraft sensed Belichick's desire to fill Parcells's shoes. The owner was fond of New England's assistant head coach, but Kraft's animosity toward Parcells tainted his view of Belichick as the team's next leader. In a case of guilt by association, Kraft was unwilling to hire the person with the most experience under Parcells, presumably his closest assistant. After wrestling with the decision, Kraft and Myra took Belichick and his spouse, Debby, out to lunch to explain things.

"I had lost the trust with Parcells," Kraft says, "and he and Bill [Belichick] were tied at the hip. They were together for so long. Could I trust him? I decided I couldn't at the time. Everything in life is timing."

Parcells and Belichick got along best when working for separate franchises, but Kraft was oblivious to the dynamic. Also, a perception existed in some NFL front offices that Parcells's lieutenant was an excellent defensive coordinator and a subpar head coach. So Kraft decided on a clean break from his nemesis and targeted George Seifert, who in mid-January had surprisingly resigned as 49ers head coach with two Super Bowl titles.

To obtain Parcells's services immediately, the Jets offered New England two second-round picks. But Kraft declined, insisting on the first overall selection. Tennessee upperclassman Peyton Manning, considered a once-in-a-generation quarterback, was a good possibility to enter the 1997 NFL draft. Kraft also wanted a slew of talented young Jets players, like defensive end Hugh Douglas, cornerback Aaron Glenn, and wideout Keyshawn Johnson. Parcells was strongly opposed to Leon Hess's relinquishing the top overall pick to New England. With free agency's start only a couple of weeks away, negotiations stalled, so the Jets switched to Plan B, as in Belichick, interviewing him for their head-coaching opening.

After being turned down by George Seifert, Kraft hired Seifert's defensive coordinator, Pete Carroll, as the new Patriots head coach. Carroll's only experience at the position had come in 1994 with the Jets, when he finished 6-10 before being dismissed, leading to Rich Kotite's appointment. However, while introducing Carroll to Patriots Nation on February 3, 1997, Kraft described the ex-49ers coach as someone he could "relate to."

Meanwhile, Jets team president Steve Gutman came up with a shrewd idea to circumvent Parcells's contractual impediments, if not pressure Kraft to lower his demands. On February 4 the Jets named Bill Belichick head coach for one season, and Bill Parcells a "consultant" until February 8, 1998. Freed from the Patriots on that date, Parcells would take over as head coach and chief of football operations while Belichick ran the Jets defense with a guarantee of succeeding Parcells in a few years.

Naturally, Kraft attacked Gang Green's contractual end-around, calling it a "transparent farce." His strong objections prompted Tagliabue to step into the latest entanglement and place an embargo on Parcells's services until a resolution could be reached. With key junctures in the off-season fast approaching, Belichick was allowed to exert his authority as a head coach. He immediately hired three of his ex-Browns underlings: Scott Pioli as pro personnel director, Eric Mangini as an entry-level defensive assistant, and a secretary, Linda Leoni. Belichick also contacted yet another of his former Browns employees, Mike Tannenbaum, to discuss a position negotiating player contracts.

Tagliabue ordered a meeting between the Patriots and Jets to be held in Manhattan at Skadden, Arps, a midtown law firm employed by the league. On Monday, February 10, representatives of both teams, including Kraft and Hess, gathered on the building's forty-seventh floor. Hess's presence was especially noteworthy given the eighty-two-year-old's public distance regarding Jets matters. Tagliabue put the two sides in a penthouse conference room to agree on compensation that would allow Parcells to coach in 1997. After more than five hours of discussion, Kraft jotted down New England's final offer on one side of a piece of paper, while Hess put Gang Green's last proposal on the other side. Wide differences remained, resulting in a stalemate, so Kraft and Hess shook hands on allowing Tagliabue to make a binding decision.

The commissioner took only twenty minutes to arrive at his ruling: New England obtained Gang Green's third- and fourth-round choices in April's draft, a second-round pick in 1998, and a first-round selection in 1999. Also, Gang Green was required to pay $300,000 to a Patriots charity. Tagliabue believed that New England deserved significant compensation for relinquishing its rights to perhaps the NFL's top coach, but he wanted to preserve Gang Green's ability to draft players over the next few years. Presuming that Parcells lived up to his reputation, the Jets would be surrendering their most valuable picks when they were an improved team, at a time when New England was likely to be losing key veterans to the salary cap.

The resolution allowed Parcells to sign a six-year, $14.4 million contract, during which he would serve the first four years as head coach.

Giving voice to the euphoria of Jets fans, the *New York Daily News* declared Parcells's hiring the franchise's "greatest triumph since Super Bowl III in 1969." Parcells became the only person in NFL history to guide both the Giants and the Jets. After a six-day stint in the lead role, Belichick, who was named assistant head coach overseeing the defense, quipped about "stepping down with an undefeated record, untied and unscored upon." His unique contract as Parcells's heir apparent paid him the highest salary of any NFL assistant coach, averaging $750,000 annually.

On Tuesday, February 11, 1997, the Jets introduced Bill Parcells at Weeb Ewbank Hall, the team's headquarters on the campus of Hofstra University. Hess made one of his rare appearances at a press conference. His colorful remarks indicated that the franchise would grant Parcells, its fourth head coach in five years, the unfettered authority he had craved in New England. "I just want to be the little boy that goes along with him and pushes the cart in the supermarket and lets him fill it up. He's going to run the show, and it's not going to be two or three cooks in the kitchen. It will be just him."

Born in Asbury Park, New Jersey, in 1914, Leon Hess came from humble beginnings. In 1933, his Lithuanian father, Mores, an ex–kosher butcher who delivered oil around the state, filed for reorganizational bankruptcy. A recent graduate of Asbury Park High, Leon Hess, eighteen, ran the reconstituted company while occasionally digging for clams for extra income. "Everybody was broke in those days," he recalled.

Leon used a small, 615-gallon truck to deliver home-heating oil in town. Despite his youth, Leon developed a reputation for toughness, shrewdness, and frugality. Most oil bids were typewritten submissions. To save on costs, Leon scrawled his company's bids in black ink. Within five years his company was a major bidder on government fuel contracts in the state.

World War II prompted Leon to join the army, where he exploited his background to become George Patton's oil-supply officer in Europe, a critical role in the general's mechanized Third Army. Leon Hess was discharged as a major, and received a Bronze Star before returning to civilian status, where he envisioned turning his business into a major integrated company similar to Shell's. Hess soon began importing oil, and by 1957 his company was handling 38,000 barrels daily. He built three refineries, including one each in Texas and the Virgin Islands. In 1960 the company expanded into retail gasoline sales, starting with twenty-eight stations. Within years he would own more than five hundred stations, spurring a merger with the Amerada Corporation, one of the world's largest producers of crude oil.

Hess became part owner of the Jets in 1964 as part of a four-man group spearheaded by entertainment impresario Sonny Werblin, purchasing the franchise out of receivership. Hess got involved largely as a favor to Werblin, one of his business partners in New Jersey's Monmouth Park Racetrack. One of the original eight AFL teams that included the Patriots, the franchise had been called the New York Titans. Hess's group renamed the team the Jets because it played near LaGuardia Airport at Shea Stadium.

Werblin and Hess held the biggest stakes, at roughly 25 percent each, and Werblin served as Jets president until 1968, when his partners bought his shares for nine times their original value. Don Lillis became team president but died two months later, causing another part-owner, Phil Iselin, to step in. Hess, who had increased his stake to a majority share of 33 percent, was named vice president.

On December 28, 1976, Iselin died of heart failure in his Jets office. Hess bought out Iselin's widow to own half the team, and reluctantly took on the club's presidency in February 1977. During seven years as Jets president, Hess quietly boosted his team shares to 100 percent. At the time *Forbes* estimated Hess's net worth to be at least $320 million, enough for the former clam digger to host the shah of Iran in his Park Avenue apartment during trips to New York. But Hess kept a low profile, retaining a public-relations man to keep his name *out* of newspapers. As a boy, he said, his parents had repeatedly warned him to "let my actions speak for me."

Hess stayed away from the league's annual meetings until 1982, five years after taking control of the Jets. The first time Parcells met Hess was at one of the powwows in the mid-1980s, after an introduction from Giants owner Wellington Mara. The few times that Hess and Parcells had crossed paths at league meetings, they engaged in pleasant chitchat. Parcells admired Hess's league-first ethos, also shared by old-school owners like Wellington Mara, Pittsburgh's Dan Rooney, and Buffalo's Ralph Wilson.

Despite Hess's apparent detachment from overseeing a bumbling franchise, he longed for a winner, and privately held strong convictions about the team. Since Iselin's death Hess had been intent on extricating the Jets from an unpalatable lease at Shea Stadium. Hess detested his team's secondary status to the Mets, for whom the stadium had been built in 1964. Dissatisfied with the city's plans to upgrade it, Hess made Giants Stadium his franchise's new home in 1984.

When Leon Hess stepped down as CEO of Amerada Hess in 1995, he was eighty-one. His worth had reportedly grown to $720 million, but that paled next to his desire to reward long-suffering Jets fans with a championship. After repeatedly turning down exorbitant offers from potential buyers, the octogenarian owner pounced at the first chance to land Bill Parcells.

In 1 BP, or one year Before Parcells, the Jets had more cash over cap than any other NFL team. In other words, the 1996 Jets spent the league's highest amount on personnel, about $70 million in long-term contracts that Hess had green-lighted to improve the club. That splurge had resulted in one victory, so on the day he signed Parcells, Hess expressed fatigue with being embarrassed by Gang Green. He told Parcells, "You know, I'm not gonna be around much longer, so I want you to do everything you can right now."

Parcells replied, "I understand that, Mr. Hess."

During that conversation, Parcells revealed to Hess the first time he had heard of the oil magnate, more than forty years earlier while Duane "Bill" Parcells and his father gazed at seaplanes roaring above the Hackensack River. The Hess oil tanks across the river had spurred the kid to ask about the name. In the press conference announcing his new coach, Leon Hess offered a slice of autobiography that went back even farther. "I was born and brought up in Asbury Park, New Jersey. Bill Parcells is in love with Sea Girt, New Jersey. They're eight miles apart. Seventy years ago, as kids in the summertime, at low tide, we used to have a little shovel and we'd go and dig up clams and sell them.

"The big ones would go for clam chowder at the restaurants. The little ones went to clam bars. We were lucky to make fifty or seventy-five cents a day. Little did I think that seventy years later, eight miles away in Sea Girt, would be a Tuna. It's all the same ocean. Little did I think the Good Lord would favor me and I would marry that Tuna."

19

Driving from Cleveland to Boston in January 1996, Mike Tannenbaum cruised the New York State Thruway on his way to his parents' home. The Tulane Law graduate had just lost his job as a personnel assistant with Bill Belichick's Browns because of the franchise's move to Baltimore. Tannenbaum's mother called his cell phone to check on his progress on the road, and to inform him that Tulane's first student-loan bill had arrived in the mail.

Mike Tannenbaum said to himself sarcastically, "This is great. You're twenty-seven years old. You're moving back home to live with your parents. And you're sixty thousand dollars in debt. Law school was a really good decision, Mike."

That degree, though, was about to start reaping benefits. Not in his next job, an entry-level spot in the Saints personnel department with a salary of $20,000, but in the one after that. In late February of 1997, Bill Parcells, heeding a recommendation from Bill Belichick, called to offer Tannenbaum a position as director of player contract negotiations with an annual salary of $85,000. The move was part of a major restructuring, in which Parcells dismissed ten of Rich Kotite's thirteen assistants and hired a slew of his own disciples. Beyond his coaches, Parcells brought in Carl Banks, his ex–Giants linebacker, as a player adviser in areas such as life skills. Mark Bavaro agreed to become a consultant to tight ends coach Pat Hodgson. And Matt Bahr, hero of the 1990 NFC Championship with five field goals, accepted a part-time role dispensing technique to Gang Green's kickers.

Two front-office members from the previous regime who kept their jobs were personnel director Dick Haley and his son Todd, a scout. Despite Gang Green's struggles over the years, Parcells valued Dick Haley, who was highly regarded around the league. From 1971 to 1990, Haley had served as the Steelers' personnel director, playing a key role in building their 1970s dynasty of four Super Bowls. Pittsburgh's 1974 draft class, among the best in NFL history, included four future Hall of Famers: linebacker Jack Lambert, center Mike Webster, and wideouts John Stallworth and Lynn Swann. In 1991 Dick Haley switched to the Jets, and four years later he helped Todd land an entry-level job in the organization as a scouting assistant.

Todd Haley, a former Steelers ball boy who used to watch game film alongside his dad, wanted to move into the coaching side of the game. When Parcells arrived, Todd made his case for an unfilled position as offensive assistant for quality control, opposite Eric Mangini, who held the defensive post. "Coach, I appreciate you keeping me on as a scout, but I want to coach, and I'll take a pay cut to do it. I'll do it for nothing, if I have to." The lowest rung of an NFL coaching staff, the position paid substantially less than a scout's salary of roughly $80,000. Won over by Todd's passion, Parcells gave him the gig with a $40,000 salary plus a company car.

Parcells's penchant for riding his coaches, especially the neophytes, was well-known around the league. "I give it to them the worst," Parcells says, "because I want to get them where they want to go—just faster. It's almost like coaching a player." Nonetheless, Dick Haley supported the move, believing that his high-strung son would be a better fit as a coach.

After his first trip to Weeb Ewbank Hall, Bill Parcells was adamant about upgrading the team's security. So he turned to Steve Yarnell, his former defensive lineman at Army, and the man he had asked to direct Big Blue's security during the week of the 1991 Super Bowl in Tampa. Until then Yarnell had only attended Giants games in the stands. "Until you get down on the field," Yarnell says, "you don't realize how fast everybody is. It's exciting."

Yarnell knew plenty about excitement. After becoming an infantry officer, he graduated from the Army Ranger School, a sixty-one-day combat program designed to physically stress students just short of death. Then, for almost two decades, Yarnell worked as an FBI special agent focusing on terrorism. He provided security for high-level informants, and played a role in solving the World Trade Center bombing of 1993. "I wouldn't want to get on his bad side," Parcells says, chuckling.

Yarnell intended to improve team security for road games by coordinating with law-enforcement officials at various cities. But his first objective after being hired was retrofitting Jets headquarters with an access control system instead of having the franchise rely on Hofstra's public-safety employees. "Bill used to kid me: 'When are we getting the burning moat?'" recalls Yarnell. "He wanted the place impregnable if necessary. Bill was also concerned about his own safety. Why wouldn't he be? He's a high-profile individual."

Parcells says, "I wanted him to cultivate sources in law enforcement, and to get a protocol in place if an incident happened. I also wanted to be able to advise players about criminal violations, and matters like having guns registered. Those things can be problems." An important aspect of the new job description also involved Yarnell's researching draft prospects and disclosing any red flags. Few NFL clubs employed anyone full-time to oversee security, but within the next several years other teams would start emulating Parcells's approach.

After identifying thirteen areas on the Jets as needing substantial improvement, Parcells wasted no time getting ensconced in his new corner office on the second floor of Weeb Ewbank Hall. He placed a black elephant figurine with gold markings at the edge of his oversized desk, not far from a toy convertible plastered with Red Sox logos. To the right of his desk Parcells used a small whiteboard to organize roster maneuverings. When Mike Tannenbaum walked in on his first day, Parcells told him, "Mr. T, this board has to be updated every single day."

Then Parcells sat, drapes drawn, to begin watching film of Tennessee's star quarterback, Peyton Manning. For hours Parcells scrutinized every throw made by the twenty-year-old in a season that had cemented his status as the best quarterback in college. Having set multiple NCAA, SEC, and school records, Manning was scheduled to graduate in the spring with a bachelor of arts in speech communication. However, finishing his studies early gave Manning another year of football eligibility, generating uncertainty about whether he would turn pro. Even though Parcells believed that the Volunteers quarterback would stay in school, the new Jets chief was preparing for the alternative.

To make his decision Peyton Manning consulted several sports stars, including quarterbacks Troy Aikman and Drew Bledsoe, plus NBA icon Michael Jordan. Phil Simms, now an NFL analyst for NBC, tried playing matchmaker between Manning and his former Giants coach. Simms told college football's premier quarterback and Parcells that they would make an ideal combination because they both saw the game of football the same way.

With suspense building on the decision in late February, Peyton Manning's father telephoned Parcells to gather intelligence on Gang Green's plans for the top overall pick. Himself a former star quarterback for the New Orleans Saints, Archie Manning was friendly with Parcells, but during this conversation, the two men tiptoed around the elephant in the room: If Peyton Manning declared for the draft, would the Jets keep their top overall pick and choose him?

Cognizant of Parcells's responsibilities as a GM, which included keeping all options open going into the draft, Archie didn't press for explicit assurances, and Parcells avoided asking for inside information. He indicated that the Jets saw Peyton Manning as a future Pro Bowl quarterback meriting the top overall selection, but the circumspect GM did not guarantee that Gang Green would keep its opening pick, especially given Peyton's undecided status. The Jets already had quarterback Neil O'Donnell, who was only one year removed from guiding Bill Cowher's Steelers to a Super Bowl appearance, playing under a franchise-record $25 million contract. So the don't-ask-don't-tell conversation ended with neither the Mannings nor Parcells getting a true sense of the other's plans.

About a week later, on March 5, Peyton Manning revealed his decision in a nationally televised press conference at the Volunteers' field house. Poker-faced, he used the past tense in describing his happy experiences at Tennessee to the overflow crowd, which included teammates and family. After making it seem as if he would be joining the NFL, Manning smiled and revealed that he was remaining at Tennessee for a final year. When the thunderous roar subsided, Peyton Manning informed the gathering that the possibility of playing for Bill Parcells had been perhaps the most difficult aspect of his deliberations. "At one point," Manning said, "I made up my mind to stay in school, but Parcells shook things up. I have a lot of respect for Coach Parcells. It made my decision a lot harder."

The Jets head coach was not surprised by the development, having been tipped off by a phone call from Archie Manning just before the press conference.

Parcells told Peyton's father, "Heck, we may have a chance at him next year."

But Archie Manning, alluding to Parcells's reputation for turnarounds, replied, "I don't think you're going to *have* the first pick next year."

"You haven't seen our defense."

Both men were laughing as they hung up.

Parcells now concedes what he had refused to confirm to Archie Manning: Gang Green would likely have drafted Tennessee's quarterback if he had come out in 1997. However, although Peyton Manning turned into one of the greatest quarterbacks in league history, Parcells expresses no regret for refusing to nudge him toward the draft. "You can't make a decision like that for the player," he says, adding that the league frowned on the influencing of underclassmen to enter the draft.

Gang Green still retained an exciting opportunity to select the top college prospect after Manning: left tackle Orlando Pace had been so dominant at Ohio State that he hadn't allowed a sack in two seasons. However, millions of dollars in Jets cap space was tied to offensive tackles David Williams and Jumbo Elliott. More important, Gang Green had recently sent its third- and fourth-round choices in April's draft to New England as part of the compensation for Parcells. With two more picks owed to the Patriots in future years, the Jets decided to stockpile selections in the 1997 draft, so Parcells traded the first overall choice to the St. Louis Rams, parlaying it into a total of seven selections by moving down multiple times through other exchanges.

Leon Hess granted Bill Parcells permission to construct a state-of-the-art, all-weather practice bubble, as part of a $3.5 million makeover of the team's facilities. The Jets upgraded their gym while adding substantially more free weights and aerobics-based equipment. The team also tore apart its three playing fields, replacing them with new gridirons in line with Parcells's specifications: artificial turf was installed next to two grass fields.

During a conversation among Jets officials about the resodded fields, Parcells awed them with his knowledge of grass. It came partly from grilling groundskeepers, particularly "grass guru" George Toma, who worked for the Kansas City Chiefs and baseball's Kansas City Royals. The NFL had assigned Toma to every Super Bowl since the first one. His résumé included stints supervising ground crews for the 1984 Olympics, 1994 World Cup, and 1996 Olympics. So Parcells picked Toma's brain at every opportunity. "That's part of the game, the surface you play on," Parcells explains. "There are different kinds of grass: bluegrass, Bermuda grass, blank grass. Some are weak and dislodge easily. Some have a good base. Others are more slippery when they get wet. You have to know all that." Parcells also knew about the different types of synthetics used for Astroturf, and occasionally compelled his players to wear certain shoes depending on the stadium.

Several weeks before conducting his first spring practice, Parcells called a mandatory team meeting at Jets headquarters. Addressing his players in a packed auditorium, Parcells informed them that he was sharply increasing the length of the voluntary off-season program, which emphasized weight lifting and conditioning. By stressing the importance of the program, Parcells essentially made attendance *in*voluntary.

He later met in his office with the team's top receiver, Keyshawn Johnson, drafted first overall in 1996 out of Southern California. Despite being one of Gang Green's few beacons during its dreary previous season, Johnson had a reputation as a loudmouth and prima donna. Shortly after Parcells was hired, Johnson released a book, *Just Give Me the Damn Ball!: The Fast Times and Hard Knocks of an NFL Rookie*. In the autobiography he described Rich Kotite as incompetent while calling offensive coordinator Ron Erhardt, sixty-five, "an old fool" and Neil O'Donnell "a stiff puppet." Johnson also complained that too many passes went to teammate Wayne Chrebet, an undrafted wideout from Hofstra once cut by a Canadian Football League team. In just two NFL seasons Chrebet had caught 150 balls for 1,635 yards while becoming the Jets' most popular player. But *Just Give Me the Damn Ball!* described the five-ten, 188-pounder as "a short, little white guy" and "team mascot." The book was co-written by ESPN's Shelley Smith, who had helped Johnson during his troubled youth in Los Angeles's notorious neighborhood of South Central.

One of six children of a single mother, Keyshawn Johnson grew up poor in the shadow of Memorial Coliseum. A skinny seven-year-old in 1979, he began to attend USC's football practices by entering the premises through an unlocked gate. Keyshawn was so omnipresent that he became an unofficial member of the powerhouse program, whose players included All-American safety Ronnie Lott and tailback Marcus Allen. Keyshawn helped stuff envelopes in the sports information office and lug the bags of Coach John Robinson's assistants to their cars. Occasionally he slept at their homes while dreaming about one day playing for the Trojans.

But Keyshawn couldn't escape the realities of South Central, infamous for its poverty and gang violence between the Bloods and Crips. After he turned eleven in 1983, Keyshawn's family became homeless, and slept in a car. By 1985 he had stopped spending time at USC, succumbing to his environment while trying to support his mother and his siblings. For the next three years, Keyshawn sold marijuana and cocaine. As an eighth-grader he was arrested for possession of a handgun and drugs, charges that led to a nine-month sentence at a juvenile facility. But Keyshawn began to turn his life around after joining Dorsey High's football team, where he blossomed into one of the nation's best wideouts.

Writer Shelley Smith met Keyshawn Johnson in the summer of 1992, working for *Sports Illustrated* on a profile of the team and the surrounding gang culture. Despite having recently graduated, Johnson was hanging around the sportswriter daily to offer stories about his exploits, and to try getting mentioned in *SI*. The white suburban mom and black inner-city kid bonded.

To improve his college-entrance scores and qualify for a top football program, Johnson attended West Los Angeles College. Meanwhile, Smith took on a supportive role in Johnson's life. She hired him to babysit her five-year-old daughter, Dylann, and found him other odd jobs. After a stint at the junior college, Johnson accepted an athletic scholarship from USC in 1994. The six-four wideout flourished, earning All-American honors. The following year, 1995, Shelley Smith wrote an *SI* article about Johnson for the magazine's college football preview, which splashed him on the cover. The Trojans went on to reach the 1996 Rose Bowl, where he led them to a 41–32 victory over Northwestern. Johnson finished with 12 receptions, including a touchdown, for a game-record 216 yards. However,

Duane Charles Parcells at age two. Duane grew to dislike his birth name, deeming it unusual and perhaps feminine. When in the eighth grade he was constantly mistaken for someone named Bill, he declined to correct anyone. Within a year, only Ida and Charles called their son by his real name. *Courtesy of Bill Parcells*

Four-year-old Duane in Juliet, Illinois, where his father had moved the family for one year while working as a corporate attorney for the United States Rubber Company. *Courtesy of Bill Parcells*

Don, seven, and Duane, nine, outside their home in Hasbrouck Heights, New Jersey, in 1950. Four years earlier, their father, Charles, had paid $8,000 for the single-story house in the New York City suburb, converting its attic into a bedroom for his boys. Just a few blocks away, the vocalist Frank Sinatra lived with his wife, Nancy, and a newborn girl. *Courtesy of Bill Parcells*

Eleven-year-old Duane, a sixth grader in Euclid Elementary School, where he was one of its biggest students, weighing more than 160 pounds. *Courtesy of Bill Parcells*

Members of the Hasbrouck Heights Peanuts: *(from left)* Danny Astrella, thirteen; George Swede, thirteen; Don Parcells, nine; Duane Parcells; eleven, in 1952. George's eight-year-old brother, Jerry, kneels in front of the baseball gang. After a tryout, Duane made the team as a second baseman—his first organized competition. The peewee club had been created in 1950 because Little League hadn't yet reached Hasbrouck Heights. *Courtesy of George Swede*

Mickey Corcoran, head coach of River Dell High's basketball team, gathers his charges on their home court in Oradell, New Jersey, circa 1958. Power forward Bill Parcells (#50), the Golden Hawks' best player, possessed a soft shooting touch, slick post-up moves, rebounding prowess, and an explosive temper that Corcoran had to suppress. Like his father, Bill emerged as one of the best hoopsters in North Jersey and a three-sport star. *Courtesy of Mickey Corcoran*

Bill's parents, Ida and Charles, in 1962. Despite a slender frame, Charles earned the nickname "Chubby" as a high school star in football, basketball, and track during the late 1920s. He focused on football at Georgetown as one of the top halfbacks in the East. *Courtesy of Bill Parcells*

Bill Parcells on Army's practice field in 1967, his first year as defensive-line coach for the Black Knights. The twenty-six-year-old was the youngest member of a talented staff containing several future head coaches. At West Point, Parcells met Bobby Knight, in his third season as Army's head basketball coach, and the two formed a deep bond that would last a lifetime. In these formative years, ending in 1969, Parcells learned the importance of a strong staff and how improving special teams was perhaps the quickest way to revitalize an entire football team. *Courtesy of Bill Parcells*

Bill Parcells in 1968 with one of his charges, Steve Yarnell. The high-strung yet charismatic Parcells related well to his players, some of whom were only a few years younger. Yarnell spent almost two decades as an FBI special agent before accepting Parcells's offer in 1997 to oversee Jets security. *Courtesy of Bill Parcells*

The Parcells family—Bill and Judy with daughters Suzy, Jill, and Dallas—outside their new home in Lubbock, Texas, after Bill joined Texas Tech in 1975 as linebackers coach. During his college coaching career, Bill, who once described Lubbock as being "in the middle of nowhere," would move the family every two years or so for a new job. *Courtesy of Judy Parcells*

Air Force head coach Bill Parcells with his father, Charles, and brother, Don, at Boston College's Alumni Stadium, September 16, 1978. The pair would watch Air Force defeat Boston College, 18–7, but the Falcons lost their next five games to finish 3-8. Parcells quit after only one season, accepting Ray Perkins's offer to oversee Big Blue's linebackers. *Courtesy of Bill Parcells*

Two of Bill Parcells's favorite players of all time, linebacker Harry Carson (#53) and defensive end George Martin (#75), at their final regular-season appearance in Giants Stadium, December 11, 1988, versus Kansas City. The co-captains announced their NFL retirement after combining for twenty-seven years with Big Blue. Carson, who would make the Hall of Fame in 2006, wears jeans because of an injury. *Harry Hamburg,* New York Daily News

Danny Astrella, one of Bill Parcells's closest friends, with the Giants head coach during a rare break at training camp, July 12, 1985. The pair had grown up together in Hasbrouck Heights, two of the biggest boys in the neighborhood. When Parcells was in elementary school after just moving to town, his sandlot fight with Danny taught him the benefits of being confrontational. *Courtesy of Bill Parcells*

Football royalty: Giants leader Bill Parcells whispers to Steelers legend Chuck Noll, the owner of four Lombardi Trophies, before the 1985 regular-season finale at Giants Stadium. Noll was among several top football minds whom the young Giants head coach would seek out for pointers. *Harry Hamburg,* New York Daily News *Archive, Getty Images*

Short shorts: Three future Hall of Famers chat during Giants training camp in August 1986, many years before the popularity of baggy shorts. Lawrence Taylor stands between head coach Bill Parcells and defensive coordinator Bill Belichick. *Jerry Pinkus*

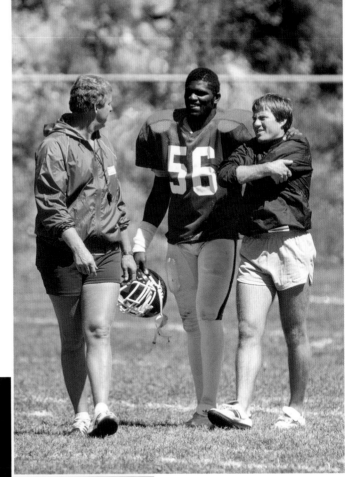

Archrivals Bill Walsh and Bill Parcells side by side during pregame activities at Giants Stadium on October 5, 1987. On *Monday Night Football*, Walsh's 49ers would defeat Parcells's Giants 41–21. Their high-profile rivalry produced some of the NFL's most memorable games, occasionally leading to Super Bowl titles. By 2006, roughly three-fourths of NFL head coaches were linked to one man or the other. *Michael Zagaris, Getty Images*

Parcells strategizes with starting quarterback Phil Simms (#11) during an October 22, 1989, game at San Diego's Jack Murphy Stadium. Simms's powerful arm had guided the Giants to Super Bowl XXI, and reserve quarterback Jeff Hostetler (in the background) often felt like an outsider. Nonetheless, when Simms suffered a

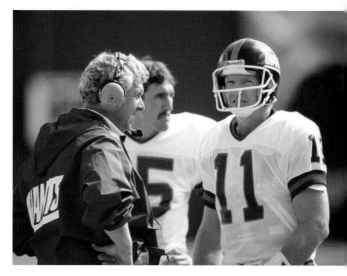

season-ending injury on December 15, 1990, versus Buffalo, Hostetler got the starter's job. The West Virginia product helped Parcells capture his second Lombardi Trophy by completing 20 of 32 passes against Marv Levy's Bills, concluding the playoffs without an interception. *Ron Vesely, Getty Images*

In snowy conditions with windchill temperatures of 21 degrees at Mile High Stadium, on December 10, 1989, Parcells guided Big Blue to a 14–7 victory over Denver. During a sit-down with Woody Hayes in early 1978, the Ohio State legend told the then rookie head coach of Air Force, "If you're gonna play in the Atlantic, you gotta train in the Atlantic!" Several years later, when Parcells joined forces with Giants GM George Young, the pair targeted athletes capable of excelling in inclement weather. *John Leyba,* Denver Post, *Getty Images*

Bill Parcells and L.T. celebrate after Big Blue won its regular-season finale at home, in subzero temperatures, over the Los Angeles Raiders, 34–17, Christmas Eve 1989. The 12-4 Giants clinched the NFC East and a home playoff appearance. However, in the opening round of the postseason, a different L.A. team, the Rams, would stun Big Blue, 19–13, in overtime. *Ray Stubblebine, AP*

Mickey Corcoran (left) was much more than Parcells's high school basketball coach, acting "like a second father," Parcells recalls, and teaching the future legend many lessons he had received as a prep hoopster under Vince Lombardi from 1939 to 1941. Corcoran helped Parcells land a football scholarship at Wichita State and a coaching job at Army. While gaining NFL glory, Parcells constantly kept his mentor close by, whether on the sidelines, at practice, or as a seatmate on plane rides to road games. *Courtesy of Mickey Corcoran*

Bill Parcells gets a lift from his linebackers Lawrence Taylor, Carl Banks (#58), and Pepper Johnson (behind the Tuna) following their Super Bowl XXV triumph over Marv Levy's Bills at Tampa Stadium, January 27, 1991. Unable to shake hands with Levy amid the celebration, Parcells waves at him. Parcells's legacy-securing ride would become a defining moment, replayed countless times. Steve Yarnell (far left) worked security for the event. *Mike Powell, Getty Images Sport Classic*

ABOVE: Looking like a championship couple, Parcells and wife Judy pose with the Lombardi Trophy on January 28, 1991, the day after the Giants' victory in Super Bowl XXV. *Courtesy of Judy Parcells*
RIGHT: Patriots head coach Bill Parcells with Tom Coughlin, the new boss of the Jacksonville Jaguars, on July 25, 1994. After a strong recommendation from Parcells in January 1994, Coughlin was named head coach and GM of the expansion franchise. But with Jacksonville one year away from operating, Coughlin spent substantial time observing Patriots practices in Smithfield, Rhode Island. When Coughlin previously guided Boston College, Parcells sometimes attended his disciple's practices in Chestnut Hill, Massachusetts. *Jim Davis*, Boston Globe, *Getty Images*

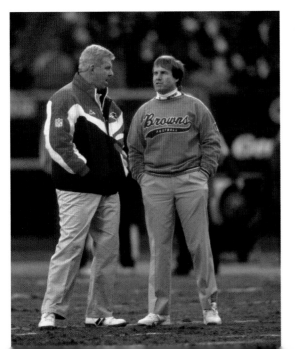

Patriots leader Bill Parcells and Browns head coach Bill Belichick at Cleveland Stadium before their teams clash in the opening round of the playoffs, New Year's Day 1995. Little Bill had grown closer to Big Bill after leaving the Giants for the Browns in 1991, suddenly sharing more in common with his mentor. In the only postseason contest between the long-time comrades, Belichick's team would prevail, 20–13, as Drew Bledsoe tossed three interceptions against Nick Saban's top-ranked defense. Parcells recalls, "In some respects, I thought I was playing myself defensively." *John Iacono*, Sports Illustrated, *Getty Images*

Patriots owner Robert Kraft and head coach Bill Parcells talk during a morning practice on July 22, 1996, in Smithfield, Rhode Island. Kraft had purchased the franchise from James Orthwein in 1994, but Parcells bristled at the new ways of doing things, which diluted the sweeping powers he'd been given under the previous owner. Irreconcilable differences with Kraft would prompt Parcells to leave for the Jets in early 1997 despite having guided New England to Super Bowl XXX. *Tom Landers,* Boston Globe, *Getty Images*

Bill Parcells and Jets owner Leon Hess at the team's headquarters in Hempstead, New York, on February 11, 1997. The reclusive oil baron made one of his rare appearances to introduce Parcells as head coach and director of football operations. The latter title granted the Big Tuna final say in all football decisions, unlike in New England, where he had complained about being unable to "shop for the groceries." Hess told the media: "He's going to run the show, and it's not going to be two or three cooks in the kitchen. It will be just him." *Kathy Willens, AP*

Keyshawn Johnson, the top overall pick of the 1996 draft, with his new head coach during a 1997 Jets practice. Pundits had predicted that the headstrong, loudmouth wideout would clash with the authoritarian, no-nonsense leader. Instead, Johnson would turn into one of Parcells's favorite players and people. The six-four, 212-pounder embraced Parcells's instruction to be a "great giraffe" instead of a "gazelle"—to use his size and strength rather than try to emulate speedy, smallish wideouts. *AP*

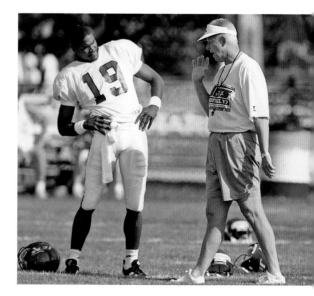

Jets chief Bill Parcells and Vinny Testaverde during an introductory press conference in Clifton, New Jersey, on June 24, 1998. Gang Green signed the bazooka-armed thirty-four-year-old after releasing Neil O'Donnell, who'd refused to renegotiate his contract. Parcells told the media that although the Jets planned on giving Glenn Foley "the benefit of the doubt" as their starter, Testaverde would get a shot at the role. Parcells considers Testaverde, who'd been waived by Baltimore, one of the best pure passers he's ever seen. *Mike Derer, AP*

Bill Parcells leads his cocksure, charged-up players, including center Kevin Mawae (#68) and special-teams ace Corwin Brown (#44), at the Meadowlands for their 1998 regular-season finale on December 27. Gang Green would trounce Pete Carroll's Patriots, 31–10, concluding a historic year highlighted by the franchise's first-ever division title. Only a couple of seasons removed from ignominy, the Jets took most of their club-record twelve victories by at least a touchdown, and strutted into the playoffs. *Thomas E. Franklin*, Bergen Record

Jets defensive coordinator Bill Belichick instructs outside linebacker Bryan Cox during an October 17, 1999, victory over Indianapolis at Giants Stadium. Head coach Bill Parcells stands close by. The two football gurus, with disparate personalities, have a mutually beneficial but complicated relationship. As part of a succession plan, Belichick was elevated to Jets head coach on January 3, 2000, but quit the next day, citing the uncertainty created by Leon Hess's recent death as one of the reasons. But after spending 14 of the previous 19 seasons under Big Bill, Little Bill seemed to want to escape his mentor's shadow. *John T. Greilick, AP*

Bill Parcells walks atop the storied Cowboys logo at San Antonio's Alamodome on August 5, 2003. *Bob Rosato*, Sports Illustrated, *Getty Images*

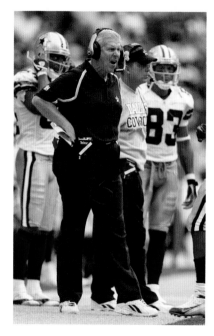

Bill Parcells barking instructions next to acolyte Sean Payton during a Cowboys game. Among his numerous lessons on leadership and football, Parcells taught his play caller about the benefits of confrontation. Starting in 2006, Payton would use Parcells's methods to rejuvenate the New Orleans Saints in the aftermath of Hurricane Katrina and capture the 2010 Super Bowl. USA Today *Sports Images*

Cowboys wideout Keyshawn Johnson enjoys a light moment at training camp in Oxnard, California, on August 3, 2005. Parcells had acquired Johnson before the 2004 season in a trade that sent wideout Joey Galloway to Tampa Bay. Jerry Jones switched training camp from San Antonio, Texas, to the coastal city thirty-five miles west of Los Angeles. Parcells favored a balmy climate to reduce the risks of dehydration and allow more repetitions as his athletes played themselves into shape. *Tony Gutierrez, AP*

All smiles among Bill Parcells's dearest: Bobby Green (far left), one of his closest friends; Mickey Corcoran, his lifelong mentor; and girlfriend Kelly Mandart at a Saratoga Springs restaurant in 2006. *Courtesy of Bobby Green*

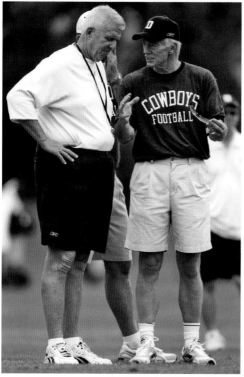

Bill Parcells and his boss, Jerry Jones, on July 29, 2006, the opening day of training camp. During their four-year partnership, the larger-than-life characters with outsized egos enjoyed defying predictions about an inevitable clash. *Matt Slocum, AP*

Bill Parcells at his introductory press conference as the Miami Dolphins' executive vice president of football operations, December 27, 2007, in Davie, Florida. Hired by Wayne Huizenga, Parcells quit in the summer of 2010, twenty-one months after real-estate magnate Stephen Ross became majority owner. Despite Miami's 20-16 record under his watch, the Big Tuna faced criticism for an inability to land a franchise quarterback or meet his goal of putting a structure in place led by GM Jeff Ireland and head coach Tony Sparano. *Joe Rimkus Jr.*, Miami Herald, *MCT, Getty Images*

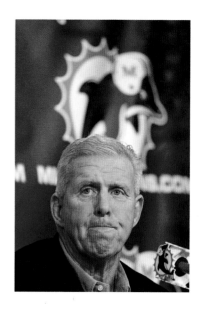

Curtis Martin and Bill Parcells flank a bust of Boy Wonder at the Hall of Fame on August 4, 2012. The former Patriots and Jets tailback felt bittersweet on February 4, 2012, when he learned the news about his election into the Hall, because Parcells had failed to make the final cut. Martin explained, "There's God and there's Parcells as far as the impact they've had on my career." The pair had fantasized about being enshrined as part of the same class. *Gene J. Puskar, AP*

Two "enemies" embrace and share laughs at the Hall of Fame ceremonies on August 2, 2013, in Canton, Ohio. Joe Gibbs and Bill Parcells sat at the same table during the Ray Nitschke Memorial Luncheon and spoke more to each other that day than they had done in decades as NFC East rivals: Parcells's Giants and Gibbs's Redskins underwent epic clashes that determined championships and legacies. Parcells explains, "You learn to respect your enemies but execute all traitors, and that's how I felt about Joe. I always held him in high regard."

Ben Liebenberg, AP

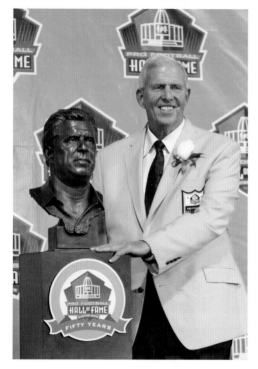

Bill Parcells grins while posing with his stern-faced bust during his Hall of Fame induction on August 3, 2013. Parcells entered football's most exclusive organization on his fourth bid for enshrinement. Despite his credentials, the polarizing figure had generated the most discussion among voters. The Class of 2013 was one of the strongest in recent memory, including offensive lineman Larry Allen, wideout Cris Carter, offensive tackle Jonathan Ogden, and defensive lineman Warren Sapp. *Rodger Mallison,* Fort Worth Star-Telegram, *MCT, Getty Images*

Ex–Giants defensive lineman George Martin poses with Bill Parcells shortly after helping unveil his bust as only the twenty-second coach inducted into the Hall of Fame. Parcells chose his former co-captain to present him largely because of Martin's career-saving support, especially during a pivotal 1984 season. *Jason Miller, Getty Images*

Bill Parcells and Lawrence Taylor at Fawcett Stadium on August 3, 2013, before the Big Tuna's enshrinement. Early in his induction speech, Parcells would express the desire for his bust to be placed near L.T.'s sculptured portrayal "so I can keep an eye on that sucker." USA Today *Sports Images*

The only men to have captured Lombardi Trophies as Giants head coaches—Bill Parcells and Tom Coughlin, each of whom won two Super Bowl titles—stand next to their glistening prizes on June 10, 2014, at team headquarters in East Rutherford, New Jersey. Parcells dislikes comparing his disciples but concedes that Coughlin is the most similar to him. The Giants wideouts coach from 1988 to 1990 describes Parcells as the person who taught him far more about football than anyone else: "The best." *Evan Pinkus, AP*

when Parcells joined the Jets, pundits predicted that he wouldn't be able to stomach the brash wideout.

Instead of relying on perception, Parcells telephoned USC head coach John Robinson for insight. Despite Johnson's NFL reputation for rebelliousness, Robinson told Parcells, the young second-year wideout ached for guidance that would help make him a star on a winning team. So in their first time meeting, Parcells skipped the introductory pleasantries. "What's the best game you ever played, Keyshawn? The Rose Bowl?"

Johnson responded, "Yeah."

"Well, how much did you weigh in the Rose Bowl?"

"212."

"What the hell do you weigh now?"

"220."

"Well, get down to 212. That's the guy I want. I don't want this fat guy I see in front of me. You look like you've got the mumps." Continuing his offensive, Parcells told Johnson that he would be required to weigh in every Friday during the season, and face consequences if he ever went over the 212 pounds. The high-strung receiver remained unruffled, agreeing to drop almost ten pounds in time for training camp. Parcells was pleased that his insults hadn't fazed Johnson, seeing his reaction as a sign of competitiveness. Conversely, the cocksure wideout welcomed Parcells's no-nonsense approach.

"I liked the dude right away," recalls Johnson. "I didn't need to hear a guy tell me that I was good and I'm the man—I already knew all that stuff. I needed to hear what was going to make me a better person and football player. He realized that I wanted to be great and to be challenged, so I embraced his attitude. I was like, 'Man, we're going to win a championship. We've got the right cat.' The previous regime was a joke. It was like Pop Warner football. I had gone from playing in a major college football program right back to Pop Warner."

Once the off-season program commenced in the spring, Parcells began scrutinizing the work habits of his players. Now starting linebacker Mo Lewis no longer dared ask a teammate to sign in for him at weight-lifting sessions. Parcells substantially lowered the air conditioner's temperature in the training room to prevent players from congregating there without legitimate injuries. He ignored their complaints, joking to his predominantly black athletes that "the brothers don't like it too cold in there."

Parcells emphasized attention to detail. During full-uniform stretching drills he required every player to place his helmet to his right. Step by step, with small changes and large, the new head coach started to revamp the culture of a team coming off 33 losses in 37 games. The biggest jolt took place during Parcells's first few practices, just as it had with the Patriots, where he established his standards for conditioning, preparation, and execution. During one such session Parcells had been going over to each unit performing its drills, screaming about flaws in technique and fundamentals, when he suddenly blew his whistle to halt the practice. After commanding his coaches to gather around him, he unleashed an expletive-laced tirade about the session's sluggishness. Longtime staff members like Bill Belichick and Romeo Crennel, who were among six Jets coaches formerly with Parcells, were used to being rebuked for lackluster performances by their groups, but Jets players were dumbfounded to see Parcells berate his staff for *their* actions. When practice resumed, the energy increased and the execution sharpened, but the new head coach never let up.

During 11-on-11 sessions, he sometimes fired questions at players about precise situations they might face on game day. Parcells yelled, "Okay, we're up three points with four seconds left to play. We've got the ball on our 20. It's fourth-and-10. What's the call?"

Punting seemed the obvious response, but some players aware of Parcells's approach in that situation shouted, "Pass out of bounds!" Parcells nodded approvingly. He ruled out punting in that situation. Instead, Jets quarterbacks were instructed to throw the ball high and toward the stands. Parcells explains, "The pass takes four seconds. Game's over. So even though you don't have another down, you can burn all the time on the clock."

In revamping the roster, Bill Parcells kept only 29 of the 61 Jets players from the previous season. He acquired a handful of his former players, so-called Bill Parcells Guys, including Pepper Johnson, to start at linebacker. Offensive lineman William Roberts, who had reached three Super Bowls with Parcells, signed as a key reserve. Parcells saw the thirty-five-year-old as a "hold-the-fort guy," providing competence for the time being.

To jump-start Gang Green, Parcells focused on its special teams, which contained mostly inexperienced players. The ex–Army coach had never forgotten what he'd learned in 1967 under Tom Cahill—that special teams marks the quickest way to revitalize a struggling program. Assembling a special-teams unit was one of his favorite aspects of football. And as a coach who often repeated Red Blaik's exhortation **"Let's put the 'foot' back in football,"** Parcells found it deplorable that Gang Green's punt- and kick-returning units were collectively the NFL's worst.

Perhaps the most talented member of the revamped special teams was rookie tailback Leon "The Natural" Johnson, drafted in the fourth round via North Carolina after setting the ACC mark for all-purpose yards. Slippery at six feet and 220 pounds, Johnson aimed for the lead role as punt and kick returner. Kicking and kick defense seemed like the best parts of Gang Green's special teams: Rookie John Hall, undrafted out of Wisconsin, possessed a powerful leg, and delighted teammates by occasionally punishing returners with a haymaker. Reserve defensive back Corwin Brown, a kamikaze tackler during Parcells's tenure in New England, also brought his act to the Jets.

The unit's most intriguing member, however, was an ex–college quarterback with only two games on his NFL résumé as a Patriots rookie in 1996 on special teams. Undrafted out of Rutgers, Ray Lucas had practiced at wideout, defensive back, and quarterback, but failed to excel in any of those positions, prompting Pete Carroll's Patriots to release him. Parcells, however, loved his multidimensionality and determination.

"I don't know what to do with you yet, Lucas, but I want you."

To enhance his knowledge of so many new personalities, Parcells mined the team psychologist, Charles Maher, whose duties included compiling profiles on every player. Maher was astonished by how thoroughly Parcells digested his assessments. During their meetings to discuss the reports, Parcells showed his relish for personal details. "He wanted to know the psychological DNA of each individual," Dr. Maher recalls, "what makes the player tick."

Parcells still contacted past coaches to flesh out information, but his favorite way to assess personalities remained having conversations with players and studying their mannerisms, especially during downtime. He noted whether they were introverted or extroverted, assertive or diffident, self-assured or self-doubting, meticulous or sloppy, cerebral or impetuous. In time, Parcells customized his methods to get the most out of each player.

"Even in a steel door, there are hinges, and there are cracks," says Ray Lucas. "Maybe on the bottom, maybe on the side. Maybe there's one on top. That sonofabitch finds it somehow, and gets into your head. And then he can either break you or he can build you up."

When Joe O'Donnell visited Parcells at Jets headquarters during summer minicamp, the stadium-food CEO marveled at the way his friend used both management tools of motivation on players—sometimes only moments apart.

"In business, you call it 'Theory X' and 'Theory Y,'" explains the former dean of Harvard Business School. "Theory Y is, 'We're in this together. Great job. Love the way you're thinking.' Theory X is, 'Do better or else. You're not cutting it.' Now, you can't say one is better than the other. Certain people respond to the stick; certain people respond to the carrot. Bill was so smart, he understood which guys needed him to snap a towel off their asses."

Following one afternoon practice, Parcells took Joe O'Donnell into the locker room. When tight end Kyle Brady walked by, Parcells tapped him on the shoulder and growled, "You dropped a pass at the 5 today. You'll drop it in the game if you don't catch it in practice." Brady agreed, and walked away. As linebacker Pepper Johnson entered the room, Parcells broached a conversation about the player's eleven-year-old son, Dionte, a lighthearted exchange between friends. When another veteran passed by, however, Parcells didn't bother acknowledging him. Joe O'Donnell considered the range of interactions to be managerial brilliance.

"I could see how much individuality was involved," remembers O'Donnell. "I went to college and played for one coach who had a clipboard and never talked to any of us. It's a lot more work to coach the individual. 'Okay, what do I say to him? He had the worst game of his life.' I think Bill's only consistency is in keeping people off guard. He does that all the time. He did it with his wife. He'll do it with me. He'll do it with you."

Before 1997, the last time a wideout had been drafted first overall occurred in 1984, when New England selected Irving Fryar. As a rookie, Keyshawn Johnson had failed to live up to the hype, despite catching eight touchdown passes among his 63 receptions for 844 yards. During one of Parcells's staff meetings to evaluate players, several coaches criticized Johnson's speed and ability to create separation from defenders. Johnson's staunchest supporter was the lowest man on the totem pole: Todd Haley, the entry-level assistant who worked with wideouts, pointed out many of Johnson's attributes, including size and strength. Parcells preferred his coaches to emphasize "what a player can do, not what he can't." So the Jets boss liked the ex-scout's observations, and believed that Johnson was undermining his talents by imitating smaller wideouts who possessed a different skill set.

During one practice, Parcells pulled Johnson aside. Mentioning some of the NFL's explosive wideouts, Parcells said, "You're not Marvin Harrison or Terry Glenn. You're Keyshawn Johnson. You're big, strong, and mentally tough. You can snatch the ball. You're not fast. You're not a gazelle; you're a giraffe. Got me? Don't try to be a gazelle. Convince the quarterback to throw you the ball when you're covered, because you're going to be covered. You can't get away from *anybody*, so be a great giraffe."

Although Johnson felt that Parcells was overstating his speed limitations, he embraced the analogy. Instead of continuing to emulate his faster counterparts, Johnson demanded that Neil O'Donnell throw him the damn ball regardless of tight coverage. The ultracompetitive wideout responded by using his length to make tough catches. When running across the middle, an area that invited punishing hits, Johnson never showed so-called alligator arms, but reached for the ball fearlessly in heavy traffic. And as a blocker on run plays, the powerfully built wideout delivered some wallops of his own. After shedding some weight, Johnson started to move with more burst, though still not exactly like a gazelle. Heading into the regular season, the wideout was falling in line with Parcells's vision of the player he could be.

Parcells also spent considerable energy defining the roles of his lesser-known players. He planned to sign fullback Richie Anderson, twenty-five, to a long-term extension, but only if the 1993 sixth-round pick set aside his aspirations of becoming a feature back. At six-two and 225 pounds, Anderson wasn't the prototypical bruising blocker like Maurice Carthon for Big Blue or Sam Gash with Parcells's Patriots. Nonetheless, Parcells valued Anderson's versatility, which was highlighted by his pass-catching skills. Parcells envisioned Anderson as an offensive cog, specifically a change-of-pace runner, for at least the next five years, while also contributing on special teams.

Almost every afternoon at around 5:30, Tannenbaum and Parcells met in the boss's office to discuss important topics involving players' contracts, personnel transactions, and salary-cap implications. Parcells dubbed that critical part of the day "family business time." Tannenbaum's duties included negotiating with agents once the Jets had established his financial parameters. So when Richie Anderson's extension came up, Parcells instructed Tannenbaum to stress the fullback's new role in upcoming talks with his representative. Tannenbaum took notes from Parcells, using bullet points for key phrases: "• Change-of-pace back. • Know his role. • Can play on this team for a long time."

During a telephone conversation the next day, agent Tony Agnone asked Tannenbaum about Gang Green's plans for Anderson. Tannenbaum followed Parcells's script, glancing at his notes. Several hours later, at family business time, Parcells asked Tannenbaum to describe the exchange as closely as possible. After Tannenbaum complied, Parcells said, "That's a good job, Mr. T. That's *exactly* what I wanted you to say."

Tannenbaum recalls, "I'm thinking in the back of my mind, 'I'm being complimented for writing something down and reading it to someone else. A well-trained monkey could do that.'"

Parcells's controlling approach extended to the team's new media policies: he limited access to players, barred reporters from regular-season practices, and required all interviews with staff members to be cleared by him.

Dallas Parcells worked as an event planner for Sharp Electronics in Mahwah, New Jersey. Before training camp the company initiated a sports marketing campaign with the Jets, giving Dallas an opportunity to visit her father at the team's headquarters. As she entered Parcells's office, Scott Pioli was just leaving, so Parcells introduced the personnel director to his daughter. Within hours, Pioli, smitten by Dallas, started discreetly questioning a few of his colleagues about her. Parcells's secretary, Linda Leoni, was friends with Pioli from their stint together with the Cleveland Browns, so she invited Dallas to a midtown get-together for a handful of Jets employees that included Pioli and Tannenbaum. Before the group met at Mickey Mantle's Restaurant, Leoni praised Pioli to Dallas while mentioning that he was single.

At the eatery Pioli made sure to sit next to Parcells's daughter, whereupon the two engaged in a long conversation ending with an exchange of telephone numbers. Because of Pioli's heavy traveling schedule, they spoke over the phone daily without making plans to see each other. "It was a long, slow process getting to know him," Dallas says, "but I liked him a lot." When they did eventually start dating, they did so without disclosing it to Bill Parcells. The deepening romance was not widely known at Weeb Ewbank Hall, but a couple of coaches who had heard the whispers needled Pioli for having the chutzpah, or the shrewdness, to date the boss's daughter.

Temperatures approaching one hundred degrees at the start of training camp on July 18 didn't save Parcells's players from a 300-yard shuttle to test their conditioning. Parcells wore a Jets T-shirt emblazoned with "WHO SAYS WE CAN'T?!!" Large crowds had begun to gather regularly at Hofstra University to watch practice, indicative of the optimism enveloping Jets Nation. Despite the previously disastrous season, a club-record 99 percent of season-ticket holders had renewed their seats. Occasionally, when Parcells upbraided a player or coach, spectators chanted, "Tuna! Tuna! Tuna!"

During preseason the Jets performed with a new sense of purpose and sharpness, going undefeated for only the third time in franchise history. Although outcomes in NFL exhibition games tended to be deceptive, Parcells placed importance on them, especially for a team with a losing culture. Sure enough, Gang Green's new winning habit spilled over into its season opener at the Kingdome. Against the Seattle Seahawks, considered to be a solid team, the Jets took a stunning 27–3 lead at halftime. The offensive explosion came on three touchdown passes from Neil O'Donnell and John Hall's two field goals, including a 55-yarder on his first NFL attempt, marking the second-longest field goal by a rookie.

Addressing his players at intermission, however, Parcells acted as if it were *his* team that was down by 24 points. Instead of focusing on the sharp first half, Parcells reminded his players of the 1996 Jets' knack for imploding, which had made the team a laughingstock. In a locker room with roughly 30 returning Jets, Parcells boomed, "They say you can't hold a lead. They say you blew six games last year after leading at halftime. Let's see what you're made of."

His players responded to the challenge by maintaining their stellar play in the second half, shutting out an offense quarterbacked by Warren Moon for the most lopsided opening-day victory in team history: 41–3. Neil O'Donnell finished with five touchdown passes, including two to wideout Wayne Chrebet, as Gang Green matched its win total from the previous season. The outcome confirmed the optimism surrounding Parcells's Jets, while bringing the franchise only its fifth victory in thirty-eight games.

When the league announced its regular-season schedule in April, top billing went to the September 14 clash between Bill Parcells's Jets and Robert Kraft's Patriots at Foxboro Stadium. The "Tuna Bowl" became one of the most anticipated non-playoff games in NFL history, the interest heightened by Shakespearean elements of betrayal, hubris, pride, and retribution.

Roughly five hundred journalists, one hundred fifty more than usual for a Patriots home game, descended on Foxboro Stadium to chronicle the Sunday-night affair. The nationally televised game marked the first time a head coach coming off a Super Bowl appearance faced his old team the next season. All around the Boston area, T-shirts that said "Can the Tuna" and "Grill the Tuna" expressed the betrayal felt by Patriots supporters As fans debated whether Parcells should be fried or seared, Boston's premier sports-radio station, WEEI, carted around a sign with an image of Parcells as a whale, urging fans to "Harpoona the Tuna."

Part of the visceral reaction stemmed from Boston's ignominious sports history involving New York teams: the Yankees' purchase of Babe Ruth from the Red Sox in 1919, shortstop Bucky Dent's monumental homer in the 1978 American League East playoffs, and Bill Buckner's tectonic error in the 1986 World Series against the Mets. Acknowledging the charged atmosphere caused by Parcells's return, the Patriots hired two hundred extra police officers. Parking-lot gates opened four hours before kickoff instead of the standard three. When Parcells took the field for warm-ups, the thousands of fans who'd arrived early drowned out scattered applause with boos. Their reaction encapsulated the polarity over the man who had resurrected a dying franchise yet bolted to a division rival over differences with the new ownership.

Among several snarky signs permitted in the stands, one asked, "Bill, was your butt too big for that plane?" It alluded to Parcells's decision against returning with the Patriots on their charter plane following the loss in Super Bowl XXXI.

When the Patriots jogged from the tunnel onto the gridiron, no player showed as much bounce as Curtis Martin, who wore blue gloves while swinging his arms. Meanwhile, Parcells paced among his Jets players, who sat on the gridiron in an organized fashion. Although the 2-0 Patriots appeared formidable once again, Parcells's Jets suddenly seemed respectable at 1-1 following a hard-fought 28–22 loss against Buffalo. On a mild evening with light winds, the Big Tuna wore a green jacket with "Jets" on the back, tan pants, white sneakers, and a steely expression. Defensive lineman Mike Jones was the first Patriots player to venture into enemy territory and greet the Jets leader. Next came Parcells's former defensive assistant, Dante Scarnecchia, who had declined his offer to join the Jets, then tight end Keith Byars, one of Parcells's favorite Patriots.

About an hour before the 8 p.m. kickoff, Pete Carroll offered his predecessor a handshake. The two men, opposites in both coaching style and demeanor, chatted briefly with an ease that belied the charged atmosphere. One overlooked subplot in this game was that it represented Carroll's first contest against the club that had fired him after the 1994 season. Explaining the reason for the decision, Leon Hess had said, "I'm eighty years old. I want results now."

Drew Bledsoe, who had publicly ripped Parcells for the way he left New England, and Curtis Martin were among the Patriots conspicuously skipping the niceties. Bledsoe entered the game with eight touchdowns and zero picks, intent on proving that New England would thrive sans Parcells.

On the opening kickoff by Gang Green, the anticipatory roar of 60,072 exploded into exhilaration as rookie Chris Canty produced a 63-yard return. Moments later tight end Ben Coates made a nifty 32-yard reception, despite linebacker Mo Lewis's wallpaper coverage. Only two minutes into the Tuna Bowl, New England led 7–0, feeding the fervor of its sold-out crowd.

For the first time in his life, Boy Wonder turned demonstrative for an entire game. Whenever he was tackled near the Jets sideline, Martin got up and scowled at Parcells before returning to the huddle. After each brilliant run, and there were many, Curtis Martin paused to glare at his former coach. Neil O'Donnell's 2-yard sprint punctuated a Jets drive, tying the score in the first quarter, but soon enough, Bledsoe marched New England down the field to reclaim the lead, 14–7, on Martin's 2-yard dash. He stared.

In his brief NFL career, the self-effacing runner had generally avoided shows of emotion. Teammates once joked that Martin was only animated when leading a group prayer. But Parcells's departure had unleashed Boy Wonder's feelings. Martin recalls, "I had this you-are-the-enemy look: 'I am going to *destroy* your team just because you're the one who's coaching them, and you're not coaching us anymore.'"

Parcells's new team responded with similar determination. In cutting New England's lead to 14–10 entering halftime, the Jets made two of three attempts to go for it on fourth down. Then, surprisingly, Gang Green charged ahead, 17–14, on Drew Bledsoe's first pass of the second half: Jets linebacker Mo Lewis intercepted it and sprinted 43 yards for a touchdown. Four years later, Lewis would change the course of Bledsoe's career and Patriots history: the linebacker's haymaker against Bledsoe in week two of the 2001 season caused internal bleeding that forced Tom Brady into the lineup, leading to New England's first Super Bowl title.

At the Tuna Bowl, with about two minutes left in the final quarter, Kraft's team reclaimed the lead, 24–17, on Bledsoe's pass to tight end Lovett Purnell. But the relief felt throughout Foxboro Stadium was brief. Gang Green capped a 72-yard drive when Keyshawn Johnson snatched a pass in the end zone, securing the ball tightly as he fell. Headed into overtime tied at 24, the Tuna Bowl lived up to its hype as the lead tied or changed seven times.

In contrast to many players, Curtis Martin exuded energy late in the game. On a nine-play, 62-yard drive by New England, he accounted for 42 yards, setting up the denouement: Adam Vinatieri's 34-yard field goal concluded the drama, 27–24, causing Parcells to grimace. Boy Wonder had used everything he had learned from the Tuna, including the importance of physical conditioning, and in one of the most riveting games at Foxboro Stadium, Martin finished with a career-best 199 yards on 40 carries.

With a play-calling sheet rolled up in his left hand, Parcells walked across the gridiron as Patriots Nation celebrated his defeat and its unblemished record. By the time the Jets leader reached midfield, he was met by several of his ex-players and an armada of photographers and cameramen. Boy Wonder, helmet in hand, elbow pads muddy, slipped through a hole to Parcells's right. The Jets coach slowed after spotting his former runner extending his right hand. Bulbs flashed and tape rolled while the two shook hands.

Martin and Parcells walked a few yards together. Parcells, still glum, asked, "Boy Wonder, who do you think you're growling at? Who are you making those faces at?"

Martin responded sheepishly, "Coach, it was just my competitive spirit."

Parcells's grimace turned into a smile, then Boy Wonder and the Big Tuna laughed. Martin moved closer to whisper in Parcells's right ear, "Coach, all jokes aside, I don't really remember telling any other man this in my life, but I really love you. And if it weren't for you, I don't know where I'd be."

Martin started heading in the opposite direction to catch up with his teammates. Parcells's lip quivered as he pointed his forefinger at Martin. "I love you, too, Boy Wonder."

Gang Green's competitiveness against New England wasn't a fluke, as indicated by their drastic improvement to 4-3. A rematch took place on October 19 when Pete Carroll's 5-1 Patriots visited Giants Stadium. Most of the 71,061 spectators wore green firefighter helmets as part of a game-day promotion, but they found little to cheer about in the first half as New York's offense struggled under Neil O'Donnell.

With his team down 5–3, at intermission Parcells approached backup quarterback Glenn Foley in the locker room. "Get ready. You're going to start the second half. We need a spark." The switch to the 1994 seventh-round pick startled Jets players, since Neil O'Donnell was among the league's highest-paid quarterbacks. However, Parcells's knowledge of Foley went beyond the NFL: during his Patriots tenure Parcells had attended some of Tom Coughlin's practices at nearby Boston College and had admired Foley's pluck.

Drew Bledsoe opened the second-half scoring with an 8-yard strike to tight end Ben Coates for a 12–3 lead. But unleashing quick-trigger darts, Foley guided Gang Green to touchdowns on three consecutive possessions. The final one occurred with New England up, 19–17, early in the fourth period, when Foley capped a 76-yard drive with a 5-yard touchdown pass to fullback Lorenzo Neal. New York's 24–19 lead spurred the green-helmeted spectators to chant, "Foley! Foley! Foley!" To their delight, Foley had outdueled Bledsoe, completing 14 straight passes along the way. In the final period Gang Green contained one of the NFL's top offenses, ensuring the outcome after a stunning comeback. The Jets' most significant home victory in a decade spurred hopes of postseason play.

Parcells never regained confidence in O'Donnell, putting the Jets in a revolving-door situation at quarterback. However, with Bill Belichick's feisty defense led by cornerback Aaron Glenn, and stellar special teams play featuring Leon Johnson, the Jets competed in every game. Their largest margin of defeat would end up being only 11 points versus Jimmy Johnson's Dolphins on October 12. Regardless of who played quarterback for Gang Green, Keyshawn Johnson backed up his huge ego by proudly playing like a "great giraffe." His performances helped mend the locker-room schism caused by his autobiography, while self-effacing Wayne Chrebet provided an ideal complement, using his Velcro-like hands for clutch receptions.

After leading the NFL in no-shows the previous season, Jets fans had turned their home stadium into a deafening mosh pit of overflow crowds, and what had once been an oft-used headline, "Same Old Jets," had vanished from the tabloids. Nonetheless, Parcells guarded ruthlessly against complacency. Former personnel director Dick Haley recalls, "He prodded the coaches to 'press the players.' That was one of his favorite terms. He had his thumb on everybody."

Parcells constantly tweaked the bottom of the roster during "family business" with Mike Tannenbaum, habitually releasing underachieving players and signing new blood wherever he found it, including the Arena Football League. "As human beings," Parcells explains, "we generally respond to one thing, and that's pressure—whatever circumstances create a feeling of necessity. Now, maybe some psychologists would disagree with that. But I have found that to be true in my life experience. Some of us respond favorably to pressure, and others respond unfavorably. But like it says in *The Coaches*, you just can't do a bad job in this business and hope nobody notices, because everybody's going to notice."

Kept on edge despite their tremendous strides, the 7-4 Jets faced the 8-3 Vikings at Giants Stadium with a chance at leading the AFC East. New York went up 7–0 the first time it touched the ball, with Leon Johnson returning a punt 66 yards for a touchdown. Neil O'Donnell started because of a knee injury to Foley, and Gang Green raced to a 23–7 lead.

The Vikings, however, put on an impressive final period, showing why they were co-leaders of the NFC Central. Brad Johnson's touchdown pass at the end of regulation cut Minnesota's deficit to 23–21. With no time left, the Vikings attempted a two-point conversion instead of an extra-point-after, trying to send the game into overtime. Most of the 70,000-plus spectators rose from their seats, exhorting the Jets defense. After taking a handoff from the 2, tailback Robert Smith bounced to his right, but defensive end Rick Lyle penetrated Minnesota's line and grabbed Smith's ankle, allowing his teammates to gang-tackle the runner.

The pivotal stop upped New York's record to 8-4, ensuring a non-losing season for the first time since 1993. Jets fans exploded with a sustained ovation, bringing Leon Hess to tears in the owner's box. Several minutes later, Parcells declared to a raucous locker room, "They can't call us losers anymore."

The Jets lost two of their next three, but with a 9-6 mark entering the regular-season finale, a victory at Detroit would guarantee Gang Green's first playoff appearance since 1991. Parcells's team also maintained an outside shot at capturing the franchise's first division title since the merger. The 8-7 Lions, with home-field advantage, likewise faced a win-and-they're-in situation. Detroit boasted a high-powered offense behind league co-MVP Barry Sanders, only 131 rushing yards short of the lofty 2,000-yard barrier.

At the late-December afternoon matchup, temperatures inside the Pontiac Silverdome reached 72 degrees, while it was 34 outside. New York's Neil O'Donnell performed with renewed confidence and effectiveness as the Jets went up 10–0 on Adrian Murrell's 14-yard run in the first quarter, quieting the 77,624 spectators. Gang Green led 10–3 at halftime after holding Barry Sanders, the focus of Bill Belichick's defense, to only 20 rushing yards.

On New York's opening drive of the third quarter, however, Neil O'Donnell's pass to Richie Anderson ricocheted off the fullback's hands, leading to an interception. Detroit parlayed the gaffe into a field goal, cutting the lead to four. For Gang Green's next series, Parcells replaced O'Donnell with special-teamer Ray Lucas, who had made brief quarterback appearances in the first and second periods. Parcells intended to occasionally recharge an offense showing modest production since O'Donnell had reclaimed his starting role.

Although Lucas had spent most of the season on the practice squad, the ex–Rutgers quarterback completed three straight passes. Throwing short strikes after rollouts that exploited his mobility, Lucas guided his team to Detroit's 19. But on third-and-4 from the 29, his pass into the end zone was intercepted by safety Ron Rice. On the last play of the third quarter, Barry Sanders finally showed his Houdini-esque moves, scampering 47 yards to New York's 17. A few plays later, he dashed 15 yards for a touchdown that put Detroit ahead for the first time, 13–10. The Motor-City mob raised the decibel level so high that Parcells's team struggled to hear its signals.

Although O'Donnell reentered the game, Parcells didn't hesitate to yank him on key possessions as Gang Green undertook a long drive to Detroit's 9. With less than eight minutes left, O'Donnell stood on the sideline in frustration while on first-and-goal, Parcells called for a halfback option from Leon Johnson, a former high school quarterback who had attempted only one NFL pass. Johnson rolled far right to the edge of the sideline before unleashing a wounded-duck pass toward wideout Jeff Graham, double-teamed in the end zone. Cornerback Bryant Westbrook snagged the pigskin, juggling it before tumbling out of bounds. Although the grab was ruled an interception, TV replays confirmed that Westbrook had controlled the ball only after he struck the ground, a sequence that would factor into the NFL's reinstitution of instant replay.

Sanders secured Detroit's three-point lead with a 53-yard run late, sending New England to the playoffs instead of Gang Green. He finished with 184 rushing yards for a season total of 2,053, becoming the third back to break the plateau, after O. J. Simpson and Eric Dickerson. Attempting a gimme field goal to force overtime, instead of a botched halfback option by a rookie, might have propelled the Jets to their first playoff appearance since 1991, but criticism of Parcells was muted. His risky decisions and derring-do, including early in the game, had led to a transformative season. Gang Green's 9-7 record represented one of the sharpest turnarounds in league history. And Jets fans, experiencing their first winning season since 1988, were responding with record-breaking attendance.

The eight additional victories had come despite the Jets dropping to sixteenth in personnel spending after having been tops in the NFL. Cornerback Aaron Glenn was the team's only player voted to the Pro Bowl, but sharper execution and better discipline led Gang Green to drastically reduce turnovers (from 46 to 22) and penalties (110 to 83). Leon Hess, constantly thanked by New Yorkers when they spotted him in public, was no longer embarrassed by his franchise.

Bill Parcells, however, craved more than respectability.

20

In mid-January 1998, Mike Tannenbaum and Bill Parcells met in the organization's boardroom to assess the team's roster needs and prioritize them. The most conspicuous hole was at starting quarterback. When free agency started about a month later, on Friday the thirteenth, Curtis Martin's representative, Eugene Parker, phoned Tannenbaum to gauge interest in his client. Boy Wonder's status as a restricted free agent allowed the Patriots to match any offer, and even if New England permitted its tailback to depart, the new club would have to relinquish first- and third-round draft picks. No free agent with such restrictions had ever switched teams, so Tannenbaum relayed news of Eugene Parker's inquiry to Parcells in a dismissive manner. "I know we're not interested in Curtis Martin, so—"

Parcells interrupted. "Whoa, whoa, whoa. What do you mean? We've got to get this guy."

Tannenbaum was befuddled. "Well, wait a second. I thought running back was our eighth need."

Parcells responded, "You don't understand something. If our best player is our best person and our best worker, he'll make everybody on the team better." The exchange provided an important lesson to the aspiring GM: assembling a team involved both art and science. "That's where Bill's genius lay," Tannenbaum says.

For the next fifteen days, Mike Tannenbaum and Eugene Parker secretly worked toward a contract that would require creativity to prevent New England from matching it. Parker, an agent since 1984, had long expressed frustration that NFL contracts only included *team* options, which empowered clubs to nullify terms at a specified date. With Parcells's blessing, Gang Green's offer included a *player* option, permitting Martin to unilaterally void the long-term deal after the 1998 season and become an unrestricted free agent.

Tannenbaum also inserted a provision barring the Patriots or Jets from using the franchise tag or transition tag on Martin in the 1998 off-season. Those designations allowed clubs to retain a valued free agent for one season by offering a non-negotiable high salary established by the league. The two key clauses in Gang Green's offer, essentially poison pills, were unprecedented. And the six-year contract, potentially worth $36 million, was the richest in NFL history for a runner. If Martin exercised the player option to return after one season, he would trigger a five-year extension for $27.7 million in a deal with an average salary of $5.5 million. "Tons and tons and tons of money," Tannenbaum says.

The salary-cap whiz entered Parcells's office to break down the numbers, and sitting across from his boss, he delivered some bad news: with $18 million guaranteed to Martin, the offer easily exceeded the club's personnel budget. The Jets had recently made Kevin Mawae, twenty-seven, the NFL's highest-paid center in their first major move of the off-season. Parcells envisioned the six-four, 300-pounder helping Gang Green to dominate the middle of the line. Mawae, a Seahawks free agent, commanded a five-year, $17 million contract that included a $5 million signing bonus.

Referring to Martin's deal, Tannenbaum told his boss, "We don't have the money to do this."

Parcells responded, "Mr. T, we've got to get this guy, but this *is* a lot of money. What the heck are we going to do here?"

Tannenbaum said, "I don't know. Call Mr. Hess?"

Parcells's face tightened, but he reached for the phone to dial the oil magnate. Mr. T sat clinging to Parcells's words while the Jets coach conveyed their predicament. Tannenbaum tried without success to read Hess's decision until Parcells laughed hard before hanging up.

Parcells, grinning, said, "Mr. T, Mr. Hess will have to sell more oil. Go get the guy!"

The good news prompted Curtis Martin to sign Gang Green's offer on March 20, 1998, but New England still had one week to decide on whether to match it. Within a few days Martin and his agent met the Jets' head coach and Tannenbaum for dinner at Parcells's regular eating spot on Long Island, B. K. Sweeney's Uptown Grille. Parcells's favorite waitress, Kelly Mandart, a vivacious and curvaceous twenty-eight-year-old, sat the quartet at a corner booth perennially reserved for him. During the meal, Martin sought Parcells's advice on the long-shot possibility of New England matching the deal. Alluding to the clause permitting him to opt out of the contract in early 1998, Martin asked, "What would you do if you were me?"

Tannenbaum perked up because it was the only scenario that Parcells hadn't discussed with him. "Lookit, Curt," Parcells replied. "I think you'd be a great fit here. But as much as I hate to say this, you'd have to exercise that option because it's a lot of money. And you never know if that's going to come around again."

"I love you, man."

"Don't love me. Love the end zone."

The Patriots now faced a wrenching decision involving one of the league's best young players, but matching the offer made little financial sense given Martin's ability to become an unrestricted free agent after one season while negatively affecting New England's salary cap. Robert Kraft protested the contract to no avail before deciding to accept Gang Green's eighteenth and eighty-first overall picks. Despite approving the Jets' offer, the NFL agreed with Kraft's contention that they had ignored the spirit of the collective bargaining agreement by inserting poison pills. Going forward, the league barred similar inventiveness: the "Curtis Martin Rule" prohibits neutering of the franchise tag via an offer sheet.

Given his team's salary-cap issues, Parcells asked Neil O'Donnell to take a significant pay cut from his salary of $4 million. After the quarterback refused, Parcells released him in late June, and signed twelfth-year veteran Vinny Testaverde to a salary of only $1.5 million. The top overall pick in 1987 via the Miami Hurricanes, Testaverde had been inconsistent during his pro career, which included playing for Belichick's Browns from 1993 to 1995, before the team moved to Baltimore. However, Testaverde was capable of making every type of throw, much like Drew Bledsoe, and at six-five and 235 pounds, he was both strapping and superbly conditioned. His bazooka arm produced spurts of brilliance, which he had sustained during a Pro Bowl season in 1996.

While studying film of Testaverde before acquiring him, the Jets detected a major flaw: when his primary receiver was wallpapered, he too often ran around in the pocket before throwing an interception. That habit aside, Parcells believed the former Heisman Trophy winner was one of the game's best pure passers. So after hiring his close friend Dan Henning as quarterbacks coach, Parcells banned Testaverde from throwing on the run. The Jets coaches instructed him instead to sprint for yardage when no one was open, or fling the ball out of bounds. They also planned to reduce the chances of a relapse by giving him extra protection.

Parcells declared Glenn Foley the starting quarterback, but left open the possibility of Testaverde commandeering the job during training camp.

Following the free-agency frenzy, Parcells drove to his winter home in Jupiter, Florida, for a respite in advance of the draft. He still had no idea that one of his scouts was seriously dating his middle daughter, but the romance had become an open secret at Jets headquarters. When Dallas discovered that Charlie Weis had been discussing the relationship, she grew alarmed because of his reputation for gossiping. "I was *really* concerned that Charlie knew," Dallas says. She certainly didn't want her dad to find out from someone else.

Pioli suggested that she ease her mind by telling her father at the next opportunity. Dallas agreed and, after arranging a visit to her parents in Jupiter, found a quiet moment with her father. "I have something to tell you, Dad. I've been dating someone, and you know him."

Mystified, Parcells asked, "Well, who is it?"

"I'm dating Scott Pioli. I just wanted to tell you because I really like him." Dallas chuckled nervously, waiting for her father's reaction.

"Oh, okay. That's fine. I'm glad you told me."

Parcells was surprised by the news but, to his daughter's relief, quickly accepted the relationship because he liked Pioli. Dallas recalls, "I felt a little ridiculous. Here I am, a thirty-three-year-old woman, and I'm telling my dad I've got a boyfriend as if I'm twelve."

In early April, Parcells returned to Long Island in time for Pioli's first day back from a scouting trip. Reluctant to broach the subject first, Pioli went about his business at Weeb Ewbank Hall, spending much of the day in Gang Green's war room working on the draft board. When Parcells entered, Pioli braced himself. His boss wasted no time. "So, I hear we're dating."

Pioli quipped, "Oh, we are? That's news to me. But I do like you a lot, Bill."

The humor broke the awkwardness, and before long Parcells gave his blessing to wedding plans that would make Scott Pioli his son-in-law in 1999.

Gang Green's off-season after a historic turnaround further lifted expectations as the franchise headed into the thirtieth anniversary of its greatest triumph: Super Bowl III. The Jets announced their players would wear a tweaked version of the green-and-white uniform and logo from the bygone era: instead of the green helmet with "JETS" in white below an airplane wing, the franchise reintroduced a white helmet with "NY JETS" superimposed on a green oval.

With the franchise flaunting a retro look, Parcells conducted another grueling training camp at Hofstra. Actor Al Pacino visited for two days to research his lead role as a pro football head coach in *Any Given Sunday*. Director Oliver Stone based the character on a composite that included Vince Lombardi and Bill Parcells. The film, set to open in late 1999, would feature an ensemble cast that included legendary NFL players Jim Brown and Lawrence Taylor with cameos from Dick Butkus, Emmitt Smith, Y. A. Tittle, and Johnny Unitas.

In their introductory exchange at Weeb Ewbank Hall, Parcells couldn't resist telling Pacino, "Just this one time, I'm going to let you ask about the

family business." Pacino grinned at Parcells's twist on the actor's famous line to Diane Keaton, who played his wife, Kay Corleone, in *The Godfather*. At Jets practices, Pacino unsuccessfully tried to stay inconspicuous, prowling the field in a light trench coat while scrutinizing Parcells's interactions with players. Occasionally, the NFL's version of the Godfather sidled up to his special guest to explain things. "He generally knew what was going on," Parcells recalls of Pacino, "but I tried to give him some insight. He was a nice man. I enjoyed meeting him."

Glenn Foley performed well enough during the camp to remain the incumbent quarterback. Opening the season at San Francisco, he amassed a career-high 415 passing yards in a passing duel with Steve Young, but Gang Green lost in overtime, 36–30, when Garrison Hearst dashed 96 yards to score on his team's longest-ever run from scrimmage. In New York's next game, against the Ravens at Giants Stadium, Foley tossed three interceptions and hurt his ribs during a 24–10 loss.

Foley's injury put Testaverde in the starting lineup for a home game versus Indianapolis, quarterbacked by rookie Peyton Manning. The rifle-armed veteran threw four touchdowns in New York's 44–6 rout of the Colts, ending his team's early-season doldrums. Gang Green followed up with another sharp performance at home, defeating the Dolphins, 20–9, as Belichick's defense intercepted Dan Marino twice.

His ribs mended, Foley returned to a starting role for an October 11 contest at St. Louis, but he was performing poorly as the Rams trampled New York, prompting Parcells to yank him in the third quarter. Testaverde entered the game and threw New York's sole touchdown in a 30–10 loss. At 2-3, the Jets faced a familiar opponent for their most important game of the season to date: the undefeated Patriots at Foxboro Stadium on *Monday Night Football*.

Trying to squash a quarterback controversy, Parcells named Testaverde the starter indefinitely, but during Friday's practice, three days from the October 19 showdown, Parcells's team looked undisciplined and uninspired. Players executed even the basics poorly, as linemen continuously jumped offside. About half an hour into the scheduled ninety-minute session, Parcells whistled it to a stop.

He rounded up his staff and said, "That's it. Let's get the hell out of here."

Perplexed, Parcells's coaches looked at each other, prompting him to reiterate, "We're leaving practice *right now*." He ordered the coaches to head into the building for an impromptu meeting. Players milled around on the field, talking to one another, hesitant to leave. Back inside, Parcells

sat at the head of a table and spent the next several minutes railing about specific players.

Todd Haley recalls, "As a young coach I don't know anything, so I'm wondering to myself, 'What is going on?' We're about to play the game of the year, and here he is going down the whole roster, venting about all the players he can't stand. Finally, I just can't take it anymore. I say, 'So, are we just quitting?' Well, *that* drives him crazy."

Parcells ordered the neophyte coach to shut up and go see whether the players were still on the field. When he did, Haley found fullback Richie Anderson and linebacker Bryan Cox overseeing a lively practice, using a script left behind by one of Parcells's assistants. After receiving Haley's intelligence, Parcells returned to his office, peeking out his window to confirm it. His players were even running sprints, knowing that Parcells would have ended practice with the dreaded exercise. Their actions stood in stark contrast to the way Texas Tech's defensive players had reacted in 1975, when they were so quick to get off the field after a similar outburst by Parcells.

More than two decades later, Parcells had come a long way from being a young defensive coordinator disliked by many of his new players. Nonetheless, cutting short Gang Green's practice before a monumental game posed a big risk for a team only two seasons removed from a 1-15 record. Romeo Crennel, Parcells's former colleague at Texas Tech, says, "I was surprised by Bill's decision, but he felt that he really needed to get the players' attention. He didn't know how it was going to turn out. Either they were going to try to make things right, or they were going to fall apart and not finish practice. The episode ended up pulling the team together."

The Monday-night affair at Foxboro Stadium lacked the fervor of the Tuna Bowl, but with eight ex-Patriots, including Curtis Martin, sporting throwback Jets uniforms, the showdown was once again laden with emotion. Following pregame fireworks, most of the 60,062 spectators booed Boy Wonder each time he touched the ball. During a competitive, hard-fought contest, he showed the hecklers his familiar mettle and shiftiness. New England was leading 14–10 in the final period when Martin's 12-yard run put the Jets on his former team's 1. Then, with less than nine minutes left, Jets tight end Kyle Brady caught a short pass for what would be the game winner. Gang Green triumphed, 24–14, as Testaverde finished with three touchdowns passes, including two to Brady, and Boy Wonder collected 107 rushing yards in an I-work-hard-for-my-money performance.

The upset victory marked a turning point, as Gang Green pivoted into a hot streak near midseason. Vinny Testaverde cemented his starting role, thriving in a well-balanced offense that featured Keyshawn Johnson, Wayne Chrebet, and Curtis Martin. Belichick's defense, starring corner-back Aaron Glenn and linebacker Mo Lewis, was transforming into one of the league's stingiest units. But even as Gang Green won four straight, center Kevin Mawae noticed a dynamic he had never experienced during his first four NFL seasons: winning streaks, a salve when he played for the Seahawks, failed to generate a kinder, gentler atmosphere for this team.

"You did not want to get caught in the hallway with Bill," Mawae says, "because you never knew whether he was going to say hi to you or he was going to rip you. One day, I'm walking down the hallway. Bill is going one way; I'm going the other. The first thing I think is: 'Crap!' Because no matter what you do, you can't win with him."

Mawae was heading to a meeting that included watching film.

Walking past Parcells, he said, "Coach, how are you doing?"

Parcells snapped, "You don't worry about me! You just worry about blocking your goddamn guy Sunday."

The big offensive lineman kept walking as his heart raced.

Mawae laughs now. "That was Bill's way of saying hi."

Brusque or eloquent, hilarious or dyspeptic, charming or caustic—players never knew which side of Parcells's personality he would flash. "He's like a kaleidoscope," Judy says. Dan Henning agrees. "You talk to five people, they see him five different ways. And their assessments are all correct, because he *can* act five different ways. He *plans* to be different."

Whether Parcells chose his silver tongue or the acid-edged alternative, uncanny timing gave his utterances maximum impact. He knew which subjects constituted an athlete's third rail, and often zapped players at their most vulnerable moments.

A November 15 setback at Indianapolis seemed to justify Parcells's crusade against complacency. Despite entering the game with just one victory, the Colts halted Gang Green's streak, 24–23, at the RCA Dome after tailback Marshall Faulk led a 13-point comeback. Boy Wonder, though, continued to justify Parcells's bold decision to sign him to an unprecedented contract, gaining 134 yards on 28 carries.

The Jets proved that the meltdown was merely a hiccup by earning a 24–3 road victory versus Jeff Fisher's Oilers, who were also in the playoff hunt. Gang Green's record stood at 7-4 for Leon Hess's annual Thanksgiving chat, the one time each year that the owner directly addressed his players. On Thursday, November 26, Hess attended practice to give his twenty-second consecutive pep talk. Wearing a knitted green hat, the owner sat on a folding chair on the sideline.

At the end of a spirited session, Hess signaled his readiness to Parcells, who called his players over to gather around their owner. In characteristically brief remarks, Hess told his team that it had been performing well enough to make the playoffs, and wished the players luck in their upcoming game versus the Carolina Panthers. He added that he was pleased at the way his guys were representing the franchise and avoiding trouble off the field.

During the three-minute chat, the tired players stood rapt, hanging on every word. Many of them were intrigued by Hess's quiet persona. "A speak-quietly-but-walk-with-a-big-stick guy," Mike Tannenbaum says of Hess. "He was a man's man. All he really wanted to do was win. And as long as we didn't violate the U.S. Constitution, he really didn't care how we did it."

After his nasty divorce with Robert Kraft, Parcells found the self-effacing owner to be an ideal partner. Despite an age difference of more than a quarter century, Hess and Parcells shared many qualities, including a biting sense of humor. They also possessed the sensibilities of New Jersey natives familiar with the state's cushy as well as seamy sides, and their Jersey experiences made them comfortable among varied ethnicities and social classes. Hess spoke with a gravelly voice even deeper than Parcells's, and unless women were present, they often accentuated their remarks with expletives. They were both obsessively organized: Parcells's tendency for detail extended to his home, where the clothes in his closet were arranged by size, shape, and color. Hess was fanatical about cleanliness, and regularly inspected his oil facilities; Hess gas stations, painted green and white, were known for their neatness.

Parcells ached to capture a Lombardi Trophy for Hess more than he had for any owner, and by late in the 1998 season the Jets resembled a contender, regularly defeating playoff-bound opponents, even on the road. Another gauge was taken on December 31 when the 9-4 Jets faced Jimmy Johnson's Dolphins, AFC East leaders at 9-3. Parcells's team triumphed, 21–16, in Pro Player Stadium after linebacker Chad Cascadden strip-sacked Dan Marino with less than two minutes left, and returned the fumble for a touchdown.

One memorable play in the third quarter involved Boy Wonder's balletic moves in perhaps the most electrifying run of his young career. After taking a handoff in the backfield, Martin eluded three Dolphins defenders despite committing two Parcells no-nos: running backward and zigzagging before crossing the line of scrimmage. He made would-be tacklers look like human pretzels during a nine-yard run to give his team a 14–3 lead. Almost every defender whiffed one time or another while attempting to corral him. The display of pure talent caused teammates on Gang

Green's sideline to act like enthralled fans. The next day at Jets headquarters, they would giddily replay the sequence in slo-mo while counting the number of defenders attempting to halt Martin. Nonetheless, in the moment, when Boy Wonder trotted back to New York's sideline, an angry head coach awaited him.

Parcells yelled, "Didn't I tell you about that? Stop trying to make everybody miss! I don't want a running back that dances! I don't want a running back that wears high heels!" Parcells punctuated the tongue-lashing by barking, "And you're carrying the ball in the wrong goddamn arm!" Late in the spectacular run, Martin had carried the pigskin with the arm closest to defenders. Proper form required cradling the ball farthest from a defender's line of pursuit, reducing the odds of another Parcells bugaboo: fumbling.

Seeing that Boy Wonder was confounded by his harshness, Parcells lowered his decibel level to explain. "Usually those habits are not going to end well. If you don't eliminate them, they'll be detrimental to your team."

But why nitpick such a sublime play?

"Because," Parcels says now, "I was trying to train him to be the best that he could be. You can't always judge the wisdom of choices by the results. We have a saying in football. It's '**NATO: Not Attached to Outcome.**' You may do something that turns out well, but it's still not the most prudent choice. I wanted him to learn every single thing that I know about the running-back position. So whenever I saw him starting to use a habit that I knew was not good based on my experience, I got on his ass about it.

"In this case he made some judgment calls that usually result in being thrown for a loss. But his unique ability"—Parcells chuckles—"just happened to take over, and he was able to make every defender miss. So my hat's off to him on that, but you can't count on it happening consistently."

Parcells compares the memorable run to an arcade game he used to play on the Jersey Shore as a kid: Skee-Ball. "You try to roll a ball up a ramp into these holes. The smallest hole's worth 100. If you keep aiming for the 100-hole, chances are you're not going to get a high score. In Skee-Ball, once in a long while the ball's going to go in that hole."

Parcells admired Cowboys great Emmitt Smith for his downhill style, toughness, and savvy. So the Jets coach urged Martin to emulate the way Smith moved to the line of scrimmage before making his cut at the last moment. Parcells noted that only a handful of tailbacks possessed this ability. The pointer was yet another way to galvanize Boy Wonder to greatness.

Leon Hess's club was positioned to capture its first AFC East title when the Jets visited Buffalo for their next-to-last game of the regular season.

On a damp, gray afternoon, Vinny Testaverde tossed two touchdowns, including a 71-yard strike to wideout Dedric Ward that snapped a 10–10 tie in the fourth quarter. With a 17–10 victory at Rich Stadium, Gang Green became the final team from the 1970 AFL-NFL merger to claim a division crown. Wideout Wayne Chrebet and defensive end Bobby Hamilton dumped a bucket of ice water over Parcells on the sideline as the head coach's intense look softened into a smile. He hugged several players and coaches before heading toward the tunnel for the visitors' locker room. Bryan Cox chest-bumped teammates as Mo Lewis, who'd endured several losing seasons since being drafted in 1991, screamed, "Thank you, Jesus!"

Fifteen minutes after creating Jets history, Parcells stood among his boisterous players, who wore green caps emblazoned "AFC East Champions." Parcells called for a hush to address them inside a semicircle.

"You hear, 'Same old Jets. Same old Jets—'"

Unable to complete the sentence, Parcells choked up, stopping for a minute to gather himself. Some players got teary-eyed seeing their cantankerous coach react that way. "That's all I remember. The pause," cornerback Ray Mickens says. "It sent chills through my body to see him like that because he was always a tough sonofabitch."

Several players cheered the moment, giving Parcells time to pull himself together. The tough-nosed leader continued forcefully. "Well, now you're the champs and nobody can take that away from you. You have a responsibility to keep playing that way." Parcells then rewarded his players with two days off, which drew the loudest whoops of all. He added that the game ball would be given to their ailing owner, who had been unable to make the trip.

The Jets won their regular-season finale, 31–10, over New England, underscoring the altered fortunes of both franchises. Testaverde threw four touchdowns to set a Jets season record with 29, three more than Joe Namath in 1967, although teams played two fewer games back then. Testaverde averaged 7.4 yards rushing, evidence that he had adhered to Parcells's ban against throwing on the run. The quarterback's altered approach helped bring the most remarkable aspect of his year: just seven interceptions. In Testaverde's sophomore NFL season as a Buccaneer, he had thrown 35 interceptions, the second most in NFL or AFL history. His own striking reversal mirrored that of his team.

Gang Green's twelve victories, including five straight, established a franchise mark that earned the club an opening-round bye and its first playoff game at home since 1986. Having won most of their games by at least one touchdown, the Jets, a bumbling team BP (Before Parcells), strutted into the postseason.

• • •

During the 1990s Tom Coughlin had transformed Jacksonville into one of the conference's best teams. In the wild-card round of the playoffs, the AFC Central champions defeated New England, 25–10, leading to a contest against Gang Green. So for the second time in three postseasons, Coughlin and Parcells matched wits. A cold afternoon brought a wind-chill factor of 16 degrees, yet Giants Stadium bustled with 78,817 spectators, the most ever in the building for a sporting event. They cheered while Gang Green's opening possession, a 70-yard touchdown drive capped by Keyshawn Johnson's 21-yard catch, set the tone for the game. The giraffe looked more like a gazelle during a chicanery-generated 10-yard run that gave New York a 17–0 lead.

That cushion helped Gang Green overcome a late comeback attempt by Mark Brunell, who would toss three touchdowns, including two in the second half, but also three picks. New York triumphed, 34–24, controlling the clock for more than 39 minutes in classic Parcells fashion.

With his virtuoso performance Keyshawn Johnson tied a team playoff record of 9 catches for 121 yards. He made a key fumble recovery and, in the game's waning moments, became an impromptu safety to intercept Brunell's desperation pass. Boy Wonder rushed 36 times for 124 yards while scoring 2 touchdowns. Showcasing his soft hands, he also made 6 receptions for 58 yards.

Gang Green's first postseason victory in twelve years triggered explosions of confetti over Giants Stadium. Just two years removed from ignominy, the Jets were headed to the AFC Championship in Denver's Mile High Stadium. Hess's team needed just one victory in their retro jerseys to reach the franchise's first Super Bowl since 1969.

Wearing a blue suit, a green tie, and an incandescent smile, the owner entered his team's locker room to celebrate. Parcells took pleasure in observing him. Hess moved gingerly while interacting with players and coaches, but the eighty-five-year-old behaved like the giddiest person in Gang Green's sanctum. "The joy on his face was like that of a happy little kid," Parcells recalls. "It meant so much to him, to win at home, to make those loyal Jets fans happy. He lived for that moment. I know he did."

To Hess's chagrin, doctors barred him from traveling to Denver because of their concerns over his health. The Broncos constituted a formidable team as defending Super Bowl champions and the AFC's top seed at a franchise-record 14-2. But Parcells's confident team certainly wasn't the same old Jets. *His* version boasted the NFL's second-ranked defense with Pro Bowl seasons from Aaron Glenn and Mo Lewis, reborn under the new regime; the team's fifth-ranked offense featured bona fide stars in Keyshawn Johnson, Curtis Martin, and Vinny Testaverde.

Swirling winds in Mile High Stadium gusted at unpredictable moments as the opening kickoff approached for the AFC Championship. Amid blustery conditions that felt much colder than the 30-degree thermometer reading, New York and Denver struggled in the first half to look like the AFC's top two seeds. Both teams, especially the Jets, squandered scoring opportunities: Keith Byars and Curtis Martin uncharacteristically fumbled the ball away in Broncos territory, and John Elway threw an incompletion on a fourth-down attempt at New York's 1.

John Hall's field goal moments before intermission put the Jets up 3–0, rendering Denver scoreless at halftime for the first time since 1995. Early in the third quarter, Jets rookie tight end Blake Spence, a reserve appearing in only his sixth NFL game, blocked Tom Rouen's punt. Gang Green recovered it at Denver's 1. On the next play, Boy Wonder, bottled up all afternoon, plunged into the end zone, giving New York a 10–0 lead that stunned the 75,483 spectators whose team had won eighteen straight at home. Leon Hess, watching in his Park Avenue apartment, felt a sense of Super Bowl destiny. Elway, though, responded on Denver's next offensive snap with a 47-yard completion to wideout Ed McCaffrey. Two plays later, the thirty-eight-year-old quarterback tossed an 11-yard touchdown to fullback Howard Griffith.

Jason Elam's kickoff became momentarily trapped in 25-mile-per-hour winds of Mile High Stadium. As if the pigskin had hit an invisible wall, it dropped from the sky almost 20 yards short of returner Dave Meggett, who was waiting in front of the end zone. Then the ball ricocheted toward the Broncos. The bizarre trajectory essentially turned the play into a long onside kick. In the ensuing scramble Jets linebacker James Farrior lost the pigskin, which bounced to Broncos linebacker Keith Burns at New York's 31, where he corralled it.

Following the eerie development, momentum shifted to Denver, as Elam's 44-yard field goal tied the score at 10. He soon added a 48-yarder, giving Denver its first lead. The Jets, seemingly still deflated by the Twilight Zone kickoff, went three and out. Then Terrell Davis, the league MVP after rushing for 2,008 yards, scored a 31-yard touchdown late in the third quarter, sending the crowd into a tizzy. In just one period, New York's 10-point lead had evaporated into a double-digit deficit that would prove impossible to overcome.

During the 23–10 setback, the Jets committed six turnovers, including four lost fumbles. The rags-to-riches-and-back-to-rags twist on the championship stage came after a magical season of disciplined play and sharp execution. In one of the worst games of his career, Boy Wonder eked out only 14 yards on 13 carries. And Vinny Testaverde, voted by teammates as Jets MVP, tossed two interceptions late, although he performed well overall. Gang Green held Elway to 13 of 35 passing for only 173 yards in the final home contest of his career, but Terrell Davis, who Parcells had feared would be nearly unstoppable, rushed for 167 yards, including 78 in the pivotal third period.

The team flight from Denver International Airport on the night of January 18 was long and gloomy. When the Jets landed at LaGuardia Airport at roughly 2 a.m., Parcells was the first to exit from his front-row seat. Walking down the ramp into a wintry rain mixed with snow, he was surprised by the sight of a familiar, lean figure standing at the end of the staircase. Leon Hess wore a yellow topcoat with its collar up. His uncovered neck revealed a green-and-blue tie over a white shirt. The owner's hat shielded his ears but failed to prevent sleet from whipping across his face.

When Parcells reached the bottom of the ramp, Hess greeted him with a strong handshake. The ailing owner thanked Parcells for engineering the franchise's best season in decades. "We came up a little short, but you did a good job."

For several minutes Hess stood in the cold exchanging pleasantries as his team's coaches and players deplaned. He didn't leave until he had finished shaking hands with the entire Jets family, including the scouts and equipment guys.

"I'll never forget that. It made me feel even more appreciative of him," Parcells recalls, "because I know how disappointed we both were."

21

Despite the heartbreaking loss, Leon Hess and Bill Parcells were pleased with the franchise's direction. Their roster included several young, talented players who had helped win seven games versus teams that reached the playoffs, matching an NFL record. Vinny Testaverde, thirty-five, had delivered a stellar season while going 12-1 as a starter, solving the club's quarterback problems.

On the coaching staff, Todd Haley epitomized Parcells's batch of green yet promising assistants, and earned a promotion to wideouts coach. Novice scout Trent Baalke, the future architect of Jim Harbaugh's 49ers, was entering his second year with the Jets. Mike Tannenbaum, the cum laude graduate of Tulane Law School, proved to be invaluable in navigating salary-cap complexities, and his work ethic matched Parcells's renowned indefatigability. Tannenbaum didn't take a day off from the Jets until his wedding in Philadelphia, and even then he heeded Parcells's suggestion that the honeymoon occur on the Jersey Turnpike so that the cap whiz could make it back to work the next day.

Hess prized such devotion, and paid his loyal employees accordingly. Team president Steve Gutman had joined the Jets in 1977 as corporate treasurer and administrative manager. With a master's degree in corporate finance from New York University, Gutman spent much of his time monitoring Hess's money. From 1988 to 1996, Steve Gutman's first nine seasons as team president, Gang Green made only one playoff appearance while going 48-96-1. So Jets fans had vilified him as a bean counter in team president's clothing. Hess, however, included Gutman in his will for a small percentage of the franchise.

A few days after the AFC Championship, the Jets owner approached Parcells about his capologist.

"This Tannenbaum guy . . ."

Parcells responded, "Yes, Mr. Hess?"

"I want to double his salary."

"We don't have to do that."

"I'm telling you, Parcells, I want to double his salary."

"Mr. Hess, I'm the GM. I don't want to do that."

"Well, what can we do? I don't want to lose this guy."

Parcells, an enthusiastic investor, remembered that when he had once asked Tannenbaum to name some of his favorite stocks, the cap specialist had responded that he didn't play the market because his law school student loan was such an albatross.

So Parcells told Hess, "We're not going to lose Mr. T. He owes almost $60,000 to his law school. Let's pay off his law-school debt."

Hess replied, "Let's do it. I still want to give him a raise."

"Let's stick with the law school loans this year."

"Okay."

The next afternoon, Parcells stepped into Tannenbaum's office to announce the organization's plans for him. First, Parcells disclosed that Tannenbaum would receive a full share of the team's playoff money, a custom most NFL teams followed for key members of their front office. Tannenbaum thanked his boss for the $47,500. Then Parcells delivered the kicker: because of Tannenbaum's contributions to Gang Green's historic season, Leon Hess had approved payment of his student-loan bill—in full.

Tannenbaum grinned in delight. "Bill, I can't thank you enough! This is going to change my life!"

Parcells replied calmly, "Look, Mr. T, just promise me this. Each month I want you to take the money that you were paying for your loans and put it in a savings account."

"No problem!"

After providing student-loan details to Gutman, Tannenbaum received a check for almost $105,000.

"It was such an emancipating feeling getting out of debt overnight," Tannenbaum says. "It was like hitting the lottery."

Leon Hess's appearance despite his deteriorating health touched Parcells. And as the owner neared his eighty-fifth birthday, on March 14, the head coach felt an urgency to collect the missing pieces for a Super Bowl title. However, Gang Green still owed New England its first-round pick for the right to sign Parcells. To enhance the roster the Jets leaned on free agency, including acquisitions of Ravens tight end Eric Green and Patriots punter Tom Tupa—whose quarterbacking skills also appealed to Parcells. Green and Tupa commanded bonuses that totaled $3.4 million, and the Jets allocated a substantial outlay to retain some of their starters, most notably Vinny Testaverde, who signed a new four-year, $16 million contract with $11 million guaranteed.

The heavy spending came only one year after the club had doled out record deals to Curtis Martin and Kevin Mawae, so Gang Green's 1999 budget was almost drained when Rams linebacker Roman Phifer sparked Parcells's interest by becoming available after his free-agent talks with St. Louis stalled. The thirty-one-year-old was one of the NFL's most versatile linebackers, an ideal fit for a coach with a win-now mentality. Since Detroit was also courting Phifer, only a strong offer from the Jets would suffice. Parcells instructed Tannenbaum to devise a multimillion-dollar contract with the club's remaining cap space, and to the head coach's delight, Phifer agreed to a three-year, $8.9 million offer.

Only minutes after the deal was finalized on March 6, Steve Gutman walked into Parcells's office with a pained expression. The team president seemed jumpy, and stammered uncharacteristically.

"Bill, this has to stop. Are we . . . ? Are we . . . ?"

Gutman exhaled, pausing to gather his words.

"Are we trying to win at all costs?"

Parcells replied, "Yes, Steve. Those were my marching orders, so that's exactly what I'm trying to do."

"Do you mean at *all* costs?"

"Yup. That's pretty much what I mean, Steve."

Parcells promised the fidgety team president that there would be no more expensive acquisitions, but the awkward exchange prompted Parcells to confirm the owner's mandate. Parcells typically phoned Hess twice a week around 8 a.m. to touch base; the oil baron's phone policy required football matters to be discussed before the start of business. Breaching protocol for the first time, Parcells dialed Hess immediately.

"Mr. Hess, we've been spending money on free agents. And I just spent another couple million dollars on—"

Hess interrupted, "I don't give a shit. If you run out of money, come over here to the oil company, and we'll get some more for you this afternoon."

Parcells thanked the owner. Leon Hess had come through for him again. Before hanging up, Hess told Parcells, "Kid, you're doing a great job. Keep it up."

The fifty-seven-year-old head coach beamed.

About a month later, as April's NFL draft neared, Hess broke a hip and required hospitalization. He went back home for a few days, but his worsening condition prompted a return to Manhattan's Lenox Hill Hospital, where he fell gravely ill. In the early morning of May 7, Leon Hess, who had been a part-owner of the Jets since 1963 before taking full control in 1984, died of complications from blood disease. Around 5 a.m., Steve Gutman telephoned Parcells to break the news. Before picking up the phone, Parcells intuited the bad news. As Gutman confirmed it, the Jets boss's eyes welled up, and after hanging up, he bawled. Despite their relatively brief partnership, he considered Hess one of his favorite people in a storied football career.

Parcells says, "He put so much into the Jets. And I was just sorry we couldn't get in the [1999] Super Bowl. We were very close to doing so, and winning it for him. Of all the things that happened in my career, *that* might have been the most satisfying."

On Monday, May 10, Parcells and several Jets players were among the approximately one thousand mourners for Hess's funeral at the Park Avenue Synagogue. The Jets fraternity also consisted of former players, including Joe Namath, and even one fired coach: Rich Kotite. Mayor Giuliani led a contingent of area politicians that included former senators and governors. Business titans paid their respects, from hotelier Leona Helmsley to investor/philanthropist Robert "Woody" Johnson IV, whose namesake great-grandfather co-founded Johnson & Johnson.

Hess was survived by his wife, Norma; son, John; daughters, Connie and Marlene; plus seven grandchildren. Parcells cried while listening to John's funeral remarks when he said his father would be watching Gang Green's 1999 season "from a different place." Although the forty-five-year-old was replacing Leon Hess as chairman of Amerada Hess, he expressed zero interest in NFL ownership, and his father's will required a sale of the team. More than twenty suitors contacted the Hess estate to express interest, so Goldman Sachs was hired to find a potential buyer by December 15, fostering uncertainty about the future of Gang Green's front office and coaches. However, Parcells was considered a franchise asset, which presumably would provide at least short-term stability.

A few days after the funeral John Hess visited Bill Parcells at Weeb Ewbank Hall to assure him that no decisions involving a sale would affect the team's upcoming season. The interim owner also confirmed Parcells's authority as football boss until 2003. Parcells's contract made him head coach of the New York Jets through the 2000 season, with a clause that triggered Belichick's promotion. In that legally binding scenario, Parcells would remain chief of football operations for another two years while ceding day-to-day control to Belichick. Some pundits expected Parcells to quit after the 1999 season, accelerating the succession plan.

Following the AFC Championship, Bill Belichick had declined interview requests from Kansas City and Chicago for their head-coaching openings. Hess had responded by giving the heir apparent a $1 million bonus. The gesture was a dramatic shift from the previous off-season, when Belichick had angered Hess by entertaining interest from other teams, prompting the oil baron to instruct Parcells to fire his lieutenant if such behavior ever happened again.

Not long after Hess rewarded Belichick, Bill Parcells and Will McDonough signed a book deal with William Morrow, an imprint of HarperCollins, to chronicle the 1999 season. They planned to write in diary form about an NFL coach's day-to-day doings while facing the inherent pressures of a football season that Parcells hoped would conclude with the Lombardi Trophy. The publisher would title the book *The Final Season: My Last Year as Head Coach in the NFL*.

The Jets embraced predictions from NFL experts who named Parcells's team a favorite to win Super Bowl XXXIV. On the wall outside the club's training room, a green picture frame said "NEW YORK JETS" on top; and "SUPER BOWL CHAMPIONS??" at the bottom. In place of a photograph stood three sentences:

"Are you in the picture?"

"When will it be taken?"

"It's a team picture only."

But that picture darkened on September 12 during the season opener versus the Patriots at Giants Stadium. Gang Green trailed 10–7 in the second quarter while marching to New England's 25-yard line. Vinny Testaverde handed off to Curtis Martin, who sprinted toward a hole to his left. Despite being blocked, linebacker Willie McGinest reached out to slap the ball from Boy Wonder, sending it bouncing behind the line of scrimmage. Only a few yards away, Testaverde darted toward the pigskin. In midstride he crumpled to the ground, writhing in pain from a ruptured Achilles tendon. Testaverde pounded the recently installed Astroturf with his fist several times before team trainers carted the 1998 team MVP off the field, leaving Jets Nation shell-shocked.

The freak accident meant that the Pro Bowl quarterback would miss the rest of the season—a crushing blow, if not a death knell, to Gang Green's championship aspirations. At age thirty-five, Testaverde was perhaps the team's best-conditioned athlete, but a team doctor would explain to Parcells that in launching off his left heel, Testaverde had placed tremendous pressure on his Achilles tendon, causing it to snap.

Parcells had traded backup quarterback Glenn Foley to Seattle in March because of his disgruntlement on being replaced by Testaverde. So when Green Bay waived quarterback Rick Mirer during training camp, Parcells had acquired him for depth. Seattle drafted Mirer second overall to Drew Bledsoe in 1993, but the Notre Dame grad struggled in the NFL after a promising rookie season.

In New York's season opener, former Patriots punter Tom Tupa was listed as the backup quarterback. The punter/passer entered the game for the first snap following Testaverde's injury, and zinged a 25-yard touchdown to Keyshawn Johnson, putting the Jets up 14–10. It marked Tupa's first touchdown since 1992, when he had played for Indianapolis prior to focusing on punting. The ex–Ohio State Buckeye delivered another scoring pass before linebacker Bryan Cox returned an interception to give New York a 28–27 lead. Then Rick Mirer, Gang Green's true backup quarterback, replaced Tupa late in the fourth quarter and committed two costly interceptions. Patriot Adam Vinatieri's field goal in the final minute handed the Jets a deflating loss in more ways than one.

During his postgame Q&A, Keyshawn Johnson banged the podium with both fists, causing a can of Slice to jump off the table. He unleashed expletives, conveying the sentiments of Jets fans everywhere. "Shit! Vinny is irreplaceable. Not in a million years did I think I'd lose my starting quarterback for the year. There's nothing you can do. We can't do shit. We couldn't throw. We threw interceptions." Cutting his session short, Johnson threw a towel in disgust before bolting from the interview to the hallway. On the way to the locker room he pounded the walls, continuing to curse; his career-high 194 receiving yards was the last thing on his mind.

Gang Green's quarterback situation, the team's Achilles' heel before Testaverde's arrival, overshadowed other key injuries suffered during the 30–28 loss. While returning a kick, Leon Johnson tore left-knee ligaments to end his season; nose tackle Jason Ferguson, the team's best defensive lineman, sprained an ankle and a knee, sidelining him for a month; and tight end Eric Green strained his neck, missing an even longer stretch.

The Jets had been the NFL's least-injured club during the season that placed them at the doorstep of Super Bowl XXXIII, but that good fortune had turned into buzzard's luck beginning in preseason, when starting cornerback Otis Smith broke his collarbone. Then, in Gang Green's exhibition finale, Wayne Chrebet fractured his left foot without anyone touching him after cutting during a route on Giants Stadium's new turf. Coming off a career season of 1,083 receiving yards, only 48 less than his much louder teammate, Chrebet would miss the season's first five games.

After Gang Green's ominous season opener, Parcells told his players, "All the excuses are in place if you want to use them. But if we play the way we're capable of playing, we can be the most dangerous opponent in the league."

With Rick Mirer starting the next four games, the Jets failed to become that dangerous opponent, particularly on offense. Mirer reenacted the interception-prone performances that had prompted his departure from three NFL teams. Against the Jaguars on *Monday Night Football*, the Jets lost 16–6 at Giants Stadium, dropping their record to 1-4. Parcells was furious with the team's regression, especially its weak offense. With the Indianapolis Colts up next at home, he felt compelled to replace Mirer, despite having no appealing options.

Consternation over Gang Green's dire straits caused Parcells to barely sleep. At the team's next meeting, he walked through the entrance in the back of the room just to announce the new starting quarterback. The bleary-eyed coach told his players, "You see that kid sitting in the front row? He's starting for the rest of the season. I don't give a shit if any of you don't like it. Either you get behind him or we'll lose every game."

The quarterbacks typically sat at the front of the room, so Ray Lucas looked down his row to locate Mirer's replacement: Tom Tupa? Or perhaps a new acquisition? When he realized that Parcells was talking about him, Lucas's heart raced with nervousness and excitement. He was finally getting the opportunity he'd ached for while being a role player. Lucas's pro résumé contained only seven passes, most notably an interception with playoff ramifications during the 1997 finale at Detroit, but Parcells was looking beyond Lucas's inexperience and pedigree: the undrafted twenty-seven-year-old out of Rutgers had been outperforming Mirer in practice.

Returning to the locker room following the meeting, Lucas found a box of Huggies on his seat. Attached to the disposable diapers, an unsigned note asked, "Are you going to need these?" He guessed the source immediately—the item bore all the earmarks of Bill Parcells. As Lucas erupted in laughter, his jitters vanished. The new starting quarterback placed the diapers inside his locker compartment, planning to keep them there for the rest of the season.

"His point was, 'Don't shit in your pants; don't be scared,'" Lucas recalls of Parcells. "That was motivation to me; that was a challenge. I knew he believed in me, but that little diaper thing hit a nerve. Does he think I'm scared, or can't handle it? I'm going to show him from day one that I can do this."

When Lucas saw Parcells later at practice, the former third-stringer grinned as he mentioned the diapers. But Parcells, in no joking mood, growled, "Are you going to need those?"

Lucas sobered. "No sir."

In his debut as a starter, Ray Lucas guided the Jets to scoring drives on three of their first four possessions. His maiden NFL touchdown, on a pass to fullback Richie Anderson, put New York up 13–0 in the second quarter. But the promising start disintegrated after the Colts tied the score in the final period. Gang Green reached Indianapolis's 3-yard line late when Lucas's pass into the end zone was intercepted, leading to kicker Mike Vanderjagt's game winner. Adding injury to insult, Lucas seriously sprained an ankle on the final play of New York's 16–13 loss.

The mishap forced Rick Mirer back into the starting lineup for two games. Despite a 17-point lead at Oakland in the third quarter, the Jets lost 24–23 to the Raiders on Rich Gannon's touchdown pass during the final minute. After the season's most disheartening setback, the fourth straight loss with a final-period collapse, Parcells's team dropped to 1-6. However, the outcome seemed like an afterthought to Parcells by the next afternoon, Monday, October 25.

TV reports indicated that golf star Payne Stewart, forty-two, had been a passenger on a Learjet that veered off course minutes after departing Orlando and crashed in a remote part of South Dakota, leaving no survivors. Parcells felt bad about Stewart, whom he had known through their mutual agent, Robert Fraley. But when CNN disclosed that five others had been on board, Parcells grew fearful that one of those unnamed people was Fraley. He immediately telephoned his agent's Orlando office, which relayed back information that shocked him: Fraley, forty-six, and a business associate were also passengers.

The two-pilot flight had been destined for Dallas so that the group could attend a PGA tournament, but the Learjet lost cabin pressure before cruising on autopilot over the South and Midwest. Everyone on board died from hypoxia, lack of oxygen. Military planes scrambled to monitor the wayward aircraft, which ran out of fuel roughly four hours after takeoff, nosediving into a field near Aberdeen, South Dakota.

A former backup quarterback for Bear Bryant, Fraley had represented major sports figures, from Steelers head coach Bill Cowher to baseball ace Orel Hershiser. But Parcells considered the prominent agent, whom he had known since 1982, to also be one of his best friends. Despite practices scheduled for his team's bye week, Parcells took a rare day off from football to attend Fraley's funeral in Orlando. Mourners included several of the agent's clients, like Joe Gibbs, Dan Reeves, Seahawks defensive tackle Cortez Kennedy, and baseball slugger Frank Thomas.

After returning to Jets headquarters, Parcells found it difficult to focus on football. His close friend's dying tragically so soon after Leon Hess left him more despondent than at any time since losing both parents near the end of his first season as an NFL head coach. He forced himself to watch video of the practice he had missed, and the next day he told backup fullback Jerald Sowell, "You could have put two goddamn eggs in your helmet for yesterday's practice, and they still would have been there when practice was over."

The Jets halted their three-game skid by defeating Arizona, 12–7, in Giants Stadium, as Boy Wonder rushed for 131 yards and Keyshawn Johnson snagged a 43-yard touchdown in the final period. Despite being ravaged by injuries, Parcells's club kept playing hard while his special-teams unit remained a force. The big difference from the previous season, caused by Testaverde's absence, was Gang Green's offense. Still, even with their poor record, the Jets were among the NFL leaders in turnover differential, generally the indicator of a good team. Of course, you *are* what your record says you are.

Ray Lucas's ankle healed in time for a Monday night affair at Foxboro Stadium, where the 2-6 Jets and 6-2 Patriots entered as teams headed for opposite fates in the postseason. But against the club that had waived him during training camp, Lucas tossed two touchdowns in the second quarter. The undrafted quarterback outplayed Drew Bledsoe as the Jets upset New England, 24–17. Gang Green's injury hex, though, continued when one of right tackle Jason Fabini's knees buckled after a play.

Even without his best offensive tackle the following game, Lucas delivered another solid performance in a 17–7 home victory versus Buffalo. The outcome gave Parcells's team its third straight triumph for a 4-6 record. Nonetheless, Gang Green's playoff hopes essentially evaporated after a 13–6 loss at Indianapolis's RCA Dome. To no avail, New York held the Colts, an offensive juggernaut in Peyton Manning's second NFL season, to their lowest output of the year.

Several hours later, on the night of November 28, the Jets landed at Newark Airport. Center Kevin Mawae maintained his habit after road games of spying on Parcells's movements while heading to the Wyndham in Garden City, a condominium complex about two miles from Jets headquarters where Kevin Mawae, Bill Parcells, and Curtis Martin lived.

Access to Parcells's condo necessitated using a ground-floor elevator near Mawae's apartment, 111. To avoid bumping into his head coach, particularly following a loss, Mawae often hustled to retrieve his car from the airport garage, then sped on the highway to reach home first. But after Gang Green deplaned from Indianapolis, Mawae got stuck behind Parcells while attempting to exit the airport. So the offensive lineman trailed his head coach's green Cadillac, driving slowly enough to escape detection.

Moments after Parcells reached their condominium parking lot, Mawae pulled in at the opposite end. Mawae hid in his car while waiting for Parcells to step into the lobby and presumably walk down the hall to get in the elevator.

After a few minutes, Mawae entered the building and asked the doorman, "Hey, Joe, did Bill make it through yet?"

Receiving a confirmation, the six-four, 300-pounder exhaled before walking to his apartment.

Mawae says now, "Sometimes I'd wait until I heard the elevator ding. That's a true story; you can't make that stuff up."

On December 5, the Jets faced Jim Fassel's Giants in a matchup between Meadowlands tenants. By halftime any fantastical thoughts about Gang Green's reaching the playoffs had evaporated as Belichick's defense gave its worst effort of the season. Behind quarterback Kerry Collins and wideout Amani Toomer, Big Blue led 27–7 at intermission after scoring their team's most points in a half since 1993. Ray Lucas prevented further embarrassment by delivering a career game, tossing four touchdowns, including three in the final period. After his last one cut the deficit to 41–28 late, Lucas walked to the sideline as self-assured as ever about quarterbacking in the NFL. Parcells, though, found nothing redeeming about heading to a record of 4-8, especially when his team allowed more than 40 points. Even Boy Wonder had been held to a career-low 4 yards on 6 carries.

Bothered by Lucas's body language, Parcells got in his face. "You think you know everything now, don't you?"

The quarterback knew Parcells well enough to respond, "Coach, I don't know shit."

Parcells nodded, and sneered, "That's goddamn right. You don't know *shit* until I tell you."

At the time of Leon Hess's death, the Jets franchise was valued at roughly $250 million, but with his replacement likely to obtain a new stadium after the team's lease expired in 2008, the Jets were expected to sell for as much as twice that amount. Charles F. Dolan, the cable television magnate who owned Madison Square Garden, the Knicks, and the Rangers, was seen as the prime candidate, having made serious attempts to purchase the Cleveland Browns in 1998 and the Washington Redskins in 1999. His pursuit of Hess's team became so frenzied that Stephen Ross, a New York real-estate developer who was among the final three suitors, dropped out after bidding exceeded $500 million. When the process reached the final stage in early December, investor Woody Johnson, an heir to the Johnson & Johnson fortune, was the only person aggressively competing against Dolan.

Meanwhile, in all four of its final games Gang Green faced teams headed to the playoffs. Rebounding from their season's most embarrassing performance, the Jets defeated Miami, 28–20, at the Meadowlands amid a windchill of zero degrees. Ray Lucas tossed two scoring passes to Keyshawn Johnson in the final period, and Belichick's defense returned to form by denying Dan Marino any touchdown passes.

While breaking out of his slump with 49 rushing yards in the final period, Curtis Martin continued to display his high threshold for pain. Late
in the game he wriggled free for a few yards along the Jets' sideline when
Miami's attempt to corral him caused Martin to spin into an about-face.
Instinctively he kept his legs churning, and as Boy Wonder ran blind a
linebacker torpedoed him, slamming his head into the Astroturf. Parcells,
who was standing only a few feet away on the sideline, saw Martin's eyes
close as blood streamed out his nose.

"I thought he was dead," Parcells recalls.

To the head coach's immense relief, Martin opened his eyes a moment
later, and rose gingerly to his feet. In an era before concussion awareness,
Martin immediately returned to the huddle, oblivious to the blood gush-
ing onto his green-and-white uniform. The 78,246 fans cheering his resil-
ience couldn't quite see the gory details, but a few teammates in the huddle
recoiled, with one saying, "Are you all right, Curt? Go to the sideline,
man. You're bleeding bad."

Looking down at his uniform, Martin saw how much blood he'd lost,
and hurried off the field, where trainers squeezed cotton gauze inside each
nostril. "Like a tampon for your nose," Martin says.

The Jets ran their next play while Boy Wonder received treatment,
but a few moments later Martin glanced at Parcells before jogging to the
huddle without waiting for his coach's approval. On the next play, Boy
Wonder took a handoff, leading to another tidy gain.

"He was a rare human being. He still is," Parcells says. "Rare, rare, rare."

After coaching many tough, talented athletes for more than twenty
years, Parcells was used to their willingness to play with pain, but Martin's
response to the bloodletting wallop showed a determination that Parcells
had witnessed from less than a handful of his players, among them Mark
Bavaro and Lawrence Taylor.

Parcells says of the bloody sequence involving Martin, "That shook
me up. I have that memory of him forever. I see him lying there. It takes
an unusual human being to take a shot like that and keep going, and if
you've been part of that experience, it bonds you. That kid knows if he ever
needed anything, all he would have to do is call me." Paraphrasing a term
he first heard from NBA legend Pat Riley, Parcells says, "It's a blood kinship, and it doesn't ever fade."

Next, Parcells's hardy group traveled to Texas Stadium for a December
19 contest versus Dallas. About two hours before the 3:15 p.m. kickoff,
Parcells spotted Cowboys owner Jerry Jones and a trainer lightly working
out players recovering from injuries, notably Larry Allen, the NFL's top
offensive lineman. Jones's presence seemed to overshadow that of Dallas's

head coach, Chan Gailey. Troubled by the scene, Parcells wrote his observation down for his book *The Final Season*.

"Now I've never seen that anywhere in my life," he penned. "Jerry Jones is very involved. I know at one time he played college ball and coached a kids team or something like that, but the NFL is supposed to be a little bit different. They tell me Jerry has a phone in his box that goes directly to the bench, and he'll call during the game with some message; or [call] if he wants to talk to certain players about their performance. If an owner wants to come around during the week and encourage players, root for them, and let them know he is with them, that's fine with me. But once the owner wants to coach, I'd be out of there the next day. I couldn't [work] in that situation myself."

Jerry Jones's hands-on approach went for naught as John Hall's 37-yard field goal with about a minute remaining lifted the Jets, 22–21. Ray Lucas finished with two touchdown passes, while Curtis Martin gained 113 rushing yards.

A rematch with the Dolphins took place on *Monday Night Football*, December 27 at Pro Player Stadium. This time the soon-to-be-retired Marino threw three touchdowns, but he was picked off three times in his final game against the Jets. Incongruously, Ray Lucas proved to be the more efficient passer, tossing three scoring passes without an interception during New York's 38–31 triumph. In the third straight contest the undrafted quarterback produced a better passer rating than a future Hall of Famer. The streak of upset victories provided the Jets an opportunity for a non-losing record, despite their disastrous start.

While Gang Green was closing out the season with a flourish, the Patriots were unraveling with three consecutive losses for a 7-8 mark, notwithstanding their hot start. New England's collapse meant that Kraft's team would miss the playoffs for the first time since 1995. Rumors surfaced regarding the owner's interest in Bill Belichick. Disenchanted by his franchise's regression since Parcells's departure, Kraft remarked to his inner circle that he should have retained Belichick in 1997.

Will McDonough investigated the scuttlebutt, and then telephoned his buddy Bill Parcells with more concrete information. The Patriots planned to dismiss Pete Carroll after the season and offer their head-coaching job to Belichick. Kraft had supposedly signaled to Belichick, through intermediaries, that he would have complete control of football operations at a salary of up to $2 million. Parcells, who had been contemplating whether to continue coaching in 2000, was disturbed by the development, especially since Belichick was under contract to replace him for the Jets.

On Friday, New Year's Eve, Gang Green practiced for its finale at home versus Seattle, leaders of the AFC West. As the Jets completed the session in their indoor bubble, Parcells made up his mind to retire from coaching. Despite feeling a sense of relief, Parcells chose not to tell anyone. After Saturday's walk-through, however, he called Belichick into his office. Parcells told Belichick that he was "99 percent sure" that Sunday would be his final day as an NFL coach.

"By contract, you're the next head coach."

Belichick replied, "I've been waiting for this."

Parcells said that he would inform Steve Gutman of his decision after the upcoming game. The next day New York maintained its torrid stretch with a 19–9 victory as Boy Wonder rushed for a season-high 158 yards and John Hall drilled four field goals. During the exclamation-point victory, 78,154 spectators aired their feelings about Parcells's coaching future, chanting, "One more year! One more year! One more year!"

Gang Green ended up with the same record as the Patriots, who dismissed Pete Carroll after their finale. Parcells considers the 8-8 season to be perhaps the best coaching performance of his career, given the Jets' 1-6 start and serious injuries to fifteen players, overwhelmingly starters.

Roughly an hour after the January 2 finale, Parcells told Gutman of his decision to retire, asking the team president to inform John Hess. The next morning at roughly nine o'clock, a Jets official at Weeb Ewbank Hall spotted an overnight fax from New England seeking permission to interview Belichick for the position of head coach and GM. After reading the transmission, Parcells crumpled it up and threw it in the wastebasket. He declined the request, informing the Patriots and the league that his resignation at 5 p.m. on Sunday had contractually made Belichick his replacement as Jets head coach.

22

In a staff meeting later that morning, Bill Parcells informed his coaches of the big transition. He left the room early to allow Bill Belichick to start acting as the new Jets head coach, and Parcells's former lieutenant stepped in with information about the upcoming Senior Bowl, and scheduled the next staff meeting.

Parcells soon gathered his players into Weeb Ewbank Hall's auditorium, used for team meetings and press conferences. Holding a microphone at the front of the room, he told the group that he no longer desired to be an NFL coach. Despite still possessing the requisite energy, Parcells lacked the commitment that he himself had always demanded from his players. He didn't want to fool himself, or anyone else, by returning to an all-consuming job. To more eloquently convey those feelings, Parcells concluded his resignation speech by reading Dale Wimbrow's poem "The Guy in the Glass."

> When you get what you want in your struggle for self,
> And the world makes you king for a day,
> Then go to the mirror and look at yourself,
> And see what that guy has to say.
>
> For it isn't your Father, or Mother, or Wife,
> Whose judgement upon you must pass.
> The feller whose verdict counts most in your life
> Is the guy staring back from the glass.
>
> He's the feller to please, never mind all the rest,
> For he's with you clear up to the end,
> And you've passed your most dangerous, difficult test
> If the guy in the glass is your friend.

With four lines left, Parcells's booming voice started cracking as his eyes welled up. But he read the poem's final lines with power.

> You can fool the whole world down the pathway of years,
> And get pats on the back as you pass,

But your final reward will be heartaches and tears
If you've cheated the guy in the glass.

Parcells released the microphone and stepped away from the stage. In previous emotional addresses Parcells had tried to fight off tears. But this time he cried unabashedly as he headed out of the auditorium. Walking out, Parcells felt a love from his players, many of them teary-eyed, as they remained in their seats. The players glanced at each other, uncertain of what to do or say. And for a few minutes, no one spoke.

During the afternoon, Parcells announced his resignation to the public, becoming the first head coach in franchise history to step down with a winning record: 30-20. He informed reporters that Bill Belichick was empowered to make all football decisions, while he himself would stay on as a confidant and consultant. Although the contract language lacked preciseness regarding ultimate authority, Parcells, still technically director of football operations at a $2.4 million salary, vowed not to overshadow Belichick. Big Bill insisted that New England's interest in Little Bill was no factor in the development, although it certainly seemed to accelerate matters.

Around the same time, Woody Johnson raised his offer for the Jets from roughly $600 million to $625 million, vaulting over the latest exorbitant proposal by Charles Dolan. Johnson's bid was the highest ever for a New York sports franchise. Having exchanged increasingly breathtaking offers with the Knicks season-ticket holder since early December, Dolan now needed to go up another notch. Meanwhile, Belichick seemed to embrace his new duties, scheduling his first "family meeting" with Mike Tannenbaum and discussing preparations for free agency with Scott Pioli. In the late afternoon, Gutman and Parcells sat in on Belichick's meeting with the head trainer to discuss injured players.

A couple of hours later, at roughly 6 p.m., Parcells was in the coaches' locker room when Belichick walked in and asked to revisit New England's fax. Startled by the query, Parcells reminded Belichick of his apparent eagerness on Saturday to finally take over. Belichick countered that uncertainty about the Jets ownership was giving him second thoughts. Those remarks angered Parcells, who warned Belichick that the club wouldn't allow him to interview with the Patriots, or any other team.

Having spent fourteen of his nineteen NFL seasons under Big Bill, Little Bill believed that, given the circumstances, his mentor owed him the opportunity to look into New England's attractive opportunity. Belichick was apparently drawn to the possibility of being a GM and head coach under a familiar owner like Kraft, as opposed to working for a neophyte owner like Charles Dolan or Woody Johnson while Parcells hovered with an unclear role. Parcells reminded Belichick about his contract, noting that Hess had paid the heir apparent a king's ransom during the previous off-season. Parcells ended the conversation by stressing that if Belichick bailed out of his three-year, $4.2 million contract, the organization intended to seek compensation.

Parcells recalls, "He made a deal, and then tried to get out of it. A deal's a deal. You want out? You're going to pay. Simple."

Despite the testy exchange, when Belichick departed the coaches' locker room, Parcells assumed that his former lieutenant had been merely exploring his options. Belichick's behavior, however, changed dramatically the next morning, several hours ahead of a 2:30 p.m. Q&A to introduce him as Parcells's replacement. He appeared nervous and agitated while interacting with colleagues, which was odd for an ex–head coach groomed to guide the Jets. In Tuesday's staff meeting, Belichick couldn't prevent his hands from shaking. He ended the caucus early, telling his coaches that he would get back to them to reschedule.

After Parcells taped a weekly TV show with Phil Simms, the erstwhile head coach returned to his office at roughly 2:15 p.m. About five minutes later, Belichick swung by to deliver a bombshell: the new head coach intended to use his introductory press conference to announce his resignation. Parcells was surprised though not quite shocked, given Belichick's recent behavior. Still, the Jets chief seethed, reiterating that the club would bar Belichick from interviewing elsewhere, putting him in coaching limbo.

Minutes before his press conference Belichick passed by the offices of several colleagues to give them a heads-up. He spotted Steve Gutman standing by his doorway after the team president had caught wind of the shocker. Belichick handed Gutman a loose-leaf sheet of paper containing three handwritten sentences. The first line read, "Due to the various uncertainties surrounding my position as it relates to the team's new ownership, I have decided to resign as the HC of the NYJ." Stunned and angry, Gutman followed Belichick to the auditorium to hear more details of the surreal switcheroo. Parcells, though, remained in his corner office down the hall, working on a short list of candidates to replace Belichick.

Wearing a dark-gray suit, light-blue shirt, and navy patterned tie, Belichick took the podium. The forty-seven-year-old removed several sheets of paper from his suit's left inside pocket. Reading a script that included the first line from his resignation letter, Belichick astonished a full house of journalists and TV cameramen. His opening statement ran for twenty-five minutes in a voice that occasionally cracked. He often gestured with his hands as sweat glistened on his brow.

Belichick said, "The agreement that I made was with Mr. Hess, Bill Parcells, and Mr. Gutman, and that situation has changed dramatically. And it's going to change even further." He noted that the franchise had been expected to find a new owner by December 15, 1999. "There are a lot of unanswered questions here," he told reporters. "I have been concerned about it since Leon Hess died."

To Parcells's chagrin, Belichick revealed a slice of their private conversation from the previous day. "He told me, 'If you feel that undecided, maybe you shouldn't take this job.' I took Bill's words to heart—thought about it last night." Belichick evaded questions about his coaching future while expressing contentment about the opportunity to spend more time with his wife, Debby, and their three children. Nonetheless, he conceded that he had hired a noted sports-labor attorney, Jeffrey Kessler, to extricate him from his contract.

After Belichick departed the auditorium, Steve Gutman took the podium. The team president tried to make sense of the organization's losing two head coaches within twenty-four hours, a period that included perhaps the strangest resignation in sports history. Referring to Belichick, Gutman said, "We should have some feelings of sorrow and regret for him and his family. He's obviously in some inner turmoil."

The partnership between Belichick and Parcells had held together well during their sole season under Kraft, but the relationship had regressed during three seasons with the Jets. Despite Belichick's substantial growth in the NFL under Parcells, and a guaranteed position as head coach, he ached to prove himself without his primary mentor and occasional tormentor. As Gang Green overcame a disastrous start in 1999, Parcells's words had been as harsh as ever.

Further complicating their partnership, the Jets organization contained a so-called Cleveland mafia, employees who had worked under Belichick with the Browns. The group, which even included Parcells's son-in-law, Scott Pioli, seemed more loyal to the heir apparent than to the incumbent football chief. After Hess's death, members of the coterie quietly realigned themselves with Belichick, while offensive coordinator Charlie Weis also started getting closer to his future boss. The dynamic created tension between the ex–Browns contingent and most of the coaches with deep ties to Parcells, like Dan Henning. So Belichick's resignation upended the organization well beyond the head-coaching position.

A few hours after the shocker, Belichick contested his inability to interview with other NFL teams by filing a grievance with the league office. Gang Green countered by sending the NFL copies of his contract.

The next day Commissioner Paul Tagliabue faxed every club that until a final ruling, Belichick remained unavailable for employment consideration without Gang Green's consent. The back-page headline of the *New York Post* mocked, "Belichicken: Jets Better Off Without Quitter." Another headline punned, "Belichick Arnold." Belichick recalls, "I knew I did the right thing, and I didn't know where my career was going."

The Jets couldn't postpone the Senior Bowl or free agency because of their internal dysfunction, so Parcells conducted an emergency staff meeting, outlining steps the organization would be taking in the upcoming weeks. While showing zero desire to reclaim head-coaching duties, Parcells withheld his thoughts about a replacement. When the meeting ended, Charlie Weis lingered to seize a private moment. Making sure no colleagues lurked within earshot, Weis implored Parcells to pick him as the new head coach.

"I can do this job. I'm your guy."

Parcells, though, was already targeting a colleague he had valued since the late 1960s, with whom he had worked at two colleges and three NFL teams. By lobbying zealously Weis was jeopardizing a spot on any new coach's future staff, so Parcells firmly rebuffed the offensive coordinator he had elevated from wideouts coach in 1997, cutting the conversation short.

One week later, on January 11, Robert Wood Johnson IV won the right to purchase the Jets for $635 million, the third-highest price ever paid for a professional sports team. Based on Leon Hess's will, the transaction meant $5.1 million for Steve Gutman beyond his salary. Known for donating money to autoimmune-disease research and Republican campaigns, Johnson ran a private investment firm on Fifth Avenue named after him. Much of the fifty-two-year-old's wealth, though, came from Johnson & Johnson stock.

His football jones stretched back several decades. While attending the University of Arizona, Johnson co-published *Touchdown,* a guide for *Monday Night Football,* which dissolved after three issues. But he was known more for his carousing, once reportedly falling eighteen feet off a darkened bridge in Tempe and breaking his back after pulling his car over to urinate. During his late twenties, Johnson had coveted the Tampa Bay Buccaneers as an expansion team. Now he had landed the Jets after Dolan declined to raise his latest bid of $612 million. Only hours after the cable TV magnate ceded, Johnson telephoned Parcells to introduce himself.

Taking the call with Mike Tannenbaum in the room, Parcells remarked, "Congratulations. **Being in pro football is not for the well-adjusted.**"

Johnson replied, "That's good, because I'm not well-adjusted."

Parcells shared Johnson's riposte with Tannenbaum. At the least their new owner had a good sense of humor. Or was he being serious?

Johnson and his football chief soon met for a brief discussion focusing on Belichick. The owner agreed with Parcells that Gang Green shouldn't free Belichick without obtaining at least a first-round pick. Their follow-up meeting was wide-ranging, with Johnson sharing his vision for the franchise. He implored Parcells to return to the sidelines, but the director of football operations declined. Johnson expressed an inclination to conduct a league-wide search for a top candidate, but Parcells insisted on continuity for a team only one season removed from an AFC Championship appearance. Parcells suggested promoting a talented disciplinarian with deep ties to him: linebacker coach Al Groh. The tough-nosed assistant's only experience as a head coach had come at Wake Forest from 1981 to 1986, and based on his 26–40 record at the ACC school, Groh seemed like an improbable choice for head coach. Nonetheless, Johnson deferred to the franchise's mastermind.

Belichick's grievance hearing came Thursday, January 13, at the Times Square headquarters of Skadden, Arps, the NFL's counsel. Charlie Weis and Bill Parcells were required to appear at a thirty-eighth-floor office after Jeffrey Kessler, Belichick's attorney, named them as witnesses along with his client. The Jets, represented by Steve Gutman and the club's counsel, didn't designate any witnesses. With Paul Tagliabue present for the 9:45 a.m. start, the opposing groups sat across from each other at a conference table. Each side made fifteen-minute opening statements. Then Kessler called Parcells as the first witness for a Q&A that lasted forty-five minutes.

Charlie Weis started testifying next, and his statements jolted Parcells even more than Belichick's resignation. During four minutes of testimony Weis supported Kessler's main argument that Parcells had no intention of ceding true authority to Belichick. The offensive coordinator claimed he had overheard Parcells telling Gutman that Belichick wouldn't quite gain the power he was contractually due. Parcells had known that Weis would testify, but never imagined him speaking so forcefully on Belichick's behalf. Dan Henning recalls the situation: "Bill [Parcells] decides to go with Al; Belichick can't coach for a year. Charlie [Weis] realizes that he has nothing. So that's when he goes and thinks that he can get Belichick out of trouble by putting Bill [Parcells] in trouble."

Weis's NFL coaching career had started in 1990 when Parcells hired the Jersey high school coach to an entry-level position. Impressed by Weis's offensive acuity over the years, Parcells had promoted him multiple times with the Patriots and Jets. Parcells could only conclude that now Weis was ingratiating himself with Belichick, hoping for a position in New England.

Kessler called his client as the third and final witness before a Jets lawyer cross-examined Belichick. The grievance hearing ended after roughly seven hours, and a ruling was expected within a week. Weis returned to his office the next day, but that move proved foolhardy when Parcells spotted him in the hallway. Incensed, the Jets chief immediately banned his offensive coordinator from the premises. "Charlie, you need to get your shit and leave the building." Watched closely by Jets employees, Weis took only a few minutes to gather some items before scuttling out of the building. Moments after he exited, the team packed up the rest of his belongings and shipped them to his home.

Parcells says, "I've told many coaches that friendship and loyalty is going to be more important than ambition. Some guys don't realize that until after they're done. I don't bear any animosity toward Charlie. I can say that with a straight face because I know what he is. When somebody shows me what he is, I usually believe it. His actions back then don't bother me anymore."

On January 21, Tagliabue ruled for the Jets, reasoning that Belichick had breached his contract by quitting. The league prohibited him from coaching in 2000 without the Jets' consent or compensation. Tagliabue's explanation echoed the one in 1997 that had prevented Parcells from joining Gang Green without New England's permission.

Three days after Belichick's setback, the Jets named Al Groh as their new head coach with a four-year contract averaging $800,000. The fifty-five-year-old promoted Dan Henning to offensive coordinator, and hired Mike Nolan as defensive coordinator. Other notable additions included tight-ends coach Ken Whisenhunt and secondary coach Todd Bowles. Groh picked his son, Mike, as a quality-control assistant on offense. On the day of Groh's official elevation, Belichick made a last-gasp attempt to overcome Tagliabue's ruling by filing an antitrust lawsuit in federal court against the Jets and the NFL.

By gaining 1,464 rushing yards to help his injury-ravaged team avoid a losing season, Curtis Martin had been voted Jets MVP. He planned to give the trophy to the person who most shaped him as a football player and person: Bill Parcells. On January 24, Boy Wonder found out exactly when the Jets chief was meeting with the new coaching staff. That afternoon, Martin slipped into Parcells's corner office while carrying his trophy and a one-paragraph letter with neat penmanship: seven sentences in blue felt-tip ink summed up his feelings about Parcells. Boy Wonder placed the items on Parcells's desk before slipping out undetected.

After the meeting Parcells walked into his office and immediately noticed the tall, gleaming trophy. "What the hell is this?" Parcells said aloud. He walked closer to inspect it, and spotted a white sheet of paper next to the trophy. As Parcells sat down to read it he received a phone call from his youngest daughter. Picking up the receiver to greet Jill, Parcells remained mesmerized by Martin's note, quickly reading it through to the end. A few moments later, Jill heard her father quietly sobbing.

"Dad? Are you okay? What's wrong?"

The letter, dated January 24, 2000, in the bottom left corner, read:

> Coach,
>> This award is the best and most
>> gratifying I've ever received.
>> It means more than the pro bowls,
>> the rushing title and the team records.
>> You've given me and football some of your
>> best years—and as a little token
>> of my appreciation I give to you my best.
>> I thank you from the bottom of my heart
>> for all that you are and all that you have
>> done for me! You're like a father to me.
>>> Love ya!
>>> Boy Wonder

Late that night, Parcells headed home with the trophy and letter. He would laminate the note, and keep both in a glass case among his most prized possessions. The gift provided a much-needed salve amid the upheaval of Bill Belichick's departure.

On Tuesday, January 25, a federal judge denied Belichick's request for a temporary restraining order, ruling that his Jets contract was valid. Accepting the futility of his situation, Belichick withdrew his antitrust lawsuit against Gang Green and the NFL. The development enhanced the team's leverage, prompting Parcells to consult Woody Johnson about brokering a deal with Kraft on compensation for Belichick's services.

Parcells found the notion distasteful given his acrimonious divorce from Kraft; the two essentially hadn't spoken since the week following the 1997 Super Bowl. Nonetheless, Parcells knew a deal would benefit both sides, and he believed that, as a savvy businessman, Kraft would embrace the opportunity to bolster his franchise. Furthermore, talks would signal a truce in what Parcells termed the "border war" between New England and New York.

So that same day Parcells telephoned Kraft's office and identified himself to the owner's secretary. Surprised by the call after years of smoldering silence, Kraft gave the go-ahead to pipe him in. When the owner picked up, Parcells said, "Hello, Bob, this is Darth Vader."

Kraft laughed, easing some of the tension.

When his nemesis broached the possibility of a resolution involving Belichick, the Patriots overlord was immediately receptive. Before going further, however, Parcells expressed regret for some of his actions in New England. Kraft responded by conceding that his inexperience as an NFL owner had exacerbated the situation.

Getting down to business, Parcells informed Kraft that the Jets would allow Belichick to coach New England in exchange for compensation via draft picks. Kraft offered a third-round pick in 2000 and a fourth-rounder in 2001. Parcells quickly countered that a deal required at least a first-round selection in 2000. The conciliatory conversation ended after forty minutes, with plans for further talks in the morning.

In their next session, Kraft increased his offer to a second-round pick in 2000 and a third-rounder in 2001, but Parcells insisted on a first-round selection. The two men hung up politely without a deal. Later that afternoon, Kraft interviewed Jaguars defensive coordinator Dom Capers for more than four hours. Parcells expected New England to hire Tom Coughlin's lieutenant as their new head coach, leaving Belichick in limbo and Gang Green without compensation for his departure. However, as Parcells headed to bed around 11 p.m., Kraft surprised him with a phone call.

"I'm going to make a decision here that I don't want to make, because I want this guy as my head coach."

Parcells replied, "We can work this out. Let's do it."

Kraft agreed to relinquish his upcoming first-round pick if the teams exchanged a couple of lower-round selections in future years. Sealing the deal, the Jets chief made an unusual suggestion: that they place a two-day window on Belichick's contract negotiations with New England in order to prevent him from holding either organization hostage. Kraft loved the idea.

Knowing about the earlier stalemate, Belichick was flabbergasted when Parcells called him at 7 a.m. to reveal the agreement he'd reached with

Bob Kraft, contingent on Belichick's signing a contract with the Patriots in less than forty-eight hours. Parcells also granted Belichick permission to hire two Jets staffers with whom he shared links to the Cleveland Browns: Eric Mangini and Scott Pioli. After all but firing Weis, Parcells gladly allowed the banished coach to join Belichick, too. Jets PR assistant Berj Najarian, who had grown close to Belichick at Weeb Ewbank Hall by perennially staying there late, was also on his wish list, to which Parcells also gave his approval.

Around 10 a.m., Kraft called Bill Belichick to confirm the arrangement and start negotiating a contract. After hanging up, Belichick telephoned Mangini, Pioli, and Najarian about heading to New England. Within a few hours Belichick drove the three men to Foxboro Stadium, where he reached a handshake agreement with Kraft on a contract to be finalized later.

At 6 p.m. that same day the Patriots introduced Bill Belichick as their new head coach, with more power over personnel decisions than Kraft, as a neophyte owner, had permitted Parcells. Belichick took the opportunity to reiterate that he had quit the Jets mainly because of the franchise's fluid ownership at the time, and Parcells's unclear role. Addressing the issue of escaping his mentor's shadow, Belichick noted that Parcells had also left a vast one in New England.

Parcells says of Belichick, "At the end of the day, he didn't want to be the Jets head coach. Then he expected me as the general manager of the organization to just say, 'Okay, I'll get somebody else.' Well, eventually, I did that. But I got compensation because I knew what Kraft was doing before the season ended. I didn't begrudge Bill getting another job somewhere else. In fact, I'm probably the one that got it for him."

Reflecting on his decision to quit the Jets, Bill Belichick says, "At that point in time, in that situation, I did what I felt I needed to do, and I don't have any regrets about that. Certainly a lot of things could have been handled differently."

Beyond losing Belichick, Gang Green faced a dilemma involving one of its top players: Keyshawn Johnson was expected to hold out during training camp if the Jets failed to upgrade his rookie contract, which had two years remaining on it. The six-year, $15.4 million deal, which had been reached after a holdout lasting almost a month, included the largest bonus for a rookie receiver: $6.5 million. However, after two consecutive Pro Bowl seasons, the loquacious wideout felt underpaid by the $2.4 million due in 2000, when lesser receivers were earning substantially bigger salaries.

During the previous off-season Parcells had tried to restructure Johnson's deal in a way that would both avoid the salary-cap consequences of an extension and keep the wideout long-term. The NFL, however, ruled that the unusual proposal was in violation of cap rules. Gang Green suspected that the decision involved fallout from Curtis Martin's controversial contract. To further complicate matters, Jets policy prohibited renegotiating deals with at least two years left on them, and Parcells disliked the scorched-earth tactics of Johnson's Los Angeles–based agent, Jerome Stanley, who demanded a new deal that included a $12 million bonus.

Parcells met with Al Groh, Dick Haley, and Mike Tannenbaum to weigh the team's options: force Johnson to stay, despite the disruption of another holdout; trade him to the highest bidder; or grant him a lucrative extension, setting a precedent that would hamper Gang Green's efforts to retain key players. Eager to start his tenure without distractions, Al Groh favored jettisoning the wideout, so Parcells consulted Keyshawn Johnson about reaching a mutually beneficial decision. In Parcells's office they spoke about the possibility of finding a team willing to meet Johnson's contractual demands.

Johnson noticed a thick binder on Parcells's desk used for organizing his personal and financial life. After the football talk, he asked Parcells if he could take a closer look. The Jets chief obliged, and explained its purpose as Johnson leafed through the binder, which included a wide range of sections: property tax estimates, book deals, endorsement contracts, horse racing, income statements, correspondence, donations, investments. When Parcells suggested that Johnson get something similar to help organize his own life, the wideout latched on to the idea, and responded with deep appreciation. The heartfelt exchange put an unusual coda on their strategy session for navigating the cutthroat business of football.

"Keyshawn can be full of shit, but he's a good listener," Parcells says. "When you're talking about something serious, he's paying attention."

On April 12, the Jets made one of the most stunning trades in franchise history, sending their star wideout to Tampa Bay, an offensively challenged team with Super Bowl expectations based on a dominant defense, for two first-round picks in the upcoming draft. The Buccaneers agreed to extend Johnson's contract by six years and $52 million, including a team-record $13 million bonus that made him the highest-paid wideout of all time. Despite losing a major offensive weapon, Gang Green ended up with an NFL record four first-round choices, including the one acquired for Belichick's services.

The Jets used those selections to draft defensive lineman Shaun Ellis (twelfth overall) of Tennessee, defensive end John Abraham (thirteenth) of South Carolina, quarterback Chad Pennington (eighteenth) of Marshall, and tight end Anthony Becht (twenty-seventh) of West Virginia. Gang Green's next selection didn't come until the third round, when the team was considering drafting Florida State wideout Laveranues Coles, whose stock had dropped because of a rap sheet. As a college senior, Coles was arrested with fellow wideout Peter Warrick for shoplifting at Dillard's, prompting the Seminoles to remove him from the team. A prior incident in 1998 had brought Coles a simple battery charge, triggering a one-game suspension. Nonetheless, Steve Yarnell advocated for Coles because the security chief's background check, which included a visit to Tallahassee, found extenuating circumstances in the wideout's troubles. With Coles still available for Gang Green's seventy-eighth overall choice, Parcells tersely asked Yarnell in the draft room whether the wideout would end up embarrassing the organization.

Yarnell pushed back. "I'm telling you, this is our guy!" The security chief's conviction helped sway Gang Green to pick Coles. Its 2000 draft class would bolster the roster for years, and the talented five-eleven, 200-pounder performed well while behaving like a model citizen.

Despite the tumultuous off-season, Al Groh's Jets captured their first four games with Vinny Testaverde back at quarterback. The first such streak in franchise history included two stirring comebacks: 20–19 at home versus Bill Belichick's Patriots on two final-period touchdowns by Wayne Chrebet, and 21–17 on the road against Tony Dungy's Buccaneers, after Boy Wonder threw the game winner to Chrebet while Keyshawn Johnson finished with just one catch for a yard.

Instead of attending games in his new role, Bill Parcells drove from his home in Seagirt, New Jersey, to Weeb Ewbank Hall, where he watched Gang Green on TV. The decision stemmed from Parcells's desire to keep from overshadowing his rookie NFL head coach, especially on game days. At most Parcells might telephone Mike Tannenbaum to chat before a contest while navigating the Jersey Turnpike past Giants Stadium, heading for Long Island. Mr. T's game-day responsibilities placed him in the Jets coaches' booth.

Less than two hours before Gang Green hosted the Dolphins on *Monday Night Football*, Parcells telephoned from the highway. "All right, Mr. T, what's going on?"

Tannenbaum replied, "Nothing much; usual pregame stuff. Are you coming?"

"Hmmm. No."

With the Jets playing Miami for first place in the AFC East, Parcells's superstitious nature reinforced his decision to stay on the periphery. Gang Green improved to 6-1 after the "Monday Night Miracle," the greatest comeback in franchise history and on the prime-time series. Down 30–7 in the fourth quarter, Gang Green tied the game with 1:20 left on Testaverde's 3-yard pass to left tackle Jumbo Elliott, who made a juggling catch while falling in the end zone. The improbable reception, the only touchdown of Elliott's career and Testaverde's fifth of the night, led to overtime. The Jets triumphed, 40–37, in a stadium that ended up being half empty mainly due to the departure of fans who had given up hope.

Groh's team, however, failed to sustain the magic, subsequently losing three straight. The slide tortured Parcells, given his vow not to micromanage. Although the Jets chief had observed some reasons for Gang Green's troubles, he felt that steering Groh would undermine him. However, Parcells was spending more time than ever discussing how to build a team with Mike Tannenbaum, who ended up receiving his boss's private complaints about Groh's decisions.

Perplexed by the information, Tannenbaum asked, "Bill, why don't you tell Al instead of me? He's the one who needs to make the changes you're talking about."

Parcells replied, "Mr. T, I just can't tell Al. He has to do things in his own way."

Tannenbaum says now, "Bill never really found his stride being the GM because he didn't want to overstep his bounds."

The director of football operations still found ways to motivate his favorite Jet, Boy Wonder. During one conversation after the sixth-year veteran described his rigorous training regimen that dated back to his rookie season, Parcells replied, "Son, **don't confuse routine with commitment**, because you've got to do more the older you get, or you're losing ground. A lot of people fall into a routine in their life's work, and as time goes on they eventually confuse that with being committed to their job. The only thing they're committed to is the routine."

Martin suddenly realized that his workouts had fallen into a rut. Despite a reputation for being Gang Green's hardest worker, Boy Wonder decided to revamp his routine. He recalls of Parcells's advice, "That sparked a new flame, a higher flame."

A three-game winning streak boosted Gang Green to 9-4, positioning the club to make the playoffs with just one more victory. Nevertheless, Groh's team collapsed again, losing three straight down the stretch.

On December 30, only one week after the season finale, Al Groh abruptly quit the Jets to accept his dream job: head coach at his alma mater, the University of Virginia, where his son Mike had starred as a quarterback in the mid-1990s. Al Groh, who had been an assistant coach at the school in the early 1970s, signed a seven-year contract worth more than $5 million in a deal that provided more long-term security than he had with the Jets. Reminiscent of Ray Perkins bolting the Giants for Alabama, Groh replaced George Welsh, sixty-seven, who had retired after nineteen seasons at Virginia.

The third Jets head coach to bail in a calendar year guaranteed that the franchise would experience another disruptive off-season, and only ten days later, on January 9, an even more powerful tremor shook the team. Bill Parcells announced his retirement from the NFL, citing reasons similar to those he'd given when he had quit as head coach, and admitting that he had experienced difficulty transitioning to his new role. As a replacement Parcells recommended that Woody Johnson decide among three of Parcells's former Giants scouts: personnel executives Terry Bradway of the Chiefs, Jerry Angelo of the Bucs, and Rick Donohue of the Giants. Interviewing them only two days after Parcells's resignation, Woody Johnson chose Bradway, a Giants scout from 1986 to 1992. The owner kept Mike Tannenbaum on, positioning the contract negotiator to be next in line to run the team.

On Parcells's final day at Weeb Ewbank Hall, he secretly placed a bottle of Grey Goose on Mr. T's desk with a note: "At some point, you're going to need this."

23

Retirement in early 2001 made Bill Parcells a serious Hall of Fame candidate for the first time. Although players were required to wait five years after retirement in order to be eligible, former coaches could qualify for induction after only one year away from the sidelines. Each Super Bowl Eve, wherever the game was being played, the Hall's board of selectors met to consider fifteen modern-era candidates before whittling them to no more than five finalists, who would then need 80 percent approval for induction. The panel also considered two so-called senior candidates for enshrinement; they had to be at least a quarter century removed from their final season.

A few days before the selection process began on Saturday, January 27, 2001, in Tampa Bay, a newspaper story speculated that Parcells would return to the NFL as Tampa Bay's head coach. Despite the team's transformation under Tony Dungy, the ownership family saw the franchise as underachieving, particularly in the playoffs. The article resonated with the Hall of Fame's thirty-eight voters, most of whom believed that Parcells, at age fifty-nine, was likely to coach in the NFL again. The possibility was anathema to the board, which mainly worried that an enshrined member might stain his legacy with an unsuccessful return to the sidelines. So Will McDonough, perhaps the most influential voter on the board of selectors, telephoned Parcells.

"Look, Bill. You're my close friend. You have to give me your word that you're absolutely not going to come back to the game, because I'll be sticking my neck way out when I go to bat for you."

After several less than definitive remarks, Parcells finally told McDonough, "Will, as a friend I can't make that promise to you. Right now, I'm retired. That's all I can say."

Later that night, McDonough called their mutual buddy, Joe O'Donnell, to express his frustration. "I think he's staying retired, but I'm not sure. Talking to Bill about this was like sumo wrestling. He moved to the right; he moved to the left. I couldn't get him to commit to staying retired."

Given the ambiguity about his future, Bill Parcells failed to make it out of the first round of the three-stage selection process. The class of 2001 consisted of linebacker Nick Buoniconti (the senior candidate), coach Marv Levy, offensive guard Mike Munchak, offensive tackle Jackie Slater, wideout Lynn Swann, offensive tackle Ron Yary, and defensive end Jack Youngblood. Levy's selection over Parcells underscored the committee's thinking on the former Jets boss. Levy had led Buffalo to a record four straight Super Bowls, but had never triumphed; Parcells had captured two Lombardi Trophies, including one against Levy's Bills, and he led New England to a Super Bowl appearance before guiding Gang Green to the AFC Championship. No NFL coach had taken three different franchises, struggling before his arrival, to such heights.

Still, it would have been unusual if Parcells had been selected on the first try. George Halas and Curly Lambeau were members of the Hall's 1963 inaugural class; since then only three coaches had gained entry in their first year of eligibility: Tom Landry (1990), Chuck Noll (1993), and Don Shula (1997). Hall voters had forced Bill Walsh (1993) to wait four seasons before induction, and Joe Gibbs (1996) three, because of concerns that they would return to the sidelines. Now their rival Bill Parcells would wait at least a year.

Even in retirement, Parcells still needed the NFL in some form. Instead of going cold turkey, he returned to the broadcast booth. The former NBC expert took on a guest role with ESPN as a studio analyst during the football season. As a head coach, Parcells had gained renown for turning his press conferences into must-see TV. He flashed intelligence, humor, and belligerence while sometimes making reporters cower the same way his players did. Despite often showing a disdain for the media that would have pleased Woody Hayes, Parcells relished the give-and-take. He established friendly, symbiotic relationships with select reporters, although no one penetrated his circle quite like Will McDonough had done.

In broadcasting, however, Parcells lacked the comfort level he had shown as a coach dominating Q&As and captivating observers. Several months into the part-time TV job and a weekly radio show, Parcells suffered from both ennui and coaching withdrawal. Such feelings came as no surprise to his spouse of almost four decades.

"Some guys like to do little things around the house. He never had any interest in that," says Judy, who notes Parcells's limited hobbies and aversion to traveling by plane. "And he was never really home all that much. He didn't know what to do with himself when he was, unless there was some sports to watch on TV. What else was he going to do but go back to the NFL?"

Late in the 2001 season, Tampa Bay patriarch Malcolm Glazer gave staff lawyer Nathan Whitaker a confidential assignment: prepare biographical sketches of potential replacements for Tony Dungy. Atop the Buccaneers' wish list was ESPN's guest analyst Bill Parcells, who had jilted the team's previous owner a decade earlier. Despite occasionally crossing paths with Dungy at the team's fitness center and exchanging small talk, Whitaker couldn't disclose the information.

In 1997, only one season after being hired, Dungy had guided the Bucs to their second playoff victory in franchise history. His 1999 team reached the NFC Championship, losing to the St. Louis Rams, 11-6. Dungy's turnaround brilliance, based largely on his defensive concepts involving safeties in deep coverage, the Cover 2, made him the best coach in team annals. But the following postseason, an opening-round setback at Philadelphia, 21–3, troubled the Glazer family, whose club that year had fielded nine Pro Bowlers. Critics deemed Dungy's offense, consistently among the NFL's worst, too conservative.

Despite being viewed as Super Bowl contenders going into the 2001 season, the Bucs won only three of their first seven games. So even as Dungy's team reversed course, speculation intensified that he would be replaced by Bill Parcells, who had once unsuccessfully wooed him as a Giants assistant. Malcolm Glazer, whose sons Bryan and Joel ran the team's daily operations, avoided comment.

During the first two weeks of January, amid all the Parcells-replacing-Dungy scuttlebutt, Chargers GM John Butler tried persuading Parcells to coach in San Diego. Although the former Jets boss listened to San Diego's pitch, he couldn't fathom leading an NFL team so far away from his home bases of Florida and New Jersey. The Chargers then decided to pursue Marty Schottenheimer, who'd been dismissed by Redskins owner Daniel Snyder.

Dungy first heard the rumors through a heads-up from someone with strong ties to Parcells: Lions offensive coordinator Maurice Carthon, who had departed Gang Green at the same time as Parcells. Perhaps feeling empathy for one of the NFL's only black head coaches, Carthon quietly offered Dungy some intel: a few coaches linked to Parcells were ready to join him in Tampa Bay for the 2002 season. After another coaching friend made similar remarks, Dungy called Joel Glazer about the rumor that he was a Dead Coach Walking.

"I asked the guy," Dungy says, "and he told me point-blank, 'No, there's nothing to it.' So I just accepted him at his word and moved on."

But on Friday, January 11, five days after Dungy buried his mother, a flurry of reports surfaced that he would be dismissed if his 9-7 team lost Saturday's wild-card affair, and that an agreement with Parcells was in place. Andy Reid's Eagles trounced Tampa Bay, 31–9, at Veterans

Stadium, once again knocking out the Bucs in the wild-card round. Afterward, Keyshawn Johnson wept in the locker room, torn between his closeness to Parcells and his fondness for Dungy.

On Monday, January 14, GM Rich McKay stunned Dungy with a phone call conveying that he was being dismissed by the Glazers. Dungy says now, "I never realized the gossip was legit until the day I got fired." The next day Mike Tannenbaum flew to Tampa Bay to interview for the Bucs's GM job after receiving permission from Gang Green, and the Glazers officially acknowledged having talks with Parcells. Tampa Bay reassigned Rich McKay, its respected personnel executive, to team president, and on January 17 he publicly expressed confidence that Parcells would accept a four-year deal worth $17 million.

Meanwhile, Jets GM Terry Bradway suspected that his organization's coaches were being contacted about joining Tampa Bay without formal approval. Despite its residual ties to Parcells, Gang Green complained to the league office, and the NFL sent letters to the Bucs and Parcells, warning them that their actions were being monitored. Parcells denied recruiting employed coaches to join Tampa Bay, protesting that as someone unaffiliated with any team his communication with former colleagues shouldn't be construed as violating NFL policies. However, Parcells quietly reached an unofficial agreement with the Bucs ahead of an announcement, its date to be mutually determined.

Confronting the issue head-on, the Jets gave Mike Tannenbaum a specific deadline to make a decision on his offer from the Bucs: Friday, January 18, at 5 p.m. Mr. T used almost all the allotted time, and late Thursday afternoon he surprised league insiders by declining Tampa Bay's offer. Only a couple of hours later Parcells shocked the Glazers by informing them that he was no longer interested in joining the Bucs. His explanation echoed the one he'd given the Bucs more than a decade earlier, when he reversed his verbal agreement with Hugh Culverhouse: ostensibly lacking the energy to coach at age sixty, he didn't want to regret the move after a season or two in Tampa.

Despite Parcells's penchant for reversals, almost no one had seen this one coming.

While the Glazers shifted their attention to Raiders head coach Jon Gruden, Parcells's actions spurred criticism, particularly given Tony Dungy's ouster. Agent Leigh Steinberg says now, "If you're part of the football fraternity, you're not supposed to do certain things. There's a code. But there's a swashbuckling nature to Parcells. He'll do what he wants, when he wants." Tony Dungy, though, refused to join Parcells's castigators. Dungy and Parcells would remain friendly over the years, chatting more than ever whenever they crossed paths at league events, but the topic of Parcells's flirtation with the Bucs and Dungy's intertwined dismissal never came up.

"To this day, I don't know whether they were courting him or he was trying to get my job," Dungy says. "If the Bucs came after him, I don't think he had any obligation to say, 'Well, I'm not going to talk to you until you fire your coach.' But if he went after my job, I might feel differently. It's like this: If my wife has an affair, I might not know how it got started, but I will know who could have stopped it. And [in Tampa Bay], that was the owner."

The contenders for the Hall of Fame's class of 2002 lacked the strength of those from the previous year, bolstering Parcells's second chance at football immortality. But this time he faced criticism from some voters for leaving the Bucs at the altar. Each candidate traditionally had an official advocate on the selection committee. On February 2 in New Orleans, Vinny DiTrani of the *Bergen Record* made the presentation for Parcells. The sportswriter, closer to Parcells than most in the media, tried his best to convince his fellow voters that the ex-coach would stay retired, adding that he was more certain of this than he had been in 2001. Will McDonough concurred; after having rebuffed Tampa Bay, Parcells was less ambiguous during their conversations.

Such support proved helpful as Parcells survived the first cut from 14 to 11, and then made it to the final round of six players and one coach. Having made it to the penultimate step, Parcells needed 80 percent approval. At this stage, finalists typically won selection, but this time enough committee members blocked Parcells while approving coach George Allen as a senior candidate voted upon separately. Allen had never captured a Super Bowl and owned a postseason record of 2-7. Former offensive guard Bob Kuechenberg, considered a relatively weak finalist, also fell short of final approval.

The Hall of Fame Class of 2002 consisted of George Allen, tight end David Casper, defensive lineman Dan Hampton, quarterback Jim Kelly, and wideout John Stallworth. Parcells, who heard the news on his car radio in New Jersey, was disappointed for the second straight year. His omission was apparently a backlash from his flirtation with Tampa Bay, plus lingering suspicion by a bloc of voters, apparently from the West Coast, that he intended to coach again after boosting his value through enshrinement. Following the selection process, Ira Miller of the *San Francisco Chronicle*, an unabashed skeptic of Parcells's candidacy, told the *New York Daily News*, "A year of two from now, if he stays out, I'll look at him again, and I may feel differently, and may be convinced."

· · ·

Judy Goss and Bill Parcells had gotten married as college sweethearts on March 3, 1962. While Parcells pursued a college coaching career that required frequent relocations, Judy knew that she was not the only woman attracted to her husband's blue eyes, curly blond hair, and Cheshire-cat smile. She also suspected that he was accommodating them. When Parcells was coaching linebackers at Florida State during the early 1970s, Judy discovered incriminating evidence of an affair for the first time. Called out on it, Parcells promised to change his behavior. As a housewife with an expanding brood, Judy felt she had little choice except to offer her husband a mulligan. "I had three little kids; Jill was a year old," she says. "What was I going to do?"

More than a decade later, after the Giants made Parcells successor to Ray Perkins in 1983, Judy still found it difficult to endure groupies who chased NFL head coaches. The home-wreckers unabashedly engaged her husband at public spots such as restaurants, particularly as he transformed Big Blue into champions. Parcells took "mystery vacations" by himself, Judy recalls, during the annual six-week break before training camp. Once Parcells told her he would be away for a few days at a golf tournament, but when Judy's skepticism prompted her to check on it, the organizer informed her that the event was still weeks away. "It made me feel sick," she recalls. She felt worse when Parcells blamed her for being paranoid and stirring up trouble.

During Parcells's final season with the Patriots, Judy and her husband agreed to build a home in Seagirt, New Jersey, so that they could live by the beach. The couple moved into the new beachside home just before Parcells joined the Jets in February 1997, causing him to rent a condominium on Long Island.

Almost every night after leaving Jets headquarters, Parcells patronized B. K. Sweeney's, not far from his condo. He usually arrived by himself between 7:00 and 7:30 p.m. to have dinner, most often with a friend. Kelly Mandart, a waitress and manager at the steakhouse, frequently served Parcells. Only a casual football fan, she knew the level of his celebrity from coworkers and patrons. Mandart informed her husband of two years, Terry Scarlatos, about her special customer. The New York City cop and fan of the legendary coach reacted with excitement, and when Scarlatos visited his wife at the restaurant, Parcells thrilled the officer with small talk.

During Judy's sporadic stays on Long Island she sometimes joined Parcells at B. K. Sweeney's. On Thursdays Mickey Corcoran drove from Jersey to dine with Parcells. By generally arriving several minutes before his friends, Parcells provided a window for the steakhouse employees to engage him in a running dialogue. Mandart and Parcells got to know and like each other, especially in 1998 when Judy rarely showed up.

On Thanksgiving week Mandart spent several days in Pennsylvania visiting her father-in-law. When she returned to work, Parcells asked her, "Where were you? I missed you." Mandart confessed to having similar feelings, and in that moment the two became aware of just how much they enjoyed each other's company. Parcells started giving Mandart Jets tickets, which she would pass on to her brothers; Terry Scarlatos's police shift, stretching until midnight, prevented him from attending the games.

By late 1998, the friendship between the famous coach, fifty-seven, and his chatty waitress, twenty-nine, had turned into a romance. The unlikely couple attempted to be discreet by patronizing far-flung restaurants on the island. "She wasn't divorced for some of that time," Parcells says of Mandart, "and neither was I. So I'm not proud of that."

As his extramarital relationship with Mandart deepened, Parcells asked his wife not to visit Garden City anymore. "I'm just making us both unhappy." Judy grudgingly heeded the request, given the deteriorated state of their marriage. Although Parcells still phoned her almost daily at Sea Girt to check in, he stopped making his weekend visits. Judy assumed that her husband was involved in an affair meaningful enough that he was effectively initiating a separation.

By December 1998, Judy had learned of Kelly's identity after Dallas got the scoop from a friend in the know. Parcells's daughters tried to lift their mother's spirits while researching Mandart. The three adult children found it particularly baffling that their father, having stressed education and financial independence throughout their lives, would end up with someone who had chosen not to attend college. In one undercover mission, Jill visited the restaurant and ordered from the bar while Parcells was working at Jets headquarters. Mandart remained oblivious that her customer was Parcells's youngest daughter.

"He would probably fall off a chair," Jill says, "if he knew how much we had figured out."

Judy Parcells's divorce from her husband of almost forty years produced headlines on January 30, 2002, just two days before Bill Parcells spurned Tampa Bay. But the ex-spouses and their children considered the marriage's dissolution inevitable, if not anticlimactic. Bill Parcells had been essentially separated from his wife for the past few years, mostly living with his new girlfriend while running the Jets. Nonetheless, Parcells and Judy both felt sadness about the official end of their marriage. Their communication, though, remained unchanged. "Nothing really seemed different," recalls Judy, who doesn't blame football for their split, "because he was never around anyway."

During their separation Parcells had telephoned his wife almost daily to touch base. To Kelly Mandart's chagrin, he maintained the habit even after the divorce, citing the need to discuss his three children. But Parcells lacked a close relationship with Suzy, Dallas, and Jill, so his idiosyncratic bond with Judy went beyond their mutual interest in the kids.

The day before news outlets reported their breakup, the new divorcees met for lunch at a popular restaurant in Sea Girt. "I have feelings for Judy," explains Parcells, who was a twenty-one-year-old junior at Wichita when he got married. "I want her to be well, so I try to ensure that if there's something she needs, I'm there for her." Neither Parcells nor Judy truly wanted a divorce. Despite marital issues that had originated during his peripatetic college career, Parcells had ruled against ever ending their union. Perhaps the most serious threat came in 1979, when Judy declined to move from Colorado for Parcells's first NFL opportunity.

Over the decades Judy had periodically contemplated dissolving her marital ties, but she loved Parcells too deeply to follow through. In late 2001, though, Judy felt compelled to file for divorce as he intensified his romance with Mandart. While the affair was not his first, Parcells kept his wife at arm's length more than ever before. "He wasn't going to give up his other life," she recalls, choking up before she pauses, wipes away a tear, and apologizes. "So, you know, I had no choice."

Parcells no longer tried to dissuade her, yet he insisted that she would have to be the one to initiate a divorce. When Judy finally took the step, Parcells considered it the most disappointing development of his late-adult life. "I was never happy about that," he says. In early December 2001, Parcells agreed to relinquish their seaside home to Judy. A judge in Monmouth County, New Jersey, granted the divorce on January 16, 2002, after Judy stated that her husband had grown "cold and distant" while not "communicating meaningfully." But such a description could have been made years, if not decades, earlier.

Parcells accepts the fault for his failed marriage. "I could have done *way* better there," he says. "I had a good wife; she was a good woman. I was just irresponsible in some ways. I was messing around and doing things wrong. It got to a point where it was aggravating to everybody. It was just time. But when you make a commitment, for better or for worse, you try to make things last."

He adds about straying outside the marriage, "It just got out of control. I just wasn't paying enough attention to her. She got sick of it, and I don't blame her. I take all the responsibility."

Their oldest daughter, Suzy, expounds. "The divorce probably came thirty years too late. My mother truly loved my dad, and he just hurt her over and over and over. Of course when we were kids, we didn't know all this. My mother kept it well hidden. Because we'd move so much, things would be okay for a while. Finally, it got to the point where my mom was going to go out of her mind. She just couldn't cope."

Unlike their parents, Suzy, Dallas, and Jill were thrilled by the divorce. "We were excited," Jill says. "We didn't have the ideal childhood, and they didn't have the ideal marriage. It was too long in coming, but if my dad had his choice, he would still be married to this day, just kind of living his own life."

During May 2002, Kelly Mandart and Bill Parcells moved into a new home in Manhasset, Long Island. Mandart soon filed for her divorce as the couple, no longer hiding their relationship, planned a future together. Expanding his duties on ESPN, Parcells inked a multiyear, multimillion-dollar deal for a full-time role on *Sunday NFL Countdown*, the network's flagship pregame show. The contract's fine print indicated that his coaching career still lacked closure: despite barring him from appearances on other networks, ESPN permitted an escape clause for a return to the sidelines.

While Parcells hadn't quite done his colorful persona justice during four guest appearances on *Countdown*, ESPN honchos valued his credibility and insight, so the show's crowded studio of six analysts notwithstanding, the network created a spot for Parcells. His full-time debut took place at Giants Stadium, when the NFL regular season opened on Thursday, September 5, with Big Blue hosting the 49ers.

About an hour before the opening kickoff, *Countdown*'s new producer, Seth Markman, visited Parcells in ESPN's trailer to review an earlier production meeting. Instead, Markman got a big surprise from his major on-air talent. "Seth, I can't go on; I'm not going to do it."

The ESPN producer replied, "Bill, what's wrong?"

"I don't think I can do this. I'm not going to be any good."

"You've coached Super Bowls. You've been in the most intense environments in the world. You're nervous about this?"

"It's different, Seth. I don't want to look like an ass out there."

"This is nothing compared to what you've been through. This is easy. Just be yourself and answer the questions. Forget the camera. Just talk to the guys."

Although Parcells never truly intended to bail because of anxieties, he enjoyed such reassurances. Once the camera lights flashed, the ex-coach gave a sharp performance. Chris Berman hosted *Countdown* with a panel composed of Parcells, reporter Chris Mortensen, and three former NFL stars: Tom Jackson, Sterling Sharpe, and Steve Young. All possessed healthy egos, and their strong opinions generated spirited debates. But no one spoke with the gravitas of Parcells. While his colleagues occasionally interrupted one another, he became the show's E. F. Hutton: everyone hushed for his insights.

Parcells transitioned successfully into his new full-time profession. He showed a strong work ethic, studying film extensively for pertinent analysis. But his circumspection during some segments clashed with the freewheeling culture of ESPN's talk shows. At production meetings, Parcells occasionally complained about receiving too much airtime, and requested to avoid discussing certain subjects.

"He was very good. He got really close to being great," says Markman, who earned the nickname "Weasel" from Parcells. "But I think something held him back. If you have the thought in the back of your mind that you may want to coach again, you don't throw all your punches."

In late November 2002, the University of Kentucky contacted Bill Parcells about its head coaching opening, stirring his dormant longing for the sidelines. NCAA violations involving cash payments to Wildcat recruits had caused the school to forfeit nineteen scholarships during a three-year probation. The SEC program had gone 2-9 the previous season under interim coach Guy Morriss. With Morriss staying for one last year of bowl-ineligibility, Kentucky had targeted pro football's turnaround-meister as a candidate to replace him.

The school's associate athletic director, John Cropp, had a link with Parcells. They had worked together at Vanderbilt under Steve Sloan in 1973 and 1974. Parcells, though, hadn't been a college coach since 1978, when he left Air Force. Nonetheless, the Wildcats urged him to seriously consider an attractive offer with benefits involving the Kentucky Derby that appealed to the horse-racing aficionado. Despite the team's albatross of NCAA sanctions, Parcells felt invigorated by the challenge.

"I really didn't have much to do," Parcells explains. "It was like, 'Well, let me go try and do this.' That's really what it was." But Parcells also wanted his girlfriend comfortable about the move. Mandart had never lived outside of Long Island, so Parcells accentuated the positives.

"You know, we'd be treated like royalty. You'd be the First Lady."

Mandart replied, "Well, are you sure you want to be a college coach? Isn't that a big difference from the NFL?"

"Yeah, I've got to really think this through, and see if I can get a staff together."

After Mandart said she was willing to move, Parcells telephoned some college head coaches and athletic directors for recommendations. The name Mike MacIntyre consistently surfaced as an ideal secondary coach and recruiting coordinator. Parcells recalled that a Vanderbilt colleague, George MacIntyre, had a kid named Mike. "That can't be Coach Mac's Mike, can it?"

Mike MacIntyre, thirty-seven, oversaw wideouts and defensive backs at the University of Mississippi. Just as important, George's son had earned a reputation for being a strong recruiter in the ultracompetitive SEC. With his help, Ole Miss was undergoing a renaissance led by players like quarterback Eli Manning and tailback Deuce McAllister.

For a possible offensive coordinator, Parcells targeted Arkansas quarterbacks coach David Lee, who had played the position at Vanderbilt during Bill's tenure there. While climbing the college-coaching ladder during the past twenty-five years, Lee had written or telephoned Parcells annually to convey an interest in pro football. Parcells had responded with encouragement and guidance.

Now, during a telephone conversation about Kentucky, Parcells told Lee, "David, there's something in me that says we can win."

Lee replied, "Coach, it's hard. Look at Bobby Bowden. He's down there in Florida. How many years did it take him to win one at Florida State?" Despite his success after taking over the Seminoles in 1976, Bowden didn't win his first national championship until 1993.

But Parcells seemed undeterred. "We've got to get a quarterback."

On Friday, December 6, 2002, David Lee traveled to Dallas for a high school game featuring a top quarterback targeted by his Razorbacks. There Lee read a story in a local paper quoting Cowboys owner Jerry Jones about his postseason plans to reevaluate his team, which was 5-7 under Dave Campo. Jones described the season as being his most disappointing since purchasing the Cowboys in 1989. Knowing that such remarks were management-speak for an impending staff overhaul, Lee dialed Parcells.

"Coach, I just want to read something to you here before you take the Kentucky job."

After doing so, Lee added, "I don't know if you know Jerry Jones, or if you would even entertain working for him, but I just thought I'd pass that along to you."

Parcells replied, "Hmmm. Jerry Jones."

Parcells's expanded ESPN duties included a weekly column for its website, and on December 11, 2002, his "QuickHits" section included two points related to the Cowboys:

- Dallas will have a good defense next year.
- Cowboys safety Roy Williams reminds me of a young Ronnie Lott.

. Later in the week, Parcells was sitting with colleague Chris Mortensen in an ESPN studio, preparing for a telecast, when footage of Jerry Jones appeared on one of several monitors. Parcells turned to Mortensen and said, "You know, I could work for that guy."

ESPN's lead NFL reporter expressed shock. Jones was a more proactive owner than even Robert Kraft, and had come in for special criticism in Parcells's recent book, *The Final Season*. Although the Cowboys owner never read it, he had been made aware of the pertinent quotes.

On December 15, 2002, Big Blue trounced Dallas, 37–7, at Giants Stadium, dropping the Cowboys to 5-9 and firming Jones's resolve to make a coaching change. The next day he telephoned Parcells's new agent, Jimmy Sexton, in Memphis, seeking a clandestine meeting with his client. After receiving the message, Parcells asked Jones to travel to New Jersey's Teterboro Airport and immediately contacted Kentucky, unequivocally declining the school's offer.

Parcells told Mandart, "Jerry Jones called. I don't know why, but he wants to talk to me."

Mandart replied, "He wants you to be the coach, Bill. Do you think I was born yesterday?"

"No, but I'm just going to see what he has to say."

24

The October 2001 issue of *Texas Monthly* splashed a caricature of Jerry Jones on its cover: with red horns protruding from his forehead, the Cowboys owner held a pitchfork as fire exploded in the background. The headline asked, "Is Jerry Jones the Devil?" Jones's nine-year-old granddaughter, Jessica, bawled when she saw the magazine, prompting him to console her. Published with the Cowboys at 0-4, the cover article skewered Jones for the outsized ego that had spurred Jimmy Johnson's departure, despite his having captured a second consecutive Super Bowl title. Echoing the sentiments of many Cowboy fans, the magazine asserted, "The most disheartening aspect of the way Jones runs his team is the way he treats his coaches. He controls them as if they were puppets."

Johnson's replacement, Barry Switzer, had won the 1996 Super Bowl with a roster containing key Johnson holdovers like future Hall of Famers Troy Aikman, Michael Irvin, and Emmitt Smith, but after that high-water mark Dallas had regressed under two obscure head coaches with reduced powers. Although Chan Gailey's Cowboys made the playoffs in 1998 and 1999, the second appearance came with an 8-8 record. And in Dave Campo's first season, the start of which had factored in the *Texas Monthly* skewering, Dallas finished a dismal 5-11.

As the 2002 season neared its end, Jerry Jones ached to blunt the relentless criticism. "I needed to hire someone," he says, "who was perceived to be stronger than me." On the team plane following yet another embarrassing loss, Fox broadcaster Pat Summerall opined that the franchise needed a respected disciplinarian "like Parcells," who happened to be his friend. Jones was surprisingly open to the idea, prompting Summerall, who was based in Dallas, to telephone Parcells and express confidence that his two domineering pals could coexist. Parcells praised Jones's reputation for salesmanship, knowing that the compliment would likely get back to the maverick owner.

On Wednesday afternoon, December 18, Bill Parcells and Jerry Jones met at Teterboro Airport, the retired coach's home turf since childhood. With two games left in the regular season, Jones and Parcells wanted to avoid being seen together, so they spoke for almost three hours in a private boardroom. Jones asked Parcells, who had never led an NFL team that was based outside the Northeast, why he was open to coaching the Cowboys.

Parcells replied, "There are lounge acts in Vegas, and then there is the big room where Elvis and Sinatra play. The Cowboys are the big room, which is one of the reasons I'm excited about coaching again."

The pair discreetly boarded Jones's private jet, parked on the runway, and spoke for another two hours. Despite the cloak-and-dagger, reports about the meeting surfaced by Saturday. Forced to respond, Jones and Parcells described the get-together as a discussion about football philosophy and the NFL, similar to meetings Jones had arranged with retired gurus like John Madden and Bill Walsh. Still, speculation regarding the improbable union swirled among NFL colleagues and pundits, most of whom were skeptical that the two alpha males could get along. But in a follow-up conversation over the telephone, the proactive owner, sixty, and the dictatorial coach, sixty-one, shared laughs while acknowledging that they needed each other.

As stunned as anyone by the prospect, Jimmy Johnson dialed Parcells. "Are you really thinking about doing this?"

Parcells replied, "Yes, I am."

Johnson paused, weighing his next words. "Well, I think it will be good. Right now, I think Jerry's ready for somebody like you." Then Johnson added a caveat—that the partnership would last "for a short time." Even that, he said, would require Jones to be circumspect in his public remarks about the Cowboys.

During the first of his two years as Eagles quarterbacks coach, starting in 1997, Sean Payton had learned the complex, script-laden West Coast offense under coordinator Jon Gruden. In 1999, Payton took the same position with Jim Fassel's Giants, where after one season he was promoted to offensive coordinator. On off days, Payton frequently slept in Giants Stadium, studying film and immersing himself in the playbook before crashing on his office couch. But seven games into the 2002 season, after the Giants offense had scored only seven touchdowns, Jim Fassel stripped Sean Payton of his play-calling duties. Fassel allowed the thirty-eight-year-old offensive coordinator to keep his title, but feeling professionally emasculated, Payton approached GM Ernie Accorsi. "I want to resign."

Accorsi replied, "Sean, you can't. You don't want to be known as the assistant who walked out on his head coach. You're young and you haven't established a reputation yet. But I promise I'll let you out of your contract after this season." Sean Payton heeded Accorsi's advice, but when

Big Blue's offense turned explosive with Fassel calling the plays, Accorsi permitted his disgruntled staffer to at least communicate with potential employers.

Around ten o'clock one night in late December, Beth Payton picked up the phone at home in northern New Jersey. When she told her husband that the caller was Big Blue's legendary ex-coach, he reacted with surprise. The two men had never spoken before. Nonetheless, with almost all of Parcells's disciples under contract for the 2003 season, he needed talented coaches for a possible Cowboys staff. And Payton had been recommended by someone whose opinion Parcells valued: Chris Mara, the Giants personnel executive and son of the team's owner, Wellington Mara. During Parcells's stint as Big Blue's head coach, Chris had been among his best scouts, showing a strong work ethic and sharp eye that earned respect beyond his bloodlines. The former colleagues had stayed in touch over the years as Chris Mara rose in his organization's personnel department.

During the phone conversation with Payton, Parcells said, "There's a job I might be interested in, and if I take it I'll be looking for coaches. If things fall into place, you're someone I'd be interested in visiting with." The interest seemed incongruous given Parcells's adherence to offensive simplicity: Payton relied on intricate playbooks heavy on the pass.

When Ernie Accorsi learned of Parcells's interest in Payton, the GM told him, "I'll let you out of your contract because I'm going to live up to my word. I *am* worried because we have to compete against Dallas, and you're a good coach. But I'll tell you this: If Parcells takes that job and hires you, that's going to be your master's degree. That education is going to help make you a tremendous head coach. You'll get lessons in everything from toughness to leadership."

The second meeting between Jerry Jones and Bill Parcells occurred on Long Island on December 27, two days before the Cowboys' season finale. With talks becoming more concrete, the owner's lieutenant/son, Stephen Jones, participated, along with Parcells's new agent, Jimmy Sexton, in a session that lasted six hours. Since naming himself GM following Jimmy Johnson's departure in 1994, Jerry Jones had overseen generally poor drafts. Given Parcells's deep-seated desire to shop for players, personnel power became a crucial issue. As owner, president, and GM, Jones declined to relinquish final authority, but he agreed to give Parcells more sway than any Cowboys head coach since Jimmy Johnson: the new partners agreed on mutual veto power over what players made the roster. Unlike his predecessors, Parcells required autonomy in choosing a staff, and Jones uncharacteristically acquiesced on the matter.

As the negotiating pas de deux continued by telephone, Oakland's Al Davis, longtime friend of both men, acted as an intermediary. The NFL's elder statesman believed that although his buddies both wanted credit for a championship, reaching the goal would generate enough kudos to satisfy their outsized egos. Jones and Parcells agreed to a formula on publicly dispensing recognition if Dallas captured a Super Bowl, and to confirm it during the final stages of negotiations, the two read each other the protocol. Then Jones offered Parcells a four-year contract worth $17.1 million, which would give the new head coach an annual salary larger than that of his four predecessors combined.

"I knew I had run out of the benefit of the doubt, and I got scared," Jones admits, alluding to mounting criticism of his micromanagement. "That motivated me to make a significant change—not just a coaching change, a philosophical change. When you come right down to it, hiring Bill represented a change in philosophy for me."

Jones imposed a signing deadline for the offer that would require Parcells to decide by the New Year. Meanwhile, though, Joe O'Donnell came to Parcells with an alternative possibility that intrigued his close friend. The Boston-based concessionaire believed that Parcells would mesh better with an NFL owner O'Donnell had known well since the 1980s: Wayne Huizenga of the Miami Dolphins. O'Donnell, whose company sold concessions at Pro Player Stadium, often visited Huizenga in Florida for business and pleasure.

Huizenga's team had also experienced a disappointing 2002 season, although to a lesser extent than Jones's Cowboys. Under Dave Wannstedt the Dolphins finished 9-7, missing the playoffs for the first time in six years. This was a letdown for a talented team that had won eleven regular-season games in both 2000 and 2001, so O'Donnell urged Huizenga to hire Parcells, noting that the former Jets boss spent winters in Jupiter.

O'Donnell recalls, "I said, 'Look, this guy's the greatest.' Wayne said, 'Well, he may very well be the greatest coach in the world'—and this is what you've got to love about Wayne—'but I've committed to let Wannstedt run this out.' Basically, that's when Bill took the Cowboys job. Otherwise, he would have been coaching the Miami Dolphins."

The night before Jerry Jones's deadline, Jimmy Sexton slept over at Parcells's home in Manhasset with plans to check into the Garden City Hotel the next day. In the morning, just a few hours before Jones's cutoff, Parcells empowered Sexton to accept the offer, but as the agent started dialing Cowboys officials anxious for a decision, Parcells stopped him. Wanting to be certain, Parcells volunteered to drive Sexton to his hotel, with Mandart coming along, and to decide before reaching their destination. A few minutes into the ride, Parcells gave Sexton the go-ahead and then almost immediately retracted it, invoking Mandart as the reason.

"Kelly isn't going to be able to make it with me if I take the job."

Parcells explains the seesawing more candidly. "My father used to have an expression: '**The time to worry is before you place the bet—not after the wheel is spinning.** There's nothing you can do about it then.' In every decision I make, I worry before."

Parcells remained worried until the moment he pulled his car into the driveway of Sexton's hotel. Turning to his exasperated representative, Parcells said firmly, "All right, all right, Jimmy. Call them, and tell them all right."

Within a week of their telephone introduction, Sean Payton and Bill Parcells boarded Jerry Jones's private jet in New York. The sixth head coach in Cowboys history and his new quarterbacks guru sat together on the Dallas-bound flight discussing football for almost three hours. Parcells dominated the conversation, intermittently diagramming plays using a ballpoint pen and several napkins. Occasionally Sean Payton drew up some of his favorite designs, but mostly he soaked up Parcells's preliminary lessons.

In Irving, Texas, the area's obsession was illustrated by its street signs: Avenue of Champions, Touchdown Drive, Dorsett Drive, Meredith Drive, Staubach Drive. Although Tony Dorsett, Don Meredith, and Roger Staubach had been Cowboys stars, the streets were also dotted with names more likely to be recognizable only to passionate fans of the team. Outside Valley Ranch, the Cowboys headquarters in Irving, a topiary took the star shape of the team's logo.

During an introductory press conference there on January 2, 2003, Jerry Jones described Parcells as the "most qualified coach in our sport that you could draw up if you were drawing your own Rembrandt." Parcells wore a dark-gray suit, white shirt, and tie striped with Cowboys silver and blue. The two men of the hour expressed optimism about their partnership and the franchise's future, but *Sports Illustrated* captured the skepticism of people who knew both bigwigs well. "Are You Kidding Me?" asked the magazine in a headline the following week.

Just as Parcells was starting this new, intriguing chapter in his football life, he lost yet another close friend. Late Thursday, January 9, Will McDonough died of a heart attack at his home in Hingham, Massachusetts, while watching ESPN. Despite McDonough's history of heart trouble, which had included a mild attack in December, his death rocked Parcells. The *Boston Globe* columnist had recently passed the same stress tests that Parcells once took before heart surgery, clearing the sportswriter to maintain his record of covering every Super Bowl. With Parcells's handful of close friends dwindling, the sixty-one-year-old coach needed football more than ever.

Parcells and Mandart moved into an apartment building in the suburb of Las Colinas, a few miles from Valley Ranch. Entering his new team's headquarters, Parcells snaked through corridors filled with pictures of Cowboys greats and reminders of the franchise's glorious past. One navy-and-white sign read, "World Champions: 1971, 1977, 1992, 1993, 1995." Parcells's new office was the same one where Tom Landry had last hung his fedora. The upgraded furniture included cherry-paneled walls, a leather couch, and a metal desk that held a framed photograph of Landry and Parcells snapped in the mid-1980s. The opposing head coaches are talking near midfield at Texas Stadium, minutes before their Giants and Cowboys battled.

Parcells had formally met Landry in the early 1980s following an introduction from Wellington Mara. One of the most innovative coaches in NFL history, Landry was at the tail end of his league-record twenty consecutive winning seasons, a stretch from 1966 to 1985, with capstones of Super Bowl VI and XII.

Whenever Parcells saw Landry during pregame warm-ups, the young head coach solicited whatever information he could get. How many days per week did the Cowboys practice in pads? How physical were their Friday sessions? Despite the Giants being archrivals, Landry educated Parcells, and Big Blue's leader, seventeen years younger than his counterpart, cherished every tidbit. Parcells says of Landry, "The most genuine, forthright, caring guy, and very straightforward with me."

While Parcells's stature rose toward the late 1980s, highlighted by a Super Bowl ring in 1987, Landry's Cowboys stumbled. On November 6, 1988, Dallas brought a five-game skid to the Meadowlands while the Giants were aiming for their fourth straight victory. Nonetheless, Parcells viewed the only head coach in Cowboys history as a football god. Both men maintained their pregame ritual of chatting, and Landry ended the conversation by praising his counterpart for revitalizing Big Blue. Parcells says, "You know what that means to a guy like me?"

That meaningful exchange would be their last one on the gridiron. Dallas lost, 29–21, en route to the league's worst record at 3-13, and a few months later an oil magnate named Jerry Jones purchased the franchise and shocked the nation by firing Landry that same day.

Parcells's new Cowboys office already contained three family photographs: his daughters in their preteen years wearing dresses and pigtails;

his grandson Kyle and granddaughter Kendall. Glued to the cabinet was a brass plate from Al Groh that repeated the succinct advice Parcells had given him as a rookie NFL head coach in 2000, guidance that originally came from Al Davis during Parcells's tumultuous 1983 season.

"Just Coach the Team."

The Tampa Bay Buccaneers were waiting on a claim filed with the league office seeking draft picks from the Cowboys because Parcells had agreed to join Tampa Bay in early 2002. Paul Tagliabue ruled against the Bucs, however, saving Parcells from needing a second straight employer to relinquish compensatory picks for his services. Now his immediate concern was to assemble a strong staff, despite a pool largely devoid of his disciples. One exception was the only person to have ever both played and coached for him: Maurice Carthon, coming off his first season as Detroit's offensive coordinator. Parcells persuaded Carthon to join him in Dallas by offering him the same plum position.

The first time the pair entered Valley Ranch together, early one morning, Carthon shook his head after a few steps, turning to Parcells. "Bill, can you believe we're coaching the Dallas *Cowboys*?" Their laughter echoed through the hallway.

After due diligence, Parcells kept on Mike Zimmer as Cowboys defensive coordinator, notwithstanding the forty-six-year-old's inexperience with the 3-4 scheme. Zimmer had fielded solid defenses amid Dallas's recent struggles. Parcells still wanted some familiar faces, however, so he targeted his Jets wideouts coach, Todd Haley, who had joined the Bears in 2001, and in the next season helped Marty Booker become the franchise's first Pro Bowl wideout since 1971. The Bears, though, declined to release their promising coach from his contract, which had one more season left on it.

Three days before Parcells's introductory conference, the Jacksonville Jaguars had fired Tom Coughlin, the only head coach and GM in its eight-year existence. He turned down Parcells's offer to reunite them in Dallas, having decided to sit out at least one year before pursuing head-coaching opportunities. But Coughlin recommended Tony Sparano, describing the forty-one-year-old as one of the best assistants he'd ever had. Such effusive praise from Parcells's even-keeled alter ego convinced him to hire Sparano as Dallas's tight ends coach.

Parcells decided to keep several of his predecessor's defensive assistants, including linebackers coach Gary Gibbs, the former head coach of the Oklahoma Sooners. Parcells also hired the two young coaches he had planned to bring to Kentucky when mulling that job: Mike MacIntyre and David Lee. When MacIntyre stepped into Parcells's office to learn that he had beaten out several candidates for the job of overseeing Dallas's defensive backs, Parcells told him, "Mike, I'm hiring you. Work your butt off. Don't worry about me patting you on the back, or saying anything to you. If you do a good job, I'll promote you and keep you. If not, I'll fire you."

MacIntyre's heart raced with nervousness and excitement. "Yes, sir."

Shortly thereafter, David Lee sat in the same chair to discuss being a quality-control coach for offense and assisting Sean Payton with quarterbacks. Despite more than two decades of pleasant conversations, Lee's new boss skipped the small talk.

"Here's your contract, here's your salary, and here's a pen. Sign it."

As Lee picked up the pen, Parcells eased up a bit. "Actually, go ahead and read it over."

Lee signed anyway. "No. I don't need to read it over. I trust you." The rookie NFL coach rose and shook Parcells's hand. "Coach, I'm going to bust my butt for you."

"David, that might not be good enough. This business is all about production."

Lee nodded, turned around, and left the room. Heading down the hall, he thought to himself, "This is a different deal. This isn't the same relationship. Things have changed."

During the first staff meeting to detail plans for 2003, Parcells warned the group, "I like confrontation; it clears the air. I don't want or need coaches who are the player's best friends. I want coaches who are demanding, who can make the player better and take him where he can't go by himself."

The remarks captivated Sean Payton as he took careful notes. Dallas's new quarterbacks coach had never heard anyone articulate the benefits of confrontation before. Since entering the profession at San Diego State in 1988, nine years before his first NFL gig in Philadelphia, Payton had generally avoided brutal honesty with players.

Only a few days into the job, Parcells confronted a major problem involving quarterback Quincy Carter, who had started seven games for Dallas the previous season: the twenty-six-year-old was about to enter a drug treatment clinic in the Boston area. The NFL had reportedly placed Carter in its substance-abuse program because his urine tested positive for marijuana, triggering multiple unannounced tests each week. His agent,

Eugene Parker, knowing Parcells well, instructed Carter to discuss the issue with Dallas's new leader or risk dismissal from the team, so the quarterback visited Parcells's office at Valley Ranch for a frank conversation.

Quincy Carter told Parcells, "You know, I've got this little problem, which is why I'm going to go away to rehab."

Parcells replied, "You go ahead. But I'm not having drugs on my team. So when you come back, you'd better be attending after-care and all that, because if you don't follow through, forget about playing on this team. I can lose games without your ass."

Since confronting the Giants' drug problems in 1984, Parcells had given players like Carter an opportunity to rehabilitate with his club's support, but he would only tolerate a slim margin for error. Recalling the advice from the addiction expert who had educated him, Parcells says, "I can't be nice to these guys. I'm not trying to be a smart-ass. Jane Jones told me to bust their balls. It's etched in my mind."

Parcells adds, "Jerry was the greatest enabler there was. He said he was going to help Carter and test the player himself. Jerry didn't know shit about that."

After quarterback Troy Aikman's retirement following the 2000 season, the Cowboys had sought a replacement, so in 2001 Jerry Jones drafted Carter in the second round, fifty-third overall, via Georgia. Before his standout college football career, which included becoming a starter during his freshman season, the fleet six-two, 220-pounder had struggled in minor-league baseball, playing outfield for a Chicago Cubs affiliate. As an NFL rookie with the Cowboys, Carter became the first black quarterback to be named a starter. Injuries, however, limited Carter to eight games. He returned as starter in 2002, but after going 3-4 he lost the job to another ex–baseball player: Chad Hutchinson, who had entered Stanford in 1995 as an elite pitcher and quarterback. Hutchinson had spent four seasons with the St. Louis Cardinals organization.

Like Tom Coughlin in his inaugural year under Parcells, Sean Payton quickly discovered his boss's distaste for scripted plays. During one of Parcells's first minicamp practices he lambasted his offensive coaches for being preoccupied with their scripts instead of teaching important details to their players. Parcells commanded an equipment guy to collect the sheets from his staff; setting them aside, Parcells barked, "Okay, now call the goddamn plays against the defense."

Forced to watch the action more closely, the offensive coaches became better attuned to nuances and passed them on to the players. In sum, Parcells's diktat led to improved instruction. He continued to acculturate, or deprogram, his new coaches, especially Sean Payton. During the first few weeks of spring practices, the offense worked on specific runs and passes. When coaches inserted new wrinkles every day the execution lagged, so Parcells laminated the playlist and banned any additions. The decision frustrated Payton, who relished experimenting from a comprehensive playbook, but the offense soon responded with sharper execution. For the first time in his football life, Payton saw the benefits of a streamlined offense.

25

Jerry Jones once heard Bill Walsh opine on TV that the Cowboys owner and Jimmy Johnson had grown careless in managing their relationship. Deeming Walsh's assessment correct, Jones intended to avoid making the same mistake with Parcells. So in early 2003, the owner assigned his son Stephen and PR chief Rich Dalrymple to the task of enhancing communication and maintaining harmony. At a meeting Jerry Jones told the two men, "I want you guys to help us work out this relationship. Always let me know where I might be going a little bit over the line, and let Bill know where he might be doing the same."

When informed of the arrangement, Bill Parcells considered it a smart idea.

Since joining the organization in 1995, Dalrymple had seen how relationships could deteriorate between management and coaches because of miscommunication or perceived slights. Stephen Jones, who held the franchise's second-highest title as executive vice president, understood his father's idiosyncrasies as well as anyone; Stephen had demonstrated a knack for defusing combustible situations in the Cowboys organization.

Jerry and Bill were also working hard to be sensitive to each other's feelings. Unlike in previous years, the owner kept his head coach in the loop on every consequential development related to the franchise. Their candid yet respectful discussions helped Stephen Jones and Rich Dalrymple in their role as intermediaries. The primary potential for trouble between the larger-than-life figures involved personnel decisions. This made Larry Lacewell—Jones's top scout, consigliere, and longtime pal—a key figure in the partnership.

After spending four decades in college football, mostly as a defensive coach, Lacewell had joined the Cowboys in 1992 for his close friend Jimmy Johnson's fourth season. As director of college and pro scouting, Lacewell oversaw the franchise's drafts. His first coaching job had come in 1959 at Alabama as a graduate assistant for Bear Bryant, who'd been a high school teammate of his father's in Fordyce, Arkansas. In Arkansas, Lacewell met Jerry Jones, a star tailback at North Little Rock High, leading to a long friendship.

Over several years Lacewell jumped from school to school while moving up the coaching ladder. Named Wichita defensive coordinator in 1967, he hired Jimmy Johnson two years after a neophyte coach, Bill Parcells, had overseen his alma mater's linebackers. Lacewell helped Johnson land jobs at multiple schools as the pair grew close enough for Johnson to be best man at Lacewell's wedding.

In 1970, Lacewell became Oklahoma's defensive coordinator under Chuck Fairbanks, and again brought Johnson along. When Fairbanks left for the Patriots three years later, Barry Switzer took over, and Oklahoma captured national championships in 1974 and 1975. Lacewell's only stint as a head coach occurred at Arkansas State from 1979 to 1989, a stretch in which he set the school's all-time mark for victories.

Mulling retirement after the 2002 Cowboys season, Lacewell sold his Dallas home and purchased property in Hot Springs, Arkansas. However, the prospect of working with Bill Parcells excited Dallas's chief scout, so he decided to stay put for the anticipated turnaround. Lacewell advised Jones, "Give Bill anything he wants. Period. If I'm part of the problem, get rid of me. Don't let you be the excuse for him quitting."

In their first major roster move, Jerry and Bill agreed to release tailback Emmitt Smith, the NFL's all-time leading rusher, who had played all thirteen seasons of his pro career in Dallas. Despite Smith's insistence on remaining a starter, his productivity had declined for three straight seasons, including the previous one, when he'd amassed 975 rushing yards while averaging 3.8 yards. The February 27, 2003, transaction provided Dallas with substantially more spending money for free agency, set to commence the next day. Shortly thereafter Emmitt Smith would ink a two-year contract with the Arizona Cardinals.

Smith, thirty-three, represented the franchise's final link to future Hall of Famers Troy Aikman and Michael Irvin; together the "Triplets" had helped Dallas capture three Lombardi Trophies during the 1990s. The media speculated that Parcells had been behind the move, but the first time the new head coach and his boss had gone over the roster, Jones said, "You don't need to worry about Emmitt. I'll take care of that. We need to be moving on." Darren Woodson, a five-time Pro Bowler and the league's most versatile safety, remained the only player on the roster tied to Jimmy Johnson's Cowboys.

The top candidate on the Cowboys to replace Smith had been signed in 2000 as an undrafted player out of Savannah State: Troy Hambrick doubled as a fullback. He showed promise as Smith's backup but was better known for special-teams contributions. As always, Parcells added former players to his new team. He acquired Terry Glenn from the Packers by relinquishing only a sixth-round pick.

New England's decision to jettison Glenn came after a four-year stretch of inconsistency, personal difficulties, and disputes with Bill Belichick, culminating in a postseason suspension while the Patriots went on to capture Super Bowl XXXVI. But Glenn had won Parcells over in New England with his brilliant rookie season, and the start of Glenn's troubles coincided with Parcells departing the Patriots. So they both saw a reunion as mutually beneficial. Parcells also signed Jets fullback Richie Anderson to a multiyear contract by outbidding New England.

Jeff Ireland, an up-and-coming scout in the organization, generally acted as the point man on personnel acquisitions. After identifying a need, Ireland approached Parcells to discuss it, and vice versa. Typically Ireland then relayed any request to Stephen Jones before it reached Jerry. Then, in keeping with his resolve to constantly communicate, the owner sometimes walked into Parcells's office to discuss the matter. Occasionally Jones came up with his own personnel ideas, which he ran by the scouts and coaches, especially Parcells.

"Jerry doesn't have a football philosophy," Parcells says, "but I like what he does. He tries to get all the information he can. He's not a talent evaluator. Now, some days he thinks he is. Some days I think I'm an oilman, but I'm not. He's an oilman." Still, if the oilman expressed reservations about one of Bill's personnel requests, the head coach reacted with openness to the owner's counterargument. Whenever Bill remained steadfast, Jerry held a roundtable of his front-office brass, and the group, including Parcells, discussed all aspects of the potential acquisition before Dallas pursued it. In rare instances Jerry and Bill reached an impasse.

"If there was a little flare-up," Larry Lacewell says, "Stephen Jones would go in and talk to both of 'em, and settle 'em down. And he did a marvelous job of that." Knowing this, Bill sometimes bounced ideas off Stephen first, an approach that facilitated requests to the ultimate boss.

The 2003 draft in late April illustrated the early compatibility of the dictatorial partners. Despite Jerry Jones's retaining final approval, the Cowboys' selections reflected Bill Parcells's emphasis on defense and power running. The Cowboys selected cornerback Terence Newman of Kansas State in the first round, center Al Johnson via Wisconsin in the second, tight end Jason Witten of Tennessee in the third, and linebacker Bradie James via Louisiana State in the fourth. During down moments in the late rounds, Bill and Jerry engaged in good-natured betting: If a certain prospect made the roster, Jerry would owe Bill two trips on the owner's private jet; if not, Parcells needed to cede a fraction of his big salary.

"Bill never encroached on Jerry's position as the owner, president, and general manager," recalls Jim Garrett, a Cowboys scout from 1987 to 2004, whose son Jason became the team's head coach in 2010. "Bill was kind and considerate to Jerry. If there was something controversial Bill needed to talk about, he whispered it to Jerry. It was a great combination."

Before the draft, Parcells had dyed his graying hair platinum blond. And as if reimagining the Cowboys based on bygone glories, he envisioned Jason Witten being a major contributor like Mark Bavaro with Big Blue and Ben Coates in New England. Jason Witten would end up being among the best draft picks in Cowboys history, a perennial Pro Bowler, smashing virtually all the franchise's records at tight end. Terence Newman would turn into a top NFL cornerback, while Bradie James would develop into a tackling machine and playmaker.

For the late rounds of the 2003 draft, Sean Payton lobbied the Cowboys to select a shifty, quick-trigger quarterback named Tony Romo from his alma mater, Eastern Illinois. While breaking some of Payton's school records, Romo had earned the Walter Payton Award for being the top player in Division I-AA. Even as Dallas used sixth-round picks on defensive back B. J. Tucker (Wisconsin) and wideout Zuriel Smith (Hampton), Payton assured Romo by telephone of the Cowboys' interest. Jerry and Bill, though, used their final, seventh-round pick on guard Justin Bates (Colorado), leaving Romo undrafted.

Mike Shanahan's Broncos were among several teams bent on signing the six-two, 235-pound gunslinger as a free agent. Like Payton, Shanahan had played quarterback at Eastern Illinois, but his college career came to an end as sudden as it was dramatic. Shanahan almost died during a 1972 practice after a linebacker's spearing tackle ruptured his kidneys. Shanahan's heart reportedly stopped for thirty seconds as the team summoned a priest to read last rites.

On May 1, 2003, Mike Shanahan offered Tony Romo the biggest signing bonus, $25,000, but Payton convinced his fellow alum to join the Cowboys for $15,000, stressing the opportunity offered by the team's unproven quarterbacks. Romo also felt a kinship with Payton, who still held several Eastern Illinois records, including 509 passing yards in one game. Payton had graduated in 1987 before joining the Chicago Bruisers of the Arena Football League in its inaugural season. His only NFL experience had come as a replacement player for the Bears during the 1987 strike. In three games, Payton completed 8 of 23 for 79 yards and produced a rating of 27.3, numbers that Tony Romo intended to far exceed.

During rookie minicamp, Parcells began employing the methods that had proven so effective in eradicating losing cultures at his previous stops. He instructed the Cowboys' equipment manager to remove the blue stars from player helmets, and told the newbies that they would have to earn the storied logo. If a rookie failed to correctly answer a random question about strategy, the group was forced to run sprints. Parcells instituted new rules that included banning eating and cell phone use in the locker room, while decorating its white cinder-block walls with some of his maxims.

DON'T CONFUSE ROUTINE WITH COMMITMENT.

BLAME NOBODY, EXPECT NOTHING, DO SOMETHING.

**THERE ARE MANY EXIT DOORS IN PRO FOOTBALL.
DON'T TAKE THEM.**

**LOSING WILL TAKE A LITTLE FROM YOUR CREDIBILITY,
BUT QUITTING WILL DESTROY IT.**

**DUMB PLAYERS DO DUMB THINGS. SMART PLAYERS
VERY SELDOM DO DUMB THINGS.**

**LOSERS ASSEMBLE IN LITTLE GROUPS, AND BITCH ABOUT
THE COACHES AND THE SYSTEM AND OTHER PLAYERS IN
OTHER LITTLE GROUPS. WINNERS ASSEMBLE AS A TEAM.**

After spotting an offensive lineman devouring pizza in the trainer's room, Parcells also banned eating there. He had already lowered the air-conditioning to 55 degrees.

Dave Campo hadn't pushed his players to attend off-season voluntary workouts, out of concern that they would complain to the players association, so a slew of key Cowboys had typically stayed away. Parcells, on the other hand, stressed the importance of the program, especially for conditioning. When necessary, he held one-on-one meetings with players to extract assurances that they would attend, and for the first time in recent memory, few players skipped the voluntary sessions.

The team weight room overlooked the gridiron, and its tinted windows eliminated the ability to see in from outside. Parcells frequently exploited the vantage to observe which players were doing extra work on the gridiron. When the head coach was away from Valley Ranch, he often telephoned strength-and-conditioning coach Joe Juraszek for updates. Parcells also persuaded Jerry Jones to build a new $4 million indoor practice facility instead of continuing to use a local high school's bubble whenever the weather turned inclement.

By the start of training camp in San Antonio's Alamodome, players had smartened up about their new leader's premium on toughness and durability. Once during practice a defensive player fell on the back of left tackle Flozell Adams's legs. Parcells only glanced at the prone offensive lineman before walking past him to conduct the next drill. Unless a fallen player had suffered a serious injury, Parcells wanted the player out of the way as soon as possible so that the session went uninterrupted.

Just in case such ruthlessness failed to send a message, Parcells cut the first two Cowboys to report injuries at the opening of camp. Although they were both backups, the move reiterated the value he placed on sturdy, reliable athletes, and when the Texans and Cowboys scrimmaged on August 3 in San Antonio, zero Cowboys were listed as injured, compared to eleven for Houston. Perhaps the most striking difference from the previous regime could be found in the trainer's room. Few players showed up there, whereas in 2002 the cozy room had bustled with athletes deemed too hurt to practice.

Parcells placed a stranglehold on almost every aspect of his team. He persuaded one Cowboys official who administered drug tests on players to give him a heads-up about any positive results. Circumventing the protocol of the collective bargaining agreement, Parcells said to the official, "If one of these guys is dirty, I want to know right away."

The test administrator replied, "Don't worry about it. You'll know."

Parcells admits now, "Then I would go after their asses. They'd say, 'Well, I'm going to the players association.' I said: 'Go ahead. I'm going to the newspapers, and telling them I've got a pothead on my team who's crying about his civil rights. Who do you think they're going to side with? Me or you? I'm not smoking the dope. *You* are.'"

By the end of camp Quincy Carter beat out Chad Hutchinson to enter the season as Dallas's starting quarterback for the third straight time. Tony Romo was behind Carter and Hutchinson on the depth chart, but Parcells's stream of motivational zingers indicated his recognition of the undrafted quarterback's potential. One time Parcells told Romo, "You're never going to get it. You know what you are, Romo? You're a ball in high grass."

Parcells eagerly awaited the rookie's request for an explanation.

"What does that mean?"

"*Lost.*"

Bill Parcells lost his first official league game as Cowboys coach, 27–13, versus Atlanta at Texas Stadium after a poor second half, especially from kicker Billy Cundiff. Dallas's regular-season opener particularly galled Parcells because it represented the worst indictment of a coach: succumbing to an opponent with inferior personnel. His lifetime body of work reflected the opposite tendency, and he took pride in that.

A chance for redemption came on *Monday Night Football* against Big

Blue at the Meadowlands. The September 15 affair marked Parcells's first return to Giants Stadium since he had guided Gang Green there in 1999. Parcells downplayed that story line, noting his multiple appearances at the Meadowlands since departing the Giants. Nevertheless, his homecoming as head coach of the despised Cowboys overshadowed Sean Payton's return after being demoted and leaving Big Blue. Dallas had lost 26 of its previous 32 road games, whereas Payton's former club looked poised for a playoff return after winning its season opener, 21–13, versus St. Louis. Parcells told his team that it faced one of the NFL's most difficult challenges: a road game on Monday night versus a formidable opponent.

The Cowboys stayed over at the Hilton Hasbrouck Heights hotel. About four hours before the 9 p.m. kickoff, he took some of his former Giants players to Bischoff's ice-cream parlor in Teaneck, where Ida had often brought him on family outings. Later, when Parcells settled into the visitors' locker room at Giants Stadium, a parade of Big Blue royalty swung by the coaches section to greet him, including Harry Carson, Wellington Mara, Phil Simms, and Lawrence Taylor. A few feet away Cowboys coaches watched the exchanges, better appreciating the impact their boss had made on Big Blue.

Parcells also received a warm reception from most of the 78,907 spectators. His team seized a 20–7 lead before collapsing, to the home crowd's delight. Matt Bryant's 30-yard field goal gave Big Blue its first lead, 32–29, with only 11 seconds left to play. Jim Fassel, however, had decided against running another offensive play before Bryant's apparent game winner, so instead of only one tick being left on the clock, the Cowboys possessed 10 extra seconds to attempt a miracle.

Bryant's kickoff boomed toward a coffin corner of Dallas's end zone, but showing poise, rookie returner Zuriel Smith let the pigskin hit the ground; it tumbled out of bounds less than two yards short of the end zone. The nervy decision gave Dallas a last-gasp opportunity to position itself for a field goal. By rule, the ball was placed on Dallas's 40-yard line.

With time for just one offensive snap, Parcells called for a shotgun play involving three receivers bunched on the right side. Wideout Antonio Bryant lined up on the opposite end, where he could avoid being jammed while facing Big Blue's zone defense. After sprinting several yards downfield, Bryant cut left toward the sideline, creating an oh-so-slight separation. Quincy Carter darted a 26-yard pass that Bryant snagged, tiptoeing before falling out of bounds. The scintillating play positioned Dallas for a 52-yard field-goal attempt, and Billy Cundiff's kick sailed through the uprights, tying the game as Parcells punched the air.

During overtime, Dan Campbell, an ex–Giants tight end whom Parcells had signed based on Sean Payton's recommendation, snagged a 23-yard pass to set up a 25-yard field-goal attempt. Dallas triumphed as Cundiff made his seventh kick of the contest.

In the coaches' locker room following the 35–32 thriller, Bill Parcells smiled at Sean Payton. "I know this was especially big for you." But several minutes later, as the Cowboys bus pulled out of a parking lot at Giants Stadium, Payton noticed Parcells scowling.

"What's wrong, Coach?"

Parcells snarled, "My relatives didn't use some of the fifteen tickets I left."

"Coach, we just beat the Giants."

"That's the last time I get them goddamn tickets! Don't they know I paid for them?!"

The Cowboys received a bye week before returning to Giants Stadium on September 28 to face the 0-3 Jets. The NFL seemed to be displaying a wicked sense of humor by having Parcells play two straight games at the Meadowlands. Although Gang Green fans cheered him before the 4:15 p.m. kickoff, their reaction lacked the exuberance of Big Blue supporters two weeks earlier: a segment of Jets Nation remained upset that Parcells had quit as coach after the 1999 season. His return against Gang Green also lacked the drama of the previous week as the Cowboys triumphed 17–6, with Troy Hambrick rushing for 127 yards. By defeating two of his former teams in back-to-back games, Parcells gave Dallas its best start in four seasons.

The flight from New York reached Dallas around 3 a.m. central time, but Parcells told his staff to be at Valley Ranch by 6 a.m. David Lee took a two-hour nap at home before arriving at Cowboys headquarters around 5:30 a.m. With some time to spare, Lee sat in his office and opened the newspaper's sports section. Meanwhile, Parcells entered the building and walked down the hall. Noticing signs of life, he looked into Lee's office.

Parcells screamed, "You better get your ass in gear, and put your mind on next week's opponents! Start breaking down Arizona right now!" His heart racing, the rookie NFL coach quickly closed the newspaper as Parcells continued walking down the hall. Though angered by the outburst, Lee didn't dare point out that he had arrived earlier than anyone else— including the head coach!

Lee recalls, "He couldn't enjoy those two wins because he was so concerned about us losing our focus. I hadn't been in pro football very long, and he was sending a message: you don't have time in this league to enjoy your successes. You better get ready for the next game 'cause everybody in this league competes. It's so hard to get a win."

• • •

With a vastly improved defense and solid if unspectacular quarterbacking from Quincy Carter, Dallas won five straight to take a surprising lead in the NFC East at 5-1. Given his inherited personnel, including multiple undersized linebackers, Bill Parcells kept the team's 4-3 defense instead of immediately installing his cherished 3-4, designed for bigger, taller linebackers. Mike Zimmer's unit, showcasing a splendid back seven, regularly battered quarterbacks and forced turnovers, and midway through the season Dallas's defense led the league in fewest yards allowed. The stingy unit starred nose tackle La'Roi Glover, free safety Roy Williams, and two linebackers who stood five-eleven or under: Dexter Coakley and Dat Nguyen.

Meanwhile, Jerry Jones remained in the background more than he had at any time since purchasing the franchise. He had put an end to his habit of attending team meetings, giving locker-room speeches, and viewing game film with players. The owner occasionally watched film with Parcells, but only at the head coach's convenience. Jones continued strolling "my sidelines," though much less than in the past. His most conspicuous involvement took place in the locker room, where he occasionally gave pep talks to individual players.

After the Cowboys' winning streak ended with an October 26 loss against Tampa Bay, they defeated Washington and then Buffalo, limiting both opponents to a total of 10 points. Dallas improved to 7-2 as Parcells entered his final game of the season against one of his former teams. Bill Belichick's Patriots, also at 7-2, awaited the Cowboys at Foxboro with a five-game winning streak.

Robert Kraft's risky decision three years earlier, trading draft picks to Parcells's Jets for Belichick's services, was paying off. Belichick had guided New England to its first Super Bowl title on February 3, 2002, upsetting the St. Louis Rams, 20–17, at the Louisiana Superdome. Game MVP went to quarterback Tom Brady, a sixth-round pick in 2000 who had thrived after replacing a seriously injured Drew Bledsoe early in the 2002 season. Belichick's staff included offensive coordinator Charlie Weis, defensive coordinator Romeo Crennel, and defensive backs coach Eric Mangini, while Parcells's son-in-law Scott Pioli oversaw the personnel department.

Following Super Bowl XXXVI, Parcells had telephoned Belichick to offer congratulations. However, the call lasted less than a minute, a sign of the lingering feelings from their divorce involving Gang Green. The previous time the football connoisseurs had crossed paths was in late March 2003, at the NFL owners meeting in Phoenix, where the new Cowboys leader and his ex-lieutenant exchanged polite though stilted remarks.

Adding to the hype about the upcoming game, the two men were both Coach of the Year candidates. They hadn't been on the same gridiron since Belichick's shocking resignation as "HC of the NYJ."

Several days preceding the November 16 showdown, Belichick instructed his players to avoid being distracted by the media's focus on the estranged coaches. "We're both assholes. We started coaching together when some of you were in diapers. The last time we coached together was five years ago. Think about how much has changed in the last five years." He added, "Don't get into Belichick versus Parcells. If you want the easy way out, tell them I won't let you comment." Belichick also stressed that his club was facing a daunting opponent with all of Parcells's trademarks: along with a strong defense, Dallas ran the ball substantially more than most teams, and dominated time of possession.

Parcells addressed his players about the hype, too, telling them to concentrate on the enormous task at hand: traveling to Foxboro and attempting to halt New England's hot streak.

The showdown marked Parcells's first trip to Gillette Stadium, which had replaced Foxboro Stadium in 2002, providing the cornucopia of luxury suites and club seats lacking in New England's old building. Accommodating a crowd of 68,436, the Patriots had maintained a home sellout streak dating to 1994, Parcells's second season with the franchise.

During warm-ups for the 8:30 p.m. kickoff, Big Bill and Little Bill stood on their sidelines directly opposite each other. Wearing a blue Cowboys windbreaker on the cloudy, chilly night, Parcells looked across the field, seemingly trying to catch Belichick's eye, but Little Bill, in his familiar gray hoodie, appeared to be preoccupied with observing his players. After a minute or so Big Bill gave up, turning away to also focus on pregame details. Parcells's actions were similar to those preceding other contests, but given the story line, the media seized on the moment. Regardless, the scene marked a sharp contrast with the three times Belichick's Browns had faced Parcells's Patriots during the 1990s, when the two head coaches had greeted each other with hugs—chatting, smiling, and laughing.

The 2003 Tuna Bowl saw both offenses struggle, with the deciding factor being Quincy Carter's three interceptions, two picked off by cornerback Ty Law. As New England led, 12–0, in the game's waning moments, the only drama left involved the customary postgame handshake. Broadcasting the contest live, ESPN mentioned the pregame lack of contact between Belichick and Parcells. The network's sideline reporter, Suzy Kolber, told viewers, "Well, we have to wonder what happens in the postgame. Do they acknowledge each other? I don't think there's ever been this much intrigue regarding a handshake in the postgame."

After Parcells was handed only the third shutout of his career, photographers and cameramen surrounded the head coaches as they walked
toward each other at midfield. Instead of a routine handshake, though,
Parcells embraced Belichick, who returned the gesture. As cameras
flashed and films rolled, Parcells whispered into Belichick's right ear, congratulating him on the victory. Little Bill complimented Big Bill about reviving the Cowboys, and wished him luck. Following the brief exchange,
Belichick trotted to the stadium's tunnel while Parcells remained on the
field, greeting linebacker Willie McGinest and some of his ex–Patriots
players. Despite the prime-time hug, however, the relationship would remain strained for the foreseeable future.

Living in Texas allowed Bill Parcells to rekindle a relationship with Gordon Wood, the legendary high school coach whose indefatigability at age
sixty-two had left an indelible mark on the then Texas Tech defensive coordinator. Parcells had discovered that long-term success in the profession
required devotion that went well beyond human nature. While becoming
a household name in football, Parcells had strived to emulate the Texas
icon who had traveled several hours daily just to scrutinize the Red Raiders' defense for ideas. Now, as the Cowboys taskmaster at age sixty-two,
his legacy secured, Parcells in many ways had grown into a mirror image
of the coach he had first met in Lubbock. At eighty-nine, Gordon Wood
maintained his football passion despite having endured a stroke, skin tu-
mors, a hip replacement, and triple-bypass surgery. Eighteen years into
retirement, he remained active in the profession, traveling the country to
give speeches to spellbound coaches.

In late November, Wood asked Parcells to join him for a high school
playoff game at Texas Stadium involving the Brownwood Lions, the team
he had transformed into a dynasty before stepping down at age seventy-
one. Parcells agreed despite the inconvenience of rushing from Valley
Ranch on Thursday night after a staff meeting and driving to the arena.
As Parcells and Wood walked to their press-box seats, spectators greeted
the men with equal reverence: "Coach" or—to differentiate—"Coach
Wood" and "Coach Parcells."

Their conversation inevitably turned to football strategy, with Wood
providing details of the run-oriented Wing T formation that had helped
him become the winningest coach in the history of high school football.
Parcells asked Wood, "What are your best trick plays?" Known for his
innovations and gimmicks while going 396-91-15, Wood spent the next
several minutes giving examples.

Parcells now recalls, "He was the same kind of guy as Mickey," referring to Mickey Corcoran.

It would be the last time that the two football lifers got together. A few
weeks later, on December 17, Gordon Wood died of a heart attack.

Deep into the season, a genuine friendship was forming between Jerry
Jones and Bill Parcells. During one visit to Jones's home in Highland Park,
a wealthy enclave of Dallas, Parcells spotted the Vince Lombardi Trophies
from 1993, 1994, and 1996. The sight of them confounded Parcells, who
had often spotted the franchise's crown jewels in Jones's office at Valley
Ranch. Parcells asked the owner, "Where did you get those trophies?"

Jones replied, "I had 'em made."

"There's a patent on that trophy. You can't just have it made."

"Well, I did. Don't you have one of yours?"

"No."

Parcells had resigned himself to owning eighteen-inch versions of his
Super Bowl XXI and XXV trophies, and bought the miniature knock-
offs for his players and staff. Each team that captured the Lombardi Trophy was allowed to purchase an extra one, which required seventy-two
hours of labor supplied by Tiffany & Co. in Parsippany, New Jersey. Being
friends with one of the trophy makers, Jones turned to his connection, and
at Christmas the owner surprised his head coach with full-sized replicas
of Big Blue's trophies. Handcrafted in sterling silver, they each weighed
seven pounds and stood twenty-two inches.

Recalling the gesture, Parcells says of Jones, "He's a good man, he's
honest, and he's benevolent. He's done some wonderful things for people
that no one knows about. He's still paying medical bills for some former
Cowboys coaches who've been out of football for a long time."

The Cowboys bounced back from their shutout loss to the Patriots with
an impressive home victory against Carolina, 24–20, as Quincy Carter
tossed two touchdowns. Then Parcells's team suffered blowout losses versus Miami and Philadelphia, but Dallas's defense returned to form with a
19–3 victory over Big Blue at Texas Stadium. The December 21 outcome
improved Parcells's Dallas Cowboys to 10-5, and secured the team a wild-
card berth—the franchise's first playoff appearance in four years. A loss in
the regular-season finale against New Orleans left the Cowboys second in
the NFC East to Philadelphia.

Having defeated only two opponents with records above .500, Dallas
entered the playoffs, facing Carolina on the road, far from being a powerful team. The Cowboys' strength lay in their defense, ranked first in the

NFL after allowing the fewest yards per game, 253.5, and the second-fewest points, 16.3. The unit often kept Dallas in games despite an inconsistent offense that averaged only 18.1 points.

Quincy Carter's 3,302 passing yards gave him the fifth-highest total in franchise history, but his 21 interceptions versus 17 touchdowns dismayed Parcells. One major plus about Carter's season occurred off the gridiron, where he had passed a slew of unannounced drug tests.

On January 3, 2004, the Cowboys' flaws were exposed at Ericsson Stadium in their rematch against the Panthers. With temperatures in Charlotte reaching the sixties, Dallas's offense stayed cold throughout the game, collecting only 204 yards as Carter faced constant pressure, particularly from blitzes. Troy Hambrick's 29 yards on 8 carries illustrated Dallas's need for improvement at starting tailback. Against Carolina, Dallas's defense turned into a weakness as cornerback Terence Newman constantly permitted big plays: wideouts Steve Smith and Muhsin Muhammad combined for 238 receiving yards on Jake Delhomme's throws. Dallas's season ended with a 29–10 loss, extending the franchise's streak to seven years without a playoff victory. Carolina would reach Super Bowl XXXVIII before losing to New England, 32–29, giving Bill Belichick the same number of Lombardi Trophies as his mentor.

Despite ending the season on a down note, Parcells had orchestrated the second-biggest reversal in team annals. He also made NFL history as the only coach to guide four different teams to the playoffs. Affirming his turnaround touch, Parcells restored respectability to a franchise coming off three consecutive 5-11 seasons, and Jerry Jones's Cowboys began to reap the financial benefits. Pepsi re-upped its pouring-rights deal at Texas Stadium, reportedly for a record $33 million.

Parcells's efforts were particularly impressive given an offense using stopgap pieces at crucial positions, and a staff almost devoid of his acolytes. He had started molding new ones, but given the team's tremendous strides, they quickly attracted attention for head-coaching positions among suitors that included an iconic NFL owner.

26

On January 7, 2004, Joe Gibbs announced his NFL return after an eleven-year absence. Despite the lengthy break, Parcells's memories of his sideline rival remained fresh, so on the day of the stunning news Parcells sent a one-sentence fax to Redskins Park. "Does this mean we can't talk for another five years?"

Reading the communique at his office desk, Joe Gibbs laughed loudly.

He recalls, "I thought that was pretty good. He was joking because we never talked before. I didn't answer, but he knew the answer was 'Yes!' I didn't want to talk to him, and he didn't want to talk to me."

Parcells and Gibbs were mutual admirers from afar, but considered each other enemies on game day, so interactions were limited to routine postgame handshakes and pregame nods. Their brilliant careers had intertwined in the NFC East while it dominated the league, often pitting Big Blue against Washington in epic clashes that determined both championships and legacies. The ultracompetitive division featured smashmouth football while regularly producing Super Bowl victors. During the stretch that they were opposing head coaches, from 1983 to 1990, Parcells reached the Super Bowl twice, triumphing each time; Gibbs got there once, obtaining his second of what would be three Lombardi Trophies.

Washington's storied offensive line, the Hogs, was the NFL's bulkiest; New York's defensive front seven, starring Lawrence Taylor, was the biggest. So the Giants and Washington often engaged in explosive goal-line stands. "Hammer city," recalls Gibbs. The Giants and Redskins banged away at each other in classic battles at the Meadowlands and Robert F. Kennedy Memorial Stadium. Although Parcells won most of them, including six straight, he considered Gibbs his most formidable counterpart. "Ninety percent of those games," Parcells says, "could have been won by either team." When they went head-to-head, Parcells's Giants averaged 22.1 points and Gibbs's Redskins 21.4.

Perhaps the most memorable showdown was the NFC Championship on January 11, 1987, at Giants Stadium, under windy, freezing conditions. Big Blue triumphed 17–0, the first-ever shutout against a Gibbs-led team. But one of Parcells's favorite contests took place on September 11, 1989, at RFK Memorial Stadium—his only game versus Gibbs that was settled on the final play. The Giants won, 27–24, when Raul Allegre booted a 52-yard field goal as time expired. Parcells had relished silencing Washington's rabid crowd of 54,160.

When Parcells quit the sidelines in 1991, Gibbs predicted that his rival would return sooner than later. After the Redskins icon retired in early 1993, partly from exhaustion, Parcells expressed empathy for Gibbs. Now, as Parcells entered his second year in Dallas, he knew that Gibbs's presence would make the division even tougher—and that the Cowboys leader needed to keep his talented staff as intact as possible.

Having played a key role in helping his mutual friends consummate an improbable marriage in Dallas, Al Davis took special note of the team's turnaround. The Raiders boss was particularly impressed with Quincy Carter's progress in an offense lacking a top runner or a first-rate wideout. So on firing his head coach, Bill Callahan, after a 4-12 season, Al Davis gained permission from the Cowboys to interview their top two offensive coaches: Mo Carthon and Sean Payton. Despite preferring to keep them, Parcells felt compelled to let his assistants pursue a head-coaching opportunity, and even recommended the duo to his longtime consigliere.

Bill Callahan happened to be Sean Payton's friend and ex-Eagles colleague, but only two years removed from being demoted as Giants offensive coordinator, Payton was thrilled by Davis's interest. One of five candidates discussing the head coach opening with the Raiders chief in early January, Payton arrived at the team's headquarters in Alameda, California, with a bad case of the jitters. A few moments before meeting pro football's éminence grise, the forty-year-old coach walked into the bathroom and took three deep breaths while saying to himself, "I belong here. I belong here. I belong here."

In mid-January Payton was the only candidate flown back to Oakland for a second round of interviews with Al Davis and personnel executive Mike Lombardi that spanned four days. By the end of Payton's trip, Davis all but officially offered him the job. Despite his inclination to accept, Payton needed to fulfill his promise to discuss the matter with his wife.

Heading to the airport for a flight to Dallas on Tuesday, January 20, Payton checked his voice mail, which included three messages from Parcells bent on finding out his quarterbacks coach's decision firsthand. As Payton walked toward his flight gate a TV monitor airing ESPN showed his face next to the Raiders logo while reporting that he was set to sign a four-year deal with Al Davis. Later that night Beth Payton expressed reluctance to her husband, but after sleeping on it, Sean Payton awoke early in the morning aching to be a head coach. After persuading his wife,

Payton purchased a black suit and silver tie—Raiders colors—in anticipation of his introductory press conference. He also contacted some coaches to gauge their interest in being part of his imminent new staff.

The switch to the Raiders seemed so inevitable that Dallas's equipment manager cleaned out Payton's locker, but when he arrived at his office the next day, Payton checked in with three head-coaching friends who had ties to Al Davis: Carolina's John Fox, Tampa Bay's Jon Gruden, and Bill Callahan, recently hired to guide the Nebraska Cornhuskers. Fox had been the Raiders' defensive coordinator in 1994 (under Art Shell) and 1995 (Mike White), Gruden their head coach from 1998 to 2001, and Callahan had guided the Raiders to the 2003 Super Bowl in his rookie season. After Payton heard their takes, he received a phone call from Parcells.

"Listen, Sean, I want to talk to you for a minute like you were my son, not like I'm the head coach and you're my assistant. These other people that you're close to in the industry: what do they think you should do?"

Payton indicated that the three opinions he'd solicited tilted toward his remaining in Dallas.

Parcells wanted to hear each individual response. "What about Gruden?"

Payton replied, "He doesn't think I should take the job. Absolutely not."

"Fox?"

"He doesn't think I should take the job."

"Callahan?"

"He doesn't think I should take the job either."

"Well, put my name behind those three. You're going to get your chance. This just isn't the right one, kid."

Bill Parcells had described Sean Payton to Al Davis as being energetic and driven with an unusually sharp offensive mind. But in attempting to dissuade his quarterbacks coach, Parcells told Payton that he needed more grooming. A few minutes after Payton hung up, he received a call from Jerry Jones requesting his presence at the owner's mansion in Highland Park. When Payton arrived, the two went into Jones's library. During their conversation the owner focused on how much the organization valued its quarterbacks coach. By the end of the get-together, Payton's desire to join the Raiders had evaporated.

Driving home, Payton called his wife about his change of heart, eliciting tears of delight. Then he telephoned Parcells about his final decision, followed by a call to Jerry Jones. The next morning, minutes after Payton arrived at his office, Stephen Jones walked in with a new contract; it included a $500,000 raise, part of a three-year deal worth $3 million as an assistant head coach keeping the same duties.

After Al Davis found out, he dialed Bill Parcells to complain. "Why didn't you just tell me you wanted to keep him?"

Parcells replied, "Coach, who would want to lose one of his top assistants? I didn't know Jerry was going to pay him the extra money. But he really didn't want to come out there. I don't know exactly why."

"All right, I'll just have to get somebody else."

Davis hired Dolphins offensive coordinator Norv Turner for Oakland's lead job, and Parcells was delighted about keeping Maurice Carthon, too. The Cowboys also avoided a significant staff loss by persuading Mike Zimmer to ignore interest from the Nebraska Cornhuskers about their head-coaching opening. Zimmer's decision came after the Cowboys gave him virtually the same raise as Payton, doubling his salary to $1 million.

Lastly, after waiting one season for Todd Haley to be free from his contract with the Chicago Bears, Parcells hired him as wide-receivers coach.

In March, Jerry Jones acquired the rights to former baseball player Drew Henson from the Texans in exchange for a 2005 third-round pick, then handed him a contract guaranteeing $3.5 million. The twenty-four-year-old hadn't played football since 2000, when he flourished as a junior at Michigan, earning distinction as one of the nation's top passers. Henson, who had backed up Tom Brady for two seasons, quit football by his senior year, inking a six-year, $17 million deal with the Yankees to become their future third baseman. After three years of mixed results, mostly with the club's affiliates, Henson ended his baseball aspirations, relinquishing the $12 million left on his contract. With the addition of the six-five, 230-pounder, the Cowboys now had three former minor leaguers at quarterback.

Parcells further altered Dallas's roster by adding two more of his former players. He traded wideout Joey Galloway to Tampa Bay for Keyshawn Johnson, and signed quarterback Vinny Testaverde, a Jets free agent, as insurance behind Quincy Carter for one season. Parcells described Testaverde, turning forty-one in November, as someone who would have a dynamic arm until he died of old age. Mostly backing up Chad Pennington in 2003, Testaverde had looked sharp, throwing seven touchdowns and two interceptions before Gang Green released him for salary-cap reasons. His presence signaled Chad Hutchinson's imminent release, while casting doubt on Tony Romo's future in Dallas, given the young gunslinger's status as a fourth quarterback.

The Cowboys aimed to use April's draft to address the need for a workhorse tailback to replace Troy Hambrick. In a draft pool with several talented runners, Oregon State's Steven Jackson was considered the best. But a knee injury during his final year with the Beavers caused him to slip toward the end of the first round. Pundits expected Dallas, which owned the twenty-second overall pick, to pounce on the all-purpose back. Instead, Jones agreed with Parcells on trading their first-round choice to Buffalo for a second-round selection, a fifth rounder, and a 2005 first-round pick. The Cowboys believed they could still land a franchise back in the second round by selecting the best runner still remaining.

With the twenty-fourth overall pick, the St. Louis Rams selected Jackson, the first back drafted. And by the time Dallas's turn came for the forty-third overall selection, four runners already had been picked. The Cowboys chose Julius Jones, a five-ten, 210-pounder out of Notre Dame.

But his Cowboys career, notwithstanding flashes of brilliance, would be hampered by injuries while Jackson turned into an elite NFL tailback. Dallas's most productive player in its poor draft class would be a seventh-rounder, wideout Patrick Crayton of Northwestern Oklahoma State. Another seventh-round pick, Rutgers cornerback Nathan Jones, would contribute as a solid reserve.

Starting in the late 1990s, Jerry Jones had explored plans for a new arena, if not a significant renovation of Texas Stadium, the franchise's home since 1971. Politics and financing issues had caused various possibilities to fall through in Dallas and the suburbs of Grapevine and Las Colinas. But in July 2004, seizing on momentum from the Cowboys' playoff appearance, Jerry Jones announced negotiations with Arlington for a new stadium near the Texas Rangers' ballpark. The city council agreed unanimously on a referendum for tax increases to collect half the stadium's projected cost: $325 million. Voters soon approved raising taxes on car rentals, hotel occupancy, and retail sales to help construct the world's largest domed arena, and the NFL's most extravagant building. Cowboys Stadium was expected to open in time for the 2009 season.

Jones had initially conducted preliminary talks with Arlington during the 1990s, but Parcells's inaugural year in Dallas helped the owner seal the stadium deal. Parcells and Jones "needed each other at the same time," says John Lucas, the Cowboys' player counselor during Parcells's tenure, who ran substance-abuse treatment centers in the Houston area. "You lose your house, you want to get it back. Sometimes you have to bring somebody in to get your house back." Cowboys Nation exuded confidence about getting back to the playoffs; all of Bill Parcells's previous NFL teams had shown tremendous improvement in his second season.

Aiming to build on Dallas's turnaround season after giving Quincy Carter more weapons while starting to phase in a 3-4 defense, Parcells opened training camp on July 31 in Oxnard, California. The change marked the team's return to the Los Angeles area, where for twenty-seven years Tom Landry's Cowboys had held camp in nearby Thousand Oaks; in 1990, one year after Jerry Jones purchased the franchise, he switched camp to Texas, with the thinking that sultry conditions would better prepare players.

But Parcells's opinion factored into a switch from San Antonio to the coastal city thirty-five miles west of Los Angeles. Although the Alamodome provided air-conditioning, Parcells favored a balmy climate for camp, to reduce the risks of dehydration and allow more repetitions as athletes played themselves into shape. So the Cowboys stayed at Marriott's Residence Inn in Oxnard, and practiced on two gridirons near a golf course.

Jerry Jones always remained conscious of the bottom line. So both sides of the fields at Oxnard were dotted with oversized signs from the team's sponsors: Deja Blue, Ford, Miller Lite, and Tostitos. Throngs gathered behind fences that offered optimal views of the advertisements as much as the action.

Only five days into a tough yet uneventful camp, Bill Parcells and Jerry Jones shocked the NFL by releasing Quincy Carter. The move ended his Cowboys career at 16-16, including the postseason. During an August 4 press conference, Jones described the move as "team policy, Bill's philosophy, and what we are about." Given the NFL's confidentiality rules on substance abuse, such cryptic remarks, echoed by Parcells, indicated that the quarterback had failed a drug test.

In early July, Carter had checked into the John Lucas Treatment and Recovery Center in Houston, and then followed up by seeing a drug counselor. Nevertheless, shortly before camp, the quarterback reportedly tested positive for marijuana. Another failed urinalysis would have resulted in a mandatory four-game suspension, a risk the Cowboys decided not to take. Looking back, Parcells believes that the addition of Testaverde adversely affected Carter's psyche. "This guy was afraid of success," he says. "That's the only way I can put it. Black Dallas Cowboys quarterback, the first in history. He got his team into the playoffs and was as smart as a whip."

Parcells elevated Testaverde to the starting role, citing the eighteen-year veteran's experience. Given Jerry Jones's investment in Drew Henson, the former third baseman became Testaverde's primary backup. More significant, it would turn out, the bombshell kept Tony Romo from being waived due to a logjam at quarterback.

· · ·

Quincy Carter's stunning departure haunted the team far beyond training camp. Typically playing from behind because of defensive struggles, the Cowboys lost seven of their first ten games, upending their postseason goals early. Despite Testaverde's preternatural throwing arm, his lack of mobility behind inconsistent protection often made the forty-one-year-old look his age. However, the biggest discrepancy between this season and the last lay in the defense, hampered by the loss of safety Darren Woodson to a herniated disc in his lower back, and the free-agency departure of cornerback Mario Edwards. While dropping to 3-7, the Cowboys suffered four losses by at least 20 points, underscoring their poor play.

Meanwhile, every Monday, Larry Lacewell was attending meetings with the team's defensive assistants and scouts in a role that had been welcomed by Cowboys head coaches dating back to Jimmy Johnson. Lacewell's background made him a guru of the 4-3, although he also possessed good knowledge of the 3-4. Two of Parcells's defensive coaches were former college players under Lacewell: linebackers coach Gary Gibbs at Oklahoma, and defensive-tackles coach Kacy Rodgers at Tennessee.

Several of Parcells's inherited assistants admired Lacewell for his football intellect, passion, and storytelling flair. Lacewell was increasingly troubled by Parcells's incorporating elements of his favored 3-4 scheme while still using the 4-3 as the base defense. Jones's consigliere blamed the approach for some of the unit's issues. He sensed that several of the coaches shared his outlook but were afraid to speak up. Exasperated, in one meeting of defensive assistants Lacewell blurted, "Bill keeps screwing up the defense!"

Word reached Parcells, angering him. He complained to Jerry Jones that the defensive coaches seemed to be more influenced by Lacewell than the head coach, undermining his authority. Lacewell says, "I was guilty of saying it, and as a head coach I wouldn't have liked it either. But it was the truth. Bill probably should have fired me that moment—or tried. I don't blame Bill for our conflict. I probably created much of it."

Their discord stemmed from opposing philosophies, extending to the scouting department. Parcells had graduated from the bigger-is-better school of thought, and Lacewell had experienced success with small yet explosive players, especially as a college coach. "Who's right?" asks Jeff Ireland. "Lacewell was part of the Cowboys' Super Bowls, but he was also part of some 5-11 teams, which is the reason Bill was there. We had been great on defense, but they didn't share the same vision, and Bill felt like he was fighting that a bit."

The sixtysomethings took disparate approaches to constructing a draft board, too. Lacewell, sixty-seven, targeted players purely based on scouting grades, while the sixty-three-year-old head coach put more value on size, character, and other intangibles. Parcells had learned from Bucko Kilroy to limit, if not eliminate, players who failed to meet the team's standards, using the maxim "Well, they're good, but they're not good for us." Or, as Tom Landry once warned him, "Bill, do not draft exceptions, or pretty soon, you're going to have a team full of exceptions." Parcells believed that the Cowboys' personnel setup kept their scouts from finding players that fit the head coach's philosophy.

The differing mind-sets inevitably caused Lacewell and Parcells to butt heads in the draft room. Seeing himself as the most independent-minded voice in Valley Ranch, Lacewell often questioned Parcells's assessments when they went against the majority, and Lacewell didn't hesitate to tell Jerry Jones when he felt that Parcells was off base.

Lacewell's attitude had reversed since the start of Bill's tenure, when he had advised Jerry to give the new head coach carte blanche, but Lacewell explains that he had underestimated Parcells's conviction on personnel assessments. "If there were four scouts saying, 'I want this,' and he was saying, 'I want that,' he didn't yield to the four," Lacewell says. "He believed his opinion totally. Bill *enjoyed* intimidating people, but he couldn't do that to me. First of all, I'm older than Bill. I was a defensive coordinator before he had even started coaching. I didn't need his recommendation to move up in the NFL. Frankly, I felt it was my role to challenge him. He *had* to be challenged, but he didn't want that."

Parcells counters, "I felt like **he was retired, but hadn't announced it**. His intentions were good, and he was close friends with Jones. But our philosophies didn't mesh. He did not know the prototypes required for a 3-4 defense in the NFL."

Injuries had delayed rookie Julius Jones's debut as a starter until November 21 at Baltimore, where the Ravens handed Parcells's team its seventh loss, one more than the previous season. During the final period of that 30–10 setback, Dallas's third straight, Testaverde took a hit that forced him out because of a sore shoulder. With the outcome decided, Drew Henson made his NFL debut, overcoming a fumble on his first snap to complete 6 of 6 passes, including a touchdown. Julius Jones finished with 81 yards on 30 carries against Baltimore's punishing defense, anchored by über-linebacker Ray Lewis. Parcells showed little hesitation turning his rookie runner into a workhorse despite Jones having missed the first part of the season.

Testaverde's injury limited his practice reps heading into a Thanksgiving affair at home versus the Bears, whose starting tailback was Julius's older brother, Thomas. With only one victory in the previous seven games, Parcells hesitated to name Drew Henson the starter, but Testaverde's situation forced Parcells's hand, to the delight of Jerry Jones and most Cowboys fans.

Henson had last started in the Citrus Bowl on New Year's Day 2001, when Michigan edged Auburn, 31–28, as he tossed two touchdowns without an interception. During player introductions on Thanksgiving, Henson drew the loudest cheers from the Texas Stadium crowd of 64,026. The applause turned deafening when Dallas took an early lead after the former Yankee prospect guided his team on a five-play, 62-yard drive, highlighted by Julius Jones's touchdown gallop of 33 yards. However, during the rest of an ugly half, the only points came from Chicago's defense: Cornerback R. W. McQuarters intercepted a pass by Henson and returned it 45 yards for a touchdown.

With the contest tied 7–7 at halftime, a desperately needed victory hung in the balance. Henson had collected only 31 yards on 4 of 12 passing, so Parcells approached the twenty-four-year-old rookie and said, "Good job," before adding that the nicked-up Testaverde would start the second half. Spotting the forty-one-year-old on the field for Dallas's first offensive sequence, the home crowd booed and groaned. The sight also dismayed owner Jerry Jones, watching from his suite.

Offensive woes for both teams continued with a scoreless third quarter, but early in the final period several shifty runs by Julius Jones helped advance the Cowboys to Chicago's 5. Then Testaverde capitalized on the situation, tossing a touchdown pass to fullback Darian Barnes. Midway through the final period, Dallas's rookie tailback added his second touchdown burst, a 4-yarder, to close out the scoring, 21–7.

Julius Jones finished the game with 150 yards on 33 carries, while Testaverde went 9 of 14, helping the Cowboys halt their skid. Thomas Jones, who led Chicago with 94 yards running and receiving, embraced his younger brother on the field and whispered congratulations. Julius's rushing total was the second-most by a rookie in Cowboys history. Mike Zimmer's struggling defense held the Bears to 140 yards, the lowest output against Dallas since 1996. Nonetheless, Parcells's decision involving Henson sparked the first signs of friction between Dallas's owner and its head coach.

Jimmy Johnson had warned Bill Parcells that their compatibility would require Jerry Jones to be careful in his public remarks. Minutes after the victory against Chicago, the "really surprised" owner second-guessed his head coach, though with some diplomacy. "We cannot let that potential escape," Jerry Jones told reporters, alluding to Henson. "I would want to see us have a game like that, ideally with Julius Jones having the night he had, with a young quarterback in there."

At any other juncture in Parcells's head-coaching career, such remarks would have provoked him into withdrawing from his owner regardless of the consequences. But having clashed with Robert Kraft proved beneficial to Bill Parcells during this second stint under a proactive owner.

So he decided to remain respectful of Jones publicly and privately. Despite the setback, both men enjoyed disproving the notion that a clash between monster egos was inevitable. As was their habit, in the days following a game, the owner and head coach met to discuss the team, and they spent extra time sharing their perspectives on Drew Henson.

Bill Parcells named Vinny Testaverde the team's starter for the rest of the season, and this time Jerry Jones calibrated his public comments to echo Parcells's rationale. The owner even publicly broached the improbable scenario of re-signing Testaverde to play the starting role at quarterback in 2005, at age forty-two.

Jones and Parcells were able to navigate the land mines threatening their partnership partly because of a genuine friendship. "I found Jones to be a compassionate person, a trustworthy person," Parcells says. "A handshake was good with Jerry Jones. He was running the show. There wasn't any doubt about that. I was an employee; I was working for him. And he had a lot more experience with football than Kraft did when he bought the Patriots, so there was a stronger basis for communication."

The relationship also thrived because the two accomplished commanders found themselves learning new things from each other. Before Bill met Jerry he generally used conservative methods to manage his money; Charles Parcells had conveyed to Bill a thriftiness that remained with the sixtysomething. As a millionaire by the mid-1990s, Bill Parcells had largely ignored advice from his accountant, Mike Lanni, to diversify his portfolio beyond municipal bonds. Although Parcells invested in stocks, he adhered to the principles of Warren Buffett and owned large, concentrated positions in a few value stocks. Even when it meant missing out on substantial gains, Parcells focused on his savings. Through his partnership with Jerry Jones, Parcells discovered the advantages of financial risk-taking.

Parcells explains, "If you told Jerry, 'Give me $10 million this November, and by next November I'll give you $12 million,' he'd have no interest in that proposition. But if you said, 'Jerry, you give me $10 million, and next year at this time, there's a 15 percent chance you'll have $100 million,' he's in. Now, I could never understand that, but that's the kind of guy he is; he's a risk-taker."

Over time, Parcells grasped the benefit of Jones's approach, and found him to be one of the most astute businessmen he had ever encountered. When Parcells complimented Jones on high-risk deals that panned out, the former oil-and-gas baron replied with humility. "I've got two legal pads full of deals like that which didn't work out, Bill. You want to see them, too?" But Parcells noticed that Jones's risk tolerance helped generate revenue that more than offset those failed endeavors. And the head coach soon caught a strain of venture capitalism late in life.

Conversely, Jerry Jones learned things from Bill Parcells about structure and organization that the Cowboys had lacked during his fifteen years of ownership. For example, the club no longer relied on just one college scout assigned to a geographic area, making sure his evaluation was cross-checked. Jones also heeded Parcells's advice to end any overlap in the personnel department between his college and pro scouts. After one conversation with Jeff Ireland, Jerry Jones told the scout, "Gosh, Bill has brought so much more to the Cowboys than just coaching. We've learned a lot from him."

The quarterback debate quickly took a backseat to Julius Jones's virtuoso performances. He led Dallas to a 43–39 upset victory at Seattle on *Monday Night Football* by rushing 33 times for 198 yards, while scoring three touchdowns. The Notre Dame product became only the second player in NFL history, after Earl Campbell, to carry the ball at least 30 times in three consecutive regular-season games. Despite Steven Jackson's thriving in St. Louis on limited opportunities behind the great Marshall Faulk, Dallas's draft-day decision to drop twenty-one spots seemed solid. Julius Jones was among the Cowboys' few bright spots as they finished 6-10, losing three of their last four games. Starting in only seven games, the rookie amassed 819 rushing yards while scoring seven touchdowns.

Jason Witten looked even more impressive, emerging as a star in his second season. He snagged 87 passes, the most in franchise history by a tight end, equaling Keyshawn Johnson for the team lead with six scoring receptions. The team's disappointing record bucked Parcells's string of producing at least a three-game improvement in his follow-up season steering a team.

Dallas's defense plummeted from being the second-ranked unit in points allowed to twenty-seventh, confirming Darren Woodson's value. The injured thirty-five-year-old announced his retirement as the franchise's all-time leading tackler, most coming on punishing hits. Woodson, perhaps the best safety in Cowboys history, ended up being the only player to experience both Bill Parcells and Jimmy Johnson. Having learned new things from Parcells even as a twelfth-year veteran, Woodson deeply regretted being unable to play more than one season under him. Woodson deemed Parcells a coaching mastermind.

The team's oldest player, Vinny Testaverde, accumulated 3,532 passing yards while throwing 17 touchdowns and 20 interceptions. But even with a rifle arm that was the envy of quarterbacks half his age, Testaverde's best days were behind him. Drew Henson and Tony Romo were deemed too raw, so the franchise wanted another veteran signal caller to help reverse its course. An off-the-field issue also gnawed at the head coach: he could no longer tolerate the team's chief scout. So Parcells approached Jerry Jones to tell him that Larry Lacewell's presence had grown unbearable.

The owner summoned his consigliere and chief scout into his office.

"We can do this the hard way or the easy way."

Lacewell replied, "What are you talking about?"

"Well, if we go the hard way, I fight Bill and you can stay. The easy way means you can retire."

"How did you know I wanted to retire?"

Jerry Jones laughed. "Because of those two houses you've already bought in Arkansas."

Lacewell roared. "Hell, let's make this easy. I'm outta here."

On January 5, 2005, Larry Lacewell announced his retirement after thirteen seasons in Dallas. One month from turning sixty-eight, Lacewell added that he would remain a part-time consultant while staying away from Valley Ranch. With Jerry Jones's blessings, Parcells promoted Jeff Ireland to chief scout.

"I'm not mad at Bill at all over what happened," Lacewell says. "I don't blame him. Shit, I was a head coach, too, so I understand. He was a very good coach. You write that down. But he wasn't Bear Bryant. You write *that* down."

27

Bill Belichick crossed his arms over his chest on New England's sideline, watching the waning moments of Super Bowl XXXIX in Jacksonville, Florida. His team held a three-point lead over the Eagles, who were backed up against their end zone on third down. When safety Rodney Harrison intercepted Donovan McNabb's desperation heave with 17 seconds left, Belichick raised both hands, grinned, and then leaped a few times, pumping his right fist. Steve Belichick, bespectacled in a Patriots windbreaker and baseball cap, sidled over to his son; Little Bill, wearing his game-day hoodie, embraced his father as the Patriots celebrated their 24–21 triumph at Alltel Stadium, earning the franchise's third Lombardi Trophy in four seasons.

Hovering behind the Belichicks, linebacker Tedy Bruschi interrupted the moment by emptying a Gatorade bucket on them. Father and son released their hug, cringing and shivering from the cold, but nothing could dampen their joy. Bill Parcells was among the millions of TV viewers watching the moment on February 6. And his heart was tugged more than most because Steve Belichick, eighty-six, had lived long enough to witness his son's crowning achievement.

"I could see the pride in his dad's face," Parcells recalls.

The Cowboys coach also felt sadness because *his* father, Charles, had died three years before Big Blue won its first Super Bowl. At the time Bill's childhood friends remarked on how much Charles Parcells would have enjoyed witnessing the achievement. Bill Parcells never stopped wishing that his father could have been present for his defining triumphs.

A few days after Super Bowl XXXIX, Big Bill sent a note to Little Bill, in his latest attempt at reconciliation. Parcells expressed happiness that Steve had been around to witness his son's Super Bowl triumphs. But Parcells decided against mentioning his inner thoughts about Charles's absences for Super Bowl XXI and XXV. Steve Belichick would die at home in Annapolis, Maryland, of heart failure on November 19, 2005, nine months after Parcells's gesture.

With Dallas's quarterback situation unsettled, Bill Parcells again reached into his past, acquiring Drew Bledsoe on February 23, just one day after

Buffalo had released the ex–Patriots star. The swiftness with which Bled-soe was signed to a three-year, $14 million contract indicated the strong mutual interest to reunite more than a decade after Parcells had drafted the bazooka-armed quarterback.

When he was setting several passing records in his first four NFL sea-sons, Bledsoe had bristled at Parcells's scathing style. As the years passed, however, the quarterback increasingly appreciated Parcells's methods, an experience Bledsoe shared with many of the coach's former players.

NFL agent Brad Blank had twenty clients who played under Parcells. "Every one of them said it was hard," Blank says, "but for some reason as soon as they were out of the league they gravitated back toward him, and told me, 'This is the best coach I ever had. He got the best out of me.' That, in my mind, makes him a genius when it comes to dealing with football players."

John Lucas, the Cowboys' player counselor, adds, "I've spoken to more than a dozen guys who played for Bill, and they all said basically the same thing: 'At the time I hated the experience, but he helped me be-come a man.'"

During the 2001 season, Parcells had disarmed Bledsoe with a phone call when the 1993 top overall pick lost his job to Tom Brady. After New England dealt Bledsoe to Buffalo in 2002, Parcells made a follow-up call wishing him luck. That year Bledsoe delivered one of his best seasons, amassing 4,359 passing yards, to earn his fourth Pro Bowl appearance. But over the course of three years with the Bills he went 23-25, while show-ing too much inconsistency. However, the Cowboys, with two first-round choices and substantial cap space for free agents, envisioned Bledsoe help-ing to make them contenders.

In early March, Jerry Jones paid a total of $29 million in signing bonuses for contracts worth $66.5 million to just three players: nose tackle Jason Ferguson, cornerback Anthony Henry, and right guard Marco Rivera. The Cowboys expected Rivera, who had made three consecutive Pro Bowls while protecting Brett Favre, to help the relatively immobile Bledsoe stay upright. As Jets chief in 1997, Parcells had drafted Ferguson in the seventh round. Despite being the eighteenth nose tackle chosen, he became a key reserve on Belichick's stingy unit during Gang Green's his-toric turnaround. And the following season, Ferguson seized the starting job at nose tackle, a difficult yet crucial position in Parcells's 3-4.

The Cowboys saw Ferguson and Henry bolstering their once-mighty defense, to which Parcells added yet another of his former players, corner-back Aaron Glenn, thirty-three. He intended to complete the installation of the 3-4 defense, free of an influential skeptic in Larry Lacewell. Former linebacker Carl Banks and ex–nose tackle Jim Burt agreed to help Parcells teach the scheme's intricacies during training camp. Burt and Parcells had reconciled after their falling out in 1988.

Dallas's influx of top free agents transformed its roster, and the franchise awaited April's draft to address more needs. Parcells's staff also underwent significant changes after offensive coordinator Maurice Carthon departed to take the same position with new Browns head coach Romeo Crennel. Forced to reshape his staff, Parcells decided against giving Carthon's title to anyone. Instead, Parcells named Sean Payton passing-game coordinator, and made the forty-one-year-old Dallas's primary play caller. The striking move illustrated Parcells's respect for his young lieutenant after only two years together. Parcells hadn't ceded his play-calling role since 1993, his first season in New England, when Ray Perkins ran the offense.

After having spent two years emphasizing to Payton the need to control the game's tempo, Parcells trusted him with the offense. The two agreed on the approach of running the ball about thirty-five times per game and bleeding the clock, while helping to keep the Cowboys defense relatively fresh. Sean Payton's new duties would free Parcells to spend more time working with Zimmer on the 3-4.

Parcells elevated tight-ends coach Tony Sparano to overseeing the offensive line as running-game coordinator. He also promoted quality-control assistant David Lee, who'd spent twenty-seven years coaching in colleges, to quarterbacks coach. Three new assistants also joined Parcells's staff: Anthony Lynn, a running-backs coach with the Jaguars, accepted the same position in Dallas, taking many of Carthon's duties. Todd Bowles came from the Cleveland Browns to guide Dallas's secondary. And Paul Pasqualoni, Syracuse's head coach for fourteen years, inherited Sparano's former duties involving the tight ends.

Before long, Anthony Lynn glimpsed a secret to Parcells's success in creating a huge coaching tree. During staff meetings, the new running-backs coach took meticulous notes; seeing his eagerness to learn, Parcells started dropping by Lynn's office to exchange thoughts.

"A guy this brilliant values your feedback. He would pick your brain," Lynn recalls. "But at the end of the conversation, there was a lesson in there. You thought you were giving him something, but he was really teaching you."

Lynn laughs at the recollection. The former special-teams ace had been a player or assistant under Wade Phillips, George Seifert, Mike Shanahan, and Jack Del Rio. "They're all great coaches in my book, but when I got to Parcells I could see the difference," Lynn says. "He's a teacher, and you don't have to beg to get lessons out of him. Other coaches know the game, but they don't always go out of their way to teach it."

Despite being born and raised in Abilene, Texas, Jeff Ireland grew up a Chicago Bears fan because of his grandfather, Jim Parmer, the team's director of college scouting from 1978 to 1985. During each of those summers, Parmer picked up his grandson in Abilene for long trips to colleges like Missouri and Oklahoma. And the pair sometimes slept in dormitories, where Parmer scrutinized soundless 16-millimeter tape. Young Jeff watched from the edge of his bed, dozing off after a few hours while his grandfather kept at it. The kid, who sometimes worked as a Bears ball boy, relished the scouting sessions.

Jim Parmer had played halfback for the Philadelphia Eagles from 1948 to 1956, winning the NFL championships in each of his first two years, with Bucko Kilroy as his teammate. After his playing career ended, Parmer joined the franchise as a scout. Moving to the Bears, Parmer put his personal stamp on their roster, especially the 1985 team, one of the best in NFL history.

Several years later, Jeff Ireland attended Baylor University, where he played placekicker. After graduating, Ireland broke into coaching, joining North Texas in 1992 to oversee its special-teams unit. He lost his job after two seasons when the entire staff was dismissed. Following a conversation with his granddad, Ireland decided to pursue scouting. He sent résumés to several NFL teams, working as a wildcatter for his father while awaiting responses. With Ireland receiving no sniffs, Parmer helped his grandson land a scouting job with the Indianapolis-based NFL combine. Jeff Ireland worked for the organization until 1997, when the Kansas City Chiefs hired him as an area scout. Then, in 2001, Larry Lacewell lured Ireland to the Cowboys with a better gig: national scout.

While overhauling the way the Cowboys evaluated prospects in 2003, Parcells broke down his personnel philosophy with Ireland. Instead of having the team's scouts simply find the best players, Parcells wanted the department to target talented prospects who fit with the head coach's philosophy. One preference went beyond physical attributes: Parcells liked "beavers," explaining their single-mindedness while cutting trees—in other words, players who shared his football passion.

Parcells told Ireland, "Look, if I can just leave you with one thing, it's my eyes. What do my eyes see?" In the 2003 draft, Ireland initially saw Tennessee junior Jason Witten as a weak blocker, but Parcells told his top scout to re-examine two specific games. After heeding the suggestion, Ireland came away seeing the tight end's potential.

He told Parcells, "That's a totally different player as a blocker. Totally different."

The head coach smiled.

Parcells admired Ireland's football passion, work ethic, and conviction when it came to personnel assessments. Their first discussions about the 2004 draft sparked an argument over Iowa safety Bob Sanders. The Cowboys scouts had given him a first-round grade, but Parcells felt that Sanders's five-eight frame made him too small for consideration. "He doesn't fit our team. Take him off the board. You can eat peanuts off his head!"

Ireland countered, "Who cares about that? He's a good player; he's a good kid. He's explosive. He can cover."

When Jerry Jones sided with Parcells, the Cowboys removed Sanders from consideration, but the head coach respected his top scout for standing firm. Parcells recalls, "I was trying to get across to the Dallas scouting staff that I wanted prototypical players. They were bringing me exceptions. You get too many, then all of a sudden you have a team of exceptions. And I'm the one that has to coach those little guys." The contrasting takes on Sanders would bear out during his eight-year NFL career. A hard-hitting safety, he made the Pro Bowl three times for the Indianapolis Colts while helping them capture the 2007 Super Bowl. But Sanders also became known for constant injuries; only twice did he make it through more than six games in a season.

Despite the occasional disagreement, Parcells and Ireland generally saw talent the same way. The head coach trusted his top scout's judgment, and took extra time to study film of prospects recommended by Ireland. With help from the new personnel chief, Parcells gained extensive knowledge of the roughly 120 players on Dallas's 2005 draft board. Parcells once told Ireland, "I wish I'd have met you when I was younger. We would have had a helluva time. I'm sorry I came along so late, but your grandfather laid an egg, and it hatched thirty years later."

Jim Parmer died on April 20, 2005, only three days before Ireland oversaw his first draft, but the seventy-nine-year-old had lived long enough to watch his grandson earn the position of Dallas's chief scout.

With the Cowboys switching to a 3-4, the organization targeted outside linebackers and defensive ends who fit Parcells's super-sized specifications. Dallas owned the eleventh and twentieth overall picks, providing a tremendous opportunity to land two top players for the new scheme. Jeff Ireland's scouts were focusing on LSU defensive end Marcus Spears, and on Troy's DeMarcus Ware, who was projected to be an outside linebacker after having played mainly defensive end.

Spears entered the draft as a first-team All-American following his senior year under Nick Saban, Bill Belichick's most successful disciple and a friend of Parcells's. Spears had also excelled as a junior, helping LSU capture the national championship. DeMarcus Ware, perhaps the best defensive end in college, posted prolific numbers during four years at his small school in Alabama. The six-four, 253-pounder was expected to become an ideal rush linebacker in a 3-4 defense.

Parcells considered Ware an attractive prospect, but saw Spears, a rugged, prototypical defensive end, as being integral to Dallas's 3-4. During evaluation meetings leading up to the draft, Parcells raved about the six-four, 300-pound Spears. He insisted that the Cowboys choose Spears first, and use their second pick to land Ware. "People say that he wanted Spears instead of Ware. That's not true," Ireland says of Parcells. "He just wanted to make sure that he got Spears. Period. If it was at the expense of Ware, so be it. But he liked Ware a lot."

The consensus among Dallas's scouts was the opposite. Having graded Ware markedly higher than Spears, they believed that the Troy product would definitely be gone by the twentieth pick. Seeking another trusted pair of eyes, Jerry Jones sent tape of both prospects to Larry Lacewell in Hot Springs, Arkansas. Then Jones visited his retired consigliere. Lacewell told him, "Jerry. There's no question that Spears is good, but Ware might end up great."

The night before the draft, Jerry Jones and Jeff Ireland studied film together of Ware and Spears one last time. The session clinched the owner's decision. The next morning, Jerry and Stephen walked into Bill's office for a closed-door meeting that included Jeff Ireland. Stephen Jones announced, "Coach, we're going to pick Ware." The verdict angered Parcells, who stayed upset for hours after the Joneses left his office. Ireland tried to calm him, suggesting he take a different perspective. "Coach, don't look at it as Ware over Spears. It's Ware *and* Spears. I think we can get both of 'em."

Parcells responded, "I don't think you're right, but we'll see."

Ireland's confidence stemmed from familiarity with the needs of every team; his only worry involved San Diego, with the twenty-eighth pick, which might try to leapfrog Dallas via a trade to snag Spears. Inside the Cowboys draft room during the first round, Ware's availability after the tenth pick prompted cheers, smiles, and hand slaps. However, Bill Parcells sat stone-faced, stewing at having been overruled. Nine picks later Marcus Spears was still there, prompting Parcells's first smile all afternoon. He leaned over and whispered to Ireland, "You're just lucky!"

Dallas used its second-round pick on another powerful, hard-hitting linebacker, Tennessee's Kevin Burnett. Lacking a third-round choice, the Cowboys put two fourth-round picks to good use: tailback Marion Barber of Minnesota, the team's first offensive player, and another defensive end in Chris Canty of Virginia. A pair of sixth-round picks brought Ball State defensive back Justin Beriault and Pittsburgh offensive tackle Rob Petitti. Using six of eight selections on defensive players, Dallas concluded the day by selecting defensive end Jay Ratliff of Auburn in the seventh round.

Dallas's 2005 draft haul would be among the greatest in franchise history, and the NFL's best in several years. It formed the nucleus of a perennial playoff team for almost a decade. Ware ended up being the best pick by any team that year, setting the Cowboys' all-time record for sacks while occasionally drawing comparisons to Lawrence Taylor. Despite lasting until the 224th choice because he was undersized at his position, Jay Ratliff became one of the NFL's premier nose tackles, anchoring Dallas's defensive line for eight years, four as a Pro Bowler.

Unlike Ware, or even Ratliff, Spears never developed into a star during his eight seasons in Dallas. However, after overcoming injuries at the outset of his NFL career, the defensive end proved durable while contributing by creating rushing lanes for outside linebackers; at one stretch he started eighty-eight consecutive games.

Marion Barber emerged as a dangerous third-down runner who excelled in the red zone. He gained a reputation for being the NFL's toughest tailback to bring down because of a running style that punished defenders. By Chris Canty's second season, he had seized the starting job at right defensive end. Kevin Burnett turned into a valuable reserve at linebacker. But before any of them even took their first NFL snap, Ireland was generating media praise for Dallas's 2005 draft.

Parcells needled him. "Everybody says you had a good draft. Are you accepting kudos now?"

Jeff Ireland, smiling, replied, "I'm not accepting kudos."

"I want to know who the top fifty players are in next year's draft."

"We'll figure that out here in a couple weeks."

"Hey, most personnel directors know that right now."

Sighing at Parcells's relentlessness, Dallas's chief scout left the head coach's office to start on his new assignment.

Parcells's 3-4 scheme marked the first time since the franchise's founding in 1960 that its base defense had varied from the 4-3 put in place by Tom Landry. With that drastic switch untested, and a revamped offense quarterbacked by Drew Bledsoe, Dallas opened the season as heavy underdogs at San Diego versus the AFC West champions. In a roller-coaster affair that featured Drew Bledsoe and Drew Brees trading touchdowns, the Cowboys triumphed 28–24, taking their first season opener in six years.

Although the upset victory was only one game, it increased optimism while seeming to address questions about the new defensive approach and Parcells's latest retread quarterback. Despite Brees's two touchdowns, Dallas intercepted the Pro Bowler twice while limiting him to 209 yards, whereas Bledsoe finished with three touchdowns, including two to Keyshawn Johnson, and no interceptions. He became only the tenth quarterback in NFL history to amass at least 40,000 passing yards in a career.

During their second stint together, Parcells detected a striking change in Bledsoe's personality: instead of being laid-back, the quarterback seemed crankier at practices and games, often getting upset over the slightest offensive mistakes. Parcells told Bledsoe, "You're starting to act like me." Bledsoe replied with a smile, "I'm going to retire if that ever happens."

The promising developments on the field did little to shield the head coach of America's Team from an ugly side of celebrity. A male stranger somehow obtained Bill Parcells's cell phone number and left him an obscene message related to football. Parcells erased the voice mail, which had come from a restricted number. A few days later, the unidentified caller left a similar rant when the Cowboys coach failed to pick up the call. After checking his messages, Parcells once again deleted it without much thought.

The next call resulted in a much more disturbing message: a threat to knife Parcells to death. During his NFL career Parcells had occasionally received death threats, most of which he had decided not to investigate. "It is what it is," he says. "There are a lot of sickos out there." But this time the head coach saved the voice mail, intent on reporting it to law enforcement.

When Parcells had coached the Jets, handling the sickos had fallen into Steve Yarnell's bailiwick. But with the former G-man still employed by Gang Green, Parcells turned to NFL security, essentially a law-enforcement arm of the league. By the early 2000s the NFL had institutionalized Parcells's brainchild by assigning each team one person, typically a former member of the FBI, CIA, or DEA, to oversee security. The Cowboys' point man was Ben Nix, an erstwhile FBI special agent, so Parcells played him the voice mail at Valley Ranch.

Restricted numbers could be traced only through the police department or telephone company. With their help, NFL security tracked the call first to eastern Pennsylvania, then to a small city, Bethlehem, and finally to the owner of the phone, presumably the perpetrator: a man in his mid-twenties employed by his father's company. Parcells recalls, "We sent some FBI guys over to talk to him about his behavior." The man, stunned by having been located, expressed contrition. Nix then contacted the perpetrator's father, who reacted with embarrassment and shock. Nix told Parcells, "I don't think you're going to have any more trouble with that fellow."

As the Cowboys climbed atop the NFC East at 4-2, the new-look defense showed sharp improvement from the previous season, especially in the secondary. On the road October 23 versus the NFC-leading Seahawks, Mike Zimmer's unit stifled the league's top offense powered by Shaun Alexander, an MVP candidate. During the rainy afternoon, the Cowboys led 7–3 early in the fourth quarter when their kicker, Jose Cortez, shanked a 29-yard field goal. In training camp the team had released Billy Cundiff, its kicker from 2001 to 2004, due to a quadriceps injury, but inconsistency plagued his emergency replacement. With about two minutes left against Seattle, Cortez's 21-yard field goal increased Dallas's lead to 10–3. Mike Holmgren's team tied the score with 40 seconds to go on Matt Hasselbeck's 1-yard touchdown pass.

Despite Dallas getting a final possession, overtime seemed like a given with 14 ticks left. On a last-gasp attempt, however, Drew Bledsoe tossed an interception that safety Jordan Babineaux returned 25 yards to Dallas's 32. Seahawks kicker Josh Brown rushed onto the field and nailed a 50-yard field goal as time expired, handing Parcells perhaps the most painful setback of his tenure. Parcells released Cortez and signed rookie kicker Shaun Suisham.

A more monumental, real-world loss came two days later, when Giants patriarch Wellington Mara, eighty-nine, died at his home in Rye, New York, after battling blood cancer. Bill Parcells and Jerry Jones attended Mara's funeral at St. Patrick's Cathedral on Friday, October 28. More than two thousand mourners watched Mara's black casket as it was wheeled down the aisle accompanied by a bagpiper playing "Amazing Grace." Jerry Jones was among the twenty-one NFL team owners in attendance, none of whom were alive when Mara, the last link to the league's founding days, served as ball boy for his father's franchise.

Saddened by Mara's passing, Bill Parcells hoped for the opposite outcome for his younger brother Don, who had been fighting brain cancer since 2001. The American Cancer Society had named Don 2004 Man of the Year. Only days after Mara's death, though, Don's condition took a turn for the worse. Bill received nightly telephone updates from his youngest brother, Doug, in Oradell. On his calendar, Parcells circled a November 14 game at Philadelphia as the ideal opportunity to visit Don, a retired banker, in Short Hills, New Jersey. But on November 9, a Wednesday night, Doug called with the sad news that their sixty-one-year-old brother, the relative to whom Bill felt closest, had finally succumbed.

Bill decided to skip Don's wake on Sunday, November 13, while the Cowboys flew to Philadelphia for *Monday Night Football,* planning instead to spend several hours on Monday morning at his brother's funeral and burial.

28

Monday, November 14, brought a caressing breeze, cloudless skies, and balmy sun to Philadelphia and northern New Jersey. The mild weather made for an incongruously beautiful day, given that Bill Parcells needed to bury a brother. Don's funeral service was scheduled for 11 a.m. in Short Hills, but Bill left his Philadelphia hotel early to spend private time with Don. Around 7 a.m. Bill Parcells and Kelly Mandart stepped into the backseat of a hired limousine, while Rich Dalrymple, the Cowboys PR chief, rode shotgun.

For the first part of the ninety-mile drive, no one made even small talk, but midway to the funeral parlor, Parcells finally broke the silence.

"There's the exit for Monmouth Park, Rich. That's where the horses run." He described Monmouth Park Racetrack before everyone returned to being quiet for several minutes. Then, as the limo hurtled past exit signs in North Jersey, Parcells rattled off the names of football figures who came from that part of the state: Cowboys secondary coach Todd Bowles, Elizabeth; former quarterback Joe Theismann, New Brunswick; ex-wideout Drew Pearson, South River, succeeding Joe Theismann as starting quarterback at South River High. During the season Parcells and Dalrymple, a Pittsburgh native, had enjoyed a competition trading pronouncements that linked NFL athletes to their hometowns in Pennsylvania or New Jersey. The Englewood-born head coach never squandered an opportunity whenever the name of a Jersey native surfaced.

"Bill is Mr. New Jersey," Dalrymple says, "and he loves his state as much as anybody loves their state that I've ever met."

Parcells's recitation helped lighten the somber ride, but when the limo reached its destination, he seemed nerve-wracked and depressed. Still sad about Mara's passing, Bill was hurting even more over Don's death. Noticing her boyfriend's pain, Mandart told him, "It's okay, I'm here."

Parcells, who was twenty months older than Don, sighed. "I can't believe he's gone, Kel. I can't believe this got him. I thought I'd be gone before him."

Mandart asked, "Bill, do you want to go in by yourself?"

"No. Come with me."

"Okay."

Dalrymple remained outside.

At 8:30 a.m., the funeral home wasn't officially open, but the couple was ushered in. An employee wheeled a brown wooden casket into one of two rooms decorated with photographs of Don. Spotting the open casket, Bill turned teary. Don, who had lost substantial weight from cancer, was dressed in a blue blazer and matching tie. Bill Parcells felt that his brother's face, though a tad gray from makeup, looked good.

As Bill stared at Don, memories of their times together, especially as boys, swept over him. In a cracking voice he told Mandart, "We slept in the same bed growing up." Parcells began sobbing, prompting Mandart to hug him. Mandart headed next door to view more photos set on easels and tables, while Bill remained alone with his brother, and shut his eyes to say a silent prayer. Then he looked at Don and said firmly, "I love you, and I'm grateful for our time together."

Dalrymple soon entered the funeral parlor and chatted with Mandart to give Parcells more time alone. She vented that Parcells had discouraged her from attending in order to avoid drama with his ex-wife. "I put up with all of his nonsense every week. I deal with his mood swings, and he thinks I'm not going to be here for this? He's crazy. How can I deal with the way this game beats him up, then not be there for this?"

Dalrymple was unsurprised by Mandart's pugnacity. She was one of the only people whom he had witnessed occasionally standing up to Parcells. "She can buck up to him sometimes," Dalrymple says. "Bill is a classic worrywart. Half the time, some of the things he's worried about, they just resolve themselves."

The night before, Parcells had left the decision to attend the funeral up to Mandart, assuming that she would want to avoid being in the same space with his ex-wife. "I don't care if you come. You do what you want." But when Mandart woke up early and started getting dressed, Parcells asked in a testy voice, "What are you doing?"

"I'm getting ready."

"So, you're really going to come, huh?"

"Yeah."

Mandart, who had been friendly with Don and his wife, Elaine, pointed out that Don's widow had requested her presence.

Parcells responded, "It's just going to cause a lot of shit for me, Kelly."

"You're worried about the wrong person's feelings!"

Recalling the exchange, Mandart says, "He reads into things too much, and it paralyzes him to a certain degree. Thinking about how he was going to handle the situation with his ex-wife was really giving him anxiety. But I had to go. It wasn't like they just got divorced the month before."

Mandart and Dalrymple rejoined Parcells in the room with Don's casket. His eyes red, Parcells told Dalrymple, "This is hard, Rich. This is really hard." Then Bill Parcells collected himself by turning the conversation to sports, and Don's athleticism. "Rich, you should have seen him. He was fast. He was *really* fast."

The threesome walked into the next room, where Bill talked about the various photographs of Don: the athlete as an Army fullback wearing the number 31 on his jersey; the banking executive visiting his brother at Patriots headquarters; the family man with his first wife and three children; the family man with his second wife and their three kids; the world traveler on an annual trip to Italy with close friends. By 10 a.m., Don's wife and all his children from both marriages had arrived for the final visitations. Parcells hugged his sister-in-law, nieces, and nephews, happy to see them despite the sad occasion. Two of Don's sons were beefy football players for the University of Maine: Christopher, a six-four, 270-pound offensive lineman, and Craig, a six-six, 270-pound tight end. Parcells asked his nephews how their Black Bears were faring.

A few blocks away, the Catholic church holding the funeral mass bustled with an overflow crowd that included many of Don's ex-teammates at Army. Roughly fifteen minutes before the service, Judy and her daughter Dallas walked into the vestibule, where they ran into Bill's other brother, Doug; Doug's wife, Joanne; and their daughter, Laura. Don's relatives planned to follow the casket down the aisle before taking their seats near the front. Doug told Judy and Dallas to sit with his family, who planned to share a row with Bill.

As the church door swung open to let someone in, Judy spotted a limo across the street. "Oh, that must be Bill." The guess was correct, but when the car door opened Judy Parcells was stunned to see Kelly Mandart step out. Sadness about Don's death turned into rage at the presence of her romantic rival. Judy announced to Doug, "Oh my God! Kelly's here. I'll go find a seat somewhere else."

Doug, equally surprised, responded, "No, stay here."

Judy felt self-conscious about being seen in the same place as Mandart, but with the church filled to capacity, she was forced to stay put. When Parcells and Mandart entered the church, confronted by the prickly situation, Parcells greeted his daughter and nodded at his ex-wife. Dallas hugged Mandart, prompting Judy to shake in anger.

Mandart looked at Parcells's ex-wife. "Hi, Judy." Head down, Judy didn't reply, but nodded a frosty acknowledgment. While Parcells and Dallas chatted, Judy seethed in silence. When that conversation ended,

Judy whispered to her daughter, sardonically asking if she was going to sit with Mandart. Dallas, flabbergasted, replied softly, "Are we really having this conversation?"

Soon Don's casket was wheeled into the vestibule for the service. Parcells leaned over to his daughter and in a shaky voice said, "This is the worst part." Dallas wasn't surprised to see her father breaking down. Throughout the years she had seen him cry, especially when he reminisced about his parents. "I felt very sad for my father," Dallas recalls, "because I really think that Don was the person he was closest to. There's only a handful of people that he's ever been really close with."

Don's wife and children trailed the casket down the aisle as Parcells and Mandart followed, ahead of Dallas and Judy. Parcells and Mandart sat in a pew two rows behind Don's family. From left to right, it contained Judy, Dallas, Parcells, and Mandart. One of Bill's best friends, Bobby Green, sat in a nearby row, along with Jets executive Mike Tannenbaum and agent Jimmy Sexton, while Rich Dalrymple watched from the balcony. Although the PR chief had never met Don, he cried, moved by the all the love and sadness in the packed church. The service's most stirring moment was Don's eulogy, delivered by his oldest child, Sean, flanked by his five siblings. Following the forty-five-minute service, mourners gathered at a cemetery behind the church, and after a brief ceremony Donald Craig Parcells, an army veteran, was lowered into the ground while an American flag fluttered atop his casket.

In the service's aftermath, Dalrymple was struck by the tableau that brought together mourners for a Jersey native with an Italian mother and an Irish father. "You had guys coming out of the church looking like they were extras from *The Sopranos*," Dalrymple recalls, chuckling. "They wore dark blue suits with big pinstripes. It was an interesting mix—a New Jersey funeral right out of central casting. Mickey was there with his sports coat on, but underneath his sports coat, he had on a golf shirt that he maybe got for free somewhere, and double-knit slacks that a coach would wear."

Despite so much grief, much of the chatter afterward concerned the crucial game on *Monday Night Football* roughly six hours away. Outside the church, Mickey Corcoran asked Bill Parcells, "Are you guys going to be able to pull it off tonight?" Parcells's team was going into the game at 5-3, which included a 33–10 romp over Philadelphia at Texas Stadium for Dallas's most impressive victory of the season. However, the 4-4 Eagles hadn't lost to the Cowboys at home since 1998, the year before the arrival of head coach Andy Reid and quarterback Donovan McNabb.

As Mandart and Parcells headed to the limo waiting down the block, Judy spotted the couple and beckoned Parcells over with her head. While

Parcells turned back, Mandart, annoyed, kept walking. In his only words to Judy that day, Parcells apologized. "I didn't want to make you uncomfortable, but she had a relationship with Don, too."

The two exchanged warm good-byes. As Parcells got into his limo at almost 3 p.m., his brother Doug walked over and stuck his head into the car. He looked at Bill and said firmly, "You better go do what you do."

Bill Parcells's return trip was even quieter than the drive to Short Hills. Even the bumper-to-bumper traffic starting at the midway point failed to spur any chatter. Dalrymple thought, "I'm exhausted, physically and emotionally. I'm ready to go home and go to bed."

The limo arrived at the team hotel in Philadelphia around 5 p.m., giving Parcells an hour before the bus ride to Lincoln Financial Field. Suddenly realizing that he hadn't eaten anything all day, Parcells went to the room for pregame meals. Dalrymple walked in and saw Parcells alone at a table, munching a bagel and drinking iced tea. "He just switched into football mode," Dalrymple recalls, "although it wasn't his normal game face."

Meanwhile, four hours before the 9 p.m. kickoff, the parking lots outside Lincoln Financial Field buzzed with activity. One street vendor sold T-shirts emblazoned with derogatory slogans about Eagles wideout Terrell Owens. Before their previous game, the Eagles had suspended Owens indefinitely because of several inflammatory incidents, including his public criticism of quarterback Donovan McNabb and management. A loudspeaker blared an expletive-laced song ripping Owens, while fans carried signs with insults such as "There's No T.O. in Eagles."

On Monday afternoon at the stadium, a local radio station, WIP-AM, had staged a funeral signifying Owens's departure. Fans placed their number 81 jerseys and even cash into a casket, mocking T.O.'s contractual demands. One of the station's hosts, Howard Eskin, burned one of the jerseys before spreading its "ashes" in an end zone. Given Don Parcells's funeral that morning, the display unwittingly showed poor taste, but Dallas's head coach hadn't even told his players about his brother's death.

As the Cowboys buses entered Lincoln Financial Field, Eagles fans kept their unruly, gauntlet-like tradition involving the vehicles of visiting teams: Philadelphia supporters pelted the team buses with objects, banged on them, and shouted R-rated insults. Sitting in a front seat, Parcells remained subdued. "I was just thinking to myself, 'I really don't want to deal with you assholes today,'" he recalls. "I was just in one of those moods: 'Don't mess with me right now.' Of course, they had no way of knowing where I had spent my day."

The heckling and pelting lasted only a couple minutes, but it briefly took Parcells's mind off his grief. "I was going back to the real world," he says.

The temperature at Lincoln Financial Field was a comfortable, cloudy 54 degrees. Wearing a thin blue sweater emblazoned with "Dallas Cowboys," Bill Parcells observed the pregame activity with a tired yet determined gaze. His blond-dyed hair lacked its usual well-coiffed look. Six minutes into the game Philadelphia opened up the scoring on a 15-yard gallop by Brian Westbrook. Moments later, Al Michaels, *Monday Night*'s play-by-play man, told the national TV audience about Parcells's personal loss. "If you see an unusually pained Bill Parcells tonight, he had to bury his brother today."

ABC aired a black-and-white photograph of Don Parcells in an Army football uniform, smiling without a helmet among three teammates. Then the network cut to an action photo of the former fullback/defensive back clutching a ball in his right hand. Michaels informed viewers that Don "played right on this ground because this is where the old Municipal Stadium/JFK Stadium was. That was torn down to make room for this [arena]."

After Philadelphia went up 20–7 on a field goal with about nine minutes left to play, the contest looked like it would not provide Dallas's careworn head coach even the slightest balm. Then, with roughly three minutes left, Drew Bledsoe tossed a rainbow pass off his back foot toward the right side of the end zone. Wideout Terry Glenn sprinted past cornerback Lito Sheppard to snag the pigskin, cutting Philadelphia's lead to 20–14 and giving the Cowboys a flicker of hope. But Bill Parcells's team still needed a miracle after the Eagles took possession with an opportunity to run out the clock.

With the ball on Philadelphia's 38, John Madden, *Monday Night*'s color commentator, made a prediction based on his long experience covering Andy Reid's Eagles: Within the next two plays, Donovan McNabb would run for a first down to essentially seal the deal. On the next snap, McNabb looked to pass toward the right side of the field, where safety Roy Williams faked a blitz before retreating into zone coverage. McNabb locked on to wideout Reggie Brown sprinting along the sideline covered by cornerback Terence Newman.

Unleashing the ball, McNabb never saw the lurking safety: Roy Williams, often maligned for pass-coverage deficiencies, dashed in front of Brown, leaped up to snag the pigskin at Philadelphia's 46, and sprinted down the left sideline. McNabb loomed as an obstacle, but linebacker

Bradie James shoved the quarterback aside, opening a clear path to the end zone.

Roy Williams was only a few yards away from pay dirt when Parcells zeroed in on the back of his jersey: 31, the same number Don wore when he played for Army. Absorbing the coincidence, Parcells flashed one of his few smiles of the day. "It was just unbelievable," he recalls. "I said, 'Holy God, he's here!'"

Williams scampered into the end zone with 2:43 left as fellow safety Keith Davis, trailing the play, unleashed a primal scream. Donovan McNabb limped off the field in anguish from a sprained knee, and suddenly the Cowboys led the Eagles 21–20, having scored two touchdowns in 21 seconds. Jerry Jones and his family turned giddy in their guest suite, trading high fives and grins. Parcells says of his Cowboys safety, "That's why I'll never forget Roy Williams."

With less than a minute left, backup quarterback Mike McMahon replaced McNabb and positioned Philadelphia for a desperation 60-yard field goal attempt. Parcells folded his play-call sheet for the night and removed his headset to watch. The kick by David Akers boomed straight and high. However, it lost steam and dropped close to the goal line, well short of the uprights, prompting Parcells to smile and shake his head. Quickly turning somber, he jogged toward midfield to shake hands with Andy Reid.

The stunner improved Dallas to 6-3 for a first-place tie with New York on top of the NFC East. Jerry Jones's franchise both swept the Eagles and defeated them on the road, for the first time in seven years. As Rich Dalrymple walked to the visitors' locker room to retrieve Parcells for the postgame press conference, the PR chief marveled at Parcells's fortitude. "What he went through that day and that night," Dalrymple says, "was one of the most physically and emotionally challenging things I've ever seen anybody do."

Entering the coaches' dressing room, Dalrymple flashed back to Don's funeral. As the Cowboys' PR chief remembered a photograph of Don's Army jersey and its number, Dalrymple smiled and said to Parcells, "Somebody was looking out for us today. Number 31."

Parcells replied, "Yeah, Rich. Can you believe it? Let's go do this press conference."

The gathering of reporters was especially deferential to Parcells during a brief Q&A. In his only remarks touching on Don's death, he told the gathering, "There was a lot of emotion for me today. I don't mean to dwell on that, but I got a message today that said, 'Don't have a troubled heart.' And I don't. I've got those guys in there." He gestured toward the visitors' locker room, where word about Don's jersey number had reached

Roy Williams. The safety told reporters, "Maybe that was his brother in me, telling Coach Parcells that everything was okay."

The parallels stretched even further. As Al Michaels had pointed out, John F. Kennedy Stadium, née Municipal Stadium, had existed from 1926 to 1992, hosting Army-Navy games for most of those years. President John F. Kennedy went to the contests whenever possible. On December 1, 1962, only thirty-four days after negotiating the end of the Cuban Missile Crisis, he attended the sixty-third annual affair. Kennedy presided over the pregame coin toss, flipping a silver dollar before the ex–navy lieutenant watched from the stands on the Midshipmen's side, one of 98,616 spectators.

Army's favored Black Knights failed to score until late in the second quarter, when fullback Don Parcells burst into the end zone on a short run, cutting Navy's lead to 15–6. Kennedy applauded diplomatically.

At intermission, an honor guard of cadets and midshipmen created an aisle on the gridiron for the president to cross to Army's side for the second half. Roger Staubach, Navy's quarterback, finished with 10 of 12 passes, including two touchdowns. In a performance that propelled him to national recognition, he also scored on a run, leading Navy to a 34–14 upset victory.

Kennedy died November 22, one week before being able to fulfill plans to attend the 1963 contest. The following year, Philadelphia renamed Municipal Stadium after him. Graduating from West Point in 1965, Donald Parcells—number 31—considered his touchdown dash, with President John F. Kennedy in the stands, to be his fondest memory as an athlete.

The Philadelphia trip marked the first of three games in an eleven-day stretch, culminating on Thanksgiving versus the AFC West–leading Broncos. "You don't have time to feel sorry for yourself," Parcells says. "You've got work to do, and you just do it." Arriving at his condominium at 4:30 a.m., Parcells slept for just an hour before waking, worried about his team being overconfident for its next game against the 4-5 Lions at Texas Stadium. At 6 a.m. Parcells drove to Valley Ranch with an idea for keeping his players focused.

When Tony Sparano arrived, Parcells enlisted his help with an unusual chore. The Cowboys players returned to Valley Ranch the next day to find oversized blue mousetraps all over the building—in the lobby, hallways, and locker room. Introducing that week's refrain, Parcells urged his players, "**Don't eat the cheese.**" In other words, ignore the media attention for winning four of five, and avoid getting full of yourself.

With Billy Cundiff recovered from his training-camp injury, Parcells waived Shaun Suisham. In only two games, the rookie had made both field-goal attempts, but Parcells preferred a veteran for a playoff push. Shortly thereafter, Dallas responded to Parcells's motivational props with a 20–7 victory over the penalty-ridden Lions. Marion Barber ran for two short touchdowns to help Dallas overcome Drew Bledsoe going without a scoring pass for the first, and only, time all season. And in his 2005 debut, Cundiff booted a 56-yard field goal that set a franchise record. The outcome lifted the Cowboys to 7-3, one more victory than they'd earned the previous year. Parcells's team entered its Thanksgiving home game with a chance for the NFC's best record.

Mike Shanahan's Broncos, Super Bowl contenders at 8-2 thanks largely to splendid play by quarterback Jake Plummer, marked Dallas's toughest test of the season. The Cowboys looked sharp throughout the tense showdown between first-place teams. Although Dallas trailed most of the way, Denver never led by more than a touchdown. With his team down 21–14 early in the fourth quarter, Drew Bledsoe tossed a 4-yard pass to Jason Witten that tied the game. But midway through the period, Billy Cundiff missed a 34-yard field goal, blowing an opportunity to give Dallas its first lead.

Neither team scored during the rest of regulation, leaving the game tied at 21. On just the second play of overtime, tailback Ron Dayne sprinted 55 yards to Dallas's 6, setting up a gimme field goal. Jason Elam's 24-yarder gave Denver a 24–21 victory, snapping the Cowboys' three-game streak. Their four setbacks, all decided late, were settled by a combined 13 points. The contest with Denver would encapsulate the Cowboys' season: promise undermined by untimely gaffes, particularly missed kicks, that led to too many close losses.

After having skipped the 2003 NFL season and declining Bill Parcells's offer to join him in Dallas, Tom Coughlin had taken over the Giants in 2004. Like the Cowboys, after a six-win season Big Blue had bounced back in 2005. Now, at 7-4, the teams shared the NFC East lead. New York's losses included a 16–13 overtime setback at Dallas in week six on Jose Cortez's 45-yard field goal. In the December 4 rematch Big Blue prevailed 17–10 during a sloppy affair at Giants Stadium. However, Dallas rebounded at home with a sharp performance versus Kansas City, winning an offensive thriller, 31–28, as Bledsoe tossed three touchdowns.

Next, Dallas had suffered a letdown at Washington, 35–7, in one of the worst blowout losses of Parcells's NFL career. His Cowboys, though, kept their playoff chances alive with a comeback victory, 24–20, at Carolina, highlighted by Julius Jones's 194 rushing yards on 34 carries. Despite the outcome, Parcells waived Billy Cundiff the next day for his split-personality production. Maintaining Dallas's revolving door at kicker, Parcells re-signed Shaun Suisham for the team's regular-season finale versus the 5-10 Rams. To secure a wild-card spot, Parcells's team needed to win in Texas Stadium, and the struggling Eagles had to defeat the white-hot Redskins. Just minutes before their 8:30 p.m. kickoff, the Cowboys learned that Washington had beaten Philadelphia, sealing Dallas's fate. In the absence of postseason possibilities, Parcells's team looked listless, falling to St. Louis, 20–10.

Dropping four of its final six games, Dallas finished 9-7 for third place in the NFC East. The up-then-down season disappointed Cowboys Nation, but at least Dallas's quarterback quandary seemed to be resolved. Drew Bledsoe amassed 3,639 passing yards while leading the NFL in game-winning drives (five) and fourth-quarter comebacks (four). His 60.1 percent accuracy was among the best of his career, helped by Sean Payton's canny play-calling. Being entrusted to direct Parcells's offense, and delivering on the big responsibility, only increased Payton's stock around the league.

Dallas's 3-4 defense proved successful, too, especially during the first half of the season. Mike Zimmer's unit improved dramatically from 2005, finishing the season ranked twelfth in points allowed.

The Cowboys experienced the same year-to-year uncertainty regarding Parcells's status that had been endured by his previous clubs. He stuck to an annual evaluation of his mind-set and the team. "Starting in my first [Cowboys] season," Haley recalls, "he kind of gave me the same line: 'Hey, I don't know what I'm going to do.' I kept telling him, 'Bill, I didn't come down to Dallas for just one year.'"

A few days after the lackluster effort versus St. Louis, Parcells halted speculation that he might quit by announcing his return in 2006, the final year of his $18 million contract. However, to avoid the problem of a lame-duck coach, Jerry Jones extended the deal through 2007, and increased Parcells's salary to $5 million, a raise of $1.5 million. Parcells joked to his girlfriend, "It'll allow us to keep eating baloney sandwiches, Kel." The sweetened contract included an option for 2007 at $6 million, which required that both sides agree on a return.

The partnership between Parcells and Jones remained strong, but the two football titans ached to use the contractual language for dispensing credit after a Super Bowl victory.

29

Bill Parcells's prediction about Sean Payton's future in the profession materialized after just one season. The Cowboys play caller had agonized before declining his first head-coaching opportunity with Al Davis's Raiders, but by early 2006 other NFL teams had come calling. Payton's contributions to the Cowboys included helping one unproven quarterback and two past their prime.

Green Bay made him a top candidate for its opening before hiring Mike McCarthy. The New Orleans Saints targeted Payton following their tumultuous 3-13 season under Jim Haslett. The Saints' interest occurred less than a year after Hurricane Katrina, which had forced the franchise to evacuate New Orleans and kept it from playing in the Louisiana Superdome. During the 2005 season, the Saints split their "home" games between San Antonio's Alamodome and Baton Rouge's Tiger Stadium.

With only one playoff victory in its forty-year history, the franchise was adrift, and top-notch leadership skills were considered essential to put it on course. GM Mickey Loomis courted Sean Payton, placing a premium on his discipline-oriented training under one of the top coaches in NFL history, whose disciples had often flourished as head coaches.

Three seasons with Parcells *had* given the offensive-minded assistant unique preparation for becoming a head coach. While transforming from a football geek into a confrontational coach, Payton had substantially expanded his knowledge of such critical areas as personnel evaluation. Parcells had also taught him the best way to structure a staff, and how to organize an off-season program. Payton even recognized the benefits of his mentor's quirkier methods, like keeping the temperature in the trainer's room uncomfortably cold.

In the late afternoon of January 17, 2006, Sean Payton reached an agreement to join New Orleans. He soon telephoned Ernie Accorsi, reminding the GM about his graduate-school analogy for working under Parcells. "Boy, were you right!" When Payton visited Parcells's office to bid his mentor farewell, the two coaches ended up having a lengthy, wide-ranging discussion about the NFL. As it drew to a close, Parcells tempered Payton's giddiness about his new opportunity by noting that head-coaching openings often occurred because of challenges inherent to the organization.

"You've got to figure out what has kept the Saints from winning. Figure it out quickly, or three years from now they'll be having a press conference announcing that they're hiring somebody else."

Parcells added that Payton would be part of a group of ten new head coaches, representing almost two-thirds of the NFL total. "Of those ten, only one or two of you will have some success. The others will fail. Those are just the statistics you'll find if you do your research."

The Cowboys allowed Sean Payton to take linebackers coach Gary Gibbs with him to run New Orleans's defense, but Parcells considered an attempt to poach Tony Sparano to become an offensive coordinator as going a step too far. He emphatically denied permission. Parcells had promoted Sparano from tight-ends coach in early 2005, and considered the running-game coordinator too valuable to lose so soon. Sparano, though, was interested in joining his friend Sean Payton at a position that increased his chances to become a head coach. "I asked myself, 'How many chances will I get to be offensive coordinator?'" Sparano recalls.

After a Saints official telephoned the Cowboys, Parcells walked into the coaches' locker room, where Sparano was showering. Poking his head into the shower stall, Parcells snapped, "New Orleans called today. I'm not giving you permission to go. If you want, come and talk to me about it later." With other assistants watching the exchange, Sparano replied, "Okay. I *do* want to talk about it." After getting dressed, he went to the head coach's office, where Parcells explained his stance, while predicting other big career opportunities for Sparano. "Tony, I have to do what's right for the Dallas Cowboys this time. I can't worry about what's right for every assistant. But trust me, this is all going to work out for you."

Sparano left Parcells's office feeling dismayed but still determined to help the Cowboys make a playoff run. Sean Payton, realizing the headache he'd created for his mentor, telephoned Parcells to apologize and avoid damaging their relationship. Parcells barked, "Are you trying to take my whole goddamn staff?" But the conversation ended with Payton and his old head coach affirming their bond.

Bill Parcells promoted Tony Sparano to assistant head coach, a move that positioned Sparano to take on new play-calling responsibilities. Todd Haley switched from wideouts coach to passing-game coordinator, inheriting most of Sean Payton's duties. And Parcells exploited the availability of a former assistant, hiring Chris Palmer as quarterbacks coach. Palmer had been the Houston Texans offensive coordinator for the previous four seasons. David Lee's title reverted to offensive quality control despite little change in responsibility.

In March 2006 the Saints and Cowboys faced another potential competition, this time for Drew Brees, twenty-seven, the top quarterback in free agency. He had suffered a serious right-shoulder injury in the San Diego Chargers' season finale, but finished the year with a career-high 3,576 yards. Two seasons earlier Brees had made the Pro Bowl with the league's third-best passer rating at 104.8. It was unusual for a top young quarterback to be available without an interested team having to relinquish draft picks or players to get him, but the Chargers were heavily invested in quarterback Philip Rivers. Assuming that Brees recovered from his torn labrum, his best years lay ahead, providing a rare opportunity for whoever landed him.

The Cowboys considered signing Brees as a long-term solution at quarterback, but were deterred by Bledsoe's resurgent season and Brees's exorbitant contract requirements. Preferring to use the team's salary-cap flexibility to fill other personnel holes, Bill Parcells and Jerry Jones decided to stick with Bledsoe. The Saints, however, lacked a reliable starting quarterback: in late 2005, Aaron Brooks, the club's talented yet erratic passer, had been replaced by Todd Bouman, thirty-three, an undrafted journeyman via St. Cloud State.

Brees was also generating strong interest from Miami. Before making a decision on him, Payton offered the Cowboys a third-round pick for Tony Romo, but Parcells and Jones refused to part with Bledsoe's backup unless New Orleans relinquished at least a second-round selection. The Saints considered the price too steep for the talented yet unproven backup.

The Dolphins essentially abandoned their pursuit of Brees, citing medical concerns, and focused on acquiring Daunte Culpepper, who had demanded a trade from Minnesota. New Orleans's interest in Brees, however, remained strong. The team's last, and only, Pro Bowl passer had been Archie Manning, during the late 1970s. Payton figured that the shortcoming at quarterback was a big reason for the franchise's struggles ever since. Heeding Parcells's advice, in his first major decision as a head coach Sean Payton put his weight behind signing Drew Brees to a six-year, $60 million contract.

Having decided not to pursue Brees, the Cowboys contemplated another bold off-season move: signing Terrell Owens. Philadelphia had waived the elite wideout because of his outlandish and divisive behavior, but Jerry Jones believed that acquiring T.O. would propel the Cowboys to a Super Bowl title. The unabashed risk-taker explained to reporters that his three Lombardi Trophies had come with contributions from another flamboyant star wideout, Michael Irvin. Jones also noted Parcells's success with such supposedly incorrigible players as wide receiver Keyshawn Johnson and linebacker Bryan Cox.

Despite some reservations due to Owens's history of recalcitrance, Bill Parcells was open to acquiring him, given Jerry Jones's wishes. Parcells started to do his homework by calling Eagles wideouts coach David Culley, whom he had successfully recruited in 1973, when Culley became Vanderbilt's first black quarterback. The inquiry focused on Owens's work ethic, and Culley described it as being unmatched among Eagles players. Parcells also contacted several of T.O.'s former teammates from his first NFL club, the 49ers. Now the Cowboys leader was most interested in learning about Owens's competitiveness, for which T.O.'s former teammates gave him high marks.

Terrell Owens was represented by Drew Rosenhaus, infamous among fellow agents for targeting players with inner-city backgrounds, stroking their egos, and representing them in an aggressive and unorthodox style. But Parcells respected Rosenhaus as a self-made millionaire who possessed a maniacal work ethic that had helped him gain the most clients in the NFL. Based in Miami with his brother and partner, Jason, Drew Rosenhaus usually picked up his business phone on one ring. He'd co-written a book, released in 1998, titled *A Shark Never Sleeps: Wheeling and Dealing with the NFL's Most Ruthless Agent*. Because Parcells had experience dealing with the Rosenhauses, he introduced the agent and his brother to Jerry Jones and his son, Stephen.

During the Indianapolis combine in late February, the four men held a meeting on Jerry Jones's luxury bus, which the owner used for travel to the annual event. After a second get-together to discuss T.O., Parcells stepped aside while the Joneses continued preliminary negotiations. He was at home in Jupiter, Florida, on March 20 when he received a phone call from the Cowboys with surprising news: Jerry Jones had signed Owens to a three-year, $25 million deal that included $10 million for his first season. Parcells had expected to participate in at least one more meeting, preferably including Owens, before the Cowboys pulled the trigger. Parcells recalls of the process, "It kind of took on a life of its own, and the next thing I knew, he was signed. I was never able to talk to the player face-to-face, although I'm sure Jerry did at some point. I can't say that I wasn't pissed off."

Part of Parcells's anger stemmed from salary-cap consequences that required the release of Keyshawn Johnson, one of his favorites. "I didn't feel too good about it," Parcells admits, "but I was determined to make things work. I wanted to show respect to Jerry, and make sure our relationship remained solid. I wasn't going to make waves, so I said, 'Hey, this is an organizational decision, and I'm going to support it.'"

Jerry and Bill made another significant move through free agency, although it lacked the sizzle of the T.O. deal. Putting an end to their pattern of employing inexperienced or inexpensive kickers, the Cowboys signed Mike Vanderjagt to a three-year deal worth $5.4 million, including a $2.5 million bonus. The most accurate placekicker in NFL history, with a success rate of 87.5 percent, Vanderjagt had become available after Indianapolis signed Patriots free agent Adam Vinatieri. The Cowboys believed that their revolving door of kickers in 2005 was responsible for three of the club's seven losses. Parcells envisioned Vanderjagt, who had set the NFL record for consecutive field goals at forty-two, turning Dallas's problem area into a strength. The move showed the franchise's sense of urgency about making a Super Bowl run in Bill Parcells's fourth, and possibly final, season.

Every midsummer during his football respite, Bill Parcells rented a home in Saratoga Springs, New York. He enjoyed the upstate area, with its opportunity to enjoy Thoroughbred racing at the city's storied course. Parcells often described the small yet culturally rich locale as "the happiest place on Earth." Its residents found him affable and approachable, in contrast to public perception. On January 26, 2004, Parcells paid $160,000 for land five houses down the street from his rental, and began constructing a house for his retirement. In June 2006, he and Kelly Mandart moved into the custom-built 7,500-square-foot home.

Several neighbors decided that Parcells's celebrity shouldn't exempt him from a welcoming tradition called "The Flocking." One night a group of them approached his front yard, where they placed dozens of flamingos wearing football helmets and horse-riding gear. One male neighbor unfurled a banner almost the length of Parcells's twenty-foot porch that read: "Welcome to the Neighborhood." When Parcells stepped outside, he smiled at the gesture, thanking the well-intentioned intruders several times.

He made plans to drive to Nantucket, Massachusetts, in early July to visit his daughter Dallas and son-in-law Scott Pioli. Like Bill Belichick, the couple owned a home on the island retreat just off the southern shore of Cape Cod. Since leaving Parcells's Jets in early 2000, Pioli had straddled a fine line as husband to Bill Parcells's daughter and personnel chief to his New England nemesis, Robert Kraft, and estranged disciple, Bill Belichick.

"We both knew where the boundaries lay," Parcells says. "I couldn't ask him questions about what he was going to do in the draft, and he didn't ask me that type of question, either. I inquired about players on his team if they were available, and he did the same, but certain things didn't come up because they would have meant crossing the line. I didn't ever find us on a slippery slope at all. We just didn't go there."

Parcells adds, "He's a good husband to my daughter and a good father to my granddaughter. That's what I give a shit about."

NFL lifers like Romeo Crennel, who had deep connections to both Big Bill and Little Bill, hoped that the coaching greats would make peace. These mutual friends occasionally reminded Belichick and Parcells about their achievements as partners. "Most people didn't want to see us at odds," Parcells recalls. "They'd say, 'Hey, you guys did a lot of good things together.' They wanted to see things okay."

No one wanted to see things okay more than Scott Pioli, so the Patriots executive informed Belichick about Parcells's trip to Nantucket, planting the seeds for an opportunity. More than a year after Parcells's conciliatory step involving Steve Belichick, Bill Belichick reciprocated by inviting the Cowboys leader to play golf at the Nantucket Golf Club during his stay. Delighted by the offer, Parcells jumped at it. He guessed that Pioli had played a role in Belichick's friendly gesture, but decided to go with the flow instead of grilling his son-in-law.

The afternoon on the links was by far the most time that Belichick and Parcells had spent together since their messy divorce following the 1999 season. The two enjoyed catching up so much that they decided to keep it going with dinner hours later. Football naturally dominated the conversation, and they reminisced about the rigorous practices that Parcells had conducted with the Giants, Patriots, and Jets. Both old-school coaches lamented the NFL's shift toward shorter, less intense practices. After Parcells opined that an obsession with preventing training-camp injuries was inhibiting proper preparation, the head coaches vowed to return to tougher sessions in the upcoming season.

Belichick told Parcells, "I used to get mad at how you made us practice. Now I'm going to do the same thing." Parcells roared.

When dinner ended, Belichick promised to stay in better touch. Parcells says now, "There was a time when we just had a difference of opinion on some things. But that's okay. You know, I wasn't happy that we were kind of at different ends of the spectrum for a while. I wouldn't say we're buddy buddies, but we get along."

On returning from Nantucket, Parcells looked forward to spending a few days at the track when it opened in late July. As the time to resume his coaching duties neared, Parcells told Kelly, "I wish we could just stay here longer." Once back at Valley Ranch, however, Parcells fully reverted to the side of him that was so familiar to his players and staff: agitated, hard-charging, irascible, and unappeasable.

His mood got no better when Jerry Jones informed him of plans to move training camp back to San Antonio starting in 2007; Bill tried dissuading Jerry, to no avail. Conceding Parcells's points about the merits of Oxnard, Jones explained that moving America's Team would benefit its sponsors, and ultimately its coffers. "You know, Ford sells more trucks in Texas than in any other state. They like to have our training camp in Texas so they can put up their displays. And Dr Pepper is very popular in Hispanic communities like San Antonio. Dr Pepper—"

Parcells interrupted. "Jerry. Now, let me get this straight. We've got a billion-dollar corporation. The Dallas Cowboys. *One billion*. And we're worried about selling soda?"

Jones laughed. "You don't know how right you are. You are *really* right. We shouldn't be worried about selling soda. But selling soda allows us to sell potato chips, and to do other deals." Although Bill increasingly disliked catering to sponsors, the football purist understood that Jerry's business savvy provided financial flexibility. And unlike many NFL owners, Jones redirected most revenues to his team, including the head coach's big salary.

Bill Belichick and Bill Parcells affirmed their rapprochement by phoning each other almost weekly. With Dallas and New England in different conferences and no games scheduled between them for 2006, the ex-comrades felt virtually uninhibited about discussing football. But now that Little Bill owned more Super Bowl rings than Big Bill, a new dynamic was emerging. Parcells showed some deference, while using his former lieutenant as a sounding board more than ever. Ahead of Dallas's preseason cuts, he sought Belichick's take on the ideal number of players at each position on a fifty-three-man roster. After several years of radio silence, Belichick also relished the opportunity to once again pick Parcells's brain.

The public learned of the reconciliation in late August at Oxnard, after a reporter asked Parcells about the team's practice routine. Parcells casually mentioned having had a recent conversation on the topic with Belichick, and added that the two coaches concurred on the need for tougher sessions to better prepare their players. Reporters seized on the revelation, generating headlines on August 28 about the thaw between football heavyweights following a six-year chill. Parcells savored the newspaper clips the next morning.

Meanwhile, in Jackson, Mississippi, another acolyte was unabashedly imitating Parcells's methods during his inaugural training camp as an NFL coach. New Orleans's two-a-day practices were organized in much the same way as Cowboys sessions. Sean Payton removed the fleur-de-lis from the helmets of rookies, requiring them to earn the Saints logo. He used the careful notes he had taken from Parcells's staff meetings in Dallas, but also telephoned Parcells whenever necessary to confirm details. Although New Orleans was scheduled to face Dallas on December 10 at Texas Stadium, Parcells continued tutoring his former lieutenant regularly over the phone.

Parcells's leadership skills were difficult to re-create, but the Saints head coach had picked up enough of Parcells's mannerisms for his wife, Beth, to nickname him "Bill Parcells Jr." During training camp, the former nerd's glare could now induce fear in his players and coaches, and Payton seldom went long without uttering one of Parcells's maxims. He turned into a control freak, persnickety about every aspect of the organization. Like Parcells, Payton generally barred coaches from speaking to the media, and often upbraided reporters he deemed to be off base.

The Cowboys' orthopedist, Andrew Dossett, knew about Bill Parcells's habit of researching the personal lives of players in order to tailor his motivational methods. During a visit to the head coach's office, the doctor, a former USC gridder, handed Parcells an article about narcissism from a medical journal.

"You need to read this. This is what we've got with Terrell Owens."

Parcells wasted no time reading the five-page article on the personality disorder. He came away surprised and intrigued by the information, which prompted him to discuss it with team doctors. "The best way to describe it," Parcells says, "is that there's a hole in the bucket. And no matter what you put in there—money, fame, attention—it leaks. It's never enough."

During training camp, Terrell Owens had missed fourteen consecutive practices because of a sore hamstring, but even while riding a stationary bike on the sidelines, he managed to glom the media spotlight. At one open workout Owens emulated Lance Armstrong, wearing the rider's signature blue uniform, crash helmet, and shades; T.O. grinned as photographers and cameramen clicked and whirred while his teammates underwent a grueling workout.

Owens wore a rubber bracelet on his right wrist, etched with his name and website, terrellowens.com. His locker stall contained two towels with an embroidered "T.O." in oversized letters. Jerry Jones often engaged Owens in animated discussions, partly to ensure that the star receiver kept the antics to a minimum. Although Jerry sometimes conveyed displeasure to T.O. about his behavior, Parcells felt that the disproportionate attention only reinforced the theatrics.

"You have to understand," Parcells says, "that they have similar characteristics. And I say that respectfully. I've never told Jones that, but it's obvious to me."

The head coach stopped using Owens's name during press conferences, and referred to him as "the player." Parcells's tactic gnawed at the perennial Pro Bowler, who considered it dehumanizing. John Lucas, the Cowboys' player counselor, recalls, "That was a subtle thing, but it had so much effect. Bill's insight into people reminded me of what I had wanted to be as a coach."

Owens never cursed in front of Parcells, and avoided raising his voice to the head coach. In a league with athletes who occasionally appeared on the police blotter, "the player" lacked an arrest record. So Parcells considered T.O. to be a decent person with a troubled soul. The main challenge in handling Owens was that it required expending additional energy on routine matters like punctuality. Parcells had never coached an athlete who was perennially late to meetings. Owens often overslept, which prompted Parcells to fine him a total of $9,500 by the end of preseason. "It was just one constant stream of drama," Parcells recalls. "You never knew what was going to happen next."

In the season opener at Jacksonville on September 10, Owens showed why employers tolerated his soap opera, at least temporarily. The Cowboys lost, 24–17, as Drew Bledsoe tossed three interceptions to undermine his team's 10–0 lead, but despite having missed most of training camp, T.O. finished with a team-high six catches, including one touchdown, for 80 yards. Even more impressively, the sharp performance came in Owens's first game since October 2005.

Back at his condominium after a return flight, Parcells tried to get a few hours of shut-eye, but following several minutes of uneven sleep, he awoke to a blazing sensation in his throat. Choking on bile, Parcells hopped out of bed while trying not to disturb Kelly. He rushed to the bathroom to vomit, then swigged water and exhaled to calm himself.

Parcells was unsurprised by the regurgitation; it had been taking place every football season since he joined the NFL. Instead of returning to bed, he checked his cell-phone voice mail. One message came from his ex-wife. "Please don't let the loss affect your health."

The mid-sleep vomiting had been most frequent late in his Giants tenure, but Parcells had decided against mentioning it to a doctor, seeing the problem as an indication of stress—the cost of doing football business. "It wasn't a disease," he says. "It was just a condition."

That problem had often disrupted Judy's sleep, particularly on Sunday nights. Their shut-eye returned to normal for a couple of years during Parcells's first NFL retirement, but after the Patriots hired him in 1993, Judy started taking two tablets of Tylenol PM at bedtime. "I got a little smarter," she says, chuckling, "because I was tired of not being able to sleep."

Although Parcells slept worse after losses, even his post-victory slumber remained choppy; he might stir after an hour, enthusiastic about a new idea for practice. Regardless, Parcells generally awoke by 5 a.m., preoccupied by play designs and depth charts.

His sleep would be no different than usual on September 17, 2006, after the Cowboys captured their home opener, 27–10, versus Washington. Drew Bledsoe bounced back with two touchdowns, while Mike Zimmer's defense allowed none. Early in the contest, Owens broke a finger, forcing him out of the game after three catches for 19 yards. The wideout underwent surgery a few days later, with team doctors expecting him to miss at least two games.

The 1-1 Cowboys entered their bye week expecting an uneventful stretch. However, on the morning of September 17, Terrell Owens generated national news by overdosing on pain medication at his Dallas condo. His publicist called 911, and an ambulance rushed Owens to a hospital just four blocks away. Released within hours, T.O. denied reports of attempted suicide, but conflicting information from the wideout, the police, and his publicist fueled the media firestorm. Owens participated in practice the next morning, then held a press conference at Valley Ranch amid a carnival atmosphere.

Parcells saw the incident as a narcissist's cry for attention, so he never asked T.O. about it. "When you sign a player like that, you have to expect certain things to happen," Parcells says. "Once I found out he was okay, that's all I needed to know. As long as he's fine, then I'm happy."

The silent treatment, which stood in such sharp contrast to the public's fascination, bothered Owens. Despite his broken finger, T.O. returned to the starting lineup for Dallas's next game at Tennessee. He helped the Cowboys triumph, 45–14, by catching five passes for 88 yards, while Terry Glenn snagged two touchdowns. The final period of the blowout prompted Tony Romo's first NFL appearance at quarterback. Primarily the holder on field goal attempts, Romo spent Dallas's final two drives strictly handing off, or running himself.

Tony Romo had thrived during preseason: playing in 10 of 16 quarters, the Eastern Illinois product led the NFL with 833 passing yards, and although he hadn't yet thrown a pass in a real game, Parcells aimed to give him some meaningful snaps. But Dallas's leader wanted to manage Romo carefully to minimize the chances of damaging the undrafted quarterback's confidence.

"You plug a young guy in too early, and if he's not ready you can destroy that player," Parcells explains. "You don't want to throw him to the wolves and have the wolves bite so hard that he loses his self-confidence—or the fans or the press get on him. If I had put in Romo in his first year and just let him play, he would have been out of football in a year and a half. He was just a gunslinger. He was indiscriminate. And he would do shit that you just can't succeed doing. But after a year or two of practicing in the preseason, getting his [reps], you could see he had a real good chance to come along."

Romo's first NFL pass came against the Houston Texans on October 15, another blowout by Dallas that he entered late: the play resulted in a 33-yard completion to wideout Sam Hurd. Romo's only other attempt produced a 2-yard touchdown to Owens, putting the Cowboys up, 34–6, the final score. With Bledsoe committing maddening mistakes while being sacked too much because of his immobility, Romo's talents weighed on Parcells's mind.

30

With only one playoff appearance going into his fourth season with Jerry Jones, Bill Parcells seemed more intent than ever on improving the Cowboys. But close friends like Bobby Green, familiar with his maniacal approach at previous stops, voiced concerns about his health. Although Parcells sometimes conducted practice with bloodshot eyes, fatigue hardly slowed the sixty-four-year-old taskmaster. "He did not take his foot off the pedal," says Todd Haley, the Cowboys' passing game coordinator. "And I could see what effort that he put into it, from the off-season through the regular season, did to him."

Returning home in the early evenings, Parcells went from hard-charging, loud, and brusque to withdrawn, subdued, and taciturn. He typically brooded for much of the night, and declined to eat dinner. "Bill was a depressed, unhappy individual," Mandart recalls. "That's not the way to live your life." One salutary pleasure at Valley Ranch came through an exercise regimen with Cowboys trainer Joe Juraszek. Every other day the pair underwent a workout that slightly boosted Parcells's spirits and energy. In an effort to address his poor eating habits, Parcells even gave up candy and cookies. Although he no longer ate an entire box of Fig Newtons each day, Parcells maintained his lust for peanut butter, consuming it directly from the jar.

Despite their inconsistency the 3-2 Cowboys played for first place in the NFC East against the 3-2 Giants at Texas Stadium. Trailing 12–7 just before halftime, Dallas had taken the ball to New York's 4, with a chance for the lead. But Bledsoe tossed a weak pass intended for Terry Glenn in the left flat, where cornerback Sam Madison intercepted it. The miscue ended both Dallas's promising opportunity and Parcells's patience with his veteran quarterback. Such bad decisions, the head coach felt, were coming too frequently from a quarterback experienced enough to know better. So Parcells decided on the major change he'd put in motion since preseason: Tony Romo replaced Drew Bledsoe to start the second half.

The backup quarterback attempted a pass on Dallas's first offensive play, but it was tipped by Giants defensive end Michael Strahan, and ended up in the hands of linebacker Antonio Pierce. Exploiting the interception only three snaps later, Big Blue went ahead 19–7 on Eli Manning's

13-yard toss to tight end Jeremy Shockey. Bledsoe stood on the sideline scowling as Tony Romo ended up with three interceptions, including one returned 96 yards for a touchdown that sealed the outcome.

Big Blue's 36–22 victory earned Coughlin's team first place in the NFC East, while rendering Dallas a .500 club yet again. Despite the interceptions, Romo's 14 of 25 passing, including two touchdowns, intrigued Cowboys Nation. In sharp contrast to Bledsoe, Romo scrambled adroitly to avoid pressure before zinging his passes.

Watching the blowout at home in New Jersey, Jim Burt was surprised by his former coach's body language. Burt noticed an unfamiliar lack of fire from Parcells on the sidelines, so the next morning he telephoned the Cowboys coach to express concerns about his well-being.

"Bill, what's wrong with you? You're white as a ghost, you're not moving [around on the sideline much]. What are you doing? What's going on?" Burt made plans to visit Parcells at the Cowboys' next game, against the Carolina Panthers at Bank of America Stadium.

Parcells wasted no time naming Romo the starting quarterback for the October 29 contest on *NBC Sunday Night Football*, the network's inaugural season of prime-time NFL telecasts. He told his players at Valley Ranch, "I don't enjoy doing this to Drew, but you've got to rally around Tony." On game day Jim Burt arrived at the stadium about an hour before the 8:15 p.m. kickoff and walked into the Cowboys locker room. In a role reversal, Jim Burt exhorted Parcells, and then delivered a pregame speech to his players before heading to the Cowboys' sideline.

Although Jerry Jones believed that his team's best chances for making the playoffs lay with Drew Bledsoe, the owner supported his head coach's quarterback decision. Jones's assessment seemed accurate late in the first quarter when Romo tossed an interception that the Panthers parlayed into a 14–0 lead. But Romo led a dramatic turnaround in the second half while Jim Burt, wearing Cowboys gear, cheered and chest-bumped Parcells's players. The young quarterback guided Dallas to 35 unanswered points, including a franchise-record 25 in the fourth quarter. In his brilliant starting debut, Romo connected frequently with Terrell Owens (9 catches for 107 yards) and Jason Witten (6 receptions for 80 yards).

Moments after the 35–14 triumph, Parcells kissed players on the cheek, although T.O. received a pat instead. On the team plane, Parcells took a few phone calls from good friends like Tony La Russa, the St. Louis Cardinals' baseball manager, who congratulated Bill for the impressive comeback. In the next game, though, Dallas maintained its win-loss pattern, falling 22–19 at Washington in perhaps the most bizarre finish that either Joe Gibbs or Bill Parcells had ever experienced.

The score was tied at 19 with only 35 seconds left when the Redskins' Nick Novak missed a 49-yard field goal. Leading a hurry-up offense, Tony Romo completed three passes, including a 28-yarder to Jason Witten, positioning the Cowboys for their turn at a field-goal try with six seconds left. However, Mike Vanderjagt's 35-yard attempt never had a chance—it was blocked by safety Troy Vincent. Safety Sean Taylor plucked the bouncing ball at Washington's 26 before zigzagging through tacklers to reach Dallas's 44. Time had run out, however, so the game was headed for overtime.

Hold that thought. The Cowboys were called for a face-mask penalty against Taylor, tacking 15 yards on to the return. By rule, regulation play couldn't end on a defensive penalty, so Washington got one more play. With no official time left, Nick Novak booted a 47-yard field goal that slipped inside the right upright as 90,250 spectators roared at the surreal finish. In a silver-lining performance, Tony Romo tossed two touchdowns without an interception while gaining 284 yards on 24-for-36 passing.

Retired from coaching since late 1994, Bill Walsh enjoyed visiting Dallas in the fall, so he surprised Bill Parcells with a telephone call from his California home, requesting their first get-together. Parcells loved the idea, and arranged for Walsh to swing by Cowboys headquarters for some quality time. While leading the 49ers from 1979 to 1988, Bill Walsh had enjoyed a high-profile rivalry with Bill Parcells, one that produced some of the NFL's most memorable games. Playoff showdowns between their teams occasionally led to Super Bowl titles. And in a sense, the rivalry continued decades beyond the Giants-49ers classics via their enormous coaching trees: by 2006, roughly three-fourths of NFL head coaches had ties to Walsh or Parcells; most of the rest were linked to Marty Schottenheimer.

After Parcells had taken over the Giants in 1983, his main communication with Walsh amounted to exchanging trade proposals over the telephone. Despite being football adversaries, they considered each other natural trade partners, and were unhesitant to cut deals. Occasionally Walsh had irked Parcells by reneging on oral agreements after getting a better proposal within hours, but the two kept negotiating ploys to a minimum.

During his special trip to Valley Ranch, Bill Walsh spent more than two hours with Parcells in Landry's old office. Sitting across from each other, the football legends reflected and looked ahead. Their topics mainly dealt with the league, from its direction to new strategies on the gridiron. Parcells and his guest agreed that the NFL possessed a cyclical nature that made some of the new trends essentially retro. For several minutes, Walsh reminisced about key clashes between San Francisco and Big Blue in the stretch during the 1980s when both men led two powerful franchises that espoused diametric philosophies.

Parcells recalls of the get-together, "That was a precious time for me."

While capturing two Lombardi Trophies in four years during the 1980s, Bill Walsh's 49ers opened their postseasons with victories over Big Blue. But Parcells's Giants crushed San Francisco, 49-3, on the way to his first Super Bowl title in 1987, and the rout helped define him as a coach.

Walsh recalled to Parcells, "We were young and vibrant guys." The remark spurred Parcells to retrieve a piece of literature he cherished and kept close by: General Douglas MacArthur's "Youth Is Not a Period of Time," also known as MacArthur's "Creed on Youth." Parcells removed it from his personal organizer in a section with his laminated preface of *The Coaches*. The sixty-five-year-old head coach read the poem to his seventy-four-year-old guest.

"Youth is not a period of time. It is a state of mind, a result of the will, a quality of the imagination, a victory of courage over timidity, of the taste for adventure over the love of comfort. A man doesn't grow old because he has lived a certain number of years. A man grows old when he deserts his ideal."

Walsh sat riveted as Parcells paused for a moment before continuing with the poem's final lines. "You will remain young," he boomed, "as long as you are open to what is beautiful, good and great; receptive to the messages of other men and women, of Nature and God. If one day you should become bitter, pessimistic and gnawed by despair, may God have mercy on your old man's soul."

The passage captivated Walsh, as Parcells had thought it would. So the Cowboys coach made his guest a copy. The poem, apparently an adaptation of Samuel Ullman's "Youth," gained popularity after MacArthur kept a framed copy on his office desk in Manila, Philippines, while serving as supreme commander of the Allied Forces after World War II. On MacArthur's seventy-fifth birthday, January 26, 1955, he quoted from the poem during a dedication of his monument at Los Angeles's MacArthur Park.

Well acquainted with the workload of an NFL head coach, Bill Walsh volunteered to let Parcells return to his Cowboys duties. The two NFL legends shook hands firmly before Bill Walsh departed for Woodside, California.

On November 10, several weeks after the get-together, Walsh made his battle with leukemia public. He'd been diagnosed with blood cancer in 2004, a decade after coaching his final game at Stanford. Walsh had kept his condition quiet, but he decided to disclose it in late 2006 through two sportswriters who had once covered his 49ers. Reading the newspaper coverage about Walsh's illness, Parcells flashed back to their precious time at Valley Ranch, convinced that it related to his rival's mortality. "I guess he knew he was dying, and just wanted to talk," Parcells says somberly. "We shared a lot of competition together."

Bill Walsh would succumb to leukemia on July 30, 2007, at age seventy-five.

After losing the heartbreaker in Washington, Tony Romo amassed a career-high 308 passing yards in a 27–10 road triumph versus the Cardinals, then outplayed Peyton Manning at Texas Stadium as the Colts suffered their first loss of the season, 21–14. Despite Romo's emergence and Dallas's latest impressive victory, Parcells went to sleep that night concerned about Mike Vanderjagt, who'd missed two medium-range field goals against his former team on his only attempts. During training camp the thirty-six-year-old had pulled his groin, causing him to miss most of preseason. He'd returned for the Cowboys' exhibition finale, and uncharacteristically missed two gimmes. Having expected Vanderjagt to be worth three additional victories, Parcells began to instead worry about him as a potential liability.

Still, with the Cowboys improving to 6-4, Jerry Jones upgraded his expectations for reaching the postseason, and on Thanksgiving Day, Tony Romo removed any doubt about his ascendancy during a nationally televised game at Texas Stadium versus Tampa Bay. The undrafted quarterback led Dallas to a 38–10 triumph by tossing five touchdowns, tying a franchise record last reached by Troy Aikman. Several giddy fans placed a sign displaying Romo's name in the arena's Ring of Honor. Romo drew effusive praise from all corners, especially the team's owner, but the person whose bold decision had led to the euphoria preached caution. Alluding to the Aikman comparisons, Parcells snapped at reporters, "We've got a ways to go here. **So put away the anointing oil**, okay?"

In a surprise move, the next day Parcells released the player whom he himself had anointed to solve the team's placekicking troubles. Mike Vanderjagt left the Cowboys after making only 13 of 18 field goals, the lowest success rate of his NFL career. To replace him for Dallas's stretch drive, Parcells signed Martin Gramatica, thirty-one. Once a top kicker for Tampa Bay during the early 2000s, Gramatica had been released by Indianapolis in 2004 for decreased production. He'd sat out 2005 while recovering from abdominal surgery, and in 2006 Gramatica rejoined Indianapolis for three games, while Adam Vinatieri nursed a groin injury.

Against Big Blue in his next game, Romo finally delivered a subpar performance with two interceptions and no touchdowns. However, the

Cowboys still triumphed 23–20, on Martin Gramatica's 46-yard field goal with one second left. The four-game streak gave the 8-4 Cowboys an upper hand in the NFC East, but it did little to reduce Parcells's grumpiness or boost his energy. And his press conferences started to lack his typical verve and animation.

Regardless of the team's outcomes, Parcells felt increasingly conflicted about whether to return in 2007 for a final season. And he vacillated at night to his girlfriend.

"What should we do, Kel? Should I give this up?"

Bill Parcells Jr.'s New Orleans Saints were one of the NFL's most surprising teams. At 8-4, New Orleans was thriving under the leadership of Sean Payton and quarterback Drew Brees, a league MVP candidate regularly posting gaudy numbers. With an upcoming showdown at Texas Stadium against his mentor and former team, Sean Payton had positioned the Saints to capture the NFC South. The improbable turnaround provided a salve to a region still slowly recovering from Hurricane Katrina. The captivating story played out as Sean Payton continued spreading the gospel according to Parcells. Payton put mousetraps in his players' locker room, and awarded Louisville Sluggers to defensive players for pivotal haymakers in games.

Five Saints players had been on the Cowboys the previous year: wideout Terrance Copper, kicker Billy Cundiff, linebacker Scott Fujita, offensive tackle Rob Petitti, and linebacker Scott Shanle. Given the franchise's transformation, Sean Payton's players and coaches, including defensive coordinator Gary Gibbs, welcomed his constant channeling of Parcells. The clash between master and pupil leading two of the NFC's best teams merited a *Sunday Night Football* appearance, but the Cowboys looked unready for prime time during a humiliating 42–17 loss, as New Orleans's offense showcased Drew Brees plus tailbacks Reggie Bush and Deuce McAllister, amassing 536 total yards.

A native of Austin, Texas, Drew Brees tied his career high with five touchdowns despite spending almost the entire the final period handing off. His 384 passing yards gave him 4,033 on the season. With Sean Payton demonstrating dynamic play calling, third-year fullback Mike Karney scored the first three touchdowns of his career. In a sign of Payton's respect for Parcells, New Orleans took a knee from Dallas's 5 with about three minutes remaining on the clock.

Sean Payton and Bill Parcells shook hands on the field during an exchange that lasted only a couple seconds. Parcells told his former lieutenant, "Good job," then grimly kept walking. Despite the embarrassing setback, Parcells deemed it an aberration and urged his players to move past it. They took heed, defeating Atlanta, 38–28, at the Georgia Dome behind two touchdown runs by Marion Barber in the second half.

The outcome, improving Parcells's team to 9-5, kept the NFC East title in sight. And on Christmas, Dallas hosted the 8-6 Eagles with a chance to clinch the franchise's first division title since 1998. However, Parcells's team squandered the opportunity, losing 23–7, on its worst offensive production of the year. Romo collected a season-low 142 passing yards while the Eagles contained their nemesis, T.O., for the second time, despite his touchdown catch. Dallas's hot streak near the middle of the season had assured Parcells's team a playoff spot in a conference lacking superpowers. But with one game left, Philadelphia now controlled the division title, with its reward of opening the postseason at home.

Instead of exploiting their outside chance to capture the NFC East, the Cowboys ended their regular season with a stunning 39–31 setback against the punching-bag Lions at Texas Stadium. It was only Detroit's third victory of the season, ending a seven-game skid. Despite amassing 321 passing yards, Romo struggled to hold on to the ball. He fumbled four times, losing it twice, confirming Parcells's reluctance to anoint him based on his tiny body of work. Lions Quarterback Jon Kitna's four touchdowns helped prevent his team from receiving the upcoming draft's top selection, which went to the 2-14 Oakland Raiders.

In a repeat late-season collapse, Dallas allowed 132 points over its final four games. The Cowboys' defense, after being stingy for much of the season, turned porous down the stretch, and the high-powered offense under an obscure backup turned Pro Bowl quarterback couldn't make up for the slide. Stumbling into the playoffs at 9-7, Dallas earned a wild-card berth against the Seahawks at Qwest Field, perhaps the league's loudest stadium.

Throughout his NFL career, Bill Parcells had constantly preached to his teams that by qualifying for "the tournament," a championship lay within reach despite regular-season struggles. So the Cowboys hit the reset button January 6, 2007, in Seattle on a brisk, overcast afternoon with temperatures in the upper thirties.

For most of the first half, both offenses managed to produce only field goals, including a 50-yarder by Martin Gramatica, as Seattle took a 6–3 lead. Mike Zimmer's unit returned to its early-season form, stifling tailback Shaun Alexander. Dallas delivered the matchup's first touchdown moments before halftime on Tony Romo's 13-yard pass to wideout Patrick Crayton. The completion capped a length-of-the-field drive, putting Dallas up 10–6. With about six minutes left in the third quarter Seattle reclaimed the lead on Matt Hasselbeck's 15-yard completion to tight end Jerramy Stevens.

On the kickoff Dallas wideout Miles Austin, an undrafted rookie via Monmouth, dashed 93 yards to score, pushing the Cowboys ahead, 17–13. The play marked their first-ever kickoff return for a touchdown in the playoffs. Then, early in the final period, Martin Gramatica's 29-yard field goal increased Dallas's lead to 20–13. Midway through the fourth quarter, the Seahawks threatened to even the score by reaching Dallas's 1. A defensive stand, though, derailed them after Hasselbeck's pass fell incomplete on fourth-and-goal from the 2.

Tony Romo sought more breathing room on Dallas's first snap, whipping a screen pass to Terry Glenn, but rookie cornerback Kelly Jennings raked the ball loose, causing a fumble into and out of the end zone for a safety. The Seahawks seized the momentum and a slim lead on the ensuing drive, when Jerramy Stevens produced another touchdown with a 37-yard reception. A failed two-point conversion kept the score at 21–20 with just over four minutes left.

In keeping with the theme of the wild-card game, Tony Romo orchestrated a drive from Dallas's 38 to Seattle's 2. His third-and-long pass to Jason Witten, who caught the ball before being hit by linebacker Lofa Tatupu, was initially ruled a first down. But Mike Holmgren's challenge led to a reversal, making the situation fourth-and-1 from the 2 instead of first-and-goal from the 1.

So with 1:19 left, Bill Parcells sent in his kicking unit for the potential game winner, only 19 yards, or essentially an extra-point attempt. Romo remained on the field as the holder. Although the job generally belonged to backup quarterbacks, Romo kept it because he excelled at the duties: catching the snap and placing the pigskin on the ground with its laces facing away from the kicker, while slightly tilting the tip toward him.

Martin Gramatica, with his long hair flowing, jogged from the sideline as NBC flashed a statistic: over his career, Gramatica was 8 of 12 (67 percent) on lead-changing field goals in the final two minutes of the fourth quarter and overtime. Gramatica made the sign of the cross twice while Parcells, wearing a blue-and-white windbreaker, paced the sideline, staring at the ground. After several steps, he looked up, sighed, and licked his upper lip. No one stood near him as he zeroed in on Gramatica. With his arms crossed against his chest, Parcells ached for Dallas's first playoff victory since 1996.

Tony Romo took a knee at the right hash mark of Seattle's 10, waiting to put the ball. Despite catching a clean snap, Romo bobbled the pigskin while trying to place it down. Shocked at the sight, Gramatica aborted his windup. Chaos ensued. Romo regained control of the ball and sprinted to his left toward the corner of the end zone. Watching in disbelief, Holmgren thought the blunder might turn into a Cowboys touchdown, but cornerback Jordan Babineaux, trailing Romo, brushed aside Gramatica's desperation shove before diving into the holder's ankles. Romo went tumbling at the 2—one yard short of a first down.

Describing the action, Al Michaels, NBC's play-by-play announcer, screamed, "Oooooooooooooh! And it's fumbled by Romo. And then Romo's gonna run to the end zone, and he's gonna get tackled by Jordan Babineaux. Amazing!"

Color analyst John Madden added, "Unbelievable!"

Michaels agreed. "How crazy is this?"

Surrounded by giddy Seahawks players, Romo sat on the gridiron tugging his face mask in disbelief, blood dripping from his left hand. A Cowboys offensive lineman trudged over to lift the forlorn quarterback.

Madden said, "There's nothing automatic in football. The ball just slipped out of his hands. It was a good snap. He went to put it down, and it just slipped . . ."

Michaels added, "Wow."

Madden commented, "Your whole season comes down to that."

Instead of Dallas's first playoff victory in a decade, one of the worst blunders in playoff history punctuated the team's tailspin and heightened the uncertainty about Parcells's future.

Anguish marked Bill Parcells's face around midnight as he buckled his seat belt on the team plane for the three-and-a-half-hour flight to Dallas. Several minutes after takeoff from Sea-Tac Airport, Parcells draped a red blanket over the upper half of his body and shut his eyes. Sitting next to him, Jeff Ireland noted that Parcells seemed to be skipping his ritual of entering the cockpit early in the flight. After several minutes, Parcells cast the blanket aside and stared ahead. Ireland saw pain, and sensed that his boss's mind was racing.

On the aircraft after a loss, Ireland would typically wait for Parcells to make the first remark. This time, Parcells stayed quiet much longer than usual before finally turning to Ireland. "Did you see that shit? Can you believe that shit?"

Ireland didn't know how to respond. "Yeah, sorry, Coach. You're right." The reply ended their conversation for the rest of the seemingly interminable flight.

Parcells realized that details of the setback would remain etched in his mind for the rest of his life. One drawback of his preternatural memory was vivid recollections of losses from decades ago, some as far back as his high school years. "The games you remember most are on the negative side," Parcells says. "I don't know why. You'd have to speak to a psychologist about that. But the time you enjoy a win is minimal compared to how long you feel disappointed by losing."

Sitting in silence next to Ireland, Parcells replayed the mishandled snap in his head several times, but he spent equal time on the play beforehand: third-and-7 from Seattle's 8 with 1:53 left. Instead of calling a conservative play, Parcells allowed Romo to throw. After Jason Witten leaped to snag the ball at the 2, a referee initially signaled first down, spurring disbelief from the Seahawks and delight from the Cowboys. With Seattle down to its last timeout compared to Dallas's three, new downs would have allowed Parcells to milk the clock before a gimme field goal. Or just as likely, Mike Holmgren would have let the Cowboys score in order to gain possession while down no more than seven. Midway through the flight, Parcells kept wondering whether Witten had been shortchanged by a measurement putting him eighteen inches shy of a first down.

Finally abandoning his exercise in self-administered torture, Parcells headed to the cockpit and commandeered one of the twin seats behind the pilots. Used to his presence, they commiserated with him for several minutes. During a quiet moment Parcells gazed out the cockpit window into the darkness. He sensed his career fading to black, and said to himself, "This is probably going to be my last football trip."

Since Parcells joined the NFL in 1980, his off-season workload had multiplied. Downtime eventually almost disappeared thanks to the Senior Bowl, the combine, free agency, the draft, minicamps, and training camp. Coaches also needed to factor in time to deal with unpredictable developments, or as Donald Rumsfeld, the former secretary of defense, might call them, known unknowns.

Before the twilight of his NFL career, Parcells had especially relished his off-season football activities. But now at sixty-five, he had little appetite to prepare another team, especially given the chance of ultimately being undermined by a player flubbing a routine task in a game's pivotal moment. "That was what got me," he says, "because now it's another year; we've got to go through a whole new cycle, when we were right there. We had a chance to win it and go to Chicago and beat the Bears. They weren't that good."

To guard against a snap decision from his mercurial partner, Jerry Jones set a distant February 1 deadline for a decision. Despite Parcells's inclination to leave the Cowboys, he intended to deliberate, knowing that his third retirement would almost certainly be his last. Back at Valley Ranch he offered no sign of impending departure as he conducted discussions with the front office about free agency and the draft. The taskmaster also pressed his coaches about their off-season duties, with the Senior Bowl just a couple of weeks away.

"He was in it to win it," Anthony Lynn recalls. "He worked like he was going to be coach of the Cowboys for the next decade." Until Parcells made an official decision, however, Cowboys headquarters crackled with suspense. Hoping for his mentor's return, Jeff Ireland refused to broach the topic. But when the chief scout discussed a schedule that included the 2007 draft, Parcells reminded him, "Hey, I might not even be here."

Ireland replied, "Oh, yeah. Right, right."

One clue to Parcells's leanings could be found in the way he approached Cowboys coaches whose contracts were set to soon expire. Instead of insisting that they ignore other employment possibilities, Parcells emphasized the uncertainty of his situation. "I just don't know if I have the energy to do this. I don't know if I *want* to do this. I may want to get on with the rest of my life."

David Lee informed Parcells that he had received an attractive offer from Arkansas head coach Houston Nutt to be his offensive coordinator. Parcells responded, "Let me call Houston Nutt right now. I want to ask him to give you another week, and then I'll know for sure what I'm doing." Obliging Parcells, Nutt gave Lee a one-week extension. When it expired on January 16, Parcells, still conflicted, walked into Lee's office and said, "David, it may be in your best interest to take that Arkansas job." The next day the Arkansas Razorbacks named Lee their offensive coordinator and quarterbacks coach, increasing speculation about Parcells's departure.

On Friday, January 19, Ireland spoke to Parcells about the team's arrangements for Senior Bowl activities, which were starting in three days. Parcells told Ireland that he would deliberate one last time over the weekend, while the chief scout headed off to Mobile, Alabama. On Sunday night Parcells and Kelly Mandart ate dinner at the Italian Cafe, a favorite spot across from their apartment building. Early on in the conversation, Parcells was upbeat about the Cowboys, emphasizing their pluses, which included a young franchise quarterback for a team on the upswing. He seemed bent on staying for the 2007 season, in order to attempt a Super Bowl run. Several minutes later, however, Parcells acted deflated, ticking off reasons to quit, including his team's most recent flameout.

Kelly, exasperated, said to Parcells, "I can't make this decision for you. Do you like the man that you are when you're coaching?"

Parcells replied, "No, I don't."

"Well, there's your answer."

The table turned silent.

Before they left the restaurant, Parcells told Mandart that in the morning he would give Jerry Jones the news that he was quitting. The decision did not surprise Mandart.

In a striking parallel to his departure from the Patriots, Parcells was leaving a young, loaded team entering its prime, quarterbacked by a star twentysomething. "It was hard in only one respect," Parcells says of his choice. "I knew this time when I did it, it was over for good. When you're giving up your life's work, it's never easy. I love the game. The game's been good to me. I've said it about players, but the same is true for coaches: eventually, you don't want to go into the huddle anymore. The battle is over. You don't want to fight. I was fighting for forty years."

So on Monday, January 22, Bill Parcells arrived at his office characteristically early, and contacted Jerry Jones to come by for the verdict. When the Cowboys owner entered the room, Parcells cut to the chase. Showing no traces of vacillation, the head coach firmly conveyed his decision.

"Jerry, I'm done. I just don't want to go through another year."

Jones replied, "Well, I kind of had an inkling this might be coming." The two men, who had defied all predictions about an inevitable clash, weren't sentimental during a brief exchange. The owner expressed gratitude for Parcells's tenure; Parcells wished Jones and his organization well. As soon as Jones walked out, Parcells telephoned Jeff Ireland in Mobile. "Hey, I'm hanging up my cleats."

Bill Parcells ended his Dallas tenure at 34-32, including losses in both postseason appearances, for an NFL career mark of 183-138-1. Beyond his own middling numbers, Parcells was leaving the team with a revamped culture and a roster containing the talent of a Super Bowl contender. But, he says, "It was time to go. It didn't have anything to do with Jerry. It was me. The energy was gone. It comes back to looking at the man in the glass."

31

Retirement kept football from intruding on Bill Parcells's summers at "the happiest place on Earth." Obliging Mike Tannenbaum, who'd been promoted to Jets GM in 2006, Parcells became an unofficial adviser to the team, but when the weather turned warm on the East Coast, he drove from Jupiter to Saratoga Springs, untethered to the NFL. His Colonial home stood on a cul-de-sac across a lake separating it from the Saratoga National Golf Club. As a member with an 8-handicapper, making him an above-average golfer, Parcells hit the links whenever the weather allowed. And just as conveniently, his off-yellow two-story mansion was also only a couple of miles from the Saratoga Race Course.

Quitting the Cowboys finally allowed Parcells to stay for the entire Saratoga meet, which ran for forty-two days starting in late July. Parcells sat with friends in a seasonal luxury box that contained five seats, not far from the one used by Buffalo Bills patriarch Ralph Wilson. Parcells owned horses with football-related names like Gameday News, a colt trained by his pal D. Wayne Lukas. He sees parallels between Thoroughbreds and gridders, describing the animals as athletes with their own personalities, attributes, and work ethics. Parcells also likens trainers to coaches.

Every morning during horse-racing season, Parcells visited the Oklahoma Training Track, known as the barns. He relished standing near a guardrail watching the ponies gallop, often gathering intelligence from longtime friends who happened to be Hall of Fame trainers: D. Wayne Lukas, Shug McGaughey, and Nick Zito. "This is one of my favorite places to be, period. Out here in the morning," Parcells says early one day, observing horses go by. "Now, there's some sadness out here, too. One summer, I saw a horse right in front of this pole drop dead: heart attack. But I like it here more than almost anywhere."

Lukas, galloping on a horse, parked it next to Parcells for a wide-ranging conversation about topics from ex-wives to Thoroughbreds. Parcells asked about one of the trainer's horses. "Where's my Sweet Sugar?"

Lukas replied, "Oh, he's coming. He's on the way."

After several minutes, Nick Zito also stopped by to chat. The retired coach surprised his friend with conviction about a horse whose promise the trainer thought had been under wraps: "I'm betting that horse with both fists."

Zito responded, "Who told you about that horse?"

"I don't know."

"Seriously. What did you hear?"

"Nobody told me anything."

"Now, tell the truth."

"I watched the horse! You think I can't tell fast when I see fast?"

"You won't help me out here."

"I don't know nothing."

"I'm going to put you on trial."

"On my mother's grave, nobody told me."

"Okay, if you say that, then forget I asked."

For the third and perhaps final time, Bill Parcells was transitioning into life away from football. Without a secretary, he took on mundane tasks like heading to Kinko's for photocopies, but everyday life didn't allow him to escape celebrity. Parcells couldn't go for long in public without someone asking for an autograph or cell phone photograph, sometimes during dinner at a restaurant; despite the intrusiveness of the requests, Parcells generally obliged. Strangers often walked up to his home to gawk, while others slowly drove by, scrutinizing the property. Although such behavior disturbed Kelly Mandart, her boyfriend, the licensed owner of a firearm, reacted with nonchalance.

During his Cowboys tenure, Bill Parcells saw his daughters perhaps once per year. Now that he had more free time as a retiree, Parcells aimed to redeem himself as best he could for the biggest regret of his personal life: being an absentee father. "I try to be a benevolent person; I try to help people," says Parcells, known to many beneficiaries for his discreet charity. "But there are some things I'm not proud of. I could have been a better father. My kids are all productive members of society, and I taught them core values, but I wasn't there for them when it counted. As a result, my relationship with my children is okay, but it's not like that of a super-tight family.

"I feel a little guilty about the things that I just didn't do—simple things. When I could have been there, many times I wasn't. It was always something at my job that kept me away, but it didn't keep other coaches away. So my family saw that other guys with the same job I had would do things that I wouldn't. I didn't pay enough attention to my children's individuality. I was not as good a husband as I could have been. A lot of coaches did both of those things very well. I just didn't. That's my biggest regret."

Parcells's conspicuous absences began with the birth of his first child,

Suzy, in October 1962 at a Wichita hospital: the Shockers' junior line-backer was in Cincinnati for a game on Saturday, October 6. Before Parcells's team lost to the Bearcats, 27–15, Judy telephoned her husband of eight months with the news that she had just given birth to a healthy girl.

Parcells returned to town with the Shockers in the early morning, intent on seeing his newborn right away. To help him overcome nursery access limitations, the team doctor drew a map of the hospital. Parcells used it to sneak into the maternity ward at 4:30 a.m., when he pressed a card against a window to identify himself, and a nurse obliged him by wheeling out Suzy Parcells to meet her proud daddy.

However, after Suzy was joined by sisters Dallas and Jill, Parcells rarely went out of his way for the girls. When Dallas attended elementary school he declined her request to appear at a father-daughter dance, which she found upsetting because he was around at the time. To blunt the pain from such rejections, and try to prevent any emotional scars, Judy constantly covered for her husband. She mainly blamed his job as a college coach, emphasizing the long hours. "I used to make excuses for him all the time when our kids were little," Judy says, "because they'd be crying about him not doing this or that."

After the girls grew old enough to understand the demands of their father's job, they still remained baffled by his obsessiveness. Dallas was a teenager in 1980, during Parcells's first NFL season as New England's linebackers coach. One fall Saturday afternoon, Parcells packed up his suitcase, preparing to join the Patriots at a nearby hotel because the team was scheduled to play at Foxboro Stadium the next day. Dallas heard her father's voice in the family room. She was surprised to walk in and find him alone, sitting in a recliner and talking out loud. Dallas watched her father for about two minutes before being noticed.

Snapping out of his trance, Parcells said, "What's the problem?"

Dallas replied, "You were talking to yourself, Dad."

"Oh yeah, I was just running through some plays."

Dallas played on her high school softball and tennis teams, but Parcells's attendance was so rare that she remembers the two times he showed up. One was at a softball game where, with Parcells watching, Dallas played poorly, trying hard to impress. "It was a big deal for him to be there," she says. In 1980, Suzy graduated from Air Academy High in Colorado Springs. Judy and her parents flew west for the ceremonies, but Parcells decided against coming along because of the distance and Patriots minicamp.

Parcells did attend two of the girls' high school graduations. In Dallas's case, however, he soured her mood by making a snide comment about her appearance. After the criticism, he gave Dallas a rare hug, slightly amelio-rating the damage. "I don't think I was an overly warm parent," Parcells concedes. "I think my kids knew that I loved them, but . . ."

His voice trails off.

Early in his Giants tenure, instead of heading home to spend time with his family, Parcells often decompressed by drinking beers at Manny's restaurant in Moonachie, New Jersey. He began feeling regretful on the mornings after, remembering his father's warning against alcoholism. So to de-stress, Parcells took to drinking more moderately.

During summer afternoons, he occasionally drove two hours from Giants headquarters to the Jersey Shore. He enjoyed sitting on a board-walk bench, watching the waves while still thinking football, sometimes dozing for a couple hours. He gave his staff the phone number at a nearby pay phone in case of an emergency. Parcells's appearances at the Jersey Shore during the NFL season surprised cops patrolling the boardwalk, who would often stop to talk. He ended up hiring one of them, Michael Murphy, for Giants security, based largely on an hour-long conversation.

Occasionally Parcells changed into his bathing suit and jumped into the Atlantic Ocean for a swim, bringing back fond memories of family outings as a child. Afterward, feeling rejuvenated, the Giants coach often returned to the Meadowlands, putting in a few more hours at work, instead of going home to spend time with his children. Like many of his players, Suzy, Dallas, and Jill feared incurring his wrath by saying or doing the wrong thing, so they gave Parcells his space while growing inured to his de-tachment. "It was uncomfortable being alone with him," Jill says, "because he didn't really know us that well. We just didn't have much to talk about."

Much of the time and energy Parcells spent with his children involved discipline or hounding them about their grades. Judy used her children's fear of her husband to get them back in line whenever they misbehaved. So in that way, at least, even when Parcells failed to show up, his presence still loomed large.

Nonetheless, he missed all of his daughters' college graduations. When Suzy obtained an Idaho State degree in 1984, her father used distance as the reason. But in 1988, he failed to attend Dallas's commencement at East Carolina University, a short flight from New Jersey. Only a few months after Big Blue captured the 1991 Super Bowl, Jill graduated from Gettysburg College, and although Parcells had announced his retirement weeks before the ceremonies in Pennsylvania, his track record prompted Jill's skepticism about his showing up. Parcells confirmed her low expecta-tions, in a decision she describes as "hurtful."

Suzy explains, "He had always stressed education. He drilled that into our heads forever. And then he didn't go to any of our college graduations."

With Judy's constant assurances, though, Parcells's children ultimately knew that he loved them. Asked if he had preferred to have a son, Parcells dismisses the notion. He stresses that all he ever wanted was healthy offspring. But Judy says, "I don't think he knew what to do with girls." She laughs.

John Lucas, who worked with Parcells in Dallas, had been an NBA head coach from 1992 to 1996 and from 2001 to 2003. Like Parcells, Lucas had mentored many of his players, a father-figure role that only increased after he retired to establish rehabilitation programs. A former drug addict, Lucas also gained renown as a professional life coach. In Parcells he saw a coach who was peerless in taking a paternal role with his players. When Parcells discovered that one of the Cowboys receivers was spread thin financially despite a multimillion-dollar salary, he got involved in a way more typical of a financial planner. The head coach designed a budget to drastically reduce the player's monthly expenses, which had totaled $36,000 because of payments for a new home and luxury cars.

"If somebody was having family trouble or money issues, he knew about it," says Lucas. "How he dealt with it was so different from most coaches. Bill had a gift. The curse involved sacrificing his own family relationships, but the blessing went to the hundreds of people he helped. It's so ironic. I would tell his daughters today, 'He was a father of the masses.'"

During the late 1990s, this irony was brought home to Suzy while she was watching a TV special about her father. After hearing a former NFL player describe Parcells's strong parental influence on him, she wept.

Former defensive end Leonard Marshall sums up the familiar sentiment. "In a way, Bill fathered dozens of Giants players, and a good number of us turned out to be pretty good eggs ourselves." Even former players who weren't Parcells Guys cite his influence beyond football. The ex–Patriots linebacker Chris Slade says, "When it's all said and done, people are going to look back and say, 'Parcells meant a lot to me, and I didn't even realize it until later on in life.' That's going to be his biggest legacy.

"He was a passionate guy. He cared about his players, and you learned probably more from Parcells than you learned from your father. I still sometimes hear his sayings in my head. I apply them to my everyday life, running my business, or even raising my children."

Suzy was twenty-seven when she gave birth to her first child, Kyle. As she raised him, memories of Parcells's neglect triggered anger. "A lot of stuff surfaced because of the way I parented my children," explains Suzy, whose daughter, Kendall, came later. "It made me realize how much I missed out on from my dad as a child."

Suzy waited until her late thirties to confront Parcells about the issue. When her father visited her home in Dillsburg, Pennsylvania, in 1999 as he and Judy were headed for divorce, Suzy felt compelled to scold him for his inattentiveness. He responded by conceding fault. "Yes, I know I should have done things differently. Yes, I know I wasn't the best father. I should have been there for you, and I wasn't. But I can't change that now."

In time Parcells had similar conversations with his other daughters, all of which proved cathartic. Dallas, who had her only child, Mia, in 2005 after several miscarriages, stresses that her relationship with Parcells has significantly improved during his NFL retirement.

Jill appreciates certain aspects of having grown up as the daughter of a famous NFL coach, perks like Giants season tickets and substantial help with purchasing an apartment in lower Manhattan. "In many ways we were fortunate as kids," she says, "especially me, because I was there during the good days. And my parents were very generous with us."

But Jill still envies the relationships some of her friends have with their fathers. She adds about Parcells, "He's done a lot of disappointing things, but he's my dad. You try to put them in the past."

After Parcells retired from the Cowboys, his daughters were among his first sleepover guests at Saratoga Springs during the summer. He also spent quality time with his grandchildren: taking Kyle, seventeen, golfing and Kendall, thirteen, to ride horses with D. Wayne Lukas at the barns. And, of course, they all watched the races from Parcells's box.

During one long conversation with Jill, Parcells put his extraordinary memory to good use. "How are your girlfriends Amy and Stephanie? How's Robin? How many kids does she have now?" The questions stunned his youngest daughter.

Jill explains, "I don't think my dad had ever asked me how my girlfriends were. I was so excited to find out that he cared about something other than my job, or how much money I had in the bank. He was getting personal, which he'd never really been before."

Parcells adds of his new, late-life approach, "I wish I had done more. I could have been more of a caring father. I didn't take enough time to get to know them. What's done is done. You can't go back. I just try to do what I can *now*, as best I can."

32

While enjoying retirement, Bill Parcells maintained his mentoring role, which extended beyond football. On July 17, 2007, Nets head coach Lawrence Frank visited him in Saratoga Springs. Frank had originally met Parcells as a student manager for Bobby Knight's Hoosiers. From 1989 to 1992, Frank chauffeured Parcells during the coach's visits each March to Bloomington while he was in the area for the Indianapolis combine. As a gesture of appreciation, Parcells gave Frank an open invitation to Giants training camp. The Indiana University student showed up one summer with his buddy and future NBA agent Andrew Miller. After graduating in 1992, Frank joined Marquette's basketball team as an assistant. His zeal helped spur his swift rise in the profession.

Frank earned the Nets' top job in 2004, and three years later he contacted Parcells, asking for time to discuss being a head coach. Parcells obliged with an invitation to Saratoga Springs, thrilling the thirty-six-year-old. Throughout the years Parcells had entertained similar requests from NBA coaches like John Calipari, Mike Fratello, and Jeff Van Gundy, and had given considerable time to disciples of his pal Bobby Knight.

At the get-together in Saratoga Springs, Frank impressed Parcells with his passion, a requirement for maintaining such access. Raised in Teaneck, New Jersey, Frank also connected with Parcells by affirming the timeless greatness of Bischoff's ice-cream parlor, located in his hometown. The Jersey-bred coaches smiled at each other knowingly as they described their favorite flavors.

The sit-down at a restaurant stretched for a few hours. Near the end of it, Parcells gave Frank permission to call anytime for more guidance, and volunteered to watch some Nets games to enhance his feedback. "He's one of the most generous people in sharing insight that I've ever met," says Frank, who decorated the Nets locker room with Parcells's sayings. "It's not like we go back a long way. That just shows you the generosity of the guy's spirit."

The rookie NBA head coach was joining the ranks of Parcells acolytes who regularly used him as a soundboard. The inquiries from NFL coaches spiked in late July, near the start of training camps. Perhaps the most frequent caller in the summer of 2007 was Todd Haley, who'd been hired as offensive coordinator of the Arizona Cardinals. Familiar voices included not just young disciples like Haley and Sean Payton but also veterans like Chiefs defensive coordinator Romeo Crennel and new Giants quarterbacks coach Chris Palmer. Personnel executives like Mike Tannenbaum also regularly dialed the NFL oracle.

Sean Payton made a special request, imploring Parcells to spend time at Saints training camp in Jackson, Mississippi, as an extra pair of eyes. Payton remembered that each Cowboys season, Parcells had recruited an outsider with a high football IQ to help evaluate the team's players. His close friend Ron Wolf, who had retired as Packers GM in 2001, had played the role multiple times. Parcells declined Payton's request in order to avoid slighting another disciple with much longer ties. Tom Coughlin had also sought his mentor's presence at Giants camp.

Todd Haley's switch from Dallas to the Cardinals' staff only added to the team's strong connections to Parcells. They included running-backs coach Maurice Carthon and offensive quality control assistant Dedric Ward, a former Jets and Cowboys wideout under Parcells. Even Cardinals head coach Ken Whisenhunt was indirectly linked to Parcells, having been Gang Green's special-teams coordinator under Al Groh in 2000. Sensitive about playing favorites, Parcells limited his help to telephone conversations and rare get-togethers in Saratoga Springs.

A major change in the NFL's media policy illustrated Parcells's influence. For most of his head-coaching career, Parcells had banned his assistants from speaking to reporters, seeking to mute self-promotion and eliminate contradictory public viewpoints. Sean Payton, who would coach for three years in Dallas virtually without being quoted, was the latest acolyte to follow suit with his own team. Greg Aiello, the NFL's public relations chief, concluded that too many head coaches had instituted Parcells's approach, creating an access problem around the league. So to enter the 2007 season, the NFL required media availability of assistant coaches at least once per week.

Not interested in full-time employment, Parcells declined an opportunity to be a color commentator for *Monday Night Football*, whose rights ESPN had acquired in 2006. The network had wanted to pair Bill Parcells with Tony Kornheiser, the *Washington Post* columnist in his second year on the job. Parcells sated his football appetite, and earned $1.5 million, by returning to ESPN as a part-time analyst. The network chauffeured him from upstate New York to Bristol, Connecticut, on Saturday morning, then back on Monday night. He starred on *Sunday NFL Countdown* and *Monday Night Countdown,* and his segments, including "Ten Quarterback Commandments," earned kudos.

At Saratoga Springs, Parcells repeatedly expressed his satisfaction to Kelly Mandart with having escaped the stresses of being an NFL head coach. He loved spending time outdoors at the racetrack or focusing on his golf game. But by November 2007 the Saratoga meet had long since been over, and cold weather limited his opportunities on the links. Less than a year after abandoning the sidelines, Parcells was turning into a restless homebody.

Despite regularly affirming his decision to quit coaching, Parcells had not mentioned one lingering desire: he was still passionate about constructing an NFL team, not as a coach, but as an executive. Parcells disclosed the feeling to Joe O'Donnell, one of the few people with whom he shared such inner thoughts. Since having met in 1994 through Will McDonough, O'Donnell and Parcells had grown close. During the criticism of Parcells in New England after his departure, O'Donnell forcefully defended him. And when O'Donnell's attempt to purchase the Red Sox in 2002 fell short, Parcells stopped rooting for the baseball team that had been his favorite since childhood.

On hearing Parcells's private thoughts, the high-powered concessionaire who shunned the media spotlight made a second attempt at playing matchmaker. In late November, O'Donnell traveled to Florida for a business meeting with Wayne Huizenga. After the stadium food powwow ended, conversation turned to Huizenga's 0-11 Dolphins, a source of embarrassment for him. Already out the playoffs for the sixth consecutive year, Miami was flirting with NFL ignominy by threatening to finish the regular season without a victory.

Huizenga revealed his intention to make drastic changes in 2008, implying that they would include dismissal of head coach Cam Cameron and GM Randy Mueller. O'Donnell pounced. "Who are you going to hire? What's your thinking? You know, Bill Parcells is ready to go back into football."

The news surprised Huizenga. "Well, that's very interesting."

Huizenga expressed regret that he had decided not to pursue Parcells in early 2003. The Cowboys were now leading the NFC East under Wade Phillips, headed toward a 13-3 mark, and Huizenga noted that before retiring Parcells had helped to provide Jerry Jones with a championship-caliber team. Nonetheless, the Dolphins boss voiced skepticism about Parcells agreeing to join his organization.

"I doubt he'll come here. He's always retiring and unretiring. And I've got to move on this."

O'Donnell replied, "If you're serious, you should talk to him. If it doesn't happen, you've lost nothing."

Wayne Huizenga owned a golf club in Palm City with only two members: him and his wife, Marti. On three hundred acres of lush greenery, the Floridian Golf & Yacht Club consisted of four guest cottages, two helicopter pads, a marina, and a clubhouse. Huizenga extended honorary memberships, at no charge, to close friends like O'Donnell, relatives, and associates. High-profile honorees included actor Michael Douglas, actress Catherine Zeta-Jones, and businessman Jack Welch.

In early 2001, O'Donnell had introduced Parcells to Huizenga after bringing the former Jets boss to the eighteen-hole course as a guest. Within weeks the Dolphins owner sent Parcells an invitation letter conferring an honorary membership. The privilege required annual renewal via the letter, which Parcells kept receiving. "So I must not have driven into the flowers," he jokes, "or anything like that." Occasionally, Parcells took friends, or his grandson, Kyle. Through infrequent and casual encounters at the club, Parcells and Huizenga became friendly.

"My impression of Bill Parcells had been that he was a hard-ass coach, boisterous, loud, pounding on everybody all the time to make things happen," says Huizenga. "But when I met him, he was different. He was nice, quiet, soft-spoken. I guess that's the old saying: 'Speak softly and carry a big stick.' You expect the big guy to be a bear, roaring all the time."

During the six years that the bearish ex-coach and the Dolphins owner interacted at the Floridian, their conversations were virtually sports-free. The exception took place soon after Miami acquired quarterback Daunte Culpepper over Drew Brees. Curious about the Dolphins' decision, Parcells asked Huizenga about the organization's medical evaluation of Brees.

Wayne Huizenga and Bill Parcells had never spoken on the phone until the owner called on December 5, 2007. Huizenga got straight to the point. "Hey, Bill, we're going to get rid of a lot of coaches here. We're going to create a different mind-set. Joe said that that's something that would interest you."

Parcells replied, "I'm kind of burned out from coaching. I'd rather do something more on the acquisition-and-development side. I'm getting too old for the coaching stuff."

"Well, how about if I fly out and come see you?"

"Fine."

In anticipation of Huizenga's visit, Parcells spent a few hours analyzing the Dolphins. He researched their roster, salary-cap situation, and draft positioning. Surprised at the depth of Miami's problems, Parcells described the team as being like a "dog's lunch." He added, "It's a mess. You ever see a dog eating lunch? Shit slopped all over the bowl and out on the floor? That's what it is."

Parcells viewed the likelihood that the Dolphins would receive the top overall pick for the 2008 draft as a double-edged sword, "because if you make a mistake, you can hinder the team for five more years." Despite management's having allocated an inordinate amount of cap space to the defense, the unit was one of the NFL's worst. And in a league increasingly reliant on passers, Miami lacked a franchise quarterback. Nonetheless, Parcells felt intrigued by the challenge.

One appealing aspect of the job was that it wouldn't require regular appearances at the stadium. He viewed the Dolphins as his final chance at a unique position in the NFL before permanent retirement. Acknowledging that he was an acquired taste—"I'm not for everybody," he says—Parcells felt compatible with Huizenga. "For all his success in business, Wayne is very down-to-earth," Parcells says. "He's one of the guys. He's also a good listener. I like to talk to him because his viewpoints are interesting. He's been around the block and accomplished a lot, but he's a very common-sense guy. I like guys like that."

Parcells had learned some hard lessons about ownership changes, so he intended to seek a contractual contingency clause to protect him should Huizenga sell the team or die. If negotiations fell through, Parcells had a backup plan: accepting a proposal to star as a judge in a reality TV show, beginning in 2008, about obscure football players training to make an NFL roster. If things worked out, Parcells intended to court his close friend Dan Henning, whose football IQ he had long respected, for a senior management position. The sixty-five-year-old was available, retired after being dismissed as the Panthers' offensive coordinator earlier in the year.

First, though, on December 8, Parcells telephoned Jeff Ireland. "I want to ask you a hypothetical question. What if I go somewhere and I offer you a general manager's job?"

Ireland replied gleefully, "I'm in."

"It might be Calgary."

"I'm in!"

Parcells loved the response, and instructed Ireland to keep the possibility secret, even from his wife. "If you tell Rachel, I'll kill you. When it comes to secrets, one and one makes eleven."

The next morning, Parcells tipped off Mandart. "Kelly, you might have to start looking for a house in Florida."

Mandart replied, "What are you talking about? Here we go again, Bill."

The first four months of 2008 could be demanding and intensive, Parcells told her, while he started putting a structure in place and prepared for the draft. However, Parcells emphasized that during the regular season his hours would be reasonable compared to his coaching days. He expected to be home each day by 7 p.m., and by skipping team travel, he'd be around on weekends, too.

Kelly Mandart was up for the new endeavor so long as her relationship with Bill Parcells progressed toward marriage and offspring. The subject had caused tension because of Parcells's reluctance to father children at his age. Meantime, Parcells insisted that Mandart not tell anyone, even relatives, about the Dolphins possibility. She recalls, "He tells me, 'Don't even tell your mother.' I said, 'Don't you tell me what I can and cannot tell my mother.'"

One week later, Parcells's agent Jimmy Sexton received a call from the Atlanta Falcons inquiring about his client's services. Their head coach Bobby Petrino had quit with three games left, one day after quarterback Michael Vick received a twenty-three-month sentence for involvement in a dog-fighting ring. The feeler surprised Parcells mainly because he had no ties to owner Arthur Blank. However, with the Falcons headed to a 4-12 finish, Blank had done extensive homework on Parcells, including consulting Jerry Jones.

Parcells updated his girlfriend on the latest employment possibility, adding, "But I'm not doing anything that you don't want me to do." Mandart was not quite buying it. She knew that Parcells, the quintessential control freak, added the caveat to deflect pressure, or to charm her.

Mandart replied, "Well, if it's something you really want to do—"

Parcells interrupted. "Well, I don't want to coach."

"You say that now, but are you going to be able to stay in the background when you don't like what the coach is doing?"

"Yeah, I think so."

"It's so nice that these people still want you, and that now they're even fighting over you."

Parcells beamed. "Yeah, it is."

Mandart recalls the exchange. "He's human, and he has insecurities. He definitely likes to be liked, and wants to be wanted."

On Tuesday, December 11, Wayne Huizenga flew to Albany on his private Boeing 737, which Parcells likened to a "luxury hotel." Then the

Dolphins owner drove to Saratoga Springs for lunch at Parcells's favorite restaurant: the West Side Stadium Cafe. When he was informed of the meeting, Sexton admonished his client for arranging it at a public place. At least the billionaire owner, sixty-nine, looked inconspicuous in a zip-up jacket and khakis, and the resident coaching legend, sixty-six, wore a sweater and corduroys.

Most of the two-hour talk covered Parcells's past football stints. Parcells expanded on the reasons he no longer wanted to coach. When Huizenga suggested that Parcells become Dolphins GM, the ex-coach declined. Huizenga wanted to know what aspects of football still excited Parcells after such a lengthy career, and Parcells quickly responded that it was building a team, specifically the talent-acquisition area. Huizenga said, "Well, how about being head of our football operations, not as a general manager or as coach. Both of them would report to you."

Parcells replied, "Well, that's interesting."

"We'll make you executive vice president of football operations. The only thing you're not in charge of is suites and ticket sales."

Parcells laughed. "I'd like to do something like that."

The Dolphins owner suggested a three-year deal, but a potential hurdle entered the equation when Huizenga revealed that he was considering selling part of the team for estate reasons: his death before a sale would cost his family, including his four children, an estimated $450 million in estate taxes.

While understanding the importance of such a consideration, Parcells voiced concerns about working under a new owner. Huizenga insisted that even with a partial sale he would maintain control of the team, shielding Parcells from any interference. NFL rules required at least one owner to hold a majority stake in the franchise for ultimate authority.

Satisfied with the assurances, Parcells told Huizenga that he would make an official decision on Tuesday, December 18. The meeting ended with both men optimistic about a future together. However, just two days after the lunch meeting, a real-estate mogul based in New York who'd grown up in South Florida stunned Huizenga with a gigantic offer to buy the entire club. The proposal came from Stephen Ross, chief executive officer of the Related Group, who had been among the finalists for the Jets after Leon Hess's death in 1999. Ross offered Huizenga more than $1 billion, whereas Huizenga had paid $138 million for the Dolphins in 1994 after having acquired the home arena from the heirs of owner Joe Robbie. Ross's heady offer complicated Huizenga's discussions with Parcells.

Parcells recalls, "So I get to thinking, 'Well, I'm not going there if he sells this team.' But deep down, that's where I wanted to go: Miami. I knew Wayne already; I didn't know Blank. And I had a place down in South Florida."

On December 13, Arthur Blank telephoned Parcells to discuss a position with the Falcons. When Parcells conveyed his lack of interest in coaching or becoming a traditional GM, Blank made a proposal similar to Huizenga's: sign as Atlanta's vice president of football operations. Near the end of the phone call, Parcells revealed his recent sit-down with Huizenga, prompting Blank to insist on a face-to-face meeting the next day. With Parcells's blessings, Blank traveled to Saratoga Springs on December 14.

Parcells met with Blank for several hours at the West Side Stadium Cafe, and once again Parcells focused on obtaining a role that would empower him to hire a GM and head coach. Once Blank accepted the parameters, Parcells revealed his December 18 deadline, only five days away, to decide on which job to take. After a December 17 appearance on *Monday Night Countdown*, Parcells left Bristol, Connecticut, with Jimmy Sexton. Given the impending deadline, Sexton planned to sleep at his client's home; their attorney was flying overnight from Memphis to vet any contract offer. During the ride, Parcells telephoned O'Donnell to find out the latest information on the Dolphins.

"Joe, what the hell is going on here? Is Wayne selling this team?"

O'Donnell responded that unfortunately the situation had turned fluid.

Early the next morning—deadline day—Parcells telephoned Huizenga to seek confirmation about reports of an imminent sale. The owner conceded that circumstances had changed because of Ross's aggressive bid for the entire club. Parcells asked, "So they may make you an offer you can't refuse? And you might take it?"

Huizenga replied, "Yeah, that might happen. But I'll know by tomorrow at eleven o'clock."

"Well, you understand that I have to do what I have to do, too."

"Well, I'm hoping you can hold off until tomorrow."

After hanging up with Huizenga, Parcells telephoned Blank to talk further about joining the Falcons. Key aspects of a potential agreement needed clarification, including finding a new role for GM Rich McKay. Parcells told Blank, "Look, I'm still not one hundred percent sure, but what we talked about last Friday sounds pretty good."

Blank pounced. "I want to fly up there tomorrow, and bring my attorney."

"You don't have to do that."

"No, I want to do it."

"Okay."

That night, Blank e-mailed Parcells a boilerplate contract covering four years, one year longer than Huizenga's proposal. Meanwhile, the *New York Daily News* and ESPN.com posted articles quoting Parcells on the likelihood of his joining Atlanta. Parcells publicly revealed that he would be meeting Blank the next day, December 19, to iron out details on a contract.

Wednesday morning at around 10 a.m., Blank phoned Parcells to say that his private plane had landed in Albany; the owner and his attorney would be at the house in about thirty minutes. After hanging up, Parcells called Huizenga.

"Lookit, Blank is on the way."

Huizenga responded, "Can you hold him off? I'm going to know about a sale shortly."

Parcells replied, "I can't stop the guy from coming. This is a free country. He's en route; he's on the ground. He's told me, 'I'll be there in a half hour.'"

Huizenga promised to call Parcells by 11 a.m.

Uncertainty about Huizenga's situation made everyone in Parcells's household jittery. The group hoped that Huizenga would telephone shortly with news that the sale had collapsed. Parcells wanted to buy time, so he decided to temporarily leave the premises with Sexton and his attorney. He instructed Mandart to stick around for Blank.

"If Arthur comes, tell him we'll be right back—that I just took Jimmy for a tour of the town."

The threesome left in Parcells's black Cadillac at 10:15 a.m. Almost forty-five minutes later a black SUV with Arthur Blank in the front passenger seat pulled into Parcells's driveway. Stepping out of the car in a brown leather jacket, Blank held a paper shopping bag. When he rang the doorbell with his attorney, Kelly Mandart greeted them. She explained that Parcells was giving Sexton, on his first trip to Saratoga, a tour of downtown, and that they would return within a few minutes.

Blank reached into the shopping bag and removed three packages, gift-wrapped in white paper.

"My wife and I went shopping for you last night. We wanted to get you some books on Atlanta so you can learn about the city."

Mandart replied, "Oh, thank you. That was so nice. And please thank your wife for me."

Parcells and company returned shortly after eleven. After everyone exchanged introductions and handshakes, Kelly told Parcells, "Arthur and his wife bought some books for me to familiarize myself with Atlanta."

Parcells replied, "Oh. That was nice."

A few minutes later, Parcells cornered Mandart within earshot of Sexton. Handing his cell phone to her, he whispered, "If you see area code 954, answer it. It'll be Wayne. Don't call me out of the meeting; that's disrespectful. Just tell Jimmy the phone's for him."

For a meeting place, Mandart suggested the dining room, which contained a cherrywood table, Oriental rug, and chandelier. As the men left the kitchen, Jimmy Sexton stayed behind momentarily. After taking a deep breath, he told Mandart, "I can't believe Huizenga didn't call. I can't believe Blank is here." Sexton laughed nervously while shaking his head, then headed off to the dining room.

Every few minutes Parcells's cell phone or the home line rang, interrupting Mandart's attempt to make everybody lunch. In a Seinfeldesque scene, Mandart hustled to check the ID for each call. Not seeing the pertinent area code, she went back to tossing salad, chopping vegetables, and grilling chicken. Occasionally both phones rang at the same time, as reporters on friendly terms with Parcells tried to get the scoop. Mandart had lowered the ring volumes, so Blank and his attorney were oblivious to the calling frenzy.

Exploiting one moment of phone silence while taking the risk of missing a call, Mandart hustled into the dining room with a platter of chicken Caesar salad, sliced peppers and cucumbers, and dill dip. Parcells was at the head of the table; Sexton and his lawyer sat to Parcells's right, Blank and his attorney to Parcells's left. Just five minutes into negotiations, Sexton expressed qualms about language in the contract involving game tickets and access to a company car.

Around the same time, Wayne Huizenga telephoned Joe O'Donnell.

"Well, great try, old friend. I appreciate your effort, but I've lost Parcells."

O'Donnell was surprised. "How's that? He wants to go to Miami. He likes you."

"We couldn't get in touch with each other. And he's signing with Arthur Blank."

"What are you talking about?"

"Blank is meeting with him today to sign a contract."

"Why don't you just call Bill and talk to him?"

"I tried. I can't get through. And he hasn't called me back."

"I've got his girlfriend's number. Let me call."

Mandart answered her cell phone.

"Kelly, where's Bill?"

She whispered, "He's in the dining room with Mr. Blank."

In an urgent tone, O'Donnell asked, "Jesus, what's he doing?"

"I think they're about to sign a contract."

O'Donnell implored, "Kelly, get Bill out of there!"

She put the concessionaire on hold, entered the dining room, and told Sexton that she had an important call for him. Reading the situation, Parcells's agent excused himself, took the phone, and stepped out onto the back porch, ignoring the chilly weather to avoid being overheard. With Sexton out of the room, Blank asked Parcells for permission to use his home office to discuss the initial contractual issue with the team attorney. Parcells walked the pair to the room, and shut the door to give the Atlanta duo privacy.

Meanwhile, O'Donnell spoke on the phone with Sexton. "Look, Wayne is waiting with a pen in his hand. Miami's where Bill wants to go. So get him out of that damn meeting."

Sexton replied, "Shit, I'll see what I can do." After hanging up, he stepped back in the house and said to Mandart, who was standing at the entrance of the back porch, "This is something. Huizenga's not selling the team. And he wants Bill."

Mandart replied, "Oh, thank God." But quickly realizing the dilemma, she added, "Oh, no. What are we going to do?"

Sexton, smiling tensely, said, "I don't know. It's going to get interesting. I have the prize bull at the county fair, and two billionaires are fighting over him."

Blank's closed-door conference gave Sexton the opportunity to brief Parcells, and to allow the prize bull to walk up to his master bedroom and call Huizenga. "Look, Wayne, this guy's here right now. He's getting ready to close the deal."

Huizenga responded, "Send him home! I'm not selling the team. Send him home! I'm keeping the team. You've got my word." The owner added that he might still sell part of the club, but no more than 49 percent. Even in that scenario, Huizenga stressed that he would remain general managing partner with ultimate authority.

Parcells replied, "If you're not the owner, I'm not sure how this is going to go, based on past experience."

Huizenga countered, "We'll just add a clause giving you a thirty-day window to leave with full pay if I sell. If you don't want to stay, you won't have to." Huizenga's lack of hesitation and the golden parachute were convincing.

Parcells told Huizenga, "I have to call you back, Wayne. Give me until three o'clock." After hanging up, Parcells took a deep breath.

Kelly told him, "We need to get Blank out of the house. This is too much."

Sexton advised candor, so Parcells walked to his home office and asked to speak with Blank privately. As the Falcons attorney returned to the dining room, Parcells said to the team owner, "Something's happened here. The Dolphins aren't going to sell. I just need a little time to think about things. So please just take a little ride or go to lunch. I need an hour and a half to myself. When you come back, we'll get this all straightened out one way or another."

Blank replied, "Good. I'm going to go and have lunch." The assertion contradicted his worried look. After getting a restaurant recommendation from Mandart, Blank left the house around 12:30 p.m.

Weighing his decision with Sexton and Mandart, Parcells said he felt the contractual issue at the start of negotiations with Blank was ominous. He also disagreed with the owner's philosophy of making Atlanta's black fan base a factor in football decisions. African-Americans constituted more than half the metropolitan area's population of five million, leading to the NFL's largest such base. However, the main reason for Parcells's inclination to join Miami was his relationship with Huizenga.

Sexton asked Parcells, "What do you want to do?"

Parcells replied firmly, "I want to go to Miami."

With the decision made, Parcells and company finally got a chance to have lunch at roughly 12:45 p.m. After a few minutes, Parcells left the group to phone Huizenga and confirm things. The Dolphins owner promised to sweeten his proposal by matching Atlanta's four-year contract. "Here's the deal if you want it. We'll work everything else out."

Parcells said, "Wayne, I'm going to put my faith in you that we've got a deal."

"Yep, we do. You got any other important questions? Let's answer 'em right now."

Parcells inquired about a company car, an early sticking point with Blank.

Huizenga replied, "You know, we're not in the car business, but we'll work that out."

Parcells said, "Okay, we've got a deal. Don't announce it. I've got to tell this guy that I'm going to go to Miami."

By 2:10 p.m., Blank and his lawyer still hadn't returned, increasing the tension in the house. Mandart wondered aloud whether the Falcons owner had decided to get on his plane. "Oh God, I can't take any more tension." As if on cue, Blank rang the doorbell. Parcells answered it, then led Arthur Blank to his home office for a private talk. Without delay, Parcells revealed that he had decided to join the Dolphins.

Blank responded, "I'm disappointed. I thought we had a deal."

Parcells countered, "You know that we really didn't have a *deal*. I just think it's probably better if I go to Miami. I told you maybe you shouldn't come up today, but you insisted, and I didn't want to stop you. I really had a genuine interest in your team. I wish you luck, and I hope it goes well for you."

Blank's face twisted in anger as he turned around to leave the room. Bumping into his attorney in the hallway, Blank snapped, "Let's go." Surprised, the lawyer responded, "Oh, okay."

Blank headed to the closet to get his jacket, trailed by his attorney. Opening the front door for them, Mandart said, "It was nice meeting you. Sorry things didn't work out."

Blank replied, "Yeah."

Holding the paper bag containing Blank's gift, Mandart asked, "Would you like your books back?"

In a polite tone, Blank responded, "No, you just keep them."

"Okay, thank you."

As Blank entered his SUV, a sense of relief spread throughout the house. Sexton exhaled, saying to Parcells and company, "That's it. I'm done with this kind of stuff." A few hours later, Arthur Blank issued a public statement declaring that Parcells had broken an agreement in principle and instead signed a revised contract with the Dolphins. Blank's stance angered Parcells, and made him feel that he'd made the right decision.

33

Stephen Ross and Joe O'Donnell first met in 2002 at a Massachusetts gubernatorial fund-raiser for the foodie's pal Mitt Romney. Stephen's uncle, Max Fisher, an oil magnate and philanthropist known as "the dean of Jewish Republicans," had heavily supported the political career of George Romney, Mitt's father. And Mitt briefly dated Fisher's daughter Mary when they attended a top boarding school in the Detroit area, Cranbrook, which also served as the Lions' training camp site until 1963. Mitt was named after his cousin Milt, who had played quarterback for George Halas's Bears during the 1920s.

After an introduction through Mitt Romney, Stephen Ross and Joe O'Donnell stayed in touch and developed a friendship. O'Donnell's business partner, mall developer Steve Karp, entered several real-estate deals with Ross. Karp and O'Donnell were perennially on *Boston Magazine*'s annual list of the city's fifty wealthiest and most powerful residents. More than once the publication named O'Donnell the city's most powerful person, with friends like President George W. Bush, whom he occasionally visited at the White House. Through business deals, fund-raisers, and social events, O'Donnell got to know Ross almost as well as the food mogul knew Wayne Huizenga.

On January 3, 2008, Bill Parcells named Jeff Ireland the Miami Dolphins' new GM, replacing Randy Mueller. Within two weeks, as expected, the pair announced that Tony Sparano, forty-six, would be the team's new head coach, choosing him over a handful of candidates to replace Cam Cameron. Chiefs offensive coordinator Todd Haley and running-backs coach Maurice Carthon were angry at their mentor, deeming the interview process a sham. Despite the bruised feelings, Parcells, with Ireland's official blessings as GM, saw Sparano as the best fit. Interviewees like Baltimore's defensive coordinator Rex Ryan and Minnesota's defensive coordinator Leslie Frazier had also impressed Parcells, but Sparano was a known quantity, having coached four seasons under Parcells. He was also being considered for head-coaching openings in Atlanta and Baltimore.

Parcells's NFL tentacles sometimes caused him to face complicated or contradictory feelings. The 2008 Super Bowl pitted Bill Belichick's undefeated Patriots versus Tom Coughlin's Cinderella-like Giants, and before the February 3 showdown, Parcells was asked which team he favored. The new Dolphins chief was vague, alluding to his daughter Dallas and son-in-law Scott Pioli. "Would you root against your own family?" But by the opening kickoff, Parcells expressed neutrality to his girlfriend because of his deep connections to the Giants. Parcells enjoyed seeing Tom Coughlin reach the big game after he'd withstood heavy criticism and demands for his ouster. Parcells said before the Super Bowl, "That bandwagon has got to get some more tires on it. It's collapsing."

Parcells and Mandart watched the showdown at the Jupiter condominium. When New England pulled ahead, 14–10, in the back-and-forth contest, Parcells's demeanor remained even. He grew excited when the heavy-underdog Giants charged back, and smiled at Eli Manning's late touchdown in the 17–14 thriller. It marked Big Blue's first Super Bowl triumph by a head coach not named Bill Parcells.

Starting in February, Wayne Huizenga visited Parcells at Dolphins headquarters at least once per week, arriving around 3 p.m. The main topics of discussion involved players the club intended to release, free-agent possibilities, and the upcoming draft. Huizenga showed more inquisitiveness about football specifics than Leon Hess had done with the Jets, but he lacked Jerry Jones's proactivity. The happy medium pleased Parcells, confirming his decision to join Miami. Because of the executive vice president's curiosity about the Dolphins owner, their conversations sometimes extended into Huizenga's other business endeavors. Parcells enjoyed getting financial pointers from his boss, and looked forward to a long, fruitful relationship.

While Sparano started assembling a Cowboys-heavy staff, Stephen Ross reignited talks with the Dolphins, conveying his desire to buy a significant stake, if not the entire franchise. *Forbes*'s list of richest Americans ranked Ross at 68th with $4.5 billion, and Huizenga at 165th with $2.5 billion. Again Huizenga expressed willingness to sell no more than 49 percent of his franchise, but the real-estate mogul insisted on buying half immediately and getting an option to purchase up to 95 percent within several years. Huizenga warmed to the idea, as long as he retained ultimate control. Ahead of an agreement in principle, Huizenga and Ross discussed Parcells's new role at length.

Joe O'Donnell had been friends with Huizenga for more than two decades. And on the issue of selling half the team, the Dolphins owner valued his opinion, especially given his closeness to Parcells. After having been the matchmaker for Parcells and Miami, O'Donnell quietly switched gears to acting as a facilitator between Huizenga and Ross, who also leaned on the concessionaire's insight. O'Donnell recalls, "Huizenga called me and said: 'What do you think about Ross?' I said, 'I like Ross.' Then Ross called me. He said, 'What do you think about Huizenga?' I said, 'I like Huizenga.' And in the middle of it all is the Tuna."

Huizenga agreed to sell Ross virtually 50 percent of the team plus its stadium for $550 million. The deal projected the value of the Dolphins at $1.1 billion, the highest amount ever paid for an NFL franchise; the previous year *Forbes* had deemed the team worth $942 million. Just as important, Huizenga gave Ross no less than four years to increase his stake to 95 percent and become managing general partner—and Parcells's boss.

On Friday morning, February 22, 2008, a few hours before a press conference to announce the deal, Huizenga walked into Parcells's office at Dolphins headquarters in Davie, Florida. "I just sold half the team. I sold it to that guy, Stephen Ross, from New York. I may sell him some more at some point. I just had to do this." Due to contingencies in the deal, Huizenga couldn't provide a precise timetable on relinquishing control to Ross. Early 2010 was the soonest Huizenga envisioned Ross increasing his stake. Huizenga seemed reluctant to cede control, and Parcells was pleased to hear the seventy-year-old convey his intention to own part of the team until his death.

At the press conference, Huizenga said, "My heart does not want me to do this, but my head tells me it's the right thing to do." Despite the uncertain situation, Parcells assumed that it would be a few years before Ross took over as managing general partner. In the worst-case scenario of an incompatible new owner, Parcells intended to exercise his contractual right to leave with full pay. Ross, who had attended Dolphins games while a student at Miami Beach High, told reporters, "You can't help but respect the track record of Bill Parcells." Minutes later he cracked, "Other than playing quarterback, I don't see myself as a hands-on owner."

Within the next few days Parcells made several phone calls to gather intelligence on Wayne Huizenga's heir apparent. He heard generally good things from contacts in Florida and New York, who described the real-estate billionaire as being a good person who excelled in his sphere. Parcells especially valued O'Donnell's take. The concessionaire told Parcells, "He's a tremendous guy; he's generous. He's like Wayne in that he's kept all his old friends, but he's more of an extrovert. He loves life. He's sixty-seven, a little younger than Wayne, and he lives with gusto."

Two weeks after the press conference, Huizenga brought Ross to Parcells's office for an introduction. The executive vice president used his break-the-ice line to new owners: "Football isn't for well-adjusted people."

To which Ross responded, "I'll fit in great, then." The cordial ten-minute conversation ended with Parcells saying, "Hey, I like what I'm doing. I'm comfortable here. Don't worry about me leaving."

Parcells considered his role in Miami to be similar to the one he had held with the Jets in 2000 after quitting as their head coach. The main difference was the need to start over in several areas while revamping the football department to his specifications. "We had a new owner with the Jets," Parcells says, referring to Woody Johnson, "but I was familiar with all the people in the organization. A lot of things were in place."

One of the key scouts for the Dolphins, Chris Grier, had been a Patriots intern in 1994, when Parcells was head coach. Chris's father, Bobby Grier, had recommended drafting Terry Glenn in the 1996 draft, exacerbating Parcells's differences with Robert Kraft. But Parcells considered the matter old news, and kept Chris in the new regime. The Dolphins also hired Brian Gaine, who'd scouted for Ireland and Parcells in Dallas and for two seasons with Parcells's Jets.

As the new Dolphins GM, Jeff Ireland officially controlled personnel decisions, and Parcells underscored the authority of the ex–Cowboys scout. However, Parcells's unique position gave him ultimate power because he controlled the purse strings. All expenditures required approval by the executive vice president of football operations, so Parcells could block any ostensibly bad ideas by his GM or head coach, and, of course, terminate their employment. Weeks after joining the Dolphins, Parcells said, "If they fail, then I get rid of their asses, and we get somebody else, just like they'd get rid of me when I was doing it." Nevertheless, Parcells saw the triumvirate as being on the same wavelength.

By mid-January, Ireland and Parcells started watching film together of impending free agents. During one session on a Bills defensive player, Parcells asked Ireland, "What am I thinking about doing with this guy?"

Ireland responded quickly, "You're thinking of turning him into an offensive player." Parcells nodded, pleased at his GM's telepathic reply.

Since both Jeff Ireland and Tony Sparano were rookies in their high-pressure positions, Parcells encouraged them to lean on his expertise whenever they desired. His long-term goal was to put a new structure in place while using his personnel philosophy to revitalize the franchise. Parcells intended to gradually loosen oversight and retire, once he saw Ireland and Sparano taking Miami in the right direction. For the time being, Parcells cast himself as more of a guidance counselor than a micromanager. Parcells told Sparano, "Tony, I'm not looking over your shoulder. You take this staff, and you put it together."

In one example of Sparano's independence, the rookie head coach hired at least two assistants who Parcells felt were far from being ideal candidates. Still, Sparano chose to heed Parcells's recommendation to make Dan Henning his offensive coordinator.

The football executive had hired one assistant before Sparano came on board: Ole Miss offensive coordinator David Lee as quarterbacks coach. The move showed Parcells's ongoing respect for the ex–Vanderbilt signal caller, whose diligent work with Tony Romo had helped propel the gunslinger into stardom. Nonetheless, one thing Lee had done more than three decades earlier still bothered Parcells. After offering Lee the Dolphins gig, Parcells asked him in an irritated tone, "Why'd you get married the week before the Peach Bowl, anyway?"

Lee laughed. Seeing that Parcells was serious, however, he replied, "Well, Coach, we had the wedding planned for six months. Vanderbilt never went to bowl games."

Early on, Bill Parcells delivered an introductory address to Dolphins players in the team's auditorium. Among other comments meant to convey a new culture, he told the gathering, "I don't want any punks. I don't want any troublemakers." Hearing those words, tailback Ricky Williams fully expected to be traded or released, a sentiment shared by many pundits and fans. The promising NFL career of the 1999 Heisman Trophy winner and fifth overall pick that year had been controversial, his career marred by multiple suspensions for marijuana use.

Two hours after Parcells's inaugural speech, Ricky Williams got word that Bill Parcells wanted to see him, reinforcing the runner's concerns. When Williams walked into Parcells's office, the new boss opened the conversation without any pleasantries. "Do you feel trapped here? Are you just playing because you've got to play? Because you don't have enough money? Tell me if you feel trapped here."

Williams replied, "No, no. I don't feel trapped, Coach. I play football because I like playing."

Parcells's response startled the runner. "Ricky, you can bounce back and do great things. God gave you the talent. If you're not a lazy-ass, you can surprise everybody. Now, you can't recoup all your abilities because you blew some of your best years, but you can thrive here." Williams, who'd been diagnosed with social-anxiety disorder, felt inspired by the new regime's desire to make him a key player. And despite the former Longhorn's reputation as enigmatic, Parcells found him to be "stone-cold honest."

In one of the NFL's most infamous trades, Mike Ditka had relinquished all of New Orleans's draft picks in 1999, plus first- and third-round choices in 2000, to Washington for the opportunity to select Ricky Williams. The athletic introvert experienced only modest success with the Saints, however, before being dealt to the Dolphins on March 8, 2002, for three draft choices, including two first-rounders. Williams then began to live up to his billing, leading the NFL with 1,853 rushing yards and scoring 16 touchdowns as Dave Wannstedt's team went 9-7. He followed up with another strong season, with 1,372 rushing yards as Miami improved by one game.

But in 2004, Williams faced a four-game suspension plus a $650,000 fine when a drug test revealed marijuana in his system. Just two days before the start of training camp, the twenty-seven-year-old announced his retirement. After the abrupt departure of their best player, the Dolphins started 1-8, prompting Wannstedt's dismissal. They finished with their first losing season since 1988, earning only four victories. Williams returned to the Dolphins a year later, and apologized to teammates before completing his suspension for drug use.

In February 2006, though, the NFL banned Williams for the entire season for violating its drug policy a fourth time. He turned to the CFL, playing that year for the Toronto Argonauts while the Dolphins retained his NFL rights. Then Williams failed another drug test just before the 2007 season, imperiling his NFL career. He won reinstatement from commissioner Roger Goodell in October of that year, but in his November 26 debut at Pittsburgh, Williams suffered a season-ending injury to his right shoulder, just days before Wayne Huizenga showed an interest in Bill Parcells.

Given that six years had passed since Williams's masterful season in 2002, his value was questionable, but Parcells considered the five-ten, 230-pounder a better pure runner than the talented Ronnie Brown because of his sledgehammer, north–south style. And Tony Sparano felt that the smashmouth offense he planned on would benefit from having both tailbacks.

Lawrence Taylor lived in Pembroke Pines, Florida, less than ten miles away from the Dolphins complex, so when the team's voluntary workouts commenced in March, Parcells asked L.T. to make an appearance in the team's weight room. "Just cruise in there for a minute. Then I'll let you go. You don't have to say anything or do anything. Just let 'em see what somebody like you looks like."

Dolphins players were exercising and chatting in the weight room one afternoon when Parcells entered with L.T. Even at age forty-nine, the former superstar appeared to be near his playing weight of 240, belying the sprinkles of gray in his facial hair. As Bill Parcells and Lawrence Taylor scanned the room, the Dolphins players seemed to increase the intensity of their workout.

L.T. whispered to Parcells, "We got any real players in here?"

Parcells replied, "I'm not sure."

"Well, we better get some."

Taylor's choice of pronoun delighted his former coach. Parcells recalls, "He said '*we.*' He was already in there with me."

The two Giants icons spent a few minutes interacting with the Dolphins players. Linebacker Jason Taylor, the only player from the 1-15 team to make the Pro Bowl, was conspicuously absent from the voluntary session, angering Parcells. The thirty-three-year-old had secretly demanded a trade through his agent, insisting that he intended to play only one more season, and wanted to do so on a Super Bowl contender. So instead of attending team workouts, Taylor, who had two years left on his contract, participated in *Dancing with the Stars,* the ABC series that paired celebrities with professional ballroom dancers. The Dolphins linebacker had raised his national profile by finishing in second place with Edyta Sliwinska.

Parcells scoffed. "The bus station is full of these Hollywood wannabes. You want names? Jim Brown, O. J. Simpson, Joe Namath, Brian Bosworth. You think they were really successful in Hollywood? The most successful guys were Merlin Olsen and Fred Dryer."

Two days later, Parcells bumped into L.T. at the Grande Oaks Golf Club, a few blocks from team headquarters. L.T. played golf there almost every morning, and Parcells happened to be at the establishment early, honing his swing before work. L.T. was with several friends, one of whom pointed to Taylor and said, "You know, Bill, this guy loves you. He's told us so many stories about you."

Parcells replied, "Yeah, well, I've got a few good things to say about him, too." A few minutes later, as Parcells prepared to swing his club, L.T., still quick as a cat, snuck up behind Parcells and kissed his nape. Even before turning around, the Dolphins chief smiled, knowing the perpetrator's identity. L.T. told Parcells, "I've got to go. We're teeing off here at nine o'clock." The intimate gesture remains a ritual, particularly when the two men haven't seen each other for at least a few months. "It means a lot," Parcells says. "That's his way of telling me. 'Hey, I love you.' It's a special thing to me."

For predraft meetings, Bill Parcells sat at a round table in the team's conference room, along with Jeff Ireland, Tony Sparano, and several of their scouts. The bespectacled GM held a small black gadget attached to a Dell laptop that controlled video enlarged on a wall. Watching tape of the prospects, Parcells jotted his observations in a notebook, using a black pen and orange and yellow markers to keep his take color-coded, occasionally sipping from a cup of iced tea.

Video compilations for each prospect were often watched in silence, but sometimes they led to heated, healthy debates. One such meeting was under way when Jason Taylor chose to make his first appearance at the team's complex since the regime change. After learning the location of the Dolphins brass, Taylor, on break from his Los Angeles–based TV gig, headed for the so-called war room. The franchise's most recognizable player opened the door, smiled, and took a few steps inside.

Parcells glanced sternly at Jason Taylor before quickly returning his gaze to the monitor. Everyone else in the room followed suit; nobody spoke as the silent tape kept running. Unacknowledged, Taylor turned around and walked out, looking incensed. GM Jeff Ireland turned to Sparano and gestured with his head as if to say, "You'd better address this situation." Sparano got up and stepped into the hallway to speak with the humiliated TV star.

Ireland recalls, "He walked in at the most inopportune time for a homecoming. Our purpose was to get through the draft meeting. If one of us needs to go pee, we run out and come back, 'cause we're not stopping. The only time we do is when Parcells wants to break. Jason should have told us he was coming, so that we could do things the proper way."

Parcells adds, "He's a sensitive guy that's used to getting attention, and if you don't give it to him, he doesn't like it. I don't mean he's a bad guy, but he has a sense of entitlement, and his ego gets bruised. He can't take his feelings being hurt."

Reporters soon got wind of Jason Taylor's chilly reception, prompting newspaper articles about a rift between Parcells and the franchise's most popular player. The media focused on Taylor's decision to participate in *Dancing with the Stars* instead of attending voluntary workouts, and speculated on the possibility of his being traded. However, the real drama went undiscovered. While publicly professing his love for the franchise that drafted him in 1997 via Akron, Taylor had issued the Dolphins an ultimatum: unless they traded him, he would skip training camp or quit the NFL to pursue an acting career, leaving the team with nothing in return. The previous season, fans had voted the former third-round pick onto the Dolphins' all-time team. Taylor, a pillar of the community, concealed the threats by operating through his agent, Gary Wichard.

Parcells believed that the thirty-three-year-old's overriding goal was to secure one final jackpot before his NFL career ended, by playing for any team willing to provide him with a rich extension. Taylor's current contract, averaging about $8 million annually, was set to expire after the 2009 season. Although the linebacker had double-digit sacks for the sixth time in his career, Parcells saw him as a player past his prime. During the early 1980s Tom Landry had conveyed to Parcells the wisdom of jettisoning such players a year too soon rather than a season too late.

The Dolphins chief, however, planned to keep Taylor until the franchise received good value from a suitor. Parcells said, "If I cut him today, he'll sign a three-year deal with somebody else—even after all this dramatic bullshit that he's not going to play. At the end of the day, he'll have to choose whether he wants to earn his money or go on with a different aspect of his life. And if that's the case, so be it."

While plummeting to the NFL's worst record in 2007, the Dolphins had used three quarterbacks who produced just a dozen touchdown passes among them. Only the Tennessee Titans had tossed fewer. So Miami's new front office spent considerable time and resources analyzing the top three quarterbacks in April's draft: Boston College's Matt Ryan had earned distinction as the best passer in college, while Delaware's Joe Flacco rated ahead of Michigan's Chad Henne.

Bill Parcells's due diligence included sending his GM, head coach, offensive coordinator, and quarterbacks coach on three trips to scrutinize each prospect in rigorous workouts. The executive vice president spent countless hours alone in his office reviewing film of every throw made by Ryan, Flacco, and Henne during their senior seasons. The Dolphins brass came away uncertain about Matt Ryan's chances to be a franchise quarterback. While breaking Doug Flutie's school record with 31 touchdown passes during his senior season, Ryan had finished with a troubling statistic: 19 interceptions, the second most in the nation.

Ultimately the Dolphins' coaches and front office reached the consensus that there was not much difference in NFL potential among Henne, Flacco, and Ryan, so the Dolphins switched gears and used their top choice on Michigan's star left tackle Jake Long, widely viewed as a future Pro Bowler, figuring they'd land a quarterback with one of their two second-round picks. The left-tackle position, which protected the quarterback's blind side, remained one of football's most important spots, and part of Miami's 2007 struggles had stemmed from poor pass protection.

Parcells applied historical perspective in reaching the Dolphins' decision: drafting an offensive tackle early contained the least margin for error, and a glaring mistake with a top pick meant salary-cap consequences that could last for several seasons. The first player drafted in 2007, quarterback JaMarcus Russell, had received a six-year, $68 million contract, including

$31.5 million guaranteed from the Raiders after he held out of training camp. The LSU product would end up being released two seasons later as perhaps the biggest bust in NFL history.

The Dolphins removed any suspense involving the top pick of 2008 by signing Jake Long four days before the draft to a five-year, $57.75 million contract, including $30 million guaranteed. Parcells had taken a similar step with Drew Bledsoe in 1993 after deciding on the Washington State product instead of Notre Dame's Rick Mirer.

When defensive end Chris Long of Virginia went second overall in the 2008 draft to St. Louis, the Atlanta Falcons took Matt Ryan, having come to a different conclusion from the Dolphins. The Boston College product would ink a rookie-record contract worth $72 million, including $34.75 million guaranteed, but by making Ryan the fourth-highest-paid quarterback in the NFL, Atlanta needed him to start—and produce— from jump.

To begin the second round, Miami selected Clemson defensive end Phillip Merling, factoring in Jason Taylor's tenuous situation. Joe Flacco had been chosen in the first round, eighteenth overall, by Baltimore, so the Dolphins used the fifty-seventh pick to make Chad Henne their quarterback of the future.

Exploiting a strong arm at Michigan, Henne had finished as the storied school's all-time leading passer. Another thing Parcells found appealing about the six-three, 230-pounder involved salary-cap flexibility: by lasting until the second round, Henne commanded a much smaller salary than that of Ryan or Flacco. He would sign a four-year deal worth $3.5 million with $1.4 million guaranteed. Parcells felt that most passers needed time to develop. Great ones like Tom Brady and Joe Montana had benefited from being middle or even late-round picks, avoiding the pressure to excel sooner than later.

In the fourth round, Miami drafted Utah State tackle Shawn Murphy, son of the ex–pro baseball slugger Dale. Three Dolphins selections in the sixth round brought the team Toledo tailback Jalen Parmele, Connecticut guard Donald Thomas, and Montana tailback Lex Hilliard. Miami's final pick, defensive tackle Lionel Dotson of Arizona, came in the seventh round, but two undrafted players would turn out to be key contributors: Montana kicker Dan Carpenter and Hawaii wideout Davone Bess.

During the 2008 draft Miami exchanged proposals with several teams interested in acquiring Jason Taylor. Tony Sparano and Jeff Ireland preferred to move on from the disgruntled linebacker instead of dealing with a possible holdout in training camp, but dissatisfied with offers that went no higher than a third-round choice, Parcells counseled against pulling the trigger. Preferring a first-round pick, Parcells said of his GM and head coach, "They just would like these problems to go away, because it makes things more comfortable for them. They haven't yet learned that by acquiescing without getting what's best for the organization, you're really opening yourself to a lot more trouble."

So after the two-day draft ended, the Dolphins stressed to the media that they planned to keep Taylor, whose leadership on the field they especially valued. In one of Parcells's few public remarks as executive VP, he declared, "The only way Jason Taylor doesn't play for the Dolphins in 2008 is if he retires." Behind the scenes, Parcells disclosed the rationale for his statement. "With a new regime, you have to establish a little law and order. One of the first rules is that a player isn't going to be allowed to shoot his way out of the place. If you let that happen, then you'll have a parade. It's monkey see, monkey do. Even if you wind up trading the player, you can always say, 'Well, I changed my mind.' Or, 'It was an offer that was much better than we anticipated.' Things like that."

At 7 a.m., Tuesday, June 3, Bill Parcells spotted a Dolphins player already on the practice field: reserve wideout Derek Hagan stood alone, sweating in the early humidity while snatching pigskins every few seconds from a jug machine. Parcells walked to the sidelines and scrutinized the six-two, 210-pounder from about twenty yards away. Although Hagan snagged every ball, Parcells detected a fundamental flaw in his form, so after about five minutes, Parcells approached the third-year player, making him nervous.

"I'm going to tell you one thing you're doing wrong while you're catching the ball."

The best way to catch the ball, Parcells said, is with the thumbs touching or barely apart. Parcells added that keeping your hands too far apart increases the chances for drops, a problem that had plagued Hagan since being a 2006 third-round pick via Arizona State. Hagan immediately heeded Parcells's instructions, eliciting an "attaboy" from the executive VP, who then spent the next forty-five minutes going over other techniques, like arching one's back on curl routes to provide crucial extra inches in fending off defensive backs. At the end of the impromptu session, Parcells teased Hagan. "Do I have to teach you every goddamn thing? Do you know *anything* at all?" Hagan, his nervousness evaporating, laughed.

Later Parcells said about the young wideout, "He wants it, so that makes me want to give it."

The next morning, Bill Parcells arrived in his office a bit after 6:30.

Ten minutes later Jeff Ireland came in with an update on Jason Taylor. In a recent telephone conversation, Gary Wichard had stressed that the linebacker's ultimatum still stood despite Taylor's public comments a few days earlier expressing a desire to remain with the team. Parcells said to Ireland, "Wichard won't talk to me because he knows he isn't getting anywhere. I've known the sonofagun since 1981. He played quarterback at C. W. Post."

At Dolphins headquarters Parcells sat at his desk considering Ireland's conversation with Wichard. The executive VP instructed his GM to save an e-mail Wichard had sent on May 16 outlining Taylor's trade demands. In case the linebacker's camp escalated a PR war, Parcells planned to retain the smoking gun. "He made the mistake of putting it in writing."

About two hours later, L.T. dialed Parcells's office, returning a call. As a resident of South Florida he had become friendly with Jason Taylor. Linked by celebrity, the linebacker position, and their last names, the football greats occasionally golfed together. L.T. had learned about the controversy between his former coach and Jason Taylor by reading the local papers.

During their telephone conversation, Parcells said to L.T., "This is a true story. My last time at Grande Oaks, I shot 74."

L.T. replied, "Bullshit."

Parcells: "No shit. I swear to you, on my mother's grave. I can't do that often, but I'm getting to where I can reach the seventies pretty regularly."

L.T.: "That's pretty good."

"Listen, you might be able to help me a little bit. I haven't ever said anything to Jason Taylor."

"So what'd you do to him?"

"Nothing. The press is just making this shit up about 'Parcells is fighting Jason Taylor.' It's not true."

"Well, I'm supposed to be golfing with him tomorrow."

"Tell him, 'You need to see Bill'; ask him to play golf with Bill, or just go out somewhere with him."

"Okay. I know that playing his whole career in Miami ain't important to him now, but it will be ten years from now. He don't know, but ten years from now, he'll know."

"That's right! If you had ever left New York, you'd have been crazy. Now you know. But some of these kids don't know that. Anyway, tell Taylor I would love to see him. Tell him we'll go somewhere, and nobody even has to know about it."

"Sure. No problem."

"Listen to me. I appreciate you sticking up for my ass in the paper the other day."

"I can't tell everybody you're a dick. Everybody already knows that."

Parcells roared. "As you told me about three years ago, I'm getting sentimental. All right, I love you. Bye."

Lawrence Taylor set up a meeting for the next afternoon in a restaurant at the Grande Oaks Golf Club. Jason Taylor and Bill Parcells spoke for the first time during a cordial sit-down that lasted about an hour. Nonetheless, the executive VP left the lunch with his sentiments about the linebacker unchanged, and Jason Taylor offered no guarantees about showing up to training camp.

On July 20, with Sparano's camp only a few days away, a team finally made a proposal for Jason Taylor that Parcells deemed acceptable. Almost two months after their get-together, the Dolphins chief dealt the linebacker to the Redskins for a second-round pick in 2009 and a sixth-rounder in 2010. The headline transaction ended Jason Taylor's stint with the Dolphins after eleven years. The Redskins had hired a rookie head coach, Jim Zorn, after Joe Gibbs's retirement, which punctuated a rare playoff appearance under owner Daniel Snyder. Confirming Parcells's suspicions, Jason Taylor reversed course about his NFL future, expressing a willingness to play in Washington for at least a few more seasons.

34

By the late summer of 2008 Wayne Huizenga informed Bill Parcells that he planned to relinquish his controlling interest in the Dolphins no later than January 2009. Huizenga blamed the presidential election for the development. Illinois senator Barack Obama was receiving surprisingly strong support versus Arizona senator John McCain, positioning himself to become the nation's first black president. Expecting a victory by the Democratic nominee, Huizenga wanted to avoid a presumptive increase in capital gains taxes from 15 percent to as much as 28 percent.

During the presidential campaign, Obama indicated that he would raise them to 20 percent, the previous rate before being lowered by George W. Bush in 2003. But Obama didn't rule out increasing capital gains taxes to 28 percent, causing many high earners to fear the worst-case scenario.

Huizenga calculated a tax hit of roughly $147 million if he sold after Obama presumably took office in late January 2009; conversely, making the $550 million transaction in February 2008 meant a tax bill for Huizenga of roughly $82 million.

Parcells was concerned by the accelerated timeline. He cherished Huizenga's approach to the franchise, and knew too well the potential perils of an ownership change. Parcells said after he got the news, "This is a bit of a tenuous situation because a new owner means an education process for him, and for his financial and legal people. None of them know shit. Most new owners are fans, too, so they have an uninformed opinion. Or some doorman at their building tells 'em something, and they swallow that worm."

During talks to finalize the team sale, Stephen Ross conveyed a bombshell to Wayne Huizenga: the impending majority owner wanted Parcells out as football czar. Ross's sentiments contradicted his public remarks after he had bought 50 percent of the club. But now, while still acknowledging Parcells's stellar legacy, Ross viewed his executive vice president as a football dinosaur. He preferred that his close friend Carl Peterson, the longtime Chiefs executive, take a lead role with the Dolphins, possibly as Parcells's replacement.

Parcells remained unaware of the new owner's true stance, and wouldn't find out about it until several years after he had left the Dolphins. Knowing the dynamics of the situation, Joe O'Donnell actively tried to reduce any tension between his two powerful friends. O'Donnell told Parcells, "Look, meet with Ross. You're going to like the guy. Yes, he's creative, and he's probably going to want ten-gun salutes after every touchdown but he'll leave you alone. He's got a hundred other things going on."

The Dolphins entered training camp with a tenuous situation at quarterback—two unproven veterans and a rookie—so Miami reacted aggressively when the Jets released Chad Pennington on August 7, one day after their bold trade for Green Bay's Brett Favre. Parcells courted the cerebral signal-caller he had drafted eighteenth overall in 2000; he envisioned Pennington, the first quarterback selected in a draft class that included Tom Brady, as being a quality starter for at least two seasons while the team groomed Chad Henne.

Pennington lacked a strong arm, and his career had been marred by injuries, including two surgeries on his right shoulder several months apart in 2005. Nonetheless, he remained one of the most accurate passers in NFL history while behaving like a coach on the gridiron. Pennington had led his teams to the playoffs in three of the four years when he started at least nine games. Parcells's presence in Miami prompted the Marshall product to choose the Dolphins over multiple suitors.

Despite optimism going into the 2008 season, Tony Sparano's Dolphins lost their first two games as the offense struggled, its receivers providing little firepower. With an upcoming road game against New England, which had won 21 consecutive regular-season games, an NFL record, Miami's outlook for 2008 turned gloomy. Although Tom Brady was out for the season with a knee injury, his backup Matt Cassell looked terrific filling in.

To jump-start his offense, Sparano wanted tailbacks Ricky Williams and Ronnie Brown, Miami's best offensive weapons, on the field simultaneously. Quarterbacks coach David Lee suggested reenacting a scheme that he had employed for a similar purpose as Arkansas's offensive coordinator: the single-wing offense, which had originated in 1907 when Pop Warner used it to exploit the talents of the great Jim Thorpe. In a formation featuring an unbalanced line, the tailback took a direct snap before handing off, running with the rock, or even passing.

David Lee dubbed Miami's version the "wildcat," with Ronnie Brown often receiving shotgun snaps while Ricky Williams went in motion after lining up wide. Dan Henning inserted the scheme into Miami's game plan to unleash on September 21. Using it six times against New England, the Dolphins produced five touchdowns, including one on lefty Ronnie

Brown's 19-yard completion to tight end Anthony Fasano: Bill Belichick's defense looked discombobulated as the Dolphins shocked the Patriots 38–13. Ronnie Brown, the wildcat's unconventional quarterback, finished with four touchdowns and 113 rushing yards.

The victory and the scheme revitalized Miami's prospects for the season. Sparano's team started causing defensive headaches for opponents by occasionally employing the quirky formation. As the Dolphins showed improvement, Stephen Ross contacted Bill Parcells in late October to set up their first extensive get-together. The impending majority owner had reversed his notion of Parcells's being passé by talking to people around the league, and by seeing the football decisions that had reinvigorated the Dolphins.

On Saturday, November 1, Parcells and Ross dined at Ke'e Grill in South Florida. Their conversation went swimmingly enough to last three hours as Ross paid respect to Parcells, and broached the possibility of a contract extension that would allow the sixty-seven-year-old to run the Dolphins beyond age seventy. While amenable to the idea, Parcells detected some red flags during their talk. For one thing, Ross conveyed his desire to still bring Carl Peterson into the organization, though not necessarily with a front-office position. The owner emphasized his long personal relationship with the Chiefs executive. He also intended to emulate Lakers owner Jerry Buss by gearing the franchise toward the entertainment industry. "South Florida is about celebrity entertainment," Ross declared. To help raise $500 million he planned to target superstar singers Jon Bon Jovi and Usher as part owners.

Parcells drove home from dinner with mixed feelings about Ross. The Dolphins executive said shortly after the meal, "He wants the team to be glitzy. If you have an organization that's run that way, eventually it filters down to the players. That's what happened in Dallas. It can have an effect. You start to wonder what's more important, the show or the game?"

But Parcells added, "I have a greater appreciation for the business end now. I look at other aspects of a franchise with a little more consideration. Jerry Jones taught me a lot about how things work together. There were some decisions made in Dallas that I wouldn't have made if I was running the show, but I understand why. I asked, and he explained."

So despite the warning signs, the get-together concluded with Parcells being open-minded about working long-term for the real-estate mogul.

At the end of one Dolphins home game, Stephen Ross left his suite with five friends and took a private elevator down to his team's locker room. Wayne Huizenga had followed a similar routine, but with one glaring difference: he never stepped into the players' domain with an entourage. The sight of Ross's group vexed Parcells, who deemed the locker room a sanctum. Even a proactive owner like Jerry Jones avoided entering "my" locker room with a retinue.

The Dolphins executive decided against asking Ross to have his friends wait in the hallway, but on getting home that night, Parcells phoned Joe O'Donnell to vent. "Ross came into the locker room with a bunch of guys. He's the owner, and he can do whatever he wants. Wayne used to come in by himself, and that was actually nice. But Ross shouldn't be bringing in so many outsiders."

O'Donnell responded, "Well, how about I give you an incredible idea, genius?"

"What's that?"

"Why don't you tell him that? Ask to sit down with him and let him know, instead of just pulling your shit and having it fester."

"I can't do that. He's the owner."

"Sure you can. He'd love to have a dialogue with you about anything. Tell him, 'Sometimes when we lose a game, or even when we win a game, the locker room needs to be kind of a private place. You can do what you want—you're the owner—but it's a little uncomfortable when you bring in so many people.'"

"I'm not going to say that."

"Then I'll tell him myself."

"You do what you want."

After hanging up with Parcells, O'Donnell dialed Ross.

"Steve, it might be a good idea to think about not bringing so many friends into the locker room. Bill mentioned it in passing last night when we talked. You may want to give him a call to straighten it out. You guys can use this to get to know each other better."

Ross replied, "Oh, gosh. I never thought about that, but he's absolutely right. We don't belong in there."

"*You* belong in there. You own the damn team, or you're about to. Bill's issue is bringing so many people with you."

The next afternoon, O'Donnell telephoned Parcells to convey Ross's contrition. "Look, I had a conversation with Ross. He's going to call you."

Parcells replied, "I already called him this morning after thinking about it. He knew my feelings because you had told him. Thanks. We're fine."

Bill Parcells avoided attending road contests, and watched home games from a booth in the media section at Dolphin Stadium. The worst aspect of his new job involved lack of direct control on game day, which brought more stress than he had expected. While viewing one televised road contest with Mandart in Jupiter, Parcells stuck out his wrist to his girlfriend.

"Here, I want you to feel my pulse. Watching this is really hard for me." Mandart expressed concern about his pulse's rapidity, which she estimated as being twice the normal rate. During Dolphins games Parcells's adrenaline surged, his mind raced, and some of his team's decisions made his blood boil, prompting loud expletives. Once, while at his office watching a road contest, Parcells vomited in the trash can after his team lost a fumble at a key moment.

Despite such anguish, Parcells avoided the temptation of contacting his underlings on game day to exert direct control. "The toughest thing is watching the action with a trained eye," Parcells said after one home game, "knowing where it's going and not being able to do anything about it. When I was coaching, I could do something about it: change pass coverage, or run a different play. I could take a chance and try to gain momentum for my team. Now I've got to watch up there like the rest of the slappies."

After his introductory press conference, the executive VP had declined virtually all interview requests. He felt that too many public remarks would undermine the GM and head coach. Parcells even chose not to appear on the cover of the media guide, the press kit distributed to journalists before each season, which featured Tony Sparano and Jeff Ireland. The rookie pair also appeared on promotional billboards throughout the Miami area. The inaccessibility of the Dolphins' highest-ranking official frustrated the local press, so in a stadium elevator after one home game, a reporter who was riding down with Parcells asked for his rationale. The football honcho responded in a manner that would have delighted Woody Hayes: "I've already served my time in hell."

One benefit of not having coaching responsibilities was that it allowed Parcells more time at the arena to engage with football people he respected or admired. Earlier in the year, Mike Holmgren had announced that 2008 would be his final season as Seahawks head coach. Although Parcells and Holmgren weren't quite NFL rivals, their teams had clashed in two memorable postseason games. Holmgren's Packers defeated Parcells's Patriots, 35–21, in the 1997 Super Bowl, and Holmgren's Seahawks triumphed during Parcells's coaching coda on January 6, 2007—the wild wild-card loss at Seattle.

Holmgren often described Parcells as the top NFL coach of his era. The admiration was mutual. Over the years Parcells had marveled at the speed of his counterpart's substitution patterns. "Mike Holmgren pressured the defense with the pace of his offense like no one else," Parcells says. "That play is in, and they're out of the huddle. Now, that's not always great for his defense time-wise, but it's a pain in the ass for *your* defense."

Although Holmgren came from the West Coast tree, Parcells intuited that they shared many outlooks on football, so when the Seahawks visited Dolphin Stadium on November 9, Parcells planned to speak to Holmgren at the game's conclusion. In the final moments of Miami's 21–19 victory, Parcells waited at the stadium tunnel. Spotting Holmgren walking from the field, Parcells felt uncertain about what to say: Seattle had dropped to 2-7 after Ricky Williams collected 105 yards on 12 carries. So Parcells hugged Holmgren for a brief exchange, declaring him one of the NFL's best minds and wishing him well in future endeavors.

"I just wanted to do that," Parcells recalls, "because I don't know whether I'm ever going to see the guy again. I wanted him to know that I was thinking about him."

Leading up to the next game, at home versus the Raiders, Tony Sparano's defensive staff was most concerned with Oakland's rushing attack. So during a Wednesday practice, Parcells employed a motivational tactic from his head-coaching days: sending a message to younger players through a veteran. He wandered over to the team's group of defensive linemen and initiated a conversation with nose tackle Jason Ferguson, who had been acquired in a trade with Dallas for his third stint with Parcells.

"Well, Fergy, you better hike up your big-boy pants this week because they're gonna run the ball, and if this center blocks you, you need to think about retiring."

Ferguson responded, "They're gonna be hiked up, don't you worry about it."

The contest also gave Parcells an opportunity to greet the iconic owner who had played an important role in shaping his own legendary career. Before the 1 p.m. kickoff, Bill Parcells visited the stadium booth assigned to Al Davis's team. Parcells hugged the Raiders owner. At age seventy-nine, Davis was using a walker, but during the half-hour conversation, as always, he impressed Bill Parcells with a razor-sharp mind, almost three years before his death.

The Dolphins triumphed 17–15 for their fourth consecutive victory. Chad Pennington gave his latest clever performance on 16 of 22 passing, Ronnie Brown gained 101 rushing yards, and Miami's defense remained sturdy while holding Oakland to only 70 yards on the ground. Despite the offense's tricky scheme, the Dolphins consistently showed sharp execution, and seemed headed toward breaking the NFL record of fewest turnovers: 14, set by Bill Parcells's 1990 Giants, who'd also captured Super Bowl XXV. With Sparano's team improving to 6-4 while averaging more than seven yards in wildcat snaps, several NFL offenses had begun incorporating the scheme into their playbooks. By the season's midway point, roughly one-third of teams in the so-called copycat league employed some version of the formation.

Nine weeks after unveiling the wildcat against New England, the Dolphins hosted Belichick's team in a November 23 rematch. At a Monday Q&A in advance of the game, a reporter asked Belichick about Parcells's role with the Dolphins. New England's head coach credited Parcells for Miami's turnaround, praising his comprehensive football knowledge, from personnel to the medical department. Belichick admitted, "I hate to see him" in the same division.

Seeing Belichick's glowing quotes the next morning thrilled Parcells. Although their beef had ended in 2006, Belichick hadn't yet publicly acknowledged the fact. For almost a decade, his responses to questions about Parcells had been lukewarm, and he occasionally downplayed his mentor's influence. Belichick's harshest remarks had come in Michael Holley's *Patriot Reign,* published in late 2004, criticizing Parcells for his behavior before the 1997 Super Bowl.

Now Parcells felt confident that they would maintain their friendship despite once again competing in the same division. Besides, the Dolphins chief viewed his head coach, Tony Sparano, as Belichick's natural adversary, not himself. Parcells was less sanguine about avoiding tension with another acolyte in the division: Jets GM Mike Tannenbaum. After joining the Dolphins, Parcells had tried to poach Jets security chief Steve Yarnell. When Tannenbaum took measures to block the move, the two football bosses drastically reduced communications. Regardless, the hallways at Jets headquarters remained unabashedly decorated with Parcells's maxims.

In a back-and-forth contest at Dolphin Stadium, Bill Belichick's defense looked prepared for Sparano's unorthodox scheme, limiting it to just 27 yards. The clubs exchanged leads six times before New England pulled ahead for a 48–28 victory. Matt Cassel tossed three touchdowns, all to Randy Moss, and amassed a career-high 415 passing yards, ending Miami's winning streak.

Just as he had done as head coach of the Jets, Bill Parcells used a whiteboard in his office to constantly adjust the team's roster maneuverings. His roster goals were broken down into "MUSTS," "NEEDS," and "WANTS." In November 2008, Parcells's board indicated his focus on the 2009 draft and free agency. "MUSTS," the highest priority, included a cornerback, wideout, and safety. "NEEDS" listed "Wildcat-QB" and kick returner, plus developmental players at tight end, wideout, and defensive lineman. "WANTS" included "3rd Down and Spread," "Offense-Cover," and "Teams-LBs."

Parcells explained the jargon. "We're seeing more spread-out offenses. We have a certain prototype for linebackers, but we may think about altering it to include a couple of guys that are a little more pass-defense oriented. They're maybe not as big as we'd like for our regular defense, but they need to be good pass defenders and good special-teams players."

One other category on the board said, "Reserve Future," with the last names of four players and their teams, including "Wake-BC Lions."

After the loss to New England, Sparano's team started another hot stretch behind Chad Pennington, whose brilliant play was generating league-MVP chatter. Miami won four straight to enter its regular-season finale against Pennington's former club, with the division title—and a playoff appearance—at stake. On an unseasonably warm afternoon of 65 degrees, Pennington returned to the Meadowlands for the first time since being released. Parcells watched the game in his Jupiter condominium with his pal Ron Wolf. While the former Packers GM ate a sandwich, Parcells was too pumped up to consider food.

Directing a storybook victory, Chad Pennington threw two touchdowns and Brett Favre tossed three interceptions as Miami triumphed 24–17. The margin of victory came on an interception by Dolphins defensive end Phillip Merling, who returned it 25 yards for a touchdown. Ted Ginn Jr., Miami's maligned wideout, the epitome of the unit's feebleness, returned two kicks for touchdowns. Despite their team missing out on the playoffs, many of the 79,454 spectators at Giants Stadium chanted, "MVP! MVP! MVP!," referring to their former quarterback.

Passing for a career-high 3,653 yards on the season while throwing 19 touchdowns versus seven interceptions, Chad Pennington earned the Comeback Player of the Year Award, and finished behind only Peyton Manning in MVP voting. He set a club record by completing 67.4 percent, eclipsing Dan Marino's mark of 64.2 percent to become the first Dolphins quarterback since the Hall of Famer to amass at least 3,500 passing yards. Pennington had stayed healthy enough to start every game for only the second time in his career, and by concluding their enchanting regular season with a victory, the Dolphins would make their first playoff appearance since 2001. A tiebreaker over the Patriots gave Miami the AFC East title and a home playoff contest, knocking New England out of the postseason.

In the visitors' locker room, Ricky Williams stood among several Dolphins players wearing gray "Division Champions" caps. Despite starting only three games, Williams had finished with 659 rushing yards, averaging 4.1 yards to reward Parcells's faith in him. Miami's running tandem flourished as Ronnie Brown amassed 916 rushing yards while scoring 10 touchdowns.

By winning nine of its final ten games of the season, Tony Sparano's team matched the greatest turnaround in NFL annals. Although the rookie head coach received kudos aplenty, much of the credit went to the self-described "guidance counselor" with a track record for revitalizing franchises. "Of course, at the very early stages, Ross told Wayne that he didn't want Parcells," recalls O'Donnell, who never told his close friend, to avoid making waves. "And then you see what happened. His team went 11-5, and Ross was begging him to stay. He was worried that Parcells might have his nose out of joint."

Sparano's team set the NFL record for the fewest turnovers at 13. The Dolphins, though, would share the new mark with a team guided by another Parcells disciple: Coughlin's 12-4 Giants also ended the 2008 season turning the ball over only 13 times.

In an intriguing playoffs showdown, the Dolphins hosted the Ravens, whose sterling defense led the NFL in takeaways. Baltimore, which had defeated Miami 27–13 on the road midway through the season, was also guided by a rookie head coach, John Harbaugh, along with a rookie quarterback, Joe Flacco; and Miami's ex-leader Cam Cameron called the offensive plays.

As usual, however, Rex Ryan's defense, featuring a ferocious pass rush, marked the difference. Linebacker Ray Lewis and defensive linemen Terrell Suggs and Trevor Pryce constantly harassed Pennington, forcing the circumspect quarterback to play out of character. He tossed four interceptions, including one that safety Ed Reed returned 64 yards for a touchdown.

The twin renaissance by Pennington and the Dolphins screeched to a halt as the Ravens forced five turnovers to triumph 27–9. With Baltimore neutralizing the wildcat, the outcome demonstrated that Bill Parcells's club needed more than a back-to-the-future scheme to sustain its newfound respectability.

35

Barack Hussein Obama's historic victory as the nation's forty-fourth president confirmed Wayne Huizenga's inclination to finish selling all but 5 percent of the Dolphins. Stephen Ross's additional 40 percent stake would trigger the thirty-day window allowing Parcells to decide whether to leave with the remaining value of his four-year, $16 million contract. "The best deal," Joe O'Donnell says, "of all time." But in anticipation of the official transaction, Parcells asked Huizenga to make the deal even better by amending the time frame to an indefinite period.

Parcells said to Huizenga during the owner's weekly visit to Dolphins headquarters, "That way I'll have more time, and the new owner will have more time. We'll get to know each other a bit longer than thirty days before anybody does anything definitive." As managing general partner, Huizenga authorized the change, and before technically selling his majority stake in early 2009, he asked Ross to sign off on the decision. The real-estate billionaire had disliked the original stipulation and felt backed into a corner by the notion of extending it. As a neophyte owner, however, Ross didn't dare chase away the great Bill Parcells, dinosaur or not, considering Miami's seemingly transformative season. So Ross rubber-stamped Huizenga's decision.

The amendment allowed Parcells to quit at any time over the ensuing three years without financial consequences. So why not cash out immediately and sign with another team? "It's hard in this business to find a job you like," Parcells replied. "And I like the people I'm working with. I like the ownership here. I like Wayne a lot." Even after the team's principal owner changed, Parcells almost exclusively spoke to Huizenga, while hoping for the best concerning Ross.

On Tuesday, January 20, 2009, the day of President Obama's inauguration, the Dolphins announced the sale: Ross became the managing general partner, or Parcells's boss, with 95 percent of both the franchise and stadium, while Huizenga kept the rest as a minority partner. At a press conference marking the transfer of power, Ross declared, "Parcells is in charge." This time, instead of stressing the Tuna's legacy, Ross described Parcells as "probably the best football mind in America."

To ease the weight of his financial commitment of more than $1 billion, the new majority owner concentrated on recruiting celebrities to buy stakes. He put on the back burner ideas like hiring Carl Peterson, who'd been forced out of Kansas City in late 2008.

Bill Belichick's girlfriend, Linda Holliday, forty-five, owned a clothing boutique in Jupiter not far from her home. For proximity to the former Miss Arkansas runner-up, Belichick, who lived in Weston, Massachusetts, was looking to buy property in the area. So in early 2009, New England's head coach heeded Parcells's recommendation to move into his six-story luxury building: Belichick purchased a condominium two floors above Parcells's unit at the Pointe at Jupiter Yacht Club. Their units contained wraparound balconies that provided spectacular views of Jupiter and the Atlantic Ocean. The Mediterranean-style building featured a vine-covered trellis, entry-court fountain, and garden deck. Amenities included a heated pool and a spa overlooking the marina. With the Jupiter inlet only a mile away, several residents parked their yachts just outside the building.

Like any other neighbors, the legendary coaches ran into each other from time to time. They also occasionally hit the links together during the off-season, and never went more than a few weeks without speaking on the phone. "I not only like him; I liked his father," Parcells says.

Todd Haley had overcome his disappointment at being overlooked for the Dolphins' head-coaching job and reestablished a relationship with Bill Parcells. The Cardinals' offensive coordinator turned into a hot commodity as Arizona reached the Super Bowl before losing to Pittsburgh, 27–23. With Scott Pioli having replaced Carl Peterson as Kansas City's GM, the Chiefs courted Haley for their lead job. During the process, Haley bombarded Parcells with phone calls seeking his counsel. Moments after receiving a contract needing his signature, he dialed Parcells for the latest advice.

Seeing Haley's number on caller ID yet again, Parcells picked up with a zinger. "Yes, honey. What is it?"

The rookie head coach also found creative ways to get guidance without constantly calling. For pointers on handling the media, Haley studied video of Parcells's Q&As as a head coach.

Going into his second season as Dolphins chief, Bill Parcells had interacted with Stephen Ross only a handful of times, including another long dinner conversation. Although Parcells remained disappointed with Huizenga's majority sale, his new partnership with Ross had gone reasonably well. The real-estate magnate showed support such as authorizing a 2009 player payroll of what would be roughly $126 million, second only to Big Blue's

$138 million. The Dolphins' outlay ballooned mainly because of a desire to re-sign several of their unrestricted free agents. The club also inked some relatively expensive hold-the-fort players, outside free agents whom Parcells deemed essential to winning while Miami's young players developed.

The executive VP occasionally met with Ross's moneyman to keep the owner posted on budgetary moves, but Ross left all football decisions up to Parcells, reinforcing his clout. Given Miami's first playoff appearance in several years, Ross did not want to be the cause of Parcells's departure. "Everybody," he recalls, "had me walking on eggshells."

The new majority owner even decided against participating in draft meetings. Instead, he made such administrative moves as agreeing on a ten-year extension for a stadium concession deal with Joe O'Donnell. During one visit to Dolphins headquarters, Ross told Jeff Ireland, "Look, don't worry about me getting in the way." The second-year GM went out of his way to connect with the new owner, and the two started to form a good chemistry.

During a Q&A with local reporters in April, Ross promised to concentrate on the team's business side, or its "margins," especially trying to lure more fans to the stadium. The Dolphins' earlier 1-15 mark had caused season-ticket sales to drop nearly 16 percent to 46,131, the lowest in more than a dozen years. Following Miami's playoff appearance, sales rose to almost 50,000, still far from the franchise's long-term goal of 62,000. Ross intended to target the Hispanic fan base, which he saw as being overlooked. He expressed disbelief that the franchise lacked a website catering to Spanish speakers. Ross's viewpoint evoked memories of Arthur Blank's conversation with Parcells about exploiting the significant black population in Atlanta.

However, in 2009 Joe O'Donnell said about Ross's attitude, "His biggest nightmare is that Parcells goes somewhere else. Ross had some other ideas about Parcells's being too old, all of that stuff. And of course, Parcells was playing his usual Greta Garbo routine. 'I want to be alone.' That's the mystery Parcells. He won't let in 99 percent of whoever he meets—just people like Tony La Russa and Bobby Knight, and a few guys from Jersey."

On late Wednesday morning, March 25, Parcells left his office, headed for the weight room. He stopped at the entrance and stared through its glass window to check out the Dolphins players inside. "Teddy Ginn is here," Parcells whispered in a tone of approval. Before long, when it became known that the Big Tuna was watching, the freewheeling atmosphere evaporated.

Parcells entered the weight room for a closer view of the roughly thirty players in team shorts and T-shirts. DMX's old rap hit "Stop Being Greedy" blared from loudspeakers as Parcells stood silently, both hands in his shorts pockets. He trudged a few feet for a different angle, but no player volunteered to be the first to break the ice.

As offensive lineman Vernon Carey walked across the room, he locked eyes with Parcells. Pleased by the attendance and effort one week before voluntary minicamp, Parcells finally lightened the mood. He slapped his right hand over his pocket, alluding to Carey's recent contract extension of six years at $42 million, including a $15 million bonus. Carey grinned. With Jake Long excelling at left tackle, the Dolphins had decided to sign the talented right tackle, securing the offensive line's bookends long-term.

Parcells noticed defensive tackle Joe Cohen and yelled a joke about his last name: "Joe, you're the only black Jew I know." Cohen, an African-American born in Melbourne, Florida, laughed loudest. Then Davone Bess walked into Parcells's crosshairs.

"Damn, I've got to read your name in the paper now. What a bunch of bullshit. The paper's calling you a star."

Bess, in a bashful tone, replied, "Oh my God. Really?" Despite being undrafted, Bess, lining up almost exclusively in the slot, had caught 54 balls, third most among rookie wideouts, and the second-most in NFL history for an undrafted rookie receiver, after Wayne Chrebet.

Parcells said, "Don't be getting too big on me now."

Bess replied, "I don't even read the paper."

"We need an athlete in the slot. Know what I mean?"

"I know, Coach."

Then Parcells caught sight of defensive end Cameron Wake standing a few feet away. After being named the CFL's top defensive player in 2008 for the British Columbia Lions, Wake had received interest from most NFL teams, but in January, the six-three, 260-pound sackster had signed a four-year deal with Miami worth $4.9 million.

Parcells yelled over the loud music, "Hey, Cameron." Wake, who'd gone undrafted out of Penn State in 2005, hustled over.

Parcells asked, "Do you like it here all right? You need anything?"

Wake replied, "I'm good. They're taking good care of me. I appreciate you asking."

"Glad to have you here, but don't be down there in South Beach too much."

"I've been down there once."

"Nothing but trouble waiting to happen."

"I've heard some stories. It's nice down here in Miami—summer all year round. I'm enjoying myself, Coach."

"Good. You making some friends here yet?"

"Yeah, so far, so good."

"Alrighty."

Finally Parcells walked over to Jake Long, who was breathing hard after bench-pressing. Alluding to the left tackle's Pro Bowl season, Parcells said, "You're farther along. I've seen quite a few guys just like you. The thing that takes some of them down is if they can't make themselves come back in here regularly. That's when you start slipping."

The Lapeer, Michigan, native replied, "I'm ready to get going again, Coach."

"It beats shoveling snow."

"I went home last week and it was snowing."

Cornerback was marked as an area of need on Tony Sparano's defense. In the 2009 draft the Dolphins aimed to land two potential starters at the position. Jeff Ireland used his top pick, twenty-fifth overall, on Illinois cornerback Vontae Davis, whose older brother, Vernon, excelled at tight end for the San Francisco 49ers. In the second round the Dolphins made a provocative selection with the extra pick they had obtained by jettisoning Jason Taylor: West Virginia quarterback Pat White went forty-fourth overall, which seemed high, especially for a passer whose six-foot, 190-pound frame violated Parcells's draft principles. Nonetheless, Parcells envisioned White adding a special element to the wildcat as a dual threat, in order to counter defenses increasingly effective against it. And Parcells's scouts, including Jeff Ireland following a trip to see White work out, had praised the quarterback's abilities.

White had enjoyed a celebrated career at West Virginia, amassing the most-ever rushing yards for a Division I quarterback: 4,480. He also made history as the only quarterback to win four bowl games, and his 34 victories as a four-year starter were among the most in NCAA annals.

The Dolphins used their original second-round choice, sixty-first overall, on Utah cornerback Sean Smith. Drawn to the size of USC wideout Patrick Turner, a six-five, 221-pounder, Miami took him in the third round. Another receiver, Brian Hartline of Ohio State, went in the fourth round. In a solid draft class, Miami would land three quality starters, including their objective of two at cornerback: Vontae Davis and Sean Smith. Brian Hartline would turn out to be the best find, developing into a number one wideout. And safety Chris Clemons, a fifth-round pick via Clemson, would turn into a dependable starter. Pat White, though, would end up as one of the worst second-round selections in franchise history, and Patrick Turner wouldn't last long with the Dolphins, or anyone else, after struggling to create separation from NFL defensive backs.

Jason Taylor's stint in Washington ended abruptly during the 2009 off-season when they released him, supposedly for declining to participate in voluntary workouts. While Miami was enjoying a rebirth, Taylor had sputtered at an unfamiliar position on the defensive line during an injury-marred season. He missed three games, just one less than he had during his entire Dolphins career. Playing mainly left end, Taylor finished with only 3.5 sacks, his lowest total since 1999. The mediocre production from a player due to earn an $8.5 million salary spurred the possibility of Washington's demanding a substantial pay cut; ultimately the Redskins decided that the trade to acquire him had been a mistake.

Taylor's agent contacted Jeff Ireland to discuss the possibility of the linebacker returning to Miami, citing the proximity to his family. The Dolphins' GM believed that the 2006 Defensive Player of the Year could still contribute to a unit with several promising young players, but Parcells, seeing an athlete in the twilight of his career, recommended that Ireland propose a drastically reduced salary for just one season. On May 13, Taylor accepted Miami's take-it-or-leave-it offer, $1.1 million plus incentives worth up to $400,000, declining similar interest from the AFC East's best team in recent years, the New England Patriots.

Stephen Ross's first major move as Wayne Huizenga's replacement came on May 8, with a novel idea involving his team's home building: the Dolphins would rename it Land Shark Stadium for the season in a partnership deal with singer Jimmy Buffett. A local icon identified with the Florida Keys, Buffett owned LandShark Lager, a niche beer distributed by Anheuser-Busch. The arena's new designation would change to Sun Life Stadium before it hosted Super Bowl XLIV on February 7, 2010. As part of the deal with his friend Ross, Buffett also created a team version of his hit song "Fins."

About a month after partnering with Buffett, Ross persuaded Cuban-born singer Gloria Estefan and her husband, producer Emilio Estefan, to purchase a stake in the Dolphins. Ross saw the move as helping to raise the team's profile in South Florida's Latin community, with its strong Cuban population. Before long, Ross attracted four more celebrities as limited partners: pop superstars Marc Anthony and wife Jennifer Lopez, and tennis stars Serena and Venus Williams. The boldfaced names all agreed to make appearances at home games in an attempt to increase attendance.

And Ross created an "orange carpet," a nod to the team's colors, welcoming VIPs before opening kickoffs.

The September 9 issue of *Forbes* placed Parcells on its cover, observing practice while wearing shades, a white Dolphins T-shirt, and a million-dollar smile. The article by Tom Van Riper, titled "Football's $300 Million Man," calculated that Parcells had helped generate that amount for each of the final three teams he coached: the Patriots, Jets, and Cowboys, each of which had gained $1 billion in value as compared to an average league appreciation of $700 million. During Parcells's Cowboys tenure, which spanned arrangements for a new stadium at Arlington, Texas, the franchise's worth jumped from $650 million to $1.5 billion. And two years after Parcells's departure, *Forbes* ranked America's Team as the league's most valuable at $1.65 billion.

Asked by *Forbes* about the figures, Parcells acted self-deprecating. "I just came along when values were on the upswing." However, Parcells couldn't wait to use the *Forbes* story to needle Jerry Jones about having been underpaid in Dallas. When the magazine hit the stands, Parcells sent his former boss a note.

"According to *Forbes,* you paid me $295 million too little. My attorney told me to settle for $150 million, and then we'll move that thing that's in the way down there at Cowboys Stadium to San Antonio, and put a big Dr Pepper sticker on it. Lawsuit to follow."

Parcells's crack about "that thing that's in the way" referred to the massive high-resolution scoreboard at Cowboys Stadium. Despite costing $1.3 billion, the new arena had experienced an embarrassing debut on August 21 when Dallas hosted Tennessee to open preseason. During the nationally televised game, a punt by A. J. Trapasso of the Titans boomed high into the air before being deflected backward. Officials ruled the ball in play until Titans coach Jeff Fisher informed them that it had struck one of the stadium's two mammoth screens. By rule, the teams replayed the down. The Cowboys had been touting the arena's scoreboard, including its twin screens at 160 feet long and 72 feet high, as the largest in the world. The organization tried to certify it in the *Guinness World Records* as the world's largest high-definition video screen. Hanging in the middle of the field, Jerry Jones's brainchild cost roughly $40 million. So in postgame comments, Jones took umbrage when reporters asked whether the scoreboard should be raised. He accused Trapasso of attempting to hit it, noting that the kick from Tennessee's 37-yard line had been higher, and more centered, than is typical from a punter.

· · ·

In his role as executive VP, Bill Parcells spent several hours each day reviewing film. During the off-season he scrutinized each practice on tape
only a few hours after having observed the session live. Detecting even
slight progress from one of the team's young players made his day. One
time, after noticing a pattern of incomplete passes by Chad Henne that
went high, Parcells explained, "When a quarterback overstrides, the ball
goes too high. It means you took too long a step. With too short a step, you
tend to throw the ball short." Parcells made a mental note to pass along the
observation to Henne at their next chance encounter.

During the regular season, Parcells's film sessions included familiar-
izing himself with Miami's upcoming opponents. He often sidled up to
players at practice, providing tips tailored to the next game. But to avoid
overshadowing Tony Sparano and his staff, Parcells preferred to wait until
he ran into players in the hallway, weight room, or cafeteria. His role as
part-time coach required a balancing act. A few players saw Parcells as a
co–head coach, so whenever they made complaints or suggestions related
to, say, a scheme, Parcells responded firmly: "Go see the coach. Don't talk
to me about that."

Tony Sparano occasionally visited Parcells's office to discuss the state of
the team, and to pick his mentor's brain. Tapping into his vast experience,
Parcells sometimes proactively warned Sparano to prepare for certain scenarios, but most of the time the football boss waited for the head coach to
reach out.

The Dolphins again started the season 0-2, but unlike the liftoff at that
juncture in 2008, their prospects nosedived on September 27 at Qualcomm
Stadium: with the game tied 3–3 early in the third quarter against the
Chargers, Chad Pennington tore his right shoulder after being slammed to
the ground by linebacker Kevin Burnett. Chad Henne replaced Pennington, and tossed a critical interception during San Diego's 23–13 triumph.

Pennington underwent a third operation on the troubled shoulder,
ending his season and, ultimately, his NFL career. At 0-3, Miami went
from being guided by one of the league's sharpest quarterbacks to being
led by a second-year player only starting to learn NFL pass coverages.
Flashing his strong arm, Henne led the Dolphins to consecutive home
victories against the Bills and Jets, creating some hope, but Miami lost
46–34 to the Saints despite having a 24–3 lead in the second quarter. A
Dolphins victory would have been momentous given the unbeaten record
of Sean Payton's team, which had scored at least 45 points in three of its

first five games. Instead, the October 25 setback foreshadowed the rest of an injury-marred season, as Tony Sparano's Dolphins seemed to keep finding ways to lose.

Even some wins came at a cost. During a November 15 victory over Tampa Bay, Ronnie Brown, the wildcat's catalyst, suffered a season-ending injury to his right ankle. With Ricky Williams thriving as a thirty-two-year-old starter, the Dolphins managed to stay competitive enough to remain in playoff contention. But after having captured the AFC East the previous season, Miami experienced a reality check with Tom Brady's return plus the Jets boasting the league's top defense under rookie head coach Rex Ryan.

The Dolphins lost their final three games in relatively close contests to finish 7-9, missing the playoffs, a huge letdown given the previous season. With an increased load due to Ronnie Brown's absence, Ricky Williams rushed for 11 touchdowns while amassing 1,121 rushing yards. He set an NFL mark by going six years between 1,000-plus-yard seasons, and his 4.7-yard average was the second-best of his career. But ultimately Sparano's team epitomized mediocrity, with an average offense and subpar defense.

The draft haul by Jeff Ireland and Bill Parcells generated little additional production. Backup quarterback Pat White saw minimal action while almost exclusively taking snaps in a spread formation. He did nothing to enhance the wildcat, failing to complete any of his five passes, and rushing just 21 times for 81 yards. Playing in only two games, wideout Patrick Turner went without a catch. Miami managed only nine completions for 30 yards or more, and continued to lack explosiveness at the receiver position. For a franchise whose new owner stressed entertainment, the Dolphins looked out of step with the rest of the pass-happy league. Amid the contrived glitz and the disappointing results, Bill Parcells could choose to opt out of his contract without financial penalty, or attempt to finish what he had started.

36

In his fourth season as a head coach, Sean Payton became the latest Parcells disciple to reach the Super Bowl, where his Saints faced the Colts on February 7, 2010, in Miami. Payton had earned kudos for guiding New Orleans to its best record in franchise history, winning 13 straight while eclipsing the NFC mark set by the great 1985 Bears team. He commanded the league's top offense, featuring Drew Brees with an NFL-record 70.6 percent completion rate. Despite such success, or perhaps because of it, Sean Payton channeled and consulted Bill Parcells more than ever. During the two-week interval before Super Bowl XLIV, Payton phoned Parcells daily for guidance, and the Monday before the big game, Parcells accepted his disciple's invitation to watch New Orleans practice at Sun Life Stadium. Parcells told Payton that his coaching mistakes against Green Bay in the 1997 Super Bowl still haunted him. The Dolphins chief urged Payton to take every step necessary to gain even the slightest edge.

On Tuesday, five Saints showed up late to media day after missing the morning bus. Payton decided to exploit the situation, à la Parcells, and set the tone for the week. He shut the doors to the Saints' locker room to address his team, and told his players and coaches that too many of them seemed satisfied with having captured the NFC Championship. Payton called out the tardy athletes by name, and claimed that their attitude risked setting up New Orleans for a blowout loss. Payton concluded his expletive-laced tongue-lashing by relaying a message from his mentor. "Here's what Bill Parcells said: 'When the band stops and the crowd stops cheering—when people stop paying to come—and it's quiet, and all you're left with is yourself, you've got to be able to answer the question: Did I do my best? Did I do everything possible to win this game?'"

By the end of Payton's address, the locker room had turned silent and the mood somber. Payton's contrived scolding helped the Saints maintain their focus for the rest of the week. Then, taking advantage of his access to one of the top motivators in NFL history, Payton asked Parcells to deliver New Orleans's pregame speech. Accepting the role as a Dolphins executive posed a conflict of interest. Also, Parcells's personal ties to the Manning family made him reluctant. Parcells explained the complications to Payton, so New Orleans turned to former NBA head coach Avery Johnson.

Jim Caldwell's Colts led, 10–6, when the Saints kicked off to open the second half, but Payton called an onside kick that his team recovered, and parlayed into a 13–10 lead. His chutzpah delivered a catalyst that led to New Orleans's 31–17 triumph, and the first Super Bowl title in the team's forty-three-year history. Giddy about the outcome, Sean Payton wasn't able to fall asleep until about 4 a.m., with the Lombardi Trophy in his bed. Later that morning Bill Parcells phoned Payton just as the Super Bowl–winning coach was heading to a mandatory media Q&A. Parcells conveyed his pride and praised Payton's bold decisions.

Bill Parcells felt disappointed that his goal of rebuilding an unprecedented fifth franchise had stalled. With two years left on his contract, the executive VP ratcheted up the pressure at Dolphins headquarters. Tony Sparano had dismissed defensive coordinator Paul Pasqualoni after his unit finished among the league's worst. As a replacement, Sparano hired Mike Nolan, whom Parcells deemed a top defensive mind, confirmed by an endorsement from Al Davis. When Parcells oversaw the Jets in 2000, Nolan had worked as Al Groh's defensive coordinator, so the Dolphins executive had some firsthand insight.

Sparano, taking a rare breather at Dolphins headquarters in March, described the atmosphere in the building. "I sit in this chair, and if Bill walks by my office, I know he's there. I can sense him. I can almost smell him. It's just one of those things. Even if I don't see him, I know he's around. It makes you work harder; it keeps you on your game."

During Miami's 2010 off-season, GM Jeff Ireland made several significant acquisitions to bolster the roster's nucleus with young stars, relinquishing two second-round picks for Broncos wideout Brandon Marshall and signing linebacker Karlos Dansby as an Arizona Cardinals free agent. Despite keeping an eye on the team's budget after the 2009 spending spree, Ross authorized a combined $46 million in guaranteed compensation to Marshall and Dansby.

Satisfied that the managing general partner was staying out of the way, Parcells remained open to Ross's idea about extending his contract. Ross, however, failed to act on his own intermittent mentions of a contract extension. The lack of follow-through frustrated his executive VP. In 2010 Parcells said, "Ross told me on about four different occasions, 'Well, I want to sit down and talk to you about the future.' He doesn't ever do it. I've been waiting for him, and he hasn't done it. I'm not pushing him, but he never seems to have the time."

Was Ross cognizant of Parcells's genuine interest in staying long-term? Parcells replied, "We haven't talked about it in any detail. He hasn't asked me."

The drama involving Jason Taylor and Bill Parcells took another twist on April 20: the Dolphins linebacker made a stunning departure to the Jets, a team whose fans he had disparaged over the years amid the AFC East rivalry. For publicly deeming them ignorant and ridiculing their "J-E-T-S!" chant, Taylor received more vitriol at the Meadowlands than any other opposing player. However, the Dolphins had decided against improving an offer that Taylor declined in late November, when he'd told them to wait until the off-season. The club's stance had come after the linebacker rebounded with a terrific season: seven sacks, an interception, and three forced fumbles, including one he returned for a touchdown against the Jets. Taylor's nine career touchdowns were by far the most in NFL history by a defensive lineman.

When Gary Wichard contacted Jeff Ireland in early April 2010 pursuing an improved offer, Parcells refused to authorize one. Instead, Tony Sparano canceled a scheduled meeting with Taylor. By contrast, the Jets had wooed Taylor. Mike Tannenbaum and Rex Ryan gave the spurned linebacker a private helicopter ride to the new home arena of the Jets and Giants, which had opened on April 10. There Gang Green played Taylor's career highlights for him on MetLife Stadium's video screen.

So the linebacker despised by Jets Nation accepted Tannenbaum's proposal for a two-year contract, joining the NFL's top defense.

The grainy, scattershot video taken in late April 2010 shows Jerry Jones sitting between two young men, strangers at a restaurant bar. The Cowboys owner is in a light-colored dress shirt, unbuttoned at the top as patrons mingle in the background. Jones, in his familiar Arkansas twang, says to his barmates, "Romo was a miracle."

One of the young men responds, "It [Romo's emergence] *was* a miracle, wasn't it?"

Jones replies, "He almost never got in, and he was almost gone." Quickly switching to another topic, Jones blurts, "[Tim] Tebow would never have—"

The second teenager interrupts. "What if you were the Jaguars? Would you just recruit—just draft him and sell fucking jerseys?"

Jones says, "That's the only reason I brought in Bill Parcells."

The owner's small audience laughs hard.

Jones adds, "Bill's not worth a shit. I love him."

Second teenager: "I know you do."

Jones: "But he's not worth a shit, but I wanted—they were on my ass so bad. 'J's gotta have a yes-man.' So to get this fuckin' stadium, I needed to bring his ass in."

On April 13, 2010, Deadspin.com, the irreverent sports site that occasionally releases unflattering information about sports figures, posted the exchange. Soon the 47-second video, shot from a hidden cell phone, went viral, prompting coverage from news organizations as disparate as ESPN and *The Huffington Post*. Embarrassed by the brouhaha, Jones dialed Parcells the same day to apologize. At Dolphins headquarters, Parcells took the call on a cell phone with a Dallas area code: 214. When Parcells had quit the Cowboys in early 2007, Jones permitted him to keep the company phone indefinitely. Even before taking Jones's call, Parcells felt that the on-camera comments were harmless.

"I knew he didn't mean it," Parcells said in his office after receiving Jones's call. "He told me he had too much to drink. I said, 'Don't even think twice about it. I know how you feel about me.' **A friend's someone that knows all about you, and likes you anyway.** That's the way I feel about Jerry being a little less than perfect, and I'm pretty sure that's the way he feels about me."

Jones's foolishness given the era of social media was pointed out, but Parcells countered by referencing his father's maxim to never discount stupidity as being a factor, because it's always in there somewhere. "Jesus Christ, you keep forgetting it. People make bad judgments every day. And you can't expect them to think like you think."

But Jones won't make that mistake again, right?

"You want to bet? He told me, 'Lucky the camera wasn't there twenty minutes earlier. I'd have had to turn off every TV set in Dallas.'"

Two days after his apology, Jones praised Parcells at a fund-raiser attended by some reporters. The Cowboy owner declared Parcells a "great" football mind with supreme people skills. Jones, who didn't mention their private conversation, described his disparaging comments as sarcasm.

Pat White's struggles reinforced Bill Parcells's rule against drafting a diminutive player. So in the 2010 draft, Jeff Ireland and Bill Parcells returned to their bigger-is-better philosophy, while particularly aiming to add bulk to Mike Nolan's defensive line. For his first time as majority owner, Stephen Ross joined his football brass in the war room, where a sign said, "No Mascot Players." The owner watched his franchise deal its twelfth overall selection to the Chargers, dropping to the twenty-eighth spot in return for an extra second-round selection.

Ireland used the lower first-round choice on defensive tackle Jared Odrick of Penn State. Parlaying the second-round pick from San Diego, the Dolphins took defensive end turned linebacker Koa Misi of Utah. To add depth to the offensive line, they selected Mississippi offensive tackle John Jerry in the third round. Except for Jerry, Miami's eight-person draft class was made up of defenders: Iowa linebacker A. J. Edds in the fourth; Maryland cornerback Nolan Carroll plus Georgia safety Reshad Jones in the fifth; finally, Miami used a pair of seventh-round choices on defensive lineman Chris McCoy of Middle Tennessee State and linebacker Austin Spitler of Ohio State.

The Dolphins would end up with another solid if unspectacular draft class that found key contributors in the lower rounds: Reshad Jones would thrive as one of the NFL's best young strong safeties, while cornerback Nolan Carroll would develop into a starter. Character concerns had prompted the Dolphins to avoid the best wideout prospect, Oklahoma State's Dez Bryant, despite his size at a chiseled six-two, 220 pounds. The decision came after Jeff Ireland grilled Bryant, whose mother had served time for dealing drugs, at Dolphins headquarters in mid-April. Parcells missed the predraft interview because of a scheduling conflict placing him out of town. So Ireland spoke alone to Bryant in the GM's office, where the wideout sat across his desk.

Bryant lasted until the lower first round, when the Cowboys selected him twenty-fourth overall, but the Dolphins received some negative fallout from their handling of the celebrated junior. On April 27, three days after the draft, Yahoo's Mike Silver reported that Ireland had asked Dez Bryant if his mother was a prostitute. The story created a national firestorm, generating heavy criticism of Ireland, even spurring accusations of bigotry. DeMaurice Smith, the executive director of the players association, blasted Ireland's line of questioning.

Despite understanding Ireland's desire to uncover pertinent intelligence, Parcells also felt that his GM had crossed the line. The executive VP, who found out about the question only after the report, immediately instructed Ireland to telephone Bryant and express contrition. Within hours the rookie wideout and GM spoke, and Bryant accepted Ireland's apology.

While acknowledging his own sharp tongue and confrontational approach, Parcells says, "My dad taught me a long time ago that you don't ask some questions that have only one answer. 'You don't need to go there.' That's what I told Jeff. The media didn't ask the question, but it takes on a life of its own. All the liberals get involved, and these organizations start demanding certain responses."

Ireland subsequently released a statement acknowledging his own "poor judgment." Stephen Ross expressed satisfaction with Ireland's apology, and promised to examine the organization's interviewing protocol. Parcells telephoned Bryant's agent, Eugene Parker, to convey remorse and make sure that their relationship remained strong.

Although Parcells considered the controversy a valuable lesson for Ireland, he took umbrage at folks who declared the GM a racist. Bryant's mother, Angela, conceived Bryant as a fourteen-year-old. Within the next three years she gave birth to another boy and a girl. Convicted in 1997 for selling crack cocaine to provide for her children, she served an eighteen-month prison term. So Dez had experienced a dysfunctional childhood in Lufkin, Texas, living in several homes while attending school. Although he lacked an arrest record, the Dolphins were among several teams concerned about his family influences.

"This isn't a nice-guy league," Parcells explains. "I wish Jeff hadn't asked that question, but I can give you twenty cases of players whose parents negatively affect them with unreasonable financial demands. I've had Polynesian players caught in a dilemma because of their family village; you can get ostracized if you don't give enough, so these kids can get caught in the middle. One kid made $1.3 million as a twenty-year-old, and had to borrow $30,000 to get through the year. Between taxes, the family, and what the village took, he didn't have anything left."

Ireland's controversial remark prompted Parcells to recall the time he apologized for uttering an ethnic slur as Cowboys coach in June 2004. During a Q&A at Dallas's minicamp, Parcells was describing how defensive coordinator Mike Zimmer and quarterbacks coach Sean Payton tried to outdo each other during practice. "Sean, he's going to have a few—no disrespect to the Orientals—but what we call Jap plays. Okay? Surprise things." The comment, referring to the Japanese attack on Pearl Harbor during World War II, brought widespread condemnation.

Parcells says, "Now, you think I meant something against the Japanese? When I was in elementary school, we had what one teacher called a 'Jap quiz.' He used the term whenever he gave a surprise quiz." Parcells received dozens of letters from Japanese people, and a few from Koreans, about his remark. He considers the episode part of his late-in-life education on acceptable language involving nationality and ethnicity.

Bill Parcells sat in his office on Monday morning, May 6, a few minutes before a scheduled appointment with Kenny Chesney. The country singer wanted an interview for his self-produced football documentary *Boys of Fall*. His close friend Sean Payton had asked Parcells to meet with the songwriter and ex–high school gridder. A doo-wop connoisseur amenable to country, Parcells obliged. While Parcells waited, his cell phone buzzed with a text: a friend at ESPN suggested that the Dolphins executive browse the Internet for urgent news involving Lawrence Taylor.

Parcells entered his password for his desktop computer, "Dolphins," before navigating the web. His face sagged on spotting a headline: "Lawrence Taylor Charged with Rape." Parcells blurted in disgust, "Get the hell out of here. Jesus Christ," shaking his head every few seconds at the troubling tidbits of the Internet report. "Lawrence Taylor arrested on rape charges. Get the fuck out of here. But that's what it says."

Finishing the article, Parcells said aloud, "Arrested on rape charges. That'll be bad if he did it." Parcells turned from the computer monitor to phone the Dolphins receptionist stationed in the lobby one floor below. "Ruby, did those country singers get here yet? He's on his way? Okay. Thank you, dear. Bye."

The Taylor bombshell had soured Parcells's mood, and he turned angry that Chesney was running ten minutes late. "This guy's supposed to be here at 10:30. We're supposed to do the interview at 10:30. Now, it's 10:40. Next they'll tell me they're ready at 11."

An observer in the room said, "You know how some of these celebrities are. They're usually—"

Parcells snapped, "He can be a celebrity somewhere else if he doesn't get here on time."

A couple of minutes later, Harvey Greene, the Dolphins PR director, peeked into Parcells's office, with Kenny Chesney behind him. Parcells stepped into the hallway to greet the country singer cum documentarian.

Greene said, "Kenny, this is Coach Parcells."

Parcells, shaking Chesney's hand, said, "Hey, Kenny. How are you doing, kid?"

Chesney, "Pleasure to meet you. I didn't mean to interrupt you."

Parcells set his cell phone on vibrate and headed to a conference room where Chesney's camera crew awaited. Following the Q&A, Parcells's cell kept buzzing. Seeing Jim Burt's number, he picked up the call. Parcells told his former nose tackle, "Can I call you in a little while? About an hour or so. Will you be around? Did you read the paper?"

"Yeah, that's why I'm calling."

"Can you tell me what the hell happened? Do you know?"

"She's underage."

"Get the hell outta here."

"Sixteen."

Parcells, voice dropping to a whisper, said, "Oh, man, he's going to the can. Is there anything we can do? Have you talked to any of the guys?"

Burt rattled off the names of some ex-teammates.

Parcells said, "Call George [Martin] too."

"Okay."

"I'll call you in a little while, Jimmy. Bye."

Parcells explained the surge of calls from Taylor's ex-teammates. "They're all mobilizing. See what happens? That's the deal. We've got to help this guy. The bond is powerful. You think I'm kidding. This kid's fifty years old."

Parcells added, "Godammit. This guy's in big trouble. The girl's sixteen. That's what Jimmy says. Maybe he didn't know."

To Parcells's relief, L.T. would avoid prison, receiving instead six years of probation after pleading guilty to misdemeanors of sexual misconduct and patronizing a prostitute. He admitted to paying for sex, but stressed his ignorance that the girl was underage. The sentence required Taylor to register as a sex offender.

For several years L.T. had avoided the negative headlines that occasionally marked his post-NFL life. Regardless of his troubles, though, Parcells maintained his unequivocal support. "I love the guy. That's the way it is. He's my guy," Parcells says. "Now, he has some characteristics that disappoint me, but he also has some that I admire. I feel that anything anybody wants to talk about with this guy is his drug problems. He had 'em. I acknowledge it. But to pass judgment on him, I'm not going to do that."

Since Parcells takes pride in the fact that many of his former athletes employed his life lessons in their post-NFL careers, he feels some guilt regarding L.T. "I failed to some degree with him," Parcells says, "but I tried very hard. And I think that's why we're still close now. He's been such an integral part of my success, I don't want to see him not be successful himself.

"He doesn't call me Bill. It's always 'Coach.' He's respectful," Parcells says. "When it comes down to it, he knows he can count on me. And if I ever need something, I know I can count on him. And that's one of his traits that I most admire."

Heading into the regular season, the Dolphins continued to make aggressive moves to rectify their mistakes of 2009. They released Pat White on September 4, 2010. Confirming Miami's reassessment of White, no team picked him up off waivers. The Dolphins also released their 2009 third-round pick, wideout Patrick Turner, prompting the Jets to claim him.

The biggest departure, however, occurred only a few days later, announced in a three-sentence bombshell from the Dolphins on September 7: Bill Parcells was handing control of football operations to GM Jeff Ireland and moving into an ambiguous consulting role. The abrupt change came only five days before Miami's season opener at Buffalo. The club's statement noted that the move had been part of Parcells's long-term plan: "This was the intent of the structure put in place." But given his recent openness to a new contract, Parcells's departure seemed to indicate a sudden decision against staying under a neophyte owner. The opt-out clause triggered payment for the final sixteen months of his deal, or roughly $6 million.

Parcells declined public comment, but he explained at the time, "I brought those guys [Ireland and Sparano] to Miami and tried to help them learn what I know about the business. The whole plan was to turn things over to them when I felt like they were ready. And I think they are. They've got to make their own way now.

"It's the end of the personnel cycle for the year—the last cuts for the season. I had thought about making the move before training camp, but I said to myself, 'Well, I better help Jeff and Tony go through the preseason and evaluate the roster while they make the final cuts.' People don't realize that the cycle for player acquisitions ends in the summer."

Parcells spent a few more weeks maintaining his role, attending practice, studying film, and engaging players. By mid-October, Parcells cleared his office of his belongings, put an end to his daily presence at the facility, and unofficially concluded his tenure. Stephen Ross's Dolphins were 3-2 after an impressive overtime victory versus the title-bound Packers at Lambeau Field. And Parcells left the building for good with a 20–16 record as executive VP and guidance counselor.

In his third season guiding the Dolphins, Tony Sparano shifted away from the wildcat scheme. He depended on Chad Henne to guide a smash-mouth offense with an upgraded wideouts corps that included emerging talents in Davone Bess and Brian Hartline. Miami's defense helped the team to a solid start, but the offense continued plodding behind its young, mistake-prone quarterback, prompting the home crowd to occasionally chant "Henne sucks!" The Michigan product finished the season with 19 interceptions versus 15 touchdowns, reinforcing doubts about his potential as a franchise quarterback, and the Dolphins repeated a seven-win mark with another flameout, this time losing their last three games, including the regular-season finale, 38–7, in New England.

At least the defense under Mike Nolan was much improved, led by two twentysomething Pro Bowlers: defensive end Randy Starks, twenty-seven, and linebacker Cameron Wake, twenty-eight. But Miami missed the play-offs for the eighth time in nine years, making 2008 seem like a distant memory, or perhaps an aberration. Despite the party atmosphere before kickoffs at Sun Life Stadium, the Dolphins produced their worst home record in franchise history: 1-7, more than offsetting the team's impressive road mark of 6-2. Tony Sparano's status, if not Jeff Ireland's, turned tenuous, especially in the absence of the powerful boss who had hired them.

After deferring to Bill Parcells during his first two years as majority owner, Stephen Ross became proactive, and Carl Peterson's role as Ross's adviser grew more public. Irate about the season, especially its conclusion, the owner spoke to several players, seeking their opinions on Sparano. Some, like Ricky Williams, criticized the head coach for micromanaging, but most players supported his methods. Despite Parcells's advice to retain Sparano, who had two years left on his contract, rumors circulated about Miami's interest in Bill Cowher and Jon Gruden.

On Monday afternoon, January 3, one day after the Dolphins' season finale, Stephen Ross met with Tony Sparano in the head coach's office, where Sparano offered a detailed plan for off-season changes. Then Ross and Jeff Ireland had a similar discussion in the GM's office. The owner gave no indication of whether he planned to dismiss either of Parcells's two disciples.

Hours later, Ross attended the Orange Bowl at Sun Life Stadium, where fourth-ranked Stanford faced thirteenth-ranked Virginia Tech. In just four seasons, Stanford head coach Jim Harbaugh had transformed his school from doormats into national-title contenders, and molded sophomore Andrew Luck into the nation's best college quarterback. Such achievements made Harbaugh the hottest coaching candidate in college or pro football, with wide-ranging suitors, from his alma mater, Michigan, to various NFL teams.

Before the opening kickoff, Ross approached Jim Harbaugh on Stanford's sidelines. Carl Peterson joined the conversation between the two Michigan alumni who were meeting for the first time: Harbaugh had starred at quarterback for the Wolverines in the 1980s; Ross had graduated in 1962, and Michigan named its business school after him in 2004, following his $100 million donation. Enamored with Harbaugh, Ross secretly arranged for a Thursday get-together in California to discuss the Dolphins' head-coaching job. Then Ross watched Stanford triumph over the Hokies, 40–12, as Luck tossed four touchdowns, giving the Cardinals their first bowl victory in fourteen years.

The next day, January 4, the San Francisco 49ers promoted their personnel executive Trent Baalke to GM. A former scout with Parcells's Jets,

Baalke had been the team's de facto GM since Scot McCloughan resigned in March for personal reasons. But before making things official, San Francisco's CEO and president Jed York wanted to consult Bill Parcells, who was still technically a Dolphins employee. The youngest team president in the NFL, York, twenty-nine, felt open to second-guessing if he named a rookie GM to a team that hadn't made the playoffs since 2002. The position included the authority to pick the head coach replacing Mike Singletary, who'd been fired after his team seemed to underachieve.

Jed York, the 49ers' chief since 2008, operated in the shadow of his uncle Eddie DeBartolo, who had owned the 49ers during their five Super Bowls victories by Bill Walsh and George Seifert. The son of former 49ers co-owners John York and Denise DeBartolo York, Jed believed that Parcells's gravitas would help reassure San Francisco's fan base that he was making the right choice, so during a national radio interview in late December, York disclosed his intention to speak to Parcells about Baalke and the league in general.

Baalke had obtained his first scouting job in 1998 after being hired by Jets personnel director Dick Haley, who assigned him to the Upper Midwest and the Pacific Northwest. During Baalke's three years with Gang Green, he impressed Parcells with an ability to find players who fit the team's personnel philosophy, especially regarding the 3-4 defense. After Parcells left the Jets in 2001, Baalke joined the Redskins, staying with them for four seasons. San Francisco hired him in 2005 as a regional scout; and by 2010 he had ascended to vice president of player personnel, second in command to the GM.

On December 28, Baalke visited Parcells in Jupiter ahead of a formal interview with York. Within a few days, the former Dolphins chief also spoke to York, confirming the owner's conviction about San Francisco's GM. After Baalke secured the job, he quietly tried to lure his first choice for head coach: Bill Parcells. York and Baalke emphasized that although the club had missed the playoffs for eight straight seasons, it contained a talented roster. The 49ers saw Parcells, even at sixty-nine and having been away from the sideline since the 2006 season, as someone who would lead the franchise to the playoffs for least a couple seasons while sharing Baalke's vision. But citing his age and the team's distance from his home base, Parcells put an end to any serious discussions. The 49ers turned their attention to the Stanford head coach on so many wish lists.

Meanwhile, Jeff Ireland obliged Stephen Ross's request to accompany him to Northern California for their own secret interview to land a head coach. On Wednesday night, Ross and Ireland boarded the owner's private jet for the scheduled meeting with Harbaugh. The trip consigned Sparano and his staff to a public limbo, as reports emerged by Thursday afternoon that Ross intended to make Harbaugh the NFL's highest-paid coach, with a $7 million salary.

Although the session between the two parties stretched for five hours, it concluded without an agreement. On a late-night flight to Miami, Ross dialed Sparano to convey that his job remained safe despite the widespread reports, but Miami's head coach had turned off his cell phone and gone to sleep. When Sparano woke up early Friday morning, January 7, he powered it on and saw about thirty text messages, mostly from Dolphins players, pleased about his survival.

Within hours Jim Harbaugh accepted a five-year, $25 million offer from the San Francisco 49ers, which made Stephen Ross realize he'd been used for leverage. The Dolphins' missteps generated derision around the league. Bill Parcells, enraged by Jeff Ireland's participation in undermining Tony Sparano, cut off communication with the GM. Given the need for damage control, the team called a press conference for Saturday, January 8, headed by Stephen Ross, Jeff Ireland, and Tony Sparano. The Dolphins announced a two-year extension for Sparano at more than $3 million annually. Lengthening Sparano's contract through 2013 after just having sought his replacement marked Ross's first major football decision as majority owner. Stephen Ross began the thirty-five-minute press conference by reading a statement that lasted eighteen minutes, chronicling the week's events. Sitting at the end of a conference table, addressing dozens of reporters, Ross conceded botching the head-coaching situation and blamed his inexperience as an NFL owner.

The owner, GM, and head coach all expressed renewed faith in one another during a press conference that seemed to be part counseling session. Like Ross, Ireland admitted error in the lack of communication with Sparano; however, the GM and head coach almost never looked at each other. Their body language and stony faces belied their conciliatory words. Ross did most of the talking, sometimes smiling and laughing in the tense atmosphere. The Dolphins, whose offense ranked thirtieth in points, also announced a mutual parting with Dan Henning, as Ross vowed to deliver an "exciting offense, a more aggressive offense, creative."

The Q&A reinforced Miami's image as a laughingstock around the NFL only a few months after Parcells's departure. The circus act created a schism between the coaching staff and the front office, sowing dysfunction. Sparano's wife reportedly asked that her skybox be moved so that she could maintain a distance from Ireland's spouse. The tension was only exacerbated while Miami lost its first seven games of 2011, as Henne continued to struggle. With ten straight setbacks dating to the previous season, Sparano's dismissal seemed inevitable, regardless of his contract extension.

Miami prevented further embarrassment with a 31–3 victory against Todd Haley's Chiefs at Arrowhead Stadium. Then Sparano's team went on a three-game winning streak, and took four of five. Nonetheless, the Dolphins fired him after a December 11 loss versus Philadelphia. With three games left, Todd Bowles stepped in as interim head coach, wining two as Miami finished 6-10.

During his brief tenure, Bill Parcells had bolstered the Dolphins with young talent, especially on defense, but unlike his stints in New England and Dallas, he'd struck out in trying to find a franchise quarterback. The main reason was Miami's lack of enthusiasm in 2008 for either Matt Ryan or Joe Flacco as the top overall pick. Despite Jake Long's making the Pro Bowl for the third consecutive season, Parcells increasingly generated criticism for passing on Ryan, and the South Florida media to which he had given the silent treatment generally skewered his tenure. Ryan was now one of the league's best young passers, although he notoriously struggled in the postseason, and Joe Flacco looked promising, having started every game since entering the NFL. He would guide Baltimore to the 2013 Super Bowl, earning the game's MVP award before parlaying his talents into the richest contract in NFL history at $120 million.

As part of the fallout involving Tony Sparano, Jeff Ireland and Bill Parcells were no longer on speaking terms, underscoring the triumvirate's shortcomings after two and a half years together. Bill Parcells felt disappointment about his rare failure to elevate a franchise to new heights.

37

Bill Parcells had proved Hall of Fame voters correct in 2003 by joining the Cowboys only one year after another unsuccessful bid for induction. Following his departure from Dallas in 2007 at age sixty-five, he
regained eligibility. However, the Hall of Fame maintained its concern
about coaches returning to the sidelines after essentially taking a long sabbatical. Joe Gibbs, who had rejoined the Redskins in 2004, was the most
prominent example, but other top coaches, such as Dick Vermeil, were
increasingly returning after some years off. Noting the trend, the Hall of
Fame in 2008 amended its bylaws, requiring a five-year waiting period for
coaches, matching that of players, instead of instant eligibility. Suddenly,
the soonest that Bill Parcells could gain induction was 2012, when he
would turn seventy-one. The development upset Parcells, who complained
to close friends about the possibility of dying before getting into Canton.

Parcells said at the time, "A lot guys who were in my corner, they're
gone, the Will McDonoughs of this world. So I'm not going to get the
same kind of support I used to have. That's the way it is. There's nothing
I can do about it."

However, the timing of the Hall's decision seemed to turn fortuitous
when Curtis Martin's second year of eligibility meshed with Parcells's
first under the new rules. The Big Tuna and Boy Wonder, among seventeen contenders for the class of 2012, fantasized about being enshrined
together. Martin had missed the final cut from ten to five in 2011, but he
seemed bound for Canton, given his career total of the fourth-most rushing yards in NFL history. If he did get inducted, Boy Wonder wanted
Parcells to be his presenter.

With coaching apparently in Parcells's rearview mirror, his own candidacy for the Hall seemed equally strong: he was a two-time Super Bowl
champion who'd also guided New England to the title game and Gang
Green to the AFC Championship. By reaching the postseason twice during his Cowboys tenure, Parcells became the only NFL coach to take four
different teams to the playoffs. He had also won four of five in the postseason versus Bill Walsh and Joe Gibbs. But perhaps the best argument for
his candidacy went beyond milestones or statistics: the modern history of
the NFL couldn't be written without Bill Parcells as a central character.

During the 1980s, Parcells had used Lawrence Taylor in a way that had revolutionized the game—as an outside linebacker in the 3-4 defense, rushing the quarterback instead of playing a conventional role in pass coverage. The scheme forced offenses to revamp pass protection, increased the value of the left tackle, and popularized the 3-4 defense. By 2012 Parcells's disciples had captured five of the past ten Super Bowls, and just one day after the Hall was to vote, Bill Belichick's Patriots faced Tom Coughlin's Giants in the Super Bowl.

Detractors, though, pointed to Parcells's solid yet unspectacular record of 172-130-1, and considered his achievements in New York and New England to be exaggerated by an East Coast bias. Other head coaches with two Lombardi Trophies, like Tom Flores, Jimmy Johnson, and George Seifert, had failed to reach the Hall.

One of the irritating arguments to Bill Parcells involved his mediocre record without Bill Belichick. Perhaps Big Bill's most impressive season had occurred in 2003, sans Belichick, guiding Dallas to the playoffs with Quincy Carter at quarterback and Troy Hambrick at tailback. Besides, as Parcells first learned at Army, finding top lieutenants was crucial to an organization's success. Other celebrated NFL head coaches had produced lesser records without specific coordinators, too.

"I thought it was the head coach's job to hire good assistants," he says. "I thought you got credit for that. Bill Walsh got credit for that. You can also say that if some of those guys hadn't been with Bill Walsh, maybe the 49ers wouldn't have been as successful either. So, yeah, I probably wouldn't have been as successful as I was without Bill Belichick. I'm not ashamed of that. How about having the vision to name him defensive coordinator? Doesn't that count for something?" What Parcells left out was that the slippery-slope contention could also be used against Belichick, given his record in Cleveland, where he didn't have Tom Brady. Beyond the numbers, some voters seemed bent on penalizing Parcells for his franchise-hopping and Hamlet-like resignations.

The forty-four-man selection committee met on Saturday morning, February 4, at an Indianapolis hotel ballroom to decide the class of 2012: up to five members from the modern era and two senior additions. Each finalist needed at least thirty-six votes for induction. Just before the session started, Curtis Martin and Bill Parcells talked on the telephone briefly, expressing their mutual affection and wishing each other luck.

The committee spent almost an hour debating Parcells's candidacy, with several dissenters emphasizing what they deemed the flaws in it. The lengthy exchange concerning Parcells's worthiness reflected the polarizing effect he had on people. By contrast, discussion on each of the other four-teen modern-era candidates took an average of roughly twelve minutes.

Parcells and Martin survived the first cut, reaching the round of ten finalists. Nevertheless, their dream scenario ended when the Big Tuna surprisingly failed to make the final five, which included Boy Wonder. Each member of the quintet then received the mandatory 80 percent of the vote to join the class of 2012: Boy Wonder, center Dermontti Dawson, defensive end Chris Doleman, defensive tackle Cortez Kennedy, and offensive tackle Willie Roaf. The modern-era inductees were joined by cornerback Jack Butler, who qualified as a senior candidate.

On hearing the news, Curtis Martin instantly thought about two people: his mother, Rochella Dixon, and his father figure, Bill Parcells. Martin explains his reaction: "There's God and there's Parcells as far as the impact they've had in my career." The new Hall of Fame runner considered the moment bittersweet: Martin told reporters he would have relinquished his place in the class of 2012 to guarantee Parcells's inclusion.

On Saturday night Parcells dialed Martin to congratulate him. "I read what you said about giving up your selection this year for me, and I want you to know that if the position was reversed, I would want the same for you." Parcells planned to visit Canton in August as Martin's presenter. After his third attempt at football immortality, he was incensed about failing to join Boy Wonder as an inductee. Within hours of the snub, however, he received a balm through a litany of phone calls from disciples like Sean Payton, who emphasized Parcells's stature as a de facto Hall of Famer.

Several excellent candidates also missed the final cut, including former wide receivers Tim Brown, Cris Carter, and Andre Reed. Carter, who had produced some of the best-ever statistics by a wideout, fell short for the fifth time. The development prompted widespread indignation from NFL fans and pundits. However, Parcells's snub gained the most attention, especially with his coaching career almost certainly over. Regardless of supposed flaws in his candidacy, Parcells seemed more worthy than many enshrined coaches, such as George Allen, Bud Grant, and Marv Levy. The omission generated scrutiny of the Hall's voters and selection process. On February 10, the website for *The Atlantic*, the cultural and literary magazine, published an article headlined, "How Did Parcells Not Make the Pro Football Hall of Fame?" The piece, by Allen Barra, an author and writer for the *Wall Street Journal* who focused on sports, echoed some common criticism of the Hall's selection process: its secrecy, the relatively small number of voters—some with terms befitting the Supreme Court—and their qualifications.

The forty-four-member board of selectors contained only sports journalists; no coaches or players, past or present, were represented. Neither individual ballots nor voting totals were released, and debates among the voters essentially remained secret. Yet because a finalist needed 80 percent approval, a strong candidate like Parcells could be denied entry by only nine dissenters. Critics often noted that, by contrast, the Baseball Hall of Fame used more than 570 voters, preventing a small bloc from wielding unusual power.

"It's an oligarchy," Allen Barra wrote. "It might be time to expand the voting body to introduce some *real* democracy to Pro Football's Hall of Fame process in the form of four or five hundred writers, historians, and former coaches and players."

On August 4 in Canton, Parcells sat behind Curtis Martin on a stage at Fawcett Stadium for inductions. Before Martin's turn, the audience watched a video clip of his first NFL game: New England's 1995 preseason opener against Detroit, when Parcells called seven consecutive run plays to teach Boy Wonder a lesson about conditioning. As Parcells smiled at the memory, the audience applauded Martin's indefatigability. Then, wearing a yellow tie to match Hall of Fame attire, Parcells unveiled Boy Wonder's bronze bust before retaking his seat.

Martin set aside his prepared text and gave a stirring speech, describing the contours of his life and his improbable path to NFL greatness. The twenty-eight-minute address included Parcells's key role in dispensing lessons about football and life, and details of the abuse Rochella Dixon had endured from her husband. Sitting in the audience at Fawcett Stadium, his mother used a tissue to wipe away her tears.

38

Sean Payton's heart was racing almost as rapidly as his mind on the morning of March 21, 2012. The Saints head coach remained in shock while driving to Louis Armstrong New Orleans International Airport, moments after learning the NFL's verdict for Bountygate. Since 2009, his defensive coordinator Gregg Williams had institutionalized the payments of bonuses, or bounties, for potentially injurious tackles during games. Because the surreptitious program, involving at least twenty-two defensive players, violated league policies and had occurred under Sean Payton's watch, the NFL had banned him for the entire 2012 season.

Having expected a suspension of only perhaps a handful of games, Payton reeled from the harshest penalty ever handed to a head coach in the league's ninety-two-year history. It included a loss of almost $6 million from his $7 million salary. At this unimaginable low point, Payton, who hadn't missed a football season since his Pop Warner days, could think of only one person to consult. Five minutes after getting the shattering news, he dialed Bill Parcells.

Speaking via cell phone from his winter home in Jupiter, Parcells calmed his former Cowboys lieutenant. During the brief conversation Parcells revisited an old lesson: collect as much information as possible before making any important decisions. Heeding Parcells's advice, Payton canceled his imminent flight to Dallas, where his wife and kids lived for most of the year, and drove from the airport to Saints headquarters. Over the next several hours, Payton carefully assessed the consequences involving management and his staff. Executive VP and GM Mickey Loomis would miss eight games, and linebackers coach Joe Vitt six. Also, key defensive players like linebacker Jonathan Vilma faced suspensions.

The penalties could only be appealed to Commissioner Roger Goodell, who was both judge and jury, by an April 2 deadline. Parcells advised Payton, who'd set the process in motion, to use the intervening time for contingency plans. Owner Tom Benson empowered his disgraced head coach to find a temporary replacement, and early the next morning, Payton dialed Parcells again, this time with an impassioned plea: fill in for him as head coach for the season. Payton emphasized his mentor's leadership qualities and his unique skill set as a former GM, head coach, and linebackers guru.

"Listen, you can help us out here. You can do all those jobs."

Parcells replied, "I'll think about it."

The 49ers hadn't been the only team in late 2011 to quietly try luring Parcells back to the sidelines. In November, Penn State contacted him after firing Joe Paterno over the child-molestation scandal involving Jerry Sandusky. Parcells responded to that inquiry by recommending Eric Mangini, whom he'd taken an increased role in mentoring since the young coach had become estranged from Bill Belichick. So Penn State interviewed Mangini before hiring Belichick's offensive coordinator, Bill O'Brien.

After having shown zero interest in the Nittany Lions and briefly contemplating the 49ers job, Parcells strongly considered accepting New Orleans's short-term gig. Despite being only five months away from age seventy, Parcells wanted to help one of his favorite pupils, someone he considered to be like a son.

Parcells's NFL staffs, including the one in Dallas, had given small cash incentives for statistics such as special-team tackles inside the 20-yard line, blocked kicks, and defensive turnovers. While those inducements technically violated league rules against salary-cap circumvention, the practice remained widespread—it was the NFL's version of jaywalking.

So Parcells expressed dismay at Sean Payton's involvement in Bountygate.

"I didn't teach him that stuff," Parcells says in a disapproving tone.

Although Payton lacked direct involvement in Gregg Williams's bounties, he had failed to halt them before belatedly admitting their existence. But Parcells detected some hypocrisy from a league exploring an eighteen-game regular season that would inevitably lead to more injuries while espousing concern for player health.

Parcells also noted that after leaving New Orleans following the 2011 season, Williams had been hired by Rams head coach Jeff Fisher, his mentor and close friend. Fisher happened to be co-chairman of the NFL's Competition Committee, which oversaw rule changes with an increased emphasis on—ahem—player safety. So while Payton faced vilification outside of New Orleans, which revered him for capturing Super Bowl XLIV four years after Hurricane Katrina, Parcells embraced the fallen coach.

Joining the Saints would mean only a six-month stint, and part of Payton's rationale on his replacement stemmed from intimately knowing Parcells's tendency to coach from year to year anyway. After Bill's Dolphins tenure, the Saints also provided an opportunity for him to burnish his legacy late by guiding an NFL-record fifth team to the postseason and, in a best-case scenario, punctuating his career with a third Lombardi Trophy.

Conversely, Parcells faced a quandary: returning to the sidelines would reset the clock on his Hall of Fame eligibility. Five years after the 2012 season would put Parcells at age seventy-seven before his next crack. After being snubbed in February, however, Parcells refused to base his decision solely on the whims of Hall voters.

On March 27, Sean Payton made his first public comments since receiving his suspension. While taking questions from reporters at the NFL owners meeting in Palm Beach, Florida, he caused a tizzy in the sports world by broaching the possibility of Parcells as a temporary replacement. Parcells's friends, his family, the media, and his former players inundated the retired coach with calls, texts, and e-mails to offer opinions or glean insight. Lawrence Taylor joined the camp urging Parcells to take the job, seeing it as ideal, but many warned Parcells about the pitfalls, including the consequences involving the Hall of Fame.

Bill Parcells lived about twenty miles away from Palm Beach, so a few hours after Sean Payton's media Q&A the sullied coach took Saints executive vice president and GM Mickey Loomis to a nearby golf course to meet Parcells for the first time. The threesome played eighteen holes, giving Loomis and Parcells an opportunity to get acquainted. In discussing the New Orleans gig with Payton, Parcells became increasingly intrigued. The Saints were an offensive juggernaut, led by one of the best passers of his generation. Parcells had reached three Super Bowls with different quarterbacks, but he'd never coached a signal caller of Drew Brees's caliber.

The Pro Bowl quarterback had heard a great deal about Parcells from his head coach, and before New Orleans played in the 2010 Super Bowl, Payton introduced Parcells to Brees. The retired coach enjoyed getting acquainted with the Purdue product, and Parcells sensed that the feeling was mutual. Brees was Parcells's type of player, based on his football passion and ultracompetitiveness.

On October 16, 2011, the Saints lost at Tampa Bay, 26–20, after Brees tossed three interceptions, his highest total of the season. The gaffes overshadowed Brees's achievement as the first quarterback in NFL history to collect at least 350 passing yards in four consecutive games. After watching the contest on satellite TV that night, Parcells dialed Payton.

"Sean, tell Brees that if he was down in the arcade throwing balls at milk bottles to win a teddy bear for his girlfriend, she would have gone home empty-handed."

Payton relayed the message the next day, but Brees found no humor in it. The Saints coach dialed his mentor to convey the quarterback's reaction.

"Drew's mad at you."

"He is, huh?"

"Yeah."

"Well, what the hell is three interceptions, two in the second half? You don't think that's worse than a line about teddy bears?"

In his next game Brees produced five touchdowns and zero interceptions during a 62–7 rout of Indianapolis on *Monday Night Football*. Completing 31 of 35 passes, Brees led New Orleans to a franchise record for points scored. Parcells quickly phoned Payton to give the quarterback his due.

"Sean, tell Brees that we ran out of teddy bears up here. They're all gone. We were forced to order some more from the factory in South Korea." This time, hearing about Parcells's crack, Brees laughed hard.

Now, with a chance to join forces, Parcells believed that New Orleans's top player would provide the support essential for a substitute head coach. He relished his first chance to coach an all-time great at quarterback, an opportunity that had benefited historic rivals like Bill Belichick and Bill Walsh. Nevertheless, Parcells maintained reservations about the job. Sure, Bountygate had upended the franchise and created turmoil, a situation that he enjoyed addressing. But New Orleans needed a leader to keep things from cratering until Payton's return, not someone to jump-start the franchise, which is what Parcells loved most.

Perhaps the most significant drawback involved Payton's staff. Parcells had no direct ties to anyone on it, a disadvantage compounded by the gig's brevity. Parcells said to himself, "So if things don't go well, people will say, 'This guy tried to change everything we were doing.' And if it does go well, people will say, 'Well, shit, he had a built-in advantage.'"

Still, Payton emphasized the pluses. For one thing, New Orleans's off-season setup and practice structure were virtually identical to Parcells's system.

After about a week of vacillation, with the media reading the tea leaves daily, Parcells remained open to the job. But he wanted to ease his nagging concern about overseeing an unfamiliar staff, one likely to view him as a lame duck. So Parcells asked the Saints for permission to hire two disciples with head-coaching experience. The organization obliged, and Parcells took steps to lure Al Groh, Georgia Tech's defensive coordinator, and Eric Mangini, an ESPN analyst two years removed from guiding the Cleveland Browns.

While Tom Benson, the Saints' owner, and Payton embraced the idea, Loomis seemed reluctant about it, perhaps sensitive to the effect on the incumbent coaching staff. Also, some reports speculated that Parcells would land an executive role in the organization after Payton's return. "Who knows what Loomis really thought? I don't have any idea," Parcells says. "I don't know Loomis; I only met him once. But guys like me threaten guys like him." In early April, the appeals process for Payton gave Parcells an extra week to weigh matters, and he focused on his reservations.

Absent from the sidelines for six years, Parcells enjoyed retirement, living in Jupiter during the late fall, winter, and spring before heading to Saratoga Springs until the weather turned cold. Parcells had a sweet deal with ESPN, too, working a few times each year on prime-time specials like *Bill Parcells' Draft Confidential*.

Finally, Parcells remained uncertain about whether he possessed the energy required to do things in his maniacal way.

"It's like an old hunting dog," Parcells explains. "He gets that smell again." Parcells sniffs a few times. "He thinks, 'Oh yeah, I know what that is. I can hunt one more time.' But he's sitting on the porch. He hasn't been out there hunting in five or six years. He's forgotten what hunting really is. He figures, 'Oh, I can do this.' But when you get down there, it's not the same. And your name is gonna be on it. You want to try to do a good job, and yet you really have no control over anything."

So on April 11, Bill Parcells informed Sean Payton that he would be staying retired, but he offered to be of assistance in any other way possible. When news broke about Parcells's decision, his friends responded with a mixed reaction that encapsulated his own ambivalence. Lawrence Taylor, representing Parcells's disappointed supporters, called. "Coach, I had never known you to bitch out on anything." Parcells tried to explain that only months from becoming a septuagenarian, he was no longer eager to dive into stormy football waters. The former linebacker refused to buy into that reasoning, but in the apparent twilight of his life, with the Hall of Fame in the back of his mind, Bill Parcells felt at peace.

"I'm at a different place in the world now."

39

In his latest bid at football immortality, Bill Parcells was one of the fifteen modern-era candidates for the Class of 2013. As the voter charged with making the case for Parcells, *New York Daily News* sportswriter Gary Myers spent January trying to size up the forty-six-man board of selectors, speaking to roughly half of them. Sentiment about Parcells had improved from 2012, but some voters still questioned his candidacy. With 80 percent approval necessary for entry, Parcells's fate remained uncertain. Leading up to the Hall's annual meeting on February 2, Parcells had characteristically downplayed his chances, but unlike with previous bids, he conceded that enshrinement would mean the world to him.

The panel of selectors met at a convention center in New Orleans for a winnowing process that began at 8 a.m. Myers, a football columnist who'd known Parcells for roughly three decades, highlighted one of Parcells's most impressive statistics: 4-1 in the postseason versus Hall of Fame coaches Joe Gibbs, Marv Levy, and Bill Walsh. He also pointed out that Parcells was tenth on the list of winningest NFL coaches of all time. Perhaps the best evidence of Parcells's impact lay in his towering coaching tree, which Parcells dubbed "those who followed." From among those followers, Myers provided the glowing statements of two potential Hall of Famers: Bill Belichick and Tom Coughlin. Finally, the sportswriter reminded the forty-five other voters that Parcells was among the best motivators in NFL history.

Back in Jupiter, Bill Parcells spent the day trying to keep his mind occupied. He worked out in the morning before running several errands. Considering how much he had ached to be enshrined with Boy Wonder, Parcells found waiting out the eight-hour meeting to be less stressful this go-around.

Once again his candidacy required the longest discussion, almost an hour. As usual, Parcells made the first cut from fifteen to ten. Former owners Ed DeBartolo and Art Modell were eliminated, which seemed to strengthen Parcells's chances, given the difficulty of two non-players being elected in the same year. Making the final five, though, remained a challenge because competition was its strongest in recent memory.

The pared-down list of ten went as follows: former running back

Jerome Bettis, ex-wideout Cris Carter, former defensive end Charles Haley, ex–offensive tackle Jonathan Ogden, ex-wideout Andre Reed, former defensive lineman Warren Sapp, ex–defensive lineman Michael Strahan, ex-cornerback Aeneas Williams, and former offensive lineman Larry Allen, who had played for Parcells's Cowboys from 2003 to 2005 before being released.

The first person propelled to the final five was Larry Allen, followed by Cris Carter and then Jonathan Ogden. Based on alphabetical order, "Bill Parcells" would be called next if he made the cut. And he was, keeping him alive as an inductee. Lastly, Warren Sapp essentially beat out Michael Strahan. Now each candidate still needed 80 percent approval, or a thumbs-up from at least thirty-six selectors.

Finally, on his fourth bid for enshrinement, Parcells entered the most exclusive organization in the sport to which he had devoted his life. His selection into the Hall highlighted the sterling class of seven, which included two senior candidates: defensive tackle Curley Culp and linebacker Dave Robinson, the eleventh player from Vince Lombardi's Packers. The final results remained secret until they were aired on the NFL Network at 5:30 p.m. the same day. Receiving the word, Parcells was overcome with emotion. His mind raced with memories from his long, storied career. Bill Parcells thought about Mickey Corcoran more than anyone else, thrilled that his ninety-one-year-old mentor was alive to share in the honor.

As the twenty-second head coach elected to the Hall, Parcells now found himself in the company of icons like Al Davis, Tom Landry, and Chuck Noll, who had helped mold him, rivals like Joe Gibbs and Bill Walsh, and football legends he revered, including Paul Brown, Don Shula, and Vince Lombardi. Head coaches made up less than 10 percent of the Hall's membership, and increasingly faced stiff competition from top players; as a football historian, Parcells relished membership in the special group of his peers.

"It's beyond comprehension," he says. "I was among my heroes."

Moments after learning he'd been selected, Bill Parcells received a congratulatory phone call from a fellow Hall of Fame coach: John Madden. In early 2006, when the broadcaster and ex–Raiders coach had learned of his selection, Parcells dialed him before anyone else. After speaking to Madden briefly, Parcells received a cavalcade of calls from family, friends, disciples, and former players. Mickey Corcoran's voice-mail message had been left just moments after the big news went public. Parcells's election also generated congratulatory statements from his five former NFL employers, including Robert Kraft, who offered praise and expressed enthusiasm about watching his former head coach's enshrinement.

In recent years, the two men had exchanged conciliatory words whenever they crossed paths at league events like the Super Bowl. They had also both conveyed regret about the behavior that led to their acrimonious divorce, and since late 2011, the Patriots owner had even advocated for Parcells's Hall of Fame candidacy. Considering the deep wounds from their battles during the 1990s, they could never quite be friends, but the old adversaries had seemed to put their animosity behind them.

A couple hours after learning of his selection, Parcells telephoned George Martin. "I need you to do me a favor."

Parcells asked his former Giants co-captain to present him in the early-August induction. Martin responded with elation and surprise. He deemed it the best post-NFL honor short of enshrinement, and had figured that Parcells would seek one of his Hall of Fame players or top disciples.

While the choice seemed surprising to many, it made sense to those with insight into Parcells's early years as an NFL head coach. During Parcells's pivotal 1984 season, Martin, then a player representative, provided indispensable support, particularly in countering Big Blue's drug problems before the NFL had established a policy. Parcells considered Martin's assistance to be career-saving. As a player, George Martin had related more to Bill Parcells, twelve years his elder, than to many of his younger teammates. The two grew so close that they once hatched an idea to buy each of their wives a baby grand piano for Christmas from the same New Jersey store. Judy cried in happiness when she discovered hers.

Parcells would be joining three Hall of Famers from his Big Blue teams: Harry Carson, Lawrence Taylor, and Wellington Mara. Unlike the Baseball Hall of Fame, which featured team caps on its plaques, the football shrine lacked club affiliations. Nonetheless, more as a gesture than anything, Parcells telephoned Giants president and CEO John Mara with a request befitting the baseball honor.

"John, I'd like to go in as a Giant, if you'll have me."

Mara replied, "We wouldn't have it any other way."

The summer ceremonies, starting on Thursday, August 1, also marked the Hall of Fame's fiftieth anniversary. To celebrate the occasion and welcome the new class, 121 of the 163 living members of the Hall gathered in Canton, football's birthplace. The largest such assembly in sports history, it featured icons from Jim Brown to Joe Namath to Deion Sanders. On the first day, Bill Parcells attended a dinner function with his ex-wife, Judy, and their daughters. Former wideout Cris Carter approached Parcells's table and handed his fellow inductee a small box containing a tie clip inscribed "278," in honor of Parcells's becoming Canton's 278th inductee.

Parcells reacted with surprise and pleasure at the gift from a former player he had never even coached. Seeing his appreciative response, Carter grew teary-eyed, and then the floodgates opened as Parcells started crying, joined by two of his daughters. The two men did have a connection that dated back to an impromptu telephone conversation on September 4, 1990. Only a few days before the regular season, Eagles head coach Buddy Ryan released Cris Carter partly because of drug and alcohol issues. Bill Parcells, whose team lacked punch at wideout despite its championship promise, dialed the fourth-year player with an invitation to Giants headquarters.

"Cris, this is Parcells. How long will it take you to get here?"

Carter responded excitedly, "Coach, I just packed my car. I can be there in a couple of hours." Parcells informed Carter that Big Blue, which had been 12-4 the previous season, intended to claim him off waivers. The revelation boosted Carter's spirits just when his pro career seemed threatened. Several minutes after their conversation, however, Carter dialed Parcells with an update: the Vikings, who were 10-6 in 1989, had also claimed him, and according to NFL rules, the team with the lesser record gained the athlete. Carter was disappointed to miss the chance to play for one of the NFL's top coaches on a championship-caliber team. Nonetheless, the Ohio State product went on to transform his career in Minnesota, setting several franchise records and emerging as one of the best wideouts in league history.

Carter never forgot the uplifting telephone call; Bill Parcells didn't grasp its impact until more than two decades later, when he received his fellow inductee's gift.

Friday at noon, Bill Parcells attended the Ray Nitschke Memorial Luncheon, an event that maintained a tradition in which enshrined members offered remarks to the new class about their experiences, as well as a description of the benefits and responsibilities of induction. Wearing the blue golf shirt given to each Hall of Famer, Parcells felt privileged to be in a private room at the Hall of Fame with football greats from multiple generations. He enjoyed seeing figures like Willie Brown, the former Bronco and Raider, whom he viewed as the best cornerback ever. "The history of pro football is right there," Parcells says, "and now you're part of it."

Curtis Martin sat next to Bill Parcells at a table that included Russ Grimm, Steve Largent, and Joe Gibbs. During that afternoon, the coaching archrivals spoke more to each other than they had in decades as competitors. "You learn to respect your enemies but execute all traitors," Parcells says, "and that's how I felt about Joe. I always held him in high regard."

As Joe Gibbs and other top counterparts like Marv Levy stood to address their new peers, Bill Parcells listened raptly. Boy Wonder also offered some anecdotes to the gathering about his year since induction. And as he ended his remarks, Martin acknowledged Parcells. "I just want to take the opportunity to thank this man. Because I'm not here talking to you guys if not for him. Parcells not only helped my career being what it was, but he helped save my life in some respects." Boy Wonder gave his former coach a meaningful look. The Big Tuna was deeply touched, but this time he managed to fight off tears.

The class of 2013 capped induction eve with a ceremonial dinner, during which its members received their golden jackets, the honorary attire for inductees. Bill Parcells grinned while trying on his new gear with help from George Martin. On Saturday morning, August 3, hours before enshrinement, Martin sat next to Parcells in an antique vehicle for the Grand Parade, highlighted by the presence of football's immortals: Dick Butkus, Earl Campbell, Joe Greene, John Madden, Barry Sanders, Gale Sayers, and others. Almost 200,000 fans lined the 2.2-mile route, cheering their heroes in the caravan, which included marching bands and floats. Not far from Parcells, Jerry Jones and Larry Allen shared a convertible.

After starting the day feeling reserved and fidgety, midway through the parade Parcells loosened up. When fans of other clubs yelled that he should coach their teams, he offered a thumbs-up sign, and he occasionally responded to questions from the crowd. Parcells especially acknowledged Giants Nation, pointing out Big Blue gear and paraphernalia to George Martin.

Almost 120 guests of Bill Parcells traveled to Canton for his enshrinement, but to reach the main event a couple hours before the 7 p.m. start, Parcells, wearing his golden jacket, took a short bus ride with the person who had influenced him more than anyone except his father: Mickey Corcoran. When they arrived, an overflowing audience sat at tables placed on the gridiron of Fawcett Stadium, adjacent to the Hall of Fame. The 22,375-seat arena contained a stage for the inductees.

ESPN personality Chris Berman emceed an introductory roundup of the 121 incumbent Hall of Famers, including Harry Carson and Lawrence Taylor. The backstage bustled with activity as the football immortals mingled while eating sandwiches and sipping soft drinks. The group included Darrell Green, Jerry Rice, Emmitt Smith, Roger Staubach, Lawrence Taylor, and Steve Young. Several of them, like L.T., decided to watch the event backstage because of its oversized flat-screen monitor and intimate setting.

Bill Belichick left his audience seat to make an appearance backstage and chitchat. The three-time Super Bowl winner joked about getting into the Hall strictly as a visitor. That morning Belichick had put his team through practice before taking a private plane to Akron with his linebackers coach, Pepper Johnson. Before returning to his stadium-floor seat, Belichick visited Parcells on the main stage for several minutes. As the two men posed together for some photos, Belichick explained that he needed to fly back to New England immediately after the enshrinement. Parcells, of course, understood the demands of an NFL head coach, especially during training camp.

Two of Parcells's other prominent disciples, Tom Coughlin and Sean Payton, also took the rare measure of leaving training camp to watch his induction. Coughlin flew on a charter plane with a large Giants contingent, missing his team's meetings on Saturday night. Belichick, Coughlin, and Payton owned a total of six Lombardi Trophies. Coughlin's second title, for Super Bowl XLVI, which had been earned by defeating Belichick in another comeback thriller, now matched Parcells's total.

Other former Parcells assistants in Canton included Maurice Carthon, Romeo Crennel, Al Groh, Fred Hoaglin, Pat Hodgson, Chris Palmer, Mike Pope, and Mike Sweatman. Although Parcells had last coached the Giants in 1991, Big Blue brought more of his supporters than any other club. They included Ann Mara, the franchise's matriarch as Wellington's wife; co-owner John Mara and his siblings Chris, Frank, and Susan; plus Parcells's former trainer Ronnie Barnes, perhaps his best friend on the team. Among Parcells's ex–Giants players who came separately were Raul Allegre, Matt Bahr, Brad Benson, Jim Burt, Rob Carpenter, Don Hasselbeck, Sean Landeta, Karl Nelson, Bart Oates, Gary Reasons, Jerome Sally, and Phil Simms.

A strong Cowboys contingent featured top players acquired during Parcells's tenure: quarterback Tony Romo, linebacker DeMarcus Ware, and tight end Jason Witten. Vinny Testaverde represented the Parcells Guys who had played for him on multiple teams. Former personnel colleagues like Scott Pioli and Mike Tannenbaum also showed up. Some of Parcells's best friends in Canton included Bobby Green, Tony La Russa, Shug McGaughey, and Ron Wolf.

After introducing Bill Parcells for enshrinement, George Martin helped him remove a blue cover to reveal a stern-faced bust. The twenty-second coach to be inducted grinned, and patted the back of the sculpted neck.

Without any notes, he took to the podium wearing a blue tie, white shirt, and flower lapel pin that matched his golden jacket. Parcells had organized his thoughts and memorized his speech during daily workouts on the StairMaster. He aimed to reflect on his almost two decades as an

NFL coach yet avoid reminiscing about any of his 183 victories, even his two Super Bowl triumphs. He had also decided against mentioning his milestones or achievements, although a jumbo screen behind him replayed career highlights.

Instead, during an assertive yet gracious and inspiring address, Parcells told some insightful stories, life lessons that he'd used to reach football immortality. He spent much of his twenty-minute address on the Giants, expressing gratitude for the people, some already dead, who'd been instrumental throughout his football life. Parcells paid tribute to his family, and thanked those who had shaped him from a brash teenager into an obscure college coach, and then, finally, into a sports icon.

Less than two minutes into his speech, Parcells made a special request concerning the placement of his bust, which remained several feet behind him. "I'd like this to be somewhere near Lawrence Taylor, so I can keep an eye on that sucker." The audience erupted in laughter and applause.

Sitting backstage next to Pepper Johnson, L.T. beamed as he told his former teammate, "I've heard that line before."

Conveying modesty, Parcells stressed that all his NFL teams had provided the support necessary for success. He expressed gratitude to the owners who had employed him, listing "the Mara family," Robert Kraft, Leon Hess, and "the great Jerry Jones and his family there in Dallas." Noting his position with the Dolphins as an "administrator," Parcells added Wayne Huizenga and Stephen Ross to the group.

"I've seen coaches go to [NFL] franchises and get fired very quickly because the situation would not allow them to succeed," he said. "Fortunately for Bill Parcells, I was never in one of those situations." Sensitive as always to showing favoritism to any one of his dozens of disciples, Parcells stressed their contributions as a group. But then he alluded to Belichick, Coughlin, and Payton. "I was lucky to have some of the top names currently as head coaches in pro football. I want them to know that I'm grateful for their support of me—very, very grateful. The nuts and bolts of a football operation are your assistant coaches. I just want to say that I take pride in their individual accomplishments, and I'm looking for a couple more championships out of some of them, so let's go."

Bill Belichick, wearing a blue short-sleeve shirt while sitting in the audience, smiled.

Then Parcells thanked a string of former peers, colleagues, and friends who had substantially helped him in the NFL: Gil Brandt, Al Davis, Mike Holovak, Bucko Kilroy, Chuck Knox, Tom Landry, Chuck Noll, Ron Wolf. "Some of the great names," Parcells noted, "in football history." He explained that because of their guidance early in his NFL career, he had vowed to mentor young coaches and scouts the same way. Parcells mentioned the death of his first agent, Robert Fraley, in the 1999 airplane crash that had also killed the golfer Payne Stewart. Fraley's many top clients included former defensive tackle Cortez Kennedy from the class of 2012. After the announcement of the class of 2013, Parcells added, Kennedy had telephoned him to say that Fraley would have been proud of them.

Parcells even credited his secretaries, who were in attendance, for handling "Blue Mondays." Regardless of Sunday's outcome, he explained, the head coach inevitably would be grouchy due to an issue like a player injury or a unit's underperforming. "But these secretaries are pretty sharp. They learn when they start hearing these short, one-word answers that a coach should not be talked to on Monday, because he's not worth talking to."

In summing up his parents, siblings, and upbringing, Parcells said, "I didn't come up the hard way, I didn't come up the easy way. I grew up in an average American family in northern New Jersey. Had a great dad. Had a lot of wisdom imparted to me. Had a mother that was highly confrontational. I probably got a little of that as well. Had two brothers, one of whom is deceased. I know he's looking down. My other brother is here tonight. And I had a sister. I know she's watching tonight. It was all good."

Judy Parcells sat in the front row of the audience, next to Jill, Dallas, Scott Pioli, and Bill's granddaughter Mia. Kelly Mandart was in the same section, not far from Suzy, but several seats away from Judy. Bill Parcells thanked his "lovely daughters" for having suffered through his peripatetic coaching career, especially during their childhoods, and found a silver lining in their being forced to move every two or three years. "I know that they travel fearlessly now; they're not intimidated by change." Parcells expressed pride in them for emerging as good parents and productive members of society.

"I love you girls," he said.

His girls responded with smiles.

Parcells also praised his ex-wife for holding the family together while coping with his football obsession. "I know full well that if it was just left to me that I wouldn't have gotten the job done. I was not only married to her, but I was married to something else as well. So I commend her for a job well done, and I thank her very much for it."

The crowd applauded, with Jill clapping harder than perhaps anyone.

Parcells kept a promise he'd made to Mickey Corcoran in 1987, just after Big Blue's first Super Bowl title: his former high school basketball coach would not be forgotten. Parcells looked down at Corcoran, who was wearing a red golf shirt and sitting in the second row behind Judy. Then the new inductee gave his most extensive remarks about anyone.

"He's pretty famous in North Jersey. He was everything that a four-teen-year-old guy needed. He was a coach, a teacher, a disciplinarian, a butt kicker. And I don't know how to characterize this relationship that we've had for fifty-eight years, but whatever adjective you could use to por-tray something good, you could use it with this relationship.

"He's been a great friend to me. He's been like a second father. He's somebody I could always talk to, my guidance counselor. He knows the love I have in my heart for him. As I said, he's ninety-two, and I've got to get ten or fifteen more years out of you, buster, so let's go."

Corcoran laughed as the audience erupted.

Parcells said that the most important lesson of his profession had come from Dean Pryor, the coach who had lured him to Hastings in 1964 for his first coaching gig. Parcells said, "He taught me one vital, vital piece of information that I took with me and preached to every organization, to every university, to my coaching staff, to my individual coaches, and I remind myself every day. That vital piece of information was, 'Bill, the players deserve a chance to win, and you have an obligatory responsibility to give it to them.'"

Pryor, sitting next to Judy, smiled and waved briefly at Parcells in acknowledgment.

Parcells then singled out the person who had brought him to the Giants: Ray Perkins. Parcells conspicuously failed to mention their GM, George Young, but he also left out some of his favorite players like Curtis Martin and Phil Simms. His only former players to receive shout-outs were "the great Harry Carson," George Martin, and L.T.

Parcells expounded on a description of the locker room he'd once heard from Steve Young, class of 2005, as being "a great laboratory for human behavior." Parcells turned to his left, glancing at the ex-quarterback, who was seated nearby. Young smiled in surprise at being credited for the analogy. Parcells noted that locker rooms embody diversity, with blacks, whites, Hispanics, Asians, Samoans, Tongans, and Native Americans. "I played and coached with them all, and the only thing that made any dif-ference is: Are you willing to help? And if you are, come on in. If you're not, get the heck out of here."

For emphasis, Parcells made a good-riddance motion.

"We've got some rules and regulations in the locker room, but they're not written down. After you've been there just a couple of days, you know what they are. If someone should deviate and violate those rules, you find out that there is a judge and jury in that room and they act decisively. Their decisions are final, because we don't have any appellate courts in there."

The best aspect of a locker room, Parcells said, is the camaraderie created by a range of experiences involving things like humor and achievement. "We've got that momentary time of exhilaration where you hoist that championship trophy over your head, and I don't know what happens, but some mystical blood kinship is formed, and although it's a fleeting moment, that kinship lasts for the rest of your life. And the thing I'm most proud of with my teams is they have it, and I know, because I lived it. Because when something goes wrong with one, all the others run to help.

"Now, on the other side of that locker room, there's darkness. There's defeat. There's despondency, there's pain. You see those players carrying those IVs onto the aircraft after a mid-summer or early-season game in a hot-weather city, and the trainers are rushing to pack them in ice, and they can't sit in their seats because they'll cramp up, so they've got to lay in the aisle." Parcells described being a longtime coach in the NFL, with its downside including tragedy and even death, as being a "priceless, priceless education."

He concluded his speech with an anecdote from the start of his Giants head-coaching stint. Roughly ten minutes after his introductory press conference, he was sitting in his office when Wellington Mara stepped in. Big Blue's patriarch told his new leader, "Bill, let's take a walk." They left the office, Parcells following Mara down the stairs toward the locker room.

Parcells recalled to the audience, "In the old Giants Stadium, the Giants players will remember that as you walk through the players entrance, there was a little room to the left, and it was like a little alcove room and had a couple chairs in it. Wellington took me over to the wall in that place, and on the wall was a little plaque and it had an inscription on it.

"Coincidentally, that inscription was attributed to the first black player ever inducted into this Hall of Fame. His name was Emlen Tunnell, and he was inducted in the class of 1967. That inscription said, '**Losers assemble in little groups and complain about the coaches and the players in other little groups, but winners assemble as a team.**'

"Well, tonight, ladies and gentlemen, I get to do just that. I'm honored, I'm grateful, and I'm thankful to every single one of you out there that had something to do with this. Thank you very much."

The audience at Fawcett Stadium rose for a standing ovation to Bill Parcells's storied and unforgettable football life.

Acknowledgments

Bill Parcells and Nunyo Demasio are grateful to everyone who helped us produce this book. Bill asked me to get more specific in acknowledging the cast of dozens.

At the earliest stage, 2008, the brilliant Kurt Andersen, who I'm fortunate to call my "pro bono consigliere," gave input on the concept, read material, and granted access to his massive Rolodex. Five years later, after I wrote most of the book with Bill's imprimatur, we hired the David Black Agency, whose namesake president teamed with literary agent David Larabell and their assistant, Sarah Smith, to adeptly fine-tune our proposal and secure a contract with an ideal publisher: Crown Archetype, an imprint of Random House.

My trusty and astute publishing lawyer, Eric Rayman, helped negotiate multiple contracts while scrutinizing the intertwined moving parts. As I once told Eric, who also gave us valuable feedback on the manuscript, it's good to have a member of the so-called Harvard mafia watching your back.

Rhahime Bell financed much of this endeavor, waiting more than half a decade for a payoff and resisting the temptation to get life insurance on me. Substantial aid also came from Dr. Kafui Demasio; Doug Lo, "the mayor of Seattle"; and Dr. Craig Moskowitz. Without this group, a book of this scope would have remained a pipe dream.

You're in good company partnering with any group overseen by Crown publisher Tina Constable, whom we nicknamed the Big Tina. Her empire contains several sharp, hard-working people like publicity director Tammy Blake, production-editorial director Amy Boorstein, managing editor Rachel Meier, and assistants Jennifer Reyes and Jenni Zellner. Regardless, the Big Tina herself displayed extraordinary multitasking abilities, which included occasionally sending inspiring e-mails. Bill and I were delighted to have someone with Tina's energy and leadership embrace our vision.

After acquiring the book, her lieutenant, Mauro DiPreta, showed a combination of both street smarts and book smarts while steering the project. He navigated Parcells's idiosyncrasies so skillfully that I warned him against leaving to run his own publishing house until after the book's release. Alas, months before *Parcells* hit the shelves, Mauro departed for the top job at a different publisher. Another of Tina's editors, Dominick Anfuso, picked a striking cover image and positioned Crown's folks for the home stretch.

Bill and I are grateful for editorial director Jacob Lewis's orchestration, judgment, and cool to help overcome a late manuscript despite the tremendous inconvenience to his crew, including Mark Birkey, a persnickety and versatile production editor. Jacob went beyond the call—even taking one during his summer vacation. Copy editor Aja Pollock's eagle eye took the book to a higher level.

Thanks goes to Matthew Martin, the associate general counsel of Random House, for vetting the manuscript. Dan Zitt, the publisher's audiobook guru, displayed passion and creativity, turning it into a quality recording.

The leader of my own editorial team, Peter Guzzardi, lived up to his reputation as a book doctor with few peers. Peter remained enthusiastic and diligent while polishing the manuscript for more than a year. Considering Bill's long, storied life, the word count threatened to reach *War and Peace* proportions, but Peter's exquisite trims under deadline pressure made the cuts virtually unidentifiable.

Much of the football insight came from our NFL historian, researcher, and fact-checker, Dan Daly, whose encyclopedic knowledge impressed even the great Bill Parcells. We were lucky to land someone like Dan, an author himself, most recently of *The National Forgotten League,* which examines the NFL's first fifty years.

Lisa Buch did yeoman's work as our photo researcher, helping us sort through so many photos, digging up some gems, giving sharp input, and allowing Crown's art department, including designer Barbara Sturman, to do its thing. Author Jamie Malanowski, an original member of my team, markedly helped organize and improve my copy and gave key editorial advice.

Eye doctor Craig Moskowitz offered the invaluable perspective of a well-rounded and well-read sports fan. We heeded many of his suggestions, like identifying the left anterior descending artery as "the widow maker" for the chapter covering Bill's heart surgery. I'm also grateful for the feedback of John Huey despite his busy schedule overseeing Time Inc.

Before Bill and I looked for the right publisher, a detailed, written critique by author Ira Berkow made us feel as if we were on the right track. I have an inkling that until Bill saw Ira's letter in early 2012 on multiple chapters, he wasn't quite sure what he'd gotten himself into.

Ann Tanenbaum, the publisher of her namesake international company, provided encouragement, candor, and wisdom, especially during the late stages. Author Steve Coll, my ex–managing editor at the *Washington Post* and now the dean of Columbia Journalism School, offered guidance.

And in an unforgettable gesture, Richard Stengel took time from his hectic schedule running *Time* to offer an opportunity for freelance work until I landed a book deal.

During an important juncture, my cousin Dr. Kafui Demasio provided housing in Westchester County. Down the stretch, though, I all but lived in the New York Society Library, an author's haven with its private rooms and numerous quiet spots. When the assistant head librarian, Carolyn Waters, first gave me a tour, I was hooked.

In one telephone conversation early on, author Michael Lewis candidly conveyed the project's challenges based on his experience penning a cover story about Bill for the *New York Times Magazine* in 2006. But even before I wrote one word, ESPN's publishing honcho Gary Hoenig expressed enthusiasm about *Parcells,* and envisioned James Gandolfini playing the lead role in a movie adaptation. Gary's boss, John Walsh, sat down with me to convey ideas for the manuscript. And author David Maraniss let me pick his brain about his methods for producing his classic book on Vince Lombardi.

Special mention must go to Bill's ex-wife, Judy; their daughters, Dallas, Jill, and Suzy; and his girlfriend, Kelly Mandart, for trusting me with sensitive information, providing insight into the man behind the icon.

George Swede gave me a tour of Hasbrouck Heights, New Jersey, where he grew up with Bill. And Army Capt. Robert McGovern, a former NFL linebacker, took me around his hometown of Oradell, New Jersey, where Bill lived during his high school years.

At least four interviewees died before the book's release: Dr. V. Paul Addonizio, former NFL coach Ron Erhardt, ex–Giants wideout Stacy Robinson, and filmmaker Steve Sabol. Dr. Addonizio, a prolific heart surgeon, explained Parcells's bypass in layman's terms, and gave me an open invitation to watch him perform surgery. Sabol provided unfettered access to the treasure trove of video at NFL Films in Mount Laurel, New Jersey.

Greg Aiello, the NFL's PR chief, answered numerous questions about the league or connected me with the right folks.

Kathleen Smith, the owner of the Saratoga Arms hotel, gave me a tour of Saratoga Springs, New York, helping to show why Bill settled down there. Thanks also goes to Kathleen's staff, including daughters Amy and Sheila and Judy Kennedy, for its hospitality during my many trips to see Bill.

Random House's Bette Graber and Regnery's Katharine Mancuso helped us cut through red tape for copyrighted material. The two daughters of late author Bill Libby, Laurie Brazzle and Allyson Tayson, granted permission to excerpt from Libby's *The Coaches* with no strings attached. A shoutout goes to Oklahoma-based Kelli Masters, the groundbreaking NFL agent and attorney for her last-minute services.

The one and only Alexa Roubachewsky tolerated my obsession with the book, although she did say that I should "marry Bill Parcells" instead of her, spurring an impromptu call from him.

For several years, Bobby Green, a member of Bill's inner circle, was a de facto assistant. A range of support came from Jarrett Bell, Kenyatta Bell (no relation), Greg Bishop, Tor Bornholdt, Anthony Brown, Damien Brown (no relation), Bobby and Milano Buckley, Les Carpenter, Lisa Chavarri, Fame Cohen, Ronard Coombs, Pierre Diaz, Mike Florio, Peter Forbes, George Francois, John Gado, Leah George, Sheldon Gilbert, Damon Hack, Tom Hamaric, Cathy Henkel, Harry Jaffe, Robert Jamieson, Joe Jeannot, Sloane Kelley, Peter King, Ken Langone, Greg Lee, Mark and Paul McCarthy, Isabel Murphy, Bill Nedoroscik, Steven O'Reilly, Julia Payne, Rob Polishook, Tim Smith, Tanya Young, Zack Secilmis, and Ned Vail.

Special gratitude goes to Richard Johnson, Rev. Dr. K Karpen, Lleanna McReynolds, Olga Obymako, Cynthia Round, Anne Scirmont, Rev. Dr. Esteen Tapp, and Hubie Toth.

I would never have gotten anywhere in my career without Seattle's incomparable Carole Carmichael, Neil Amdur, Leon Carter, Milton Coleman, Marie Davitt, Len Downie, John Huey, Terry McDonell, Norman Pearlstine, Pam Robinson, George Solomon, Barry Werner, the late Dr. Roger Wetherington, and Kevin Whitmer. I'm grateful for writing pointers from Ira Berkow, Robert Lipsyte, Bob Roe, and George Vecsey. Special thanks goes to ESPN executives Rob King and Leon Carter and *Washington Post* managing editor Kevin Merida for being role models; and to the great Donald Graham for his galvanizing notes over the years. Leon occasionally took my calls past midnight for updates on the project.

Not surprisingly, our family members played crucial roles in this endeavor. Doug, Bill's youngest brother, hosted me in the Oradell home where the Big Tuna lived as a teenager. Thanks goes to my sister Fafa, for her miscellaneous assistance; brother Bubu; niece "little" Aseye; aunt Phoebe; cousin Ezekiel; and the matriarch, Dorcas Demasio, a.k.a. Queen Dorcas.

It took almost an entire year to convince Bill to cooperate in this type of endeavor. The turning point came after I sent him a twenty-page summary about my mother's life: moving from Ghana to Harlem, USA, then working day and night to put five kids, including three boys, through college. Bill contacted me the next day, said that I should be writing *her* story instead of his, and invited me to his home in Saratoga Springs.

We wish our siblings were still around to check out *Parcells*—Bill's brother Don and my sister Aseye and brother Nana—but we know that they are watching and smiling, maybe even reading.

The Coaches

As Florida State linebackers coach in 1972, Bill Parcells read the preface for Bill Libby's *The Coaches*, published that year by Regnery. Feeling that it eloquently described his profession, Parcells condensed the 1,039-word introduction into roughly 390 words that hit home the most. The coach laminated the shortened version. Throughout his long football career, he re-read it, especially during tough times. Below is the exact wording from Parcells's sheet.

He is called "Coach." It is a difficult job, and there is no clear way to succeed in it. One cannot copy another who is a winner, for there seems to be some subtle, secret chemistry of personality that enables a person to lead successfully, and no one really knows what it is. Those who have succeeded and those who have failed represent all kinds—young and old, inexperienced and experienced, hard and soft, tough and gentle, good-natured and foul-tempered, proud and profane, articulate and inarticulate, even dedicated and casual. Most are dedicated, some more than others. Some are smarter than others, but intelligence is not enough. All want to win, but some want to win more than others, and just wanting to win is not enough in any event. Even winning is often not enough. Losers almost always get fired, but winners get fired, too.

He is out in the open being judged publicly almost every day or night for six, seven, or eight months a year by those who may or may not be qualified to judge him. And every victory and every defeat is recorded constantly in print or on the air and periodically totaled up.

The coach has no place to hide. He cannot just let the job go for a while or do a bad job and assume no one will notice as most of us can. He cannot satisfy everyone. Seldom can he even satisfy very many. Rarely can he even satisfy himself. If he wins once, he must win the next time, too.

Coaches plot victories, suffer defeats, and endure criticism from within and without. They neglect their families,
travel endlessly, and live alone in a spotlight surrounded by
others. Theirs may be the worst profession—unreasonably
demanding and insecure and full of unrelenting pressures.
Why do they put up with it? Why do they do it? Having
seen them hired and hailed as geniuses at gaudy, party-
like press conferences and having seen them fired with pat
phrases such as "fool" or "incompetent," I have wondered
about them. Having seen them exultant in victory and
depressed by defeat, I have sympathized with them. Having
seen some broken by the job and others die from it, one is
moved to admire them and to hope that someday the world
will learn to understand them.

All-Parcells Team

OFFENSE

QUARTERBACK
PHIL SIMMS, New York Giants
VINNY TESTAVERDE, New York Jets
DREW BLEDSOE, New England Patriots, Dallas Cowboys

OFFENSIVE TACKLE
JUMBO ELLIOTT, New York Giants
BRUCE ARMSTRONG, New England Patriots
MARK COLUMBO, Dallas Cowboys

GUARD
BILL ARD, New York Giants
WILLIAM ROBERTS, New York Giants, New England Patriots,
    New York Jets
CHRIS GODFREY, New York Giants

CENTER
KEVIN MAWAE, New York Jets
ANDRE GURODE, Dallas Cowboys
BART OATES, New York Giants

RUNNING BACK
CURTIS MARTIN, New England Patriots, New York Jets
O. J. ANDERSON, New York Giants
JOE MORRIS, New York Giants

THIRD-DOWN RUNNING BACK
DAVE MEGGETT, New York Giants, New England Patriots
TONY GALBREATH, New York Giants

FULLBACK
MAURICE CARTHON, New York Giants
KEVIN TURNER, New England Patriots
SAM GASH, New England Patriots, New York Jets

WIDE RECEIVER
Keyshawn Johnson, New York Jets, Dallas Cowboys
Terry Glenn, New England Patriots, Dallas Cowboys
Wayne Chrebet, New York Jets

TIGHT END
Mark Bavaro, New York Giants
Ben Coates, New England Patriots
Jason Witten, Dallas Cowboys

RETURNER
Dave Meggett, New York Giants
Troy Brown, New England Patriots
Phil McConkey, New York Giants

FIELD-GOAL KICKER
Matt Bahr, New York Giants, New England Patriots
Adam Vinatieri, New England Patriots

DEFENSE

DEFENSIVE END
George Martin, New York Giants
Leonard Marshall, New York Giants
Greg Ellis, Dallas Cowboys

NOSE TACKLE
Jason Ferguson, New York Jets, Dallas Cowboys
Jim Burt, New York Giants
Jay Ratliff, Dallas Cowboys

INSIDE LINEBACKER
Harry Carson, New York Giants,
Pepper Johnson, New York Giants, New York Jets
Dat Nguyen, Dallas Cowboys
Vincent Brown, New England Patriots

OUTSIDE LINEBACKER
 Lawrence Taylor, New York Giants
 DeMarcus Ware, Dallas Cowboys
 Carl Banks, New York Giants
 Andre Tippett, New England Patriots
 Willie McGinest, New England Patriots
 Brad Van Pelt, New York Giants
 Mo Lewis, New York Jets

CORNERBACK
 Mark Collins, New York Giants
 Maurice Hurst, New England Patriots
 Marcus Coleman, New York Jets
 Aaron Glenn, New York Jets
 Everson Walls, New York Giants

SAFETY
 Terry Kinard, New York Giants
 Darren Woodson, Dallas Cowboys
 Lawyer Milloy, New England Patriots

PUNTER
 Sean Landeta, New York Giants
 Tom Tupa, New England Patriots, New York Jets

Bill Parcells's Unsung Opponents

MORTEN ANDERSEN, KICKER
New Orleans Saints (1982–94), Atlanta Falcons (1995–2000, 2006–7),
New York Giants (2001), Kansas City Chiefs (2002–3), Minnesota
Vikings (2004)

> "I always thought he would make the kick."

WILLIAM ANDREWS, FULLBACK
Atlanta Falcons (1979–83, 1986)

> "Best blocker I ever coached against. Good, tough runner. Career
> cut short, but a man's man on the field."

RANDALL CUNNINGHAM, QUARTERBACK
Philadelphia Eagles (1985–95), Minnesota Vikings (1997–99), Dallas
Cowboys (2000), Baltimore Ravens (2001)

> "First new-wave quarterback. Dangerous as a runner. Strong arm.
> Needed to be accounted for; made defenses cautious."

LYNN DICKEY, QUARTERBACK
Houston Oilers (1971–75), Green Bay Packers (1976–85)

> "Moved an offense against almost anyone. Smart and dangerous."

ROY GREEN, WIDE RECEIVER
St. Louis/Phoenix Cardinals (1979–90), Philadelphia Eagles (1991–92)

> "He came into the league as a nickel back, and moved to wide
> receiver. Blazing fast. He kept me up at night for about eight years."

RON HELLER, OFFENSIVE TACKLE
Tampa Bay Buccaneers (1984–87), Philadelphia Eagles (1988–92),
Miami Dolphins (1993–95)

> "Rough and tumble. Great competitor; would never give in."

WALTER JONES, OFFENSIVE TACKLE
Seattle Seahawks (1997–2009)

> "Box-car type with good quickness. Capable of dominating."

CORTEZ KENNEDY, DEFENSIVE TACKLE
Seattle Seahawks (1990–2000)

> "Quick, thick, and difficult to block. Good pass rusher for an inside player."

BRIAN MITCHELL, RUNNING BACK, RETURNER SPECIALIST
Washington Redskins (1990–99), Philadelphia Eagles (2000–2), New York Giants (2003)

> "Do-everything guy. I would have loved to have him on my team. Real football player."

MIKE NELMS, PUNT RETURNER
Washington Redskins (1980–84)

> "Tough as they come. Great hands and hard to tackle."

ROD SMITH, WIDE RECEIVER
Denver Broncos (1994–2007)

> "Sneaky, productive, durable. Steady performer."

JOE WASHINGTON, RUNNING BACK
San Diego Chargers (1976–77), Baltimore Colts (1978–80), Washington Redskins (1981–84), Atlanta Falcons (1985)

> "Extremely smart, versatile back who could also catch and score. Super-elusive."

LIONEL WASHINGTON, CORNERBACK
St. Louis Cardinals (1983–86), Los Angeles Raiders (1987–94), Denver Broncos (1995–96), Oakland Raiders (1997)

> "Crafty, tall corner with good skills to disrupt wide receivers."

JAMES WILDER, RUNNING BACK
Tampa Bay Buccaneers (1981–89), Washington Redskins (1990), Detroit Lions (1990)

> "Powerful, bruising runner who could punish a defense."

Note on Sources and Book Website

Over the course of six years, Bill Parcells gave me approximately ninety interviews, about a third in person and the rest over the telephone. Dozens of these sessions took place between 2008 and 2010, when Bill was a Miami Dolphins executive, but the bulk of Q&As occurred while he was retired from the National Football League. I strove to get inside Bill's head so that *Parcells* would evince the intimate, personal voice of a memoir despite being written in the third person.

Our underlying goal was to chronicle the story of football over five decades, with mini-portraits of key characters, from Woody Hayes to Bill Walsh to Curtis Martin and more. For the sake of nuance and balance in the collaborative biography (or third-person memoir), I also interviewed more than one hundred people, including some of Bill Parcells's detractors.

No book about an NFL coach can pretend to be authoritative without the previous contributions of writers and journalists. So, considering the scope of this project, I mined fifty-six books.

Michael MacCambridge's *America's Game* and David Harris's *The League* offered the most breadth on NFL history. Parcells's multiple first-person books laid a foundation for his life through 1999. Bill Gutmans's *Parcells* painted the most comprehensive portrayal of Bill up until his Jets tenure, although being an unauthorized biography, it lacked his voice. Jerry Izenberg's *No Medals for Trying* revealed the inner workings of Parcells's Giants over a one-week period in November 1989. And Gerald Ezkenazi's *Gang Green* gave an informative take on Jets history, including the Parcells era.

Two books were indispensable in helping explain the complicated relationship between Bill Belichick and Bill Parcells: David Halberstam's *Education of a Coach* and Michael Holley's *Patriot Reign*, which also delved into Big Bill's divorce from New England's owner Robert Kraft.

The beat reporters who covered the Giants, Patriots, Jets, Cowboys, and Dolphins during Parcells's tenures at each of those franchises, between 1980 and 2010, provided the "first draft of history" for his NFL career.

Parcells aimed to retell the epic games involving Bill with vividness and immediacy while capturing their sights, sounds, and perhaps smells. So we relied on some of the footage brilliantly produced by NFL Films.

A detailed breakdown of sources, including the magazines, newspapers, video, and even audio recordings, is by itself the equivalent of a slim book. It can be found on the official *Parcells* website, parcellsbook.com. Bonus content, with exclusive material, is also available.

—NUNYO DEMASIO

Index